THINK
SOCIOLOGY

Canadian Edition

JOHN D. CARL
Rose State College

MARC BÉLANGER
Vanier College

Pearson Canada
Toronto

Library and Archives Canada Cataloguing in Publication

Carl, John D.
        Think sociology / John D. Carl, Marc Bélanger. — Canadian ed.

Includes bibliographical references and index.
ISBN 978-0-13-512283-9

        1. Sociology. 2. Sociology — Research.
3. Sociology — Methodology. I. Bélanger, Marc, 1967– II. Title.

HM585.C365 2011   301   C2010-907711-3

Vice-President, Editorial Director: Gary Bennett
Editor-in-Chief: Ky Pruesse
Senior Acquisitions Editor: Lisa Rahn
Signing Representative: Françoise Dykler
Marketing Manager: Lisa Gillis
Senior Developmental Editor: Victoria Naik
Project Manager: Marissa Lok
Production Editor: Heidi Allgair, Element LLC
Copy Editor: Kelli Howey
Proofreaders: Margaret McClintock, Susan Broadhurst
Manufacturing Coordinator: Jane Schell
Compositor: Element LLC
Photo and Permissions Researcher: Deborah Henderson
Art Director: Julia Hall
Interior Designer: Julia Hall and Element LLC
Cover Designer: Miguel Acevedo
Cover Image: Masterfile and Anzovino family

1 2 3 4 5   15 14 13 12 11

Printed and bound in the Unites States of America.

BRIEF CONTENTS

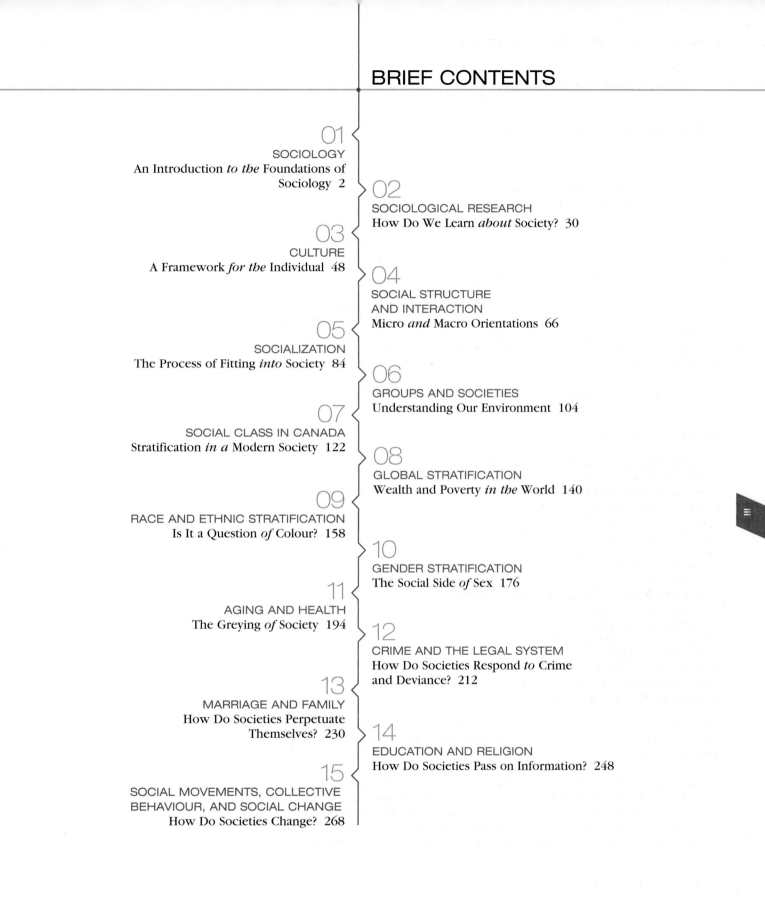

CONTENTS

14

EDUCATION AND RELIGION
How Do Societies Pass on Information? 248

15

SOCIAL MOVEMENTS, COLLECTIVE BEHAVIOUR, AND SOCIAL CHANGE
How Do Societies Change? 268

JOHN CARL'S interest in sociology grew from his interests and job experiences after college, which included working in hospitals, schools, churches, and prisons. John reflects, "In these many diverse encounters, I continued to notice how often the structures of society frequently did not support the change so desperately sought after by the individual. I began to reflect on my sociology courses from my undergraduate work and decided to return to graduate school to study sociology."

At the University of Oklahoma, he became passionate about the study of Criminology and Stratification, completing his Ph.D. while teaching full time at Rose State College. John says, "I found that every part of my life, to this point, fit perfectly with the study of sociology. It is a diverse and exciting field that helps each of us understand our world."

Today, teaching remains his primary focus. John Carl has excelled in the classroom, winning awards for his teaching and working to build and improve the sociology program at Rose State College. "I teach the introductory class every semester because I believe it is the most important course in any department. It is where students get the foundation they need for their continued study of sociology. In these classes, my goal is simple: to teach students to think sociologically so that they can consider any new event in the light of that thought."

When asked why he wrote *THINK Sociology,* the answer was simple: "This book is truly a labour of love for me. I wanted to write a book that is filled with examples used in the classroom and written in a language that students can understand without compromising the core concepts of sociology."

John lives in Oklahoma with his family: wife, Keven, and daughters Sara and Caroline. In his free time, John plays golf, gardens, throws pottery, and plays his guitar. He continues to move from the classroom to community by being active in non-profit leadership in his home community and providing training to non-profit boards so they may better achieve their goals. John suggests, "It is all part of sociology, not only to understand the world in which we live, but to take that understanding from the classroom and use it to improve the community."

MARC BÉLANGER'S natural curiosity about why people do the things they do and a passion for anything academic led to his study of sociology. Marc holds a B.A. and an M.A. from McGill University in Montreal, and is currently working on a Masters in Education from the Université de Sherbrooke. In the eight years that he has been at Vanier College, Marc has taught the introductory sociology course many times.

"When I first saw John Carl's book, like many, I was attracted by the visual format. After a closer reading, I also appreciated that there was a lot of good sociology in it. It has been an honour and a pleasure to work on the Canadian edition of *THINK Sociology.*"

Marc lives in Montreal with his wife, Denise, and their children Tommy and Katerina.

The authors welcome your comments and suggestions about this **THINK** Sociology text at jcthinksociology@gmail.com and belangem@vaniercollege.qc.ca.

To the important women in my life,
Keven, Sara, and Caroline. I love you all.

–J. C.

To my beautiful family:
Denise, Tommy, and Katerina. I love you.

–M. B.

THINK
SOCIOLOGY

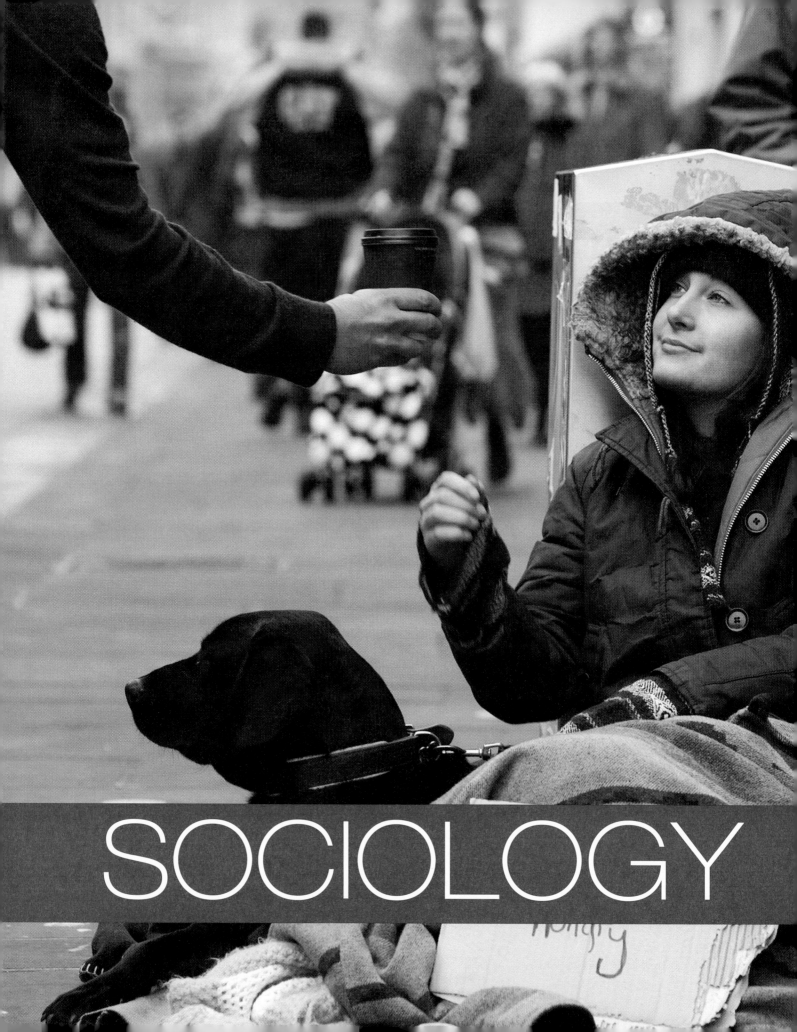

SOCIOLOGY

"It has

been known since the mid nineteenth century that living conditions are the primary determinants of health and well-being. The term *poverty* has come to stand for the situations whereby these living conditions are so materially and socially deprived as to severely threaten health and quality of life. It has also been known over this time that the incidence of poverty is primarily a result of how a society organizes and distributes its economic, social, and political resources. A century and a half of research and lived experience have confirmed these understandings. There exists no research study that demonstrates that living in conditions of poverty is good for individuals, communities, or societies. Indeed, thousands of accumulated studies have come to the same basic conclusion: The incidence of poverty is a severe—if not the most severe—threat to the health and quality of life of individuals, communities, and societies in wealthy industrialized societies such as Canada...

"An increasing body of research finds that poverty rates cannot be attributed to failings of individuals who are living in poverty. There are personal characteristics that make some individuals more susceptible to falling into poverty than others. These characteristics include being Aboriginal, having less education, living with a disability, being female, being a recent immigrant to Canada, being a person of colour in Canada, or being a lone-parent. But these characteristics by themselves do not create a situation of poverty. Poverty is more likely because the political and economic system does not provide employment wages or social assistance benefits at a level for these individuals that allow for a life outside of poverty. And these situations are worsened when public policy does not provide affordable housing, childcare, and health and social services, thereby straining the resources available to these vulnerable groups."[1]

An Introduction *to the* Foundations of Sociology

It is shameful that in a country like Canada, there are people who are poor. In *Poverty and Policy in Canada: Implications for Health and Quality of Life,* Professor Dennis Raphael provides an interdisciplinary perspective on poverty in Canada. Rather than simply asking why a particular individual is poor, Professor Raphael examines the structural causes of poverty—how society and its distribution of resources are the primary causes of poverty.

Dennis Raphael
Foreword by Jack Layton

POVERTY AND POLICY IN CANADA
Implications for Health and Quality of Life

The poor are often viewed as nameless, faceless, voiceless people loitering on street corners or huddled away in decrepit apartments. It's easy for us to turn a blind eye to the problem if we don't feel a personal connection to the man panhandling on the sidewalk or the woman standing in line at the soup kitchen with her children.

Nobody chooses to be poor, but sometimes circumstances turn against people. Poverty can happen anywhere, even on a college campus, as I found out one semester: One day, I saw a student looking through the large garbage bin behind the cafeteria. He found a sandwich, still in its wrapper. As I watched, he quickly opened the wrapper and wolfed down the sandwich. I later learned that this student lived with his mother, who was a drug addict. Often, there was no money for food, and he was forced to rummage in the garbage if he wanted something to eat. Of course, none of this was planned; it simply happened. And I was left to wonder why in a country as developed as Canada there are still young people who live like this.

Raphael's book is a blueprint of what sociology is all about. He gathers information, explains his findings, and then thinks about the bigger picture. He questions social policies and draws his own conclusions. An interdisciplinary researcher like Raphael does not try to pinpoint one specific cause of poverty in Canada. Instead, he tackles the issue from all angles.

SOCIOLOGY

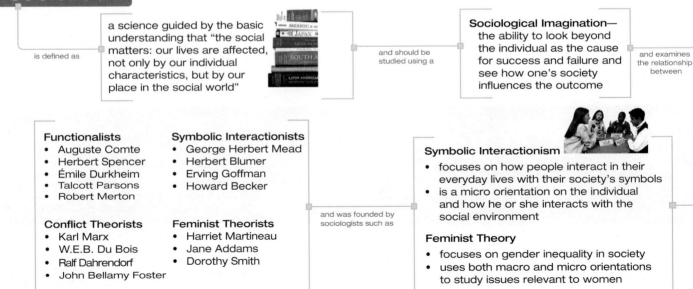

is defined as a science guided by the basic understanding that "the social matters: our lives are affected, not only by our individual characteristics, but by our place in the social world"

and should be studied using a

Sociological Imagination— the ability to look beyond the individual as the cause for success and failure and see how one's society influences the outcome

and examines the relationship between

Functionalists
- Auguste Comte
- Herbert Spencer
- Émile Durkheim
- Talcott Parsons
- Robert Merton

Symbolic Interactionists
- George Herbert Mead
- Herbert Blumer
- Erving Goffman
- Howard Becker

Conflict Theorists
- Karl Marx
- W.E.B. Du Bois
- Ralf Dahrendorf
- John Bellamy Foster

Feminist Theorists
- Harriet Martineau
- Jane Addams
- Dorothy Smith

and was founded by sociologists such as

Symbolic Interactionism
- focuses on how people interact in their everyday lives with their society's symbols
- is a micro orientation on the individual and how he or she interacts with the social environment

Feminist Theory
- focuses on gender inequality in society
- uses both macro and micro orientations to study issues relevant to women

get the topic: WHAT IS SOCIOLOGY?

Sociology Defined

How do you define sociology? You might say that it's the study of society, the study of how people live, or the study of people's interactions with one another. These are all true, but these answers only scratch the surface. Most sociologists would agree that **sociology** is a science guided by the basic understanding that our lives are affected not only by our individual characteristics but by powerful social forces and our

> **SOCIOLOGY** is a science guided by the basic understanding that our lives are affected not only by our individual characteristics but by powerful social forces and our place in the social world.

place in the social world. Like all scientists, sociologists seek to understand the facts of a situation while keeping an open mind about what they are studying. In addition to this, we strive to keep our personal opinions at bay.

MAKE CONNECTIONS

Using Video Games to Study Sociology

Have you ever wanted to control someone else's actions? Leave it to video games to allow you to act out such a fantasy. One of the most popular is *The Sims,* a strategic computer game that simulates real life. You decide when your character sleeps, eats, and even bathes. More recently, the game *Façade* has sprung forth a similar idea. While *The*

Sims and *Façade* play up the entertainment factor, they also provide a lesson in sociology.

Players of *The Sims* and *Façade* manipulate characters in a virtual world to see the effect certain behaviours have on the characters' lives. Your characters become depressed when they have little interaction with others, just like in real life.

The Sims and *Façade* allow you to study the effect people's actions have on themselves and others. The best part is that in the simulated world, the consequences are not real, so

you don't have to be afraid to test how extreme behaviours affect your characters.

>>> **ACTIVITY** Think about a real-world theory you'd like to use *The Sims* or *Façade* to test. How would you use the game to test the theory? What do you think the outcome of your study will be? Write a few paragraphs describing your proposed sociological study. If you have access to either of these video games, go ahead and test your theory!

Developing a Sociological Imagination

One of my students recently lost her job at a nearby clothing factory. She now attends classes during the day and works at a convenience store at night. Being a single mother of two, she has no one to watch her kids while she is at work. Without supervision, her children are falling behind in

school, hanging out on street corners, and getting into trouble. Like many single parents, she has no other options and no idea what else to do.

When we think of kids in trouble, many of us probably blame the parents. But, in my student's situation, does the blame rest solely on her shoulders? Famous American sociologist C. Wright Mills (1916–1962) would say no. Mills asserted that people must understand how outside forces contribute to someone's situation. In other words, Mills wanted us

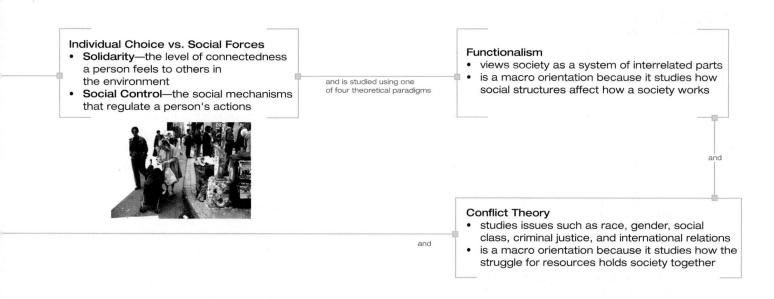

Individual Choice vs. Social Forces
- **Solidarity**—the level of connectedness a person feels to others in the environment
- **Social Control**—the social mechanisms that regulate a person's actions

and is studied using one of four theoretical paradigms

Functionalism
- views society as a system of interrelated parts
- is a macro orientation because it studies how social structures affect how a society works

and

Conflict Theory
- studies issues such as race, gender, social class, criminal justice, and international relations
- is a macro orientation because it studies how the struggle for resources holds society together

and

to develop a **sociological imagination**—the ability to look beyond the individual as the cause for success and failure and see how one's society influences the outcome.[2]

Developing a sociological imagination helps you understand your place in a complex world. We must grasp both the history and the biography of a situation to generate this imagination. Mills argued that most of us see social issues through biography; that is, our personal point of view.[3] This **micro**, or small-scale, reference focuses our attention on the individual. We must also understand how history and social structure affect the individual. By including this **macro**, or large-scale, point of view in our imagining of the social world, we can understand it more clearly. These factors influence both our individual choices and our interpretation of events. So, using the sociological imagination gives us more than an individualistic interpretation of the world.[4]

Let's consider my student's situation this time using our sociological imaginations. Is outsourcing labour to blame for her situation? When Canadian companies close because of cheaper overseas labour, workers in Canada suffer. Ultimately, the goal of most businesses is to make the biggest profit possible, so owners can't resist the lure of hiring cheap labour. With gas and food prices skyrocketing, many businesses must adjust their budgets accordingly and find less expensive

> ∧
> ∧
> ∧ **When working-class parents struggle to put food on the table, some might blame their predicament on a lack of education or motivation.** People using a sociological imagination, however, might attribute other forces, such as rising gas prices, to the parents' predicament.

ways of doing things. Some people win and others lose, as in my student's case. If my student had not lost her job, would her children still be in trouble? Probably not. She reported that when working her old job, she was home every day when they got home from school. Now, she rarely sees them. What's clear is that when thinking sociologically about an issue, simple answers rarely explain the complexities of human situations.

Émile Durkheim's Theory on Suicide

There often are several biographical, social, and historical causes for every event—from poverty to unemployment to suicide. Using a sociological imagination means that we consider the impact on the individual from these points of view. Ever wonder why someone would commit suicide? Suicide is perhaps the most personal type of death, and yet in the 1897 book *Suicide,* sociologist Émile Durkheim (1858–1917) proposed that two social forces, solidarity and social control, influence the chance of a person taking his or her own life.[5] **Solidarity** refers to the level of connectedness a person feels to others in the environment, and **social control** refers to the social mechanisms that regulate a person's actions.[6] These two social forces are independent factors that help predict the type of suicide someone might commit.

When people lack solidarity, **egoistic suicides** occur. People who commit these suicides have few social connections, feel isolated and alone, and are more likely to fall into despair. Of course, this doesn't mean that all "loners" are suicidal. It only shows that having low levels of solidarity increases the odds for egoistic suicides.

Solidarity levels also influence the likelihood of **altruistic suicides**. These suicides result when the level of solidarity is exceptionally high. Because the individual is deeply connected to a group, he or she views the best interests of the group as superior to all other interests. This particular analysis might explain the rationale behind *kamikaze* pilots and suicide bombers.

SOCIOLOGICAL IMAGINATION is the ability to look beyond the individual as the cause for success and failure and see how one's society influences the outcome.

MICRO means small-scale.

MACRO means large-scale.

SOLIDARITY refers to the level of connectedness a person feels to others in the environment.

SOCIAL CONTROL refers to the social mechanisms that regulate a person's actions.

EGOISTIC SUICIDES are suicides that result from a lack of solidarity, occurring among those who have few social connections, feel isolated and alone, and are more likely to fall into despair.

ALTRUISTIC SUICIDES are suicides that occur when the level of solidarity is exceptionally high and when the individual views the group's interests as superior to all other interests.

∨
∨
∨ **Durkheim identified four different types of suicide**—egoistic, altruistic, fatalistic, and anomic—illustrated in the graphic below.[7]

DURKHEIM'S FOUR TYPES OF SUICIDE

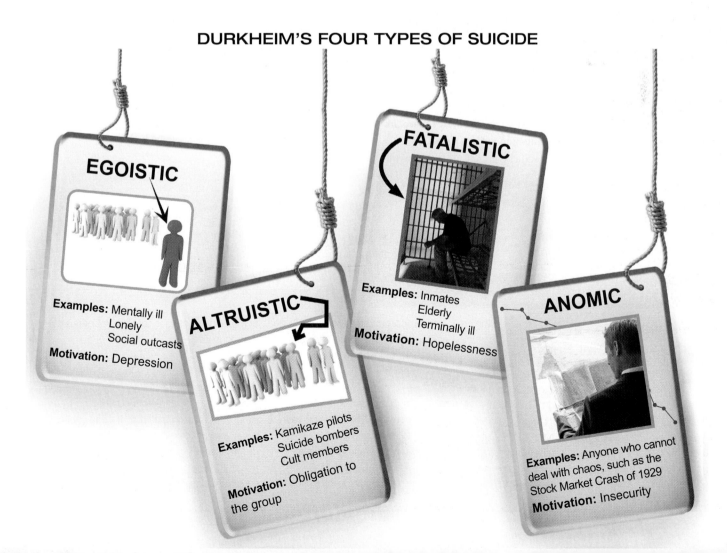

EGOISTIC

Examples: Mentally ill
Lonely
Social outcasts

Motivation: Depression

ALTRUISTIC

Examples: Kamikaze pilots
Suicide bombers
Cult members

Motivation: Obligation to the group

FATALISTIC

Examples: Inmates
Elderly
Terminally ill

Motivation: Hopelessness

ANOMIC

Examples: Anyone who cannot deal with chaos, such as the Stock Market Crash of 1929

Motivation: Insecurity

FATALISTIC SUICIDES are suicides that result from a lack of social control.

ANOMIC SUICIDES are suicides that occur as a result of social unrest.

PARADIGM refers to a theoretical framework through which scientists study the world.

FUNCTIONALISM is a theoretical framework that defines society as a system of interrelated parts.

CONFLICT THEORY is a theoretical framework that views society as an unequal system that brings about conflict and change.

SYMBOLIC INTERACTIONISM is a theoretical framework that focuses on how people interact with others in their everyday lives.

Unlike altruistic suicides, **fatalistic suicides** are related to the level of one's social control. This type of suicide happens when a person feels that his or her future is bleak and there is no way for the situation to improve. Individuals who live in hopeless environments—such as prisons and long-term health-care facilities—are more likely to commit fatalistic suicide.

During times of social unrest, **anomic suicides** increase. Anomie refers to social instability caused by a wearing away of social standards. Durkheim predicted that modernization and industrialization would bring an increase in anomic suicides because society's rules for appropriate behaviour were changing. As a result, many of the social institutions that had once regulated society, such as religion, lose their power.[8] In times of civic unrest, certain individuals will decide that living through the chaos is more than they can handle, so they will take their own lives.

Although Durkheim's theory is more than a century old, it's still an important way to consider the tension between social forces and individual choice.

Suicide might be seen as an individual decision, but there are many social factors that seem to influence suicide rates. We cannot use these factors to specifically predict who will and will not kill

themselves, but we can understand that one's environment influences the rate of suicide in a society. Other factors, such as one's family makeup and the relative size of a group of people born during the same time period, also play a role.[9]

INDIVIDUAL CHOICE AND SOCIAL FORCES

You've probably guessed by now that social factors often influence our personal choices. They provide a context in which we make decisions. Again, consider the act of suicide. Most of my students suggest that this is totally an individual choice, and in fact it is. However, certain trends arise in the data on suicides that indicate people who are at higher risk of taking their own lives.

A person's sex, age, and the province where they live all predict the likelihood of suicide. According to Statistics Canada:

- Studies have found males to be at least four times more likely than females to commit suicide. Males are also more likely to die in their first attempt.
- For both males and females, the suicide rate of those aged 30 to 59 was higher than the overall average rate by sex.
- Historically, suicide rates in Canada have tended to increase from east to west. However, since 1993, Quebec has had the highest age-standardized provincial rate.[10]

It is important for you to note that these factors do not cause individuals to commit suicide *per se*; however, they do indicate groups who are at risk of killing themselves. When sociologists examine an issue, such as suicide, poverty, or any other social event, they use their sociological imagination to help consider how social factors influence an individual's choice. How do sociologists use the sociological imagination to study the larger world? Let's examine four important theoretical perspectives and the sociologists who helped develop them.

THINK SOCIOLOGICALLY

Homelessness—Individual Choice vs. Social Factors

Have you ever heard someone argue that people choose to be poor? You might have even made the argument yourself. In *Poverty and Policy in Canada: Implications for Health and Quality of Life,* Raphael asks, "Do people become poor because they lack education, have low motivation, adopt deviant lifestyles, or live in situations where

they receive little community support? Or do people become poor as a result of public policies that create unjust and inequitable distribution of economic and social resources?"[11]

By now, you must be starting to realize that society has a powerful influence on each of us. If we want to address the issue of poverty in Canada, we have to realize that there are social causes of poverty. Until we realize this, any solutions that we propose will

only touch the surface, but will not get to the root causes.

>>> **ACTIVITY** Visit a homeless shelter in your community. Talk to the people there and find out how social factors contributed to their situation. How did they arrive at the shelter? What was their life like before? Write a paragraph describing one of the people you met and analyzing the factors that led to that person's homelessness.

think sociologically: WHAT ARE THE CHARACTERISTICS OF THE FOUR MAJOR SOCIOLOGICAL PARADIGMS?

Before I ever knew anything about sociology, I had a worldview. Being born in Canada to a middle-class family, my parents' teachings shaped my point of view. Had I been born in China, Chad, or Chile, I would likely think differently about the world. How do you view the world? What personal beliefs or ideas do you value most? It might be difficult to respond to these questions, but I bet you have some pretty definitive answers. When sociologists take in the world, they do it through a **paradigm**—a theoretical framework through which scientists study the world.

In Canada, most sociologists view the world through four major paradigms—functionalism, conflict theory, symbolic interactionism, and feminist theory. **Functionalism** is a theoretical framework that defines society as a system of interrelated parts. This paradigm is a macro approach to sociological study because it focuses on larger social structures rather than individuals. When you think about functionalism, it may be helpful to think about the human body. The body has built-in mechanisms that help it maintain a normal body temperature. If you are stranded outside in freezing temperatures, you will start shivering in an attempt to regulate your body temperature. Society is similar in many ways. When something happens to throw a social system off-kilter, certain forces step in to help balance things out again.

Conflict theory is a theoretical framework that views society as being in a constant struggle over scarce resources. This constant struggle inevitably results in an unequal system. Similar to functionalism, conflict theory is also a macro approach, as this theory is concerned with various interested groups battling for power. Inequality of wealth and power in society is often the focus of modern conflict theory. For example, conflict theorists might examine how the chasm between the rich and the poor affects people's opportunities in our society. It's no surprise that children who come from privileged backgrounds can afford to receive the best educations, participate in organized sports, and take music lessons. However, children from poorer families may not get these same opportunities, and this lack of opportunity puts them at a disadvantage.

Symbolic interactionism is a theoretical framework that focuses on how individual interactions between people influence them and how these interactions can impact society. Symbolic interactionism is primarily a micro approach to sociology because it is concerned with the individual's role in creating society. The use of "symbols," such as words, gestures, body language, and facial expressions, influences how people communicate. Our actions communicate meaning. For example, if you're having a "bad day," what does that mean? One student once told me he had a bad day every time it rained. If that is the case, could such a definition of reality influence how you behave toward others on your job or in the classroom? How might his "bad day" influence the "days" of others? Interactionists constantly seek to understand how small interactions influence the larger society.

>>> In early 2009, two leaders of the polygamous community of Bountiful, B.C., were charged with practising polygamy, which is illegal under the Criminal Code of Canada.[12] **How might being raised on a polygamist ranch influence one's worldview?**

FEMINIST THEORY is a theoretical framework that focuses on gender inequalities which are built in to the social structure.

PATRIARCHAL refers to a social system that benefits men.

SOCIAL LAWS are statements of fact that are unchanging under given conditions and can be used as ground rules for any kind of society.

SOCIAL STATICS are the existing structural elements of society.

SOCIAL DYNAMICS are the change in the existing structural elements of society.

Feminist theory has made two important contributions to sociology. First, on a theoretical level, feminist theory contends that most societies are **patriarchal**; that is, they are controlled by and benefit men. The feminist perspective emphasizes the social inequality between men and women. If we are to have true social equality, we must first acknowledge that our social structures create and perpetuate gender inequality. Feminist researchers often use both macro and micro approaches. At the macro level, feminists examine the gendered institutions of the social structure. On the micro level, many feminist researchers choose to study individuals and small groups using more qualitative methods such as interviews and focus groups. The second contribution of feminist theory is in the topics that are studied. Many feminists study issues such as lone-parenthood, domestic violence, or prostitution that have a greater impact on women.

As you can see, sociologists often approach their study of society from either a macro or micro perspective. In sociology, the macro approach is most commonly used, as it examines larger social groups and institutions and their effects on society. This is part of what separates sociology from psychology, as psychology operates on a micro level by studying the workings of the human mind. Although some sociological studies focus on the individual, the primary concern is the effect that these individuals have on the rest of society and the influence that society has on the individual. Each sociological paradigm can combine aspects of macro and micro approaches, and yet they all seek to understand the process by which people influence society and society affects them.

Sociologists from each paradigm often analyze similar issues, such as why poverty exists or how children learn about the social world. However, the questions they ask as they analyze these issues differ. The chart below illustrates how functionalists, conflict theorists, symbolic interactionists, and feminists approach learning about society.

Sociologists use these questions to help them build theories about the world. So, is one school of thought better than the others? Not necessarily. In fact, most sociologists' worldview is rather eclectic or diverse. They may use each paradigm to illuminate different issues or use all four to look comprehensively at a single issue. If you consider Dennis Raphael's work, for example, you'll see that he uses bits and pieces of each paradigm to understand poverty. Raphael finds that a society's structures create poverty (functionalism), and people with wealth and power control those structures and are generally abusive to the poorest of the poor (conflict theory). Those who experience poverty often create in themselves self-fulfilling prophecies that help them remain mired in their plight (symbolic interactionism). In Canada, women are more likely than men to be poor. Even if they are working, women are more likely to have a part-time job, and to earn less (feminism). Raphael uses each of these ideas to create a complete view of why poverty exists in our society.

Now that you have a general understanding of each paradigm and know what kinds of questions it asks, let's take a closer look at each one. We'll begin with the oldest of the sociological paradigms—functionalism.

The Functionalist's Worldview

Although philosophers have always tackled the issues surrounding how people and society fit together, it was not until French philosopher Auguste Comte (1798–1857) coined the term *sociology* that the discipline got its name.[13] The functionalist paradigm owes much to Comte, who is considered the father of sociology.

Comte felt that sociology should strive to discover **social laws**—statements of fact that are unchanging under given conditions and can be used as ground rules for any study of society. In order to discover these laws, Comte proposed that we study **social statics**, or the existing structural elements of society, and **social dynamics**, or the change in those elements. He believed that by discovering the interplay between structures and

COMPARING THE THEORETICAL PARADIGMS

	Functionalism	Conflict Theory	Symbolic Interactionism	Feminism
Level of Analysis	Macro	Macro	Micro	Macro and Micro
Core Questions	• What keeps society functioning smoothly? • What are the parts of society and how do they relate? • What are the intended and unintended outcomes of an event?	• How are wealth and power distributed in society? • How do people with wealth and power keep them? • Are there groups that get ahead in this society and why? • How are society's resources and opportunities divided?	• How do people co-create the society? • How does social interaction influence, create, and sustain human relationships? • Do people change behaviour from one setting to another, and if so, why?	• How does society advantage men and disadvantage women? • What social issues are important to women? • How can social structures be changed to benefit both men and women equally?

∧
∧ It's hard to spot the light-coloured moth in this photograph, isn't it? The
∧ moth's colouring is probably a result of natural selection. **Moths with colours that stand out in their environment often die out, leaving behind the "best fit" members of the species.**

dynamics we could develop social laws that would help improve society. To date, we have no social laws, but some sociologists are still trying to develop them. Although few people follow Comte's theories today, his basic ideas are the groundwork on which functionalism is based.

As we've discussed, functionalism is a theoretical framework that defines society as a system of interrelated parts. These parts work in concert with one another to satisfy the needs of society as a whole. According to functionalists, society is relatively stable, which means that things occur in society for a specific function and those functions help maintain stability.

Social institutions such as the family, economy, educational system, and political system are critical for society to function properly.

Understanding how these and other social institutions work in a society is of great interest to functionalists. Since these parts are interrelated, each has an impact on the others. Remember my student who lost her job? The economic system influenced the family system, which may, if her children continue to get into trouble, interact with the criminal justice system. By this example, you can see that performing functional analysis can be quite complex.

Functionalism suggests that a society's values and norms provide the foundation for the rules and laws that it creates. These norms regulate the relationships among social institutions. Therefore, general agreement on these norms must occur for a society to achieve balance.

All of the social structures, from the minor day-to-day interactions with friends to the complex cultural traditions and customs, work together to keep society running. Functionalists, however, have differing views about how these structures cooperate with one another. Some compare society to living, breathing organisms, others analyze the expected and unexpected outcomes of a social event, while still others wonder what exactly it is that holds a society together. Although it's the oldest theoretical approach, functionalism remains an important way to consider society. On the next few pages, we'll investigate some early functionalists and you can see who these ideas come from. Early theorists like Herbert Spencer and Émile Durkheim contributed to the growth and development of the functionalist perspective.

HERBERT SPENCER

Herbert Spencer (1820–1903) was a British intellectual whose ideas furthered the development of functionalism. Spencer's study of sociology was informed by Charles Darwin's theory of natural selection. Darwin argued that natural selection—a process resulting in the evolution of organisms best adapted to the environment—makes evolution occur. Spencer viewed society as a biological organism, and as such, it can evolve, thrive, or die. For him, some societies are "more fit" than others because they adapt better to changes in the environment. From Spencer, you can see a type of thinking often called **social Darwinism**—a notion that suggests strong societies survive and weak ones become extinct.[14]

Spencer's idea informs a social theory that, in essence, evaluates the superiority or inferiority of a society based on its ability to be strong and survive. For example, in a recent class discussion about poverty, one of my students stated, "Poor people can't follow the rules that everyone else does; being poor is their own fault." Do you see Spencer's ideas in her comments? How do her words reflect the idea of social Darwinism? On the macro level, do you think some societies are superior to others? Would you suggest that Canada reached its success due to its own merit? If so, you think a bit like a social Darwinist.

ÉMILE DURKHEIM

Like Spencer, French intellectual Émile Durkheim (1858–1917) also viewed society as an organism. You should recognize Durkheim's name from our discussion of suicide earlier in the chapter. Durkheim was one of the first true sociologists, in that he used data to test theories. His work provides the basis for much of functionalist thought.

Durkheim's work suggested that solidarity is a vital component that holds society together. Solidarity integrates—or holds together—a society because people see themselves as unified. Durkheim pointed out that the type of society influences the type of solidarity. He divided solidarity into two different types, mechanical and organic. **Mechanical solidarity** refers to the state of community bonding in traditional societies in which people share beliefs and values and perform common activities. It's this bond that works to keep society running smoothly.[15]

As societies become more complex, their type of solidarity changes from mechanical to organic. **Organic solidarity** occurs when people live in a society with a diverse division of labour. Division of labour refers to the many different jobs we have today; the division forces people to depend on one another for survival. Ask yourself, when was the last time you ate something you either grew or killed yourself? For most of us, the answer is never. Food is essential for survival, and yet most of us require a complex division of labour to feed ourselves. Farmers, truckers, and grocers all must do their part so we can eat.[16] This organic connection ensures that we get the things we need and holds society together. Beliefs remain important in a modern society, but what binds people together is their organic solidarity.[17]

Durkheim's ideas about solidarity are just the tip of the iceberg, though. A number of thinkers drew inspiration from Durkheim and expanded his ideas into what is known as functionalist thought. One of these thinkers was Talcott Parsons.

TALCOTT PARSONS

Functionalist Talcott Parsons (1902–1979) was a giant in the field of sociology. Parsons was interested in creating grand theories that attempted to explain every aspect of the human experience and how social systems interconnect. For Parsons, society is much like a bicycle wheel, made up of independent yet interdependent parts. When properly balanced, each independent spoke connected to the hub keeps the wheel spinning. But if just one spoke on your wheel breaks, the entire wheel will eventually fall out of balance. Similarly, society is an interrelated system, and if one part fails to work, the whole system suffers.[18]

Parsons also commented on the inertia of social systems, meaning that they tend to remain at rest, if they are at rest, or stay in motion, if already in motion. For example, when you go bowling, you must take a bowling ball and use your own force to make it roll down the lane. Once the ball starts rolling, it tends to keep rolling until the pins and the end of the lane stop it. Although the friction from the floor may slow it down, some other force must stop it. Parsons pointed out that the social world acts the same way. Thus, in order to change a society, some great force must impact the system or it will remain unchanged. This is because societies naturally will find a balance. Thus change is unlikely and often disruptive. Of course, once the process of change starts, the system will continue on that path until some counter-reaction occurs due to social inertia.[19]

<<< **Mennonite farm communities** in Ontario **have mechanical solidarity because everyone lives in much the same way, does the same things, and shares the same values.**

ROBERT MERTON

Functionalist Robert K. Merton (1910–2003), a contemporary of Parsons, sought to create a middle-range theory that could bridge the gap between grand theories and the study of individual parts of society. He did this by breaking society into parts and studying them individually to better understand the whole.[20] This idea is widely accepted in sociology today, as most sociologists have an area of expertise, be it race, gender, crime, inequality, population, or a host of other issues. It is possible to spend a career pursuing knowledge in one of these areas, seeking to create theories of the middle range that describe these issues and how they influence society. Merton's work also shows how sociologists are rarely "pure" theorists in any area.

One of Merton's greatest theoretical contributions to functionalism was his understanding that social realities have both intended and unintended functions—social factors that affect people in a society. Merton identified two types: **manifest functions**, or factors that lead to an expected conse-quence or outcome, and **latent functions**, or factors that lead to an unforeseen or unexpected consequence. Merton suggested that when looking at any social event, sociologists should ask the question, "For whom is this functional?" By doing this, we'll do a complete analysis

SOCIAL DARWINISM is a notion that suggests strong societies survive and weak ones become extinct.

MECHANICAL SOLIDARITY refers to the state of community bonding in traditional societies in which people share beliefs and values and perform common activities.

ORGANIC SOLIDARITY occurs when people live in a society with a diverse division of labour.

FUNCTIONS are social factors that affect people in a society.

MANIFEST FUNCTIONS are functions that lead to an expected consequence or outcome.

LATENT FUNCTIONS are functions that lead to unforeseen or unexpected consequences.

because we'll consider both manifest and latent functions. For example, one could argue that the manifest function of outsourcing jobs is to improve a company's profits while providing cheaper goods to consumers. However, the latent function of such a system creates tension for families whose jobs are lost, like my student. For Merton, one cannot complete a functional analysis without considering both manifest and latent functions.[21]

THE FUNCTIONALISTS—AT A GLANCE

AUGUSTE COMTE

J'aime social physics and laws!

HERBERT SPENCER

Only the strong survive!

ÉMILE DURKHEIM

SOLIDARITY

TALCOTT PARSONS

ROBERT MERTON

SO CI ET Y

CRITICISMS OF FUNCTIONALISM

In the mid twentieth century, functionalism was the dominant theoretical approach. However, its dominance has waned in more recent years. Critics of functionalism sometimes claim that this paradigm does not take into account the influences of wealth and power on the formation of soci-ety. From a purely functionalist point of view, all social structures exist because they meet some need. For example, pay phones used to be found in all public places. But recently, my daughter was unable to call me from the arena where she was skating because there was no pay phone. As more and more people have cell phones, pay phones are los-ing their social function.

Functionalists are accused of supporting the status quo, even when it may be harmful to do so. Consider the invention of the automobile. Certainly it has made society more mobile and provides freedom of movement for millions. And yet, if we fail to consider the latent conse-quences of this invention, we do not fully understand it. Thus, supporting the car means supporting the air pollution, concrete parking lots, and potential accidents that come with it.

BOURGEOISIE refers to members of the capitalist class.

PROLETARIAT refers to members of the poor working class.

FALSE CONSCIOUSNESS is a person's lack of understanding of his or her position in society.

CLASS CONSCIOUSNESS is an understanding of one's position in the class system.

Functionalists suggest that societies will naturally find a balance point on their own. If change occurs, it will do so slowly, and this is actually in the best interest of society. However, if you think about certain social problems such as poverty, is this something that should be addressed slowly or quickly? Although it is easy to point out that certain individual traits may lead some to live in shelters, is it really good for anyone to have people sleeping on the streets? The lack of affordable housing in society remains a problem. Although Raphael argues that Canada does not have enough cheap housing or high-paying work for all of its citizens, he points out that a lack of a decent wage drives much of the poverty in Canada. In this way, he criticizes the functional argument that the balance point is fair. Thus, is Canada really a land of opportunity for everyone?

As you consider poverty or other societal issues, ask yourself for whom is the system functional? Or whom does the system benefit? Functionalists might argue that society works for the greatest number of people. Change will arise when problems become "big enough." However, critics would argue that this belief results in many minorities being ignored. Who speaks for the poor? What choice did my student have about globalization and the loss of her job? The functionalist perspective often fails to recognize how inequalities in social class, race, and gender cause an imbalance in our society.

The conflict theory paradigm arose as a response to some of functionalism's weaknesses. Conflict theorists want to analyze how these social inequalities affect society as a whole.

The Conflict Theorist's Worldview

Remember, conflict theory is a theoretical framework that views society in a struggle for scarce resources. So, what is scarce? Two main concerns for conflict theorists are economic wealth and power. Such theorists acknowledge that we live in an unequal society. Why? It could be because there is not enough "stuff" to go around, or it could be because those with the "stuff" don't want to let go of it. In either case, conflict theory suggests that we're all struggling for more "stuff," whether that "stuff" is power in a marriage or wealth in the world.

Conflict theorists, like functional theorists, tend to focus on macro issues, viewing how society's structures contribute to the conflict. Modern conflict theorists often look at the inequality of a capitalist economic system. Such a system breeds inequality, as it rewards some at the expense of others. Once you have power, you want to keep it. For this reason, the wealthy elites are more likely to create advantages for themselves, even if their actions put others at a disadvantage.

In general, the essence of conflict theory suggests that a pyramid structure of power and wealth exists in society. The elite at the top of the pyramid determine the rules for those below them. Under such a system, laws, institutions, and traditions support their authority. When Raphael discusses the lack of adequate wages and the blame we all deserve because we permit poverty to exist, he is in essence suggesting that those of us who are not poor are, in part, responsible for those who are because we allow the system to ignore these people.

Many theorists who use the conflict paradigm might examine macro conflicts between different groups of society, different countries, or different social classes. The study of inequality in sociology always involves a consideration of conflict theory. Thus, you can see the paradigm applied to social class, race, gender, marriage, religion, population, environment, and a host of other social phenomena. If you believe that discrimination, ageism, sexism, racism, and classism occur in society because some people have the power to inflict their desires on others, then you think like a conflict theorist.

KARL MARX

Karl Marx (1818–1883) was a German theorist, social activist, and writer who analyzed the effects of capitalism—an economic system in which private individuals own businesses and control the economy. Believing that capitalism corrupts human nature, Marx hoped for a utopia in which equality reigned. At his core, Marx was not that different from Comte, because he wished to understand society to improve it for all.

Marx suggested that in a capitalist system, the **bourgeoisie**, or members of the capitalist class, own most of the wealth because they control the businesses. Since increasing profit is their first goal, owners pay workers as little as possible. Raphael, too, notices this when he describes poor women who actually have some form of employment, but don't make enough money to afford decent housing. Employers generally pay these women as little as possible, and the women have no way to fight the system.

Marx called the workers in a capitalist system the **proletariat**, or members of the poor working class. They do all the work and the owners reap all the benefits. The proletariat live in an unending cycle in which they work for low pay and then use those wages to survive. According to Marx, workers will never get ahead if they do not share in the wealth they create.

Why don't workers do something to change their fate? Marx suggested that it is because people have a **false consciousness**, or a lack of understanding of their position in society. The workers feel that they are alone in their plight. Marx proposed that the workers must develop **class consciousness**, or an understanding of one's position in the system. Marx suggested that most workers do not truly understand how capitalism enslaves them. They think if they work hard, they'll get by and perhaps thrive. Marx argued that these ideas are fantasy.

Marx believed that once workers recognized their positions, they would unite to end their tyranny. He proposed an overthrow of the private ownership of capitalism, and instead suggested socialism. In such a system, the government controls the economic system, ensuring that all people share in the profits generated by their own labour.

However, Marx didn't suggest that long-term government repression was necessary to enforce communism on people. He knew that the government would initially have to force the bourgeoisie to give up their wealth because it takes force to make powerful people give up their power. Consider this example: in 2007, Conrad Black, owner of the Hollinger media empire, was sentenced to $6\frac{1}{2}$ years in prison, fined $125 000, and ordered to pay $6.1 million in restitution after being found guilty of fraud and obstruction of justice. After the sentencing, Black repeatedly appealed the decision. Black did not step down willingly: Those on top do whatever it takes to stay there.[22]

Marx believed the same would be true in society. However, he believed that members of the capitalist class would willingly share their wealth once they saw the benefits of communal living. Our true human nature is to live in harmony, sharing everything equally.[23]

Sociologists' opinions on Marxist theory vary. While some may hope for a type of class consciousness to arise and replace our current system, others think Marx oversimplified class struggle. His simple system of social class is difficult to apply to a complex postindustrial capitalist society, and even if you try, where would you draw the line between owners and workers? My student actually owned shares in the company that let her go, so was she a worker or an owner? Seems like both.

Marxist theory clearly remains active in today's discussions of sociology. Marx felt that economic power should be in the hands of the people because wealth corrupts human nature.

These ideas continue to inspire sociologists. Let's next look at the work of three other conflict theorists—Du Bois, Dahrendorf, and Foster—to study how social inequalities affect a society.

W.E.B. DU BOIS

W.E.B. Du Bois (1868–1963) was an African American conflict theorist who agreed with a great deal of Marx's thinking. After attending Fisk University, Du Bois moved on to Harvard, where he would eventually complete both his under-

graduate and graduate work. His writings are vast, but he is often credited for initiating the study of race in America. He was particularly interested in issues of racial inequality in the United States.[24]

In his book *The Philadelphia Negro,* Du Bois showed that poverty among African Americans in the United States is primarily the result of prejudice and discrimination.[25] In the book, he reviewed the history of African Americans in Philadelphia and connected that history to the problems his contemporaries were facing. Implying that slavery and capitalism led to African Americans' problems, Du Bois pointed out that history was influential over the present. He also noted that African Americans of his time had to live in two worlds, a white one and a black one. In one world, they were second-class citizens, while in the other they were equals. This idea, which Du Bois termed "double consciousness," created tension and conflict for African Americans. He felt that with greater assimilation into the mainstream culture, African Americans would eventually lead better-quality lives.[26]

When Du Bois saw extreme poverty, oppressive governments, and many wars in Africa, he realized that colonizing Europeans caused many of these problems. **Colonialism was a primary way for European powers to generate wealth for capitalists while doing little to improve the lives of the African poor.** Du Bois increasingly believed that the greed of the United States and western Europe was the cause of war and poverty throughout the world. **To counter this, promoting economic justice and equality helps the world be at peace.**[27]

In many respects, Du Bois was the first and perhaps most influential sociologist to study race. He was a social activist, and he became more interested in working to improve life on the African continent and less interested in life in the United States. Du Bois eventually came to believe that African Americans would never be equal to whites because the white population would not allow this. For this reason, he left the United States and spent his remaining years in Africa.

CYCLE OF WEALTH IN A CAPITALIST SYSTEM

The Bourgeoisie

spend their wages in businesses owned by

own the wealth and exploit

The Proletariat

RALF DAHRENDORF

Ralf Dahrendorf (1929–2009) served as Commissioner for the European Economic Community, as a German Foreign Minister, and as Director of the London School of Economics. Among sociologists, he is most known for his critique of classical Marxist theory. In his book *Class and Class Conflict in Industrial Society,* Dahrendorf argued that Marx's two-class system (*proletariat* and *bourgeoisie*) was no longer relevant to describe twentieth-century society, which he described as "post-capitalist." Instead of focusing only on property ownership as the definitive social distinction, Dahrendorf recognized that other social factors divide people into groups. While still deeply inspired by the Marxist view of social interaction as being essentially based on conflict and struggle for power, Dahrendorf opened the door for subsequent sociologists to explore other arenas of social conflict.[28]

∧
∧ The studies of W.E.B Du Bois revealed inequality in the U.S. democratic system.
∧ What about in Canada? **Is the Canadian system fair for each person in the photograph?**

JOHN BELLAMY FOSTER

John Bellamy Foster, a contemporary professor of sociology, often writes using a conflict paradigm. His work is primarily concerned with the negative effects of capitalism on society and the planet as whole. In his article "The End of Rational Capitalism," he points out that purely capitalist economies, or economies in which markets are totally free, are disappearing throughout the world.

In free-market capitalism, businesses seek short-term rewards by working to expand markets. They do not care about long-term consequences. As a result, Foster argues that businesses' pursuit of wealth has created environmental and global problems, including the existence of extreme global poverty and inequality.

Foster argues that markets cannot "solve problems" because there are no profits to be had from such an endeavour. Often, people suggest that the United States is the wealthiest country in the world because it has worked harder and used the capitalist system to give opportunity and incentive to people. Foster reminds us that such a perspective ignores important parts of history, namely the period after the Second World War when most of the "industrialized world" was destroyed (except the United States), and the expansion of the U.S. economy was largely related to building up these devastated countries. This had very little to do with the superiority of the American capitalist system. Developments such as the fall of the USSR and the privatization of the Chinese economy seem to indicate that capitalism has won—and, thus,

is "superior" to socialism. However, totally free-market capitalism will result in the destruction of the environment and the exploitation of workers throughout the world.[29] The long and short of it, according to Foster, is that capitalism cannot continue to expand because we are reaching a stagnant point.

CRITICISMS OF CONFLICT THEORY

While functionalists are accused of being too conservative, critics of conflict theory often accuse it of being too radical. This paradigm often becomes synonymous with the idea that powerful people oppress the weak. However, most people seem to agree that the roles and rules of society "make sense." For example, even after we discussed globalization and the depletion of factory jobs in Canada, my student who lost her job still felt that the Canadian system was "fair." She said, "It still makes sense to me, even though I'm being hurt by it." This illustrates the reality that most people in society tend to agree with the status quo. Marx would say that this is evidence of false consciousness.

A simple reading of conflict theory can also seem to make the notion of conflict seem like a "bad" thing. However, doesn't competition breed excellence? In practice, a lot of conflict is actually institutionalized in society. When issues are debated in the House of Commons, Members of Parliament may represent conflicting viewpoints, but this conflict may result in a more equitable solution for all.

After examining the works of functionalists and conflict theorists you're probably thinking in a macro manner. Whether you're using functionalism or conflict theory, you are thinking like many sociologists. Yet sociologists can take a more micro view. If you believe that the way to change the world is through the individual, you might find symbolic interactionism appealing.

The Symbolic Interactionist's Worldview

Symbolic interactionism focuses on how communication influences the way people's interactions with each other create the social world in which we live. Symbolic interactionists believe that the root of society comes from its symbols. They suggest that the symbols we use are arbitrary, meaning that they vary from culture to culture.

Do you write with a pen or *un stylo*? Neither is wrong; one is a label in English, the other in French. **As long as you are with other people who speak the same language, you can interact.**

A long time ago, I enrolled in a language school in Mexico. I lived with a family who spoke no English, and my teachers spoke to us only in Spanish. At first, I was totally lost. I clung to the members of the family with whom I lived as if I were a little child. However, I soon began to learn the language. It is amazing how our need to communicate with others helps us learn. Although the words or accents of different languages sound different, communication is central to all human interactions.

Of course, words are not the only symbols. Consider the photograph on the next page of flags from countries around the world. The flag that probably has meaning for you is the Canadian flag. However, people from China, Brazil, Belgium, or the United Kingdom probably feel the same way about their flags as you do about yours. These symbols represent entire nations, and yet you cannot identify many of them and they probably don't hold much interest to you. This is because the importance of a symbol is rooted in the culture from which it comes. Just as languages vary between people, so, too, do their symbol systems.

As you can see, then, for interactionists society is fluid thing. It is always in a process of change because how we use symbols and what they mean to us are constantly changing. For example, when I was in school, teachers might tell ethnic jokes, such as "Polack" jokes. Of course, now most of you have not ever heard these jokes. Why? Because people began to define such humour as unacceptable.

So, our definition of what has value depends on our understanding of it. Context and setting affect our understanding of a social event. You certainly behave differently in your sociology class than you would if you were at a friend's house. Social order results when the members of society share common definitions of what is appropriate.

<<< This is a collection of flags from many countries. Which of these do you recognize? **Do any of these flags have meaning to you?**

Disputes arise when we do not share the same definitions. Think about an argument you've had with someone recently. Did the fight stem from a different interpretation of meaning? For example, if your roommate eats your food without asking your permission, you might interpret that behaviour as disrespectful and rude. However, he might feel that his behaviour shows that the two of you are friends and share everything with one another.

Symbolic interactionism is the most micro of sociological approaches, as it often studies the activities of individuals and then draws connections to larger society from these. Studies of relationships, race, deviance, and even social movements can all use a symbolic interactionist approach.

Interactionists argue that individuals have the power to co-create the world, to make it what they want it to be. People develop standards and norms through a process of interacting with others. This way, we learn what is "normal" and acceptable behaviour. Widespread social acceptance of a behaviour is the main criterion in declaring it to be normal, and we quickly learn that different situations allow for different behaviours. For example, kissing your boyfriend or girlfriend on the lips is a perfectly acceptable behaviour. However, trying to kiss a co-worker on the lips could result in your being charged with sexual harassment.

In many ways, symbolic interactionism blends sociology and psychology. Let's take a look at the work of its founder, George Herbert Mead.

GEORGE HERBERT MEAD

Symbolic interactionism was the brainchild of George Herbert Mead (1863–1931), an American sociologist from the University of Chicago. Mead's former students were so committed to him that after his death in 1931 they combined his articles, notes, and lectures into the book *Mind, Self, and Society.* This book introduced a new theory called "symbolic interactionism."[30]

In *Mind, Self, and Society,* Mead suggested that the root of society is the symbols that teach us to understand the world. We then use these symbols to develop a sense of self, or identity. It is this identity that we then take into the world, and we interact with other identities to create society. Thus, the initial building blocks of society are our minds, the place we interpret symbols.

How do you learn to interpret symbols? Mead suggested that you do this through the micro interactions you have every day. You have probably learned that in a classroom, you should raise your hand if you have something to say. When the teacher calls your name, or points to you, then it is your turn to speak. Mead argues that all these various symbols enter our minds, where their meaning is interpreted and we are told how to react. Mead suggests that this process is never-ending; therefore, we have a fluid sense of who we are. Our selves can change, and they do change based on how we interpret the symbols thrown our way.

In this way, your self develops. **Self** is your identity. It's what makes you who you are and separates you from others. According to Mead, you couldn't have a self without symbols or without someone to pass those symbols on to you. In other words, you learn who you are through others.

In high school, did you ever feel embarrassed by your parents? Do you feel the same level of embarrassment today? The answer to both questions is probably yes *and* no. When I ask this in class, most of my students report that they don't find their parents nearly as embarrassing as they used to. Why does this occur? It is because when you were younger, you didn't have a well-developed sense of self yet you were trying to develop your identity. You are anxious, taking your cues from others as to what is "cool" or acceptable. You worry that your parents' actions might reflect upon you. As you grow older, you've experienced thousands of interactions that have taught you who you are. This is why, the older you get, the less embarrassing your parents seem. You know yourself much better now.

Mead proposed that symbols build society. Symbols have meaning, and meaning directs our lives. The symbols a society uses help us understand the people in that society. In Canada, we have accepted that we need the word "homeless" to discuss people who cannot afford housing. Symbols help us define a situation and determine what we should do about it. For example, if someone told you about a homeless person, you might feel sympathy and want to help him—but if they used the terms "filthy, lazy bum" you might not feel the same desire to help.

HERBERT BLUMER

Symbolic interactionist Herbert Blumer (1900–1987), a disciple of George Herbert Mead and former chair of the sociology department at the University of California–Berkeley, established three basic premises that define the symbolic interactionist perspective:

1. Human beings behave toward things on the basis of the meanings they ascribe to those things.
2. The meanings of such things are derived from, or arise out of, the social interaction that one has with others and society.
3. These meanings are handled in and modified through an interpretive process used by the person in dealing with the things he or she encounters.[31]

What does Blumer mean? First, we all react to situations and people based on how we perceive them. Have you ever noticed that you can "dis" your mom, but if someone else does you get defensive? This is because you ascribe meaning to the act of dissing—that it's OK for someone in the family, but when outsiders join in you move to defend the group.

How did your feelings emerge? They probably occurred from the many years in which your mother cared for you. While she may drive you crazy sometimes, she once fed you, tucked you in at night, and nurtured you when you were sick. In other words, the social interactions you had with her support the meaning you ascribe to who can and cannot dis her.

Blumer proposed that the primary focus of the interactionist approach involves studying individual interactions with symbols. This micro focus places great importance on the idea that symbols have great power to affect society as a whole. The way we talk about something creates the way we deal with it. Consider this example: In the 1950s, many whites spoke using racial slurs. Today, such language is socially unacceptable. Has this change eliminated racism? Certainly not, but the level of racism in Canada has certainly declined. Are these two factors connected? Blumer would suggest that they are. Words convey meaning and meaning creates reality. Eliminating racist language moves society closer to eliminating racism.

Normally, people interpret the words and actions of those around them and determine their behaviour based on this interpretation. This results in rational behaviour, meaning that we tailor our responses to the setting after we've interpreted the reactions. However, in a group setting our behaviours are somewhat different. Blumer suggests that, generally, in a group setting we react without the same degree of thought we use in an individual decision. At some point, people stop thinking rationally and act in ways that they might not consider acceptable in a different setting. Last hockey season, our hometown team was losing an important game. A man in the stands became extremely agitated; four-letter words poured from his mouth like water over Niagara Falls. The stands were filled with men, women, and children, and I'm sure this man would never have behaved this way at a business meeting. So why did this happen? Blumer would suggest that it was the result of collective excitement, an intense emotional behaviour that makes it hard for us to think and act rationally. This is what Blumer calls **contagion**, a rapid, irrational mode in which people do not think rationally or clearly. In such a setting, they "lose their heads" and react emotionally, not rationally. In this way, you can see that individual interactions can create social realities. I was thankful at that game that I had not taken my youngest child, but someone in the crowd eventually did tell the man to watch his mouth because there were children around. Initially, the foul-mouthed man seemed angry to be scolded in public, but he quickly cooled down as he noticed that a number of people around him were watching his behaviour closely. How do we react when others are watching? Sociologist Erving Goffman developed a theory about this.

> Goffman's primary insight is that we are constantly trying to manage the impressions that others have of us. Impression management is the action we use to control what others think of us. When the angry man at the hockey game calmed down, it was probably because he was a season ticket-holder and he knew that we'd all see him again next week. He didn't want to come off as the "jerk who cusses."

SELF refers to a person's identity and what makes that person different from others.

CONTAGION is a rapid, irrational mode in which people do not think rationally or clearly.

DRAMATURGY is a theory of interaction in which all social life is like acting.

ERVING GOFFMAN

Canadian sociologist Erving Goffman (1922–1982) developed a theory he called **dramaturgy**, a theory of interaction in which all social life is like acting. Goffman uses this theory to compare daily social interactions to the gestures of actors on a stage. People are constantly "acting" in order to convince people of the character that they wish to portray to the outside world. This is not to say that people

---

▶▶▶ GO GL🌐BAL

Homeless Labels Around the World

Assigning negative labels to the homeless isn't unique to Canada—it occurs in countries all over the world. In Finland during the 1980s, homelessness became associated with alcoholism. People related the two ideas so closely that the government in Finland had to step in to prevent such nega-tive stereotyping. In China and India, people connect homelessness with a lack of governmental registration, which means that the homeless aren't seen as true citizens. In Peru, children living on the street are called *piranitas*, or little piranhas, which implies that they are dangerous and likely to resort to criminal behaviour. People in Bangladesh equate homelessness with having a lack of morals.[32]

Criminal, alcoholic, immoral—these are only a handful of labels that exist for the homeless around the world. As we noted above, negative labels make it even more difficult for poor individuals to rise above their situation. If people who are poor are given an opportunity and adequate support, they can be just as successful and stable as any other members of society.

are always faking it, but rather that people are concerned about what the rest of the world will think of them, and they adjust their social interactions accordingly.

Frequently, we alter our behaviour without much deliberate thought. For example, if you're on a first date, do you behave differently than the way you do with an old friend? Usually, on a first date you dress differently, talk differently, and eat more carefully. You may be nervous, but you will also, without thinking about it, change your behaviour. Why? Because you are taking extra care to make a good first impression, even if it means not being completely yourself. Goffman points out that managing impressions involves a complex series of actions and reactions. As a person gets older and has more practice in socializing, he or she may be better equipped to gauge the reactions that his or her actions will receive.[33] Chapter 4 provides more detail on dramaturgy.

HOWARD BECKER

Howard S. Becker (1928–), a sociologist from Chicago, suggests that human action is related to the labels attached to it. In his book *Outsiders: Studies in the Sociology of Deviance,* Becker suggests that a label is attached to a certain behaviour when a group with powerful social status labels it deviant. He suggests that deviance is rooted in the reactions and responses of others to an individual's acts.

The label of deviant—or conformist, for that matter— is applied when people see our behaviour and react to it. This sets up a self-fulfilling prophecy for behaviour as people seek an identity that will match up to the expectations that others hold of them. Becker applied these ideas to the study of deviant behaviour, but the idea of labelling theory applies to all identity issues, including gender, sexual orientation, and personal identity.

Consider the example of a five-year-old girl who has been labelled a "good girl." The theory would suggest that somewhere along the line, she did what others expected of her and that these people had power over her. Her parents asked her to take a bath and she did. She received a positive reward, "she's a good girl," and through repeated events throughout her life she developed that sense of self whereby she never does anything remotely dangerous or out of line—and always takes a bath. However, if this "good girl" becomes a "terrible teen" and her parents label her as a delinquent, she might stop bathing and start smoking. Becker would suggest that the label we ascribe to people has a major influence on their behaviour.

THE SYMBOLIC INTERACTIONISTS—AT A GLANCE

CRITICISMS OF SYMBOLIC INTERACTIONISM

Critics of symbolic interactionism suggest that this perspective ignores the coercive effects of social structure, focusing too much on the power of the individual to co-create his or her world. If, for example, you're a prisoner in jail, it doesn't matter whether you reject the prisoner label or not. If you try to leave, you'll be stopped.

Of course, we are all born into a culture and social setting; we don't create them as we go along. As a result, your parents, neighbourhood, and nation of birth all influence how you see things. Had you been born in a different time or in a different culture, you might have believed totally different things.

The Feminist Theorist's Worldview

Feminist theory, or the study of how gender affects the experiences and opportunities of men and women, often takes a conflict-oriented point of view. Women throughout the world are still subordinate to men. In some countries, this might mean women cannot choose their husbands, while in this country it may be more linked to employment opportunities afforded to women. You'd be hard-pressed to find women CEOs in the very biggest companies: women lead only 19 of the top 500 companies in Canada.[34] Feminists often suggest this occurs because men want to maintain their positions of power in society and strive to keep women out. Do you see the conflict perspective here?

The feminist perspective brings attention to the **androcentric bias** both in the wider society and in the traditional practice of sociology. The androcentric bias influences sociology in two ways. First, it assumes that the social research done on males is applicable to both males and females. Second, it focuses on issues and topics that are of greater concern to males. For example, traditional sociological studies on crime have often focused on males as the perpetrators of crimes; the findings are then generalized to all criminals, both male and female. Conversely, the feminist perspective is more likely to focus on the female victims when studying crime. While all feminists are primarily concerned with gender inequalities, many have also drawn attention to other areas of inequality—especially race and ethnicity, social class, and sexual orientation. If you believe that society is often unfair because there are many advantages for males and many injustices for females, then you are thinking like a feminist theorist.

HARRIET MARTINEAU

Harriet Martineau (1802–1876), like Karl Marx, came from a bourgeois family and received the benefits and status that came with such a class distinction. However, she hoped that capitalism and industrialization would bring greater justice and opportunity. Martineau, one of the first female sociologists, did not just examine the inequalities in the economic system: she also focused on the inequality between the sexes.

In the book *Society in America,* Martineau analyzed the impact of slavery, the position of women in society, and the social customs within U.S. political and economic systems.[35] She pointed out how these systems favour men who hold the power in society.

Martineau's studies noted hypocrisy and favouritism in the United States. For example, only white men could vote, despite the nation's democratic ideals. Enslaved people and women did not have equal opportunities for political, economic, and educational involvement. Martineau pointed out that some people did not have the same opportunities as others. She not only paved the way for other female sociologists,

ANDROCENTRIC BIAS is a focus on men which influences sociology in terms of how social research is done and which issues and topics are studied.

but also expanded people's thinking about the world, enlightening what would become the conflict paradigm.[36]

JANE ADDAMS

Laura Jane Addams (1860–1935) was born in Cedarville, Illinois. Addams's father, a businessman and politician who worked to elect Lincoln and strongly opposed slavery, raised her. Jane earned a bachelor of arts degree from Rockford Women's Seminary in 1882 and then travelled to Europe, where she saw things that changed her life.

In London's Toynbee Hall, Addams witnessed the settlement house movement.[37] The settlement house movement supported the idea that poverty results from ignorance and structural barriers, not from failings in the morality of the person. The settlement house workers actually lived and worked in the slums. Jane and a friend, Ellen Gates Starr, decided to create a settlement house in Chicago. In 1889, they opened Hull-House with these three principles:

1. Workers would live in the slums to better understand the problems there.
2. Every person has dignity and worth regardless of race/ethnicity, gender, or social class.
3. Dedication, education, and service can overcome ignorance, disease, and other problems often associated with poverty.

Offering services ranging from medical to educational, Addams also used her position at Hull-House to write articles and books on a variety of topics, like the rights of women and the poor. In many ways, Hull-House became a laboratory for the application of sociological principles. In 1931, Jane Addams won the Nobel Peace Prize for her lifetime of service and dedication to peace.[38]

Through her teaching, writing, and action, Jane Addams embodied the best of sociology principles. Along with Albion Small, she helped found the American Sociological Association and often guest lectured in sociology classes at the University of Chicago. In order to understand the poor, Addams felt that she must live among them. Once she comprehended a situation, she wrote about it to inform others. These theories impacted her work at Hull-House. These are the steps you will take in learning to think like a sociologist.

DOROTHY SMITH

Dorothy Smith (1926–) is one of the most influential and well-known Canadian sociologists. Like many sociologists, Smith understands that culture is socially constructed. But Smith recognizes that this also includes the practice of sociology, which, in its tradition, reflects a very male perspective. In *The Conceptual Practices of Power: A Feminist Sociology of Knowledge,* Smith critiqued traditional sociology for adopting an "objectifying discourse."[39] When sociologists use census data and labour statistics to describe and understand social behaviour, they are ignoring the lived experiences of individuals. By overlooking these experiences, most (male) sociologists perpetuate an ideology that justifies the existing social structure. Smith called this type of writing the "father tongue." It is a symbol of a patriarchal system that downplays the importance of individual experience and prefers to pursue objective knowledge—a typically male approach.

Smith argued that the work of the sociologist should be to recognize the everyday experiences of ordinary people, including women, workers,

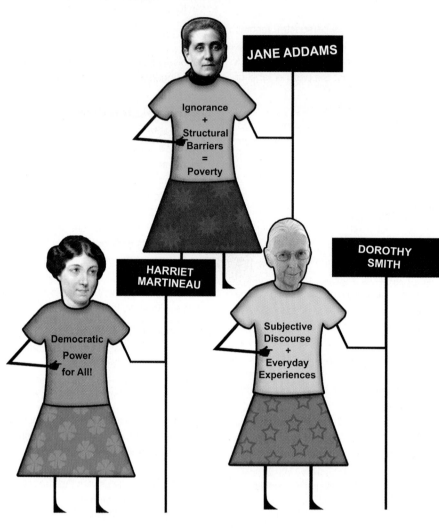

JANE ADDAMS

Ignorance + Structural Barriers = Poverty

HARRIET MARTINEAU

Democratic Power for All!

DOROTHY SMITH

Subjective Discourse + Everyday Experiences

and other marginalized groups. We should develop a sociology that is relevant for all members of society and which explains the social world, including our subjective experiences of it.[40]

CRITICISM OF FEMINIST THEORY

You have seen that some of the earliest sociologists, such as Harriet Martineau and Jane Addams, were women. Nevertheless, sociology has primarily been practised by men. The feminist perspective brought a new theoretical focus to sociology, one that recognized the patriarchal nature of society and the inequality that exists between men and women. Some have criticized feminist theory for placing too much emphasis on the impact of gender on social relations. While it is true that a hundred years ago most social institutions were explicitly biased against women, this is not necessarily the case today. Gender inequalities still exist, but there has been incredible improvement in the social, political, and economic position of women in Canadian society. It is probably due to the work of feminist sociologists that the social structure has changed.

The feminist perspective has also challenged the principle of objectivity in studying social behaviour. The quest for objectivity, it is argued, is a particularly male view. Feminists are more likely to try to understand the subjective meaning and individual experiences of the people and groups they are studying. However, this has resulted in the accusation that feminist research methods lack scientific validity.

The Four Paradigms—How Are They Interrelated?

In the sports arena, we tend to associate phenomenal players with the teams on which they play. The player's name and the team name become synonymous. Sidney Crosby and the Pittsburgh Penguins. Michael Jordan and the Chicago Bulls. Derek Jeter and the New York Yankees. You get the idea. The same is true of sociologists—we associate the theorist with the paradigm that he or she favoured or had a hand in developing. For example, Marx is a symbol of conflict theory, whereas Comte and functionalism go hand in hand. However, sometimes it can be tricky to confine sociologists to such a tight box because they might use parts of each paradigm in their analyses. In fact, I know of no colleague of mine who is a "purist" in anything. That's because no single paradigm perfectly fits every situation. To get a complete picture, many sociologists use all four paradigms. In this way, the four paradigms are interrelated and work together to help us figure out why society is the way it is.

Think about sociologist Robert Merton and his concept of latent and manifest consequences. He takes a functionalist stance, but adds to it the notion that intended and unintended results can arise. Thus, we should ask, for whom is this functional? Can you see a bit of conflict theory here? Like Merton, symbolic interactionist Howard Becker also blurs the lines between the paradigms.

OVERLAPPING THEORIES

FUNCTIONALISM

Everything in the social world exists because it has both an intended outcome and an unintended outcome.

The social structure (functionalism) is patriarchal because it benefits men more than women (feminism).

Power differentials (conflict theory) often indicate for whom things are functional and for whom they are not (functionalism).

Feminist Theory

Gender inequality is the fundamental feature of society. It exists in the social structure and affects our interactions.

CONFLICT THEORY

Inequality exists in the social world because of differences between different groups' wealth and power.

Our most important label is our gender. Gender stereotypes (feminism) can limit the behaviour of an individual (symbolic interactionism).

Labels are attached to certain individuals; this practice sets up a self-fulfilling prophecy as people try to match their behaviour to their labels.

People in power create labels and assign them to others (conflict theory) and these labels influence the outcomes of the individual (symbolic interactionism).

SYMBOLIC INTERACTIONISM

Becker's labelling theory can be linked to conflict theory because the labelling tradition suggests that those with power determine what is and is not labelled as deviant or criminal. In other words, the power of the label influences the outcome of the individual, but people with the ability to get what they want done put the label on us. Like a conflict theorist, Becker acknowledges that a system of inequality exists within our society. Consider this question: Why are cigarettes legal, while marijuana is illegal? Labelling theorists would argue that this is because people with power smoke cigarettes, but not pot. If powerful people ever started smoking pot, the practice would become legal.

We've seen how conflict theory overlaps with both functionalism and symbolic interactionism, but does functionalism ever overlap with symbolic interactionism? When Émile Durkheim suggests that values unify people, he sounds a bit like George Herbert Mead. The solidarity of a society for Durkheim is related to what it values, and he acknowledges that values change as societies become more modern.

We've said that feminism takes both macro and micro approaches. When feminists argue that the social structure is patriarchal, they are overlapping with many of the assumptions of the functionalists. You have seen that functionalists study social institutions such as the family or the educational system. Feminists draw attention to the fact that many of these social institutions have gender bias because they provide more benefits to men. When feminists focus on the subjective meaning of gender stereotypes, they are sharing a worldview with the symbolic interactionists. Our gender is an important part of who we are. You probably act differently around someone depending on whether they are male or female.

The point for you as a student of sociology is to be aware that just because a sociologist is classified as a functionalist, conflict theorist, symbolic interactionist, or feminist, that doesn't mean that he or she won't use other points of view in making an analysis of the world. In fact, at times, a theorist's point of view can be so eclectic that he or she can't be pinned down to a single category. This sentiment is especially true of sociologist Max Weber (1864–1920).

Max Weber—Theorist Who Transcends Categorization

To some sociologists, Max Weber (1864–1920) is the German counterpart of Émile Durkheim because he wrote about a great variety of topics, used data in his analysis, and laid the foundations for high-quality sociological research. In his work, students often see a variety of ideas that seem to blend different schools of thought. Yet, he wrote at a time before many of these "schools" were clearly defined or established.

Because Weber wrote partly as a response to some of Karl Marx's ideas, many consider him a conflict theorist. Weber accepted that social classes influence our outcomes; however, he felt Marx's social class system was too simple. He proposed that all people have economic, political, and cultural conflicts that are related to their relative social position. As a result, being an owner does not necessarily make you important in society. Wealth is important, but political power and social standing are also important.

In other ways, Weber appeared to take a more functional approach, particularly when he discussed how bureaucracies function in society. Bureaucracies, which will be discussed in depth in Chapter 6, are formal organizations that are organized into a hierarchy of smaller departments. You might think of a large corporation or a government agency as a bureaucracy. Weber proposed that rational and ideal bureaucracies naturally occur because we need them. They provide clear lines of authority, divide tasks so that workers can specialize, and clearly define rules and expectations. Under such a type of leadership, societies and large organizations function smoothly and improve the function of society. Although Weber was well aware that few perfect bureaucracies exist, he argued that responsible leadership will tend toward the ideal because Western society is increasingly focused on achieving goals, and a rational bureaucracy is an efficient way to achieve those goals.[41]

Others have suggested that Weber's ideas seem to lay the foundation for the symbolic interactionist school of thought. Why? Because he pointed out how values influence our goals and affect our behaviours. In his book *The Protestant Ethic and the Spirit of Capitalism,* Weber clearly linked a person's religious values to the societal creation of a capitalist economy. For him, capitalism arose in the Western world primarily because a religious value system that he called "the Protestant ethic" emphasizes the accumulation of wealth as a marker of God's favour on a person.

Furthermore, Weber also discussed how values are important to the study of sociology. For example, he understood that sociologists are at risk of approaching their profession with personal values that might influence the outcome of their study. Weber stressed that sociology should be value-free. In other words, sociologists should study society as it is, not as they would like it to be. They should put their biases aside when analyzing a topic. He implied that personal values may impact social research, and therefore sociologists must strive to put such values aside when they make their analyses.

So, where does your professor put Weber? The more you read about social theorists, the more you will find that most of them blend ideas from all schools of thought.

>>> Is Max Weber (pronounced VAY-bur) a conflict theorist? A functionalist? A symbolic interactionist? Or is he all three? **Sociologists everywhere disagree on how to classify Weber. That's because his views are so varied that he almost defies categorization.**

APPLYING SOCIOLOGICAL THEORIES

Now it's time to think like a sociologist. Thinking like a sociologist means that you understand the topic, and you examine it from one or more of the four sociological theories covered in this section. Consider the problem of poverty in a society. How might a functionalist view poverty? How might a conflict theorist view it? A symbolic interactionist? A feminist?

WRAP YOUR MIND AROUND THE THEORY

Functionalists look for the function of any issue. **Food banks, functionalists argue, make a dysfunctional system like poverty function in a society.**

FUNCTIONALISM

Functionalists suggest society works as an interrelated system. Communitarians understand that if society is to run smoothly, the government, the local community, and the business sector must all work together for the well-being of all. The root of society is the local community; it anchors this societal tree. The government carries the will of the people to the economic system, thereby functioning as the trunk of this tree. The leaves of a tree make the sugar that allows the entire plant to live. Of course, leaves without roots blow over, and roots without leaves die.

CONFLICT THEORY

Conflict theorists would view poverty as a sign of inequality in society. Conflict theorists focus on social classes and their drastic differences in wealth, power, and prestige. They believe that the upper class controls society's wealth and resources and exploits the lower class. If the upper class shared its wealth, conflict theorists argue, then poverty would be cut down dramatically.

WHAT CAUSES POVERTY IN A SOCIETY?

SYMBOLIC INTERACTIONISM

Because symbolic interactionists view things on a smaller scale, they would explore how poverty affects the way individuals act toward one another. These theorists would ask: How do individuals behave toward one another? What labels do individuals assign to the poor? How do rich people interact with poor people?

FEMINIST THEORY

Feminists would focus on how poverty affects women in particular. They might look at how social structures and policies result in more women than men being poor. What changes would have to be made to the social, economic, and political systems in order to reduce the poverty of Canadian women? When we study poverty, do we focus on the homeless man, or do we consider the single mother who is struggling to barely make ends meet?

The **inequality of wealth** in a society **is a leading cause of poverty.**

Look at each picture. **How do you think each pair of people is acting toward each other? Do you think there are differences between the pairs?**

discover sociology in action: WHY IS COMMUNITY LEARNING IMPORTANT TO A SOCIETY?

Getting Involved in Sociology— Community Learning

COMMUNITY LEARNING occurs when individuals and groups work to identify and address issues of public concern.

In one of the classes that I teach, students must complete 15 hours of community service. At the end of the semester, each student does a short presentation on what they did and what they learned. I have always been pleasantly surprised by the great insights that students gain when they are actually "out there" being active participants in the community.

It's easy for people to believe that social problems are so widespread that there is nothing we can do about them. Often, we feel so out of touch with the world around us that we do not vote, we do not know our neighbours, and we cannot name our town council members. **Community learning**, however, can help you see things with fresh eyes. Working in the community expands your understanding of sociology and your world.

Raphael's study of poverty shows us that poverty is a widespread problem, and there is plenty of blame to go around. There are too many people who don't understand the problem, just ignore it, or both. When I worked at a local day shelter during my undergraduate days, I realized I had a lot to learn. One day, while serving lunch, I noticed that one of the patrons became quite irritated. "Hot dogs again!" he screamed. Startled, I thought that he had no right to complain when he could be eating nothing for lunch. An older and more experienced volunteer must have noticed my face, because she said to me, "Sometimes, so many people look past them, that they just have to yell so you'll know they're there." That sobering comment brought me back to my senses. When you actually take a minute to view the world from someone else's perspective, you'll find it hard to just sit around and do nothing.

ACTIVITIES

1. What community learning opportunities are available in your area? Surf the Web to find local shelters, food banks, or other organizations in your community. Choose an organization and volunteer there. Write about your experience.
2. Research your local and provincial governments. Who are the important government officials? What roles do they play in the government? What policies and issues do they support?
3. Poverty is just one of many issues that plague today's society. What other social issues do you think are important to address and why? How would you try to solve these problems?

From Classroom to Community } Helping the Homeless

"Homeless people are just a bunch of drug addicts, aren't they?"

I wasn't surprised when Theo, one of my first-year sociology students, made this comment during a lecture. However, I was disappointed because I knew that many people around the world share this view. After a lively debate on the subject, I realized I hadn't changed Theo's mind, so I challenged him to volunteer at a local homeless shelter.

Day after day, Theo worked with the families at the shelter—feeding, clothing, and talking with them. While at the shelter, he met a homeless mother who had been the victim of domestic violence.

"When I looked into that mother's face and the faces of her children, I realized how narrow my viewpoint had been," Theo remarked to me later. "How did I ever think you could label an entire group of people?"

At the end of Theo's volunteer period, he wrote a paper for class revealing how much he had learned about the homeless. He even decided to continue working at the shelter. Volunteering made him feel like he was making a difference in the lives of the people he encountered, and he knew they were making a difference in his. Theo's experiences helped him realize that the people at the shelter were just like him. The only difference was that they had fallen on some bad luck.

Theo's story shows how moving out of the classroom and into the community helps people gain a new perspective. They can get out of their individual boxes and view the world as a sociologist would.

CHAPTER

01

WHAT IS SOCIOLOGY?   5

a science guided by the basic understanding that our lives are affected not only by our individual characteristics but also by powerful social forces and our place in the social world

WHAT ARE THE CHARACTERISTICS OF THE FOUR MAJOR SOCIOLOGICAL PARADIGMS?   9

functionalism: defines society as a system of interrelated parts; primarily a macro orientation because it focuses on larger social structures rather than individuals
conflict theory: views society as an unequal system that brings about conflict and change; focuses on macro issues and supports the idea that the struggle for scarce resources holds a society together; concerned with inequality as it relates to wealth and power
symbolic interactionism: focuses on how individual people interact with other people in their everyday lives; studies how the use of symbols influences how people communicate; follows a micro approach because it is concerned with the individual's role in creating society
feminist theory: views society as being based on a patriarchal ideology that benefits men and discriminates against women; focuses on issues that are relevant to women; uses both macro and micro approaches; concerned with gender inequality

WHY IS COMMUNITY LEARNING IMPORTANT TO A SOCIETY?   26

provides you with a fresh perspective and expands your understanding of sociology and your world

get the topic: WHAT IS SOCIOLOGY?

Theory

FUNCTIONALISM   10

- society is a system of connected parts working together to keep society intact
- it is important to consider the function of any issue
- society is fairly stable, which means that things occur in society for a specific function
- suggests society will find a balance point of its own

CONFLICT THEORY   14

- focuses on social classes and their drastic differences in wealth, power, and prestige
- upper class controls society's wealth and resources and exploits the lower class
- once a group has power, they want to keep it, so they are likely to create advantages for themselves

SYMBOLIC INTERACTIONISM   17

- believes the root of society comes from its symbols
- society is fluid, meaning it is always in the process of change because the symbols we use and their interpretations change
- disputes arise when people do not share the same definitions of symbols

FEMINIST THEORY   21

- focuses on gender inequality in society
- social structures are patriarchal, meaning that they benefit men more than women
- traditional sociology has ignored issues that are important to women

Key Terms

sociology is a science guided by the basic understanding that our lives are affected, not only by our individual characteristics but by powerful social forces and our place in the social world. *5*

sociological imagination is the ability to look beyond the individual as the cause for success and failure and see how one's society influences the outcome. *6*

micro means small-scale. *6*

macro means large-scale. *6*

solidarity refers to the level of connectedness a person feels to others in the environment. *7*

social control refers to the social mechanisms that regulate a person's actions. *7*

egoistic suicides are suicides that result from a lack of solidarity, occurring among those who have few social connections, feel isolated and alone, and are more likely to fall into despair. *7*

altruistic suicides are suicides that occur when the level of solidarity is exceptionally high and when the individual views the group's interests as superior to all other interests. *7*

fatalistic suicides are suicides that result from a lack of social control. *8*

anomic suicides are suicides that occur as a result of social unrest. *8*

paradigm refers to a theoretical framework through which scientists study the world. *9*

functionalism is a theoretical framework that defines society as a system of interrelated parts. *9*

conflict theory is a theoretical framework that views society as an unequal system that brings about conflict and change. *9*

symbolic interactionism is a theoretical framework that focuses on how people interact with others in their everyday lives. *9*

feminist theory is a theoretical framework that focuses on gender inequalities which are built in to the social structure. *10*

patriarchal refers to a social system that benefits men. *10*

social laws are statements of fact that are unchanging under given conditions and can be used as ground rules for any kind of society. *10*

social statics are the existing structural elements of society. *10*

social dynamics are the change in the existing structural elements of society. *10*

social Darwinism is a notion that suggests strong societies survive and weak ones become extinct. *12*

mechanical solidarity refers to the state of community bonding in traditional societies in which people share beliefs and values and perform common activities. *12*

organic solidarity occurs when people live in a society with a diverse division of labour. *12*

functions are social factors that affect people in a society. *13*

manifest functions are functions that lead to an expected consequence or outcome. *13*

latent functions are functions that lead to unforeseen or unexpected consequences. *13*

bourgeoisie refers to members of the capitalist class. *14*

proletariat refers to members of the poor working class. *14*

false consciousness is a person's lack of understanding of his or her position in society. *14*

class consciousness is an understanding of one's position in the class system. *14*

self refers to a person's identity and what makes that person different from others. *18*

contagion is a rapid, irrational mode in which people do not think rationally or clearly. *19*

dramaturgy is a theory of interaction in which all social life is like acting. *19*

androcentric bias is a focus on men which influences sociology in terms of how social research is done and which issues and topics are studied. *21*

community learning occurs when individuals and groups work to identify and address issues of public concern. *26*

Sample Test Questions

These multiple-choice questions are similar to those found in the test bank that accompanies this textbook.

1. Which of the following is a criticism of conflict theory?
   a. It overlooks the fact that many willingly accept society's rules.
   b. It does not recognize the differences between social classes.
   c. It fails to acknowledge social inequality.
   d. It is unsympathetic to poverty.
2. Which of the following questions might a symbolic interactionist ask about the social world?
   a. Why does inequality exist in society?
   b. Why do income disparities occur between the races?
   c. How do social institutions keep society running smoothly?
   d. How does a particular social setting affect a person's behaviour?
3. Erving Goffman's theory of dramaturgy suggests that
   a. people behave similarly in a variety of situations.
   b. people change their behaviour to fit the setting they are in.
   c. people's behaviour has little to do with others' perceptions of them.
   d. people's behaviour is not affected by the behaviour of others around them.
4. Who does a patriarchal social structure benefit?
   a. The poor
   b. The rich
   c. Men
   d. Fathers
5. All of the following are macro orientations *except*
   a. functionalism.
   b. conflict theory.
   c. social Darwinism.
   d. symbolic interactionism.

ANSWERS: 1. a; 2. d; 3. b; 4. c; 5. d

ESSAY

1. The four sociological paradigms often overlap with one another. Choose a sociologist discussed in the chapter. Discuss how his or her ideas connect to at least two different sociological paradigms.
2. Why is it important for a sociologist to use a sociological imagination? What consequences might arise if he or she failed to use this way of thinking?
3. What sort of attitudes concerning poverty might a symbolic interactionist discourage?
4. Why is suicide a compelling sociological issue?
5. Describe possible manifest and latent functions of a law that would legalize drugs.

WHERE TO START YOUR RESEARCH PAPER

To learn more about sociology as a scientific discipline, go to www.csa-scs.ca

To find useful information about the famous figures of sociology, go to www.sociosite.net/topics/sociologists.php and http://media.pfeiffer.edu/lridener/DSS

To find an in-depth sociology dictionary, go to www.webref.org/sociology/sociology.htm and http://bitbucket.athabascau.ca

For more information about sociology departments in Canada, go to www.mcmaster.ca/socscidocs/w3virtsoclib/cansoc.htm and www.sociolog.com/canada/links.html

To find a guide for sociological internet sources, go to www.socioweb.com

For more information about the study of symbolic interactionism, go to http://uregina.ca/~gingrich/f100.htm

To find an online journal of sociology, go to http://en.wikipedia.org/wiki/List_of_journals_in_sociology

To find a website dedicated to finding out the truth about urban myths, go to www.snopes.com

To find an excellent source for different information on sociology, go to www.trinity.edu/~mkearl/theory.html

For more information about feminist sociology, go to http://uregina.ca/~gingrich/o28f99.htm and www.sociosite.net/topics/women.php

Remember to check www.thethinkspot.ca **for additional information, downloadable flashcards, and other helpful resources.**

SOCIOLOGICAL RESEARCH

"Most social

scientists who have worked 'in the field' are aware of the impact that they might have and take this into account when they come to analyze their data. To what extent does the involvement enhance or diminish our 'scientific' study of religion? . . .

"First of all, just being there can make a difference. When I began studying the Unification Church [often called the Moonies*] in the early 1970s, it was a relatively closed community with strong boundaries distinguishing 'them' from 'us.' To have someone living in the community who was not part of 'us' threatened and weakened the boundary and, thus, the beliefs and actions associated with a strong-group situation (Douglas 1970). The very fact that a normally impermeable boundary *can* be permeated by an outsider affects the group and its members in a number of concrete ways. For example, one girl left, not because I advised her to do so but, she said, because my anomalous existence as someone who could live both within and without led her to realize that she did not have to make the stark choice between *either* a godly *or* a satanic lifestyle; there could be a middle way which would allow her to pursue an alternative way of serving God without having to deny all that was good about her Unification experience.

"At the same time, it is possible that others stayed in the movement, at least for slightly longer than they might

*"Moonies" is slang for the followers of Sun Myung Moon, founder of the Unification Church.

otherwise have done, because of the existence of a 'professional stranger' (Barker 1987). My presence meant there was someone who would neither report back to the leadership, nor go to the media, but on whom they could offload their anxieties and frustrations.

"Asking questions (in formal interviews, general discussions, or through questionnaires) that no one else has previously asked can lead to an unexpected 'raising of consciousness.' . . . Sometimes, I was told, the result was a deeper understanding of the theology, but on other occasions the consequence was a growing irritation or suspicion of the leadership. . . .

"As my research into NRMs [new religious movements] progressed, I found myself affecting the situation more consciously. First, I was being asked to mediate between members of movements and their parents, who also formed part of my data. . . .

"Once the results of my research became public it became increasingly obvious that they would not go unchallenged. . . . To the astonishment and/or amusement of anyone who knew me, I found myself being labelled a Moonie, a Scientologist, a fundamentalist Christian, or a cult lover— or, by the more benign, an innocent who was being deceived by the movements. *What* I said was rarely questioned."[1]

How Do We Learn
about Society?

In a chapter of *Cults and New Religious Movements: A Reader,* British sociologist Eileen Barker explains how doing research into a new religious movement or cult can leave a scientist "bruised and confused."[2]

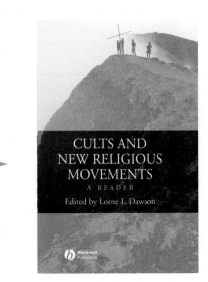

"Cults," or new religious movements (NRMs), are found around the world. In 1980s Canada, for example, Roch Thériault, who called himself Moses, set up a cult commune with his followers near Burnt River, Ontario. One of his eight wives called him a psychopath after he cut off one of her arms. After pleading guilty to second-degree murder in the death of another of his wives, who was disembowelled with a kitchen knife during a cult ritual, he was sentenced to life in prison.[3]

Sociologists study all kinds of social groups. University of Waterloo sociologist Lorne Dawson wrote in *Cults and New Religious Movements* that cults emerged as a social problem in Western societies in the late twentieth century, which helps explain why they started coming under scrutiny after that.[4]

In studying controversial groups like cults, it is even more important that the social researcher be objective and scientific in his/her study. In our ongoing quest to help you think like a sociologist, this chapter will equip you with a precise understanding of research method tools.

get the topic: WHAT ARE RESEARCH METHODS?

RESEARCH METHODS are the scientific procedures that sociologists use to conduct research and develop knowledge about a particular topic.

Hearing jargon like "sociological research" and "statistical analysis" may trigger horrid visions of crunching numbers, learning terms, and memo-rizing formulas for hours on end. However, practising the actual nitty-gritty of research methods is very different from that. While it's true that research requires dealing with data and measurements, it also allows you to delve into the behaviours of your society. **Research methods** are the scientific procedures that sociologists use to conduct research and develop knowledge about a particular topic. So, to fully understand what

Research Methods

are → the scientific process by which sociologists conduct research in an effort to develop knowledge

key concepts are →

Objectivity
means by which research is conducted without bias
Variables
factors being studied
Cause
something that brings about change in something else
Correlation
measure of how two or more factors vary under certain circumstances

which help you understand

Step 6
Share and Publish Results

now you can complete →

Qualitative
words, pictures, or photos
Quantitative
numeric form

which can be

sociology *is*, you have to be aware of what a sociologist *does*. And that means learning to think and act like a sociologist.

As we discussed in Chapter 1, the first step in thinking like a sociologist is to comprehend the topic, and part of this involves understanding certain terms and research methods.

Objectivity

The first concept in a sociologist's repertoire should be objectivity, the foundation for all sociological research. For sociologists, **objectivity** is the ability to conduct research without allowing personal biases or prejudices

to influence them. They must put their own opinions and preconceived notions aside to study human behaviour objectively. Being objective may seem simple, but it can be very difficult in practice. We all have our own opinions and prejudices, which can skew an objective point of view. For example, if you're studying the implication of ethics violations among NHL referees, your research might be swayed if you feel a particular referee has treated your favourite team unfairly.

OBJECTIVITY is the ability to conduct research without allowing personal biases or prejudices to influence you.
INDEPENDENT VARIABLES are variables that are deliberately manipulated in an experiment.
DEPENDENT VARIABLES are the response to the manipulated variable.

In that case, it's probably unwise to start this study after a bad call just cost your team a playoff game.

Whether you're studying NHL referees or researching religious communities in your area, it's important to be objective. Sociologist Max Weber (1864–1920) applied the term *verstehen*—understanding the meaning of action from the actor's point of view—to his research.[5] Weber argued that only when a researcher completely detaches himself or herself from a subject could accurate conclusions be drawn. When conducting a sociological study, you must enter your subject's world and check your personal prejudices at the door.

Variables

It may be impossible to erase your own biases, but you can become aware of them and train yourself to see beyond them. Once you've accounted for your prejudices, you can then focus on the variables you will observe. Two types of variables exist in all kinds of research: independent and dependent. **Independent variables** are variables that are deliberately manipulated to test the response in an experiment, and **dependent variables** are the response to the manipulated variable. In other words, the dependent variable *depends* on the independent variable. Let's say you want to know if there's a connection between playing a musical instrument and doing well in school. In this case, playing an instrument = the independent variable, and your grades = the dependent variable. When testing these two variables, a person's academic success, or lack thereof, is dependent upon whether or not he or she plays a musical instrument.

>>> Max Weber's idea of *verstehen* suggested that **sociologists step out of their own shoes and into their subject's shoes when conducting a study.**

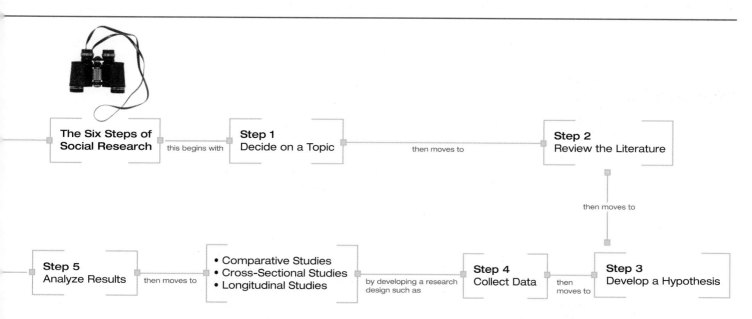

CONTROL VARIABLES are variables that are kept constant to accurately test the impact of an independent variable.

CAUSAL RELATIONSHIP is a relationship in which one condition leads to a certain consequence.

CAUSATION is the relationship between cause and effect.

CORRELATION is an indication that one factor might be the cause for another factor.

POSITIVE CORRELATION includes two variables that move in a parallel direction.

NEGATIVE CORRELATION occurs when variables move in opposite directions.

SPURIOUS CORRELATION occurs when two variables appear to be related, but actually have a different cause.

SOCIAL RESEARCH is investigation conducted by social scientists.

LITERATURE REVIEW is a study of relevant academic articles and information.

THEORY is a comprehensive and systematic explanation of events that lead to testable predictions.

HYPOTHESIS involves a suggestion about how variables relate.

To determine the effect of playing an instrument on grades accurately, though, you'll need to control these variables. **Control variables** are variables that are kept constant to accurately test the impact of an independent variable. These variables must be controlled because they might influence the results, which would lead the researcher to a false conclusion. If you compare the grades of students who play instruments to the grades of students who don't play instruments, you have to make sure that all other factors are equal. If all the students who don't play instruments also have learning disabilities, then you'll get skewed results. You'd have no way of determining whether the students' disability caused the poor grades or if it was the absence of practising and playing a musical instrument. Control variables ensure that you are testing *only* the independent variable.

Cause and Correlation

A **causal relationship** is one in which a condition or variable leads to a certain consequence. To understand causal relationships, you need to recognize the difference between causation and correlation. **Causation** is the relationship between cause and effect. Suppose I let go of a pencil. Gravity *causes* the pencil to fall to the floor. According to the law of gravity, the same cause results in the same effect every time. Correlations, unlike causes, are not laws because they do not guarantee a certain effect. Instead, a **correlation** is an indication that one factor *might* be a cause for another factor. Consider this correlation using the variable we discussed: Students who play musical instruments generally have higher grades than students who don't play an instrument. There is a correlation between the study of music and one's grades. However, that doesn't mean that playing an instrument will always result in higher grades. There are other factors that come into play, such as how much you study and whether you apply what you learn. Unlike gravity, the correlation between instrumental music and grades is not a *law*.

Causes always create the same effects; correlations don't. Although it's likely that there is a relationship between getting good grades and playing an instrument, it's not a sure thing.

There are three types of correlations—positive, negative, and spurious. A **positive correlation** involves two variables moving in a parallel

direction. In other words, you can find a positive correlation when variables increase or decrease together. Take the relationship between one's level of education and income. It has been observed that people with higher levels of education earn higher incomes.[6] This is a positive correlation because both variables trend in the same direction. A second type of relationship between variables is called a **negative correlation**, which occurs when the variables move in opposite directions. So, if you notice your grades slip as your internet surfing or TV watching increases, that is a negative correlation. The third type is a spurious correlation. Spurious means not genuine or authentic, so a **spurious correlation** occurs when two variables appear to be related, but actually have a different cause. So, if you're looking at statistical data and notice that ice cream sales and the drowning rate are both increasing, that doesn't mean that someone eating a hot fudge sundae is destined to drown in a swimming pool. Another factor is probably affecting these statistics. In this case, these increases are likely occurring in the hot summer months, when more people happen to be buying ice cream and going swimming. This proves that researchers should always be wary of spurious correlations.

Scientific Method: What Are the Six Steps of Social Research?

Doing sociological research follows many of the same procedures as any type of scientific research. After all, sociology is the scientific study of society. By requiring a logical and organized series of steps, sociologists ensure accurate results. In this section of the chapter, we will review the six steps of **social research**, or investigation conducted by social scientists. As with any type of research, you first need to decide what topic you want to find out more about.

1 **Decide on a Topic** The first stage of the research model involves determining what you want to study. In order to take this step, researchers bring to light a question they want answered. Sociologists select topics on the basis of importance, personal interest, or the availability of research.

2 **Review the Literature** After you select a topic, you'll need to perform a **literature review**, which is a study of relevant academic articles and information. This is essentially an organized effort to research your topic. Literature reviews let you know what other researchers think about a particular topic and what they have discovered through their research. For example, if you were still examining how playing an instrument affects one's grades, you might review scholarly articles written by sociologists who've examined the same idea. Viewing their methodology will help you improve upon their work and avoid making any of the same mistakes they made.

3 **Develop a Hypothesis** After you have completed the initial research of your topic, it is time to formulate a hypothesis. It's important not to confuse a hypothesis with a theory. A **theory** is a comprehensive and systematic explanation of events that lead to testable predictions. These testable predictions are the basis for what we call a hypothesis.[7] A **hypothesis** involves a suggestion about how variables relate. For example, my hypothesis that students who play a musical instrument will have high grades comes from the theory that students who earn good grades are more likely to play an instrument than students who earn bad grades, and that music is part of the reason they do better. My hypothesis is a way for me to test that theory by manipulating variables. In this case, the two variables are (1) playing an instrument and (2) the student's grades.

Concepts and Operationalizing Variables

So how are we supposed to measure these variables, anyway? You might notice that the two variables above are not very specific. What does it mean to *play* an instrument? Will playing once a week be enough? Do you have to be an exceptional musician, or can your music be mediocre? Also, what do *good* grades entail exactly? Is a B-minus a good grade? In order to create a testable hypothesis, we'll need to be a bit more specific. Right now, "playing a musical instrument" and getting a "good grade" are just **concepts**, or abstract ideas that are impossible to measure. Turning these abstract ideas into something measurable is called **operationalizing** the variables. If you operationalize "playing an instrument" into "hours spent playing the instrument," you now have a variable that's measurable in minutes. Likewise, we can change the relative idea of "a better grade" into a more measurable "grade of B-minus." Now that we have a hypothesis, we can move on to designing a research strategy.

4 **Collect Data** You have a hypothesis, so now what? Now you'll have to test that hypothesis to see whether data support or refute your idea. Collecting data means using a research design to help you. A **research design** refers to the process used to find information. Designs need to be both logical and orderly so that the research is reliable and valid. A logical, orderly design isn't the only thing that'll guarantee your research is up to snuff. For research to be **reliable**, or trustworthy, you must measure things the same way, every time. If you alter your measuring technique in any way, your results could easily change. **Validity** ensures that you're actually measuring the thing you set out to measure in the first place. In our example, you wouldn't want your professor to use your musical taste to determine what kind of grade you get in class. To collect data that are both reliable and valid, sociologists use a variety of strategies, which include conducting studies.

Comparative, Cross-Sectional, and Longitudinal Studies

Comparative studies use data from different sources in order to evaluate them against each other. International comparisons often use data from different countries and put them side by side. You should be aware, though, that comparative data across cultures might have methodological problems. For example, definitions of drug offences can differ greatly between countries (see page 37). What passes as taboo in one country might be perfectly permissible in another.

The majority of available data in sociology are the result of cross-sectional studies. Like a camera capturing a singular moment, **cross-sectional studies** look at an event at a single point in time. Researchers may use a variety of cross-sectional studies to try to track trends in society. However, these may not always include data gathered from the same people. To learn how specific people change over time with the changes in society, researchers conduct longitudinal studies.

Longitudinal studies include data from observations over time using a specific group of people called a **cohort**. These types of studies allow the researcher to provide measures of the same group over a period of time. The period of time can be extensive, and researchers frequently take multiple measures over a period of years. Although this longitudinal information can be expensive and time-consuming to gather, it is useful in illustrating trends and showing how segments of society change.

Survey

A **survey** is an investigation of the opinions or experience of a group of people. This is done by asking them questions. In sociological research, surveys are necessary to gauge valuable information. Institutions ranging

---

CONCEPTS are abstract ideas that are impossible to measure.

OPERATIONALIZING is turning abstract ideas into something measurable.

RESEARCH DESIGN refers to the process used to find information.

RELIABLE means able to be trusted.

VALIDITY assures that you're actually measuring the thing you set out to measure in the first place.

COMPARATIVE STUDIES use data from different sources in order to evaluate them against each other.

CROSS-SECTIONAL STUDIES look at one event at a single point in time.

LONGITUDINAL STUDIES include data from observations over time using a cohort.

COHORT is a specific group of people used in a study.

SURVEY is an investigation of the opinions or experience of a group of people by asking them questions.

POPULATIONS are target groups from which researchers want to get information.

PARSIMONY is extreme unwillingness to use resources.

SAMPLE is a subset of the population.

---

from government agencies to marketing teams rely on survey responses to determine how the general public feels about their policies or their products. Surveys include interviews and questionnaires. Seeing as how it would be nearly impossible to survey every single individual within a specific population, researchers need to be more focused.

How to Conduct a Survey

Sociologists generally use the following seven steps to conduct a survey:

1. Clarify Your Purpose—What do I want to find out?

2. Define Your Population—Who do I want to study?

3. Choose a Sample—I can't study everyone so I have to choose a few people to represent the entire population.

4. Prepare Questions.

5. Decide How to Collect Data—Do I want to conduct face-to-face interviews or hand out surveys?

6. Collect the Data.

7. Record, Analyze, and Interpret the Data.

Populations

For starters, researchers need to determine the specific **populations**, or target groups, from which they wish to gain information. Perhaps you're interested in discovering what commuter students think about the parking situation on campus. Ideally you'd ask every student with a car on campus, but that would take a lot of time and money. Because researchers also have limits on their resources, they have to practise **parsimony**, or extreme unwillingness to use resources, so that they get the most for their effort.

Samples

To get the most bang for their buck, sociologists give surveys only to a **sample**, or subset, of the population selected for research. In order to

Country Music and Suicide

Back in 1992, researchers wanted to study the relationship between country music and its listeners. Researchers Steven Stack and Jim Gundlach found positive correlations between country music airplay and white male suicide rates in American metropolitan areas.[8] According to their research, common themes in country music created a subculture that essentially led men to suicide. These themes include problems with personal relationships, including divorce and infidelity, alcohol consumption, and general hardships like work problems or death. Sara Evans's *Cheatin'*, Toby Keith's *Get Drunk and Be Somebody*, and Johnny Paycheck's *Take This Job and Shove It* are all songs that fit these themes.

The researchers took data from 49 different metropolitan areas in the United States. To prevent a spurious conclusion, they used poverty, divorce, gun availability, and region of the country as control variables. For example, because divorce has a strong influence on the suicide rate, the researchers had to make sure that this variable didn't affect their results. In their analysis, they showed that the white male suicide rates positively correlated with the amount of radio airtime of country music.

The conclusion was that country music contributed to an ideology that supported suicide. Because people tend to listen to songs many times, the power of their thematic message is stronger than other media. These themes help create a subculture in which individuals perceive a world full of sadness, drinking, and exploitation.

Following this research, a statistical and methodological debate raged. Sociologists Edward Maguire and Jeffrey Snipes tried to retest the data, but failed to duplicate Stack and Gundlach's 1992 results.[9] Maguire and Snipes claimed the original authors were mistaken because they did not take into account how other factors in their subjects' lives might have contributed to their actions. Stack and Gundlach stuck by their research. In a series of articles, each designed to respond to the other, these two camps argued over which side's research was valid.

Can you see problems with the research, particularly as associated with spuriousness and correlation? Is it possible that there is another relationship being depicted? For example, since white men are more likely to listen to country music than other ethnic groups are, perhaps more country music is aired in metropolitan areas with higher concentrations of white men.[10]

>>> **ACTIVITY** Pick three songs within a particular genre (i.e., hip-hop, rock, pop) and examine their lyrics. Do these songs express anything about the culture in which we live? If so, how do you think this affects people who listen to this type of music? Is there a spurious correlation?

∧∧∧ **Could country music have led** this man **to the edge?**

GENERALIZATION is the extent that what is learned from a sample can be applied to the population from which the sample is taken.

RANDOM SAMPLE is a group of subjects arbitrarily chosen from a defined population.

OVERSAMPLING is the process of taking a bigger sample if the group you wish to study makes up a small percentage of the whole population.

produce a reliable result, samples should represent an accurate picture of the population.

When sociologists study a part of the population, the percentages in the sample should reflect the percentages of women, racial minorities, and other groups that exist in the population. In short, the sample needs to look like the population so we can generalize the findings. **Generalization** is the extent that what is learned from a sample can be applied to the population from which the sample is taken. Would it be fair to say that people who join cults are representative of all Canadians with religious beliefs? Certainly not. If you were studying one particular cult, you would select a sample of members of that cult and generalize your findings to all members of that cult, but not to members of every religion. To do that, you would need a sample of members from different religious groups.

A **random sample** is a group of subjects arbitrarily chosen from a defined population. This type of sample increases the chances that the sample represents the population. Randomness means that everyone in the population has an equal chance of selection for the sample. Few true random samples exist, especially if the entire country is the target population. However, random samples are the best method for a social scientist to know that his or her sample looks like the population.

Many national surveys, therefore, rely on random samples and can, with as few as 1000 people, make predictions about what Canadians think about specific issues. Although sample size can affect the power of the predictions, after a certain point the advantage of a bigger sample becomes almost irrelevant. Thus, samples are usually as small as possible. However, if you want to use the survey for a variety of purposes, it might be a smart practice to make the sample bigger. This is called **oversampling**. You need to oversample if the group you wish to study makes up a small percentage of the whole population. Let's say exit pollers conducting a random survey of people who voted in the October 2008 federal election wanted to know how many voters aged 65 and older supported the Conservatives. Since seniors made up approximately 13.7 percent of the Canadian population at the time, a random

Serious Pot Problems: North America versus Europe

In 2010, the latest figures placed North America as the No. 1 region in the world for cannabis herb seizures, at 48 percent of all seizures, with western and central Europe at only 2 percent.[11]

Based on just that information, you might assume that North America (including Canada) has the most serious marijuana problem in the world. But figures don't always tell the whole story: they can reflect different attitudes and different government policies.[12]

Some countries in Europe have very different drug policies than those in North America. The Dutch, for example, believe the best course of action with drugs is to implement a harm reduction approach, which minimizes risks typically associated with drug use, instead of total drug suppression.[13] In the Netherlands, a harm reduction approach includes increased drug treatment and needle exchange programs. Drug use is a public health problem, not a criminal one. Since Dutch authorities believe "soft" drugs, like cannabis, are ultimately harmless and simply associated with

youthful indiscretion, marijuana is legalized in small amounts. Moreover, the predominant thinking regarding these soft drug users is that they are less likely to get mixed up with hard drugs, like cocaine or heroin. Therefore, the focus is less on incarceration and more on treatment and prevention.[14]

In North America, the issue of differing national policies raised its head when Canadian marijuana policy reform advocate Marc Emery ended up in an international tangle. For years Emery openly ran a business selling pot seeds out of Canada, until a Vancouver police raid was made at the request of the U.S. Drug Enforcement Agency.[15] Emery was extradited to the United States and sentenced to five years in prison for shipping marijuana seeds across the border. The U.S. Attorney's office estimated that 75 percent of the seeds that Emery's company had sold over 10 years ended up in the United States.[16] Ontario lawyer Karen Selick suggested that the U.S. had targeted Emery and two of his employees because they had taken a "principled, public stand against the U.S. government's war on drugs."[17]

In Canada, marijuana was banned in 1923, but control laws have been described

as "spottily enforced, with the west coast (British Columbia) being well known for its high quality cannabis and low levels of enforcement."[18] Many Canadian companies have openly sold pot seeds, using a legal loophole within the country's Controlled Drugs and Substances Act that calls "non-viable" seeds legal but fails to address the issue of "viable" seeds. One online news report noted that a seed is viable if it produces a cannabis plant containing the active ingredient THC and that viable marijuana seeds are only implied as illegal.[19]

Nevertheless, Canada and the United States have arrested hundreds of thousands of people for possession and use of marijuana over the years. In 2009, 97 666 drug offences were recorded in Canada alone, including 48 981 involving the possession of marijuana, and 16 335 for the trafficking, production, or distribution of pot.[20] The kind of possession arrests made in North America may not have been made in the Netherlands, which reflects a methodological problem. The number of drug offences generally reflects the ideologies that countries have about drug policy enforcement and prevention.

48%

North America

PERCENTAGE OF WORLD MARIJUANA SEIZURES

2%

Europe

Source: Adapted from the *World Drug Report 2010* (pp. 8–9) and the associated document on "Global and Regional Seizure Totals" for cannabis herb by 2008 (p. 1), United Nations Office on Drugs and Crime, both accessed through www.unodc.org/unodc/en/data-and-analysis/WDR-2010.html on September 24, 2010.

sample of 1000 people would include roughly 137 seniors. This sample size is too small to be meaningful; therefore, a larger one is required to increase the odds that it accurately represents the over-65 population.[21]

Selection Effects and Samples of Convenience

Even though random samples are preferred, other types of samples are often used. Researchers may use a **sample of convenience**, which is a nonrandom sample available to the researcher. These are simply people we can find to study. These samples often suffer from **selection effects**;

that is, the likelihood that a nonrepresentative sample may lead to inaccurate results.

Imagine that you have been doing field research on a new religious movement, or cult. Your questioning reveals that 56 percent of them—24 of the 43 people who belong to this cult—were recruited while they were doing summer work in a small beach town. However, your findings would not imply that more than half of all people participating in cults around the world were recruited in beach towns. Why? Because what you have is a sample of convenience. Of course, nonrandom samples can be quite valuable because they help illustrate a problem, illuminate issues, and test theories, but one cannot generalize the findings from them to the larger population. Therefore, all people who join cults probably are not mirror images of the members in your study.

Experiments

Like any good scientist, a sociologist uses experiments to test ideas. In an experiment, researchers hope to control variables in order to test

THINK SOCIOLOGICALLY

Milgram Obedience Study

Social psychologist Stanley Milgram created a series of experiments to test a subject's ability to reject the orders of a perceived superior. In the experiment, two subjects enter a room where a man in a lab coat meets them. This individual, called "the experimenter," takes on the role of the authority figure. The subjects are told they are going to be part of a study to test the effects of punishment on learning. One of the subjects role-plays as the "teacher," while the other—who is secretly one of Milgram's assistants—is the "learner."

The subjects are then led into a room where the "learner" is strapped into a chair with electrodes attached to him. The experimenter assures both subjects that while pain will result, no permanent damage will occur.

The teacher is placed in front of an electroshock machine and separated from the learner, who can be heard but not seen. If the learner fails to recall a series of paired words, the teacher is supposed to administer an electric shock. With each error, the teacher is instructed to increase the voltage. In reality, the learner is only acting and never receives a shock, unbeknownst to the teacher.

Throughout the experiment, some subjects would pause when they heard learners cry "ouch" or "I want

to quit." The scripted responses also included groans, screams, and even silence. When teachers questioned whether they should continue to inflict pain on the learner, they were told, "Please go on" and/or "You must go on."

Milgram found that 65 percent of the teachers administered up to 450 volts, even when there was no reply and despite the fact that the dial on the machine for this voltage read "danger."

Milgram pointed out that subjects would shock others to unconsciousness and even death on the command of a stranger who represented authority. Thus, Milgram suggested that when faced with an authority figure, most people follow orders even if those orders go against their better judgment.[22]

If you were the teacher in Milgram's research, **what action would you have taken based on the learner's response?**

causes and effects. Sociological experiments do the same thing, but some may test people's interactions or other social causes of human behaviour. Read the "Think Sociologically" feature to learn about a series of experiments Stanley Milgram conducted in the 1960s.

Hawthorne Effect

The seminal Milgram experiment documented what happens when a subject is unaware that he is being experimented on. But what about people who are cognizant of the experiment? In the 1930s an electric company hired researchers to test worker productivity in its Hawthorne Works factory outside Chicago. After pre-testing worker performance, researchers made the lighting brighter. They quickly noticed that brighter lights seemed to make people work harder. However, when they later turned down the lights, productivity increased once again. In fact, every step the researchers took helped boost the workers' productivity.

Why did every change, even ones that seemed likely to hinder productivity, have the same effect? Researchers believed it was because the subjects knew they were being studied. Thus, the **Hawthorne effect** was coined for occurrences in which people behave differently because they know they are being studied.[23] Unlike the experiment at the Hawthorne factory, Milgram's experiment used subjects who did not know they were being studied. When conducting experiments and studies, sociologists must make sure that the Hawthorne effect does not influence their findings. Remember that in the opening vignette, sociologist Eileen Barker observed that her presence among the Moonies did affect some of them. One member left the movement, while others began to question the leadership.

FIELD RESEARCH

It would be difficult to study a society without actually mingling with the people you're observing. Therefore, researchers need to venture out and conduct studies in a natural setting. This **field research** takes the sociologist out into the streets, or homes, or classrooms. There are three common methods of field research—participant observation, case studies, and ethnography

Participant Observation

In the excerpt from Eileen Barker's description of studying the Unification Church (page 31) she clearly was not pretending to be a Moonie herself, but if she had done so she would have been making use of covert **participant observation**.

Participant observation is a type of field research in which the researcher poses as a person who is normally in the environment. Research that deliberately misleads the public or other study participants is extremely controversial.[24] However, it does give researchers access to information that would otherwise be unavailable and decreases the chances of the Hawthorne effect because subjects do not know they are being studied.

Case Studies

Unlike participant observations, **case studies** investigate one person or event in detail. Such a study is able to illuminate a complex issue through the lens of an individual case. Isabelle, a feral child who had spent most of her six years in a dark room with minimal human contact, is an example of a case study.[25] This case study not only includes a history of both emotional and physical neglect, but also provides a compelling tale about experts who worked to develop the child's potential.

HAWTHORNE EFFECT occurs when people behave differently because they know they are being studied.

FIELD RESEARCH is research conducted in a natural setting.

PARTICIPANT OBSERVATION is a type of field research in which the researcher poses as a person who is normally in the environment.

CASE STUDIES are investigations of one person or event in detail.

ETHNOGRAPHY is a research method that aims to understand the social perspective and cultural values of a particular group by participating in or getting to know their activities in detail.

SECONDARY DATA are data that others have already collected and published.

SECONDARY DATA ANALYSIS is the process of using and analyzing data that others have collected.

When Isabelle was discovered, she could communicate using only grunts and invented gestures. Remarkably, Isabelle was able to improve her social skills and fully integrate into mainstream society. Some critics believe case studies are subjective because it's tricky to generalize the findings of an individual case to fit a larger group.[26] For example, the findings in Isabelle's case don't fit *all* feral children because some might not be able to fully develop.

Ethnography

Ethnography is a research method that aims to understand the social perspective and cultural values of a particular group by participating in or getting to know their activities in detail.

In one well-known ethnographic line of study from the 1950s and 1960s, Morris Freilich focused on Mohawk men who were drawn to dangerous jobs—as so-called skywalkers—on highrise construction sites in New York, away from their traditional homes. His research included field work in Kahnawake, the Mohawk reserve south of Montreal, and in Brooklyn, New York.[27] A bar turned out to be a good place for such field work. Freilich met with hostility when he took out his notebook there, so carried a book in his pocket and would disappear to the washroom every now and then to make notes.[28]

Mohawks are members of the Iroquois peoples. In the end, Freilich found that working in dangerous steel construction jobs was a way for Mohawk men to experience their traditional role as brave warriors in a modern world that no longer required them to go to war against non-Iroquois peoples.[29]

Secondary Data Analysis

Sociologists don't always have to collect new data. Instead, sociologists sometimes need to access **secondary data**, or data that others have already collected and published. The process of using and analyzing data others have collected is known as **secondary data analysis**. A variety of data sources exist for sociologists to use. Not surprisingly, the World Wide Web contains many of these sources. Census data, crime statistics, journal entries, and transcripts of speeches are just a few of the examples of secondary data found on the Web.

5 **Analyze Results** The fifth step of the scientific method, analyzing results, involves the dreaded "S-word." No, not *that* word. The term I'm thinking of is *statistical* analysis. Because sociological research can delve into very complex statistics, it's important that you learn a few basics that will help you confidently confront any statistics you encounter now or in the future.

> **CENTRAL TENDENCY** is the middle of the distribution of a variable.
>
> **MEAN** is an average.
>
> **MEDIAN** refers to the midpoint in a distribution of numbers.
>
> **MODE** refers to the most common value in a distribution.

MEASURES OF CENTRAL TENDENCY

You know how news outlets report on the national price of a litre of gasoline? Sometimes, the price you hear on the radio ends up being lower—or higher—than the one at the pump. This is because the reporters were only finding a measure of **central tendency**. To put it more simply, researchers look at the dis-

John's Test Scores

Test 1: 90
Test 2: 70
Test 3: 80
Test 4: 20
Test 5: 80

tribution of a variable and find the middle. There are three measures of central tendency—mean, median, and mode. Imagine that a student received the test scores listed above. How would you calculate the mean, median, and mode?

Mean

A **mean** is an average. You add up all the scores and then divide by the number of scores. John's mean score is 68. Does this average accurately measure his performance? He failed one exam, but received a C or better on all other tests. It doesn't seem fair that one bad grade leaves John with a D average for the class. That's the problem with calculating mean scores. Extremely high or low scores can have dramatic impact on statistical means.

$$90 + 70 + 80 + 20 + 80 = 340$$
$$340 \div 5 = 68$$
$$\text{Mean} = 68$$

Median

When you're cruising down the highway—after blowing your savings on that full tank of gas—you might notice the northbound lanes are separated from southbound ones by a median. In statistical analysis, the **median** refers to the midpoint in a distribution of numbers. If you line up the numbers from lowest to highest, the median is the one in the middle. The median does not vary when you have extremely high or extremely low values in the distribution. John's median score is 80.

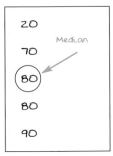

Mode

The **mode** refers to the most common value in a distribution. Extremely high or low scores do not impact this measure either. It's possible to have more than one mode in a distribution. In our simple example, 80 is the mode because it occurs twice. You will notice that the modal score in this example is the same as the median. Both give John a final grade of an A. Which measure of central tendency best shows John's performance?

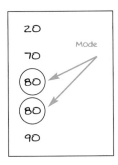

Most colleges have a policy of using averages to calculate grades. However, when I review grades at the end of the semester, I frequently take all three measures of central tendency into account. In most cases, the mean is close to the median and the mode. However, an extreme score can alter the mean score dramatically, as in John's case. If you have a low score on an exam, consider asking your professor to consider other measures of central tendency to calculate your performance. It might just raise your grade!

EVALUATING DATA

Evaluating and interpreting data are important parts of conducting research. What's the use of gathering data if you don't know what to do with them? It's vital to be able to make sense of the data you collect. The tables and graphs you will encounter during the research process may

Research Methods: How Do They Measure Up?

Method	Example	Pros	Cons
Survey	Interview	• Sampling process lets researcher apply data from a few subjects to an entire population	• Time-consuming • Difficult to find participants
Experiments	Manipulation of variables to study human behaviour	• Gives researcher specific quantitative data	• Ethical concerns put restrictions on the way human subjects can be used
Field Research	Case study	• Can study behaviour in a natural environment • Can be inexpensive	• Time-consuming • Ethical concerns put restrictions on the way human subjects can be used
Secondary Data Analysis	Another sociologist's analysis of population data	• Inexpensive • Reduces time spent to collect data	• Data not collected for the purpose in which you are using it • Data could be biased by the collector

seem daunting at first. But it's really not as complicated as you might think, as long as you know what steps to take.

HOW TO READ A TABLE

The table below provides regional HIV/AIDS statistics reported in 2009. What do the data in the table tell you?

If you struggled to make sense of the table, don't worry. You're not alone. Fortunately, the four simple steps that follow will help make reading this and other tables second nature to you.

1. Carefully read the title of the table. Ask yourself: What do I expect the table to show me?

2. Notice the structure of the table. This one is made up of columns and rows. The columns represent a specific category, such as People living with HIV and the rows list data from each geographic region.

3. This table has an important subheading. In italics, you see the phrase, *"Figures shown in millions."* In a table with large number values, it is quite common to shorten the number by placing it in a category. This means that 22.5 million adults and children are living with HIV in sub-Saharan Africa.[30]

4. Read any text and notes provided below the table.

- The asterisk next to "Oceania" in the table indicates that the word will be defined below.
- The note provides information about the data in the table. In this table, the data provided, from December 2009, are the most up-to-date data available at the time the table was created.
- The source note indicates where the original data are located.

Now review the table again. Do the data make more sense this time?

6 **Share and Publish Results** Doing research is important; however, if we don't share what we learn with others, our work is meaningless. Sharing allows others to read and use your findings in their own research, which ultimately expands the base of knowledge.

Publishing requires an appropriate writing style. There are many accepted academic and publication styles, including ASA, APA, and MLA. Check out these links: for ASA, see www.asanet.org/Quick StyleGuide.pdf; for APA, see www.apastyle.org/learn/index.aspx; and for basics on MLA, see the Canadian sources http://library.mcmaster.ca/guides/mla.pdf, www.mcgill.ca/files/library/mla.pdf, or http://library.concordia.ca/help/howto/mla.php.

Most sociology research follows the American Sociological Association style. In the ASA style guide, you'll find standards for using language and directions on how to cite sources appropriately. If you need a quick style guide, be sure to visit their website at www.asanet.org.

Region	People Living with HIV	New HIV Infections	AIDS-Related Deaths
Regional HIV/AIDS Statistics in 2009 *(Figures shown in millions)*			
Sub-Saharan Africa	22.5	1.8	1.3
Middle East and North Africa	0.46	0.075	0.024
South and Southeast Asia	4.1	0.27	0.26
East Asia	0.77	0.082	0.036
Oceania*	0.057	0.004	0.001
Central and South America	1.4	0.092	0.058
Caribbean	0.24	0.0017	0.012
Eastern Europe and Central Asia	1.4	0.13	0.076
Western and Central Europe	0.82	0.031	0.009
North America	1.5	0.07	0.026
TOTAL	33.3	2.6	1.8

* Oceania refers to the islands and archipelagos of the central and south Pacific, including Australia, Malay Archipelago, Melanesia, Micronesia, New Zealand, and Polynesia.

Note: December 2009 was the most recent update.

Source: Data based on Health Statistics under Health from OECD.Stat Extracts. Accessed at http://stats.oecd.org.

ETHICS is a system of values or principles that guide one's behaviour.

QUANTITATIVE DATA refer to data based on numbers.

QUALITATIVE DATA include words, pictures, photos, or any other type of information that comes to the researcher in a non-numeric form.

CONTENT ANALYSIS is a type of research in which the sociologist looks for common words or themes in newspapers, books, or structured interviews.

ETHICAL CONCERNS

Have you ever been asked to do something that violated your personal beliefs or values? Of course you have. Sociologists struggle with this issue all the time. Sometimes, a sociologist's findings have the potential to hurt or embarrass the human subjects of a particular study. Deciding how to protect human subjects is a major concern for sociological researchers.

Ethics is a system of values or principles that guide one's behaviour. For some, it means following the law, and for others, trusting one's gut. In Canada, the three big federal research agencies—the Canadian Institutes of Health Research, the Natural Sciences and Engineering Research Council, and the Social Sciences and Humanities Research Council—have created a document known as the *Tri-Council Policy Statement: Ethical Conduct for Research Involving Humans*, or TCPS.[31] The TCPS identifies three core principles in research ethics[32]:

1 **Respect for Persons** recognizes the intrinsic value of human beings and the respect and consideration they are due.

2 **Concern for Welfare** means that researchers should aim to protect the welfare of participants, and in some circumstances to promote that welfare. To do so, researchers must ensure that participants are not exposed to unnecessary risks.

3 **Justice** refers to the obligation to treat people fairly and equitably.

The Canadian Sociological Association's (CSA) multi-point Code of Ethics[33] reaches out into the following areas: (1) organizing and initiating research; (2) protecting people in the research environment; (3) informed consent—"As far as possible, research should be based on the freely given informed consent of those studied"; (4) covert research and deception—"Deception should not be used where another methodology would accomplish the research objectives";

(5) dissemination of findings—"Researchers have an obligation to disseminate results openly except those likely to endanger research participants or to violate their anonymity or confidentiality"; (6) relations with colleagues and the discipline; (7) faculty appointments; (8) relations with students; (9) harassment and exploitative relations; and (10) relations with institutions.

RESEARCH ETHICS IN OPERATION

Consider for a moment the scope of the above-mentioned principles and guidelines for ethical behaviour. Do you think research practices can easily be labelled as either ethical or unethical? Do you think that Eileen Barker was using unethical practices in her Unification Church study? Or do you think she succeeded in respecting her subjects' dignity and worth?

The issues raised by sociological field investigations helped create the need for codes of research ethics in the first place, and prompted federal governments to play a role in research ethics. Earlier, I mentioned the *Tri-Council Policy Statement: Ethical Conduct for Research Involving Humans* (TCPS); these days in Canada, researchers or institutions that receive funding from any of the main federal research funding agencies are obliged to use the TCPS as a condition of their funding.[34]

Nonetheless, sociologists do not all agree about the ways in which studies should be conducted. Some researchers who study deviant behaviours, for example, suggest that deception is essential in collecting accurate information. The issue of how to use deception is a critical question in field research. If you fully disclose what you are doing, how can you be sure the Hawthorne effect is not affecting your results? If you deceive, how can you protect the subjects' dignity and worth? That's why a debate on ethics rages on within the sociological research community today.

So the question is, how can you avoid ethical dilemmas? One way is to get your subject's consent. Hand out an informed consent form before the study begins. Informed consent means that the research subject understands the general purpose of the study and its main features. If the researcher is using deception, subjects deserve to know when they will find out the truth. Subjects must know that they can cease their participation at any time without risk to themselves.

>>> Despite the differences in these people's ethnic backgrounds, **sociologists should strive to value each of them equally.**

think sociologically: HOW DO SOCIOLOGISTS USE RESEARCH METHODS?

No single research method applies only to functionalism, conflict theory, symbolic interactionism, or feminist theory. But these theoretical frameworks do lend themselves to using types of data in different ways. The basis for these differences is often quantitative and qualitative data.

Quantitative and Qualitative Methods

If you were asked to rank your motivation on a scale of 1–5, with 5 being highly motivated, your response would be an example of quantitative data. Simply put, the term **quantitative data** refers to data based on numbers. Another example includes the number of students enrolled at Canadian colleges and universities. Quantitative data can be converted from people's responses to survey questions. For example, you might ask whether students prefer multiple-choice or short-answer tests. You can then calculate a proportion—say, 87 percent of students prefer multiple-choice tests.

Qualitative data may include words, pictures, photos, or any other type of information that comes to the researcher in a non-numerical form. A researcher who poses as a market researcher and interviews his subjects in their homes would be collecting qualitative data. One common type of qualitative data is a **content analysis**—a type of research in which the sociologist looks for common words or themes in newspapers, books, or structured interviews.

Both quantitative and qualitative data require evaluation. The way in which the evaluation is measured is different, but both allow sociologists to better understand an issue.

The choice to use either qualitative or quantitative data pertains to all four theoretical perspectives, but there are some general trends that appear.

Functionalist and conflict theorists tend to address more structural issues, and so they often use quantitative measurements. Conversely, symbolic interactionists might prefer qualitative data because they deal with the words and meanings attached to events. Feminist theorists may use both approaches. Whichever way you slice it, there is no hard and fast rule that connects a particular theoretical paradigm to a single research method. Both qualitative and quantitative data can be appropriate.

Think about the research methods we discussed earlier in the chapter. How would you classify those methods? Are they quantitative or qualitative?

Methods of
Qualitative Analysis

Participant
Observation

Case Studies

Ethnographies

METHODS OF QUANTITATIVE ANALYSIS

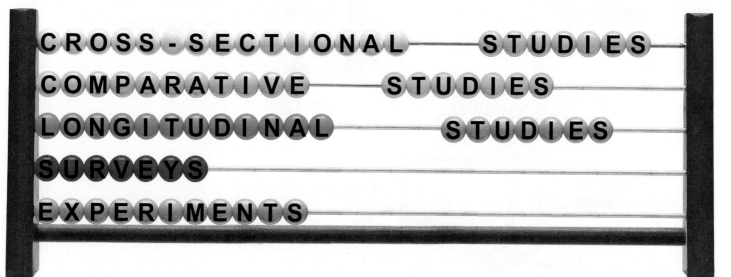

CROSS-SECTIONAL STUDIES
COMPARATIVE STUDIES
LONGITUDINAL STUDIES
SURVEYS
EXPERIMENTS

> **TRIANGULATION** is the process of using multiple approaches to study a phenomenon.
>
> **NEEDS ASSESSMENT** is an analysis that studies the needs of a specific group and presents the results in a written statement.

Triangulation

Triangulation is the process of using multiple approaches to study a phenomenon. Just as a centrist politician triangulates by considering issues from both sides of the political spectrum, sociologists often use triangulation to include aspects of both qualitative and quantitative analysis. For example, if you want to study the influence of hip-hop music on white, teenage, suburban culture, you might look at the quantitative data of hip-hop CD sales among white teens. Afterward, you'd conduct in-depth qualitative interviews with the consumers who buy hip-hop to gauge how the music influences their lives. When you follow this process, you're triangulating the issue, or studying it from multiple points of view. Triangulation allows you to better explain a social event, because you use two or more methods to study it.[35]

If you relied on only one method, you might draw an inappropriate conclusion about a social issue because all the facts are not available.

Triangulation helps researchers use **the strengths of one approach to compensate for the weaknesses in another.**

Research Methods and the Four Paradigms

Although our theoretical paradigm does not dictate the research method we use, it does affect how we interpret data. Conflict theorists and functionalists can look at the same data and come to different conclusions. Imagine that a conflict theorist and a functionalist studied data showing the rise of income inequality in a community. In other words, the gap between the "haves" and the "have-nots" in the community is widening. How might the two sociologists interpret the data? Remember, both functionalists and conflict theorists have a macro orientation, so they study how a certain issue affects the whole society and not individual people. However, functionalists examine how a certain issue functions in a society, whereas conflict theorists study how the unequal distribution of goods affects society.

Functionalists studying the data might suggest that income inequality serves the society well, as more rich people are able to start businesses and invest in long-term projects that will one day make society better for everyone. These businesses might one day be able to employ the poor members of the community and help them rise above their situation. Functionalists would not view the income inequality as a negative phenomenon. Conflict theorists, meanwhile, might suggest that the same numbers show that the rich exploit the poor and that this exploitation is only getting worse. You can see how two researchers look at the same data and come to different conclusions.

Because symbolic interactionists have a micro orientation, they might focus more on how the income inequality affected people at an individual level. These researchers might study wealthy individuals' perceptions of the poor and low-income individuals' perceptions of the rich. They might examine how being poor affects an individual's lifestyle—for example, how the lack of money affects the kind of clothes that a person wears or the place he or she lives. Like functionalists and conflict theorists, feminist theorists would also look at quantitative data on inequality, but they would focus on the inequality of women relative to men. They might also adopt a micro orientation that would examine how women in particular experience poverty. Here, too, you can see the same set of data can be interpreted differently depending on the theoretical lens through which the data are viewed.

Using Triangulation

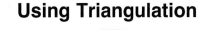

Quantitative Data

Qualitative Data

Triangulation

<<< **Here's how someone might use the process of triangulation to study an issue—a particular cult, for example.**

discover sociology in action:
HOW IS RESEARCH INVOLVED IN SOCIAL POLICY AND COMMUNITY LEARNING?

The Canadian Sociological Association's Code of Ethics calls upon sociologists to "enter into dialogue with the communities we research."[36] Working on social policies and participating in community learning projects are just two of the ways sociologists can better the community.

Social Policy and Statistics

Social policies arise because people recognize a problem and take action to deal with it. Often the first step is to get more information about the problem, which involves analyzing statistics. When consuming statistical evidence, it's important that you:

- **Beware the Headline.** Sensationalism can lead to a newspaper headline like MURDER RATE WORST IN DECADES even when the actual rate is falling. The word "rate" is shorter than "numbers" and so might be easier to use in a headline, but it doesn't mean the same thing.

- **Check Term Definitions.** Each researcher makes decisions about how to measure certain constructs. Beware of any study using value-laden terms such as "conservative" or "liberal" without properly defining them. What you consider "liberal" might not be interpreted the same way by your neighbour or a community in another province.

- **Find Out Who Funded the Study.** Groups that fund research often have an interest in the outcome. You should always consider the possibility that stakeholders want to use research to support their positions.

ACTIVITIES

1. Check out the online resources at your school's library. Which search engines does your school suggest are best for sociological research? Make a list. Then write a paragraph evaluating each one.
2. Conduct a class survey. Talk with your professor and create a 10-question survey to give to your classmates about something that interests you.
3. Have a class discussion about whether or not the end justifies the means in social research. Can a researcher truly hope to find out about a subculture without deception?

Remember, objectivity is the foundation of sociological research. Be on the lookout for groups or individuals with ulterior motives.

- **Look for Spuriousness and Selection Effects.** When reading research, ask yourself: Could something else be causing this result? Has the researcher really looked at every possible angle?

- **Look for Agendas.** Agendas are often political in nature. Many times politicians quote statistics, but that doesn't mean they're true. Regardless of party affiliation, many politicians choose to manipulate statistics to make their claims appear stronger than they actually are.[37]

Community Learning—Needs Assessments

As you consider how to assist your local communities, one research method might be exceptionally valuable: a needs assessment. A **needs assessment** is an analysis that studies the needs of a specific group and presents the results in a written statement. There are three key questions to ask when you're doing a needs assessment:

1. What information is needed?
2. What is the background of this situation?
3. How will we collect this information?

Your methodological training can help you help others in your community. But don't forget, statistics are everywhere, and you need to understand them in order to evaluate research accurately.

From Classroom to Community } Volunteering at the Rec Centre

> "I can't believe the building has changed so much within a year!"

Afroditi, one of my first-year sociology students, was commenting at the grand reopening of a local recreation centre that provided after-school and weekend activities for youth with a Greek background. As a volunteer at the centre last year, Afroditi noticed that many of the centre's rooms were empty and unused. She knew that if the rooms were put to use, the kids' attendance would skyrocket. Since she didn't know why the rooms were unused or even how the centre should use them, Afroditi decided to conduct a needs assessment.

> "I met with the directors of the centre and learned that they didn't have the funds necessary to renovate the empty rooms," she said. "But the directors agreed that giving the kids more options at the centre might beef up their interest."

After meeting with the board, Afroditi spoke to staff members to find out how they proposed to use the empty rooms. She met with potential investors and found several interested parties. A quick examination of the public records found that 40 percent of the city's population was within the recreation centre's target age group. Armed with this information, Afroditi met with the board of directors again. This time she proposed her own ideas for how to renovate the space and how the centre could fund the renovations. Afroditi worked alongside the board to create two computer rooms and a game room. Like many sociologists, Afroditi identified a need, analyzed data, and found a way to meet that need in the end.

WHAT ARE RESEARCH METHODS?   32

the scientific procedures that sociologists use to conduct research and develop knowledge about a particular topic

HOW DO SOCIOLOGISTS USE RESEARCH METHODS?   43

through analysis of quantitative data using cross-sectional studies, comparative studies, longitudinal studies, surveys, and experiments; through analysis of qualitative data using participant observation, case studies, and ethnographies

HOW IS RESEARCH INVOLVED IN SOCIAL POLICY AND COMMUNITY LEARNING?   45

through analysis of statistics and by conducting needs assessments

get the topic: WHAT ARE RESEARCH METHODS?

Key Terms

research methods are the scientific procedures that sociologists use to conduct research and develop knowledge about a particular topic.   32

objectivity is the ability to conduct research without allowing personal biases or prejudices to influence you.   33

independent variables are variables that are deliberately manipulated in an experiment.   33

dependent variables are the response to the manipulated variable.   33

control variables are variables that are kept constant to accurately test the impact of an independent variable.   34

causal relationship is a relationship in which one condition leads to a certain consequence.   34

causation is the relationship between cause and effect.   34

correlation is an indication that one factor might be the cause for another factor.   34

positive correlation includes two variables that move in a parallel direction.   34

negative correlation occurs when variables move in opposite directions.   34

spurious correlation occurs when two variables appear to be related, but actually have a different cause.   34

social research is investigation conducted by social scientists.   34

literature review is a study of relevant academic articles and information.   34

theory is a comprehensive and systematic explanation of events that lead to testable predictions.   34

hypothesis involves a suggestion about how variables relate.   34

concepts are abstract ideas that are impossible to measure.   35

operationalizing is turning abstract ideas into something measurable.   35

research design refers to the process used to find information.   35

reliable means able to be trusted.   35

validity assures that you're actually measuring the thing you set out to measure in the first place.   35

comparative studies use data from different sources in order to evaluate them against each other.   35

cross-sectional studies look at one event at a single point in time.   35

longitudinal studies include data from observations over time using a cohort.   35

cohort is a specific group of people used in a study.   35

survey is an investigation of the opinions or experience of a group of people by asking them questions.   35

populations are target groups from which researchers want to get information.   35

parsimony is extreme unwillingness to use resources.   35

sample is a subset of the population.   35

generalization is the extent that what is learned from a sample can be applied to the population from which the sample is taken.   36

random sample is a group of subjects arbitrarily chosen from a defined population.   36

oversampling is the process of taking a bigger sample if the group you wish to study makes up a small percentage of the whole population.   36

sample of convenience is a nonrandom sample available to the researcher.   38

selection effects are the likelihood that a nonrepresentative sample may lead to inaccurate results.   38

Hawthorne effect occurs when people behave differently because they know they are being studied.   39

field research is research conducted in a natural setting.   39

participant observation is a type of field research in which the researcher poses as a person who is normally in the environment. *39*

case studies are investigations of one person or event in detail. *39*

ethnography is a research method that aims to understand the social perspective and cultural values of a particular group by participating in or getting to know their activities in detail. *39*

secondary data are data that others have already collected and published. *39*

secondary data analysis is the process of using and analyzing data that others have collected. *39*

central tendency is the middle of the distribution of a variable. *40*

mean is an average. *40*

median refers to the midpoint in a distribution of numbers. *40*

mode refers to the most common value in a distribution. *40*

ethics is a system of values or principles that guide one's behaviour. *42*

quantitative data refer to data based on numbers. *43*

qualitative data include words, pictures, photos, or any other type of information that

comes to the researcher in a non-numeric form. *43*

content analysis is a type of research in which the sociologist looks for common words or themes in newspapers, books, or structured interviews. *43*

triangulation is the process of using multiple approaches to study a phenomenon. *44*

needs assessment is an analysis that studies the needs of a specific group and presents the results in a written statement. *45*

Sample Test Questions

These multiple-choice questions are similar to those found in the test bank that accompanies this textbook.

1. "Children who participate in organized sports are less likely to suffer from obesity later in life." This statement is an example of a
   a. causal relationship.
   b. positive correlation.
   c. negative correlation.
   d. spurious correlation.

2. Which of the following research steps requires developing a logical research design?
   a. Collecting data
   b. Analyzing results
   c. Deciding on a topic
   d. Developing a hypothesis

3. What kind of study tells you what other researchers think about a particular topic?
   a. Literature review
   b. Longitudinal study
   c. Comparative study
   d. Cross-sectional study

4. Which of the following is not a core principle in Canadian research ethics?
   a. Justice
   b. Concern for welfare
   c. Timeliness
   d. Respect for persons

5. Which measure of central tendency is not affected by extreme high or low scores?
   a. Mean
   b. Mode
   c. Average
   d. Median

ESSAY

1. If you were doing a study on cults, what kinds of ethical issues should you consider?

2. What caveats should you keep in mind when reading statistical evidence?

3. Suppose you were conducting a study of how people of different racial and ethnic backgrounds felt about a particular political candidate. How might you collect quantitative data for this study? How might you collect qualitative data?

4. How did Morris Freilich approach his ethnographic study about Mohawk skywalkers?

5. Provide an example of a theory. Next, explain how you would use that theory to form a hypothesis.

WHERE TO START YOUR RESEARCH PAPER

For more information on all countries, including maps and profiles, go to www.cia.gov/cia/publications/factbook

To find United Nations data on children, go to www.unicef.org/statistics

To find more information on national population projections, go to www.statcan.gc.ca/pub/91-520-x/91-520-x2010001-eng.htm

For more information on international population projections, go to http://esa.un.org/UNPP

To find more information on inequality and poverty numbers around the world, go to www.worldbank.org/html/extdr/thematic.htm (and click on "Poverty")

To find religious data on the Web, go to www.adherents.com

For comparison data on education, go to www.statcan.gc.ca (and click on "Education, training and learning")

For more information on the world population report, data, and trends, go to www.un.org/esa/population

To find summary data on topics related to population growth, go to www.statcan.gc.ca (and click on "Population and demography")

To find information on health indicators and health-related data in Canada, visit the Canadian Institute for Health Information. Go to http://secure.cihi.ca/cihiweb/splash.html (and look for the "Health Indicators 2010" report and the "Canadian Population Health Initiative")

To find international information on health indicators, health care systems, and health-related data, go to www.who.int/gho/en

To find international data and analysis of poverty and wealth throughout the world, go to www.worldbank.org

Remember to check www.thethinkspot.ca **for additional information, downloadable flashcards, and other helpful resources.**

ANSWERS: 1. c; 2. a; 3. a; 4. c; 5. d

CULTURE

"A Canadian is . . .

always unsure of what it means to be Canadian. Maybe this is a strength. Maybe it is evidence of our tolerance and pluralism and of our enlightened postmodernism. Let a thousand identities bloom! Or maybe it just reveals our hollow core—a vacuity at the centre of our soul. Outside of Quebec, at least, we do not really know who we are or what we represent—other than that we have made ourselves remarkably comfortable in a cold land, and that we are good at hockey.

"A country with a clear identity and self-understanding would find it easier to develop a consensus around its *projet de société.* To the extent that Canadians do not have a clear identity, it hampers our larger social task of deciding what kind of society we want, and then getting on with building it.

"Still, we have created an extraordinary country, one that regularly ranks among the very best in terms of quality of life. People from around the world strive to come here to enjoy our economic opportunity, social tolerance, and political freedoms. Canadians today are among the most fortunate human beings to have ever lived. But sometimes it seems to have happened almost by accident—as if we have created this remarkable country more by luck and happenstance than by consensus and design."[1]

A Framework
for the Individual

In his book *What Is a Canadian? Forty-Three Thought-Provoking Responses,* Irvin Studin has collected 43 essays from various Canadians in which they give various insights into culture in Canada.

I deliberately wrote "culture in Canada" instead of "Canadian culture." Canada is often described as a multicultural society, but does this mean that there is no real "Canadian culture"? Keep this question in mind as you read through this chapter. See if your answer changes.

get the topic: WHAT IS CULTURE?

CULTURE is the language, beliefs, values, norms, behaviours, and material objects that are important enough to pass on to future generations of a society.

MATERIAL CULTURE consists of items within a culture that you can taste, touch, and feel.

The languages we speak and the behavioural codes we follow may seem perfectly natural to us, but there's nothing "natural" about culture: It is a framework built by and for human societies. We adopt our **culture** from those who came before us.

If you want to think like a sociologist, you'll need to understand not only the definition of culture but also how culture affects our lives. Because we see the world through the lens of our culture, it's easy for us to take our cultural orientation for granted, accepting it without much thought. In fact, we're often not even aware of the ways in which culture guides (or misguides) our thoughts and actions. The fact that you may speak only English, for example, is indicative of the culture in which you grew up. Had the French run the English out of Canada in the 1600s, we might all be

saying "Salut!" instead of "How's it goin', eh!" The tangible and intangible aspects of culture have a significant impact on your daily life.

Material Culture

One category of culture is **material culture**: items within a society that you can taste, touch, or feel. The jewellery, art, music, clothing, architecture, and crafts a society creates are all examples of material culture. Of course, the natural resources available to a culture can influence that culture's creations. For example, while seven countries (Canada, the United States, Japan, Russia, Germany, France, and the United Kingdom) use more than 37 percent of the world's electricity and oil, these countries combined hold only about 12 percent of the world's population. What do these statistics tell you about material culture? On a tour of these countries, you'd be likely to stumble across plenty of cars, air conditioners, heaters, blow dryers, and a host of other modern conveniences. If you took a trip to Nigeria, though, you'd notice that a lack of access to energy also influences material culture. Nigeria is the eighth largest country in the world by population, yet it ranks 69th in the world's electricity use and 45th in the world's use of oil. Few people own a car, and many live without regular access to electricity.[2]

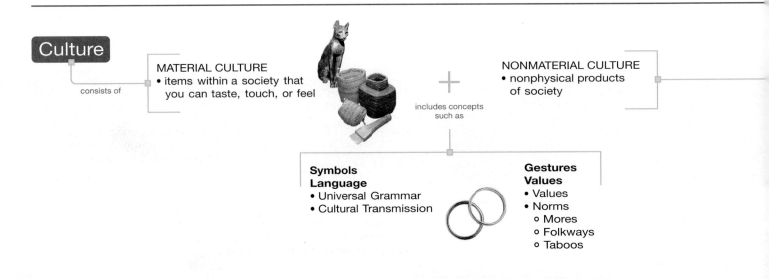

Culture

consists of

MATERIAL CULTURE
• items within a society that you can taste, touch, or feel

+

includes concepts such as

NONMATERIAL CULTURE
• nonphysical products of society

Symbols
Language
• Universal Grammar
• Cultural Transmission

Gestures
Values
• Values
• Norms
  o Mores
  o Folkways
  o Taboos

Nonmaterial Culture

Not all elements of culture are items you can touch, see, or buy at your local mall. **Nonmaterial culture** consists of the nonphysical products of society, including our symbols, values, rules, and sanctions.

> **NONMATERIAL CULTURE** consists of the nonphysical products of society, including our symbols, values, rules, and sanctions.
>
> **SYMBOLS** represent, suggest, or stand for something else.
>
> **LANGUAGE** is a system of speech and/or written symbols used to convey meaning and communicate.

SYMBOLS

What do you think of when you see the Canadian flag? To most of us, it's more than just a piece of cloth—it's a symbol. **Symbols** represent, suggest, or stand for something else. They can be words, gestures, or even objects, and they often represent abstract or complex concepts. For example, wedding rings represent a legal bond of marriage and an emotional bond of love between two people. Each culture determines the meaning of its own symbols and uses these symbols to share thoughts and concepts with others. If you know what Timbits and double-doubles are, then you recognize these symbols of Canadian culture.

In 2008, one of the recommendations of the Bouchard-Taylor Commission—which was set up to gather public input on the issue of "reasonable accommodation" in Quebec—was that the crucifix in the Quebec National Assembly should be removed because it was a symbol of one particular religious group, and the state should be neutral. However, Premier Jean Charest argued that the crucifix represents 350 years of history in Quebec, and he was not about to erase that important heritage.[3] Symbols are powerful things.

LANGUAGE

Language is a system of speech and/or written symbols used to convey meaning and communicate. Some languages exist only in

>>> **The crucifix in the Quebec National Assembly is a powerful symbol.**

the oral tradition, while other languages are expressed through both speech and writing systems, but all cultures use some form of language. The United Nations reports that currently there are more than 6000 different languages on the planet. Due to conquest, commerce, and failure to write down some languages, about half of these are in danger of extinction.[4]

Two main factors determine the number of speakers of a language: population size and colonial history. China and India are the world's largest countries by population, a fact that single-handedly explains the large percentage of people who speak Mandarin Chinese and Hindi. The English language is widely spoken throughout the world, but this has little to do with Great Britain's population size. If you've ever heard the phrase, "The sun never sets on the British Empire," you know that the British Empire once ruled territory on every continent. As Great Britain colonized countries around the world from the 1700s to the early 1900s, English was introduced to these places.

Universal Grammar

The famous linguist Noam Chomsky suggests that human beings' ability to use language comes from common roots.[5] All languages contain what Chomsky calls a "universal grammar." This term refers not to particular language rules but to the way in which languages are constructed. Chomsky theorizes that, among other things, commonalities in sentence construction and word pronunciation connect languages throughout the world. Furthermore, he says, universal grammar

The Study of Culture

may be influenced by
- Ethnocentrism
- Xenophobia
- Xenocentrism
- Cultural Relativism

and should focus on
- **Ideal Culture**—the values to which a culture aspires
- **Real Culture**—the way people actually behave

and might discuss

- **Subcultures**—subsets of the dominant culture that have distinct values, beliefs, and norms
- **Countercultures**—subcultures whose values and/or beliefs are in opposition to the dominant group

- Multiculturalism—concept that supports the inherent value of different cultures in a society
- Assimilation—process by which minority groups adapt to the dominant culture

CULTURAL TRANSMISSION is culture passing from one generation to the next through language.

SAPIR-WHORF HYPOTHESIS is a hypothesis, first advanced by Edward Sapir in 1929 and subsequently developed by Benjamin Whorf, that the structure of a language determines a native speaker's perception and categorization of experience.

GESTURES are symbols we make using our bodies, such as facial expressions, hand movements, eye contact, and other types of body language.

∨
∨ **Language influences how we perceive**
∨ **things,** which in turn influences our experience of the world. Our experiences help us develop language, **but our use of language also influences our experience.**[8]

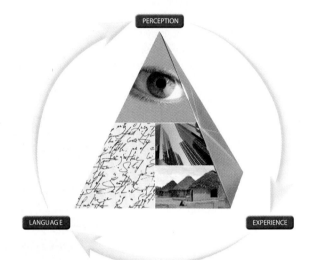

begins in children at about the same age, regardless of culture. Chomsky's observations suggest that humans have an innate need for language.

Research by Coppola and Newport supports much of Chomsky's theory. In their study of deaf subjects who were isolated and knew no official sign language, Coppola and Newport found that these people's "home sign language" (i.e., language that they developed themselves) follows a predictable grammatical style.[6] For instance, the subject of a sentence generally appears at the beginning of the statement. Such findings point to an innate logic in the construction of language and support Chomsky's theory of universal grammar.

Cultural Transmission

Language is a useful tool, but is it culturally crucial? There's plenty of evidence to support the idea that a system of communication is, in fact, a critical aspect of culture. Culture often passes from one generation to the next through language. We call this phenomenon **cultural transmission**. Thanks to cultural transmission, you can use information others have learned to improve your own life. Cultural transmission also helps spread technology: Scientific studies of electricity and the development of microwave technology and the microchip made today's cell phones and computers possible.

Language doesn't just advance our knowledge; it also brings us together by helping us create social consensus, or agreement. If you and I were to meet, we could use language to exchange ideas, debate, or decide on a course of action. Language is inherently social: It serves as a tool for sharing past memories, making plans, and building relationships.

The Sapir-Whorf Hypothesis

It's difficult to overstate the importance of language in our lives. Benjamin Whorf, a student of anthropologist Edward Sapir, suggested that language and thinking patterns are directly connected. Sapir and Whorf reached this conclusion, known as the **Sapir-Whorf hypothesis**, after studying many different languages and the people who spoke them.[7] The Sapir-Whorf hypothesis proposes two key points:

1. The differences in the structure of language parallel differences in the thinking of the people who speak languages.
2. The structure of a language strongly influences the speaker's worldview.

>>> The lyrics of rap music often prize material culture. **Why do you think this is?**

Have you ever considered how much language actually influences our thinking? Imagine that the English language had no words for right, left, front, or back. Would you still be able to understand these concepts? Probably not. An aboriginal group from Cape York Peninsula in Australia has no words for relative locations; instead, the group has words for absolute location, such as east, west, north, and south. Most members of the group do learn English, so they have an understanding of relative location. However, if they do not learn English at an early age, they struggle when asked to describe their location in relative terms.[9] Ongoing research into the Sapir-Whorf hypothesis suggests that because language influences thinking, it also influences culture.

GESTURE

Although language is a primary component of nonmaterial culture, it's not the only one. Another symbol system that differs by culture is gesture. **Gestures** are symbols we make using our bodies, such as facial expressions, hand movements, eye contact, and other types of body language. A gesture's symbolic meaning can vary widely between cultures: I once interpreted a Pakistani student's lack of eye contact as distrust or boredom until I realized that in her culture, making eye contact with someone, particularly a male teacher, is considered rude.

VALUES

Values, part of a society's nonmaterial culture, represent cultural standards by which we determine what is good, bad, right, or wrong. Sometimes, these values are expressed as proverbs or sayings that teach us how to live. Do you recognize the phrase "Life is like a box of chocolates—you never know what you're going to get"? This modern-day saying is popular today among those who embrace life's unpredictability. Cultures are capable of growth and change, so it's possible for a culture's values to change over time.

Value pairs help us define values, usually in terms of opposites. For every positive value, we have a negative one. We may also hold values that support or contradict our other values. **Value clusters** are two or more values that support each other. Let's say you value both equality and tolerance. These values form a value cluster because they are similar concepts that strengthen each other. When two or more values are at odds, however, a **value conflict** occurs. For example, equality and racism are conflicting values.

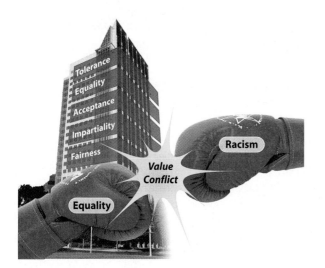

"The **differences in the structure of language parallel differences in the thinking of the speakers** of those languages."

Canadian Values

On November 1, 1990, the federal government announced the creation of the *Citizens' Forum on Canada's Future.* The Forum's task was to get Canadians talking and to listen to the people to find out what kind of country Canadians wanted for themselves and their children. The comments were collected in a variety of ways: a toll-free Idea Line so that Canadians could call from wherever they lived, group discussions held in communities all across the country, and special kits for individuals to use alone.

After analyzing and organizing the hundreds of thousands of comments, the Forum commissioners identified seven major issues facing Canada:

- Canadian identity and values
- Quebec and Canadian unity
- Official languages
- Aboriginal issues
- Cultural diversity
- The Canadian economy
- Responsible leadership and participatory democracy

The Forum commissioners also identified seven "Canadian values." Many Canadians spoke or wrote eloquently to the Forum on the subject of the core values they see as essential elements of Canadian society. The following list represents the core values that emerged very strongly from participants in all regions of Canada:

- **Belief in Equality and Fairness in a Democratic Society:** Canadians are fortunate to live in a country that allows democratic elections. This is important to Canadians. Canadians also value the principles of equality and fairness to all groups in society.
- **Belief in Consultation and Dialogue:** This Forum was an example of consultation and dialogue. Given the number of people who participated, it is obvious that Canadians value the opportunity to talk with one another, and to be consulted on important issues.

▶▶▶ GO GL🌐BAL

International Gestures Quiz

Think you know what it means to give a high five in Honduras or a thumbs-up in Thailand? Test your body language IQ to find out if you're culturally savvy.

1. How would you let a French person know he's boring you to tears?

a. Pat your mouth and let out a giant yawn
b. Mime playing an imaginary flute
c. Push your nose with your middle and index fingers

2. Your Puerto Rican friend wiggles her nose at you. What's she saying?
a. "What's going on?"
b. "I smell a rat—literally."
c. "My nose itches!"

3. Which gesture is considered offensive in Egypt?
a. Using the right hand for eating
b. Showing someone the sole of your shoe
c. Walking hand in hand with someone

Answers: 1. b; 2. a; 3. b

- **Importance of Accommodation and Tolerance:** Canada is a multicultural society. There are many different groups who wish to sustain their own culture, and even different regions of the country have different interests (this is most prominent in Quebec). Canadians said that, as a country, we should strive to be accommodating and tolerant of all groups and regions, as long as these also demonstrate their own acceptance of accommodation and tolerance as key values.
- **Support for Diversity:** Diversity in Canada has a number of facets: linguistic, regional, ethnic, and cultural differences. Canadians repeatedly emphasized that Canada's diversity is one of the most important things they value about this country.
- **Compassion and Generosity:** Canada is known for its compassionate and generous character, as exemplified by our universal and extensive social services, our health care system, our pensions, our willingness to welcome refugees, and our commitment to regional economic equalization.
- **Attachment to Canada's Natural Beauty:** While the North has long been part of Canadian myth and legend, participants indicated that Canada's unspoiled natural beauty is a matter of great importance to them, and is in their view threatened by inadequate attention to protecting our environment.
- **Our World Image—Commitment to Freedom, Peace, and Non-Violent Change:** In 1957, future Prime Minister Lester B. Pearson was awarded the Nobel Peace Prize for his role in defusing the Suez Crisis. Since then, Canada has been recognized as an international peacekeeper. This is a valued role that many Canadians believe we should maintain.[10]

Norms and Sanctions

How can people uphold and enforce their values in everyday life? First of all, they might develop rules for appropriate behaviour based on those values. We call these rules norms. **Norms** are conditional; they can vary from place to place. In 2003 the Las Vegas Convention and Visitors Authority launched the advertising tagline "What Happens Here, Stays Here." The tourism board wanted visitors to frequent their city's casinos, bars, shows, and restaurants without feeling guilty about how participation

V It's customary for players and fans alike
V to remove their hat or helmet and sing
V the national anthem before sporting events.
Why do so at an event that has nothing to do with politics, patriotism, or war?

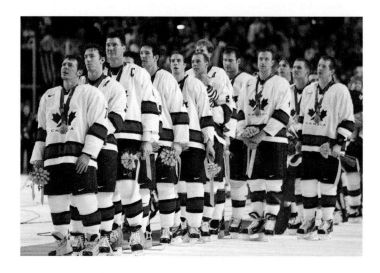

at these places may contradict their cultural values. Las Vegas is now known as a place to escape from cultural norms in other cities; the norm in Vegas is for people to enjoy entertainment without regret.

Norms provide the justification for sanctions. A **sanction** is a reward or punishment you receive when you either abide by a norm or violate it. If you do what you are supposed to do, you get a positive sanction; if you break the rules, you earn a negative sanction.

Most sanctions are informal, like when your friend rolls her eyes at your terrible joke. However, if we violate a law or some formal written rule, we receive a formal negative sanction. A speeding ticket is one example

>>> **Canada's unspoiled natural beauty is a matter of great importance to many Canadians.**

∧
∧ In 2007, actor **Richard Gere** caused
∧ a stir when he **kissed actress Shilpa
Shetty** on the cheek at a public event
in India. **While this gesture is common
in the United States, it's considered a
vulgar act in India.**

of a formal sanction. Sanctions, both positive and negative, can reinforce a culture's values by rewarding people who hold those values and punishing those who have opposing values.

FOLKWAYS

Folkways are informal types of norms. They provide a framework for our behaviour and are based on social expectations. Because they are less serious types of norms, the sanctions applied are less severe than for other types of norms. For example, if you see a person struggling with packages, you will hold the door for him or her. If you let the door slam on the person, you might be considered rude, but you won't go to jail. Folkways are often social customs that, when violated, call for minor, informal negative sanctions.

MORES

Although folkways are informal norms, mores (pronounced MORE-ayes) are more serious. **Mores** are norms that represent a community's most important values. A **taboo** is an act that is socially unacceptable. For example, if you murder a person, you've violated one of society's mores. People who violate mores are given a particularly serious type of formal negative sanction. Acts that lead us to feel revulsion, such as murder, are taboos.[11]

The Study of Culture

When you study culture, it's a good idea to consider whether a particular behaviour or event is a cultural universal, or common to all cultures. For example, funeral rites are a cultural universal because all cultures have methods of disposing of the dead. Many specific cultural norms surround funerals and death; however, these norms vary widely from culture to culture. In what is now known as Micronesia, anthropologist Bronislaw Malinowski witnessed a funeral ritual in which native islanders ate part of the dead person to maintain a connection.[12] After eating, they would vomit in an attempt to create distance from the deceased. This Micronesian funeral norm probably differs greatly from your own culture's norm.

▶▶ GO GL⦿BAL

Individualistic and Collectivistic Views

Individualism, while it may be a core Canadian value, is hardly universal across the globe; people in countries such as Japan are more apt to see things through the lens of collectivism.[13] In a collectivist culture, interdependence is valued over independence, group goals valued over individual wants and needs.[14]

How do our individualist or collectivist views affect us in practical terms? For starters, let's consider how we respond to questions. Research has shown that people from more collectivist societies, such as China and Japan, are less likely to answer with extremes on surveys. On a survey that allowed participants to strongly agree, agree, disagree, and strongly disagree, Canadian and American students were more likely to choose "strongly agree" and "strongly disagree," whereas Chinese and Japanese participants tended to choose the less extreme responses.[15]

Important cultural differences like these can inform business situations. One study compared how Canadian and Chinese executives dealt with conflict situations. The researchers found that the Chinese executives preferred to avoid conflicts in advance of their occurrence, but when conflict did arise they were more likely to use negative resolution strategies, such as ending negotiations. The authors suggested that because groups in collectivist cultures are harder to get into, stable and harmonious relationships are more important. In individualistic cultures, an individual can more easily leave the situation and join another group.[16]

ETHNOCENTRISM occurs when a person uses his or her own culture to judge another culture.

XENOPHOBIA refers to fear and hostility toward people who are from other countries or cultures.

XENOCENTRISM is perceiving other groups or societies as superior to your own.

CULTURAL RELATIVISM means making a deliberate effort to appreciate a group's ways of life without prejudice.

NORMATIVE RELATIVISM is the evaluation of a society based on that society's norms.

NOTICE TO ALL JAPANESE PERSONS AND PERSONS OF JAPANESE RACIAL ORIGIN

TAKE NOTICE that under Orders Nos. 21, 22, 23 and 24 of the British Columbia Security Commission, the following areas were made prohibited areas to all persons of the Japanese race:—

LULU ISLAND
(including Steveston)
SEA ISLAND
EBURNE
MARPOLE
DISTRICT OF
QUEENSBOROUGH
CITY OF
NEW WESTMINSTER

SAPPERTON
BURQUITLAM
PORT MOODY
IOCO
PORT COQUITLAM
MAILLARDVILLE
FRASER MILLS

AND FURTHER TAKE NOTICE that any person of the Japanese race found within any of the said prohibited areas without a written permit from the British Columbia Security Commission or the Royal Canadian Mounted Police shall be liable to the penalties provided under Order in Council P.C. 1665.

AUSTIN C. TAYLOR,
Chairman,
British Columbia Security Commission

∧∧∧ Propaganda posters popped up all over the nation after the Japanese bombed Pearl Harbor. **Thousands of Canadians of Japanese descent were forcibly sent to internment camps for the duration of the war.**

ETHNOCENTRISM AND CULTURAL RELATIVISM

When studying culture from a sociological perspective, you must not allow your personal biases to complicate your understanding. **Ethnocentrism** occurs when a person uses his or her own culture to judge another culture. Nearly all people in the world are ethnocentric, but ethnocentrism is potentially dangerous to sociologists because it can lead to incorrect assumptions about different cultures.[17]

Xenophobia refers to fear and hostility toward people who are from other countries or cultures. Despite being a multicultural society, Canada has experienced episodes of xenophobia. After Japan bombed Pearl Harbor in 1941, people in Canada began to fear Japanese Canadians and imprisoned many in internment camps.

Perspectives of a Central American Hotel Room

Not all personal biases result in a negative view of foreign cultures. Sometimes, we engage in **xenocentrism** when we perceive other groups or societies as superior to our own. When living in Mexico, I noticed that my host family watched very little television. Instead, the family spent time discussing ideas. I remember wishing that people in my own culture would follow suit and interact with one another more.

Thinking like a sociologist means striving to practise cultural relativism when studying other cultures. **Cultural relativism** consists of a deliberate effort to appreciate a group's ways of life in its own context, without prejudice. Philosophers sometimes refer to this effort as **normative relativism**, because it bases the evaluation of a society on that society's own norms. In some Islamic countries, for instance, women are not encouraged to seek education. Within the context of these countries, this practice could be interpreted as a normal function of that culture. However, if women in Canada were not allowed to get an education, the practice would seem unfair because it would violate Canadian cultural norms. When we engage in normative relativism, we evaluate acts within their cultural contexts.

Some people, however, argue that there are universal human values that are standards by which we should evaluate cultures.[18] According to this argument, women in every culture should be educated, and any culture that does not allow this is inferior and exploitive of women.

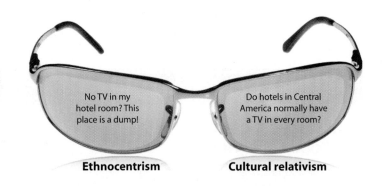

No TV in my hotel room? This place is a dump! | Do hotels in Central America normally have a TV in every room?

Ethnocentrism | **Cultural relativism**

When **travelling in Central America,** I noticed that even in very nice hotels there was **rarely a television in the room.** I viewed this observation through an **ethnocentric** lens based on my **cultural expectations,** but I was also able to view it through an **objective, prejudice-free lens of cultural relativism.**

CULTURAL LAG AND CULTURE SHOCK

Cultural lag happens when social and cultural changes occur at a slower pace than technological changes. This is often the case when new technology enters and changes a culture. In the late 1970s, scientists were concerned with the deforestation of poorer regions of the world. People used most of the felled lumber to heat stoves for cooking. To combat this problem, more energy-efficient cookstoves were developed. However, initial tests in Africa and Haiti showed that people were reluctant to use these cookstoves. After learning of the cookstoves' benefits, people's reluctance waned, and today more than 120 million cookstoves are used around the world.[19]

Have you ever been to a foreign country and marvelled at how the culture differed from your own? If so, you were probably experiencing culture shock. **Culture shock** occurs when a person encounters a culture foreign to his or her own and has an emotional response to the differences between the cultures. During my time in Mexico, I was stunned to discover that the electricity went out every afternoon. My host family planned their cooking schedule around the predictable power outages. It took some time, but I eventually accepted this cultural difference.

IDEAL VERSUS REAL CULTURE

Is there a difference between culture as we'd like it to be and culture as it really is? Often, the answer is yes. Ideal culture represents the values to which a culture aspires, and real culture represents a culture's actual behaviours. Democracy, for example, has always been part of the ideal culture of Canada, but voter turnouts for the 2000, 2004, and 2008 federal elections indicate that only about 60 percent of the eligible population showed democratic values and turned out to vote.[20]

SUBCULTURES AND COUNTERCULTURES

Groups with a common interest may form a subculture. A **subculture** is a subset of the dominant culture that has distinct values, beliefs, and norms. In complex societies, subcultures allow people to connect with

> When a subculture expresses values or beliefs that are in direct opposition to the dominant group's values, it becomes a counterculture.

CULTURAL LAG occurs when social and cultural changes occur at a slower pace than technological changes.

CULTURE SHOCK occurs when a person encounters a culture foreign to his or her own and has an emotional response to the differences between the cultures.

SUBCULTURE is a subset of the dominant culture that has distinct values, beliefs, and norms.

COUNTERCULTURES are groups with value systems that are in opposition to the dominant group's values.

MULTICULTURALISM is a concept that supports the inherent value of different cultures within society.

ASSIMILATION is the process by which minority groups adopt the patterns of the dominant culture.

other people who have similar interests. Churches, civic organizations, clubs, and even online communities can become subcultures.

When you see the term *counterculture,* images of mafia organizations and violent motorcycle gangs might come to mind. These groups are **countercultures** because their value systems are in opposition to the dominant group's values. Sometimes, countercultures can merge with and change the dominant culture. For example, in the Roman Empire, Christianity was once banned and practising Christians were fed to the lions. However, Christianity later became the official religion of the empire.

MULTICULTURALISM AND ASSIMILATION

If you move to a new country, you'll bring along not only material belongings but also concealed cultural baggage. It can be tricky to "unpack" that baggage, but you'll need to find a way to adapt to your new culture. **Multiculturalism** is a concept that supports the inherent value of different cultures within society. Proponents of multiculturalism think that immigrants should maintain links to aspects of their original culture—such as language, cultural beliefs and traditions, and religion—while also integrating into their new culture. However, opponents of multiculturalism worry that this practice keeps groups from adapting to the dominant culture. In 1971, Canada became the first country in the world to adopt multiculturalism as an official state policy.[21]

Assimilation is the process by which minority groups adopt the patterns of the dominant culture. If a minority group completely abandons its

MAKE CONNECTIONS

The Subcultures of Facebook

Are you a member of a Facebook subculture? Considering that Facebook has more than 500 million active users worldwide, you probably are. Facebook, an online social networking site, helps connect people through mutual interests. When you use this site, your friends are always at your fingertips.

When you join Facebook, you create a profile that includes personal information, interests, beliefs, or hobbies. The more information you include, the larger your world can become, because Facebook connects you to others in the system who have similar characteristics. For example, you can connect to people who have the same class schedule or belong to the same fraternity and/or sorority. You're linked to people who have similar values, or your subculture of friends.

Like any culture or subculture, Facebook has norms and sanctions. Many Facebook users believe that the more friends you have, the more popular you are. One norm for interacting with friends on the site is to "poke" a person. The person you poke may poke you back or ignore your poke. An informal sanction might occur if your poke goes unanswered. A formal sanction can occur if a friend deletes you from his or her friends list. Though nontraditional, Facebook creates a virtual community in which people interact with others who share norms and values.

>>> ACTIVITY Log on to a social networking site, like Facebook, and identify a culture.
- **Make** a list of the values of that culture.
- **How** are these values distinct from the values on pages 54–55?
- **How** are they similar?

>>> **Twitter, a social networking/microblogging device, allows users to alert their friends (with "Tweets") to their current activities via instant message or RSS feed.** Twitter, in effect, encourages users to know all the actions of their friends in real time. **Do programs like Twitter make the world feel smaller? Why or why not?**

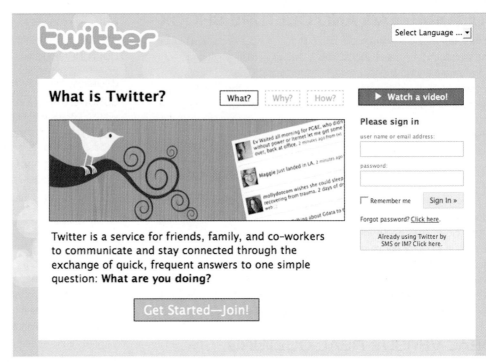

GLOBAL VILLAGE refers to the "shrinking" of the world through immediate electronic communications.

previous culture in favour of a new one, that group is likely to experience rapid assimilation. One method by which the Canadian government tried to force rapid assimilation involved taking aboriginal children from their parents and placing them in residential schools to teach them "white ways." However, many of these students left the residential schools unprepared to live in either the dominant culture or their own culture.

Global Village

In the 1960s, the noted Canadian intellectual Marshall McLuhan popularized the term **global village**, which refers to the "shrinking" of the world through immediate electronic communications.[22] McLuhan's work suggests that time and space differences are rapidly becoming irrelevant as a result of technology. But is technology really bringing people closer together?

Before the advent of the internet, Stanley Milgram conducted an experiment in an attempt to determine whether it really is a small world after all.[23] Milgram found people from different areas of the United States and sent them on a hunt for strangers. He asked them to mail a letter to a target person, whom they did not know, using only their social networks. He provided only the subject's name and town of residence but nothing else. After passing through the hands of between two and ten people, the letters eventually found their targets. Now that the internet plays such a large role in our lives, could our separation be even shorter than it was in the 1960s? How many links would it take you to connect with a student in Japan?

Dodds et al. used the internet to conduct a similar study.[24] Through email, Dodds sent more than 60 000 people on a target hunt to find 18 people in 13 different countries. Their results were astonishingly similar to Milgram's results. Although these findings certainly support the notion of a small world, they do not suggest that the world is any smaller today than it was in Milgram's time.

THINK SOCIOLOGICALLY

Technology and Cultural Change

In *Amusing Ourselves to Death: Public Discourse in the Age of Show Business,* Neil Postman discusses television's impact on U.S. culture. Television is the primary means of communication for news and information in the United States. Fewer people read newspapers and magazines. Do the media affect the message?

Marshall Fishwick would say that they do. According to him, many aspects of life that make us human are not computable.[25] Your laptop cannot feel, create beauty, or think. Your MP3 player talks to you; it does not listen. Like Fishwick, Postman argues that technology, such as television, provides a passive type of engagement for the user. Postman suggests that this creates a nation of people who cannot think. This inability increases the odds that we will accept overly simple solutions to extremely complex problems, which will destroy our culture in the long run.

Of course, not everyone believes that technology will destroy our culture. In *Culture and Technology,* Andrew Murphie and John Potts argue that technology has improved society. For example, Murphie and Potts argue that the technology of writing "transformed human consciousness" because it brought about new ways of thinking. Technological advancements, such as the internet and television, inspire creativity and innovation, and open up a world of opportunity for a society. They claim that technology does not limit a society, as Fishwick and Postman suggest, but it gives people the tools to continue to improve their lives.[26] Is our culture becoming a technopoly? A technopoly is a society that values technological change for its own sake. In such a culture, having the latest upgrade is most important. Fishwick suggests that our culture is experiencing a tyranny of technology, while Murphie and Potts argue that culture and technology are so tightly linked that we can't really separate one from the other. What do you think? Has technology really improved society?

think sociologically: WHAT DIFFERENTIATES ONE CULTURE FROM ANOTHER?

Now we will turn to the major theoretical perspectives on culture. The theoretical perspectives affect how sociologists view language, gestures, and values in a culture.

Symbolic Interactionism— Canadian vs. American Values

Symbolic interactionists explore how history, symbols, and values affect a culture. In 1990, Seymour Martin Lipset wrote *Continental Divide: The Values and Institutions of the United States and Canada,* in which he contrasted and compared these two North American nations. For Lipset, one essential difference between the two cultures is how they achieved nationhood. The Americans won their independence after fighting a revolutionary war, whereas the Canadian provinces peacefully formed a confederation (a counterrevolution) while still maintaining ties to Britain. According to Lipset, this has influenced how each country developed its identity and values. And it is the difference in values that has influenced the development of each country's social structure and activities, both within their own borders and on the international stage.

Historically, Canadians have defined themselves as being "not-American." This has been a central feature of the Canadian identity. But what of the different ideologies? Lipset examined Canadian and American literature for examples of ideology. He found that American literature was more likely to focus on themes of winning, opportunism, and confidence, while Canadian literature more often dealt with defeat and difficult circumstances. He quoted Margaret Atwood, who identified the defining symbol of the United States as "the Frontier," which represented something *new*. In Canada, the symbol is *survival* in a hostile wilderness.[27]

∧
∧ **Although we have a lot in common with**
∧ **Americans, many Canadians identify**
themselves as "not-American."

Despite being close neighbours, both geographically and culturally, Lipset's research showed how different values and ideologies created important differences between the Canadian and American cultures.

Functionalism—The CRTC

Does culture arise and develop naturally, or is it something that needs to be protected? Because culture is such a significant aspect of all societies, it may be functional to direct and support the diffusion of certain cultural values. Radio, television, and other media are powerful transmitters of culture. The Canadian government regulates these important services to ensure that they contribute to Canada's culture and economy and meet the social needs of Canadians.

In 1936, the Canadian government created the Canadian Radio Broadcasting Commission (CRBC). The CRBC regulated and controlled all radio broadcasting in Canada and provided a national broadcasting service. The number and location of radio stations was regulated by the CRBC, as well as the amount of time that was devoted to national and local programming. The CRBC was replaced by the Canadian Radio-television and Telecommunications Commission (CRTC) in 1968. Today, the CRTC supervises and regulates Canadian broadcasting and telecommunications. It reports to Parliament through the Minister of Canadian Heritage.

In 1971, the CRTC introduced a regulation that 30 percent of the songs played on the radio must be Canadian; this was increased to 35 percent in 1998. Since 1968, 60 percent of television programming has had to be Canadian shows. These regulations are known as Cancon (Canadian content). The function of these policies has been to ensure that Canadian songs and shows are seen and heard, and therefore Canadian culture is preserved and promoted. Canadian content remains a controversial issue. Some say that it artificially protects Canadian productions, so artists are not challenged to produce top-quality work. Others claim that Cancon violates the right of consumers to make their own choices about what they want to listen to and watch.[28]

Conflict Theory—The McDonaldization of Society

Conflict theorists suggest that society is united in a struggle for scarce resources. Unequal distribution of wealth means that some people win and others lose. But how do you win? Are there predictable patterns of interaction that can bring about financial success? McDonald's restaurant is successful because it prizes efficiency, practicality, and affordability. Sociologist George Ritzer suggests that many modern societies model themselves after a McDonald's restaurant through a process he calls "McDonaldization."[29]

Using a conflict theory rooted in the work of economist/sociologist/political scientist Max Weber, Ritzer notes that efficient bureaucracies succeed in business. In a capitalist system, those who follow the McDonaldization process are likely to be financially successful.

1 **Efficiency** When a business practises efficiency, consumers benefit from the low prices that the business offers. The McDonaldization of efficiency means customers do the employees' work. If you go to McDonald's, you usually carry the food to the table yourself, and in some parts of the country, you might fill your own drink as well.

2 **Calculability** McDonald's counts every item, from the pickles on the hamburger to the number of chicken nuggets in a box. Quantity is valued, and quality is less relevant. McDonaldized societies measure success by the number of tasks completed on time. If the quality of the task is mediocre, we often accept it as long as it is finished on schedule.

3 **Predictability** Finding a product that is predictable decreases the risk of business failure. In this way, our culture has taken a page from the fast-food industry. A Big Mac tastes the same whether you purchase it in Halifax or Calgary. Predictability increases reward and decreases risk to both the business owner and the consumer.

4 **Technology** Businesses gain more control over their products when they use technology to limit human error. This trend helps increase profits because business owners are able to hire fewer people.

NEGATIVE EFFECTS OF MCDONALDIZATION

Ritzer warns that the use of technology dehumanizes our culture. People use ATMs or self-checkout lines for convenience. However, using these forms of technology shows that society values speed through a checkout line over human interaction. In the long run, is this healthy for today's society?

McDonaldization trades convenience for high quality and ensures high profits for business owners. Innovation and creativity suffer, but short-term profits rise. By replacing workers with technology, wages drop and inequality increases, leading to conflict between business owners and workers.

In Canada, the Tim Hortons chain of coffee and donut shops is our home-grown version of McDonald's. In fact, Tim Hortons outlets outnumber

McDonald's restaurants two-to-one, and Tim Hortons accounts for 62 percent of the Canadian retail coffee business. A large part of Tim Hortons' success is that it copied the McDonald's process. By using this winning formula, Tim Hortons succeeded in the struggle for control of the Canadian coffee market.[30]

Feminist Theory—Gender Inequity in Hockey

On a Sunday afternoon in late February, it is estimated that 22 million Canadians—nearly two-thirds of the population—watched as Sidney Crosby scored in overtime and the Canadian team won the gold medal in Men's Hockey at the 2010 Vancouver Olympics. Just three days earlier, one-third that number of people (7.5 million) watched the Canadian Women's Hockey team also win a gold medal.

Hockey is certainly an important part of Canadian culture. In fact, it is our national winter sport. But it seems like one version of the game—the men's version—is the one that really counts. Feminist theorists are more likely to recognize this imbalance, and to try to explain it. Although women playing hockey is not a twenty-first-century event, it is only in the past 20 to 30 years that women's hockey has really become recognized and somewhat respected. In *Higher Goals: Women's Ice Hockey and the Politics of Gender,* Nancy Theberge suggests that both structural and ideological changes were necessary before women's hockey could attain the popularity and legitimacy it has today. On the structural side, the absence of teams and coaches meant there was little opportunity for girls to play hockey. The most critical resource for hockey is ice time, and the boys' teams were always given preference. On the cultural side, an ideology that viewed hockey as a tough, masculine sport discouraged many girls from crossing this powerful gender barrier.[31]

Women's hockey was first introduced as an Olympic event at the Nagano Winter Olympics in 1998. This has further legitimized and popularized women's hockey in many countries. However, as significant difference in viewership between the two Olympic gold medal games illustrated, female hockey players still have a way to go before they are considered as exciting and respected as their male counterparts.

<<< **This is a familiar sight in communities across Canada. Tim Hortons is one of Canada's most successful businesses** because it prizes efficiency, practicality, and affordability.

WRAP YOUR MIND AROUND THE THEORY

The CRTC is an independent public authority in charge of regulating and supervising Canadian broadcasting and telecommunications.

FUNCTIONALISM

Functionalists suggest that sometimes governments or other regulatory agencies can intentionally direct and control culture. In Canada, the CRTC has regulations known as Cancon which specify that a certain percentage of songs played on the radio and shows broadcast on television must be Canadian.

SYMBOLIC INTERACTIONISM

Interactionists suggest that culture is rooted in the values expressed by the people who live within it. Seymour Lipset compared Canadian and American values, and found that there were important differences between the two cultures. Americans tend to value independence and winning, while Canadians are more respectful of authority and more likely to cooperate.

CONFLICT THEORY

Conflict theorists point out that members of society struggle for what is scarce. In our society, that usually involves wealth and power because of the McDonaldization process. Short-term rewards increase power and wealth of the few. The costs to society are irrelevant.

IS YOUR COUNTRY LOSING TRADITIONAL VALUES TO SECULAR ONES?

FEMINIST THEORY

Feminists point to the gendered nature of both our social institutions and our ideologies. These are often disadvantageous to women. Female hockey players have faced many challenges. But changes to both the social structures and the gender biases that discouraged girls from playing hockey have resulted in a growing number of women's and girls' hockey teams. While more Canadians still prefer to watch men play hockey, the increased popularity of women's hockey in the past few decades has been incredible.

Slot machines and VLTs (video lottery terminals) are popular forms of entertainment **because of the lights, sounds, and interactive nature of the game.**

Although still not as popular as men's hockey, women's hockey is becoming a significant part of Canadian culture.

discover sociology in action: HOW DOES SOCIAL POLICY INFLUENCE CULTURE?

Social Policy—Bill 101

It was August 27, 1977. In Quebec, and especially in Montreal, the rich and powerful English-speaking minority was the dominant group. Bilingualism meant that francophones had to learn to speak English. The thousands of immigrants who arrived each year seemed to more naturally and easily assimilate into English culture. Camille Laurin was a psychiatrist, politician, and member of the separatist *Parti Québécois*. That summer, he was the driving force behind the passing of Bill 101, the infamous language law. The *Charter of the French Language* proclaimed that every Quebec resident had the right to work, shop, study, be administered, treated, and judged in French, everywhere, all the time. Nearly overnight, the changes were apparent. Immigrants were obliged to send their children to school in French. The use of English on commercial signs was no longer allowed, although this was soon revised so that English could be used, so long as it was smaller and less obvious than the French. In all businesses, organizations, and government offices, French was the only language allowed to be used.

Camille Laurin understood the power of social policy in cultural change. He envisioned Bill 101 as much more than a mere language law. It was a bold attempt at altering the social order. As an ardent separatist, Laurin believed that this was a first step on the road to Quebec independence. Thirty years later, we can see that Bill 101 has certainly resulted in a cultural shift in Quebec. French is now firmly established as the language of business and government. But there have been changes that neither Laurin, nor anyone else, could have anticipated. Montreal today boasts the highest proportion of people speaking three or more languages in all of North America. The forced integration of immigrant children in French schools has created a truly multicultural society, which is in stark contrast to the traditional, homogenous, and xenophobic Québécois culture, at once diluting it and enriching it. And rather than stimulating a drive to independence, the language law reassured many francophones that their culture was being protected. It was no longer necessary to leave Canada in order to protect Quebec's cultural integrity.[32]

ACTIVITIES

1. Research language laws in different Canadian provinces. Are any Canadian provinces officially bilingual?
2. Imagine that you moved to another country and were banned from speaking English. How might you feel? What would you do to adapt?
3. Visit an ESL (English as a second language) classroom in a school in your community. Ask the teacher about the importance of language in cultural transmission.

From Classroom to Community ⟩ Assisting Immigrants

"I didn't know what I was getting into."

Sonya, a 22-year-old, trilingual, Canadian-born Latina student, uttered these words when reflecting on an experience she had while working on a civic engagement project. When Sonya began volunteering at a local Latino development organization that offered legal, medical, and psychological help to Spanish-speaking immigrants, she could not imagine the life lessons she would learn.

"After the first week, I was given a case of an immigrant woman who needed help getting daycare for her children,"

Sonya recalled. The woman spoke very little English, and her husband had left her and her children about a year earlier. As a legal citizen of Canada, the woman was entitled to public assistance. However, she did not know how to get it.

The process was long and arduous, but Sonya did not falter. She followed the woman through the system. Eventually, Sonya was able to help the woman find daycare for her children, and she helped the woman collect child support from her ex-husband. The experience taught Sonya how not speaking English cripples many immigrants in Canada.

"If you can't speak English very well, you cannot really negotiate the system.

Even legal immigrants suffer in such an environment. Fortunately, the Latino society is closely knit and more collective. This helped her to survive. Without her community's support she would have had no hope to make a new and better life for herself and her children."

WHAT IS CULTURE?   50

the language, beliefs, values, norms, behaviours, and material objects that are important enough to pass on to future generations of a society

WHAT DIFFERENTIATES ONE CULTURE FROM ANOTHER?   59

language, gestures, values, perception and categorization of experiences, actions, norms, interaction of social structures, and struggle for scarce resources

HOW DOES SOCIAL POLICY INFLUENCE CULTURE?   62

culture: affects how we perceive things; guides our thoughts and actions; must be studied while keeping these differences in mind

get the topic: WHAT IS CULTURE?

Theory

SYMBOLIC INTERACTIONISM   59

- Canadian versus American values
- The American War of Independence and Canadian Confederation are two very different routes to nationhood that continue to affect each country's culture
- American literature more often contains themes of winning or "the Frontier," while Canadian authors are more likely to write about defeat or survival.

FUNCTIONALISM   59

- culture (shared values and norms) holds society together through shared values and norms
- interaction of social structures
- in Canada, the CRTC regulates radio and television to protect and promote Canadian culture

CONFLICT THEORY   59

- society struggles for resources
- societies win resources by using McDonaldization process (efficiency, calculability, predictability, and technology)
- convenience over quality
- only the wealthy benefit: wages drop, inequality increases, short-term profits rise

FEMINIST THEORY   60

- social structures can restrict the access of women and girls to certain activities, such as hockey
- gender stereotypes can also work against females participating in "male" activities
- as the social institutions and the ideologies change, the culture changes as well

Key Terms

culture is the language, beliefs, values, norms, behaviours, and material objects that are important enough to pass on to future generations of a society. *50*

material culture consists of items within a culture that you can taste, touch, and feel. *50*

nonmaterial culture consists of the nonphysical products of society, including our symbols, values, rules, and sanctions. *51*

symbols represent, suggest, or stand for something else. *51*

language is a system of speech and/or written symbols used to convey meaning and communicate. *51*

cultural transmission is culture passing from one generation to the next through language. *52*

Sapir-Whorf hypothesis is a hypothesis, first advanced by Edward Sapir in 1929 and subsequently developed by Benjamin Whorf, that the structure of a language determines a native speaker's perception and categorization of experience. *52*

gestures are symbols we make using our bodies, such as facial expressions, hand movements, eye contact, and other types of body language. *52*

values are a part of a society's nonmaterial culture that represent cultural standards by

which we determine what is good, bad, right, or wrong. *53*

value pairs help us define values, usually in terms of opposites. *53*

value clusters are two or more values that support each other. *53*

value conflict occurs when two or more values are at odds. *53*

norms are rules developed for appropriate behaviour based on specific values that are conditional; they can vary from place to place. *54*

sanction is a reward or punishment you receive when you either abide by a norm or violate it. *54*

folkways are informal types of norms. *55*

mores are norms that represent a community's most important values. *55*

taboo is an act that is socially unacceptable. *55*

ethnocentrism occurs when a person uses his or her own culture to judge another culture. *56*

xenophobia refers to fear and hostility toward people who are from other countries or cultures. *56*

xenocentrism is perceiving other groups or societies as superior to your own. *56*

cultural relativism means making a deliberate effort to appreciate a group's ways of life without prejudice. *56*

normative relativism is the evaluation of a society based on that society's norms. *56*

cultural lag occurs when social and cultural changes occur at a slower pace than technological changes. *57*

culture shock occurs when a person encounters a culture foreign to his or her own and has an emotional response to the differences between the cultures. *57*

subculture is a subset of the dominant culture that has distinct values, beliefs, and norms. *57*

countercultures are groups with value systems that are in opposition to the dominant group's values. *57*

multiculturalism is a concept that supports the inherent value of different cultures within society. *57*

assimilation is the process by which minority groups adopt the patterns of the dominant culture. *57*

global village refers to the "shrinking" of the world through immediate electronic communications. *58*

Sample Test Questions

These multiple-choice questions are similar to those found in the test bank that accompanies this textbook.

1. Norms include all of the following *except*
   a. folkways.
   b. mores.
   c. rules for behaviour.
   d. definitions of beauty.

2. Which of the following statements is *false*?
   a. Values may cluster, but they cannot contradict.
   b. Values remain the same over time.
   c. Values are often defined by their opposite.
   d. Values exist in all societies.

3. Gestures are part of
   a. assimilation.
   b. material culture.
   c. nonmaterial culture.
   d. multiculturalism.

4. How does a counterculture form?
   a. When a subculture's values differ from the dominant group's values
   b. When a group maintains links to aspects of their original culture
   c. When the dominant culture does not accept part of the group
   d. When the subculture adopts the values of the dominant culture

5. In order for sociologists to practise cultural relativism when studying polygamists in Canada, they must consider
   a. Canadian laws.
   b. Canadian norms.
   c. polygamist norms.
   d. cultural universals.

ANSWERS: 1. a; 2. b; 3. c; 4. a; 5. c

ESSAY

1. What aspects of Bill 101 have been positive for Canadian culture?
2. How does culture influence sociological theory and study?
3. How might individualism lead to conflict?
4. How can a business benefit from the McDonaldization process?
5. How did Seymour Lipset define Canadian culture?

WHERE TO START YOUR RESEARCH PAPER

To learn more about sociologist George Ritzer and McDonaldization, go to www.georgeritzer.com and www.mcdonaldization.com

To find local information about studying abroad, go to www.cicic.ca/384/Studying_Abroad.canada

To learn more about the communitarian movement, go to www.gwu.edu/~ccps/index.html

To find urban legends and myths as well as their origins and why they are not true, go to www.snopes.com

For more information on international study options, go to www.studyabroad.com, www.studyabroadlinks.com

For more information on international volunteering, go to www.crossculturalsolutions.org

To learn more about how Canada contributes to collaborative development through volunteering, go to www.cuso-vso.org

Remember to check www.thethinkspot.ca **for additional information, downloadable flashcards, and other helpful resources.**

SOCIAL STRUCTURE
AND INTERACTION

"Many

immigrants, refugees, and international students have come to Canada with the belief that the hard work, intelligence, ambition, tenacity, maturity, and other personal qualities that made them successful in their old countries and helped them survive what might have been a treacherous journey would also help them to succeed in Canada. Unfortunately, this has not always been the case. Such overconfidence has been the undoing of many an immigrant, refugee and international student. Far too many have been blindsided in the benign looking environment of Canada, forcing them to abandon their dreams and to accept conditions of life that they would never have imagined a few years before.

"Not taking the time to understand the Canadian system, the underlying rules that govern life, and strategic resources that facilitate success can be pricey in the long run. . . . The point is that it takes strategic resources to enhance one's hard work, intelligence, talents, abilities and ambition to make the stories about Canada as land of milk and honey a reality.

"Although Canada claims to be a multicultural country, the reality is that conventional rewards are located in the upper/middle class Anglo and Franco cultures of both the larger society and academia. Those who have access to strategic resources to effectively connect with the opportunity structures of the mainstream culture and/or academia are those who get most conventional rewards. New entrants to Canada who remain disconnected from strategic resources remain secluded in their minority cultures and tend to experience trapped socio-economic mobility. Real life experiences of immigrants, refugees and international

students support this claim. The fact is connecting with the opportunity structures in the mainstream Canadian culture and academia from a culture on the margins requires appropriate information and knowledge, definitive decisions on the choices the information presents, mentoring, relevant networking and a strong support system. . . .

"For new immigrants, refugees, and international students, basic skills are not enough because of the reality that unequal opportunity structures exist in Canadian society and academia that tend to work against minorities because of racism, ethnocentrism and other social injustices embedded in the Canadian social structure. Therefore racial and ethnic minorities are located in the margins of Canadian society and their success may not be determined by hard work, individual intelligence and personal ambition. Should new immigrants, refugees and international students despair and lose faith in themselves because of racism, ethnocentrism and injustices in Canadian society and academia? No! There is a way out! Many immigrants, refugees and international students have proven that there is some wisdom in the popular notion in the minority communities that says because of racism and ethnocentrism in Canada minorities need higher than average qualifications, abilities, skills, mentors, and support systems in order to achieve success. . . . The reality is that new immigrants, refugees and international students can succeed in Canadian society and academia despite the prevalence of racism, ethnocentrism and other barriers they face. *Chocolate can thrive in a Vanilla World!*"[1]

Micro *and* Macro Orientations

CHAPTER 04

By focusing on how racial and cultural minorities within Canada can succeed, **Francis Adu-Febiri and Everett Ofori illustrate that there is a clear link between the small-scale and large-scale components of a society.**

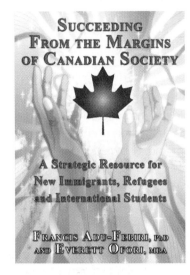

While I was a student, I also worked at the university cafeteria. One day, I came in to work to find that a new person had been hired to work in the dish-room. He ended up telling me his story. He had just recently arrived from Burma (also known as Myanmar), and he had a degree in engineering. However, his degree was not recognized in Canada, so he was obliged to take engineering courses at the university. Because his degree was not recognized, he was unable to find a job in his field, and so the engineer was working as a dishwasher.

That is the kind of social barrier that Adu-Febiri and Ofori write about overcoming in *Succeeding From the Margins of Canadian Society: A Strategic Resource for New Immigrants, Refugees and International Students.*

When you take note of differences between the lives of minority and established segments of Canadian society, you are really looking at ways in which small and large components combine to create the social world.

get the topic: WHAT ELEMENTS CREATE A SOCIAL STRUCTURE?

Macrosociology and Microsociology

When Oceanic Flight 815 crashes in the middle of the ocean on the hit TV show *Lost,* the survivors find themselves washed up on the shores of a seemingly uncharted desert island. After recovering from the initial shock of the crash, some survivors search the island for signs of life or danger. Another group scours the wreckage for food and water. Still others battle mysterious clouds of black smoke and fend off polar bears; this *is* a fictional TV show after all, but you get the idea. Very quickly, fixed social positions are established. The survivors become hunters, warriors, builders, and cooks.

It soon becomes apparent that rescue is not imminent, so the survivors find ways to deal with death, crime, and outsiders. Rules are put into place and leaders are chosen. The survivors use their various medical, outdoors, and military experiences to help one another survive.

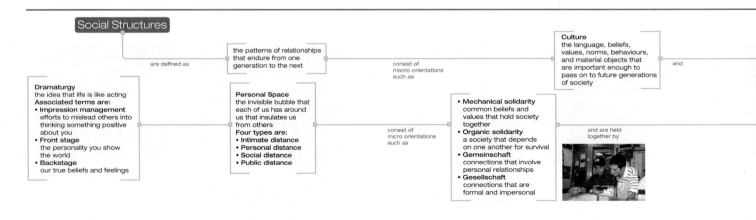

Social Structures

are defined as — the patterns of relationships that endure from one generation to the next — consist of macro orientations such as — **Culture** the language, beliefs, values, norms, behaviours, and material objects that are important enough to pass on to future generations of society — and

Dramaturgy
the idea that life is like acting
Associated terms are:
• **Impression management** efforts to mislead others into thinking something positive about you
• **Front stage** the personality you show the world
• **Backstage** our true beliefs and feelings

Personal Space
the invisible bubble that each of us has around us that insulates us from others
Four types are:
• Intimate distance
• Personal distance
• Social distance
• Public distance

consist of micro orientations such as

• **Mechanical solidarity** common beliefs and values that hold society together
• **Organic solidarity** a society that depends on one another for survival
• **Gemeinschaft** connections that involve personal relationships
• **Gesellschaft** connections that are formal and impersonal

and are held together by

What does this example show us? It draws attention to two important components of society: the macro (large) elements and the micro (small) elements. On the island, the survivors developed both macro structures to accomplish needed tasks and micro orientations to ensure that their society would run smoothly. **Macrosociology** is the study of large-scale society, focusing on the social structures that exist within a society and examining how those structures create the social world. **Microsociology** deals primarily with the small interactions of daily life.

SOCIAL STRUCTURE

You've probably never had to think too hard about the way a society functions. That's because we often have an inherent understanding of how our society is structured. **Social structures** are patterns of relationships that endure from one generation to the next. They are the arrangement of systems—such as marriage, education, and work—by which people in a society interact and are able to live together.

Consider your position as a student. When you were in high school, you quickly learned that the guidance counsellor could help you choose your courses, but was probably not much help with your math homework. You didn't expect the principal to clean the blackboards, and you would have been surprised if the janitor gave you a detention. The pattern of these relationships does not change much over time and becomes part of a school's culture.

Culture

Culture, discussed in depth in Chapter 3, is the language, beliefs, values, norms, behaviours, and material objects that are important enough to pass on to future generations of a society. The embedded structure of culture touches every aspect of our lives and is a large part of our society.

Groups

Groups are any number of people with similar norms, values, and behaviours who frequently interact with one another. Knitting clubs, government agencies, religious cults—all of these are groups. Residents living in the same apartment complex aren't necessarily a group, because they may rarely hang out together.

Sociologist Charles H. Cooley suggests that we divide ourselves into two types of groups: primary and secondary.[2] **Primary groups** are small, intimate, and enduring. Your family and close friends are primary groups to which you belong. **Secondary groups** are formal, superficial, and temporary. The group of you and your classmates is probably a secondary group. The line between these two types of groups is not always clear-cut, but we have far more secondary groups than primary ones. You'll learn more about groups and group interactions in Chapter 6.

MACROSOCIOLOGY is the study of large-scale society, focusing on the social structures that exist within a society and examining how those structures create the social world.

MICROSOCIOLOGY is the study of the small interactions of daily life.

SOCIAL STRUCTURES are patterns of relationships that endure from one generation to the next.

GROUPS are any number of people with similar norms, values, and behaviours who frequently interact with one another.

PRIMARY GROUPS are groups that are small, intimate, and enduring.

SECONDARY GROUPS are groups that are formal, superficial, and temporary.

Social Class

Social class, which will be discussed in more detail in Chapter 7, refers to a group with similar access to power, wealth, and prestige. The importance of social class varies depending upon the society. In Canada, for example, about 30 percent of the population can be considered working class.[3] The members of this social class are often the swing voters at election time.

Your social class can have a profound impact on your life, especially the length of it. Studies have shown that one's social class can affect his or her health, happiness, and life span. In England, researchers have found that the life expectancy for professional women is far longer than for women who are unskilled labourers.

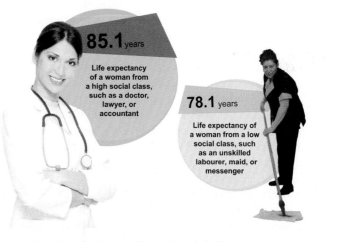

85.1 years
Life expectancy of a woman from a high social class, such as a doctor, lawyer, or accountant

78.1 years
Life expectancy of a woman from a low social class, such as an unskilled labourer, maid, or messenger

Source: Data from "Wealthy, Healthy, and Aged 85: The Women Living Even Longer" by Jill Sheerman.

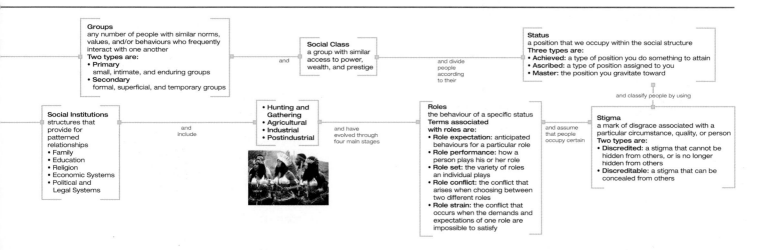

Groups
any number of people with similar norms, values, and/or behaviours who frequently interact with one another
Two types are:
• Primary
small, intimate, and enduring groups
• Secondary
formal, superficial, and temporary groups

and

Social Class
a group with similar access to power, wealth, and prestige

and divide people according to their

Status
a position that we occupy within the social structure
Three types are:
• Achieved: a type of position you do something to attain
• Ascribed: a type of position assigned to you
• Master: the position you gravitate toward

and classify people by using

Social Institutions
structures that provide for patterned relationships
• Family
• Education
• Religion
• Economic Systems
• Political and Legal Systems

and include

• Hunting and Gathering
• Agricultural
• Industrial
• Postindustrial

and have evolved through four main stages

Roles
the behaviour of a specific status
Terms associated with roles are:
• Role expectation: anticipated behaviours for a particular role
• Role performance: how a person plays his or her role
• Role set: the variety of roles an individual plays
• Role conflict: the conflict that arises when choosing between two different roles
• Role strain: the conflict that occurs when the demands and expectations of one role are impossible to satisfy

and assume that people occupy certain

Stigma
a mark of disgrace associated with a particular circumstance, quality, or person
Two types are:
• Discredited: a stigma that cannot be hidden from others, or is no longer hidden from others
• Discreditable: a stigma that can be concealed from others

Social Class in China

While some cultures don't have a rigid social class system, others have a well-established system. Take, for example, the Hukou system used in China immediately after the Communist Revolution. Under this system, once a person registered in a specific geographic area—rural or urban—he or she was not allowed to move far beyond the area. This fixed system gave city dwellers the advantages of better access to education and more opportunity for advancement than those living in rural areas.

Today, groups of workers in rural areas are predominantly male and make up emerging social classes. In the rural areas of modern China, being connected to the government is far less important than it is in urban areas, where Communist party membership can be vital to a person's success. Therefore, in urban areas class systems are significantly different than they are in rural areas. For one thing, they're much more fluid and allow for more movement than rural divisions do.

In the rigid rural class system, people do not have much freedom to move up and down the hierarchy. The rural system from top to bottom includes cadres, capitalists, managers, household business owners, professionals, wage labourers, and peasants.

For the urban class, the system is more flexible. The urban social class system from top to bottom includes capitalist entrepreneurs, intellectuals and professionals, members of the middle and working class, and the poor.

Because of the increasing fluidity of China's social systems, people are able to change the social class to which they belong. Receiving an education and owning a business are two ways that people raise their social standing.[4]

Social Status

Hollywood superstar Halle Berry, her Canadian former partner, and their baby jumped security lines at the Montreal international airport on January 4, 2010—and the headlines blared. A uniformed Montreal police officer had whisked the trio from the back to the front of the lines after Gabriel Aubrey, Berry's partner, revealed who she was and asked for help because they were late for their flight. Security at the time was extra tight. Police were later described as "embarrassed" and said they wouldn't let something like that happen again. But we all know that this is not an isolated incident.[5] In our fame-obsessed society, celebrities have reached a certain social status. Status refers to the position that a person occupies within the social structure and is often closely linked to social class. The wealthier and more powerful you are, the higher your social status will be. Often, a person's value to society does not determine his or her social status. For example, traditionally doctors enjoy high social status, while garbage collectors are looked down upon. However, if we had no more garbage collectors, a social crisis would arise more quickly than if we had no more doctors.

Sociologists divide status into two different types: achieved and ascribed. **Achieved status** refers to a type of position that someone earns or does something to attain. When you finish your college degree, you'll have *achieved* the position of college graduate. **Ascribed status** describes a position in society that is given or assigned. For example, socialite Paris Hilton's fame is an ascribed status. Because she was born into a wealthy and famous family, she draws attention at red-carpet events and enjoys the privileges of a celebrity. Hilton didn't choose to be wealthy, just like you didn't choose your gender, race, or ethnicity. Ascribed statuses are given to us at birth—we do not make a decision to choose them.

Most of us occupy a number of positions in our lives. For example, I am an author, college professor, husband, father, son, and brother, just to name a few. Since we all occupy more than one status in life we will gravitate toward one, which we call a **master status**. The master status may be what is most important to us, such as our status as a parent, or what is most important to others, such as one's ethnicity or social class.

People often perceive individuals who have high status to be experts in fields other than their professions. Julian A. Oldmeadow and colleagues found that personal status impacts others' perceptions.[6] In a study of student athletes, Oldmeadow found that team captains have a higher status than the rest of the team.[7] Thus, team members are likely to follow the advice of their captains even in areas unrelated to their particular sport.[8] The status of being a captain carries with it power. Some statuses in our society, such as judge, doctor, and professor, carry instant authority. People in other positions may be discounted when giving their opinions. For example, although a student may have more knowledge in a particular area, he or she may defer to the professor's wisdom on the topic because the professor has achieved a certain status and is deemed wise.

Status is an important social construct because the positions we occupy lead to the roles we play.

Social Roles

When you enter a classroom, you sit in the chairs designated for students. You don't go to the front of the room and stand behind the podium. You understand that your status is that of a student, and so you play the role of student, not teacher. A **role** is the behaviour of a specific status, and your status affects the role you play. If the professor asked you to lecture without any advance notice, you'd probably think something was wrong. This is because the roles we play come with certain expectations about how to play those roles.

Role expectations are the anticipated behaviours for a particular role. When you go to the doctor, you do as the doctor says, even if you have never met him or her before. This is because the statuses of doctor and patient define the roles. However, if the doctor is rude or obviously uninterested in your care, you'll say he or she has a "bad bedside manner." We tend to view people as less capable when they do not fill their role expectations as socially gracefully as we would hope.

Role expectations dominate our lives. When you refer to a "bad date," it's usually because you expected one thing and got something else. We evaluate **role performance** on whether or not a person plays the role in a manner we expect. It's important to remember that role expectations can be reasonable or unreasonable. If you expect your professor to make this course a cakewalk, you're probably going to be disappointed because you have an unreasonable expectation. If you then trash your instructor on a rate-your-professor website, it's because you judged his or her performance negatively based on your role expectation.

Robert Merton clarifies other important components of roles.[9] We all play a variety of roles, which make up our **role set**. As a college student, you might also play the role of child, employee, parent, or spouse, and when playing these multiple roles you might find you have to choose among the competing demands of those roles—a phenomenon known as **role conflict**. This happens when you need to study for a final exam to satisfy your role as a student the same night you need to attend your dad's retirement party to satisfy your role as a child.

At other times, we may feel **role strain**. This occurs when the demands and expectations of one role are impossible for us to satisfy. You might feel role strain when deciding whether to go out to a party on Saturday night or to cram for your midterm that Monday.

The ways in which status and roles influence our lives often go unnoticed. We expect the cashier at the grocery store to take our money and send us on our way. If he or she talks too much, we might get annoyed. The setting influences our expectations.

For example, in Iran the Supreme Leader of the nation is the ultimate religious authority, who is also the highest ranking authority figure in the government. Meanwhile, the president of Iran has far less political power, especially in areas of governmental policy.[10] These roles are just the opposite in Canada, where religious leaders may influence political decisions but are not allowed to implement laws and policies directly. The variety of statuses and roles depends upon the type of society.

Stigmas

Any convict who's been released from prison will tell you that life on the "outside" is no picnic. That's because people who serve time for a crime and then rejoin society carry with them the label of "ex-con" for the rest of their lives. In other words, we attach a **stigma**, or a mark of disgrace associated with a particular status, quality, or person, to the ex-convict. Sometimes, one's age, religion, sexual orientation, economic status, or race can result in a stigma.

ACHIEVED STATUS is a type of position that you earn or do something to attain.

ASCRIBED STATUS is a position in society that is given or assigned.

MASTER STATUS is the status toward which we gravitate.

ROLE is the behaviour of a specific status.

ROLE EXPECTATIONS are the anticipated behaviours for a particular role.

ROLE PERFORMANCE is the degree to which a person plays the role in a manner we expect.

ROLE SET is the variety of roles an individual plays.

ROLE CONFLICT is a phenomenon occurring when one is forced to choose between the competing demands of multiple roles.

ROLE STRAIN occurs when the demands and expectations of one role are impossible for us to satisfy.

STIGMA is a mark of disgrace associated with a particular status, quality, or person.

DISCREDITED STIGMA is a stigma that cannot be hidden from others or is no longer hidden from others.

DISCREDITABLE STIGMA is a stigma that can be concealed from others.

Sociologist Erving Goffman suggests that we all have a positive ideal identity that we hope others will accept.[11] Unfortunately, a stigma points out the differences between our ideal and real selves. There are two types of stigma—discredited stigma and discreditable stigma. A **discredited stigma** is a stigma that cannot be hidden from others, or is no longer hidden from others. A person with a physical handicap has a discredited stigma. A **discreditable stigma** is a stigma that can be concealed from others, such as sexual orientation, sexually transmitted infections, and criminal history.

For example, in *Succeeding From the Margins of Canadian Society,* Adu-Febiri and Ofori describe how racism and ethnocentrism in Canada stigmatize immigrants, refugees, and international students. The authors believe newcomers who understand what's going on can overcome social barriers and succeed in Canada.

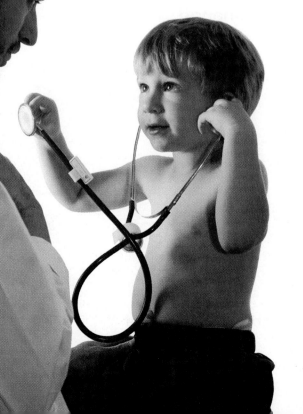

<<< Here, the roles seem to have reversed. We'd normally expect the adult to play the role of the doctor, while the child plays the role of the patient.

STAGES OF SOCIETAL CHANGE

As societies change over time, the complexity of social interaction also changes. With increasing population and technological advancement societies have become more diverse, which leads to changes in the social structures. American sociologist Gerhard E. Lenski is one of the few theorists who maintain an evolutionary view of society. According to Lenski and colleagues, the evolution of society consists of four main stages—hunting and gathering, agricultural, industrial, and postindustrial.[12]

Hunting and Gathering Societies

Have you ever wondered how you might survive if you were forced to become a hunter-gatherer? Recently, some friends and I took a camping trip into a wilderness area along the Canada–USA border. In such a place, you have only what you bring with you. And if you want to eat, you'd better learn how to fish, patiently, from a lake. I can't say we had much luck living off the land; the one fish I did manage to catch was hardly enough to feed us all. Luckily, the dehydrated food in our backpacks was enough to sustain us.

Of course, the first hunter-gatherers didn't rely on dehydrated food to survive, but they did live off the land and focused most of their efforts on finding food. Archeological evidence supports the idea that *Homo sapiens* lived as hunters and gatherers approximately 50 000 years ago. Beginning in the Neolithic period, hunters and gatherers existed in small groups of approximately 150 people for about 2000 generations. Over this period, their culture and population changed slowly.[13]

In hunting and gathering societies, an individual's status and role were closely linked. Thus, the status of tribal leader was often given to the strongest person or the best hunter. Because there were few roles for people to play in these types of societies, Lenski suggested that the division of labour in hunting and gathering societies was very limited.[14] Everyone in the society had to be involved in the production of food for survival.

Successful hunters and gatherers adapted to their environment. Geography professor Jared Diamond shows that food supply and available natural resources dictate a great deal about the form of society.[15] People living in areas with abundant food were able to hunt and gather for longer periods than those living in cold climates. Geological differences fostered human innovation. For example, farming and raising animals occurred in areas that supported crop growth and had a suitable climate for animals. This transition ushered in the agricultural stage of society.

Agricultural Societies

Roughly 10 000 years ago, people began to move from hunting and gathering to agrarian-based societies.[16] With this change, society became more complex. Lenski and colleagues divided agricultural societies into two groups: (1) pastoral and horticultural societies and (2) agricultural groups.[17]

Pastoral and horticultural societies appeared when humans learned to domesticate plants and animals. Members of these societies learned to use simple hand tools to till the soil and plant seeds in order to grow grains for food. They figured out that certain grains could be planted in soft ground. Likewise, they developed ways to raise certain types of animals in captivity, such as cows, goats, and chickens, which increased their food supply and allowed them to become less nomadic.[18]

Around 5000 to 7000 years ago, some groups took yet another step in the evolution of society. With the invention of the plough, agricultural societies arose. The simple technology of the animal-drawn plough—a sharp, hard piece of stone, wood, or metal that tills the soil—helped people cultivate lands that were previously unusable. The dramatic increase in food production promoted the growth of cities.[19] These agrarian city-states were often quite large, with up to one million people. Humans lived for approximately 500 generations in agrarian cultures.[20]

The Stages of Societal Change

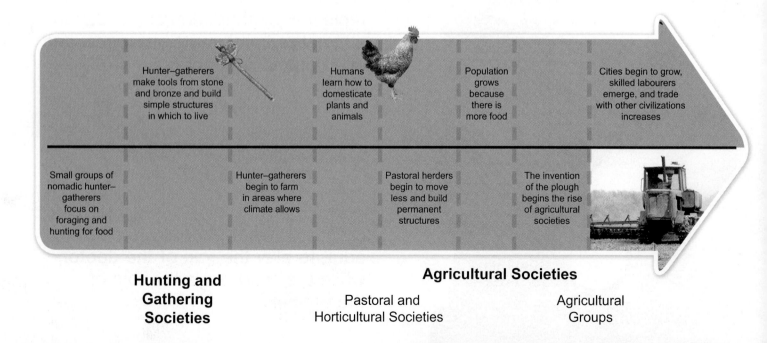

Hunter–gatherers make tools from stone and bronze and build simple structures in which to live

Humans learn how to domesticate plants and animals

Population grows because there is more food

Cities begin to grow, skilled labourers emerge, and trade with other civilizations increases

Small groups of nomadic hunter–gatherers focus on foraging and hunting for food

Hunter–gatherers begin to farm in areas where climate allows

Pastoral herders begin to move less and build permanent structures

The invention of the plough begins the rise of agricultural societies

Hunting and Gathering Societies

Agricultural Societies

Pastoral and Horticultural Societies

Agricultural Groups

Industrial Societies

During the seventeenth and eighteenth centuries, the Western world experienced an industrial revolution. Complex machines, such as the steam engine, encouraged the growth of industry. Steam-powered machines made human labour more efficient because the machines could perform a simple task quickly and repeatedly without rest.[21] The steam engine revolutionized the clothing industry, for example, because fabric no longer had to be hand-woven. Machines mass-produced fabric, which reduced the cost of labour.

This basic idea, using technology to create goods, greatly expanded the surplus of industrial societies. Farming techniques improved through mechanization, and early tractors expanded the farmable land even more. Fewer people were required to produce sufficient food for the population, which allowed for even more specialization of labour. As a result, more new types of jobs were created that ultimately led to new statuses and roles.

Lenski and colleagues suggested that industrial societies actually have less social inequality than agrarian societies.[22] This is largely because the increasing technology and surplus improve the standard of living. Even the poorest people in industrial societies have access to goods and services that are unavailable in agrarian societies.

The industrial society lasted only nine generations in some parts of the world, although it continues in others. The change occurred in some areas as a new form of society began—the postindustrial society.[23]

Postindustrial Societies

The term *postindustrial society* refers to the societal change that occurs when people move from an economy based on manufacturing to one based on service and technology. Such societies still require basic food and manufactured goods, but seek them from other countries. Before this stage, it's possible for a society to live off its natural resources. Since postindustrial societies can no longer meet their own needs, energy, food, and goods must be imported. These societies have become societies vested in a technology that grew exponentially with the invention of the microchip.

Sociologist Daniel Bell suggested three key characteristics of a postindustrial society: (1) a shift from manufacturing to services, (2) the centrality of the new science-based industries, and (3) the rise of new technical elites. These characteristics bring about changes in status and power.[24] The creation of wealth is no longer rooted in controlling land or building factories. Power and wealth are associated with who controls and develops the latest technology. Thus, Bill Gates became the richest man in the world by developing computer software.

Postindustrial societies have great surpluses of wealth and goods. Their material culture is the most developed of all societal forms. Consider the fact that even the poorest person in your neighbourhood probably owns a phone or a television. These societies do not provide dramatic changes in where people live or how they are governed, but the advances of technology expand divisions of labour and increase international interdependence.

SOCIAL INSTITUTIONS

> **SOCIAL INSTITUTIONS** are structures that provide for patterned relationships.

Although hunting and gathering, agricultural, industrial, and postindustrial societies are very different, they all share social institutions. **Social institutions** are structures that provide for patterned relationships.

In other words, the roles and statuses are already established and the members of society merely need to step into them. It's important to note that the specifics of these institutions change with the type of society and the culture of the people being studied.

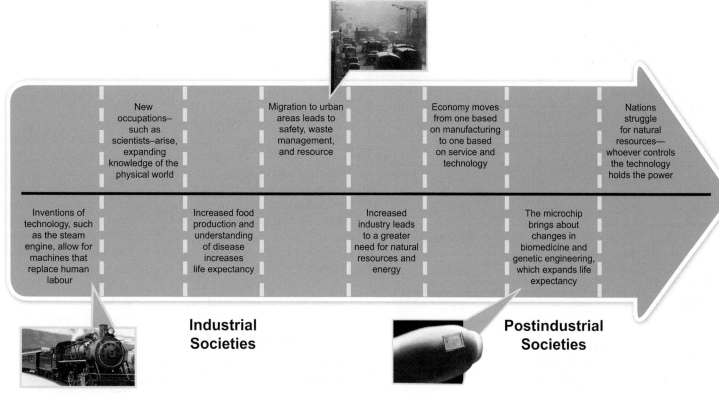

Industrial Societies		Postindustrial Societies
New occupations—such as scientists—arise, expanding knowledge of the physical world	Migration to urban areas leads to safety, waste management, and resource	Economy moves from one based on manufacturing to one based on service and technology	Nations struggle for natural resources—whoever controls the technology holds the power
Inventions of technology, such as the steam engine, allow for machines that replace human labour	Increased food production and understanding of disease increases life expectancy	Increased industry leads to a greater need for natural resources and energy	The microchip brings about changes in biomedicine and genetic engineering, which expands life expectancy

Family

Families are a cultural universal. The form of the family may have changed a great deal throughout human history, but the institution of family has remained constant.[25] Families teach the value of sharing and mutual support. They provide safety and security needs for their members, pass on important values, and offer a safe haven for raising children and caring for the elderly.

Educational and Religious Systems

Two more cultural universals, education and religion, assist in socialization. Educational systems transfer the knowledge and information of the society to new members and can be both formal and informal.

Religious practice varies a great deal depending upon a person's culture, but most religions unify people through an organized system of beliefs. By bringing people together, religion stabilizes society and provides a framework for people to live their lives.

Economic Systems

From the time of the earliest hunters and gatherers to today, societies have required a system that helps people get what they need. Economic systems allow for the consumption, production, and orderly transition of goods from one person to another. If, for example, you want a new TV, you understand how to trade money to get it. Without an economic system, people either do without or steal. Either option would make for a dangerous and chaotic society.

Every region has some type of educational system, *even though every child does not always participate in that system.*

Secondary School Net Enrollment Rate in World Regions, 2006

Developed Regions	**92%**
Developing Regions	**54%**
Sub-Saharan Africa	25%
Oceania	33%
Southern Asia	54%
Western Asia	58%
Northern Africa	60%
Southeastern Africa	63%
Latin America & the Caribbean	67%
Eastern Asia	68%
Transitional Countries in South and Eastern Europe	84%

Source: Data from the United Nations, *The Millennium Development Goals Report*, 2007

Early economic systems involved bartering—the trading of goods from one person to another. As societies became more complex, the currency of coins and money became the default value source, allowing for quicker and easier transitions of goods and services. Although bartering is often thought of as an ancient system, there are modern-day examples of the barter system on websites such as Craigslist. Craigslist gives users a forum to post free classified ads for jobs, internships, housing, and personals.

To keep a society's economic system running smoothly and efficiently, rules must be established. That's why every society has political and legal systems to help establish rules for society at large.

Political and Legal Systems

Ever since the first chief in the first hunter-gatherer tribe was named, people have been involved in politics. Political systems distribute power in a society, and power is the key component of any political system, whether a dictatorship or democracy. As you consider the importance of political systems, it's crucial to understand how power is used.

Political power is used to create laws or rules that dictate right and wrong in society. So, the political and legal systems are integrally linked. When someone with power sees something that's wrong, he or she is likely to create a law to fix it. The legal system serves the vital function of enforcing those laws to maintain social order and promote unity.

Although the form may vary, family, education, religion, economics, politics, and legislation exist in every form of society. That makes these institutions social facts. As we have seen, societies become more complex as they develop; this complexity results in the replacement of many of the old ways of living and thinking.

HOLDING SOCIETY TOGETHER

In January 1998, icy rain fell upon Quebec and surrounding areas for five days in what came to be known as the ice storm of the century. In Quebec alone 900 000 households lost power, and damage was estimated to be in the billions of dollars. At least 25 people died. The extreme weather forced about 100 000 people to leave their homes and take refuge in temporary shelters.[26] As a sociologist, I was amazed to see people's generosity—we learned that throughout the affected area friends and family threw open their doors and otherwise helped thousands of people to stay warm. What exactly holds a society together? Solidarity. That's the "glue" that binds a society.

Mechanical and Organic Solidarity

Think back to Chapter 1, when you first learned about Émile Durkheim and solidarity—the shared values, needs, and beliefs of a society. Durkheim suggested that simple forms of society have mechanical solidarity, whereas organic solidarity holds more complex societies together. In societies with mechanical solidarity, people's common beliefs and practices help bind them together. On the other hand, the interdependence of the people is what holds organic societies together. Durkheim's idea led German sociologist Ferdinand Tonnies to investigate how the form of society affects the interactions that we might have.

Gemeinschaft and *Gesellschaft*

Society can be classified into two distinct groups: *Gemeinschaft* (or community) and *Gesellschaft* (or society).[27] **Gemeinschaft** connections involve personal relationships based on friendship and kinship ties, such as the family. A society's form can also influence the type of group. For example, small bands of hunters and gatherers live in communal societies because they have very little division of labour. This creates a group that exists with shared values, goals, and beliefs.

Often we also engage in groups considered as *Gesellschaft*. These relationships are more formal and impersonal. Urban life is filled with many impersonal interchanges, so groups living here are more likely to occur in industrial and postindustrial societies. In such a society, social status, role, and social class become very important. Are you interested in knowing the janitor who cleans the classroom? You're probably only aware that the seats and floor are clean. Tonnies suggested that as societies grow more complex, many of our interactions invariably become more impersonal.

As you review these ideas, you can see that large cities tend toward *Gesellschaft* relationships, while smaller ones tend to be more *Gemeinschaft.* That means the size of your immediate area influences your daily life.[28] This idea leads sociologists to look for other common behaviour patterns. To do this, we turn from large-scale observations and review the sociological study of small orientations.

∧
∧ Since people have virtually the
∧ same job, **mechanical solidarity** creates a common moral order that **holds people together.**

GEMEINSCHAFT refers to community connections involving personal relationships based on friendship and kinship ties, such as family.

GESELLSCHAFT refers to societal connections that are more formal and impersonal.

THINK SOCIOLOGICALLY

Social Class and Character Traits

Many people believe that a person's social class implies specific traits. A story in a 1994 book on Upper Canada College by Toronto writer James FitzGerald illustrates the point.[29] UCC is an exclusive boys' school whose students have included the sons of the rich and famous upper class in Canada, and some people regard it as snobbish. (Indeed, FitzGerald quotes author James Bacque as saying, "In my day, UCC was very

snobbish."[30]) Trial judge Frank Kelso Roberts recalls in the book that when he was a young lawyer, another young lawyer—after being scolded by senior partners in their firm for making a mistake—confided that he had come up "through a poor family." The young lawyer used derogatory terms for the senior partners and mentioned in the same sentence that the senior partners were "all Upper Canada College graduates." Roberts didn't mention that he too had attended UCC. Instead, he agreed with the young lawyer's assessment.[31]

It's clear that the lawyer from a poor family regarded everyone who had graduated from the privileged halls of UCC as uniformly unpleasant. He was so sure of it that he didn't even consider that a lawyer he looked up to might have attended the same school.

When people hear the terms *working, middle,* and *upper class,* they don't always think about character right away—the terms are generally first associated with occupation and salary. Do you think these terms also imply specific personal characteristics?

PERSONAL SPACE is the invisible bubble that each of us has around us that insulates us from others.

INTIMATE DISTANCE is distance reserved for those with whom we are very close.

PERSONAL DISTANCE is distance that ranges from 45 centimetres to 1.2 metres; this distance is for normal conversations.

SOCIAL DISTANCE is distance that ranges from about 1.2 metres to 3.6 metres and is usually reserved for formal settings.

PUBLIC DISTANCE is the zone of interaction that is used in highly formal settings; this distance includes everything greater than 3.6 metres.

Micro Orientations: Social Interactions

Generally, macro orientations take for granted that society exists. Micro orientations place more emphasis on the ways in which societies are held together. Thus, symbolic interactionists tend to study the "how" of society, as opposed to the "what." Instead of observing what binds a society together, these sociologists seek to discover how that society is held together.

Communication is one component of the "how" of the social world. However, communication involves more than simply having conversations. From verbal interaction to physical distance, effective communication requires knowledge of the things that inform how we communicate with one another. One of those things, **personal space**, refers to the invisible bubble that each of us has around us that insulates us from others.

Just as you adjust the personal distance between yourself and others depending on the situation, you probably also adjust your behaviour so that it's appropriate for the setting you're in. **When you're in public, you often show off your best self to others and hide what you don't want them to see.**

PERSONAL SPACE

How do you feel when someone stands very close to you during a conversation? It's a little uncomfortable, right? Even if the person is a friend, your natural impulse is to back away.

Our feelings about personal space often depend upon the setting and the person with whom we are interacting. For example, in order for a doctor to properly examine you, she needs to enter your personal space. In a different setting, you would never allow such behaviour. Although socially appropriate amounts of personal space vary between cultures, Edward Hall suggests that people in North America have four discrete zones of personal space.[32]

1 We reserve **intimate distance** for those with whom we are very close. This zone covers roughly from 0 to 45 centimetres. We generally reserve this distance for intimate encounters, but these conditions may vary depending on setting.

2 **Personal distance** ranges from 45 centimetres to 1.2 metres. Normal conversations occur at a personal distance. When you share secrets with a friend, you automatically lean in to an intimate distance. Once the whispering is over, though, you will automatically return to a personal distance.

3 **Social distance** ranges from about 1.2 metres to 3.6 metres and is usually reserved for formal settings. When you go on a job interview, for instance, you generally sit at what sociologist Edward Hall called "social distance."[33] Social encounters at this distance are not very personal. This distance allows the speaker to be heard, but does not presume any friendship.

4 **Public distance** refers to the zone of interaction that is used in highly formal settings. This distance includes everything greater than 3.6 metres. When you sit in the back of the classroom, you guarantee that you will maintain a public distance from your professor. Public distance also occurs during political speeches, at churches, and at formal events. Speakers are separate from the listener, and, generally, the audience shows respect and deference to the speaker.

Zones of Personal Space

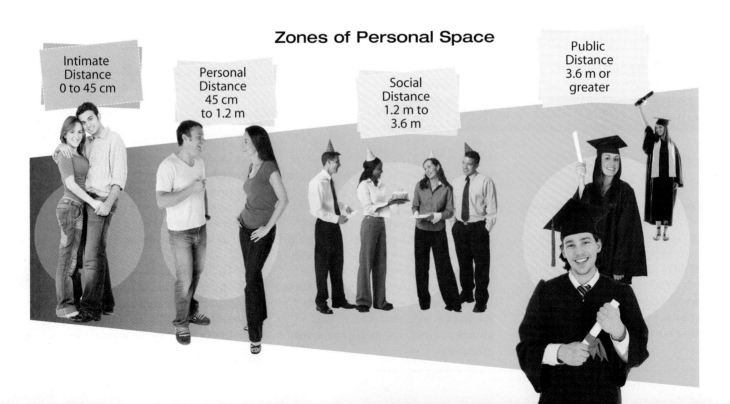

Intimate Distance 0 to 45 cm

Personal Distance 45 cm to 1.2 m

Social Distance 1.2 m to 3.6 m

Public Distance 3.6 m or greater

DRAMATURGY

"All the world's a stage," Shakespeare wrote in *As You Like It*. Though he wasn't technically a sociologist, the Bard may have been more accurate than he realized. Erving Goffman developed a theory of interaction called dramaturgy, which suggests that life is like acting.[34] Social actors enter every situation with two possible selves. The first, the performer, attempts to manage the impressions that he or she makes on others. Goffman termed this effort **impression management**.

For example, if you think someone having an iced mocha at the corner coffee shop is attractive, you might want to make contact with him or her. As you approach, hoping to look "cool," you are entering the **front stage**. This is what the audience sees. Most of us live our lives on the front stage.

Of course, we are more than our front stage acts. **Backstage** demeanour incorporates our true feelings and beliefs. Most people do not show their backstage personas very often. We usually save that version of ourselves for our very closest family and friends.

Returning to our coffee shop example, let's assume that as you approach this person, you trip and fall. Obviously, you'll be embarrassed. **Embarrassment** occurs when we realize our act has failed. It's hard to pull off looking cool and tripping at the same time. When this type of mismatch happens, we engage in **face-saving work**. People generally choose one of three different options when they engage in face-saving work: humour, anger, or retreat.

Using humour, you can turn an embarrassing situation into a self-deprecating joke. This gives you the chance to impress upon the person that you have your act together because you can laugh at yourself.

In an angry reaction to this embarrassing situation, you may start cussing. This reaction is an attempt to say to the audience, "I'm powerful, even though I'm on the floor."

Efforts to retreat when we become embarrassed involve simply an attempt to escape. After all, our act has failed, and we want to leave the stage as soon as possible.

Goffman suggests that we would be wise to distrust most of what we see in other people because almost every interaction is front stage behaviour. A wise student of Goffman can use impression management to get ahead in the world. Look at the Make Connections box and review the research there by Wayne and Liden.[35]

IMPRESSION MANAGEMENT is management of the impression that the performer makes on others.

FRONT STAGE is what the audience sees, or the part of ourselves that we present to others.

BACKSTAGE is the demeanour that incorporates our true feelings and beliefs.

EMBARRASSMENT is a state that occurs when we realize our act has failed.

FACE-SAVING WORK is a reaction to embarrassment in the form of either humour, anger, or retreat.

<<< In September 2010, Manitoba judge Lori Douglas stepped down from active duty to await results of a federal review—immediately after news broke that naked photos of her engaged in bondage had appeared on the Web.[36] Politicians try to craft their front stage selves to appear family-oriented and honest; however, their backstage selves may tell a different story. What other types of occupations require a person to have a highly controlled front stage demeanour?

MAKE CONNECTIONS

Using Impression Management to Get Ahead in the Workplace

No matter where you start your career, you probably hope to climb the ladder of success while you're there. You can impress your boss and chart your course to the corner office of your dreams by following the simple steps below.

Sandy J. Wayne and Robert C. Liden showed that successful impression management techniques positively affect an employee's performance rating.[37] They found three components that influence successful performance reviews: demographic similarity, supervisor-focused impression management, and self-focused impression management. **Demographic similarity** means that you share characteristics such as race, gender, or age with your boss, coworkers, or others you encounter. **Supervisor-focused impression management** techniques involve flattering your boss and agreeing with your boss's opinions (or at least avoiding disagreements whenever possible). **Self-focused impression management** techniques include acting modest about your accomplishments (even if that modesty is false), boasting occasionally about your successes, and showing your friendliness and self-assuredness through smiles and eye contact.

Most of us like people who are like us, and bosses are no different. By using either self-focused or supervisor-focused impression management techniques, you can advance your career and look forward to the day when your employees use impression management techniques to impress *you*.

>>> ACTIVITY The next time you hang out with a friend, act as though your friend is your boss and use the impression management techniques listed above. Record how he or she responds and share it with your class.

think sociologically: HOW DO THE FOUR PARADIGMS VIEW SOCIAL STRUCTURES?

Now let's turn our attention from the specific terms and concepts of the macro/micro world, and look at it through the lens of the four sociological paradigms.

An Example of Symbolic Interactionism: The Thomas Theorem and the Social Creation of Reality

From the interactionist point of view comes the Thomas Theorem: "If men [sic] define situations as real, they are real in their consequences."[38] This statement describes the social construction of reality.

Remember reading earlier in the chapter about the man with an engineering degree who was working as a dishwasher? That situation and the one I am about to describe illustrate how social barriers can help dictate your own personal reality. A colleague told me that one winter, this unforgettable wintry story was doing the rounds in Edmonton, where she worked at the time. It was about a black mathematician from a warm country who had a foreign degree and had been unable to find work in his field since arriving in Canada. Whenever he applied for a job, he was told to "get Canadian experience." So he started driving a cab in Ottawa. During his first winter on the job, there was a heavy snowstorm. He was sitting waiting for a fare when a white woman with a "Canadian" accent knocked on his window, calling "Help!" He rolled down his window. The woman said her car was stuck in the snow and she needed him to help her get it out. The cab driver stared at the woman, then slowly turned away and rolled up his window, saying: "I'm sorry, lady. I don't have any *Canadian* experience." On this day, that man claimed his own personal power. The social creation of reality emphasizes personal power; however, it does not deny the importance of social structures and their effects on us. We attach the meaning of events to them.

An Example of Functionalism: Studying Essential Features of Functional Social Structures

When functionalists study a topic, they often ask how various elements fit together. Social institutions and structures serve essential functions in a society. As you study social structures in later chapters, you will see a general functional framework that applies in virtually all cases. Durkheim (1858–1917) called these essential features "functional requisites."[39] Consider the five primary tasks of society that create social structures: (1) adaptation and replacement, (2) socialization and orientation, (3) production and economy, (4) social order, and (5) unity and purpose.

Adaptation and Replacement Effective and functional societies must get their needs met to survive. Jared Diamond suggests that societies collapse unless they can accomplish certain tasks, including adapting to changes in the environment.[40] Adaptations are also essential for accommodating the changing relationships that a society has with the world around it.

Besides adapting to environmental and political changes, societies must also replace people who either die or leave the group. Without continually replacing people, societies cannot carry on.

Socialization and Orientation Closely tied to replacement are socialization and orientation of new members. When children are born, they need to be socialized into the group. Socialization and orientation are vital to the continuation of a society because these processes allow new members to join and assign them roles. In "traditional societies," this assigning of roles might include gender-specific tasks such as men hunting or women caring for children. In a postindustrial society, socialization and orientation can be much more formal and include teaching related social norms.

Socialization is not possible without some means to communicate. Societies create a system of symbols that include language and gestures to orient new members and to pass on information to the next generation. Socialization takes place in schools and families as well as through media, religion, and other structures found in various forms of society.

Production and Economy The ability of a society to meet its needs through its environment is the most important idea associated with this task. Simple societies create a material culture based on the resources at hand, whereas more complex societies trade with other groups to get the goods and services they need.[41] People within complex societies require an economic system to simplify the trading of goods and services. Although the exact nature of the economic system differs between societies, people always need a way to make or acquire the goods and services they need.

Social Order Because every society has people who cannot follow the rules, social norms and sanctions must be created to deal with these lawbreakers. In simple societies, force and strength might rule the day,

∧
∧ **According to Durkheim, there are**
∧ **"functional requisites" that hold society together.** Think of the five tasks listed as puzzle pieces; if you're missing one, the puzzle isn't complete.

whereas in complex societies, people settle disputes through legal battles. Not all societies have written laws, but they all socialize their members to promote social order.

Unity and Purpose Unity is achieved through common thoughts, beliefs, and attitudes. Canada is built on common ideals, not common heritage. Those shared thoughts united people, leading them to create a new country. Unity is also achieved through a sense of purpose, which gives a society some goal to achieve. This purpose holds people together, causing them to work together in times of trial.[42]

An Example of Conflict Theory: Deliberate Efforts to Weaken the Structure and Culture of First Nations Peoples

In order to understand the interaction of micro and macro components, consider the conflict perspective of the interaction of First Nations Peoples with European settlers in what is now Canada.

The Europeans started to explore the land in the sixteenth and seventeenth centuries, and from their earliest contact with the aboriginal peoples it was clear that the French and English would determine how Canada developed.[43] Striving to change both micro and macro components of life for the First Nations Peoples, the goal was to teach them the ways of the white people.

By the early nineteenth century, church-run mission schools were trying to teach First Nations Peoples to read English so they could study the Bible and convert to Christianity.[44] The British colonial government started to work with the churches, and around 1864 set up a residential school system; they suggested that if they did not intervene, "native people would be left behind" in a modern Canada.[45] In 1876, nine years after the Dominion of Canada came into being, Parliament passed the first Indian Act, and now "the government was required to provide aboriginal peoples with an education and to integrate aboriginal peoples into Canadian society."[46] By 1931, there were about 80 residential schools in Canada.[47] In 1969, it was decided that the schools should be closed; the last one closed in 1996.[48]

In the residential school system, First Nations children were sent (or taken) away to schools that might be very far from their homes. Excessive punishment, sexual abuse, and the fact that aboriginal languages were forbidden in most school operations were among the harsh realities of life.[49] "It is generally accepted," states the Indian Residential School Survivors Society website, "that the forced removal of children from their families was devastating for aboriginal individuals, families, communities and cultures."[50]

The IRSSS notes that estimates suggest as many as 60 percent of the students died while in the schools, and the aftermath in First Nations communities has included higher rates of violence than elsewhere in the country, sexual abuse, suicide, drug abuse, unemployment, and poverty.[51] In 2008, Prime Minister Stephen Harper, on behalf of the federal government, offered an apology to all former students of residential schools in Canada.[52] Under the Indian Residential Schools Settlement Agreement—the largest class action settlement in Canadian history—$1.9 billion was set aside to directly benefit former residential school students. Each could potentially receive $10 000 for the first school year and $3000 for each subsequent year.[53]

What happened to the First Nations Peoples in Canada is not unlike what happened elsewhere in North America. In the United States, the structures of family and the entire Native American population were weakened because the children were removed to boarding schools, thus leaving

DEMOGRAPHIC SIMILARITY refers to shared characteristics such as race, gender, or age.

SUPERVISOR-FOCUSED IMPRESSION MANAGEMENT refers to techniques that involve flattering your boss and agreeing with your boss's opinions (or at least avoiding disagreements whenever possible).

SELF-FOCUSED IMPRESSION MANAGEMENT refers to techniques that include acting modest about your accomplishments (even if that modesty is false), boasting occasionally about your successes, and showing your friendliness and self-assuredness through smiles and eye contact.

parents with no role to fill and children without the support they needed. Consequently, a generation of people were unschooled in their own culture. Whites viewed all this as a social program designed to help aboriginal peoples to assimilate, but aboriginal peoples saw it as an example of cultural genocide.[54]

An Example of Feminist Theory: The Gender Wage Gap in Canada

In August 2010, in Canada the average hourly wage for a man was $24.07; for a woman, it was $20.56.[55] Why is there a difference? Feminist theory argues that in Canada, as in most countries, the social structure is patriarchal; that is, it benefits men more than women. One area in which women have long been disadvantaged—and still are—is in the wages they earn. Despite a growing number of women participating in the labour force, and increases in women's levels of skill, educational attainment, and work experience, there is still a noticeable and persistent difference in wages. One explanation for the difference is that women are more likely to work in lower-paying jobs, such as retail or childcare. Of course, this leads to the question, Which came first? Are these jobs lower-paying because they have traditionally been held by women, or are women's wages lower than men's because they are more likely to choose those jobs that pay less?

Because the Canadian social structure has developed according to a patriarchal ideology, the differences in pay that have been deeply entrenched in the employment system reflect gender bias. The social structure is fundamentally designed so that work done mainly by women is paid less than work done mainly by men. Occupational segregation ensures that males will generally earn more than females.[56]

What about when men and women work in the same job? There is still a discrepancy in their earnings, with men earning slightly more than their female coworkers. Part of the explanation comes from the fact that it is women who have babies. When a man and a woman start a new job together, they will probably earn the same salary. However, it is more likely that the woman will at some time have to leave her job if she has a child. This will have long-term consequences on her earnings. While a woman is off on maternity leave, she is probably not developing her work skills. But her male coworker will likely continue to acquire more skills, which will result in promotions and raises for him.[57]

As a society, we can choose how we view women who leave the workforce to have children. In Canada, there is a growing trend toward offering "parental" leave rather than "maternity" leave. With both mothers and fathers eligible to take the same amount of time off when a child is born, what impact might this have on the gender wage gap?

WRAP YOUR MIND AROUND THE THEORY

How do you think **these two people** from *Crash* might **define their situations?**

FUNCTIONALISM

Social institutions and structures are essential functions for society. Sociologists believe that there are five basic structures necessary for a society to function. However, just because society is getting its needs met, this does not mean individual members of society are also having their needs fulfilled. Canada has a stable social structure, but millions of people are living at or below the poverty level. Functionalists might suggest that for both the rich and the poor, the economic system rewards those with ability and drive, while the system allows those who are less motivated to fall behind of their own merits.

CONFLICT THEORY

Conflict theorists study issues such as race, social class, and inequality. After Hurricane Katrina hit the Gulf Coast and flooded parts of Louisiana, Mississippi, and Alabama, the U.S. federal government's response to the citizens there was widely criticized. Many people alleged that aid was delayed because a majority of struggling citizens were poor African Americans. Did the citizens' social class really affect their treatment? The book *Succeeding From the Margins of Canadian Society,* highlighted at the start of this chapter, includes a section on racial profiling. It mentions a *Toronto Star* finding that African Canadians in that city are much more likely to be charged with traffic offences than the mainstream population.[58] The 2002 newspaper article was headlined "Police target black drivers: Star analysis of traffic data suggests racial profiling."[59] It said that Toronto police traffic offence data that the newspaper had obtained and analyzed "shows a disproportionate number of blacks ticketed for violations" that police had routinely only become aware of once they had pulled motorists over (e.g., driving without insurance). Do you think people's race affects their treatment much – even in Canada?

SYMBOLIC INTERACTIONISM

Symbolic interactionists believe that a person's social creation of reality may take into account social issues such as job opportunities, welfare policies, and unemployment. Experiences with these issues can have an effect on people, causing them to alter their creation of reality. Recall how impression management can be used to help you get ahead on the job. Bosses may take demographic differences into account. For example, in the 2004 movie *Crash,* Farhad, a Persian shop owner, incorrectly assumes that his Hispanic locksmith looted his shop. Farhad's belief that Hispanic men cannot be trusted leads him to take matters dramatically into his own hands.

FEMINIST THEORY

Feminists perceive the social structure to be overtly patriarchal. More opportunities are available to men within the structure because the structure has been built to benefit men. If it were mainly men who worked in childcare facilities, how much do you think childcare workers would earn? The gender wage gap in Canada is evidence that the social structure of work in Canada benefits men more than women.

DOES THE SOCIAL STRUCTURE IN CANADA REALLY HAVE A "GLASS CEILING"?

Even though we are living in a stable society, millions of Canadians are living in poverty. How should society adapt to help these individuals?

Does society tip the scale in **favour of certain segments of the population?**

discover sociology in action: HOW CAN SOCIAL POLICIES IMPROVE SOCIETY?

In our culture, social policies are applied in an effort to improve society. High-quality preschool is one area that is still going through much change in Canada.

Social Policy—Childcare in Canada

Preschool childcare is a controversial subject in Canada. It's widely used, and levels of funding vary across the country.

Seven out of 10 preschool children with an employed or studying mother now use regulated childcare (including kindergarten) in Quebec, and 4 out of 10 do so in the rest of the country, a major report prepared for the non-profit Institute for Research on Public Policy revealed in 2008. That means the Quebec figures tripled and the figures for the rest of Canada doubled, to 72 percent and 40 percent, respectively, in the space of a decade.[60]

This gives you a good idea of how important high-quality preschool childcare has become in Canada. It also reflects the fact that Quebec is regarded as a leader in providing universal daycare (even though there have been some problems with waiting lists to get into subsidized daycare programs in Quebec).[61]

When kindergarten is not counted, just over a third of all Canadian preschool children with employed or studying mothers now attend regulated care services, and just under a third receive exclusively parental care, the IRPP report said.[62] Kindergarten is part of the compulsory school system only in New Brunswick.[63] It is free for five-year-olds, and in Ontario also for four-year-olds. Most regulated childcare is expensive, the IRPP report notes, adding that "Low-income (particularly single-parent) families in Canada may be eligible for childcare subsidies for children of any age. As a result, those in the lowest income quintile are not less likely to use regulated care than those with middle incomes."[64]

The federal government has been proposing to make some changes to its childcare benefits.[65] However, in 2009 the Child Care Advocacy Association of Canada said the government had "simply failed to meet the child needs of Canadian families."[66]

From Classroom to Community Giving Kids a Good Start

Nasreen, a student in a sociology course, decided to volunteer at a local daycare centre.

She told our class, "The first thing I noticed was that the entire program was about socialization. The teachers taught the kids about rules and how to fit in. The children and parents both attend different classes designed to help them adapt to school and eventually be successful in it."

During her time as a volunteer, Nasreen helped set up classrooms, file necessary papers, and supervise the children during free time. "Playing with the kids was my favourite thing to do. I discovered that many of the things with which I was raised are rare for these children. For example, their clothes and toys were often used and torn. Some came for lunch because their parents could not always afford food for them."

Nasreen saw her time as a volunteer through the lenses of both functionalists and conflict theorists. I couldn't help but think that this program was really there to help teach children how to fit into school and the larger society. In that way, it supports social control components of society and socializes children.

"However, the lack of staff and funding seemed to be the major issue facing my placement. I couldn't help but wonder why the program was so underfunded. It seems like people should be able to do more to help these kids learn."

get the topic: WHAT ELEMENTS CREATE A SOCIAL STRUCTURE?

Theory

SYMBOLIC INTERACTIONISM   78
- a person's social creation of reality may take into account social issues such as job opportunities, welfare policies, unemployment, and access to a living wage
- experiences with these issues can have an effect on people, causing them to alter their creation of reality

FUNCTIONALISM   78
- social institutions and structures are essential functions for society
- five primary tasks of society that create social structures: (1) adaptation and replacement, (2) orientation and socialization, (3) production and economy, (4) social order, (5) unity and purpose

- just because society is having its needs met does not mean that individual members of society are also having their needs fulfilled

CONFLICT THEORY   79
- studies issues such as race, social class, and inequality
- social class and race may play a part in such different situations as receiving aid after a hurricane and being pulled over by police

FEMINIST THEORY   79
- in most societies, the social structure is patriarchal
- gender inequality is a significant feature of the social structure

Key Terms

macrosociology is the study of large-scale society, focusing on the social structures that exist within a society and examining how those structures create the social world.   *69*

microsociology is the study of the small interactions of daily life.   *69*

social structures are patterns of relationships that endure from one generation to the next.   *69*

groups are any number of people with similar norms, values, and behaviours who frequently interact with one another.   *69*

primary groups are groups that are small, intimate, and enduring.   *69*

secondary groups are groups that are formal, superficial, and temporary.   *69*

achieved status is a type of position that you earn or do something to attain.   *70*

ascribed status is a position in society that is given or assigned.   *70*

master status is the status toward which we gravitate.   *70*

role is the behaviour of a specific status.   *70*

role expectations are the anticipated behaviours for a particular role.   *70*

role performance is the degree to which a person plays the role in a manner we expect.   *70*

(continued)

role set is the variety of roles an individual plays. 71

role conflict is a phenomenon occurring when one is forced to choose between the competing demands of multiple roles. 71

role strain occurs when the demands and expectations of one role are impossible for us to satisfy. 71

stigma is a mark of disgrace associated with a particular status, quality, or person. 71

discredited stigma is a stigma that cannot be hidden from others or is no longer hidden from others. 71

discreditable stigma is a stigma that can be concealed from others. 71

social institutions are structures that provide for patterned relationships. 73

Gemeinschaft refers to community connections involving personal relationships based on friendship and kinship ties, such as family. 74

Gesellschaft refers to societal connections that are more formal and impersonal. 75

personal space is the invisible bubble that each of us has around us that insulates us from others. 76

intimate distance is distance reserved for those with whom we are very close. 76

personal distance is distance that ranges from 45 centimetres to 1.2 metres; this distance is for normal conversations. 76

social distance is distance that ranges from about 1.2 metres to 3.6 metres and is usually reserved for formal settings. 76

public distance is the zone of interaction that is used in highly formal settings; this distance includes everything greater than 3.6 metres. 76

impression management is management of the impression that the performer makes on others. 77

front stage is what the audience sees, or the part of ourselves that we present to others. 77

backstage is the demeanour that incorporates our true feelings and beliefs. 77

embarrassment is a state that occurs when we realize our act has failed. 77

face-saving work is a reaction to embarrassment in the form of either humour, anger, or retreat. 77

demographic similarity refers to shared characteristics such as race, gender, or age. 77

supervisor-focused impression management refers to techniques that involve flattering your boss and agreeing with your boss's opinions (or at least avoiding disagreements whenever possible). 77

self-focused impression management refers to techniques that include acting modest about your accomplishments (even if that modesty is false), boasting occasionally about your successes, and showing your friendliness and self-assuredness through smiles and eye contact. 77

Sample Test Questions

These multiple-choice questions are similar to those found in the test bank that accompanies this textbook.

1. In what kind of society is the economy based on service and technology?
   a. Industrial
   b. Agricultural
   c. Postindustrial
   d. Hunting and gathering
2. Craigslist is an example of a modern-day
   a. social institution.
   b. political system.
   c. barter system.
   d. religious group.
3. Which of the following systems distributes power in a society?
   a. Legal
   b. Political
   c. Economic
   d. Educational
4. Which of the following groups is the best example of a *Gemeinschaft* relationship?
   a. A large city
   b. A soccer team
   c. A government
   d. A large corporation
5. Which of the five tasks of society allows new members to join and assigns roles to the new members?
   a. Socialization and orientation
   b. Adaptation and replacement
   c. Production and economy
   d. Unity and purpose

ANSWERS: 1. c; 2. c; 3. b; 4. b; 5. a

ESSAY

1. What are the differences between an industrial society and a postindustrial society?
2. How do societies demonstrate adaptation and replacement for survival? Give examples.
3. Why is it important to observe the conventions of personal space?
4. Explain how a group might change from a *Gemeinschaft* to a *Gesellschaft*.
5. Which systems would a conflict theorist target when addressing the issue of cultural integration? Why?

WHERE TO START YOUR RESEARCH PAPER

For more information on sociological theories, especially the works of Durkheim and Marx, go to

http://socserv.mcmaster.ca/w3virtsoclib/theories.htm

To learn more about the agricultural revolution and its transition from hunting and gathering, go to

www.wsu.edu/gened/learn-modules/top_agrev/agrev-index.html

For a detailed view of hunting and gathering in New Guinea, go to

www.climatechange.umaine.edu/Research/projects/NewGuinea.html

To learn more about how elevated social status may help people live longer lives, go to

www.canada.com/health/Canadians+living+longer+Study/2602046/story.html, www.newscientist.com/article/dn10972-social-status-helps-you-live-longer.html

For more information on impression management as an important factor in business success, go to http://changingminds.org/index.htm

Remember to check www.thethinkspot.ca for additional information, downloadable flashcards, and other helpful resources.

SOCIALIZATION

"The Marines. . .

draw their recruits from the most extravagantly individualistic civilian society in the world and turn them into elite combat soldiers in twelve weeks.

"It's easier if you catch them young. You can train older men to be soldiers; it's done in every major war. But you can never get them to believe that they like it, which is the major reason armies try to get their recruits before they are twenty.

"Young civilians who have volunteered and been accepted by the Marine Corps arrive at Parris Island, the Corps's East Coast facility for basic training, in a state of considerable excitement and apprehension. Most are aware that they are about to undergo an extraordinary and very difficult experience. . . .

"During a period of only seventy-two hours, in which they are allowed little sleep, the recruits lay aside their former lives in a series of hasty rituals (like being shaven to the scalp) whose symbolic significance is quite clear to them even though they are deliberately given no time for reflection, nor any hint that they might have the option of turning back from their commitment. . . .

"The first stage of any conversion process is the destruction of an individual's former beliefs and confidence, and his reduction to a position of helplessness and need. . . . The training, when it starts, seems impossibly demanding for most of the recruits—and then it gets harder week by week. . . . But it is all carefully calculated by the men who run the machine, who think and talk in terms of the stress they are placing on the recruits. . . . The aim is to keep the training arduous but just within reach of most of the recruits' capability to withstand. One of the most striking achievements of the drill instructors is to create and maintain the illusion that basic training is an extraordinary challenge, one that will set those who graduate apart from others, when in fact almost everyone can succeed."[1]

The Process of Fitting *into* Society

CHAPTER 05

In this excerpt from *War: The New Edition,* Gwynne Dyer describes the arrival of new U.S. Marine Corps recruits at Parris Island, South Carolina.

GWYNNE DYER

In 2002, I had the opportunity to visit Parris Island and to work there for one week. As someone who had studied sociology and was familiar with the terms *resocialization* and *total institution,* I was still deeply affected by what I saw, and the overall design and efficiency of the training that these young men and women were undergoing. Every day that I was there, I would think about the enormity of the transformation that was happening before my eyes. The Marine Corps has trained hundreds of thousands of recruits to do something that, for most of us, is the most terrible thing we could ever do—to kill.

get the topic: WHAT IS SOCIALIZATION?

SOCIALIZATION is the process that teaches the norms, values, and other aspects of a culture to new group members.

How do you know what language to speak? What does a red light mean? From the minute you are born, you are being socialized into the world around you. At a baseball game I recently attended, a young man did not remove his hat during the national anthem. Offended, an older man reached over and snatched the hat off the young man's head. Each man's values, in terms of respect for his country, were miles apart. How did they learn these differing values? Through socialization, of course.

Socialization is the process that teaches the norms, values, and other aspects of a culture to new group members. As such, it is a lifelong process of creating and maintaining group membership. Countless sociologists and psychologists have studied how people become socialized, which has led to the development of several socialization theories.

Socialization theory claims that the person we become is the result of our environment. According to sociologist Talcott Parsons, introduced in Chapter 1, socialization requires people to learn and internalize society's values.[2] In other words, we accept and integrate the values of the group as our own. These social values constantly surround us, but they often go unexamined.

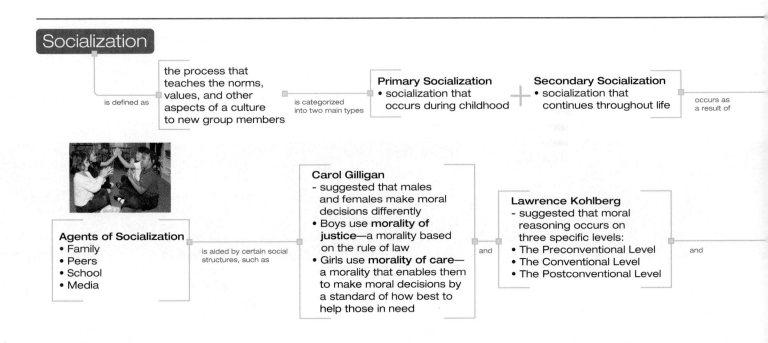

Socialization

is defined as **the process that teaches the norms, values, and other aspects of a culture to new group members**

is categorized into two main types

Primary Socialization
• socialization that occurs during childhood

Secondary Socialization
• socialization that continues throughout life

occurs as a result of

is aided by certain social structures, such as

Agents of Socialization
• Family
• Peers
• School
• Media

Carol Gilligan
- suggested that males and females make moral decisions differently
• Boys use **morality of justice**—a morality based on the rule of law
• Girls use **morality of care**—a morality that enables them to make moral decisions by a standard of how best to help those in need

and

Lawrence Kohlberg
- suggested that moral reasoning occurs on three specific levels:
• The Preconventional Level
• The Conventional Level
• The Postconventional Level

and

At what point in our lives does socialization take place? Parsons and Robert Bales argue that most socialization occurs during childhood.[3] Orville Brim refers to this early socialization as **primary socialization**.[4] Parents are their children's first teachers; they pass on values, rules, language, religious beliefs, and an unending list of social norms. However, socialization is reciprocal because children also influence their parents. Before I had children I thought I knew about parenting, but each child teaches me something new as I try to socialize them. Because socialization is an unending cycle, we are at times the "socializer" and at other times the "socialized."[5] This dynamic whereby socialization continues throughout our lives is considered **secondary socialization**.[6] As you experience life-changing events—like going to college, beginning a career, or getting married—new socialization occurs. At each stage of life, we encounter new norms, values, and expectations. We learn to accept and integrate them as we adapt to our environment. In a sense, the socialization process makes us who we are.

The Nature vs. Nurture Debate—What Makes Us Who We Are?

As one theorist said, "We, and all other animals, are machines created by our genes."[7] Pure **nature** theorists believe that the genes we get from our parents at conception are the primary causes of human behaviours—in short, our genetic makeup determines who we are.

In the twentieth century, social scientists began to fight biologists' belief that nature is the sole determinant of who we are. Those who believe in **nurture**, like philosopher John Locke, propose that our environment influences the way we think, feel, and behave.[8] Supporters of this idea assert that socialization moulds us like pieces of clay, particularly during early childhood. Many nurture theorists believe that a social process teaches people who they are and how they fit into their world. Without such nurturing, a person's ability to cope within society could be greatly affected.

Extreme proponents on both sides of the nature/nurture debate have difficulty sorting out this issue. Although it is true that our genes do not

PRIMARY SOCIALIZATION is socialization that occurs during childhood.

SECONDARY SOCIALIZATION is the dynamic whereby socialization continues throughout our lives.

NATURE THEORY states that the genes we get from our parents at conception are the primary causes of human behaviours.

NURTURE THEORY states that our environment influences the way we think, feel, and behave.

necessarily dictate our destiny, it's also true that our biological makeup is what interacts with the environment in the first place. Noted biologist and author Paul Ehrlich supports a blended point of view. He notes, "We can't partition the responsibility for aggression, altruism, or charisma between DNA and upbringing. In many such cases, trying to separate the contributions of nature and nurture to an attribute is rather like trying to separate the contributions of length and width to the area of a rectangle, which at first glance also seems easy. When you think about it carefully, though, it proves impossible."[9]

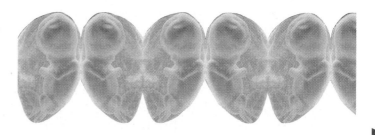

∧
∧ **Does our genetic makeup really deter-**
∧ **mine who we will become? Or do other factors come into play, such as the way our parents care for us?** Where do you stand on the nature vs. nurture debate?

Nature
• the belief that genetic and biological heredity are the primary causes of human behaviours

or

Nurture
• the belief that the ways in which we think, feel, and behave are the results of our environment

has inspired many theorists to explain how people become socialized, such as

Charles H. Cooley
- proposed the theory of "looking-glass self," which states that the self develops through a process of reflection

and

George Herbert Mead
- proposed that the self consists of two parts, the "I" and the "me"
- suggested that the self develops in three stages:
• The Imitation Stage
• The Play Stage
• The Game Stage

and

Jean Piaget
- proposed that people go through a four-stage process of cognitive development:
• The Sensorimotor Stage
• The Preoperational Stage
• The Concrete Operational Stage
• The Formal Operational Stage

and

Erik Erikson
- proposed that people develop a personality in eight psychosocial stages
- at each stage we experience a crisis that upon resolving will have an effect on our ability to deal with the next one
The Eight Stages:
• Infancy
• Toddlerhood
• Preschooler
• Elementary School

• Adolescence
• Young Adulthood
• Middle Adulthood
• Late Adulthood

Rhesus Monkey Study

Which is more important to our survival—nature or nurture? To find out, researchers Harry and Margaret Harlow conducted numerous experiments with rhesus monkeys.[10] One of the most famous was designed to test which need is greater: the need for physical contact or the need for biological sustenance. The Harlows raised monkeys in isolation and eventually presented them with two artificial "mothers." The first "mother"—which was simply a hard wire frame with a wooden head—

provided food. The other "mother" provided no food at all but was made of soft, cuddly material. The Harlows noticed that frightened baby monkeys sought comfort with the soft "mother" and not with the "mother" that fed them. They drew the conclusion that the key component of infant–mother bonding is not the providing of food, but the presence of comfort. The Harlows' findings, while not directly applicable to human development, support the idea that socialization—that is, nurture—is a key building block in normal development.

The conclusion made by the Harlows supports what happened to "Genie," the famous girl discussed in the section below. The Genie team concluded that Genie was not developmentally challenged from birth, but due to deprivation early in life she would never be "normal." Her arrested development proves how sustenance is actually secondary to comfort as a necessary component for human development. Genie's growth as a person was stunted due to her lack of socialization.

FERAL AND ISOLATED CHILDREN

Tales of **feral**, or wild, children raised by animals are not limited to works of fiction like *Tarzan* or *The Jungle Book*. Newspapers and tabloids often feature sensational headlines about the discoveries of such children. Unfortunately, there are too many stories about children held captive at the hands of abusive and/or mentally unstable parents. Although these stories may be shown on the nightly news, we rarely explore or even think about what happens to these children as a result of their isolation. How does human contact, or the lack thereof, affect the people we become?

In April 2008, the story of Josef Fritzl—an Austrian father who had imprisoned his daughter in a basement dungeon for 24 years—attracted worldwide news coverage. Fritzl repeatedly abused and raped his imprisoned daughter Elisabeth, even impregnating her seven times. One child died; Fritzl and his wife were raising three children; and the remaining three were left in the dungeon with little human contact. Until the rescue, the three isolated children had never seen the light of day, and they communicated using only simple grunts and gestures.[11] The future of the Fritzl children and their mother remains to be seen. They've surely got intense therapy and a long struggle ahead of them. Will the children ever become socialized?

Some clues might be found in the story of Genie, who was discovered in Los Angeles in 1970 at the age of 13. The news media said she had been locked in a room and tied to a potty chair for most of her life, with little to look at and no one to talk to for more than 10 years.[12] When authorities removed the child from her home, they immediately began to care for her.[13] A group of experts, known as the "Genie team," observed that Genie could not walk normally and understood only a few words. Additionally, she had problems eating solid food and still needed diapers. However, after her rescue, Genie made rapid progress. She quickly learned to dress and go to the toilet herself. She also learned to walk more normally. Her language skills began to develop, and within a few months her vocabulary of only five to ten words had expanded to more than 100 words.[14]

Unfortunately, despite the massive efforts to help Genie, she never caught up with her peers.

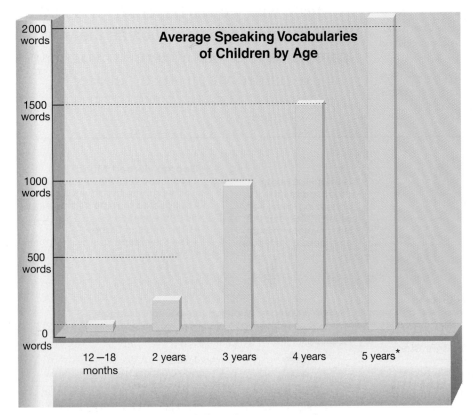

Average Speaking Vocabularies of Children by Age

| 2000 words |
| 1500 words |
| 1000 words |
| 500 words |
| 0 words |

12–18 months • 2 years • 3 years • 4 years • 5 years*

*Five-year-olds have a speaking vocabulary of over 2 000 words.

<<< **Shortly after Genie's rescue, she developed a vocabulary of more than 100 words.** How does Genie's vocabulary compare to that of children raised in a more typical way?

The Genie team concluded that her delayed progress was the result of missing key points in her social development. Because this lack of socialization kept her brain from fully developing, Genie must now live in a home for adults with intellectual disabilities.[15]

Not all feral children have such difficulty becoming socialized. Isabelle, a feral child whose grandfather locked her in a darkened room with her deaf-mute mother, was discovered at age six. She communicated only through gestures, which her mother taught her. Experts put Isabelle through a rigorous socialization process. Surprisingly, Isabelle learned quickly. After two months she was able to speak in sentences, and after about 18 months she had a vocabulary of 1500–2000 words. Ultimately, Isabelle was able to go to school and function normally with children her own age.[16]

Humans need other humans in order to live and to develop normally. Our human nature is not necessarily instinctual. If it were, Genie would have been able to catch up developmentally to her peers.

Deprivation of human interaction is perhaps more detrimental to humans than being underfed or physically abused. If we are to achieve our full potential, we need others to socialize us. The nurturing we experience in our early lives ultimately affects who we are and who we will become.

Theorists on Socialization

Socialization is a process that theorists have been studying for decades. Many of these theorists, from sociologists to psychologists, have made significant contributions to our understanding of the development of self and the development of morality. Like a never-ending college course, we're enrolled in "socialization" until the day we die. In that sense, we're constantly learning about ourselves.

COOLEY'S LOOKING-GLASS SELF

Charles H. Cooley is one of the central theorists of the development of the self. His notion of the **looking-glass self** proposes that, like a mirror, the self develops through a process of reflection. That said, one's self is also established through interactions with others. According to Cooley, this process contains three steps:

1. We imagine how our behaviours will look to others.

2. We interpret others' reactions to our behaviours.

3. We develop a self-concept.[17]

Although Cooley's ideas were developed more than a century ago, modern scholars remain interested in them. King-To Yeung and John Levi Martin, contemporary sociologists who study the processes of the looking-glass self, used Cooley's theory to test the internalization of self-understanding.[18] Their research found general support for the theory that our self-concept involves interpreting and internalizing others' perceptions about us. Yeung and Martin showed that the importance of our relationships is the key factor in determining how we internalize others' perceptions of us. This is why our parents influence us more than, say, our local bank tellers do.[19]

FERAL means wild.

LOOKING-GLASS SELF is the theory that the self develops through a process of reflection, like a mirror.

"I" SELF is the subjective part of the self.

"ME" SELF is the objective part of the self.

IMITATION STAGE is Mead's first stage of development, which is the period from birth to about age 2, and is the stage at which children merely copy the behaviours of those around them.

PLAY STAGE is Mead's second stage of development, which occurs around the ages of 2–4 years, during which children play roles and begin to take on the characteristics of important people in their world.

GAME STAGE is Mead's third stage of development, which never truly ends, and is the stage in which we begin to understand that others have expectations and demands placed upon them.

GENERALIZED OTHER is our sense of others.

GEORGE HERBERT MEAD—THE THREE STAGES OF THE "I–ME" SELF

Another theory about how humans develop the self was explored in symbolic interactionist George Herbert Mead's *Mind, Self, and Society*. For Mead, the self is that part of personal identity that has both self-awareness and self-image.[20] Like Cooley, Mead agreed that the development of self involves interaction with others.

For Mead, though, the self consists of two parts: the "I" and the "me." These two parts essentially create the self through their interaction. The **"I" self** is the part of us that is an active subject, our subjective sense of who we are. It seeks self-fulfillment, asking, "What do *I* want?" In contrast, the **"me" self** is the objective part of the self; the part of our self-concept that questions how others might interpret our actions. The "me" understands the symbols that others give us, and seeks to find favourable reactions to our behaviours from others.[21]

According to Mead, the self develops in three stages. The first is the **imitation stage**, which is the period from birth to about age 2. At this stage, children merely copy the behaviours of those around them. They don't attribute meaning to their actions, nor do they understand the implications of their behaviour. For instance, when you see your baby sister clapping her hands, she's probably just imitating something she's seen and not actually giving you a round of applause.

Children enter the **play stage** around the ages of 2–4 years. Here, children play roles and begin to take on the characteristics of important people in their world. By playing roles, children see others as separate from themselves. They understand that their actions can affect other people, and vice versa. Mead claimed that, through play, children learn to find a sense of who they are and how best to interact with others in their society. At this stage, you're likely to see little boys tie blankets around their necks and pretend to be superheroes.

During our early school years, we enter what Mead called the **game stage**, a stage that never truly ends. It is in the game stage that we begin to understand that others have expectations and demands placed upon them. Mead termed this sense of others the **generalized other**.

Through understanding others we are able to adjust or evaluate our own behaviour based on factors such as culture and society. Developing a concept of the generalized other helps us understand other people's roles, norms, and expectations. This concept is important if we are to fit into society and live intimately with others.[22] The idea of children's organized sports best represents this stage.

PSYCHOSOCIAL CRISIS is a crisis occurring during each of Erikson's stages that will be resolved either positively or negatively, and each outcome will have an effect on our ability to deal with the next one.

COGNITIVE DEVELOPMENT is a person's ability to think and reason.

SENSORIMOTOR STAGE is the stage (birth to 2 years) at which infants learn to experience and think about the world through their senses and motor skills.

PREOPERATIONAL STAGE is the stage (ages 2 through 7 years) at which the ability to speak grows rapidly.

CONCRETE OPERATIONAL STAGE is the stage (ages 7 through 12 years) at which children can think about objects in the world in more than one way and start to understand causal connections in their surroundings.

FORMAL OPERATIONAL STAGE is the stage (ages 12 years and above) at which people become able to comprehend abstract thought.

When children are involved in a team sport like baseball or hockey, they must understand each position's roles and responsibilities in order to play the game. Not everyone can hit or shoot; everyone has a job to do or we can't play the game.

ERIK ERIKSON'S EIGHT STAGES OF DEVELOPMENT

Erik Erikson proposed that humans develop a personality in eight psychosocial, or psychological and social, stages. (See page 91 for a complete list of each stage.) During each stage, we experience a particular **psychosocial crisis** that will be resolved either positively or negatively, and each outcome will have an effect on our ability to deal with the next one.[23]

According to Erikson, the crisis at each stage of development must be resolved positively before we can successfully master subsequent stages. Think back to Genie. She was imprisoned from the infancy stage through the elementary school stage, so did she ever truly become socialized? The answer is no. Although Genie did make some initial progress, she regressed after her first foster parents severely punished her for vomiting. Genie refused to open her mouth for fear it might happen again and responded in the only way she knew how: silence.[24] Genie's case helps illustrate Erikson's theory that failing to master one stage can mean that a person will fail the subsequent stages.

JEAN PIAGET'S THEORY OF COGNITIVE DEVELOPMENT

While Erikson's research focused on personality development, the work of Jean Piaget focused on **cognitive development**, which relates to a person's ability to think and reason. Since the way we think helps shape our self-concept, cognition (thinking) plays a significant role in socialization. Simply put, Piaget found that children don't think like adults. His four-stage theory of cognitive development has become an important basis for much educational theory, particularly as it applies to teaching young children.

When my daughter was an infant, nearly everything she touched went directly into her mouth. It didn't matter if it was a stuffed panda, a board book, or a long red millipede. If she could reach it, it was going in her mouth. According to Piaget, this is the way babies learn. At the **sensorimotor stage** (birth to age 2 years), infants learn to experience and think about the world through their senses and motor skills. During this period, children develop a sense of "object permanence," the understanding that objects outside themselves still exist even when they are not in view.[25] For example, play "peek-a-boo" with an infant and you'll notice that the baby expresses surprise when you cover your face, followed by great joy when you reveal it. Near the end of the sensorimotor stage, peek-a-boo loses its allure and object permanence exists.

At the **preoperational stage** (ages 2 through 7 years), the ability to speak grows rapidly. Although children have already learned some words and phrases, their ability to use and interpret symbols is limited. Children will generally identify objects by a single characteristic. If you show a child the letters C-A-T, for example, the child is likely to read each individual letter aloud. It is unlikely that she will link them together into the word *cat*. Linking multiple symbols together is difficult for a preoperational thinker. By the end of this stage, however, a child can say the word *ball,* draw a picture of a ball, point to a ball on the floor, and understand that all of these mean the same thing.[26]

During the **concrete operational stage** (ages 7 through 12 years), children can think about objects in the world in more than one way and start to understand causal connections in their surroundings. They can think logically about some objects and events. For example, they learn that even though a plain sheet of white paper is folded into a paper airplane, it is still that same piece of white paper. Children at this stage can also imagine what other people might be thinking or feeling. Piaget believed we can't understand the "position" of others until we have passed through some developmental state. Children gain this ability during the concrete operational stage.[27]

Only at the **formal operational stage** (ages 12 years and above) do people become able to comprehend abstract thought. Because they're testing their ability to reason and comprehend the complexities of their world, children at this stage often argue with those in authority. Unsure of themselves, they're testing their thinking. Understanding abstract mathematical principles, such as algebra, becomes possible at this stage, and we become able to understand more deeply the interactions of concrete reality with abstract ideals.[28]

Piaget argued that it could be frustrating and traumatizing to force children to learn ahead of their cognitive capacities. In other words, it serves no purpose to try to teach geometry to a child in grade one. Expecting a child to act like an adult is both impossible and unfair.[29]

> Each of the theorists—Cooley, Mead, Erikson, and Piaget—provides a different view of the development of self. **All these theorists agree that a person's development continues throughout life. These theories present human development as a type of staircase process.** Children who miss one or more stages of socialization generally fail to reach successful completion of their development, as was the case for Genie.

ERIKSON'S EIGHT STAGES OF DEVELOPMENT

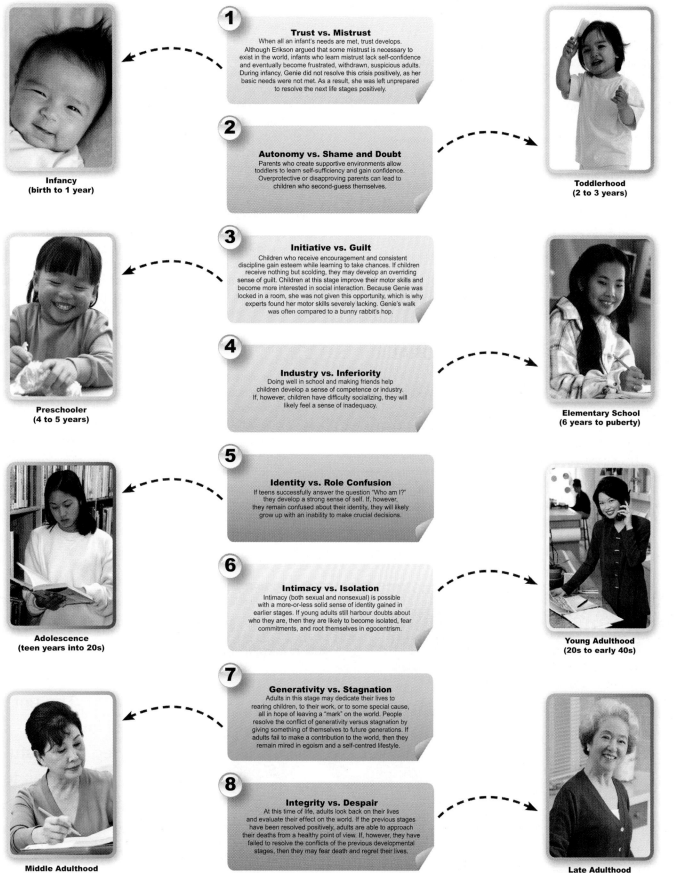

Infancy
(birth to 1 year)

1

Trust vs. Mistrust
When all an infant's needs are met, trust develops. Although Erikson argued that some mistrust is necessary to exist in the world, infants who learn mistrust lack self-confidence and eventually become frustrated, withdrawn, suspicious adults. During infancy, Genie did not resolve this crisis positively, as her basic needs were not met. As a result, she was left unprepared to resolve the next life stages positively.

Toddlerhood
(2 to 3 years)

2

Autonomy vs. Shame and Doubt
Parents who create supportive environments allow toddlers to learn self-sufficiency and gain confidence. Overprotective or disapproving parents can lead to children who second-guess themselves.

3

Initiative vs. Guilt
Children who receive encouragement and consistent discipline gain esteem while learning to take chances. If children receive nothing but scolding, they may develop an overriding sense of guilt. Children at this stage improve their motor skills and become more interested in social interaction. Because Genie was locked in a room, she was not given this opportunity, which is why experts found her motor skills severely lacking. Genie's walk was often compared to a bunny rabbit's hop.

Preschooler
(4 to 5 years)

4

Industry vs. Inferiority
Doing well in school and making friends help children develop a sense of competence or industry. If, however, children have difficulty socializing, they will likely feel a sense of inadequacy.

Elementary School
(6 years to puberty)

5

Identity vs. Role Confusion
If teens successfully answer the question "Who am I?" they develop a strong sense of self. If, however, they remain confused about their identity, they will likely grow up with an inability to make crucial decisions.

Adolescence
(teen years into 20s)

6

Intimacy vs. Isolation
Intimacy (both sexual and nonsexual) is possible with a more-or-less solid sense of identity gained in earlier stages. If young adults still harbour doubts about who they are, then they are likely to become isolated, fear commitments, and root themselves in egocentrism.

Young Adulthood
(20s to early 40s)

7

Generativity vs. Stagnation
Adults in this stage may dedicate their lives to rearing children, to their work, or to some special cause, all in hope of leaving a "mark" on the world. People resolve the conflict of generativity versus stagnation by giving something of themselves to future generations. If adults fail to make a contribution to the world, then they remain mired in egoism and a self-centred lifestyle.

8

Integrity vs. Despair
At this time of life, adults look back on their lives and evaluate their effect on the world. If the previous stages have been resolved positively, adults are able to approach their deaths from a healthy point of view. If, however, they have failed to resolve the conflicts of the previous developmental stages, then they may fear death and regret their lives.

Middle Adulthood
(40s to early 60s)

Late Adulthood
(late 60s to early 80s)

Source: Based on *Childhood and Society* by Erik Erikson.

Theories of Moral Development

How do we know what's right and what's wrong? Do girls learn about morals differently from boys? These are just two of the questions that theories of moral development seek to answer.

KOHLBERG'S THEORY OF MORAL DEVELOPMENT

Building upon the work of Piaget, the prominent theorist Lawrence Kohlberg suggested that moral reasoning occurs on three specific levels: preconventional, conventional, and postconventional. Each level describes different ways in which we make moral decisions.[30]

During the **preconventional level**, which lasts through the elementary school years, children make their moral judgments within a framework of **hedonism**—seeking pleasure over pain.[31] In other words, children judge right from wrong on the basis of what feels good or right to them. If a little boy notices that drawing on the walls results in a visit to the "naughty stool," chances are he won't take the crayons to the walls again.

The **conventional level** arises before puberty and uses the lens of norms and rules to determine what is right and wrong.[32] Basically, what is "right" is obedience to the rules. Rather than question the logic behind why those rules were established, a child simply does what he or she is told. The child may not understand *why* kicking his sister is wrong; he just understands that he shouldn't do it because "Mommy says so." Following the expectations of the family or group is valuable in and of itself. Doing your duty and respecting authority are the hallmarks of this level of development.

Kohlberg's third stage of moral development, the **postconventional level**, refers to a morality based on abstract principles. These may be rooted in political beliefs, religious beliefs, or a combination of both. Kohlberg suggests that the "good" includes adherence to agreed-upon principles rather than rules.[33] Such principles guide all decisions and provide a seamless web of morality for us all. For example, during the civil rights movement of the 1950s and 1960s, countless African American college students held sit-ins at segregated lunch counters, museums, libraries, and many other public places. Although their behaviour broke the Jim Crow laws of the time, these students believed their behaviour was "right" because they were drawing attention to laws that were morally wrong. ("Jim Crow" was the name of a man in a nineteenth-century song and is used as shorthand for segregation in the United States.[34])

Although Kohlberg's own research supported his theory, more recent scholars question some of his assumptions. For example, Charles Helwig and Urszula Jasiobedzka found that children's moral judgments about law and lawbreaking occur earlier in life than Kohlberg's theory proposed.[35] Preschoolers may abide by the rules because they believe rule-breaking is wrong. In addition, moral reasoning doesn't always correlate with moral behaviour. Using Kohlberg's schema, Colby and Damon showed that people at the highest levels of moral development act the same as people at lower levels of moral development. Instead, the situation influences people's behaviour.[36] Take speeding, for example. Although everyone knows it's against the law, many people speed when they believe they won't be caught. These and other questions about Kohlberg's theory of moral development led Carol Gilligan to propose another point of view in 1982.

<<< It's hard to imagine that the simple act of sitting at a lunch counter could be illegal. **The unfairness of laws** such as these **led many students of all races to hold peaceful sit-ins across the southern United States in hopes of abolishing segregation laws.**

CAROL GILLIGAN AND THE "MORALITY OF CARE"

Carol Gilligan suggested that Kohlberg's theories were valid, though only when discussing the development of male morality. To Gilligan, his conclusions were biased against women because Kohlberg only studied men initially.[37] This, in turn, led him to erroneously assume men and women developed moral decisions similarly without actually studying women. Do men and women approach moral decisions differently?

I recently faced a moral decision while shopping at my local discount store. The cashier gave me $10 too much change. Being a bit of a miser, I immediately noticed her mistake. I'm human, so I considered keeping the money, but then I began to wonder what might happen if I took the money. Was it my fault that the cashier made a mistake? Would she get in trouble when she came up short at the end of her shift? All of these thoughts ran through my mind. Of course, I gave her the money back. Gilligan would argue that my gender influenced the way I approached my decision; women would follow a slightly different process.

After investigating women's experiences with morality, Gilligan concluded that moral decisions arise from two different principles: the morality of justice and the morality of care. She agreed that boys primarily follow what she called a **morality of justice**, a morality based on the rule of law. However, girls learn a **morality of care**, which enables them to make moral decisions by a standard of how best to help those who are in need.[38]

To study the differences between moral development in boys and girls, Gilligan proposed a real-life moral dilemma to young male and female subjects. Gilligan used the story of "Mr. Heinz and the Druggist," a tale that Kohlberg also used in his research. The general idea of the story is this: Mr. Heinz's wife is sick with a potentially fatal disease. Luckily, their small-town pharmacy is the only place around that carries the life-saving medication that his wife needs. The problem is the drug costs an astronomical $10 000, and the druggist refuses to sell it for any less. Should Mr. Heinz steal the drug?

Gilligan found that most male subjects used logic when answering the question. Many boys believed that Mr. Heinz should steal the medication, even though it's legally wrong. Boys reasoned that the judge would likely be lenient on Mr. Heinz because of the circumstances. In short, the boys answered the question like a math problem: $x + y = z$. The girl subjects, however, considered the personal relationships involved. Girls worried that Mr. Heinz might go to jail, which could make his wife sicker and leave no one around to care for her or provide her with medicine. They also tried to think of other ways for Mr. Heinz to get the drug so that he would not have to leave his wife. Girls were more concerned about how Mr. Heinz's actions would affect the dynamic between him and his wife.

Modern research provides mixed support for Gilligan's assertion of gender differences in moral reasoning. In short, it appears that girls and boys learn *both* morality of care and morality of justice. The two types of

> **"Both boys and girls go through the same three stages— preconventional, conventional, and postconventional— to develop their morality."**
> **— Lawrence Kohlberg**

> **"Boys and girls develop their morality differently. Boys generally develop a morality of justice, while girls develop a morality of care."**
> **— Carol Gilligan**

morality are not exclusive to one gender over the other.[39] Some findings show that since girls advance through the stages of moral development faster than boys, they actually develop postconventional morality at earlier ages.[40] The most important aspect, perhaps, is the link between ego development and the moralities of care and justice. Because girls develop faster than boys, they present a morality of care more quickly than boys.[41]

Either way, Gilligan and Kohlberg both agree that moral reasoning follows a developmental process and that the surroundings affect that process. Although the precise gender differences may not be as clearly distinguished as Gilligan initially believed, and Kohlberg's age groups may be more flexible than he proposed, both theories show that we learn to make moral decisions in different ways.

Agents of Socialization

We learn socialization with outside help from different **agents of socialization**, which are the people and groups that shape our self-concept, beliefs, and behaviour. So what social structures, or agents, help us become socialized?

THE FAMILY: PARENTING STYLES AND RECIPROCAL SOCIALIZATION

Few things in life shape us more than our parents. Because both my parents worked full time, I learned at an early age that one must work to live. I started working at 13 and am still working today, as evidenced by my writing this book on nights, weekends, and summer vacations. My parents also valued education. My sister, my brother, and I all went to university. Sometimes, I wonder what my life would have been like if I had had different parents. What if my parents were drug addicts? Or illiterate? Or members of the wealthiest elite in the country (my personal favourite)? My point is merely that children don't select their parents, and yet family is one of the most important agents of socialization.

When parents socialize their children, they do so in two different ways. First, they create safe environments by providing emotional support through love, affection, and nurturing. Second, parents provide social control by teaching their children appropriate behaviours. Parents do this by using force, coercion, threats, or rewards.[42] If parents are not successful at providing these things for their children, the results can be disastrous. Genie's father, for example, locked her in a dark room on a potty for days on end. She didn't receive the love and nurturing she needed as a child, which led to socialization problems after she was rescued.

Sociologist Diana Baumrind explored how parental discipline affects children. Although disciplining children is a cultural universal, the manner in which it occurs varies by culture and family style. Baumrind observed that parenting styles have a substantial effect on individual socialization outcomes.[43] Parents who practise an **authoritative style** listen to their children's input while consistently enforcing the preset rules. Children reared in such an environment integrate into the world with the most ease because they exhibit high levels of self-esteem and possess the capacities for independence and cooperation with others.

Whereas authoritative parents practise a balanced style of child-rearing, permissive and authoritarian parents represent opposite extremes, and neither produces positive outcomes. **Permissive-style** parents provide high levels of support but an inconsistent enforcement of rules. This results in a child who does not understand boundaries and expectations. The teenagers on MTV Canada's *My Super Sweet 16* who are showered with lavish gifts and extravagant parties by their affluent parents may be ill-equipped to deal with the disappointments and responsibilities that are sure to come later in life.[44] Conversely, children reared by **authoritarian-style** parents experience high levels of social control but low levels of emotional support. Such children understand the rules but have no relational reasons to obey them when their parents are not looking. Often, the most rebellious youths are by-products of very strict households. Baumrind suggests that these two styles of parenting produce children with lower self-esteem and less self-assurance.[45]

Three Parenting Styles

Permissive Style | **Authoritative Style** | **Authoritarian Style**

Source: Based on *Current Patterns of Parental Authority* by Diana Baumrind.

▶▶▶ GO GLOBAL

Parenting in Asian Cultures

Do the parenting styles that Baumrind describes apply in all cultures? Ruth Chao studied how the parenting styles of Chinese families affect children.[46] In order to explore the stereotype of Chinese schoolchildren as successful and well behaved, Chao observed how parents interacted with their children.[47] The mothers she observed provided high levels of control, but also high levels of sacrifice and personal closeness to their children. Parents in China expect their children to meet high standards of both individual achievement and social conformity. In general, Chinese children meet these standards. The parents in this culture are authoritative; children receive adequate emotional support and know that their hard work will gain the family's approval.

In another study, sociologist Min Zhou proposed that Confucian philosophy, with its emphasis on family loyalty, acts as a social control mechanism that supports Asian children's success.[48] Studies of Vietnamese immigrant children living in enclaves in the United States show similar findings to those of Chao. They show that second-generation immigrant children who remain linked to their families and culture have better outcomes with regard to educational attainment and the likelihood that they will stay in school.[49] Culture plays an important role in psychologists' and sociologists' interpretations about family socialization.

Can We Be "Resocialized"? Experiencing the Total Institution

Resocialization is the process of learning new norms, values, attitudes, and behaviours and abandoning old ones. This process involves more than the kinds of secondary socialization that occur when we marry or take a new job. Yoda, the noted Jedi philosopher, says it best in the film *The Empire Strikes Back:* sometimes, "You must unlearn what you have learned."

The most effective forms of resocialization occur in **total institutions** that isolate people from outside influences so they can be reformed and controlled.[50] People may enter total institutions voluntarily, as in the case of non-draftees that enlist in military boot camps, or involuntarily, as in the case of inmates in mental institutions and prisons. Regardless, total institutions have certain characteristics:

1. There is one authority, and activities take place in specific locations.

2. Carefully structured activities control the participants.

3. Authorities carefully screen all information from outside the institution.

4. Rules and roles are clearly defined.

5. A strict hierarchy exists within the institution.

6. Total institutions restrict individual choice.

How might development inside a total institution affect a person's sense of self? Look back to the opening of this chapter and consider the implications of the reference to the "hasty rituals (like being shaven to the scalp)" that young recruits to the Marines go through in their first few days of basic training.

Sociologist Harold Garfinkel explored the similarities in the ways prison inmates and military enlistees are resocialized upon entering those total institutions.[51] Garfinkel points out that these institutions "welcome" new members through some form of degrading ceremony designed to humiliate the person. This humiliation is required to "break them down" so that resocialization is possible. Inmates and enlistees may both have their heads shaved and their "street clothes" taken away. After putting on uniforms, their individual style of dress is erased in order to look like everyone else. In boot camp and under the control of the institution, the new recruit has no choice in when he or she will eat, sleep, or bathe. Similarly, inmates receive numbers to replace their names, are given uniforms to wear, and are told where they will sleep, when they will eat, and how they will spend their allocated "free" time. In both cases, the goal is to strip away former identity and resocialize the person into someone who will be obedient to commands.

Through resocialization, the institution controls all aspects of a person's life.[52] The techniques that total institutions use change the inmate's or soldier's internal thinking, which in turn changes his or her sense of self.

AGENTS OF SOCIALIZATION are the people and groups who shape our self-concept, beliefs, and behaviour.

AUTHORITATIVE STYLE is a parenting style in which parents listen to their children's input while consistently enforcing the preset rules.

PERMISSIVE STYLE is a parenting style in which parents provide high levels of support but an inconsistent enforcement of rules.

AUTHORITARIAN STYLE is a parenting style with which children experience high levels of social control but low levels of emotional support.

RESOCIALIZATION is the process of learning new norms, values, attitudes, and behaviours, and abandoning old ones.

TOTAL INSTITUTIONS are places in which the most effective forms of resocialization can occur because they isolate people from outside influences so they can be reformed and controlled.

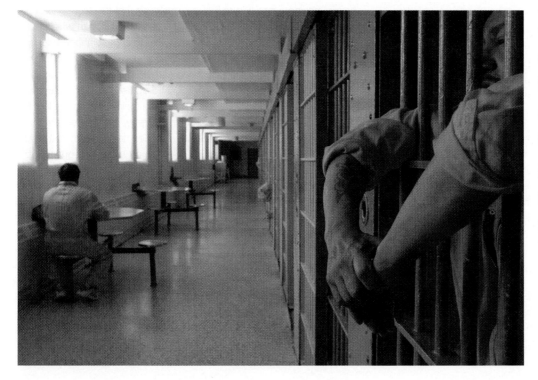

<<< Prison inmates are stripped of their individual identities so that they can be transformed into people who willingly follow the orders of those in authority.

think sociologically: HOW DO THE FOUR THEORETICAL PARADIGMS VIEW SOCIALIZATION?

Symbolic Interactionism and Peer Groups

We've seen how symbolic interactionists focus on small group interactions. It is through these interactions that people create a sense of self. After the family, the peer group is an important agent of socialization for most children. **Peer groups** are made up of people who are generally the same age and who share the same interests. They provide the important function of helping children to separate from their family and may be the first introduction to the wider society. Because they are organized by grade levels, schools provide a setting that facilitates the formation of peer groups. Young children tend to associate primarily with others of the same sex, but in adolescence, the peer group may expand to include others of the opposite sex. For many adolescents, the peer group replaces the family as the most important agent of socialization.

Functionalism

While symbolic interactionists study the effect of institutions on individuals, functionalists examine how certain institutions, such as religion and education, function in society. An institution's function, and the individual's relationship to that institution, helps determine what role it plays in the development of self.

RELIGION

From Muslim practitioners to Orthodox Jews and Buddhist monks, all world religions provide frames of reference for believers. These frameworks include beliefs, values, and behaviours in keeping with the teachings of that religion. Religions teach about life, death, and all of life's transitions in between. The religious socialization that results from this teaching process has measurable effects.

Sociologists Charles Tittle and Michael Welch studied the links between religiosity and juvenile delinquency and found that they are inversely related. The more religious the juvenile, the less likely he or she is to be delinquent.[53] Harold Grasmick and colleagues found weaker, but similar, results with respect to adults and behaviours such as tax cheating and littering.[54] This research shows that religion can play a role in forming our behaviour.

EDUCATION

Out of a typical seven-hour school day, students in secondary schools in North America might spend only about three hours doing academic activities.[55] Instead, students are learning the "**hidden curriculum**"—lessons taught in school that are unrelated to academic learning. School teaches you to deal with peers who are sometimes cruel.[56] If students successfully negotiate the dangers of their neighbourhoods and the various power struggles that go on in their schools, they feel a sense of satisfaction. Schools also socialize children by setting regulations that structure the school day. Students must show up on time, get along with others, follow teachers' expectations, wait in line, and follow the rules.[57]

When families and schools cooperate to teach children to follow the rules, they help create a society that has fewer lawbreakers. When neighbourhoods support these ideals, children grow up feeling part of something important. In the event that the family is dysfunctional, or the school does not work, or the neighbourhood is infecting them with negative ideas about the society, this too socializes children. Negative outcomes usually result. Society functions best when social institutions cooperate.

Conflict Theory

SOCIAL CLASS: OPPORTUNITIES FOR SOCIALIZATION

Family isn't the only agent of socialization; our social class also affects us. Numerous studies show connections between social class and socialization. Melvin Kohn's research found that working-class parents focus on their children's obedience to authority, whereas middle-class parents showed greater concern about the motivations for their children's behaviour.[58] Because working-class parents are closely supervised at their jobs, they are more likely to demand this same conformity from their children. Therefore, the mother who is used to punching a clock at the assembly line is more likely to expect a home environment in which her children do their chores at set times.

Our social class affects us in many ways that we do not anticipate and may not even recognize. The availability of piano lessons, art classes, and children's organized sports teams all socialize children; however, these experiences are typically available only to middle- and upper-income families. Children of less affluent families tend to miss these socialization opportunities. Social class affects not only the type of experiences we have, but also their quality and quantity.

NEIGHBOURHOOD

Anyone who's ever visited a college or university residence building before making a decision to live there believes that the "right" residence matters. The same is true of choosing a neighbourhood in which to live because your social class is often tied to the kind of neighbourhood you live in. Noted sociologist William J. Wilson looked at how inner-city poverty brought with it the disadvantages of poor schools, weak social structures, high crime rates, and rampant drug use.[59] Wilson argued that poor people are truly disadvantaged because their community offers few role models for anything else. Children who grow up in these communities are likely to make poor decisions. Studies have shown that neighbourhood has significant negative effects on IQ, teen pregnancy, and high school dropout rates.[60]

Neighbourhoods also influence economically privileged children. Children who grow up in more affluent neighbourhoods often do better in school, have lower rates of teen pregnancy, and higher IQ scores.[61] Neighbourhoods can also predict how far you may go in school, showing that the higher the socioeconomic status of the neighbourhood, the higher the educational attainment.[62] Neighbourhood effects also apply to voluntary associations for children. A predicting factor in the sport children will play is correlated to their neighbourhoods.[63] For example, a sport like skiing that requires expensive equipment is more likely to be played by children of well-to-do families because they can afford the upkeep and travel to the slopes.

Of course, just because parents are affluent does not mean that they will be great parents or that their children will be successfully socialized. The reverse is also true; a parent who has very limited financial means may be a very good parent.

Feminist Theory—The Power of Gender Socialization

Feminist theory recognizes that the patriarchal social structure has a powerful influence on all of us. Two Canadian researchers asked boys from different class backgrounds to define "masculinity" and to state what they thought about "gender transgressions" in sports—boys playing girls' sports. **Gender** refers to the expectations of behaviour and attitude that a society considers proper for males and females. To guide our actions, societies use **gender socialization** to teach their members how to express their masculinity or femininity. The researchers found that the boys answered quite differently depending on their social class. However, their answers can be understood if we consider their social context.

The upper-class boys primarily defined masculinity in terms of leadership ability and being respected by all others. This is consistent with their socialization as future owners and managers when they enter the workforce. Middle-class boys emphasized intelligence, sociability, and self-confidence as the primary masculine traits. Their socialization generally emphasizes upward mobility, and education and networking are important factors in achieving this. For working-class boys, most anticipate a life of manual labour and working for someone else. For them,

> **PEER GROUPS** are made up of people who are generally the same age and who share the same interests.
>
> **HIDDEN CURRICULUM** refers to the lessons taught in school that are unrelated to academic learning.
>
> **GENDER** is the expectations of behaviour and attitude that a society considers proper for males and females.
>
> **GENDER SOCIALIZATION** teaches members of society how to express their masculinity or femininity.

physical strength and respect through intimidation were characteristics of a "real man."

When asked about how boys who played girls' sports were viewed, the working-class boys generally voiced a powerful opposition to this, and any boy who did this would be loudly insulted and stigmatized. The middle-class boys were more accepting of the transgressions, which is consistent with their ideology of individual rights and making personal choices. The upper-class boys were also more comfortable in being more politically correct by accepting the transgressions, but were secure in the knowledge that the social system would maintain their gender and class privileges.[64]

Feminist theorists often argue that **men use their power to dominate and limit women.**

The Effect of Household Income on Participation in Organized Sports in Canada

Source: Based on *Sport Monitor*, Canadian Fitness and Lifestyle Research Institute, 2006–2007. Accessed at www.cflri.ca/eng/statistics/surveys/documents/2006_07_sport_b1.pdf, page 2

Fictional Tales and Gender

From *Aesop's Fables* to the Brothers Grimm, folktales symbolize the innocence of childhood. But a closer analysis shows how these folktales shape how children perceive gender. Most folktales follow a typical pattern in which a dependent woman relies exclusively on a strong man to save her from harm. Think about the story of Rapunzel—the girl with the long, golden hair who is trapped in a tower by a witch. In the story, Rapunzel is merely a piece of property, given away by her father in exchange for his life. While trapped in the tower, Rapunzel is dependent on the witch and unable to escape. Rapunzel, afraid of the witch's wrath, remains in the tower alone and refuses the prince's help to escape. The prince goes blind because he is unable to save the beauty. Young children, especially young girls, who read these tales internalize the idea that being submissive and reliant on men is a desired trait.

These stereotypes are not just a part of archaic folktales; they also appear in modern works of fiction. Television programs like *Grey's Anatomy* and *Desperate Housewives* feature female characters who reinforce generalizations about gender roles. That said, there are a number of stereotype-breaking characters, like those featured on *Buffy the Vampire Slayer* and *Lost*. Even in the *Harry Potter* series, Hermione Granger, Harry's sidekick, is a secondary character and yet she is always saving the day. Real life does not work as it does in fiction. Not all men can be heroes, and passivity and dependency rarely bring women success in the modern world.

>>> **ACTIVITY** Think about a movie or TV show you've seen or a book you've read recently. What gender stereotypes, if any, are depicted on the screen or the page? Does the work defy any traditional gender stereotypes? Write a paragraph analyzing the work you chose.

GENDER BIAS IN THE MEDIA

Kim Campbell, who for a few months in 1993 served as Canada's first female prime minister, has been quoted as saying that if she were to do it all again she would address the issue of gender bias in the media's political coverage head-on instead of letting it take her by surprise in the election that ended her brief time in power.[65] Campbell said she realized later that, although the media had not schemed to oust her from office, reporters had reacted to their unconscious ideals and expectations of women during her disastrous re-election campaign.[66]

Any print or electronic resource that is used to communicate to a wide audience is referred to as **mass media**.

MASS MEDIA include any print or electronic resource that is used to communicate to a wide audience.

Products of mass media—books, magazines, television, radio, movies, music, and newspapers—are everywhere, and their influence on culture is inescapable. **The media play a role in our socialization because they transmit stories, values, and attitudes.**

Consider the effect the media have in determining gendered stereotypes through sexual imagery. Kirstie Farrar and her colleagues reviewed the sexual images that aired during prime-time television hours. They found that images on shows like *The Bachelor* and *One Tree Hill* tended to reinforce the notion that women are primarily sexual objects.[67] These and other images supported the dominant male/submissive female paradigm. They also found that 64 percent of the television shows during the 2000–2001 season contained sexual messages, and that sexual intercourse occurred in 14 percent of the shows. For conflict theorists, these findings suggest that such imagery is an effort by those in power to maintain it. Men are the primary decision makers for large media corporations, so are they responsible for perpetuating these ideas about gender roles?

Because of the way gender roles are defined in society, it can take several years to see through the generalizations. I can remember realizing during my first year in college that my father and I had never hugged, primarily because of gender ideals about men touching each other. The next time I returned home, I gave him a big hug as soon as he answered the door. From that day forth, hugging was no longer taboo at our house. In this simple way, my father and I changed our gender socialization.

WRAP YOUR MIND AROUND THE THEORY

In order for a society to function, **functionalists argue that people adapt their behaviour to the norms and values of the institutions in that society.**

FUNCTIONALISM

According to functionalists, socialization occurs when people internalize society and enact its norms, values, and roles. In high schools across the country, students struggle with the choice to conform and practise "normal" behaviour or to think outside the box. Those who step outside the box are often stigmatized and labelled as "different." These individuals are not "functioning" because they don't conform to the rules set by the society's institutions. Institutions, such as religion and education, serve their function. To keep a society running smoothly, people adapt to the norms and values of their particular institutions. In short, people become socialized when they learn and accept what a society expects of them.

CONFLICT THEORY

Conflict theorists believe that the "haves" and the "have-nots" are socialized differently. Children who come from middle- and upper-class backgrounds are more likely to participate in organized sports, take music or art lessons, and have internet access in their homes. Taking part in activities such as these teaches children how to interact with others and learn what society expects of them. Impoverished children sometimes find themselves at a disadvantage because they are less likely to have these experiences. Of course, material wealth is not the only determinant of whether one becomes socialized. However, parents' material wealth does put some children at an advantage.

HOW DO PEOPLE BECOME SOCIALIZED?

SYMBOLIC INTERACTIONISM

Symbolic interactionists believe that socialization is the major determinant of human nature. People develop their sense of self by incorporating how others interpret their behaviour. The symbols we encounter, such as other people's interpretations of our behaviour, help shape who and what we become. Genie, the feral child discovered in 1970, was not given the opportunity to interact with others during her formative years. As a result, she was unable to fully develop her own identity when she was thrust into the social world. As we saw in Mead's theory of the "I" and the "me," people develop their sense of self though their interaction with others.

FEMINIST THEORY

A large part of our socialization involves gender socialization—learning how to act like boys and girls, men and women. Many parents will dress boys in blue and girls in pink. They will buy trucks for the boys and dolls for the girls. At school, there are different sports teams for boys and girls. The media constantly send us messages about how to act "appropriately," and what is a "man" and what is a "woman."

Children who participate in organized sports learn how to interact with others in the social world. **Having few or no opportunities to play sports can limit a child's socialization.**

If the students in class snicker and whisper while the child gives his report, how might the child interpret these symbols? How might he feel about himself?

discover sociology in action: HOW DOES UNDERSTANDING SOCIALIZATION HELP US IMPROVE OUR SOCIETY?

Applying Sociological Thinking in the World, Social Policy, and the *Canadian Charter of Rights and Freedoms*

Auguste Comte, the founder of sociology, urged us to use our knowledge about society to improve society. Lawmakers have used that philosophy to enact various **social policies**, deliberate strategies designed to correct recognized social problems. The 1982 *Canadian Charter of Rights and Freedoms* might be considered one such attempt to implement sociological knowledge.

The *Charter* is part of the Canadian Constitution, the top law in the country. It has a wide impact, because:

- Governments across the country use the *Charter* as a guide in making laws.
- Courts across the country use it as a guide in applying laws.
- Individuals, associations, or the government can ask courts to rule how it applies in particular cases.[68]

The *Charter* is regarded as the biggest achievement of then Prime Minister Pierre Trudeau. In September 2010, a decade after Trudeau's death, his politician son Justin noted: "When my father was fighting for the just society, it was about recognizing the rights of all individuals and that was (enshrined) with the *Charter of Rights and Freedoms*."[69]

> **SOCIAL POLICIES** are deliberate strategies designed to correct recognized social problems.

ACTIVITIES

1. What agents of socialization influenced you the most when you were growing up? What influences you the most now?
2. Read stories of feral children, such as Genie. What is the importance of early socialization on development? Have researchers made any strides in socializing feral children?
3. Visit a developmental disability hospital in your area and talk to the staff and parents. Can the best efforts at socialization overcome nature? Write about your findings.

From 1867, when Canada was founded, until 1982, the Canadian Constitution did not have a bill of rights that governments had to follow. (The federal government had introduced a Canadian Bill of Rights in 1960, but it wasn't part of the Constitution and didn't have much power.) The *Charter* had a difficult political birth, and it was decided that the easiest way to introduce it finally was to agree that the provinces would have a way of temporarily avoiding some parts of it for a while. The equality rights section was delayed until April 1985, allowing governments across the country time to make the necessary updates to their laws.[70]

For just one example of how important the *Charter* is, consider that if it had been in effect at the time, Japanese Canadians might not have been sent to internment camps and had their property taken away from them in 1942, during the Second World War.[71] The historical treatment of First Nations Peoples (some of which is described in the previous chapter) would have been very different too.

"Of all the human rights milestones in twentieth century Canada, arguably the single most significant is the passing of the *Charter of Rights and Freedoms*," the Canadian Human Rights Commission says. "With its signing, human rights became an intrinsic and irrevocable part of our Canadian identity."[72]

From Classroom to Community } Children's Hospital

When Ahmed, one of my sociology students, decided to do his service learning project at a local children's hospital for the developmentally disabled, he was not prepared for the experiences he was about to have.

"Before I started my volunteerism," he said, "I had a clear understanding of the socialization process. I'd studied Genie and knew how difficult it was to socialize children who had developmental delays."

Ahmed realized that many of the children, unlike Genie, came from loving families and had received all kinds of therapy from a very early age. But Ahmed found that despite all the assistance they received, something about their development was delayed.

"Some children had physical delays, while others had cognitive ones," he recalled. Ahmed was particularly interested in a 12-year-old boy who was born deaf, blind, and with an intellectual disability.

"He was a really difficult case because I couldn't figure out how to communicate with him. He interacted mostly through touch. Yet when you reached out to help him, he often hit you and wildly swung his arms around in the air."

Children with development delays that influence communication often experience problems with socialization.

"It seemed that about all my patient could do was hit people and eat.

"I could not help but wonder how this boy would come to know who he was and where he fit in the world. Without communication, it seems almost impossible."

WHAT IS SOCIALIZATION? 86

the process that teaches the norms, values, and other aspects of a culture to new group members

HOW DO THE FOUR THEORETICAL PARADIGMS VIEW SOCIALIZATION? 96

functionalism: institutions, like religion and education, are useful in socializing individuals

conflict theory: an individual's social statuses, such as social class, can influence how she or he is socialized

symbolic interactionism: total institutions are successful in resocializing people by altering their sense of self

feminist theory: societies use gender socialization to teach members how to express their femininity and masculinity

HOW DOES UNDERSTANDING SOCIALIZATION HELP US IMPROVE OUR SOCIETY? 100

through social policies that are designed to give equal opportunities to both genders

get the topic: WHAT IS SOCIALIZATION?

Theory

SYMBOLIC INTERACTIONISM 96

- socialization is the major determinant of human nature
- people develop their sense of self by incorporating how others interpret their behaviour
- peer groups are made up of people who are generally the same age and who share the same interests

FUNCTIONALISM 96

- socialization occurs when people internalize society and enact its norms, values, and roles
- people who don't internalize norms are stigmatized and labelled as "different"
- people become socialized when they learn and accept what society expects of them

CONFLICT THEORY 96

- the "haves" and the "have-nots" are socialized differently
- taking part in activities teaches children how to interact with others and learn what society expects of them
- children who come from middle- and upper-class backgrounds are more likely to participate in organized activities than some impoverished children who are unable to participate

FEMINIST THEORY 97

- gender socialization teaches us what is culturally appropriate behaviour for men and women
- social institutions and agents of socialization perpetuate gender stereotypes

Key Terms

socialization is the process that teaches the norms, values, and other aspects of a culture to new group members.   86

primary socialization is socialization that occurs during childhood.   87

secondary socialization is the dynamic whereby socialization continues throughout our lives.   87

nature theory states that the genes we get from our parents at conception are the primary causes of human behaviours.   87

nurture theory states that our environment influences the way we think, feel, and behave.   87

feral means wild.   88

looking-glass self is the theory that the self develops through a process of reflection, like a mirror.   89

"I" self is the subjective part of the self.   89

"me" self is the objective part of the self.   89

imitation stage is Mead's first stage of development, which is the period from birth to about age 2, and is the stage at which children merely copy the behaviours of those around them.   89

play stage is Mead's second stage of development, which occurs around the ages of 2–4 years, during which children play roles and begin to take on the characteristics of important people in their world.   89

game stage is Mead's third stage of development, which never truly ends, and is the stage in which we begin to understand that others have expectations and demands placed upon them.   89

generalized other is our sense of others.   89

psychosocial crisis is a crisis occurring during each of Erikson's stages that will be resolved either positively or negatively, and each outcome will have an effect on our ability to deal with the next one.   90

cognitive development is a person's ability to think and reason.   90

sensorimotor stage is the stage (birth to 2 years) at which infants learn to experience and think about the world through their senses and motor skills.   90

preoperational stage is the stage (ages 2 through 7 years) at which the ability to speak grows rapidly.   90

concrete operational stage is the stage (ages 7 through 12 years) at which children can think about objects in the world in more than one way and start to understand causal connections in their surroundings.   90

formal operational stage is the stage (ages 12 years and above) at which people become able to comprehend abstract thought.   90

preconventional level is the first stage of moral development that lasts through the elementary school years; at this level, children make their moral judgments within a framework of hedonistic principles.   92

hedonism is seeking pleasure over pain.   92

conventional level is the second stage of moral development that arises before puberty and uses the lens of norms and rules to determine what is right and wrong.   92

postconventional level is the third stage of moral development that refers to a morality based on abstract principles.   92

morality of justice is morality based on the rule of law.   93

morality of care is morality decided by a standard of how best to help those who are in need.   93

agents of socialization are the people and groups who shape our self-concept, beliefs, and behaviour.   94

authoritative style is a parenting style in which parents listen to their children's input while consistently enforcing the preset rules.   94

permissive style is a parenting style in which parents provide high levels of support but an inconsistent enforcement of rules.   94

authoritarian style is a parenting style with which children experience high levels of social control but low levels of emotional support.   94

resocialization is the process of learning new norms, values, attitudes, and behaviours, and abandoning old ones.   95

total institutions are places in which the most effective forms of resocialization can occur because they isolate people from outside influences so they can be reformed and controlled.   95

peer groups are made up of people who are generally the same age and who share the same interests.   96

hidden curriculum refers to the lessons taught in school that are unrelated to academic learning.   96

gender is the expectations of behaviour and attitude that a society considers proper for males and females.   97

gender socialization teaches members of society how to express their masculinity or femininity.   97

mass media include any print or electronic resource that is used to communicate to a wide audience.   98

social policies are deliberate strategies designed to correct recognized social problems.   100

Sample Test Questions

These multiple-choice questions are similar to those found in the test bank that accompanies this textbook.

1. During which of Erikson's eight stages would a person develop a strong sense of self?
   a. Trust vs. mistrust
   b. Initiative vs. guilt
   c. Industry vs. inferiority
   d. Identity vs. role confusion

2. According to Piaget, at what stage of cognitive development does a child's ability to speak grow rapidly?
   a. Sensorimotor stage
   b. Preoperational stage
   c. Concrete operational stage
   d. Formal operational stage

3. The preconventional level, conventional level, and postconventional level are stages of
   a. moral development.
   b. social development.
   c. creative development.
   d. language development.

4. Which of the following is *not* an example of a total institution?
   a. A prison
   b. The military
   c. A university
   d. A rehabilitation clinic

5. Which researcher developed the morality of care and the morality of justice?
   a. Erik Erikson
   b. Carol Gilligan
   c. Lawrence Kohlberg
   d. George Herbert Mead

ANSWERS: 1. d; 2. b; 3. a; 4. c; 5. b

ESSAY

1. How did Piaget describe the stage at which a child learns to speak?
2. What is the difference between authoritative-style and authoritarian-style parenting?
3. Why is resocialization important in total institutions?
4. Feminist theorists often argue that men use their power to dominate and limit women. Provide an example of gender bias in the media and explain how it supports this theory.
5. In the terms of Erikson's theory, how was Genie's development stunted?

WHERE TO START YOUR RESEARCH PAPER

For more information on child socialization, visit the BBC's "Child of Our Time" series website, a 20-year documentary following 25 children from across the UK who were born in 2000; go to www.open2.net/childofourtime/2010/index.html

For in-depth articles on the field of evolutionary psychology, relating the development of the brain and how social settings influence a person's development, go to www.sfu.ca/~janicki/

To find data on child socialization, go to www.childdevelopmentinfo.com

For more information on parenting from around the world, go to www.scu.edu/ethics/publications/other/lawreview/manymothers.html

For information on early childhood learning and development, go to www.eccdc.org

For information for children with a disability in Canada, go to http://disabilitystudies.ca/programs

For information on children with a disability in organized sports, go to www.specialolympics.ca/en/images/pdfs/Cdn_Sport_Policies.pdf

To learn more about how media influences society (particularly the sociological perspective on media and society), go to www.theory.org.uk/resources.htm

For more information on resources for people who have developmental delays, go to www.earlyinterventioncanada.com/home.html

Remember to check **www.thethinkspot.ca** for additional information, downloadable flashcards, and other helpful resources.

GROUPS AND SOCIETIES

WHAT ARE THE CHARACTERISTICS
OF SOCIAL GROUPS?
HOW DO SOCIOLOGISTS VIEW GROUP
LEADERSHIP?
HOW DOES A PARENT'S CIVIC ENGAGEMENT
AFFECT A CHILD'S FUTURE POLITICAL
INVOLVEMENT?

"The community

of Bountiful has been Canada's dirty secret for more than sixty years. Tucked away in the southeastern corner of British Columbia, it's out of sight and out of mind. As its founders had hoped in the mid-1940s, when they chose this remote location to raise their polygamous families, the neighbours don't really mind. . . .

"Bountiful, B.C. is the polygamy capital of Canada. You won't find it on any map because it's a made-up name. . . .

"Children—boys mainly, but also girls—are frequently used as unpaid labourers in dangerous construction and forestry jobs. To ensure that those children don't have any other choices, the leaders encourage them to leave school well before high-school graduation to become either wives and mothers or indentured labourers. It's all done in the name of God and religion by men who are aiming to be gods with dozens of wives and hundreds of children serving them for all eternity. . . .

"The Bountiful people are taught from birth to 'keep sweet.' Happiness is the only emotion that's allowed. Anger, frustration, depression and especially rebellion are not allowed. They're taught to suppress those emotions and to put all their energy into obeying the word of their prophet, who speaks directly to God.

"[They] are also taught that it's okay not to tell the truth to outsiders, especially if it means protecting the secrets of how many mothers and how few fathers there are or of how the fathers are ripping off the evil government, a practice known as 'bleeding the beast.'"[1]

Understanding Our
Environment

In *The Secret Lives of Saints: Child Brides and Lost Boys in Canada's Polygamous Mormon Sect,* **Daphne Bramham gives a history of the** infamous polygamous **commune of** Bountiful, B.C.

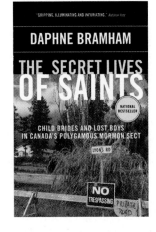

About 700 people now live in the secluded valley community of Bountiful, in the interior of British Columbia.[2] They practise a strictly fundamentalist version of Mormonism, which includes polygamy.

Although Canadian law has banned polygamy for more than half a century, it was only in recent years that the law was really tested, when the modern-day leaders of the Bountiful group—Winston Blackmore and James Oler—were each charged with one count of practising polygamy. The charges were linked to Blackmore's alleged marriages to 19 women and Oler's to three women. The B.C. Supreme Court threw out the charges against Blackmore and Oler in September 2009.

These people form a social group which is distinct from the wider Canadian society.

get the topic: WHAT ARE THE CHARACTERISTICS OF SOCIAL GROUPS?

SOCIAL GROUPS are groups that consist of two or more people who interact with one another and share a common identity.

On March 20, 2010, an estimated 75 000 public-sector workers from all across Quebec took to the streets in downtown Montreal to protest lagging contract talks. The crowd included nurses, teachers, and other public-sector workers. Among the crowd were about 30 teachers (including me) from the college where I teach. We all know each other, and see each other quite often. Within the larger crowd, we were a **social group**.

Whether we're aware of it or not, we all belong to a social group in some way or another—families, close friends, teammates, classmates, clubs, and organizations are all examples of groups to which we

<<< These people work in the same building, maybe even in the same office. **But are these people a social group?**

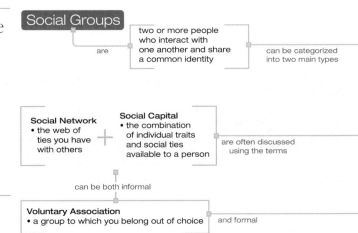

Social Groups are two or more people who interact with one another and share a common identity — can be categorized into two main types

Social Network
• the web of ties you have with others

Social Capital
• the combination of individual traits and social ties available to a person

are often discussed using the terms

can be both informal

Voluntary Association
• a group to which you belong out of choice — and formal

belong. Few of us could live totally self-reliant lives, so we find groups on which to depend. Of course, not all groups are the same. For all intents and purposes your membership in your family is permanent, but you might not work with the same people for the rest of your life. Although no two groups are alike, they do have two commonalities: the members of the group share something in common, and they identify each other as members of that group.

PRIMARY AND SECONDARY GROUPS

Classmates qualify as a social group with shared goals and values. Although you have this relationship with your class-mates, you might refrain from spilling your guts to your chemistry lab partner. Why? Because we have different types of groups that dictate how we interact within them.

According to sociologist Charles H. Cooley, groups can be divided into two main categories—primary and sec-ondary. *Primary groups* are small, intimate, and long-lasting.[3] Our most immediate relationships, such as relationships with family members and close friends, form primary groups. The Bountiful community created a primary group by sharing everything. The residents of Bountiful had a com-munal society in which a few men had several wives and dozens of children.

More importantly, primary groups help us to determine who we are. Because our primary groups are usually made up of our relatives and closest friends, their presence and influence are constant

PRIMARY VS. SECONDARY GROUPS

- Secondary relationships are transferable.
- Primary relationships are not easily replaced.
- Primary relationships play a variety of roles.
- Secondary relationships have specialized roles.
- Primary relationships are filled with emotion and involve open communication.
- Secondary relationships are impersonal and unemotional and involve limited communication.

reminders of how we see ourselves. It is through these relationships that we create our "looking-glass selves" (see Chapter 5). By reflecting their per-ceptions back to us, primary relationships provide valuable feedback.

Secondary groups, on the other hand, are formal, superficial, and last for a short or fixed time.[4] These groups generally come together to meet some specific goal or purpose. If you join a civic organization in order to help put on a parade, you are join-ing a secondary group. Such groups provide **bounded relationships** that exist only under specific conditions. For example, you and your cowork-ers might "do lunch," but you probably wouldn't invite them to a family function. Coworkers form a group that is usually of secondary importance to you.

Formal types of social norms heavily influence the way we interact in secondary groups. These norms direct our actions and frame our communication. For example, you might ask the person who brings your mail about the weather, but you probably wouldn't get into a debate about climate change. Moreover, the types of norms we follow when interacting affect the way we feel about the group. If we are close and informal, we may fit in with the group, making it feel more like a primary one. If not, we can easily feel like outsiders.

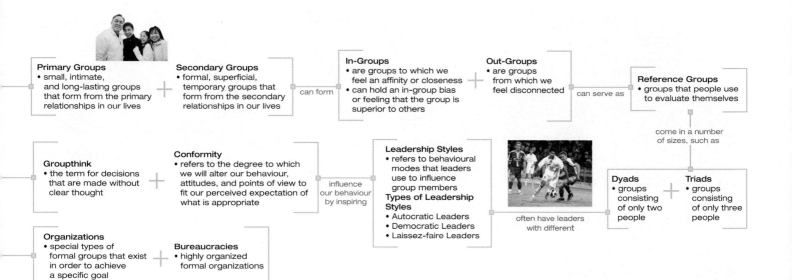

Primary Groups
- small, intimate, and long-lasting groups that form from the primary relationships in our lives

Secondary Groups
- formal, superficial, temporary groups that form from the secondary relationships in our lives

can form

In-Groups
- are groups to which we feel an affinity or closeness
- can hold an in-group bias or feeling that the group is superior to others

Out-Groups
- are groups from which we feel disconnected

can serve as

Reference Groups
- groups that people use to evaluate themselves

come in a number of sizes, such as

Groupthink
- the term for decisions that are made without clear thought

Conformity
- refers to the degree to which we will alter our behaviour, attitudes, and points of view to fit our perceived expectation of what is appropriate

influence our behaviour by inspiring

Leadership Styles
- refers to behavioural modes that leaders use to influence group members

Types of Leadership Styles
- Autocratic Leaders
- Democratic Leaders
- Laissez-faire Leaders

often have leaders with different

Dyads
- groups consisting of only two people

Triads
- groups consisting of only three people

Organizations
- special types of formal groups that exist in order to achieve a specific goal

Bureaucracies
- highly organized formal organizations

IN-GROUPS AND OUT-GROUPS

In the words of supermodel-turned-reality-show-host Heidi Klum on *Project Runway,* "One day you're in, and the next day, you're out." Klum's catchphrase, which is used to discuss whether an aspiring designer's fashions are in or out of style, is true not just of clothes, but also of social groups. If you've ever waited for what seemed like hours on the sidelines while all the popular kids were getting chosen for the team, you've hoped to be welcomed into the in-group of people who don't have to wait until last to be chosen.

An **in-group** is a group to which we feel an affinity or closeness. For this reason, we often have a strong sense of loyalty to an in-group. Most people hold an **in-group bias**, the feeling that their in-group is superior to others.[5] The ABC reality series *Wife Swap* perfectly illustrates how some families engage in in-group bias. The show, in which the mothers of two very different families exchange places for a period of time, usually features participants who believe theirs is the best way to raise a family. The mothers are then confronted by the strange interactions of another's family. Each mother considers the other family an out-group.

An **out-group** is a group from which we are disconnected. We often hold negative biases toward out-groups and may even feel very competitive toward them. We see this all the time in sports. Ask a Montreal Canadiens fan about the Toronto Maple Leafs, and you may well face unvarnished vitriol. The same will probably happen if you ask a Leafs fan about the Canadiens. In both cases, the respective fan group holds an out-group bias toward the other fan group. This is especially true in partisan politics, in which skirmishes among Conservatives, Liberals, and New Democrats can erupt over the most mundane issues. The members of the Bountiful community came together to form a type of in-group, sticking together and shunning the ways of the "outside" world.

Sociologist Robert Merton suggests that our biases come from our position in society.[6] We see the traits of our group as acceptable, while we hold the views of out-groups as unreasonable. Generally, people hold a bias toward out-groups; however, a number of factors impact whether these biases are positive or negative.[7] For example, social outcasts in high school can hold either a positive or negative bias toward the "popular" group. If the outcasts know that nothing can change their outsider status, then they're likely to hold the cool kids in contempt. If, on the other hand, an outcast hopes to one day penetrate the cool group, he or she holds a positive bias toward them. In a sense, outcasts place the in-group on a pedestal if they think they can join them, and they knock this group down if they feel joining the group is impossible.[8]

∧
∧ **Judging from the expressions** on the faces **of Heidi and crew** on the set of the
∧ fashion design competition *Project Runway,* **the designer frock** they're viewing
is definitely a fashion "don't."

Sociologists Henry Tajfel and John Turner suggest that everyone seeks a positive social identity.[9] This pursuit is the root cause of in-group and out-group biases. We may point out the negative differences in others to elevate our own identity, even if the differences are insignificant. Go to an internet message board where posters are discussing a hypothetical battle between Superman and the Incredible Hulk, and you might observe some heated wrath being spewed as each camp takes sides. This seemingly innocuous conversation can quickly devolve into a flame-throwing contest among angry fanboys. By poking fun at the other, the groups make themselves feel superior.

Position and power are other factors that can impact our perception of in-groups and out-groups. The workplace is common ground for these biases. Courtney Von Hippel studied temporary employees' out-group biases.[10] Temps who actually wanted a full-time job desired their coworkers' acceptance.[11] Meanwhile, temps who didn't expect permanent employment resented full-time employees because they didn't need to feel accepted.[12] In other words, it was highly unlikely that full-timers were taking these temps out to lunch.

REFERENCE GROUPS

In nearly every situation, we compare ourselves to another person or group. For example, you might not have a need for a new cell phone, but if one of your best friends keeps going on and on about his new iPhone, you might find yourself visiting your local wireless phone dealer so you're not left out. Since we cannot make judgments about our own behaviour in isolation, we often use others to assess our behaviour.[13] Sociologists refer to the group you use to evaluate yourself as a **reference group**.

REFERENCE GROUPS, though, are not necessarily in-groups because we don't have to belong to them. **If, for example, you are studying to be a neurosurgeon,** you might talk to surgeons at your local hospital **about the duties and challenges of the career.** But simply thinking like a surgeon doesn't make you one. **They're just a reference group to help guide who you are and who you will become.**

▶▶▶ GO GL🌐BAL

In and Out in Japan

Xenophobia, the fear of outsiders, is a powerful example of out-group bias. In Japan, only those with 100 percent Japanese lineage are considered Japanese.[14] Foreigners who move to Japan and live there for years might eventually be able to gain citizenship, but will never "become Japanese," nor will their children.[15] In this way, Japanese society alienates itself from other cultures. "True" Japanese people in Japan form an in-group, whereas all other non-native or different peoples form an out-group.

Throughout history, it's been customary for the Japanese to create out-groups, ostracize them, and then hold that group responsible for current social problems.[16] During the early 1900s, many Korean people were brought into Japan as migrant workers to meet the nation's industrialization needs.[17] Japanese society immediately began to look at the Korean population as outsiders. Association with the population was frowned upon, and cultural integration was impossible. In fact, in present-day Japan, Koreans cannot gain full citizenship. However, leaders are working to change laws in order to recognize Koreans as full-fledged Japanese citizens.

>>> **ACTIVITY** Research a country other than Japan. What in- and out-groups are part of that country's society? How are members of the out-groups treated? Discuss your findings with a classmate.

DYAD is a group consisting of only two people.

TRIAD is a group consisting of three people.

LEADERSHIP STYLE is a behavioural mode that leaders use to influence group members.

AUTOCRATIC LEADERS are leaders who determine the group policies and assign tasks.

DEMOCRATIC LEADERS are leaders who strive to set group policy by discussion and agreement.

LAISSEZ-FAIRE LEADERS are leaders who lead by absence and may in fact not want to be leaders at all.

CONFORMITY is the degree to which we will alter our behaviour, attitudes, and points of view to fit into our perceived expectation of what is appropriate.

GROUPTHINK is the term for group decisions that are made without objective thought.

large conversation became impossible. I noticed people breaking off into subgroups. Some played games, others went outside, and still others stayed in the kitchen sampling the holiday goodies. Such divisions are normal even among close families. The group was simply too large to allow for one conversation.

If you attend a concert in a large arena, you'll probably talk to only the friends you came with, right? You and others are sandwiched into tight surroundings, and you may be actually physically touching someone you don't know, yet you probably won't talk to that person. Ironically, our sense of group often gets smaller when we're in large crowds. As a population increases in size and becomes denser, our perception of group size becomes smaller.[21] As crowds get larger, they become more stressful to us. In order to reduce the stress, we retreat into smaller, safer groups, thus limiting the interactions in the group and the stress of being in the crowd.

GROUP SIZE, STRUCTURE, AND INTERACTION

Groups come in all shapes and sizes. As a group gets larger, maintaining in-group feelings becomes harder. Smaller groups tend to be more intimate and less official, which makes them easier to maintain.

The smallest and strongest form of a group is a **dyad**, a group consisting of only two people. The two members become very close, intimate, and connected. Think of a happy marriage as an example of a strong dyad. Such closeness is not possible in larger groups. Paradoxically, a dyad can also be unstable because either member can unilaterally decide to dissolve the group.[18] If someone has ever dumped you, you probably understand this principle.

When a third member enters a twosome, a **triad**, or group of three, forms. In a triad, mediation, alliances, and competition are likely. For example, if two members of the triad are at odds, the third member can act as a mediator to resolve the conflict. Triads can also allow for alliances between two of the members—potentially against the third, which weakens the group. If two friends ever teamed up against you, then you understand this principle. When alliances occur, the chance for competition among the members increases, which can lead to dissolution of the group. As a result, sociologist Georg Simmel referred to the triad as the weakest group size.[19]

As group size grows, there are greater opportunities for potential interactions, but also more formality and less intimacy. Family gatherings are great places to see this theory play out in real life. At a recent family gathering, I closely watched the interactions taking place as people slowly began to arrive. When the group size was small, people remained together, sitting in the same room and holding a single conversation. However, as the size grew to greater than 10, having one

> According to Henry Hamburger and colleagues, **the size of the group affects the group's ability to cooperate in a task.**[20] This phenomenon explains why reducing class size in public schools is a major issue in education policy. **Smaller groups accomplish more in less time than larger ones do.**

LEADERSHIP STYLES

In many groups, there are individuals who always stand apart from the crowd and become leaders, either officially or unofficially. If you've watched any season of *Survivor,* you know that often tribe leaders emerge. Tribe leaders provide food for the group, instructions for building shelter, and unity among the tribe members. Since leadership makes others more conscious of the person, leaders on *Survivor* often are at more risk of being voted out even though their contributions are usually crucial to the tribe's success.

According to Kurt Lewin and colleagues, leadership can be summarized by three distinct styles.[22] **Leadership style** refers to a behavioural mode that leaders use to influence group members. Leadership style varies among autocratic, democratic, and laissez-faire styles. **Autocratic leaders** determine the group policies and assign tasks.[23] These strict authoritarians inform you, "It's my way or the highway." Conversely, **democratic leaders** strive to set group policy by discussion and agreement.[24] They hope for consensus and are likely to ask for your opinion on matters. Finally, **laissez-faire leaders** lead by absence and may in fact not want to be leaders at all.[25] They set few goals and do only what must be done.

Whichever style you've encountered, there are some important points to remember about leadership style as it applies to social groups:

1. There is no "right" type of leadership style.
2. Successful leaders adapt the style to the situation.
3. The process of leadership impacts both the group members and the leader.
4. Leadership styles are learnable.
5. Different styles can be effective in certain situations and/or with certain groups of people.[26]

CONFORMITY

Because it takes the rare individual to stand out and be a leader, most members of a group are followers in some way. **Conformity** refers to the degree to which we will alter our behaviour, attitudes, and points of view to fit into our perceived expectation of what is appropriate. Everyone hopes to "fit in," but would you change your opinion of what you think is true in order to fit into a group?

Psychologist Solomon Asch wanted to test the impact of groups on people's perception in 1952.[27] Asch set up groups so that only one member was not aware that the rest were actors. Then, he showed the pseudo-group a series of cards like those shown below. He asked them to match the lines on card 2 to the line they saw on card 1. At first, the confidants chose correctly and the group could easily make unified decisions. However, over time the confidants began to make deliberate mistakes in order to test the desire to achieve group conformity. Amazingly, about a third of the participants went along with the group, even though it was in error. Such a phenomenon is more common than you might think. When people are in a group, they often want to conform to the majority and don't offer an opinion that goes against the grain.

>>> When you're with a crowd, **do you find that you change your behaviour to match everyone? Or do you march to your own drummer?**

ASCH'S CARDS

CARD 1

CARD 2

A   B   C

Groupthink

At times, group conformity becomes so strong that a group will not consider other ideas or influences. Extremely cohesive groups or ones with very strong leaders might make decisions using groupthink.[28] **Groupthink** is the term for group decisions that are made without objective thought. When a group is in this mode, people conform to what they believe is the consensus of the rest of the group. They often make decisions that they would not make as individuals. Extreme group conformity leads to groupthink. It frequently results in bad decisions that people later agree were a mistake. Groupthink is more likely when the following conditions are present:

- **Cohesiveness:** Groups that are highly connected are more likely to engage in groupthink. If, for example, you were to join a board of directors that the same people had led for 10 years, odds are groupthink is occurring. This group is likely to be very interconnected and to think they have ironed out all the possible solutions to the potential problems.
- **Threats:** When groups encounter an external threat, solidarity increases because common enemies unify groups.
- **A Strong Leader:** If the leader has a domineering style or is charismatic enough, groups will usually accept the leader's will. Although a strong leader is important to a group's progress, it can also increase the odds of groupthink because few will want to take on the leader.[29]

A History of Groupthink

Sociologist Irving Janis pinned down eight shortcomings that are likely to result from groupthink decisions.[30] We can use these criteria as standards to evaluate any decision and determine whether groupthink was involved. Groupthink in politics is hardly anything new. Janis points out that political leaders often run the risk of making poor decisions because of this phenomenon. The failed U.S. invasion of Cuba, known as the Bay of Pigs, fits the bill.[31] Think about past political leaders' decisions to invade nations—such as the U.S. invasion of Iraq in 2003 (discussed further below) or the Soviet invasion of Afghanistan in 1979. Was groupthink behind these decisions?

1 **Illusion of invulnerability.** Groupthink creates excessive optimism that the desired outcome will occur. Some have suggested that the just-mentioned invasion of Iraq arose from an illusion of invulnerability. When the United States launched its "Shock and Awe" campaign in 2003, media coverage gave citizens the impression that the war would be easily won.[32] The military was supposed to dominate Iraq rapidly, quickly winning the war on terror and suffering few casualties in the process.

2 **Collective rationalization.** Members ignore warnings as irrelevant and will not reconsider the assumptions of the decision. Some have suggested that the 2003 invasion of Iraq arose from collective rationalization. Critics point to U.S. President George W. Bush's "Bring 'em on" and Vice President Dick Cheney's proclamation that "We'll be greeted as liberators" as examples of such thinking.[33]

3 **Belief in inherent morality.** People in the group believe their cause is just and right. In a 2001 speech, Bush claimed, "Either you are with us, or you are with the terrorists."[34] This led many citizens to reconsider their opposition to the war.

4 **Stereotyped views of out-groups.** Groupthink is likely when members view themselves as the "good guys" and their opponents as the "bad guys." When the United States invaded Iraq to overthrow the government of Saddam Hussein, many American students held negative stereotypes of the Iraqi people, believing them to be "cold-blooded terrorists."

5 **Direct pressure on dissenters.** Members of the group who disagree are under pressure to keep quiet if they dissent. Frequently, the group will not allow any voicing of disagreement. In his 2004 book *Plan of Attack,* journalist Bob Woodward suggests that members of George W. Bush's presidential cabinet effectively isolated dissenters of the war in Iraq.[35] Moreover, many critics of the administration were labelled "unpatriotic" and accused of "not supporting the troops" if they expressed contradictory opinions.

6 **Self-censorship.** Group members squelch their doubts and fail to express reservations they may have about the proposal. When group members see dissenters punished or isolated, they will self-censor in order to avoid punishment from a strong leader. In the time leading up to the war in Iraq, many media outlets, such as *The New York Times* and NBC News, tended to downplay anti-war stories due to pressure from the Bush administration.[36]

7 **Illusion of unanimity.** The group leadership in particular mistakes a pressured majority view for unanimity. For example, in an interview with ABC News, former U.S. Secretary of State Colin Powell admitted that his public support for the war in Iraq came from his loyalty to President Bush and not his personal convictions.[37] When Powell silenced his personal convictions, he gave the appearance of unanimity.

8 **Self-appointed mind guards.** Certain members play the role of protector of the leader, shielding him or her from information and ideas that might be contradictory to the group's decision. Many American television media stations could be considered mind guards because they rarely, if ever, aired views that could be considered counterproductive to the war.

What conditions do you think **are contributing to** this **groupthink?**

>>> **ACTIVITY** Think about your own life. How has groupthink played a role in a past decision you've made? Do you regret that decision now? Evaluate your choice using the eight shortcomings of groupthink. Did all eight factor into your decision?

SOCIAL CAPITAL AND SOCIAL NETWORKS

When you think of all the possible things that brought you to this point in your life, you're basically thinking about social capital. **Social capital** is a sociological concept that refers to the individual and collective resources available to a person. Social capital includes the institutions, relationships, attitudes, and values that influence interactions among people and contribute to economic and social development. Sociological theorist James S. Coleman suggested that social capital impacts all aspects of our lives and affects the choices and options available to us.[38]

Most of us use this kind of capital to find jobs, colleges, and other opportunities. For example, my first job was repairing bicycles in a local bike shop. I got the job because my mother knew the owner. Later on, a friend helped me find my second job at a fast-food chicken restaurant. Of course, I had to do the work and keep the job, but my friends and family were a part of my social capital that helped me gain employment.

Although Coleman suggests that social capital is functional for society and individuals, Pierre Bourdieu, a conflict theorist, views it as an economic resource.[39] Consider legacy admissions: a policy in which applicants to a highly touted private school are admitted based on

their family's history with the school. Such a practice tends to benefit wealthier students because they are more likely to have family members who are alumni. In short, our social and familial contacts can help us get a foot in the door of a place to which we might have otherwise been denied access.

The social contacts that people make, when pulled together, comprise a social network, which is one component of social capital. Basically, a **social network** is the web of ties you have with others. Networks usually include people with similar values, beliefs, and identities. They allow us to gain important information and may even open doors of opportunity. In the twenty-first century, social networking has taken on an even greater importance for Web-savvy individuals. Sites such as Facebook and LinkedIn serve as virtual alternatives to traditional networks. The power of the internet allows people to expand their network exponentially.

To see the value of social networks, look at how recent immigrants are able to use them to their advantage. The Longitudinal Survey of Immigrants to Canada surveyed immigrants who arrived in Canada between October 2000 and September 2001 and who were over 15 years of age. The survey found that immigrants rely on three types of social networks:

1 **Kinship network:** consists of relatives and family members

2 **Friendship network:** includes friends and acquaintances

3 **Organizational network:** various formal and informal groups and organizations, such as community groups, religious groups, and sports clubs.

The study confirmed previous findings that social networks are very important. Six months after landing, immigrants without social networks faced worse situations than those who had some networks upon landing.[40]

Sometimes, you don't have to depend on a strong network to succeed. Even weak ties can also be immensely valuable to us. For example, you may hear about a job opening from someone sitting next to you in class. Even though your classmate isn't necessarily in your primary group, this tip could prove much more valuable than information from your family or friends. Mark S. Granovetter suggests that weak ties play a vital role in social capital because they expand our networks, thus expanding our possibilities.[41]

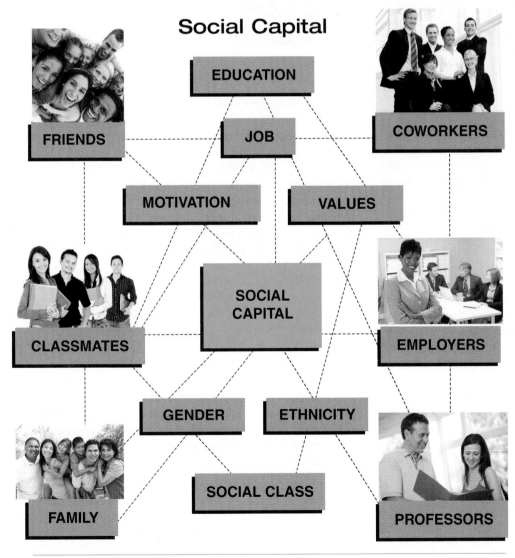

Social Capital

EDUCATION

FRIENDS — JOB — COWORKERS

MOTIVATION — VALUES

CLASSMATES — SOCIAL CAPITAL — EMPLOYERS

GENDER — ETHNICITY

FAMILY — SOCIAL CLASS — PROFESSORS

∧
∧ **Your social capital is a** network of personal characteristics,
∧ institutions, relationships, and social statuses.

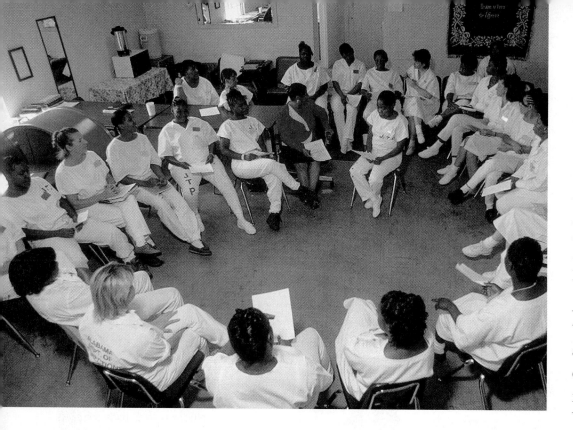

<<< **Our view of an organization depends upon our involvement with it.** For example, **a prison can be a utilitarian organization** for the prison guards, **a normative organization** for people who volunteer to lead Alcoholics Anonymous groups with the inmates, **and a coercive organization** to the inmates themselves.

Formal Organizations

When you hang out with friends or family, you let your guard down and forget about all the formal rules. That's because these social groups are informal. Other groups you're affiliated with, such as your local bowling league or hockey team, are probably formal organizations. **Formal organizations** are groups created for a certain purpose and built for maximum efficiency.

VOLUNTARY ASSOCIATIONS

Through joining a team, singing in a choir, or helping in a soup kitchen, you can make a **voluntary association**. In 1995, political scientist Robert Putnam showed that participation in these kinds of associations is declining.[42] Take bowling leagues, for example. The number of bowling leagues is decreasing, while the number of people bowling has not changed. People are joining organizations less frequently, creating a more individual and isolated society. The social capital of our entire society may be suffering from shrinking social networks, despite our using networks to increase our outcomes and improve our lives.

Voluntary associations have life-changing effects on communities. For example, in an area of Nepal where high fertility rates were an increasing problem, more individuals became involved in voluntary associations—like credit bank groups, women's groups, agricultural groups, and youth groups. As memberships increased, the likelihood of Nepalese people using contraception also increased.[43] People who lived in neighbourhoods that had a number of possible voluntary associations were more likely to use contraceptives than people who lived in relatively isolated communities. Through fostering a better sense of community among individuals, voluntary associations helped control fertility rates.

ORGANIZATIONS AND BUREAUCRACIES

Organizations come in a variety of types and sizes. Some organizations are formed to help a cause, such as Greenpeace. Others, like the popular furniture store IKEA, serve to make money. All organizations are alike in that they are formal groups that exist to achieve a desired goal. Sociologist Amitai Etzioni suggested that the type of organization ultimately determines our membership in it.[44] For example, when you get a job at a department store or office building, you're joining a **utilitarian organization**.[45] Members join utilitarian organizations because they receive wages in exchange for work. **Normative organizations**, though, exist in order to achieve a worthwhile goal.[46] If you volunteer at a normative organization, such as a soup kitchen, you do so because you believe feeding the homeless serves an essential purpose in society.

While we willingly join utilitarian and normative organizations, we do not join **coercive organizations** by choice.[47] Members of coercive organizations, like prison inmates or rehab patients, don't join voluntarily; outside forces of authority bring them into the organization.

Whether utilitarian, normative, or coercive, organizations have some important qualities that keep them running smoothly.

- **Division of labour:** Tasks are clearly defined and divided, and members understand their roles and expectations.
- **Concentration of power:** Organizations concentrate power in the hands of a few, who can then use that power to control the institution.
- **Methods of succession:** Membership in the organization allows for the replacement of all roles, including leaders.[48]

A structure exists within all organizations, though some structures may be more formal than others. **Formal structure** refers to the explicit rules, goals, and guidelines of the organization. Organization charts, policy and procedure manuals, and established titles and roles are all part of the formal structure of an organization. You can see such formal structures develop in any student organization that elects presidents, vice presidents, and other officers. **Informal structures** consist of friendships, allegiances, and loyalties among members of the organization. All organizations have informal structures, and these often make the organization run smoothly.

CHARACTERISTICS OF BUREAUCRACY

If you've ever had to wait in line for hours to renew your driver's licence, only to hear "I can't help you. You'll have to wait over there," then you know some of the frustrations that come with a large bureaucracy. **Bureaucracies** are formal organizations that are organized into a hierarchy of smaller departments. Bureaucracies often have an impersonal feel when one department doesn't have much contact with another. Since a better method of organization has not yet been found, it looks like they are here to stay.

Max Weber was one of the early sociologists to discuss the idea of bureaucracy.[49] Weber proposed that no matter what a formal organization's purpose might be, all ideal bureaucracies display certain characteristics.

Weber and the Iron Cage

For Weber, bureaucratization was a logical extension of formal rational thought.[50] **Formal rationality** refers to the reasonable actions organizations and bureaucracies take to achieve goals in the most effective way. If Weber's theory sounds familiar, it's because George Ritzer used the same theory in his discussion of the McDonaldization of society included in Chapter 3.[51]

According to Weber, any organization that grows large enough will inevitably strive toward formal rationality and bureaucracy. However, such a highly structured bureaucracy can cause the members to feel trapped in a dehumanizing "**iron cage**" that turns them into little more than robots accomplishing tasks. Weber proposed that this iron cage, while problematic from a personal level, is actually a good thing because it helps the organization thrive and places its needs above the needs of the individual.

The power of the bureaucracy often moves from the top down, meaning that the leaders of the group make decisions and those lower on the organizational chart complete these tasks. This setup forces leaders to be accountable for the actions of the bureaucracy and increases their control. However, this hierarchy strips workers of having a say in decision making.

With all the decision-making power at the top, inefficiencies can occur. If leaders don't understand what is happening at the lower levels of the organization, they can easily lead it astray. For example, while I was working as an intake social worker, the agency hired a new director. The director decided that instead of seeing a social worker first, all potentially new clients should have nurses assess their medical condition. Both the nurses and I voiced our objections, but the director overruled us. As a result, many of our new clients found out that after spending hours in the agency, they were not eligible for service. Many wasted hours resulted, and eventually the director went back to the old system.

The division of labour in a bureaucracy can also be a negative. Workers may become alienated from the organization's purpose and focus only on their specific tasks. For example, a factory worker who spends hours putting tires on cars might notice a broken windshield but not say anything because "it's not my job." Such a feeling arises from an impersonal organizational culture.

Although written rules and regulations let workers know what is expected of them, strict enforcement of these rules stifles creativity and imagination. Workers might not be inclined to speak up in order to implement a new idea or to perform tasks that do not fall under their job description.

Now that we have discussed the role of groups and group interaction in society, it's time to think sociologically about these groups.

FORMAL ORGANIZATIONS are groups created for a certain purpose and built for maximum efficiency.

VOLUNTARY ASSOCIATION is the act of joining an organization that offers no pay and that expands social networks through interaction.

ORGANIZATIONS are formal groups that exist to achieve a desired goal.

UTILITARIAN ORGANIZATION is an organization in which people receive wages in exchange for work.

NORMATIVE ORGANIZATIONS are organizations that exist to achieve a worthwhile goal.

COERCIVE ORGANIZATIONS are organizations that people are forced to join.

FORMAL STRUCTURES are the explicit rules, goals, and guidelines of an organization.

INFORMAL STRUCTURES are friendships, allegiances, and loyalties among members of an organization.

BUREAUCRACIES are formal organizations that are organized into a hierarchy of smaller departments.

FORMAL RATIONALITY is the reasonable actions that organizations and bureaucracies take to achieve goals in the most effective way.

IRON CAGE is a concept introduced by Max Weber that refers to the way in which bureaucracies make workers feel trapped and turn them into little more than robots accomplishing tasks.

Weber's Characteristics of Bureaucracy

Division of Labour

Workers are assigned specific, specialized tasks.

Hierarchy of Authority

Decision-making power moves from the top (supervisors) down to workers in lower positions.

Rules and Regulations

Rules and regulations guide a bureaucracy's actions to ensure that tasks are performed uniformly.

Impersonality

Workers perform "without hatred or passion," meaning that all clients are treated equally.

Technical Qualifications

Hiring and promotions are based on a worker's ability to perform a task.

think sociologically: HOW DO SOCIOLOGISTS VIEW GROUP LEADERSHIP?

Functionalism and Leadership

What makes someone a good leader? Influential functionalism theorist John C. Maxwell provides a model of leadership made up of five levels.[52] As you read, think about leaders you know who exhibit these qualities.

LEADERSHIP 101: WHAT EVERY LEADER NEEDS TO KNOW

The true measure of leadership is influence on others. If you lack this ability, no one will follow you. The style of leadership—autocratic, democratic, or laissez-faire—you employ does not directly affect your level of leadership. An autocratic leader can be just as influential as a democratic leader. However, Maxwell suggests that all leaders begin at the most basic level.[53]

Level 1: *Positional leaders: People follow the leader because they must.*

This level serves as the most basic type of leadership. Simply put, other people give positional leaders the reins of leadership. They don't rely on vision or charisma to lead others; instead, people follow them because of their title. When you enter the workforce, the hierarchy of your company determines who your supervisor will be, and it is part of your job to follow that person's lead. In the overall scheme of things, though, the positional leader and the people he or she oversees are just cogs in a machine. This type of leader has the least amount of influence.

Level 2: *Permission leaders: People follow because they want to.*

> Successful leaders eventually understand that there is more to leadership than merely being the boss.

Although positional leaders often lack personal relationships with their followers, permission leaders take the opposite tack. These leaders generate followers willingly precisely because they develop personal relationships with them. A permission leader doesn't merely view workers as a means to an end; instead, they work together because they enjoy each other's company. Such a leader has considerably more influence because their followers are actually invested in the relationship, and, by extension, the task that is to be completed.

Level 3: *Production leaders: People follow because of what you have done.*

At this level of leadership, goals are met with minimum effort because the leader sets the example. Production leaders spur a sense of accomplishment in the people who follow them and clearly communicate a vision of what can be. They then go out and perform just as hard as everyone else. Production leaders are also willing to make difficult decisions and take the blame for failures.

Level 4: *People development: People follow because they are empowered.*

Rather than demonstrating their own skills to set an example, empowering leaders help people meet their potential by encouraging them to accomplish tasks they might have previously felt were impossible. By developing people, an empowering leader accomplishes tasks more easily because the team members feel they are capable and competent.

Level 5: *Personhood: People follow because of who you are.*

It can take many years for people to attain this highest level of influence. Such leaders must spend a lot of time cultivating relationships with people and developing communication skills. But once this level is reached, they will be able to inspire their followers to exceed their potential and willingly sacrifice for them.

Maxwell suggests that all leaders have the potential to climb this ladder of influence, but every new leader starts at the first level. Successful leaders eventually understand that there is more to leadership than merely being the boss.

Conflict Theory—Marx, Bureaucracy, and Democratic Organizations

While Weber saw both the positive and the negative aspects of bureaucracy, Karl Marx believed that "bureaucracy [was] a circle from which one [could not] escape." For Marx, bureaucracy provided no essential function

---

THINK SOCIOLOGICALLY

Leadership in Canada

Pierre Elliott Trudeau—who was Canada's prime minister for a total of 16 years—displayed each of Maxwell's levels of effective leadership.

The charismatic Quebecker was first swept to power in a 1968 federal election, soon after winning the Liberal Party leadership in a wave of "Trudeaumania" that had turned him into a political star.[54] At this point he was a positional leader, but already showed signs of rising to Maxwell's "personhood" level.

Trudeau made bold and dramatic gestures on and off the political stage. He pirouetted behind the Queen's back and made news because of the famous women he dated and the young woman he married. As prime minister, he brought in the *Official Languages Act* (1969), invoked the *War Measures Act* (1970, after several bombing attempts and kidnappings by the Front de libération du Québec), appointed the first female Speaker and Governor General in Canada (Jeanne Sauvé on both counts), supported the enactment of the *Canadian*

Charter of Rights and Freedoms (1982), and "patriated"—or brought home—the Canadian Constitution from Britain (1982).[55]

He continued to be elected to power because people were following him because it was their choice, because of what he was accomplishing, and because they were empowered. He clearly reached Maxwell's fifth level of leadership, and is remembered, in the words of the CBC, as having "helped shape Canada with his vision of a unified, bilingual, multicultural 'just society.'"[56] Pierre Elliott Trudeau died in 2000.

∧
∧
∧
Marx believed that **bureaucracy was actually a "hierarchy of knowledge."** The **leaders trust workers** to handle all the details, while the **workers trust the leaders** to handle the general outcome. Based on this idea, **Marx believed each side deceived the other,** which ultimately **benefited the bourgeoisie.**[57] Do you agree with Marx's interpretation of bureaucracy? Why or why not?

for society. It was just another way for the bourgeoisie to exploit workers more efficiently and gain more wealth and control for themselves.

You'd probably expect workers to fight against bureaucratic systems. However, Marx's theory suggests that employees who oppose a bureaucracy's leadership are easily discovered, reprimanded, or fired. Is this the most beneficial for productivity? Studies show that a democratic, instead of an autocratic, leadership style actually increases worker productivity. Democratic leaders encourage workers to participate in production decisions, and this participation increases profits and productivity.[58] It seems that a more inclusive leadership style helps both the workers and the owners.

Greater labour participation in leadership roles does not mean that the company will succeed. In studies by Tove H. Hammer and colleagues, increased labourer participation on boards of directors does not translate to increased profits.[59] In fact, such involvement is counterproductive for future planning because workers and management tend to have differing points of view. Workers focus primarily on job protection, while managers are interested in appeasing shareholders.

Symbolic Interactionism— Creating a Just and Democratic Workplace

You probably have high hopes of landing your dream job after you graduate from college. The sad fact is that for many North Americans the daily grind is a nightmare. One in 12 workers in Canada—about 1.3 million people—is dissatisfied with his or her job, according to one study.[60] In the United States, four out of five workers do not have their dream jobs, a survey found.[61]

Negative feelings like these have symbolic interactionists wondering: How do workers' attitudes toward their jobs impact productivity and job satisfaction? This is a question that can keep a human resources administrator up at night. When people have a level of personal control over the outcomes of their jobs, they are more connected to their work.[62] For example, if a programmer has designed a software prototype and it catches her supervisor's eye, she is more likely to feel a stronger connection to the company.

Joyce Rothschild suggests that traditional bureaucracies create ineffective work environments because workers are disconnected.[63] Studying Eastern European capitalist and communist countries in the late 1970s and early 1980s, Rothschild found similar feelings of disconnection in both environments.[64] Workers experienced little ability to innovate and change their work environment in the centrally organized government-owned businesses of Eastern Europe. This top-down management style is very similar to that of Western capitalist bureaucracies. Rothschild's conclusion was clear—restrictive work environments equal inefficient and unproductive workers.[65]

In contrast, team approaches in management encourage democracy in the workplace.[66] Teams in the workplace are likely to be more connected to their jobs because individuals can connect to other team members. From the perspective of an interactionist, such a change could be linked to a changing definition of business success. As workers become more educated, they expect to have more input in the work they do. After completing your degree, you'll probably seek a job that includes you in the process of deciding how to do your work. It's a good position to strive for. Jobs like these allow people to have a sense of satisfaction both at work and in their personal lives.

Feminist Theory—New Directions

The traditional descriptions of bureaucracies and organizations have focused on objective descriptions of the structures and the rationalization of roles and relationships. For many feminists, this is a predictably male perspective.

In *The Feminist Case against Bureaucracy*, Kathy Ferguson proposes an alternative way to interpret bureaucracies. First, we need to recognize that the structures and processes of bureaucracies affect the individuals caught within them. Second, by listening to the typical experiences of women, and how they suffer persistent patterns of subordination, we can start to change the power relations and performance expectations of bureaucratic structures. This would benefit not only women, but men as well. Finally, we must recognize that the bureaucratic structure, as it exists, may not be the best formal social arrangement—alternatives are possible.[67]

Today, Oprah Winfrey is one of the most influential women in the world, but she did not start off that way. After beginning her career in 1971 at a small TV station in Nashville, TN, she worked her way through the levels of leadership. Since then, she expanded her audience so much that people have described her influence to be greater than most political and religious leaders, aside from the Pope.[68]

FUNCTIONALISM

When studying groups, functionalists might examine the group's values and behaviours, particularly those of the group's leader. Successful groups often have successful leaders, so studying a group's leadership and how it impacts other members is important. John Maxwell points out that while anyone can be a "boss," only specific people can become a leader. He created a model outlining the five levels of leadership and proposed that each level depicts an increase in influence and empowerment in workers. Pierre Trudeau—who served as Canada's prime minister for a total of 16 years—displayed each of Maxwell's levels of effective leadership.

SYMBOLIC INTERACTIONISM

Symbolic interactionists realize that along with leadership, personal attitude has a big effect on job performance and satisfaction. People feel good about themselves and their jobs when they feel they have a certain level of control over their actions. Rothschild suggests that workers feel disconnected under traditional bureaucracies, which create unproductive environments. Symbolic interactionists view a democratic work environment as more satisfactory for workers because it helps them feel connected to their jobs.

CONFLICT THEORY

Since conflict theorists focus on macro issues and their relationship to society, they would take note of the arguments surrounding bureaucracy. While Weber saw bureaucracy as an extension of formal rational thought, Marx viewed it as a tool of the rich to keep the working class down. Critics of Marx have pointed out that democratic environments actually improve productivity and profits. However, if a democratic environment is not implemented, then bureaucracy can be stifling for the worker and the organization.

HOW DO DIFFERENT PERSPECTIVES VIEW GROUP LEADERSHIP?

FEMINIST THEORY

Feminists declare that traditional theories and models of leadership are based on masculine values—hierarchy, rationalization of tasks, and objectivity. Currently, if women want to succeed in these types of organizations, they need to adopt these values as well. Feminists suggest that it is possible to introduce more feminine modes of leadership without weakening the effectiveness or the achievement of goals. As well, this can benefit everyone who works or otherwise participates in groups or organizations.

What do you see when you look at this picture? Is it an organized business, or is it a tool to maintain oppression?

When people have a certain level of control over their jobs, they are much more likely to feel connected and satisfied. This, in turn, makes them more productive in the organization.

discover sociology in action: HOW DOES A PARENT'S CIVIC ENGAGEMENT AFFECT A CHILD'S FUTURE POLITICAL INVOLVEMENT?

I always vote. Why? Primarily, because my parents did. During my childhood, they stressed the importance of being involved in my government and community. My mother always said, "If you don't care, why should anyone else?"

Adult Civic Engagement and Childhood Activities

Social capital is changing in North America. Since the 1960s, civic organizations have witnessed a sharp decline in participation in the United States, which could certainly lead to a society that is less interconnected and has a lower level of social capital.[69] Canada has experienced "relative stability of the social capital reservoir" since the 1960s, but most social capital trends have been "plummeting" since the early 1990s.[70] Lower levels of social capital mean that a number of social problems can arise, one of which is voter apathy.

Could participation in voting and politics be related to what you did when you were younger? Daniel McFarland and Reuben Thomas suggest your involvement as a child impacts your willingness to engage in political action in the future.[71] The authors tested children and controlled for a variety of factors, including the parents' socioeconomic status and education.[72] They found that involvement in activities that encouraged public speaking and/or community service increased the likelihood of political involvement in adult life.[73] Perhaps this is because participants become involved in communities and see the benefits of such involvement.

These findings have direct implications on social policies and civic engagement. Schools that encourage students to become involved in their communities build active citizens. Not only does service learning help you take what you learn in the classroom and use it in the community, but you are also more likely to remain civically engaged.

ACTIVITIES

1. Visit with a professor and discuss your ideas about leadership in the classroom and on your college campus. What does your professor do to inspire followers to his or her discipline?
2. Does your college offer courses or clubs to train you in leadership skills? If so, what are they? If not, where in your local community can you find such opportunities?
3. Do you vote? Do your classmates vote? Why or why not?

Leading Groups

As you take your learning from the classroom to the community, you may find yourself leading groups. Effective group work practice requires you to have an understanding of how groups work and a level of comfort with group leadership. How do you gain these things?

The first thing you should ask is, "What are the group's goals?" Depending on the group's goals, your work may be quite different. If you are supervising a call centre for a political campaign, your goal may be as simple as monitoring the hours other volunteers work, or you may need to keep their motivation up. No matter what type of group you lead, you need to be able to provide direction if the group gets off-track.

From Classroom to Community } Registering Voters

Indira, a student in my class, was also studying political science. She earned extra credit by helping to campaign for a local candidate for an upcoming election. In a report for her poli-sci class, she detailed how people reacted when asked if they were going to vote.

"Lots of people just walked by the table and tried to ignore me. Some people actually got mad if I asked them why they weren't going to vote.

"I couldn't understand that. My parents always voted, and so the thought that college students wouldn't care shocked me. Of course, my sociology class helped shed light on the problem. The government is such a large bureaucracy that many people feel like they don't matter. I guess they're too busy with their primary groups to care much about secondary groups."

06

WHAT ARE THE CHARACTERISTICS OF SOCIAL GROUPS?   106

two commonalities: the members of the group share something in common, and they identify each other as members of that group

HOW DO SOCIOLOGISTS VIEW GROUP LEADERSHIP?   116

functionalism: leaders are measured by their influence on others
conflict theory: for Marx, bureaucracy was a way to exploit workers, so the bourgeoisie could gain wealth
symbolic interactionism: workers' attitudes toward their jobs impact productivity and job satisfaction
feminist theory: many feminists view traditional ways of looking at bureaucracies and organizations as reflecting only the male perspective.

HOW DOES A PARENT'S CIVIC ENGAGEMENT AFFECT A CHILD'S FUTURE POLITICAL INVOLVEMENT?   119

increases the likelihood of political involvement in adult life

get the topic: WHAT ARE THE CHARACTERISTICS OF SOCIAL GROUPS?

Theory

FUNCTIONALISM   116
- examines the group's values and behaviours, particularly the group's leader
- successful groups often have successful leaders
- Maxwell's five levels of leadership

CONFLICT THEORY   116
- democratic leadership styles increase worker productivity
- if a democratic environment is not implemented, then bureaucracy can be stifling for the worker and the organization
- greater participation in leadership roles does not mean the company will succeed

SYMBOLIC INTERACTIONISM   117
- along with leadership, personal attitude has a big effect on job performance and satisfaction
- people feel good about themselves and their jobs when they feel they have a certain level of control over their actions
- democratic work environments help people feel connected to their jobs

FEMINIST THEORY   117
- traditional leadership theories and models are based on male values
- alternative, but equally effective, leadership styles that reflect female values can be introduced in organizations and bureaucracies

Key Terms

social groups are groups that consist of two or more people who interact with one another and share a common identity.   *106*

bounded relationships are relationships that exist only under specific conditions.   *107*

in-group is a group to which we feel an affinity or closeness.   *108*

in-group bias is the feeling that a person's in-group is superior to others.   *108*

out-group is a group from which we are disconnected.   *108*

reference group is the group that you use to evaluate yourself.   *109*

dyad is a group consisting of only two people. *110*

triad is a group consisting of three people.   *110*

leadership style is a behavioural mode that leaders use to influence group members.   *110*

autocratic leaders are leaders who determine the group policies and assign tasks.   *110*

democratic leaders are leaders who strive to set group policy by discussion and agreement.   *110*

(continued)

laissez-faire leaders are leaders who lead by absence and may in fact not want to be leaders at all. *110*

conformity is the degree to which we will alter our behaviour, attitudes, and points of view to fit into our perceived expectation of what is appropriate. *111*

groupthink is the term for group decisions that are made without objective thought. *111*

social capital is a sociological concept that refers to the individual and collective resources available to a person. *113*

social network is the web of ties you have with others. *113*

formal organizations are groups created for a certain purpose and built for maximum efficiency. *114*

voluntary association is the act of joining an organization that offers no pay and that expands social networks through interaction. *114*

organizations are formal groups that exist to achieve a desired goal. *114*

utilitarian organization is an organization in which people receive wages in exchange for work. *114*

normative organizations are organizations that exist to achieve a worthwhile goal. *114*

coercive organizations are organizations that people are forced to join. *114*

formal structures are the explicit rules, goals, and guidelines of an organization. *114*

informal structures are friendships, allegiances, and loyalties among members of an organization. *114*

bureaucracies are formal organizations that are organized into a hierarchy of smaller departments. *115*

formal rationality is the reasonable actions that organizations and bureaucracies take to achieve goals in the most effective way. *115*

iron cage is a concept introduced by Max Weber that refers to the way in which bureaucracies make workers feel trapped and turn them into little more than robots accomplishing tasks. *115*

Sample Test Questions

These multiple-choice questions are similar to those found in the test bank that accompanies this textbook.

1. What type of leader sets few goals and does only what must be done?
   a. Totalitarian leader
   b. Autocratic leader
   c. Democratic leader
   d. Laissez-faire leader
2. A soup kitchen is an example of a
   a. coercive organization.
   b. utilitarian organization.
   c. normative organization.
   d. democratic organization.
3. Which of the following is *not* a characteristic common to all properly functioning organizations?
   a. Division of labour
   b. Methods of succession
   c. Voluntary participation
   d. Concentration of power
4. Which organization did Weber call a logical extension of formal rational thought?
   a. Democracy
   b. Bureaucracy
   c. Coercive organization
   d. Informal organization
5. By a functionalist's standard, the greatest measure of a leader is
   a. influence.
   b. charisma.
   c. authority.
   d. intimidation.

ANSWERS: 1. d; 2. c; 3. c; 4. b; 5. a

ESSAY

1. How and why are social networks of great use to immigrants?
2. Why is groupthink a potentially dangerous method of decision making?
3. What are the potential pitfalls of the three leadership styles discussed in this chapter?
4. Which leadership style do you think Pierre Trudeau used as prime minister of Canada? Explain.
5. Why is a dyad considered the strongest form of a group?

WHERE TO START YOUR RESEARCH PAPER

To find out how you can be a leader, go to http://ildii.ca/leadership-initiatives, www.leadershipcanada.ca (click on "Resources")

To learn more about the skills needed for leadership, go to www.theglobeandmail.com/report-on-business/your-business/business-categories/leadership
www.livingskillslibrary.com/html/Leadership%201%20Models.html

To find Max Weber's notes and original texts, go to www.sociosite.net/topics/weber.php

For more information on the sociology of Georg Simmel, go to www.sociosite.net/topics/sociologists.php#simmel

Remember to check www.thethinkspot.ca **for additional information, downloadable flashcards, and other helpful resources.**

SOCIAL CLASS
IN CANADA

WHAT IS SOCIAL STRATIFICATION?
WHAT ARE THE THEORIES BEHIND SOCIAL STRATIFICATION?
WHAT SOCIAL POLICIES HAVE BEEN CREATED TO EASE POVERTY?

"One of the most persistent images that Canadians have of their society is that it has no classes. This image becomes translated into the assertion that Canadians are all relatively equal in their possessions, in the amount of money they earn, and in the opportunities which they and their children have to get on in the world. An important element in this image of classlessness is that, with the absence of formal aristocracy and aristocratic institutions, Canada is a society in which equalitarian values have asserted themselves over authoritarian values. Canada, it is thought, shares not only a continent with the United States, but also a democratic ideology which rejects the historical class and power structures of Europe.

"In a society which is made up of many cultural groups there is usually some relationship between a person's membership in these groups and his class position and, consequently, his chances of reaching positions of power. Because the Canadian people are often referred to as a mosaic composed of different ethnic groups, the title, 'The Vertical Mosaic,' was originally given to the chapter which examines the relationship between ethnicity and social class. As the study proceeded, however, the hierarchical relationship between Canada's many cultural groups became a recurring theme in class and power. For example, it became clear that the Canadians of British origin have retained, within the elite structure of the society, the charter group status with which they started out, and that in some institutional settings the French have been admitted as a co-charter group whereas in others they have not. The title, 'The Vertical Mosaic,' therefore seemed to be an appropriate link between the two parts of the book."[1]

Stratification *in a* Modern Society

CHAPTER 07

In *The Vertical Mosaic: An Analysis of Social Class and Power in Canada,* John Porter described the features of **class and stratification in Canadian society.**

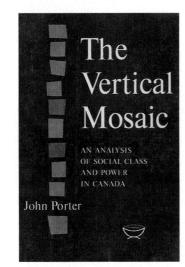

Although it was researched and written nearly 50 years ago, much is still relevant in Porter's analysis of the Canadian social structure. The term *mosaic* refers to the rich diversity of languages, cultures, ethnicities, and religions that make up Canadian society. However, as Porter pointed out, not all groups enjoy the same power and status. There is a hierarchy, and so the mosaic is also "vertical," with some groups higher than others. Being higher means having better income, better health, better education—overall, a better life. In Canada, those of British ancestry enjoy the greatest privileges, while aboriginal peoples are the most disadvantaged. How does social position affect a person's life? As sociologists, we want to find out.

get the topic: WHAT IS SOCIAL STRATIFICATION?

It seems that it's in our nature to rank things. Pick up any magazine at the end of a given year, and you're sure to find "top ten" lists ranking that year's best (or worst) movies, albums, or books. Similarly, David Letterman has made the Top Ten List his signature bit on the *Late Show with David Letterman.* Sociologists also like to rank individuals based on objective criteria, usually including wealth, power, or prestige. **Social stratification** relates to the ranking of people and the rewards they receive based on objective criteria, often including wealth, power, and/or prestige.

All forms of society have ways to rank, or stratify, the members of their populations, but the level of stratification can vary a great deal between societies.[2] Some societies may use political power to separate people by giving party members special privileges unavailable to others. Societies might use wealth to stratify people into social classes as well; the more money you have, the higher your status. Still others use birth status and family of origin as a means to divide people; certain families regarded as "nobility" hold privileged positions.

In Canada, we tend to divide groups by their access to wealth and/or income. **Income** refers to the money received for work or through investments. Whether it's the paycheque you get every two weeks or the dividends you receive from your stock investments, the money you receive regularly is considered income. **Wealth,** on the other hand, refers to all your material possessions, including income. If you were to take everything you

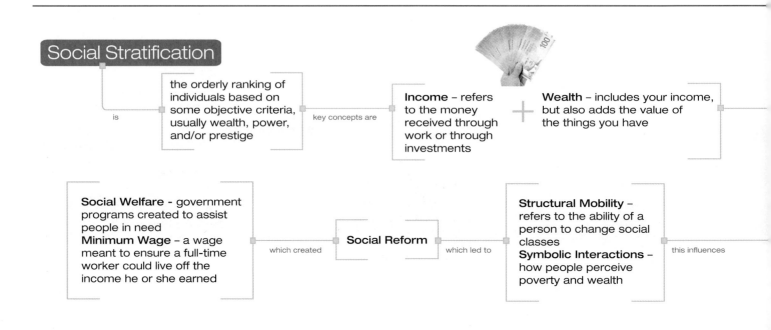

Social Stratification

is → the orderly ranking of individuals based on some objective criteria, usually wealth, power, and/or prestige

key concepts are → **Income** – refers to the money received through work or through investments

+ **Wealth** – includes your income, but also adds the value of the things you have

Social Welfare - government programs created to assist people in need
Minimum Wage – a wage meant to ensure a full-time worker could live off the income he or she earned

which created → **Social Reform**

which led to → **Structural Mobility** – refers to the ability of a person to change social classes
Symbolic Interactions – how people perceive poverty and wealth

this influences →

owned—your car, your computer, your clothes, and so on—and sell it all at a fair market value, you could probably raise a considerable sum that would be more than your monthly income. It's important to know the difference between the two and to understand how each of these factors can affect your social standing.

INCOME DISTRIBUTION

When I was a college student, I could put everything I owned in the back of my Honda Civic. I worked for 25 cents above the minimum wage, and I had few expenses. I earn much more now than I did in college, but my expenses have also increased significantly as I married, bought a house, and started a family. Statistics Canada conducts an annual survey of Canadian households that measures the distribution of income. All households are listed from poorest to richest, and then divided into five groups called **quintiles**. If income distribution trends continue, the rich are going to get richer and the poor are going to get poorer. In 1989, the lowest quintile received 4.8 percent of total income and the highest quintile received 43 percent. Compare these percentages with 2008, when the poorest 20 percent of the country's earners received only 4.2 percent of the total income, whereas the top 20 percent received 47.3 percent.[3] The median, or midpoint, household income for Canadian families of two or more persons in 2008 was $63 900.[4] However, Canadian households in the lowest quintile had incomes of just $24 700 or lower, while the top 20 percent of all households earned more than $104 100.[5] Between 1980 and 2005, earnings increased by 16.4 percent for those in the top income group, stagnated for those in the middle income group, and fell by 20.6 percent for those in the bottom group.[6]

WEALTH DISTRIBUTION

Wealth refers to the value of material possessions. For most Canadians, their most significant asset is their house. Other kinds of assets are cars, belongings, and personal pension funds, including RRSPs. The median wealth of Canadian families was $148 400 in 2005. Since 1999, all Canadian families have seen an increase in wealth, except those families in the lowest quintile. Increases were highest in the fourth and fifth quintiles, which indicates a growing inequality in Canada's wealth distribution. The 20 percent of family units with the highest net worth held 69.2 percent of all personal wealth in 2005.[7]

The wealth distribution of Canada shows other trends as well. Generally, men have more wealth than women do. In 2005, Canadian families headed by a woman had a median wealth value of $105 470 compared to $184 964 for families headed by a man. Families with an older family head typically have more wealth. After 65 years old, though, wealth starts to decline because retired people often draw on their assets to supplement their income when they retire. In 2005, older families had the

<<< Some societies use birth as a way to stratify their people. Although Japan is a democracy with a prime minister, nobility such as Emperor Akihito and Empress Michiko are among Japanese society's most elite and wealthy members.

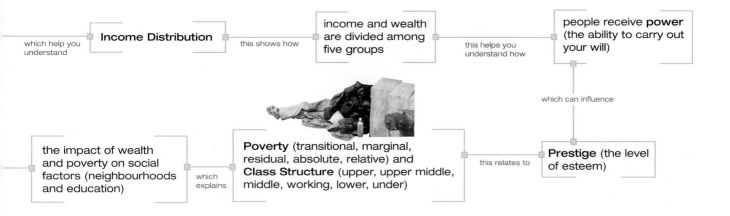

which help you understand → **Income Distribution** → this shows how → income and wealth are divided among five groups → this helps you understand how → people receive **power** (the ability to carry out your will)

which can influence

the impact of wealth and poverty on social factors (neighbourhoods and education) ← which explains → **Poverty** (transitional, marginal, residual, absolute, relative) and **Class Structure** (upper, upper middle, middle, working, lower, under) → this relates to → **Prestige** (the level of esteem)

TRANSITIONAL POVERTY is a temporary state of poverty that occurs when someone loses a job for a short time.

MARGINAL POVERTY is a state of poverty that occurs when a person lacks stable employment.

RESIDUAL POVERTY is chronic and multigenerational poverty.

ABSOLUTE POVERTY is poverty so severe that one lacks resources to survive.

RELATIVE POVERTY is a state of poverty that occurs when we compare ourselves to those around us.

highest median wealth. This is mainly because they are more likely to live in a mortgage-free home and their pension assets are higher. Single individuals, including the elderly living alone, had the lowest median wealth.[8]

How Does Canada Define Poverty?

Sociologists have several different ways of defining poverty. **Transitional poverty** is a temporary state that occurs when someone loses a job for a short time. **Marginal poverty** occurs when a person lacks stable employment. For example, if your job is lifeguarding at a pool during the summer season, you might experience marginal poverty when the season ends. The next, more serious level, **residual poverty**, is chronic and

multigenerational. People who live in a seemingly never-ending cycle of poverty that passes on to their children and grandchildren experience this type of poverty. A person who experiences **absolute poverty** is so poor that he or she doesn't have resources to survive. The people who are starving to death in the Darfur region of the Sudan are living in absolute poverty. **Relative poverty** is a state that occurs when we compare ourselves to those around us. You might experience relative poverty if you feel like your cell phone is old and insufficient compared with your friend's phone.

While there is no "official" definition of poverty in Canada, Statistics Canada uses three measures of low income. The first is the *low income cut-off* (LICO). Families that spend at least 20 percentage points more of their after-tax income on food, clothing, and shelter than the average family of the same size are counted as low income. Since it is a comparative measure, the LICO is more of a measure of inequality or relative poverty than of absolute poverty. The *low income measure* (LIM) defines low-income Canadians as those living in families that have an after-tax income lower than 50 percent of the median income for all Canadian families. This measure is often used to make international comparisons. One of the main criticisms of the LICO and the LIM is that they do not account for regional differences in the cost of living. The *market basket measure* (MBM) estimates the cost of a specified set of goods and services in 48 geographic regions across Canada. In 2006, this amount ranged from $23 781 in urban communities with populations between 30 000 and 99 999 in Quebec to $31 399 in the Toronto Census Metropolitan Area.[9]

Canada Income Distribution, 2008

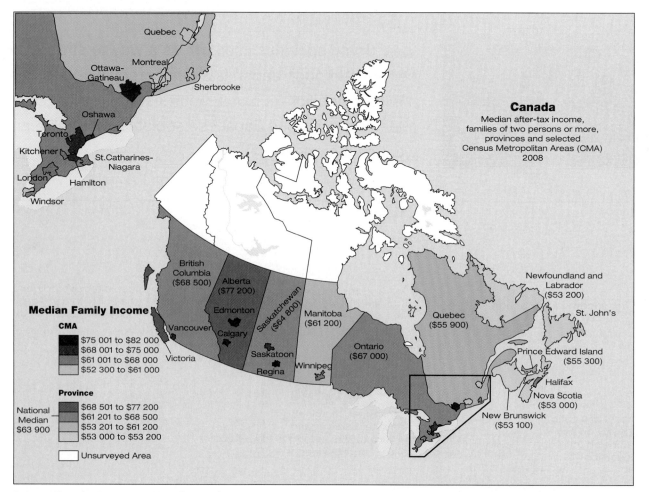

Source: Canada, Income in Canada, Catalogue 75-202-X, 2008, Figure 1. Accessed at http://www.statcan.gc.ca/pub/75-202-x/2008000/analysis-analyses-eng.htm.

POWER

Another measure of stratification is **power**—the ability to carry out your will and impose it on others. In college classrooms, teachers possess great power. They select the textbooks, the topics the class will cover, and the order in which they will cover them. In short, college instructors have a great deal of power over what happens in their classes, and students' only power is to enroll or drop the course. Why are things this way? Because the power to educate in college is **delegated**, meaning given or assigned, to faculty by the college or university. Members of the House of Commons exercise delegated power when they represent the people who elected them. They can use this power to draft new laws or steward the economy out of (or into) a recession.

Individuals have varying amounts of power, but no one has totally unlimited power. C. Wright Mills suggested that within the United States a small group called the **power elite** holds immense power.[10] Canada has its own version of a power elite. The power elite come from three distinct but related groups: economic elite, state elite, and media elite. They decide what information and knowledge to share with the rest of us, and they use their social position and influence to direct the country's decisions. For example, in Canada, six families control 723 companies: the Westons (123), the Blacks (123), the Desmaraises (121), the Irvings (121), and two branches of the Bronfmans (Charles Rosner with 118, and Edward and Peter with 117).[11]

Most politicians must be voted into power, but not all eligible voters exercise their right to vote. People with high incomes and people who've achieved high levels of education are more likely to vote than their less wealthy, less-educated neighbours.[12] So what does this mean? Older, wealthier, educated people are making key decisions for the entire country. How does this affect the kinds of politicians we elect, the social measures we pass, and the economic packages we approve?

POWER is the ability to carry out your will and impose it on others.
DELEGATED means given or assigned.
POWER ELITE is a small group of people who hold immense power.
PRESTIGE is the level of esteem associated with one's status and social standing.

PRESTIGE

Prestige refers to the level of esteem associated with our status and social standing. Most of us want others to hold us in high regard, but various types of jobs hold differing levels of prestige. Occupational prestige refers to how well a job is regarded by society. It may be based on how much the job pays, but also includes other factors such as the level of education required to gain entry to the job, the sector, the degree of autonomy, or even the perceived "social usefulness" of the job.[13] We often judge people by the job they do. When I worked as a cafeteria manager, I made pretty good money, but when I told people what I did for a living, they were not impressed. When I became a college teacher, people were much more interested in knowing more about me and what I did. Occupational prestige varies a great deal among jobs and shows the general respect our society has for certain kinds of work.

Occupational prestige is generally ranked on a scale from 0 to 100, with 0 being the lowest. Because occupational prestige is socially defined, job rankings can change over time. In 2000, John Goyder replicated a study done in 1975 in Kitchener-Waterloo. In 1975, the lowest-ranked jobs in the survey were worker in a dry-cleaner (16.7) and filling-station attendant (17.2) while physician (93.6) and architect (90.3) were the highest-ranked. In 2000, some of these jobs had changed a lot in their ranking. Architects fell to 74.5, while hospital attendants increased from 30.8 to 55.5.[14]

▶▶▶ GO GL🌐BAL

From One Extreme to Another

The United States has the greatest percentage of children living in poverty compared with other industrial democracies.[15] In the U.S., 20.7 percent of children under the age of 18 live in poverty,[16] and 21.3 percent of children live in households classified as "food insecure," which are households that change the quantity or quality of their food or frequently skip meals because of limited incomes.[17] In 2005, seven percent of the children living in the United States lived in extreme poverty.[18] These families have incomes below 50 percent of the poverty threshold.[19]

Ironically, the United States leads the world in the total number of millionaires as well as the highest percentage of new

millionaires.[20] Many of these millionaires run for positions in government or contribute large donations to political causes. In fact, of the 100 members in the 2010 Senate, 54 were millionaires.[21]

<<< Although there are government programs designed to help the poor, many **impoverished children suffer from lack of nutritious food, dirty living conditions, and poor health.**

UPPER OR ELITE CLASS is a social class that is very small in number and holds significant wealth.

UPPER MIDDLE CLASS is a social class that consists of high-income members of society who are well educated but do not belong to the elite membership of the super wealthy.

Job prestige is generally ranked on a scale from 0 to 100, with 0 being the lowest. In 2001, Canadians ranked physicians, dentists, and judges and lawyers as the top occupations. Trappers and hunters, sports referees, and door-to-door vendors were ranked the lowest.[22] A prestigious job may carry its benefits into other areas of life. For example, you might take a stock tip from the CEO of a successful start-up, but I doubt you'd take the advice of a minimum-wage-earning grocery bagger. You don't expect someone who works as a bagger to be able to give you a great stock tip; why would he or she be working in such a low-status job? Occupational prestige varies a great deal among jobs and shows the general respect we have for certain work. Few people look at their newborn baby and hope she'll grow up to become a fry cook rather than a doctor.

Wealth, power, and prestige are the basis for the stratification system used to characterize the population, so these three components can also be used to analyze the class system of Canada.

CLASS STRUCTURE IN CANADA

If someone asked you what your social class is, what would you say? You have already seen in this chapter that social class is in fact a complicated mix of income, wealth, and occupation. It also includes things like education and political ideology. Sociologists have varying opinions on how many classes there should be and what constitutes each class. For our discussion, however, let's look at six different social classes in Canada: upper class, upper middle class, middle class, working class, lower class, and underclass. Ask yourself how your membership to one class or the other might influence your perspective, opportunities, and long-term outcomes.

Upper/Elite Class

The **upper or elite class** is very small in number and holds significant wealth. The

upper class possesses much of the country's "old money," which affords them great access to the three components of class: wealth, power, and prestige. The Bronfmans, Thomsons, Molsons, and Westons have been rich for generations. This class also includes the "new rich," people such as Jim Balsillie, who made billions selling the BlackBerry, or Wayne Gretzky, the hockey superstar turned astute businessman.

In *The Vertical Mosaic,* John Porter describes the Canadian elite. "At the high end of the social class spectrum are the families of great wealth and influence. They are not perhaps as ostentatious as the very wealthy of other societies, and Canada has no 'celebrity world' with which these families must compete for prestige. . . . Almost every large Canadian city has its wealthy and prominent families of several generations. They have their own social life, their children go to private schools, they have their clubs and associations, and they take on the charitable and philanthropic roles which have so long been the 'duty' of those of high status."[23] The upper class's money affords them opportunities that most people only dream of having. However, members of the upper middle class come pretty close to matching the elite's status.

Upper Middle Class

As with all distinctions of class, the definition of the upper middle class is fairly subjective. For the purposes of our discussion, the **upper middle class** consists of high-income members of society who are well educated but do not belong to the elite membership of the super wealthy. These people occupy professional positions and have achieved a level of income that makes their lives comfortable. They own property, have high occupational prestige, and often hold positions of authority within their jobs.[24]

<<< **Geoff Molson was born into one of the richest families in Canada.** Do you think he would have been as successful if he had been born into a poor family?

THINK SOCIOLOGICALLY

Ashbury College

One of the luxuries that elite students enjoy is attending a high-quality preparatory school such as Ashbury College in Ottawa. Founded in 1891, Ashbury College is a co-educational boarding school with slightly more than 500 students in grades 4 through 12. Students

enjoy a variety of educational opportunities, from anatomy to German, and can participate in many different sports including downhill skiing and rowing. The average class size is 17 students. Students who wish to attend will pay up to $44 250 a year for the privilege.[25]

This kind of education gives the upper class the edge they need to succeed. In

recent years, 100 percent of graduates from Ashbury College have been accepted at universities such as McGill, Queen's, and the University of Toronto. The exclusive education they received ensures that they are groomed for top-paying positions that come with great power.

The two primary components of this group are occupational prestige and education. Owning a small business, having a professional career, or holding a high-status job often propels a person into this group. Your dentist, your lawyer, or the owner of a successful business may belong in this group.[26]

Middle Class

Most Canadians claim that they are members of the middle class. If you're trying to decide where you fall along the country's economic spectrum, you might think, "Well, I'm not poor, and I'm not rich, so I must be somewhere in the middle. That's middle class, right?" However, the sociological definition for middle class is a bit more complex.

In general, **middle class** people have moderate incomes. They may be lower-paid white-collar workers, such as schoolteachers, or well-paid blue-collar workers, like factory foremen. Middle-class workers generally aren't involved in manual labour, but they may be skilled labourers (such as electricians). In many middle-class families, if there are two parents present both must work in order to make ends meet. Most middle-class members have at least a high school diploma and many have technical training or college credits. Such attainment affords them a moderate level of occupational prestige. When you graduate from college and get your first job, you are likely to start out in the middle class. Members own property but generally hold much less wealth than the previously discussed groups.

MIDDLE CLASS is a social class that consists of those who have moderate incomes.

WORKING CLASS is a social class generally made up of people with high school diplomas and lower levels of education.

LOWER CLASS is a social class living in poverty.

Working Class

The **working class** is generally made up of people with high school diplomas and lower levels of education. They often hold jobs that involve manual labour or clerical skills. Blue-collar factory workers or white-collar clerical workers make up most of the working class. Unlike those in the middle and upper middle classes, members of the working class earn an hourly wage instead of a salary. Because they work by the hour and lack formal education, the working class has very limited opportunities for job improvement. Many non-traditional college students come from the working class. They understand that "good jobs" are increasingly rare and that education opens doors. However, their ability to raise their social class is hindered by the increasing number of blue-collar and even white-collar jobs that are moving overseas. There is an increasing amount of competition for work, which is a further motivation for workers to boost their marketable skills.[27]

Lower Class

A notch below the working class are the members of society who truly feel the effects of poverty: the **lower class**. Thanks to the skyrocketing costs of tuition, food, and rent, many college students might think they understand what it means to be poor. In most cases, though, the relative poverty of their situation pales in comparison to the experiences of the working poor. After all, the privileges of attending a university and receiving a higher education are designed to lead students to employment that will land them in the middle class. When I was in college, I worked at a landscape nursery doing physical labour. Our pay was low and the hours were long. For me, a college student living at home, it was a good job. For my colleagues at the nursery who were trying to feed their families, it was not.

Members of the lower class often live on meagre paycheques, if they even have a job at all. Those people who do work are often one big bill or layoff away from financial ruin.

∧
∧
∧ **Many non-traditional students are working-class adults who want to gain more skills through education.** More and more adults are going back to school for additional training and new careers.

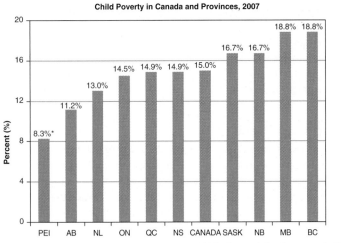

Child Poverty in Canada and Provinces, 2007

Source: Campaign 2000, a cross-Canada network working to end child/family poverty in Canada, www.campaing2000.ca
Note: * StatsCan lists data as E, meaning "Use with caution." Figures are LICO before tax.

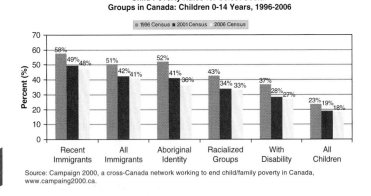

Child Poverty Rates for Select Social Groups in Canada: Children 0-14 Years, 1996-2006

Source: Campaign 2000, a cross-Canada network working to end child/family poverty in Canada, www.campaing2000.ca.

Canadians in low income after tax (In percent, 2004 to 2008)					
	2004	2005	2006	2007	2008
	prevalence in %				
All persons	11.4	10.8	10.5	9.2	9.4
Under 18 years of age	13.0	11.7	11.4	9.6	9.1
18 to 64	11.9	11.4	11.2	9.9	10.2
65 and over	5.6	6.2	5.4	4.9	5.8
Males	10.8	10.5	10.2	9.0	9.0
Under 18 years of age	13.2	12.3	11.4	9.9	9.3
18 to 64	11.3	11.1	10.9	9.7	9.8
65 and over	3.5	3.4	3.4	3.3	3.6
Females	11.9	11.1	10.9	9.4	9.9
Under 18 years of age	12.9	11.1	11.4	9.1	8.8
18 to 64	12.5	11.7	11.5	10.2	10.7
65 and over	7.3	8.4	7.0	6.1	7.6

Source: Adapted from Statistics Canada. Accessed at http://www40.statcan.ca/l01/cst01/famil19a-eng.htm, December 31, 2010.

The Underclass

Despite our country's prosperity, there are homeless people in Canada. They belong to the underclass of Canadian society. Other members of this group live in substandard housing and may be receiving government assistance. They often lack a high school diploma, and if they find a job it's usually a minimum-wage position that propels them no higher than the working-poor class.

The **urban underclass** lives in disadvantaged neighbourhoods. Many workers in disadvantaged neighbourhoods are forced to take low-paying positions that go nowhere, leaving them with little hope of escaping the neighbourhoods that are holding them down.

However, what makes them truly disadvantaged is that they are often socially isolated and lack conventional role models. These issues make life significantly more difficult for the residents and children who live in these ghettos.

NEIGHBOURHOODS AND SOCIAL CLASS

Sociologists have observed how neighbourhoods influence behaviour. Their findings have demonstrated an increase in the geographic concentration of poverty and affluence especially in large cities. Over time, poor people are living in neighbourhoods densely populated by other poor people. Simultaneously, the well-off members of society, particularly those who live in cities, tend to cluster in economically affluent neighbourhoods, such as Westmount in Montreal, Rosedale in Toronto, and Shaughnessy in Vancouver. Looking at each end of the spectrum gives us a clear vision of the dynamics between poverty and affluence in Canada.

The concentration of poverty in a single geographic area is correlated to various issues such as high crime rates, increased drug use, and increasing numbers of single-parent homes. Often, people who achieve any sort of economic advantage move out of these poor neighbourhoods. This sort of residential segregation increases the disadvantages for those left behind.[28] Children who grow up in such neighbourhoods are at increased risk for lower birth weights, poorer health, lower levels of educational attainment, and higher dropout levels.[29]

Conversely, children growing up in affluent neighbourhoods do better in school, have lower rates of teen pregnancy, and have higher test scores. Interestingly, when a poor child is raised in a more affluent neighbourhood, due to foster care or some type of rent control supplement, the child tends to do better than his or her peers who remain living in poor neighbourhoods. In short, living in a more affluent neighbourhood seems to decrease the power of the negative effect that poverty has on children. Why do you think this is the case? Apparently being "the poor kid on the block" is better for a child than being another poor kid on the block.[30] Why?

Social Mobility

Wherever we are in life, there's always the chance that something could happen to us that would change our status. Whether it's winning the lottery or investing in the right stocks, our social class could change in an instant. Likewise, the recession and corporate downsizing have sent many middle-class families plummeting into poverty. **Social mobility** is a term that describes this ability to change social classes. If social class is a ladder, social mobility occurs when we climb either up or down it. Several patterns of social mobility are possible.

Horizontal mobility, as the name suggests, refers to moving within the same status category. For example, when a teacher leaves one school to take a position at another school, horizontal mobility has occurred. The teacher is earning the same amount of money and performs the same tasks; she just happens to be doing these things at a different location. Her movement is lateral, not vertical. **Vertical mobility** involves moving from one social status to another. This type of mobility can either be upward, in the form of a promotion at work, or downward, in the form of a demotion at work. For example, if the same teacher got a master's degree and became a principal, then vertical mobility has occurred.

In Canada, the labour market has changed immensely. When was the last time you bought something that was labelled MADE IN CANADA? **Canadian citizens who previously performed this type of work find themselves out of a job, which in turn slows upward mobility.**

Intragenerational mobility occurs when an individual changes social standing, especially in the workforce. Climbing the corporate ladder is a prime example of this type of mobility. For instance, if you begin your working career as an unskilled labourer doing construction work and then 10 years later own a construction company, you are experiencing intragenerational mobility.

Intergenerational mobility refers to the change that family members make from one social class to the next through generations. If you hope to live a better life than your parents did, then you hope for upward intergenerational mobility. However, if you expect to do much better than your parents, the odds are probably stacked against you. A number of researchers have found that while intergenerational mobility does occur, children tend to climb only a little higher on the social class ladder when compared with their parents, if they climb at all.[31]

The likelihood of this kind of mobility is even less for children born into poor families. Their parents probably lack the education, skills, social networks, and other resources that would provide them with the social capital that would make mobility upward easier. Children raised in poor homes are more likely to experience poverty in adulthood. In a vicious circle called the **cycle of poverty**, poor children are more likely to remain poor in adulthood compared with other children who are not raised in poverty.

URBAN UNDERCLASS is a social class living in disadvantaged neighbourhoods that are characterized by four components: poverty, family disruption, male unemployment, and lack of individuals in high-status occupations.

SOCIAL MOBILITY is the ability to change social classes.

HORIZONTAL MOBILITY refers to moving within the same status category.

VERTICAL MOBILITY refers to moving from one social status to another.

INTRAGENERATIONAL MOBILITY occurs when an individual changes social standing, especially in the workforce.

INTERGENERATIONAL MOBILITY refers to the change that family members make from one social class to the next through generations.

CYCLE OF POVERTY refers to the vicious circle where poor children are more likely to be poor as adults.

STRUCTURAL MOBILITY occurs when social changes affect large numbers of people.

Structural mobility occurs when social changes affect large numbers of people. During economic booms, some climb the ladder and benefit from changes in the economy. Think of the success that the Chrysler company experienced during the economic prosperity of the mid-1990s.

When the economy heads into a recession, workers who have lost their jobs to outsourcing experience downward structural mobility. For example, the same Chrysler company that flourished in the 1990s was forced to close many plants and lay off more than 13 000 workers a little more than a decade later.

MAKE CONNECTIONS

Nickel and Dimed into Poverty

Before writing the book *Nickel and Dimed*, Barbara Ehrenreich spent a year living among the working class in the United States. Going from state to state, she worked as a waitress, a maid, a nursing home aide, and a Walmart salesperson. Ehrenreich's experiences led her to dispute the idea that these jobs require low-level skills. Instead, she believes that such low-wage jobs are physically demanding and actually require a great deal of interpersonal and technical skills. These jobs don't normally provide health care or sick leave, so workers who fall ill have to choose between their health and their pay. Yet despite the hurdles society has placed in their way, these workers are actually more motivated to succeed and are not depressed by a system of low wages and long hours.

>>> **ACTIVITY** Recent college graduate Adam Shepard wrote *Scratch Beginnings: Me, $25, and the Search for the American Dream* in rebuttal to Ehrenreich's book. By undertaking a self-imposed experiment, Shepard tries to demonstrate that an individual can overcome the structural obstacles to success. Read Shepard's book or search the internet to learn his findings. Which author paints a more accurate picture of life for the working poor? Why?

EXCHANGE MOBILITY is a concept suggesting that, within a country, each social class contains a relatively fixed number of people.

MERITOCRACY ARGUMENT states that those who get ahead do so based on their own merit.

FEMINIZATION OF POVERTY refers to the fact that around the world women experience poverty at far higher rates than men.

The concept of **exchange mobility** suggests that, within a country, each social class contains a relatively fixed number of people. If you move upward into a class above you, someone else must move down. When you consider the changes in income over time that we talked about earlier, you can see that such data generally support the idea that social stratification levels do not change much, though the people who make up each layer may be different.

think sociologically: WHAT ARE THE THEORIES BEHIND SOCIAL STRATIFICATION?

Functionalism

Functionalists believe that systems find equilibrium, or balance, so stratification must be the result of some kind of functional balance. Theorists Kingsley Davis and Wilbert Moore summarize the common argument that a stratification system is inevitable and aids in the smooth functioning of society.[32] This **meritocracy argument** states that those who get ahead do so based on their own merit.

Davis and Moore believe each society has important positions that must be filled. The more important the position, the more we reward those who choose to pursue it. Doctors in Canada generally get hefty paycheques because everyone needs a doctor to tend to his or her health-care needs. Society offers rewards to those who are willing to fill important positions. The rarer the skill or the longer the training period, the greater the rewards can be. If you faint at the sight of blood or if you can't stand the thought of spending a good portion of your life in school, you probably shouldn't become a doctor.

On the other hand, the reason why KFC (or PFK in Quebec) is able to pay its employees minimum wage is because they can learn to fry chicken in about two hours. I should know; I once cooked chicken for the Colonel. But why would anyone become a medical doctor considering the stress and training involved? Davis and Moore say that society has to offer greater rewards to entice people to take particularly tough or stressful jobs. To sum up the functionalist view, stratification inevitably happens because people have different abilities, and those abilities are more or less important to society.

Therefore, if you get ahead, it is based on some ability or drive you have that pushes you to get there. Delayed gratification, or the ability to wait in order to get something you want, can also determine your success. If you're willing to put in the time to go to school and work hard, you're likely to be successful.

In this sense, it means that stratification is inevitable, since we do not all have the same intelligence, drive, and desire.

Those who get ahead in this country tend to be those who use these individual forces to reap society's rewards.

After teaching sociology for many years, John Carl believes that most of his students are functionalists. They support the idea that people succeed or fail based on their own merit.

The graphic on the right provides information from student surveys that he has used in his classes. This non-scientific study yields the same results virtually every year. He asked students if they "agree with the following statements," and the percentages show those who agree with the statements. What do you think? Do individuals determine their own success?

Student Opinions on Why People Get Ahead

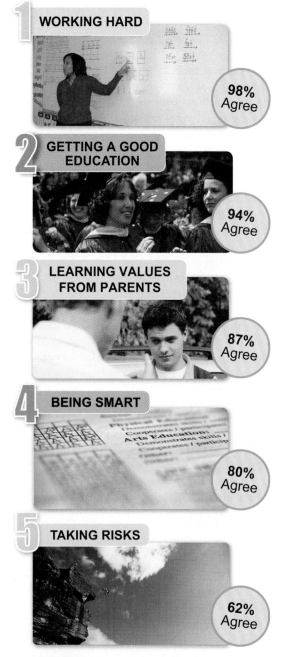

1. **WORKING HARD** — 98% Agree
2. **GETTING A GOOD EDUCATION** — 94% Agree
3. **LEARNING VALUES FROM PARENTS** — 87% Agree
4. **BEING SMART** — 80% Agree
5. **TAKING RISKS** — 62% Agree

Source: Based on informal surveys by John D. Carl of American sociology students on the reasons people get ahead in the United States.

Average Salary: $61 249[33]

Average Salary: $73 582[34]

2010 Earnings: $9 million[35]

<<< Teachers and police officers are essential for society, but professional athletes, like Sidney Crosby, are not. **Why do you think there is such a discrepancy between salaries?**

Conflict Theory

Unlike functionalists, conflict theorists focus on the role of conflict as the basis of stratification. Every society has limited resources to go around, so groups struggle with one another for those resources. Melvin Tumin offers a critique of Davis and Moore that supports the conflict point of view. For Tumin, social inequality is rooted in a system that is more likely to reward you based on where you start—not solely based on the abilities you have.[36] There is nothing inevitable about inequality, it is merely those with wealth doing the best they can to keep that wealth and pass it on to their children. In this way, social inequality is rooted in the unjust capitalist system and not the people who live under it.

Tumin also suggests that stratification is not as simple as some might suggest. First, the societal importance of a job does not seem to be the only basis for financial rewards. Think about it: Who is arguably more important to society, a police officer or a professional athlete? Now ask yourself who makes more money? Being a soldier, firefighter, police officer, or teacher requires dedication, training, and unique skills. But these groups are actually paid very little in comparison to entertainers, corporate CEOs, and professional athletes.

Conflict theorists point out that groups with power will extract what they can from the groups beneath them. The dominant group takes control of social institutions in order to preserve the best resources for itself. By extension, conflict theorists argue, the wealthy try to maintain the status quo so that access to training will remain limited to their group, thus helping them gain even more wealth and power. Why do doctors make so much money? People need them and have very little choice about it.

Students from working-class backgrounds are far more likely to talk about social class as an issue on college campuses than are upper middle-class students. **The perception of social stratification, then, comes primarily from the "have-nots" instead of the "haves."**

Symbolic Interactionism

Symbolic interactionists are interested in how people perceive poverty and wealth. They seek to understand whether people actually have a sense of social class. According to research by Edward G. Grabb and Ronald D. Lambert, our particular social class impacts how we talk about class in general. In a survey, respondents from the lower class were more likely to identify class as being based exclusively on economic criteria, while the upper-class respondents were more likely to include non-economic considerations.[37]

The higher our socioeconomic status (SES), the less we believe that social class matters. For example, upper middle-class college students tend to disregard issues of class and often don't notice that others cannot do what they can do financially. They may be socialized not to care about social class, or they might not have thought much about it.

This could be because working-class students must make financial choices that upper middle-class students don't even have to consider. In addition, students from the working class have lower expectations about future earnings and successes. Basically, the disparity in these college students' social status demonstrates how ascribed positions affect expectations.

The perception of class differences is most pronounced in the dichotomous way that people look at welfare recipients. Some students in my classes become angry when discussing the social welfare system. As one young woman put it, "If they really wanted to, they could just get a job and make money like everyone else." Putting aside the obvious problems with this statement, this woman's words certainly illustrate the difference between what the general public perceives and the reality of welfare.

Feminist Theory

Feminist theorists talk about the **feminization of poverty**—the term used to describe the fact that, around the world, women experience poverty at far higher rates than men. For example, median annual earnings for Canadian men in 2008 were $36 200, whereas the median for Canadian women was $22 800. By this measure, women earn 63 cents for every dollar that men earn.[38]

In *So You Think I Drive a Cadillac?* Karen Seccombe investigates how female welfare recipients view the welfare system and deal with the associated stigma. Some of their coping strategies include distancing and denial: Women who avoid any discussion about their situations are distancing themselves from the fact that they receive assistance at all. Others who come up with plausible excuses—such as losing a job or fleeing an abusive marriage—are denying they are similar to other welfare recipients. But, when they viewed other women on welfare, they restated common stereotypes that echoed my student's anti-welfare tirade.

Poor women realize society views them negatively, so they see accepting welfare as a last resort. Seccombe specifically shows that low wages and a lack of financial support from men are the driving factors behind female poverty. The reason why many of these individuals are poor is because they cannot earn enough to make ends meet or because they're not receiving court-ordered child support from their ex-husbands.

WRAP YOUR MIND AROUND THE THEORY

The average salary for a physician is over $202 000.[39] On the other hand, the average salary for someone earning a minimum wage of $10 per hour would be approximately $18 000 a year. What factors might have influenced such different outcomes for these two people?

FUNCTIONALISM

Functionalists suggest that social class is connected to a person's ability to negotiate the social world. Therefore, intelligence, drive, and personal choice influence a person's social class. All people are different, so it makes sense that differences in social class exist in Canada. Some people simply have more skills and abilities than others, and these skills naturally help them reap economic rewards. Have you ever heard the phrase "The cream rises to the top"? In many ways, this statement explains why stratification continues to occur.

SYMBOLIC INTERACTIONISM

Social class and our understanding of it are relative to our personal belief system. In *The Subjective Meanings of Social Class Among Canadians,* Grabb and Lambert used a different strategy to study social class in Canada. Rather than using the traditional sociological approach in which the researcher classifies individuals based on objective social conditions, they asked ordinary Canadians to give their own subjective definitions of class. Because people in the lower class have fewer financial resources, they are probably more concerned with "bread and butter" issues. More prosperous individuals might try to legitimize their prosperity by pointing to cultural and psychological explanations for their success. Because of these different perspectives, lower-class respondents were more likely to identify class as being based exclusively on economic criteria, while the upper-class respondents were more likely to include non-economic considerations.[40]

CONFLICT THEORY

Conflict theorists believe that social mobility rarely occurs in a dramatic way, largely because the Canadian system doesn't allow it. Generally, one's parents and the opportunities they can provide determine social class. Parents in positions of wealth wish to make sure their children keep that advantage, so they pass wealth to their children in the form of an inheritance, they make sure their children attend the "best schools," and they use their social prestige to help their children succeed. Children who lack such things generally remain poor.

WHAT FACTORS INFLUENCE SOCIAL CLASS IN CANADA?

FEMINIST THEORY

Feminization of poverty is the term used to describe the fact that women are far more likely than men to experience poverty. The poorest families in Canada are those headed by a single mother. Elderly women living alone are also more likely to be living in poverty. It is not that women are less capable than men. There are more women living in poverty because the social structure is designed so that it is more difficult for a woman to earn the same income as a man. Since most lone-parent households are headed by women, a significant number of Canadian children also live in poverty.

What future might lie in store for the children of these unwed young mothers?

Affluent parents often give their children opportunities, such as music lessons and access to organized sports, which can influence their social class later in life.

discover sociology in action: WHAT SOCIAL POLICIES HAVE BEEN CREATED TO EASE POVERTY?

Social Policy: Welfare for the Poor

You saw in Chapter 3 that compassion and generosity are defining values of the Canadian culture. You might expect that in a country with such values everyone would be taken care of, and no one would really be poor. The truth is that some people in Canada do suffer from poverty. If you were to make a plan so that no Canadian would suffer from poverty, what would you recommend?

This was the challenge given to the Standing Senate Committee on Social Affairs, Science and Technology. In late 2009, the committee published a report called *In From the Margins: A Call to Action on Poverty, Housing and Homelessness.* The report examined how governments,

businesses, and volunteer organizations could help poor Canadians escape poverty. In talking with various people across the country, the committee members made a startling and devastating discovery: The existing policies and programs too often trap people in a cycle of poverty. People become reliant on income security programs and even homeless shelters, making it difficult for them to escape poverty. Even when the programs are working, the resulting benefits they receive still keep people in poverty, rather than lifting them into a life of full participation in the economic and social components of their communities.

On the bright side, many of the federal programs have been effective. The Working Income Tax Benefit supplements the revenue of low-income workers. The National Child Benefit is designed to help families with children, and Old Age Security/Guaranteed Income Supplement provides assistance to seniors.

The committee identified certain groups in Canadian society who are particularly disadvantaged. These are unattached individuals, people with disabilities, aboriginals, newcomers to Canada (including immigrants and

IN FROM THE MARGINS: A CALL TO ACTION ON POVERTY, HOUSING AND HOMELESSNESS

The Standing Senate Committee on Social Affairs, Science and Technology

Report of the Subcommittee on Cities

The Honourable Art Eggleton P.C., Chair
The Honourable Hugh Segal, Deputy Chair

December 2009

<<< The report *In From the Margins: A Call to Action on Poverty, Housing and Homelessness* examined how **governments, businesses, and volunteer organizations could help poor Canadians escape poverty.**

Source: Reprinted with permission by the Senate of Canada.

refugee claimants), and lone parents. In later chapters, you will see how race, ethnicity, and gender are all significant factors in social stratification. The committee found that race and gender seriously complicated the challenge for people already in these disadvantaged groups.

The final report made 74 recommendations on how to deal with poverty in Canada. Here are a few highlights from the recommendations[41]:

- Adopt a goal that all programs dealing with poverty and homelessness are to lift Canadians out of poverty rather than to make living within poverty more manageable (Recommendation 1).
- Implement a federal minimum wage of $10 per hour, indexed to the Consumer Price Index (Recommendation 6).
- Analyze gender-based differences in designing policies (Recommendation 32).
- Increase the Guaranteed Income Supplement to seniors (Recommendation 33).
- Increase the National Child Benefit to $5000 by 2012 (Recommendation 34).

of teens aged 15 to 19 worked for minimum wage. People who did not complete high school were five times more likely than those with some postsecondary training to earn minimum wage or less. Nine percent of workers who received a minimum wage belonged to a union or were covered by a collective agreement. I saw this firsthand when I used to work in the food-service business. Although the cafeteria was unionized, many of the workers earned only minimum wage.

The first minimum-wage law was passed in 1918 in British Columbia and Manitoba, followed two years later by Ontario, Quebec, Nova Scotia, and Saskatchewan. Minimum wage is intended to reduce poverty by ensuring that full-time workers can live off the income they receive. But just about everyone agrees that a minimum wage is not a living wage. Even two minimum wages in a household will not protect it from the short-term and long-term consequences of poverty.[42]

Maybe reading about wealth and poverty has made you think about how you might use these ideas in your everyday life. One major way in which you can take action is working at a community homeless shelter. Students who lend a hand at shelters and soup kitchens get firsthand knowledge about the complexities of poverty in Canada.

Social Policy: Minimum Wage

When you were in high school, your first job might have consisted of flipping burgers at McDonald's or stocking the cereal aisle at a grocery store. Whatever the case, this job probably earned you the minimum wage.

Many of us have probably held a minimum-wage job at some point in our lives, but who really are the minimum-wage workers? The demographics that make up this particular workforce might surprise you. In 2008, over 750 000 Canadians worked at or below minimum wage, representing 5.2 percent of Canadian workers. Women accounted for 60 percent of workers who earned minimum wage. Only about 35 percent

While you might categorize a minimum-wage job as something limited to teenagers venturing into the workforce for the first time, in fact a large percentage of minimum-wage workers (29 percent) are over 25 years old.[43]

From Classroom to Community } Helping Homeless Children

Armin decided to seek some extra credit by volunteering to help at a shelter for homeless women and children.

"These kids are rarely anywhere for very long, and so the people at the shelter try really hard to make them comfortable while they're there," he said.

"I can remember meeting this seven-year-old girl whose only real toy was a stuffed rabbit. She told me that she'd kept it with her no

matter where she went. Her mom would get jobs for a short time, and then they'd move somewhere else in search of work.

"When I met the girl's mother, she was really nice, but I could tell that she didn't have much education. She was working as a cleaning person in a hotel, but the hours were long and the work was hard. She told me that the pay barely covered the costs of her uniforms and transportation to work, so she and her daughter would be staying at the shelter for as long as they could.

"Coming from a middle-class background, I

never thought about all the things I had growing up and how lucky I was to have a house with a backyard and toys. We weren't rich, but compared to this girl, I had everything. Until I volunteered at the school, I guess I really didn't understand poverty."

07

WHAT IS SOCIAL STRATIFICATION? 124

the ranking of people and the rewards they receive based on objective criteria, often including wealth, power, and/or prestige

WHAT ARE THE THEORIES BEHIND SOCIAL STRATIFICATION? 132

functionalism: stratification is the result of some kind of functional balance, is inevitable, and aids in the smooth functioning of society

conflict theory: social inequality is rooted in a system that is more likely to reward you based on where you start than on your abilities

symbolic interactionism: a person's particular social class affects how he or she discusses class in general

feminist theory: because of patriarchy women are more likely than men to suffer from poverty

WHAT SOCIAL POLICIES HAVE BEEN CREATED TO EASE POVERTY? 135

Working Income Tax Benefit, Old Age Security/Guaranteed Income Supplement, National Child Benefit, minimum wage

get the topic: WHAT IS SOCIAL STRATIFICATION?

Theory

FUNCTIONALISM 132

- social class is connected to a person's ability to negotiate the social world
- intelligence, drive, and personal choice influence a person's social class
- all people are different, so it makes sense that differences in social class exist

CONFLICT THEORY 133

- social mobility rarely occurs in a dramatic way
- generally, one's parents and the opportunities they can provide determine social class
- the higher our socioeconomic status, the less we believe social class matters

SYMBOLIC INTERACTIONISM 133

- social class and our understanding of it are relative to our personal belief system
- because people in the lower class have fewer financial resources, they are probably more concerned with "bread and butter" issues
- more prosperous people might try to legitimize their prosperity by pointing to individual explanations for their success

FEMINIST THEORY 133

- poverty is more frequent among women than among men
- the social structure, which is patriarchal, makes it more difficult for women to earn as much as men

Key Terms

social stratification is the ranking of people and the rewards they receive based on objective criteria often including wealth, power, and/or prestige. *124*

income is the money received for work or through investments. *124*

wealth is all of your material possessions, including income. *124*

quintile is one of five groups of households, ranked by income. *125*

transitional poverty is a temporary state of poverty that occurs when someone loses a job for a short time. *126*

marginal poverty is a state of poverty that occurs when a person lacks stable employment. *126*

residual poverty is chronic and multigenerational poverty. *126*

absolute poverty is poverty so severe that one lacks resources to survive. *126*

relative poverty is a state of poverty that occurs when we compare ourselves to those around us. *126*

power is the ability to carry out your will and impose it on others. *127*

delegated means given or assigned. *127*

power elite is a small group of people who hold immense power. *127*

prestige is the level of esteem associated with one's status and social standing. *127*

upper or elite class is a social class that is very small in number and holds significant wealth. *128*

upper middle class is a social class that consists of high-income members of society who are well educated but do not belong to the elite membership of the super wealthy. *128*

middle class is a social class that consists of those who have moderate incomes. *129*

working class is a social class generally made up of people with high school diplomas and lower levels of education. *129*

lower class is a social class living in poverty. *129*

urban underclass is a social class living in disadvantaged neighbourhoods that are characterized by four components: poverty, family disruption, male unemployment, and lack of individuals in high-status occupations. *130*

social mobility is the ability to change social classes. *130*

horizontal mobility refers to moving within the same status category. *130*

vertical mobility refers to moving from one social status to another. *131*

intragenerational mobility occurs when an individual changes social standing, especially in the workforce. *131*

intergenerational mobility refers to the change that family members make from one social class to the next through generations. *131*

cycle of poverty refers to the vicious circle where poor children are more likely to be poor as adults. *131*

structural mobility occurs when social changes affect large numbers of people. *131*

exchange mobility is a concept suggesting that, within a country, each social class contains a relatively fixed number of people. *132*

meritocracy argument states that those who get ahead do so based on their own merit. *132*

feminization of poverty refers to the fact that around the world women experience poverty at far higher rates than men. *133*

Sample Test Questions

These multiple-choice questions are similar to those found in the test bank that accompanies this textbook.

1. People with seasonal jobs most likely experience
   a. residual poverty.
   b. absolute poverty.
   c. marginal poverty.
   d. transitional poverty.
2. Which of the following is *not* a member of the Canadian power elite?
   a. Economic elite
   b. State elite
   c. Sports elite
   d. Media elite
3. Which of the following is true of the upper, or elite, class?
   a. Most members are newly wealthy.
   b. They have higher rates of teen pregnancy.
   c. They make up one percent of the country's population.
   d. They are generally regarded highly for their specialized skills.
4. A doctor transferring from one hospital to another is an example of
   a. intergenerational mobility.
   b. horizontal mobility.
   c. vertical mobility.
   d. exchange mobility.
5. A high school graduate who works on an assembly line in a manufacturing plant is most likely a member of which social class?
   a. Urban underclass
   b. Working class
   c. Middle class
   d. Lower class

ANSWERS: 1. c; 2. c; 3. c; 4. b; 5. b

ESSAY

1. How does prestige affect one's social standing?
2. How is the mobility of the urban underclass restricted?
3. What is the relationship between social class and education?
4. Which social policies are available to Canadians with low income?
5. How does the concept of exchange mobility conflict with the beliefs of conflict theorists?

WHERE TO START YOUR RESEARCH PAPER

For more information on current poverty in Canada, go to

www.campaign2000.ca/

www.ccsd.ca/pubs/recastin.htm

www.makepovertyhistory.ca/

For more information about hunger and poverty in the world, go to www.undp.org/poverty/, www.poverty.com/

For more information on working in homeless shelters, including a complete list of shelters, go to intraspec.ca/homelessCanada.php, www.raisingtheroof.org/lrn-youth-index.cfm

For more information about minimum wage, go to Service Canada, at srv116.services.gc.ca/dimt-wid/sm-mw/menu.aspx?lang=eng

For an article about minimum wage in Canada—now and historically, go to www.cbc.ca/money/story/2009/01/23/f-money-minimum-wage.html

Remember to check www.thethinkspot.ca **for additional information, downloadable flashcards, and other helpful resources.**

GLOBAL STRATIFICATION

WHAT IS GLOBAL STRATIFICATION?
WHAT ARE THE THEORIES BEHIND GLOBAL STRATIFICATION?
WHAT IS BEING DONE TO ASSIST UNDERDEVELOPED COUNTRIES?

"In July 2005,

I was travelling in Kenya, visiting an association of women living with AIDS in a slum suburb of the city of Nairobi. The slum was teeming with orphans, being cared for by the women left alive. In every such instance, there's always some kind of 'performance' for the visitors, as though the encounter would be incomplete or marred without it. We gathered outside one of the crumbling homes, where six children, ranging in age from five to twelve, wearing ragged green school uniforms, chanted the largely tuneless, funereal dirge of their own composition: 'Here we are, the orphans, carrying our parents in their coffins to their graves.' The song ended with the words 'Help, Help, Help.' And then there came forward a girl of ten, a translator at her side, to describe the last remnants of her mother's life. It was awful. The mother had clearly died only a few days before, and as the young girl described the journeys in and out of hospital, and her mother's final hours, she wept so uncontrollably, her words strangled in loss, the tears gushing—not falling, or streaming, or pouring, but gushing—down her cheeks and onto her sweater and then to the ground. . . .

"I have to say that the ongoing plight of Africa forces me to perpetual rage. It's all so unnecessary, so crazy that hundreds of millions of people should be thus abandoned. . . . It's important to remember that Africa was left in dreadful shape by the departing colonial powers, and was subsequently whip-sawed between ideological factions in the Cold War. But rather more decisive, it was also delivered to the depredations of the so-called IFIs—the collection of International Financial Institutions dominated by the World Bank and the International Monetary Fund (colloquially known as 'the Bank' and 'the Fund'), and including the African Development Bank and other regional development banks. The result of the IFIs' destructive power over Africa was to compromise the social sectors, particularly the health and education sectors of the continent to this day."[1]

Wealth and Poverty *in the* World

CHAPTER 08

In *Race Against Time,* Stephen Lewis gives a stark description of the terrible situation confronting the majority of people living on the African continent.

Stephen Lewis saw the poverty in Africa firsthand as Canada's Ambassador to the United Nations

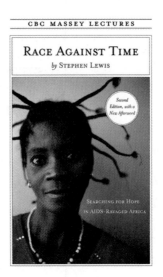

CBC MASSEY LECTURES

RACE AGAINST TIME
by STEPHEN LEWIS

Second Edition, with a New Afterword

SEARCHING FOR HOPE IN AIDS-RAVAGED AFRICA

between 1984 and 1988, and later, as the United Nations Secretary-General's special envoy for HIV/AIDS in Africa. He also saw the United Nations from an insider's perspective, and sadly realized that the very organization that professed to be helping the people in Africa was, in many ways, responsible for their dire situation.

get the topic: WHAT IS GLOBAL STRATIFICATION?

GLOBAL STRATIFICATION is the categorization of countries based on objective criteria, such as wealth, power, and prestige, which highlights social patterns and inequality throughout the world.

Global Stratification

Nearly three billion people, or half of the world's population, live on less than two dollars a day.[2] The loaf of bread on my kitchen counter costs double that. Although poverty exists in Canada and countries all around the world, the widest gap in social inequality is not within nations, but between them. Thus, when you look at the standard of living in a wealthy country, such as Canada, and compare it to a poorer nation, such as Chad, you see great disparity in the way people live. **Global stratification** categorizes countries based on objective criteria, such as wealth, power, and prestige, which highlights social patterns and inequality throughout the world.

POPULATION AND GEOGRAPHIC AREA

When comparing nations and regions, size matters. In particular, factors such as population and geographic size can determine a country's use of and access to natural resources and talented people. However, large population and large land area do not always go hand in hand. Consider the staggering population differences between Canada and Bangladesh. Among all the countries in the world, Canada is second only to Russia in geographic area, but ranks 36th in population size. Bangladesh, on the other hand, is the 7th largest country in terms of population and ranks 94th in geographic area.[3] Why the disparity? Population is not always distributed evenly. For example, Canada is dotted with lakes and mountains, and includes vast northern tracts of land where few people live. In Bangladesh, the measure of population density provides insight into life there. The cities are overcrowded and the latest population density figures show 1142 people per square kilometre, compared with 3.4 people in the same area of Canada.[4]

INCOME

To determine a country's per-capita income, you must divide the country's total gross income by the number of people in that country and assume it is equally distributed—which, of course, it is not. However, the per-capita income can provide interesting comparisons. Look at the top and bottom income-producing countries in the graphic on the next page. Most of the top ten income-producing countries are located in Europe, while most of the bottom income-producing countries are located in Africa.

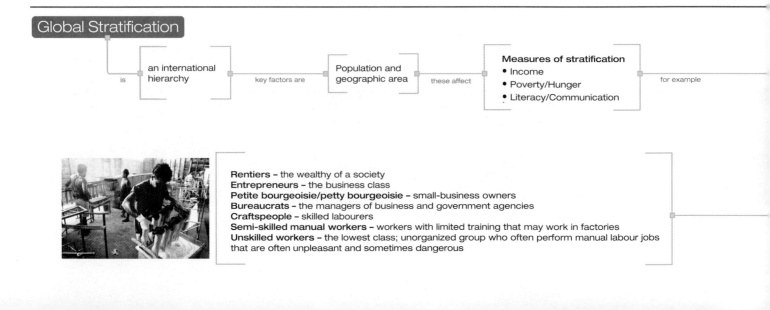

Global Stratification

is an international hierarchy   key factors are   Population and geographic area   these affect   Measures of stratification
• Income
• Poverty/Hunger
• Literacy/Communication   for example

Rentiers – the wealthy of a society
Entrepreneurs – the business class
Petite bourgeoisie/petty bourgeoisie – small-business owners
Bureaucrats – the managers of business and government agencies
Craftspeople – skilled labourers
Semi-skilled manual workers – workers with limited training that may work in factories
Unskilled workers – the lowest class; unorganized group who often perform manual labour jobs that are often unpleasant and sometimes dangerous

The average annual income of Norway is 576 times that of Burundi.

This clearly illustrates one component of global stratification: **the gulf between the richest countries and the poorest countries is extremely wide.**

Gross National Income Per Capita in 2009
(*in countries with data available*)

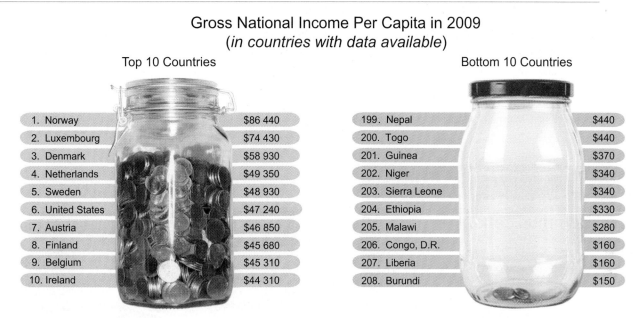

Top 10 Countries		Bottom 10 Countries	
1. Norway	$86 440	199. Nepal	$440
2. Luxembourg	$74 430	200. Togo	$440
3. Denmark	$58 930	201. Guinea	$370
4. Netherlands	$49 350	202. Niger	$340
5. Sweden	$48 930	203. Sierra Leone	$340
6. United States	$47 240	204. Ethiopia	$330
7. Austria	$46 850	205. Malawi	$280
8. Finland	$45 680	206. Congo, D.R.	$160
9. Belgium	$45 310	207. Liberia	$160
10. Ireland	$44 310	208. Burundi	$150

Source: World Development Indicators Database, World Bank, revised July 9, 2010.

Generally speaking, the wealthiest citizens in Canada enjoy a greater share of the total income of the country than do their affluent counterparts in other rich nations.

MEASURES OF STRATIFICATION IN UNDERDEVELOPED NATIONS

Underdeveloped nations are countries that are relatively poor and may or may not be in the process of becoming industrialized. The United Nations aids the least developed countries on the basis of three criteria: a country must have a low gross national income; its population must meet health and education criteria; and factors like population size and remoteness determine need.

Developing countries are those in the process of becoming industrialized. However, issues like poverty and hunger still affect these countries as they grow.

Poverty and Hunger

According to international stratification measures, sub-Saharan Africa is the most disadvantaged region of the world. This region has the highest rates of childhood death, hunger, and people living on less than one dollar a day. Sub-Saharan Africa also has the lowest rates of sanitation, which leads to higher rates of illness and death.[5]

Disadvantaged regions illustrate disparity between wealthy countries and poor ones. In 2008, a striking 99 percent of all maternal deaths occurred in developing regions—57 percent in sub-Saharan Africa, and

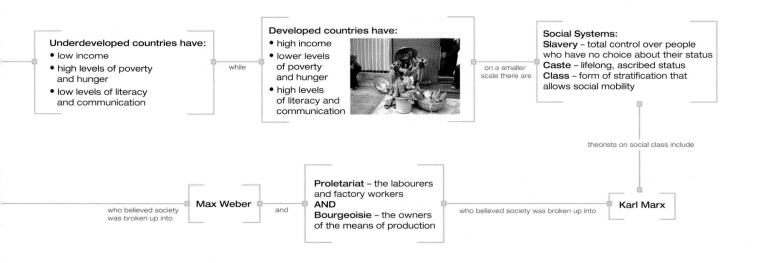

Underdeveloped countries have:
- low income
- high levels of poverty and hunger
- low levels of literacy and communication

while

Developed countries have:
- high income
- lower levels of poverty and hunger
- high levels of literacy and communication

on a smaller scale there are

Social Systems:
Slavery – total control over people who have no choice about their status
Caste – lifelong, ascribed status
Class – form of stratification that allows social mobility

theorists on social class include

who believed society was broken up into

Max Weber

and

Proletariat – the labourers and factory workers
AND
Bourgeoisie – the owners of the means of production

who believed society was broken up into

Karl Marx

30 percent in South Asia.[6] Examples of the lifetime risk of maternal death in different regions include:

- Sub-Saharan Africa: 1 in 31
- South Asia: 1 in 110
- Wealthy countries: 1 in 3900.[7]

Poverty means different things to different people. The dictionary defines it as lacking the necessities of life.[8] Sociologists, though, talk about (a) absolute poverty, where people don't have the basic needs for food, shelter, clean water, and clothing, and (b) relative poverty, or living below working-class standards.[9] Absolute poverty is deadly serious. In the words of one charity foundation: "Extreme poverty is not an inconvenience. It is a death sentence. Millions of people die from malnutrition and disease."[10]

MEASURES OF STRATIFICATION IN DEVELOPED NATIONS

Developed countries, like Canada, have a well-educated population, regular elections, diverse and abundant industry, and free enterprise. Germany, Japan, and Britain are all developed nations and share many of the same characteristics, both socially and politically, with Canada.

Poverty

When studying global stratification, it's important to consider international comparisons of poverty among developed countries. Before you look at the numbers, you'll need to understand that U.S. dollars are the standard measure of income and that poverty definitions vary depending on the country. As a result, our data use half of the median income of the country as the definition for poverty, which allows for a more standardized

MAKE CONNECTIONS

Access to Communication and Literacy

Think about different media and electronic communication devices you use every day, such as email, texting, and cell phones. You may be surprised to learn that much of the world doesn't have the same access to these communication devices as you do. These figures show selected countries' access to cell phones and the internet, as well as their literacy rates.

People living in underdeveloped countries without the ability to read or write are often forced to take unskilled, labour-intensive jobs and work long hours to help support their families. As a college student in Canada, you probably can't imagine living under these conditions. But for many around the world, other options aren't available.

>>> ACTIVITY Spend a day without using any type of communication device. This means no cell phones, computers, books, magazines, televisions, radios, journals, and so on. After spending a day without using a communication device, think about your experience. What did you spend your day doing? How did you feel? Bored? Appreciative? Peaceful? How do you think your life would be different without these items?

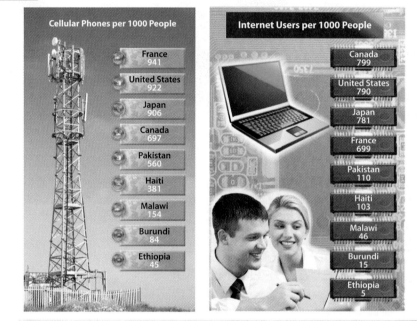

Cellular Phones per 1000 People

France	941
United States	922
Japan	906
Canada	697
Pakistan	560
Haiti	381
Malawi	154
Burundi	84
Ethiopia	45

Internet Users per 1000 People

Canada	799
United States	790
Japan	781
France	699
Pakistan	110
Haiti	103
Malawi	46
Burundi	15
Ethiopia	5

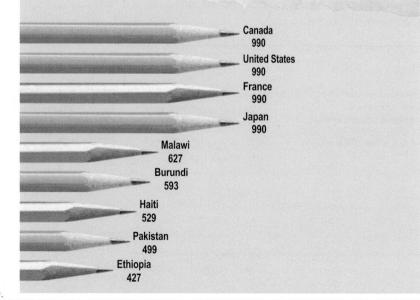

Residents Over 15 Who Can Read and Write per 1000 People

Canada	990
United States	990
France	990
Japan	990
Malawi	627
Burundi	593
Haiti	529
Pakistan	499
Ethiopia	427

Source: Data from The World Factbook 2008 and 2010.

comparison among nations. The table below shows how the poverty rates of ten developed countries stack up against one another.

Clearly, there are relatively high percentages of poverty in North America as a whole, even though Canada ranks 5.6 percentage points lower than its list-topping neighbour, the United States. The U.S. showing reflects the fact that the United States has the greatest gap between the rich and the poor of all high-income countries. What does that mean? Of the top 21 nations in the world by income, the distance between the top 10 percent of incomes and the bottom 10 percent is greatest in the United States.[11] Note that the poverty figures are consistently lower in Continental Europe than in Canada. The area where Canada stands out most positively is the percentage of the country's elderly living in poverty—5.9 percent. But when it comes to child poverty, the percentage in Canada drops nearly 8 percent when taxes and welfare transfers are taken into account; still, the end result, 14.9 percent of children in poverty, is far above the lowest on the list shown here—Danish taxes and welfare transfers reduce child poverty by more than 9 percent, to 2.4 percent.

Poverty Rates of 10 Developed Countries

Country	Percentage of Total Population in Poverty (Rank)	Percentage of Children in Poverty	Percentage of Children in Poverty After Taxes and Welfare Transfers	Percentage of Elderly in Poverty
United States	17.0 (1)	26.6	21.9	24.7
Ireland	16.5 (2)	24.9	15.7	35.8
United Kingdom	12.4 (3)	25.4	15.4	20.5
Canada	11.4 (4)	22.8	14.9	5.9
Denmark	9.2 (5)	11.8	2.4	6.6
Germany	8.3 (6)	18.2	10.2	10.1
France	8.0 (7)	27.7	7.5	9.8
Belgium	8.0 (8)	16.7	7.7	16.4
Austria	7.7 (9)	17.7	10.2	13.7
Switzerland	7.6 (10)	7.8	6.8	18.4

Source: Reprinted from The State of Working America, 2004/2005, by Lawrence Mishel, Jared Bernstein and Sylvia Allegretto. Copyright © 2005 by Cornell University. Used by permission of the publishers, Cornell University Press.

QUALITY OF LIFE

Which world city offers the best quality of life? A 2010 study shows that Vienna, Austria, is the best city to live in, and ranks five Canadian cities among the top 30: Vancouver (4th), Ottawa (14th), Toronto (16th), Montreal (21st), and Calgary (28th).[12] The Swiss cities of Zurich and Geneva are 2nd and 3rd, respectively, and the highest-ranking U.S. cities are Honolulu (30th) and San Francisco (32nd).

An associated eco-city ranking places Calgary 1st in the world and Ottawa 3rd, with Montreal and Vancouver tied for 13th spot, and Toronto in 39th position. This index is based on ecological factors such as water availability, water potability, waste removal, sewage, air pollution, and traffic congestion.[13]

So, how might one measure the quality of life in one country or another? Many use measures of health and longevity to determine a location's quality of life. Common sense follows that the quality of life must be highest in the countries in which fewer babies die and people live longer. The small Asian nation of Macau boasts the highest life expectancy (84.36 years), while Angola has the lowest (38.20 years) in a recent estimate of 2010 figures.[14] We discussed earlier in this chapter that sub-Saharan Africa has the highest rate of childhood deaths. These numbers, though, tell only part of the story about a country's quality of life.

Sociologists and economists look for variables to make international comparisons.[15] Kai Müller created a list ranking world economic and social development using a variety of measures.[16] Although income is important, it is only one of many factors to be considered. Other measures include access to telephones, televisions, and newspapers. Structural measures such as the country's debt ratio and the gross national product are also included. Finally, infant mortality, life expectancy, and literacy round out a series of items. By this method, Müller proposes that Norway is the best country in the world to live and the Congo is the worst.

Outside of Japan (2nd), New Zealand (20th), Australia (17th), and Canada (11th), all of the top 20 countries in Müller's list are located in western Europe. Furthermore, the bottom-ranked 20 countries are all in Africa. Clearly, quality of life is not equal throughout the world. Students are often surprised to see that the United States is not in the top 20. Of course, methods of weighing the factors can significantly change the ranking. For example, using older data but similar variables, Daniel J. Slottje found that Canada ranked 6th and Switzerland placed 1st.[17]

Li Lian Ong and Jason D. Mitchell provide a slightly different list.[18] By ranking 21 different countries on four criteria—economic, social, cultural, and political—they provide another view of how to compare countries. These rankings showed that some countries might rank very high in one area, but lower in others. For example, Canada ranks 8th in social and cultural components, but 19th in economic aspects and 14th overall. Ong and Mitchell combined all the tested areas to compile their quality-of-life list.

Efforts to compare and contrast different countries and measure quality of life often involve subjectivity. If you were to develop a schema, what variables would you use? Although the amount of air pollution is easy to measure, any assertion that one country has more beauty than another is very much open to debate.

Social Systems

All societies have systems by which they stratify, or rank, their members and by which those people receive the rewards of that society. Sociologists often characterize populations using wealth, power, and prestige as the basis of stratification systems. The three most common **social stratification systems** are slavery, caste, and class systems.

SLAVERY

Slavery refers to the total control over people who have no choice about their status. You may believe that slavery is a thing of the past; however, estimates suggest that there are currently as many as 27 million slaves

worldwide.[19] That number equals more than 80 percent of the total population of Canada.[20] This staggering figure is probably difficult to believe, but the important thing to remember is that today's slavery hardly resembles the slavery of the past.

In *Disposable People,* Kevin Bales discusses "old" slavery and "new" slavery.[21] **Under old systems, slavery was legal and slaves were never paid. Today, slavery is illegal,** but today's slaves may be bound by debts, rarely earning enough to repay them.

Slaves were once expensive; in 1850, a field slave sold for approximately $1000 to $1800, or about $50 000 to $100 000 today. Because of their expense, slave owners viewed slaves as long-term investments. The high price and required care of slaves meant annual profits might have been only five percent of the initial investment. Today, slaves are much cheaper and virtually disposable. Once "used up" they are sent away, which increases profits. Bales estimates annual profits from modern slaves are about 50 percent of the initial investment. Owners of modern slaves are in a win-win situation; they have a continuous supply of labour and stand to make a huge profit.

Bales suggests that several new factors drive slavery today. Apart from rapid population growth and extreme poverty, weak governments, worldwide desire for cheap labour, and capital investment can support slavery. Weak governments may tolerate bribery or cannot control the behaviour of local warlords and wealthy landowners. With rapid population growth, potential slaves abound. Many countries use their abundant labour supply to attract foreign investment, which can easily lead to the potential consequence of slavery.

Forms of Slavery

Modern slavery takes three forms: chattel, debt bondage, and contract slavery. **Chattel slavery** is the closest to the old form of slavery because

v v v **Contrary to popular belief, slavery is not a thing of the past. Modern-day slaves exist in countries all around the world.** How do you think the slaves in these pictures differ?

Source: (left image) *Returning from the Cotton Fields in South Carolina,* ca. 1860, stereograph by Barbard, negative number 47843. © Collection of The New-York Historical Society.

a slave is considered property. A chattel slave may work a lifetime for one family. Future generations will also become servants of the "owner."

Debt bondage occurs when a debtor is housed and fed by his or her lender. Debtors' wages are never enough to cover their expenses or debt. This form of slavery usually begins when someone borrows money in order to repay a different debt. The borrower then promises to work for the lender. Of course, the pay for the work is never high enough to decrease the debt while covering expenses for food and shelter. Thus, the person remains enslaved by his or her debt.

Contract slavery occurs when a person signs a work contract, receiving food and shelter through an employer. This is different from debt bondage because it is conducted under the façade of a legal contract. Workers sign contracts to work, often in another country, and the employer transports them to a job site. The employer also feeds and houses them. Employers deduct these costs, which often exceed the pay, and use fear and intimidation to keep workers from running away.[22]

CASTE SYSTEMS

Caste systems are similar to slave systems in that people have an ascribed status. However, unlike most slave systems, people are born into a caste system and the status is lifelong. Within **caste systems**, a person's position may be a position of power and privilege or of disadvantage, but in either case his or her place is permanently fixed. Caste systems do not allow people to move up and down the ranks, as the Canadian class system does. A person who is born to the lower class in a caste system will never have an opportunity to move vertically and join a higher class.

Perhaps the most widely known caste system is in India. Although now illegal, the caste system remains a powerful force in India today, especially in rural areas where the system decides whom you marry, what job you have, and where you live.[23] The Go Global box on page 148 provides a brief overview of the Indian caste system.

CLASS SYSTEMS

Unlike caste systems, class systems represent a form of stratification that allows social mobility. In fact, North Americans like to think of themselves as having a classless society. In 2000, for example, 20 percent of

> **DEBT BONDAGE** is a form of slavery in which someone borrows money in order to repay a different debt, and works off the new debt.
>
> **CONTRACT SLAVERY** is a form of slavery in which a person signs a work contract, receiving food and shelter from an employer, but is threatened when he or she tries to leave the contract.
>
> **CASTE SYSTEMS** are systems in which a person's position may be a position of power and privilege or of disadvantage, but in either case his or her place is permanently fixed.

Americans thought they would make it into the top one percent of income earners during their lifetime. Another 19 percent thought they were already there, which means that a whopping 39 percent of people thought they could become rich or were already rich.[24] Sociologically speaking, there is no "official" agreement on the number and kind of social classes within Canada. However, as we discussed in Chapter 7, it's unlikely for a person from the lower class to climb very high on the social class ladder. If a person does manage to climb vertically, he or she goes up only a few rungs.

Karl Marx on Class Systems

Recall from Chapter 1 that Karl Marx suggested that the class structure of western Europe consisted of two groups: the proletariat and the bourgeoisie.[25] The *proletariat* were the poor factory workers, while the *bourgeoisie* were the owners of the factories. They hired the workers and paid them as little as possible to help increase their own personal wealth.

> Marx pointed out that **workers willingly participate in their own exploitation because they have a false consciousness,** or a false sense of their place in society.

Marx suggested that the owners foster this ideology in order to maintain their powerful position in society. Let's say you have a lower-rung job at a major corporation and receive a bonus each year because of what your manager calls "profit sharing"; you would be operating under false

THINK SOCIOLOGICALLY

Slaves in Canada

Your first instinct may be to associate slavery in Canada with another century. After all, slavery was abolished throughout the British Empire in the 1830s.[26] But even as this textbook was being put together, modern-day slavery was in the news in Canada: in October 2010 police arrested and charged a man with running several brothels in Metro Vancouver, where police said women had been forced to work as sex slaves after being lured from Hong Kong.[27]

Slavery first raised its head in Canada hundreds of years ago. Its presence has taken different forms. For example:

- A number of aboriginal tribes practised slavery long before Canada came into existence as a country.

- Portuguese explorer Gaspar Corte-Real may have been the first European to practise slavery in this part of the world. He is known to have enslaved 50 aboriginal men and women in Newfoundland in 1500.[28]

- Oliver Le Jeune was the first black slave officially recorded in Canada, in 1628. After being captured in Africa at age six,

he was brought to Canada by an Englishman and then sold to a Canadian resident in 1629. A total of 1132 slaves of African descent were taken to the part of Canada known at the time as New France.[29]

If there is a bright spark in a discussion of slavery in Canada, it has to be the existence of the so-called Underground Railroad, which helped escaping American slaves find freedom in Canada from about 1835 until 1865, when slavery was abolished in the United States. As many as 40 000 "freedom seekers" made it to Canada.[30]

The Indian Caste System

India is often referred to as a land of castes. India's caste system has five different levels: *Brahmin, Kshatriya, Vaishya, Shudra,* and the *Harijans (Dalit).* Citizens are born, live, work, marry, and die within their caste. There is no room for movement up (or down) in the hierarchy of the system, and social order dictates that castes remain separate.

In India, *Brahmins* make up the priestly and scholar caste. *Kshatriyas* represent the warrior caste. These were the political leaders who protected the people and fought wars. Merchants, artists, and traders come from the *Vaishya* caste. Mohandas Gandhi,

∧
∧ *Dalit* protestors call for equal opportunities and
∧ treatment. **Although there are laws to protect**
Dalits' rights, much of Indian society still treats
them poorly.

the "father" of the Indian nation, was part of this caste. The *Shudra* caste represents the country's workers, such as labourers from the fields and cities. The lowest caste is "the untouchables." Gandhi referred to them as the *Harijans,* or the people of God. Today,

they are known as the *Dalit.* They were seen as unsanitary people who performed the lowest form of labour in the society. In such a system, *Harijans* were socially unacceptable. They lived outside the mainstream, remaining separate from the rest of society.[31]

consciousness if you thought you were going to get rich as long as the corporation continued to make millions of dollars in profits each year. Only through class consciousness, or an understanding of one's position in the social system, will workers unite and eventually benefit from their labour. The bourgeoisie promote false consciousness to further exploit workers for their own benefits. The only way to break through this façade is for the exploited to unite and take power from the dominant class.[32]

According to Marx, class consciousness begins the revolution, whereby the proletariat usher in a perfect society and everyone shares resources equally.[33]

Max Weber's Class System

Max Weber expanded Marx's idea that property is the sole determinant of social class. Weber's class system included class, status, and party. When Weber discusses class, he refers to wealth, much as did Marx. However, a person's position in society is not determined by only one factor for Weber. Status or prestige includes people with fame or important positions.[34] Status matters in society. Party refers to the political dimension of power. Power elevates a person's importance, which in turn causes his or her rank to rise.

Weber's class system is more detailed than that of Marx. For Weber, **rentiers** are the wealthy of a society. They come from a privileged class who own businesses and land; they are the people with "old money." **Entrepreneurs** are the business class. They, too, may have a great deal of money, but they must work to maintain their place. They are "new money." These two groups make up social classes similar to what Marx called the bourgeoisie.

The **petite bourgeoisie** own small businesses. The people who own your local convenience store might be considered members of this group. Although they own a business and have power similar to the entrepreneurs, they do not have the same wealth, prestige, or power.

Bureaucrats make up a separate class. They are the managers of business and government agencies. They own nothing, but they have great power in the corporate structure. Corporations hire accountants and middle managers to oversee their business, often with high salaries. Weber felt this class would grow along with society's tendency to become more bureaucratic.

Next, Weber turns to labourers, which he divides into three groups. Craftsmen, or **craftspeople**, are skilled labourers, such as plumbers or carpenters. They hold a special position in society because they have a needed skill that is unusual. **Semi-skilled manual workers** have some training and may work in factories. I was a semi-skilled worker when I was a bicycle mechanic. Without at least a little training, I would not have been able to perform well at my job. **Unskilled workers** make up the lowest class. They are an unorganized group who frequently perform manual labour jobs that are often unpleasant and sometimes dangerous. When I fried chicken at a fast-food restaurant, I was doing unskilled labour. The work was hot, dirty, and dangerous because the hot grease often burned me. However, it didn't take any specialized skills for me to fry chicken. Unskilled labour pays the least and frequently places the heaviest physical demands on the worker.

RENTIERS are the wealthy members of a society, as identified by Weber.

ENTREPRENEURS are the business class, as identified by Weber.

PETITE BOURGEOISIE are small-business owners in Weber's class system.

BUREAUCRATS are managers of business and government agencies.

CRAFTSPEOPLE are the skilled labourers such as plumbers or carpenters.

SEMI-SKILLED MANUAL WORKERS are the workers who have some training and may work in factories.

UNSKILLED WORKERS are the lowest class, consisting of people who frequently perform manual labour jobs that are often unpleasant and sometimes dangerous.

∧∧∧ **Weber divides the labourer group into three classes: craftspeople, semi-skilled manual workers, and unskilled workers.** Craftspeople, like the plumber shown here, have unique skills that make them valuable members of society.

For Weber, people have differing levels of wealth, power, and prestige. Those with the most of all three components make up the upper class, or the rentiers. While Weber links social class to job type, class is also related to these other factors. Marx, on the other hand, primarily links social class to business ownership. **You are either a worker or an owner. Only through class consciousness will the poor rise up and create an egalitarian society.**[35]

Now you have a solid framework for discussing global stratification and its effect on citizens around the world. Why do you think global stratification occurs?

think sociologically: WHAT ARE THE THEORIES BEHIND GLOBAL STRATIFICATION?

Global Stratification—No Longer a Third World

When I was in college, I was told the world was divided into three parts: the first, second, and third world. The first was the United States and its allies—including Canada; the second consisted of the Soviet Union and its allies; and the third world was made up of everyone else. Of course, this system bases its divisions on political and economic ideologies. Sociologists rarely use this system today. First, it's ethnocentric, inferring that the West should be first. Second, the "second world" no longer exists; the Soviet bloc has largely dissolved. Finally, lumping more than 60 percent of the world into one category hardly provides an accurate description of the included countries.

IMMANUEL WALLERSTEIN'S WORLD SYSTEMS THEORY

Immanuel Wallerstein's world systems theory presents an alternative view to the old system.[36] Wallerstein suggests that the world is divided by its connection to economic power. At the centre of the system are core nations who are constantly trying to expand their capitalist markets, decrease costs, and increase profits. The economies of these nations influence the actions of others.

All core nations eventually run out of natural resources and they constantly seek expansion, so they find ways to enter *periphery* countries. Historically, core nations made colonies of periphery nations in order to expand their influence. For example, Britain used its Indian colony to expand its market and gain access to resources. Indians had to buy salt from British companies because it was illegal to make and use sea salt. Today, core nations do not have colonies. Instead, they use multinational corporations, trade treaties, and other techniques in order to access the periphery's resources and send the wealth home. Periphery nations hope to generate wealth through the sale of their human and natural resources. Countries like Nigeria and Iraq are periphery nations because of rich natural resources such as natural gas and petroleum.[37]

If a periphery nation can use some of its wealth to build its own economy, a small group of elites will arise who build industries of their own. In that way, the country becomes *semi-periphery*. Semi-periphery nations are developing nations who use their raw materials to manufacture goods that can be sold to the core nations while keeping more wealth in the country. Investments in future services and industries mean that the country has the chance to move closer to the core. Countries like Brazil and South Korea are semi-periphery nations.

External nations are underdeveloped nations that have little interaction with the rest of the system. They have few national resources and little ability to attract investment or interest from core nations. Burundi, Chad, and many of the nations of sub-Saharan Africa fit this category. From the perspective of the world system, they exercise little or no impact on other countries.

World Systems Theory

Semi-Periphery   Core   External

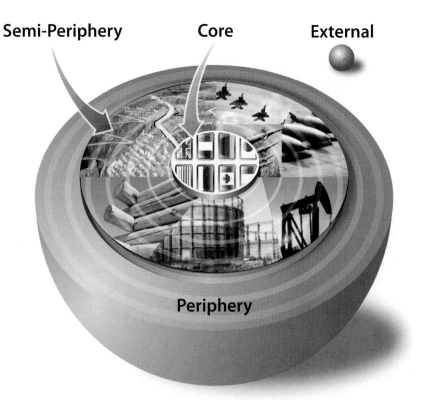

Periphery

<<< Wallerstein's theory suggests that **core nations are at the centre of the "universe," and affect all surrounding nations.** External nations, however, are unaffected because they are seen as having little to offer to the rest of the system.

Source: Adapted from Immanuel Wallerstein's *The Modern World-System,* 1974.

NEOCOLONIALISM

Most of North and South America was once under the colonial rule of various European powers. Over time, however, it became difficult to stop rebellions, so many countries gave up their colonies.[38]

Michael Harrington says countries now use **neocolonialism**, a process in which powerful nations use loans and economic power to maintain control over poor nations.[39] Through loans for food, weapons, and development, poor nations become dependent upon rich ones. Once in debt, poor countries often cannot repay the loans and so agree to alliances, sale of natural resources, and trade agreements that primarily benefit the wealthy nation.[40]

Extending the ideas of neocolonialism, some propose that wealthy nations now use multinational corporations to control poorer nations.[41] Multinational corporations offer jobs, income, and potential riches to poor nations. The corporations benefit because they may gain tax-free status, weak environmental oversight, or some other concession that may not be in the best interest of the country. These corporations may create working conditions that lead to the enslavement of the native people. Bales points out that although company executives might not want to be involved in slave labour, they probably want to maximize their profits.

Through multinational corporations, wealthy countries continue to control weaker ones with corporate investment. This may, in effect, lead countries to engage in a "race to the bottom." To win the prize of foreign investment, they cut local regulations and salaries. This "race" can lead to wage and gender discrimination and less worker safety.[42] Of course, there

NEOCOLONIALISM is a process in which powerful nations use loans and economic power to maintain control over poor nations.

GLOBALIZATION is a complex process by which the world and its international economy are becoming more and more intertwined.

BRAIN DRAIN occurs when the best talent leaves poor countries and thereby provides an even greater advantage to wealthy countries.

is another side of this: they provide jobs and incomes to workers with few other opportunities.

GLOBALIZATION

Globalization involves a complex process by which the world and its international economy are becoming more and more intertwined. Globalization connects the world through business, travel, immigration, education, health issues, and production of goods.[43] Bales argues that every consumer in the world is linked to modern-day slavery in one way or another. Workers in China put together shoes made from leather tanned in Brazil, with rubber soles from Indonesia. Frequently, rich countries recruit the best and brightest from poor countries to become doctors, scientists, and other vital occupations. This is **brain drain**—the best talent leaves poor countries and thereby provides an even greater advantage to wealthy countries.[44]

Some argue that an aspect of globalization is exploitation. Others suggest that it is the only hope for poor nations. As the world becomes more interconnected, are the various cultures around the world becoming more similar or less so? Those who believe cultures are becoming more similar suggest that the world's cultures are adopting more Western values. On the other hand, some suggest that globalization will have the opposite effect on culture as local groups work hard to maintain their own religions, customs, and languages.[45]

Multinational corporations often set up factories in countries where they can **pay lower wages to the workers in order to make a heftier profit.** The Chinese women in this image are workers in the Reebok shoe factory.

Functionalism

In 1997, Jared Diamond published *Guns, Germs, and Steel,* a book explaining how the Western world advanced so quickly while other regions of the world were left behind. Diamond points out that there was a time in history when all people on the earth were poor and lived in underdeveloped conditions. So why did some regions advance while others did not?[46]

Simply put, the fastest developing regions of the world had the climate, geography, and available natural resources that allowed them to advance. Other areas did not possess such advantages. The dawn of agrarian civilization occurred in the Fertile Crescent, an area that is present-day Iraq. The land in this region is fertile and easy to traverse. Most mountain ranges are passable, allowing for travel and trade amongst peoples. Goods and knowledge were shared throughout the region. With knowledge, civilizations became more organized, complex, and powerful because they used information to improve the quality of life. This led to greater power and wealth, which allowed for more trade.[47]

Tribal groups in Europe competed for many centuries, which built up the region's military know-how. Internal struggles led to alliances between groups, increasing trade and the transmission of information.[48]

Tribes in Europe and Asia were able to domesticate a number of animals and plants. Herders raised sheep and goats while farmers grew grains. Domesticated animals and plants allowed groups to amass more wealth and knowledge, which left people available to specialize as teachers, craftspeople, artists, and warriors.[49]

Unlike Europe and Asia, native animals that live in sub-Saharan Africa defy domestication. Although native plants can be eaten, the Africans did not have the long grains that grew in the Fertile Crescent. Additionally, because the diverse African landscape ranges from desert to mountainous, regions could not share the same technologies used to grow food.[50]

Jacques Diouf explains that countries cannot develop as their people starve and live in poverty.

These countries must produce high food quantities to sustain the increasing demands of development. **Only when a country resolves its hunger issues can it begin to prosper from the benefits of global markets.**[51]

An abundance of food allowed Europeans to thrive. They created cities where they faced another hardship, which actually helped them more than hurt them. Open sewers spread disease and created high death rates for city dwellers. Consequently, their descendents developed a strong immune system and were genetically hardier than their ancestors.[52]

Those areas with great natural resources were able to acquire the power needed to function as the wealthy power brokers in the world. Remember that functionalism studies how social structures affect society. Diamond believes that Europeans and Asians advanced because they had abundant resources, strong military skills, set trade routes, and strengthened immune systems. Geographic areas with fewer advantages developed at a much slower place.[53]

Some theorists say that globalization polarizes the world and creates gaps between groups. They predict more war, terrorism, and unrest as Western countries continue to expand. Do you share this view on globalization?

Conflict Theory

Vilfredo Pareto provides a theory of how elite members of society reach positions of power and strive to maintain it.[54] Society seeks equilibrium, and changes in one part of society cause changes in another. This creates a circulation of the elite as the old elite members are replaced by the new.

Gaetano Mosca suggests that elites seek greater power for themselves and are unlikely to give it up.[55] Leaders use position to garnish benefits for themselves and their supporters. Consider Latin America. Fernando Cardosa and Enzo Faletto acknowledge that Latin American nations follow this pattern of leadership circulation.[56] They also discuss dependency on foreign investment and exploitation by more powerful countries. Aristocrats seek short-term rewards over long-term benefits to all. These landowners control natural resources, and they influence the government to gain more wealth. This is called the dependency theory.

It's interesting that Cardosa, one of the founding thinkers of dependency theory, led his country toward free market capitalism when he was elected president of Brazil in 1995. Cardosa, originally a financial minister, said he was an "accidental president," becoming president because he was working to quell Brazilian economic woes.[57] **His two presidential terms stabilized and expanded the country's economy by increasing social programs to help the poor while opening the Brazilian economy to become a free market.**[58]

Nations are dependent because they have no other choice but to borrow from wealthy places, but this often leaves them with nothing. However, the next elected president was a man who ran against Cardosa in the previous presidential elections. President Lula stood in opposition to many of Cardosa's reforms, illustrating Pareto's circulation of elites.

Pareto suggests two primary elites: lions and foxes. Lions are leaders who are patriotic, unified, and support the status quo. People choose lion leaders because they use force to create order in times of chaos. An example of this was the military dictatorship that overran Brazil prior to Cardosa's election. Cardosa was a new type of leader. Pareto refers to this type as a fox. Foxes are clever and rational with new ideas that try to change the status quo. Societies ebb and flow between leadership run by foxes or lions, balancing the desire for change with the need for stability.

Symbolic Interactionism

After the Second World War, European nations sought ways to prevent future wars and work together. Representatives created treaties that led to what is now called the European Union. This union grew from simple trade agreements among 6 countries to a group of more than 20 nations.[59]

Taken as a whole, the countries that make up the European Union have a weak central government to handle trade disputes, a common currency (the euro), and an increasingly common language (English). Although the EU does not have military forces, there are NATO (North Atlantic Treaty Organization) troops, which often come from a variety of European Union countries, as well as the United States and Canada.

As a single nation, the European Union would be the richest country in the world. Business flourishes in the European Union, and many of the world's largest banks and corporations are centred there. The European Union also produces more scientific discoveries than any other country. Its inhabitants enjoy the highest standards of living, and Europeans work fewer hours, receiving more paid vacation time than North American workers.[60] The European Union shows how unity and cooperation can drastically benefit a region and its people. In fact, T.R. Reid suggests that many European Union residents see themselves as "Europeans," not members of a single nation. Reid suggests this collaboration could lead to a United States of Europe, becoming the world's greatest superpower.[61]

Feminist Theory

Around the world, it is women and girls who suffer disproportionately from poverty, hunger, abuse, and lack of basic human rights. Around the world, half a million women die every year from complications related to pregnancy and birth. The majority of these women live in poor countries. In some countries in sub-Saharan Africa, one woman in 50 dies during childbirth. Compare this to Scandinavia, where the rate is one per 20 000.

In countries around the world, women are increasingly the sole heads of households. Unfortunately, these families, especially those with younger children, are overrepresented among the poor, despite the fact that women on average work more than men. Persistent sexual discrimination in terms of work and wages leads to a vicious cycle of poverty and, as a result, children get less food and maternal care.

Breaking the vicious cycle of poverty will require significant social changes and targeted social policies. One requirement is to expand the access of poor women to family planning and reproductive health services. Another important strategy involves expanding access to education for girls. Women who are educated tend to have fewer and healthier children, and their children are more likely to attend school. Yet in all regions of the world except North America and western Europe, women's literacy rates are less than men's. Two-thirds of illiterate people around the world are women. Because education improves health, autonomy, and income, strategies aimed at improving access to education for girls would yield future benefits for these women and for their children. As former World Bank vice president Mieko Nishimizu has said, "If you educate a boy you educate a human being. If you educate a girl, you educate generations."[62]

Working Hours Around the World

	Annual hours	Average per week
Mexico	1857	43.6*
United States	1768	NA
Australia	1690	36.0
Japan	1714	NA
Canada	1699	36.5**
United Kingdom	1646	36.6
Italy	1773	38.0
Sweden	1610	36.3
Germany	1390	35.7
France	1554	38.0
Norway	1407	33.9

Note: * 2004 data, ** 2006 data, NA = not available

<<< On average, Europeans work fewer hours and have more paid vacation time than Canadians. Why do you think Canadian workers spend more hours at the office?

Source: Based on data from Hourly Earnings under Earnings under Labour from OECD.Stat Extracts. Accesed at http://stats.oecd.org/Index.aspx?DatasetCode=EAR_MEI.

WRAP YOUR MIND AROUND THE THEORY

Mountains and the Sahara Desert take up almost the entire north African region. **Life exists where there are reliable water sources and vegetation.** Lush fields and plentiful resources allowed European societies to advance at a much faster rate than did those in north Africa.

FUNCTIONALISM

From a functionalist point of view, global stratification is a result of geographic conditions. Diamond states that the European societies thrived because they had natural resources that helped those societies function more efficiently. Domesticated plants and animals, trade with others, warfare, and disease all played a role in increasing the advantages for western Europe. These were the result of how societies used their resources to function more efficiently.

CONFLICT THEORY

Conflict theorists believe that an imbalance of power between the elites and the poor in a country causes stratification. Pareto argues that even among elites, power changes occur. He also believes that in times of struggle, lions will rule the day, but eventually foxes will take charge. Mosca states that leaders will do what they can to remain in power because it's in their best interests to do so. How do these power struggles between the elites affect those who are not in power?

WHAT CAUSES GLOBAL STRATIFICATION BETWEEN COUNTRIES AROUND THE WORLD?

SYMBOLIC INTERACTIONISM

Symbolic interactionists look at how language and symbolic events influence society. When the European Union was created, an entirely new notion entered the lives of Europeans. T.R. Reid suggests that Europeans increasingly identify themselves as members of Europe, not the specific country in which they were born. What impact might this have on the long-term influence of that region of the world over others?

FEMINIST THEORY

Feminist theory focuses on the poverty of women around the world. Since women are largely responsible for the care of children, their poverty results in a vicious cycle in which their children suffer from malnutrition, poor health, lack of access to education, and a grim future. Social policies that serve to reduce the poverty of women, give them better access to health care, and improve access to education for all children, especially girls, would go a long way toward reducing poverty.

Poor countries and their workers are exploited by richer, more powerful countries. These workers work long, hard hours for a fraction of what workers in a richer country would be paid.

Core nations have markets with local goods, but many of the cheaper items are made by slave labour in foreign countries. **Developed nations enjoy the best standards of living in the world, but at what cost to other nations?**

discover sociology in action: WHAT IS BEING DONE TO ASSIST UNDERDEVELOPED COUNTRIES?

Social Policy: Foreign Aid

Some students get angry about foreign aid. They oppose the idea of paying huge amounts of tax dollars to help other nations when there are people in Canada in need.

"Helping the world's poor is a strategic priority and a moral imperative. Economic development, responsible governance, and individual liberty are intimately connected."[63]

The main aim of Canadian foreign aid is to promote popular welfare and overall economic improvement of underdeveloped countries around the world.[64] The world's rich countries agreed in 1970 at the United Nations General Assembly to provide 0.7 percent of their gross national product (GNP) for international development aid each year. They have since rarely met their targets, and the European Union has set a new target date of 2015.[65]

The countries' donations depend upon a percentage of the wealth of the country. An example may help you understand the difference. If you and I both donate $10 to charity but you only have $100 in the bank and I have $1000, who has actually given more? We both gave the same amount, but you gave 10 percent of your wealth, while I gave only 1 percent.

In 2009, Canada donated 0.3 percent of its GNP, or US$4.341 billion.[66] The OECD said five countries exceeded the 0.7 percent target in 2009: Denmark, Luxembourg, the Netherlands, Norway, and Sweden.[67]

ACTIVITIES

1. Check the tags of your clothes and shoes. Where were they made? Do you have any assurances that slaves were not used to make your apparel?
2. Discuss with a partner what can be done to combat slavery. If almost everything is connected to slavery, what can be done?
3. Take an internet trip to www.antislavery.org. Surf the website. Write a paragraph explaining what you learned about modern slavery, how to stop human trafficking, and the lengths to which people are going to stop slavery.

From Classroom to Community] Becoming a CUSO-VSO Volunteer

After Marie-France graduated from college, she didn't know what to do. She knew she could get a job, but she wanted to see the world and use her college education to improve the lives of others in some way. She felt her double major of sociology and Spanish could be a great asset. After joining CUSO-VSO, she took a 27-month appointment in Ecuador.

"I never really thought I could live in another country, but I fell in love with Ecuador and the people there."

Marie-France learned just how hospitable and welcoming the Ecuadorian people could be.

"The families I encountered were so close and loving. At night, it was normal to see families crowded around a television watching soap operas with one another.

"I also learned firsthand that rules about privacy are very different in Ecuador.

"As a teenager growing up in my house, it was customary for me to hole myself up in my room surfing the Web or talking on the phone, but it's considered very rude in Ecuador! The wildlife and scenery was amazing, but my favourite experience was spending time with the kids at school." "The children were so eager to learn from me. Once they got over their initial shyness, we became good friends."

While there, Marie-France taught English in a local school and provided education to women regarding health issues. In her free time, she travelled throughout the country. Once back in Canada she found a job working with abused children.

"I love my life, but a part of me will always be in Ecuador."

get the topic: WHAT IS GLOBAL STRATIFICATION?

Theory

FUNCTIONALISM   152

- global stratification is a result of geographic conditions
- Diamond: European societies thrived because they had natural resources that helped those societies function more efficiently
- Pareto: even among elites, power changes occur; in times of struggle, lions will rule the day, but eventually foxes will take charge
- Mosca: leaders will do what they can to remain in power because it's in their best interests to do so

CONFLICT THEORY   152

- an imbalance of power between the elites and the poor in a country causes stratification

SYMBOLIC INTERACTIONISM   152

- looks at how language and symbolic events influence society
- Reid: Europeans increasingly identify themselves as members of Europe, not the specific country in which they were born

FEMINIST THEORY   153

- globally, women are more likely than men to live in poverty
- since women are also the primary caregivers to children, this results in a vicious cycle of poverty
- social policies that reduce the poverty of women would go a long way to reducing global poverty

Key Terms

global stratification is the categorization of countries based on objective criteria, such as wealth, power, and prestige, which highlights social patterns and inequality throughout the world.   142

social stratification systems are slavery, caste, and class systems.   146

slavery is the total control over people who have no choice about their status.   146

chattel slavery is a form of slavery in which a slave is considered property.   146

debt bondage is a form of slavery in which someone borrows money in order to repay a different debt, and works off the new debt.   147

contract slavery is a form of slavery in which a person signs a work contract, receiving food

and shelter from an employer, but is threatened when he or she tries to leave the contract.   147

caste systems are systems in which a person's position may be a position of power and privilege or of disadvantage, but in either case his or her place is permanently fixed.   147

rentiers are the wealthy members of a society, as identified by Weber.   149

entrepreneurs are the business class, as identified by Weber.   149

petite bourgeoisie are small-business owners in Weber's class system.   149

bureaucrats are managers of business and government agencies.   149

craftspeople are the skilled labourers such as plumbers or carpenters.   149

semi-skilled manual workers are the workers who have some training and may work in factories.   149

unskilled workers are the lowest class, consisting of people who frequently perform manual labour jobs that are often unpleasant and sometimes dangerous.   149

neocolonialism is a process in which powerful nations use loans and economic power to maintain control over poor nations.   151

globalization is a complex process by which the world and its international economy are becoming more and more intertwined.   151

brain drain occurs when the best talent leaves poor countries and thereby provides an even greater advantage to wealthy countries.   151

Sample Test Questions

These multiple-choice questions are similar to those found in the test bank that accompanies this textbook.

1. Which of the following is characterized by the worker becoming property of an owner?
   a. False consciousness
   b. Contract slavery
   c. Chattel slavery
   d. Debt bondage

2. Which citizens illustrate what Marx would call an ideology of false consciousness?
   a. Petite bourgeoisie
   b. Bourgeoisie
   c. Proletariat
   d. Rentiers

3. Which of the following is *not* one of the three labour groups described by Weber?
   a. Craftspeople
   b. Bureaucrats
   c. Unskilled workers
   d. Semi-skilled manual workers

4. Immanuel Wallerstein's theory suggests that the world is divided by its connection to
   a. military power.
   b. economic power.
   c. political stability.
   d. technological innovation.

5. Nations that have wealth, technology, and strong military power, which they use to influence the entire global system, are called
   a. core nations.
   b. external nations.
   c. periphery nations.
   d. semi-periphery nations.

ANSWERS: 1. c; 2. c; 3. b; 4. b; 5. a

ESSAY

1. What are the positive and negative effects that globalization can have on underdeveloped nations?
2. What are the differences between a caste system and a slave system?
3. According to Marx, how do the bourgeoisie successfully promote false consciousness?
4. What characteristics does Weber use to determine social class?
5. How could wealthy nations be using multinational corporations to control poorer nations?

WHERE TO START YOUR RESEARCH PAPER

To learn more about efforts to curb slavery throughout the world, go to www.antislavery.org

For more information on the Asian Development Bank, go to www.adb.org

For more information about how people are ending child prostitution, child pornography, and trafficking of children for sexual purposes, go to www.ecpat.net

To learn more about international anti-slavery movements, go to www.freetheslaves.net

www.abolishslavery.org, www.un.org/depts/dhl/slavery

For interactive maps and data to visualize world issues, go to www.gapminder.org

For more information on *Guns, Germs, and Steel* and a view of the ideas contained there, go to www.pbs.org/gunsgermssteel

To learn more about human trafficking, go to www.humantrafficking.org

To learn more about human trafficking involving Canada, go to www.justice.gc.ca/eng/fs-sv/tp/p4.html

http://dsppsd.pwgsc.gc.ca/Collection/PS64-1-2004E.pdf

www.rcmp-grc.gc.ca/ht-tp/index-eng.htm

www.canadafightshumantrafficking.com

http://4mycanada.ca/HumanTrafficking.html

To learn more about the International Monetary Fund, go to www.imf.org

For information regarding health, crime, and standards of living, go to www.nationmaster.com

To learn more about the OECD and read its reports on economic development throughout the world, go to www.oecd.org

For more information about volunteering around the world, go to www.vsocan.org

For information on population problems, refugees, and reports on world poverty, go to www.worldbank.com

For more information regarding the use of cheap and child labour in the garment industry, go to www.freethechildren.com

To learn more about international aid funded by the federal government, go to www.acdi-cida.gc.ca/index-e.htm

For information on the nongovernmental organizations (NGOs) Canada works with to give international aid, go to www.ccic.ca

To learn more about bilateral and multilateral methods and how Canada distributes aid, go to www.acdi-cida.gc.ca/acdi-cida/ACDI-CIDA.nsf/eng/JUD-112911931-LY2

For national statistics and reports from Statistics Canada, go to www.statcan.gc.ca

For more information about the United Nations, go to www.un.org/english

For more information about the World Food Program, go to www.wfp.org

For more information about the World Health Organization and its data, including issues of hunger, HIV/AIDS, and other statistics from a variety of countries throughout the world, go to www.who.int/en

To research how the World Trade Organization handles trade disagreements among countries, go to www.wto.org

To learn more about Canada's economical, financial, and trade-based relationships with the rest of the world, and how the country's foreign policy is used, visit Foreign Affairs and International Trade Canada, go to www.international.gc.ca

Remember to check www.thethinkspot.ca **for additional information, downloadable flashcards, and other helpful resources.**

RACE AND ETHNIC STRATIFICATION

WHAT IS THE DIFFERENCE BETWEEN RACE
AND ETHNICITY?
WHAT CAUSES RACIST ATTITUDES, AND HOW
DO THESE ATTITUDES AFFECT PEOPLE?
HOW DOES AFFIRMATIVE ACTION HELP
MINORITY GROUPS IN CANADA?

"The

assumption that the term 'race' refers mainly to racial minorities was revealed in one classroom discussion when students were asked to talk about themselves in racial, ethnic, and cultural terms. One white participant insisted that he was Canadian, and therefore his racial and ethnic identities were irrelevant. When asked how he would feel if a Chinese person and black person both insisted that they were Canadian and therefore refused to identify themselves by their ethnicity, the participant responded by saying that he would not be satisfied by their answers because, to him, Canadians are people who look like him: 'Chinese and blacks are immigrants—they do not look Canadian.' Another participant said to me, 'I feel when you mention race you're talking about people of different ethnicities and countries.'

"Another common tendency is to equate talking about or naming a race with a display of prejudice or racism. Hence, when asked to talk about race as it relates to their identity and behaviour, white participants tend to become defensive. They responded: 'I never see race . . . I see the person, not her race . . . I don't feel uncomfortable with black people'; or 'Every time I've talked about race, it's been about stereotyping or prejudice.' Others wrote the following:

"Greg: As for my race, I am white, but I never really had to think about it before. I don't feel that it ever affected the people with whom I associated or talked to. My two best friends are black, and (Canadian) Indian. I was brought up in a family that didn't believe in prejudice and I'm proud of that. If I don't like a person, it's because of their personality, not their race or heritage.

"Henry: Concerning my race, which is Caucasian, I really don't believe that it has contributed enormously to my identity or behaviour. I feel this way because my culture is basically all Canadian.

"Laurie: I . . . cannot see how my race influences or affects me. I have always been aware of how my ethnicity influences my ideals, morals, values, and beliefs, and these personal elements have not changed. For me to say that race affects me would either show that I feel inferior or superior to other races, and this is incorrect."[1]

159

Is It a Question *of* Colour?

In *Identity and Belonging: Rethinking Race and Ethnicity in Canadian Society,* Sean P. Hier and B. Singh Bolaria have gathered together a wonderful set of essays on the complex and fascinating issue of race and ethnicity in Canada. The excerpt above was taken from Chapter 3, "Race, Ethnicity, and Cultural Identity," by Carl E. James.

"Race" is one of those words that has many powerful meanings. We might try to act like it doesn't exist, or pretend that it doesn't really mean anything, especially in a country as tolerant as Canada. And yet, there is a lot of evidence that shows that race and ethnicity (which are not the same thing) *are* still important, even in Canada. Your race or ethnicity determines your chances of finishing high school, what kind of job you will likely get, whether or not you will go to prison, and even how long you can expect to live.

According to recent science, race is purely a social construct, not a biological one. And yet, people often seek to define race solely in biological terms. Often, this mentality is instilled at an early age because we often teach children, who don't even have a concept of race, about racial differences that do not really exist. In fact, I remember when my daughter came home from preschool and said, "Ho is different than me." Ho was a Chinese boy whose father worked with me at the university. "What makes you say that?" I asked. "The kids in the class say he's different because his skin looks different than mine," she said. "Does that make him different?" I asked. "I don't know, but I still like to play with him at recess." What is telling about this story is that it took two years of schooling and outside influence to teach a five-year-old about racial differences. This is how we learn about race: from our social experiences.

RACE

is defined as **socially-constructed divisions of people based on certain physical characteristics** differs from **Ethnicity - a shared cultural heritage**

can be broken down into groups

Majority Groups - groups that have greater representation in a society and hold significant power and privilege

OR

Minority Groups - groups that hold less power than the dominant group

OR

Dominant Groups - groups who discriminate because they have greater power

Education
- schools continue to be unofficially segregated
- poorly funded schools are in poor neighbourhoods where most minority students live

and **Income** - minorities are the most likely to live in poverty

get the topic: WHAT IS THE DIFFERENCE BETWEEN RACE AND ETHNICITY?

If you walk down any street, you'll find people with different hairstyles, fashion sense, age, body type, and, yes, skin colour. Because society feels it's necessary to separate groups of people, **race** refers to the divisions of people based on certain physical characteristics. The most prominent of these characteristics is skin colour. Examples of racial categories include white, black, and Asian. **Ethnicity** is a little more complex than race because it usually involves grouping people who share a common cultural, linguistic, or ancestral heritage. Thus, there are many more ethnic than racial categories. Examples of ethnic groups in Canada include those from Chinese, Ukranian, Italian, or Haitian backgrounds.

As the population grows and intermarriage becomes more common, traits like skin colour may no longer be such a simple signifier of identity. However, sociological questions regarding race are not fixated on the

RACE is the division of people based on certain physical characteristics.

ETHNICITY is the classification of people who share a common cultural, linguistic, or ancestral heritage.

differences in looks. Instead, these questions focus on how society interprets those differences in appearance and how those interpretations affect an individual's opportunities.

CENSUS DEFINITIONS

At the time of Confederation in 1867, Canada was already a multicultural society. The first Canadian census was conducted in 1871, and asked questions about people's age, sex, religion, and race. Since that first census, the choices for "race," "ethnicity," and "ancestry" have changed many times. In the 1891 census there was no question about race, but in the next census it reappeared, and from 1901 until 1941 Canadians were asked to identify their

<<< Although these women differ in physical appearance, they are the same biologically. **Why does society see fit to place them in separate racial categories?**

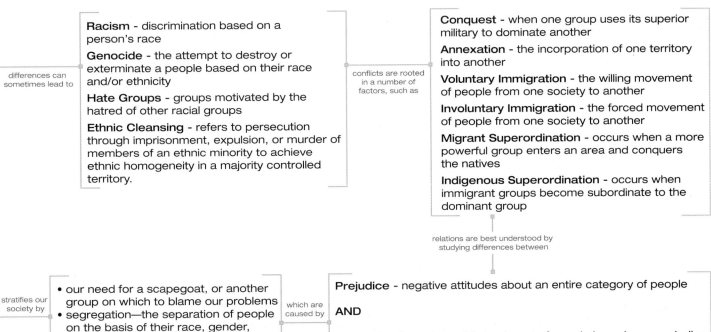

differences can sometimes lead to

Racism - discrimination based on a person's race

Genocide - the attempt to destroy or exterminate a people based on their race and/or ethnicity

Hate Groups - groups motivated by the hatred of other racial groups

Ethnic Cleansing - refers to persecution through imprisonment, expulsion, or murder of members of an ethnic minority to achieve ethnic homogeneity in a majority controlled territory.

conflicts are rooted in a number of factors, such as

Conquest - when one group uses its superior military to dominate another

Annexation - the incorporation of one territory into another

Voluntary Immigration - the willing movement of people from one society to another

Involuntary Immigration - the forced movement of people from one society to another

Migrant Superordination - occurs when a more powerful group enters an area and conquers the natives

Indigenous Superordination - occurs when immigrant groups become subordinate to the dominant group

relations are best understood by studying differences between

stratifies our society by

• our need for a scapegoat, or another group on which to blame our problems
• segregation—the separation of people on the basis of their race, gender, or ethnicity

which are caused by

Prejudice - negative attitudes about an entire category of people

AND

Discrimination - the unfair treatment of people based on a prejudice

Self-Identified Ethnic Origins of Ancestors
(2006 Canadian Census)

Ethnic Origin	Number of Respondents
British Isles	11 098 610
French	5 000 350
Aboriginal	1 678 235
Canadian	10 066 290
Caribbean	578 695
Latin/Central/South American	360 235
European	9 919 790
African	421 185
Arab	470 580
West Asian	302 555
South Asian	1 316 770
East/Southeast Asian	2 212 340
Oceania	58 500

Source: Earl Andrew, http://en.wikipedia.org/wiki/File:Censusdivisions-ethnic.png. Accessed Dec 31, 2010.
Note: Figures will add up to more than the total population (31 241 030) because respondent may identify multiple origins.

race. The race question was mysteriously dropped in 1951. By 1991, Canadians were being asked to identify their "ethnic origin," and could select from a list of 11 choices. In the 1996 census, respondents were asked to identify themselves according to population group. This data was used to derive counts of the **visible minority** population in Canada. A visible minority is someone, other than an Aboriginal person, who is non-Caucasian in race or non-white in colour. An **aboriginal** is a person who is Indian, Inuit, or Métis. For the first time, "Canadian" was included as one of the ethnic origin choices.[2]

These constant changes are good evidence that race and ethnicity are social constructs rather than biological categories. The census people at Statistics Canada are good sociologists, because on their website they state: "It must be noted that the measurement of ethnicity is affected by changes in the social environment in which the questions are asked, and changes in the respondent's understanding or views about the topic."

MINORITY AND DOMINANT GROUPS

A **minority group** refers to any group that holds less power than the majority group. Louis Wirth assigns minority group status to people who are singled out for unequal treatment. Minorities also have a collective sense of being discriminated against.[3]

In some societies, having a numeric majority isn't necessarily required to wield power or practise discrimination. Sociologists refer to those who are more powerful as the **dominant group** because even if they may not have greater numbers, they have greater power. Apartheid, the five-decades-long system of oppression in South Africa, showed how a group's numbers don't necessarily reflect a group's political and economic power. In the era of apartheid, whites, who were the numeric minority of South Africa, passed laws that forced blacks, the native majority, into segregated housing, took away their right to vote, and generally treated them like second-class citizens.[4] The idea of a minority group ruling over a majority population, especially in periphery nations, is almost always the direct result of **colonialism**, in which more powerful countries impose their will on weaker nations. More often than not, though, dominant groups tend to be a country's numeric majority as well.

In Canada, minority populations are on the rise. Between 1996 and 2001, the total population increased 4 percent while the visible minority population rose 25 percent—six times faster. Between 2001 and 2006, Canada's visible minority population increased by 27 percent—five times faster than the growth rate of the total population.[5] By 2017, around 20 percent of all Canadians will be a visible minority.[6] Migration patterns certainly influence these projections. In the future, minority group members will have greater representation in the population.

RACISM

The simplest definition of **racism** is that it refers to discrimination based on a person's race. However, there is more to racism than just discrimination. To truly understand racism, you must recognize that it involves a complex calculus of intergroup privilege, power, and oppression. According to Joseph Graves, racism has relied on three assumptions that often go unchallenged: (1) races exist; (2) each race has distinct genetic differences; and (3) racial inequality is due to those differences. Graves outlines five pillars of racist thought.

1. Biological races exist in the human species.
2. Races have genetic differences that determine their intelligence.
3. Races have genetically determined differences that produce unique diseases and cause them to die at different rates.
4. Races have genetically determined sexual appetites and reproductive capacities.
5. Races have genetically determined differences in athletic and musical ability.

An extreme example of racism is the use of **genocide**, the attempt to destroy or exterminate a people based on their race or ethnicity. The most well-known example is the Holocaust during the Seond World War. The Nazis slaughtered millions of Jews, Roma, and people with mental or physical disabilities in an attempt to cleanse Europe of people they felt were inferior. Extreme racism is not a thing of the past, either. The film *Hotel Rwanda* depicted the events of 1994, when members of two Rwandan political parties began killing opposition leaders and journalists.

VISIBLE MINORITY is a person, other than an aboriginal, who is non-Caucasian in race or non-white in colour.

ABORIGINAL is a person who is Indian, Inuit, or Métis.[7]

MINORITY GROUP is a group that has less power than the majority group.

DOMINANT GROUP is the group that has the greatest power, but not necessarily the greatest numbers.

COLONIALISM is the imposition of control over a weak nation by a more powerful country.

RACISM is discrimination based on a person's race.

GENOCIDE is the attempt to destroy or exterminate a people based on their race and/or ethnicity.

HATE GROUPS are organizations that promote hostility or violence toward others based on race and other factors.

Quickly, the violence spread to the rural areas, where members of the majority Hutu tribe slaughtered members of the Tutsi tribe. Don Cheadle received an Oscar nomination for his portrayal in the film of Paul Rusesabagina, a hotel manager who heroically saved the lives of nearly 1300 Rwandans. Demographic data show that gender made little difference in predicting who might survive—men, women, children, and the elderly were all killed.[8]

The idea of racial purity has not just been the dominion of Nazi Germany or tribal Rwanda. The history of Canada is stained by similarly horrible acts, starting with the appalling treatment of First Nations Peoples, but also including the Chinese Head Tax and Japanese internment camps during the Second World War. Most people associate slavery with the American pre–Civil War South, but slavery was also legal in Canada until it was formally abolished in 1834—just 31 years before the United States.[9]

Such behaviour has a long history and still continues today. There is an increasing use of the internet by **hate groups** in Canada and around the world. These groups are organizations that promote hostility or violence toward others based on race and other factors. They include white supremacists, neo-Nazis, and other groups that advocate hate against immigrants, gays, and other minorities. In Canada, the most active hate groups are Northern Alliance, Heritage Front, and Western Canada for Us.[10]

It's not just openly racist groups that can have significant impacts on minority groups. European settlers in Canada may not have deliberately tried to exterminate the indigenous peoples they met, but their actions often had serious consequences. The Beothuk were the original inhabitants of Newfoundland. For hundreds of years before the arrival of the Europeans, the Beothuk hunted and fished along the coast of the island. In contrast to many other First Nations Peoples, the Beothuk generally avoided any kind of interaction with the Europeans. In the late 1700s and early 1800s, there was an increase in European settlers throughout Newfoundland. The Beothuk,

<<< **Shanawdithit, the last known member of the Beothuk culture, died in St. John's, Newfoundland, in 1829.**

CONQUEST is the domination over a group of people by a superior force.

ANNEXATION is the incorporation of one territory into another.

VOLUNTARY IMMIGRATION is the willing movement of people from one society to another.

INVOLUNTARY IMMIGRATION is the forced movement of people from one society to another.

ETHNIC CLEANSING refers to persecution through imprisonment, expulsion, or murder of members of an ethnic minority by a majority to achieve ethnic homogeneity in majority-controlled territory.

MIGRANT SUPERORDINATION is the conquest of a native population by a more powerful group.

INDIGENOUS SUPERORDINATION is the subordination of an immigrant group to a dominant group.

PLURALISTIC MINORITIES are groups that enter into an area voluntarily but seek to maintain their own culture while also integrating into the dominant group.

ASSIMILATIONIST MINORITIES are groups that seek to shed their old ways and integrate themselves into mainstream society.

SECESSIONIST MINORITIES are groups that voluntarily separate themselves from the dominant group and view the dominant group with disdain, believing that it will corrupt the group's belief system.

already very few in number (perhaps just 1000 people), were displaced from their traditional hunting and fishing territories and forced into armed disputes with the settlers. By the 1820s, the Beothuk had been practically wiped out. In 1829, Shanawdithit, the last known remaining Beothuk woman, died. While the extermination of this peaceful culture was not intentional, in the territorial disputes with the Europeans, the already tiny and fragile Beothuk culture was sadly lost.[11]

PATTERNS OF INTERACTION

As we've already discussed in reference to genocide and ethnic cleansing, interracial conflict is as old as history itself. But how did all this get started? To better think like sociologists, we need to understand the origins of racial and ethnic stratification.

Conquest and Annexation

Racial and ethnic tension is rooted in a number of factors. The first is **conquest**. Throughout history, human groups have travelled and come into contact with people who have a different culture and often a different physical appearance. If one group is more powerful, it will try to dominate the other. During the sixteenth and seventeenth centuries, European powers used their superior technology and military strength to colonize Africa, Asia, and the Americas.[12]

Annexation is the incorporation of one territory into another. Under this system, members of ethnic and racial groups are forced to become members of a new society. Soon after Confederation, the newly formed country of Canada looked to add new land. In 1868, the *Rupert's Land Act* allowed Canada to annex the vast territory of the Hudson's Bay Company. The government ignored the land claims of the aboriginals and Métis who were living in the region. In 1870, Manitoba became the sixth Canadian province, followed by Saskatchewan and Alberta in 1905. Annexation often leads to tensions among groups, as those who are annexed resist the new occupiers. The Métis living in those areas organized a series of armed rebellions under Louis Riel, but were eventually defeated.[13]

Immigration

Another pattern that can create racial and ethnic tension is immigration, whether it is voluntary or involuntary. **Voluntary immigration** refers to the willing movement of people from one society to another. However, the countries receiving these people may not always welcome the new immigrants with open arms. Discrimination is more likely when the immigrants are from a different race than the dominant group. In 1871, construction of the Canadian trans-national railway began, and thousands of Chinese men came to Canada to fill the need for workers. However, when the railway was completed in 1885, the federal government tried to stop the flow of Chinese immigrants. That same year, a head tax was imposed on every Chinese immigrant. No other group of immigrants was targeted in this way. The *Chinese Exclusion Act* was passed in 1923, making it virtually impossible for anyone from China to immigrate to Canada. This law was in effect until 1947.[14]

Involuntary immigration refers to the forced movement of people from one society to another. Forcing First Nations Peoples onto reservations and

▶▶▶ GO GL🌐BAL

Ethnic Cleansing—Bosnia

Following the breakup of the former country of Yugoslavia in 1990, the Serbian majority seized control and forced large numbers of minority group members, particularly Bosnian Muslims, or Bosniaks, to leave their lands or face extermination. In 1992, the Serbian army launched an ethnic cleansing campaign against Bosniaks in eastern Bosnia. **Ethnic cleansing** refers to persecution through imprisonment, expulsion, or murder of members of an ethnic minority by a majority to achieve ethnic homogeneity in majority-controlled territory. Bosniak civilians were rounded up and detained in camps;

Bosnian civilians, men and women, were rounded up and detained in separate camps. Many were beaten or killed during capture. The surviving men were sent to concentration camps and the women were sent to detention centres known as rape camps. In July 1995, near the end of the war, the Serbs rounded up and killed an estimated 8000 Bosniaks in the region of Srebrenica. This act of genocide, known as the Srebrenica Massacre, is the largest mass murder in Europe since the Second World War.[15] The Serbian and Croatian forces carried out these tactics of torture and murder in the hope of creating ethnically pure states. During this war, armies used ethnic

differences as a justification for thousands of deaths and the forced removal of millions of people from their homes.[16]

These crimes, however, have not gone unnoticed by the rest of the world. In 1995, the International Criminal Tribunal for the former Yugoslavia in The Hague indicted former Bosnian Serb leader Radovan Karadzic. Charged with multiple counts of genocide, war crimes, and crimes against humanity, Karadzic went into hiding for more than 12 years before he was eventually captured in 2008. His trial is still ongoing. If convicted, Karadzic could face a possible life sentence for crimes committed during the Bosnian War.[17]

imprisoning thousands of Japanese Canadians in detention camps during the Second World War are both examples of involuntary immigration in Canadian history.

Superordination

Regardless of whether the migration is voluntary or involuntary, some predictable patterns of interaction can occur when people come into contact with unfamiliar groups. Often people become involved in **migrant superordination**, which occurs when a more powerful group enters an area and conquers the native population. In the sixteenth century, Spain used military strength to dominate Central and South America and to elevate their own culture above the native culture. In this case, the migrants' status was elevated, or superordinated. The opposite of this is **indigenous superordination**. When arriving immigrants enter Canada today, they are expected to learn English and subordinate their old ways to their new country. In other words, they must become subordinate to the dominant group. In the province of Quebec, French has been the only official language since 1974, when the provincial government passed Bill 22, *la Loi sur la langue officielle*. In Chapter 3, you read about Bill 101, the infamous language law, which states that immigrants must send their children to French schools. This is because the Quebec government wants new immigrants to adopt the Québécois culture.[18]

These two patterns of interaction are often justified through ethnocentric thinking. Remember, *ethnocentrism* is thinking about or defining another culture on the basis of your own. Generally, the greater the differences, the more negatively groups tend to view each other. At the same time, there is often competition between groups, which becomes more intense when resources are scarce. Consider the migrant pattern to Montreal in the first half of the twentieth century. Immigrants divided up the jobs that were available to them. Jewish immigrants took over the clothing industry, Greek immigrants established themselves in restaurants, and Italian immigrants were predominant in construction. If you were a member of one of these groups, you could find a job in those industries. But if you were a Greek immigrant who wanted to work in construction, you were unlikely to be hired. This is because ethnic groups often had differences in power. Once a group has power, it is unlikely to let it go.

Minorities

When minority groups face superordination, there are a number of ways they can choose to react. **Pluralistic minorities** are generally groups that enter into an area voluntarily. They seek to maintain their own culture, but want to integrate with the dominant group as well. Thus they hope to keep their cultural ties while participating in the political and economic system of the new society. **Assimilationist minorities**, on the other hand, seek to shed their old ways and integrate themselves into society. Groups that most closely resemble the dominant group—either racially or ethnically—are able to do this more easily.

For example, when German immigrants first came to Canada, their culture and language were generally accepted. German newspapers were printed and there was even a town named Berlin, Ontario (it was later re-named Kitchener). However, with the beginning of the First World War in 1914 came outright hostility toward almost anything German. Many German Canadians tried to camouflage their identity and to pass as Dutch, Scandinavian, or Russian. Perhaps because of this hostility, German Canadians were more likely to try to assimilate into the dominant culture. Census data confirm that even now, German Canadians are more likely than other ethnic groups to abandon their mother tongue.[19]

Sometimes, groups voluntarily decide to separate themselves from the dominant group and become **secessionist minorities**. Such a group does not seek assimilation or cultural unification. Instead, it views the dominant group with disdain, believing that it will corrupt its belief system. The Mennonites of Ontario can be considered an example of a secessionist minority. This group has carved

∧
∧
∧ **During the Second World War, nearly 22 000 Japanese Canadians were forced to relocate to internment camps.**

out a lifestyle and culture in which a form of German is commonly spoken and modern conveniences are rare. They emphasize the importance of family, religion, and a simple lifestyle. Their children are educated at Mennonite schools and a great deal of their life is exactly as it was 100 years ago. Although some Mennonite people are increasingly opening themselves up to other businesses besides farming, as well as allowing in a few modern technologies, their community remains secessionist.[20]

Ever since Confederation, there has been a secessionist element in the province of Quebec. Supporters of Quebec sovereignty point to the unique culture and the French-speaking majority in the province as rationales for Quebec having a unique relationship with the rest of Canada.

Support for the sovereignty movement has come and gone in waves. The most recent revival was in 1995, when the provincial Parti Québécois held a referendum on the question of whether Quebec should become a sovereign nation. The "No" side narrowly won, with 50.6 percent.[21]

Sometimes, minorities react to their subordination through militancy. **Militant minorities** seek to overthrow the existing system that they see as unjust. Often the militant minority is actually a numeric majority and may take the path of violence and war to fight perceived injustice, as was the case in Cuba in 1958 when Fidel Castro overthrew a government that he believed was corrupt.[22] Militants can also be peaceful, as when Mohandas Gandhi led a peaceful revolution that ended in 1947 and ultimately brought about the end of British occupation of India.[23]

Types of Minority Groups

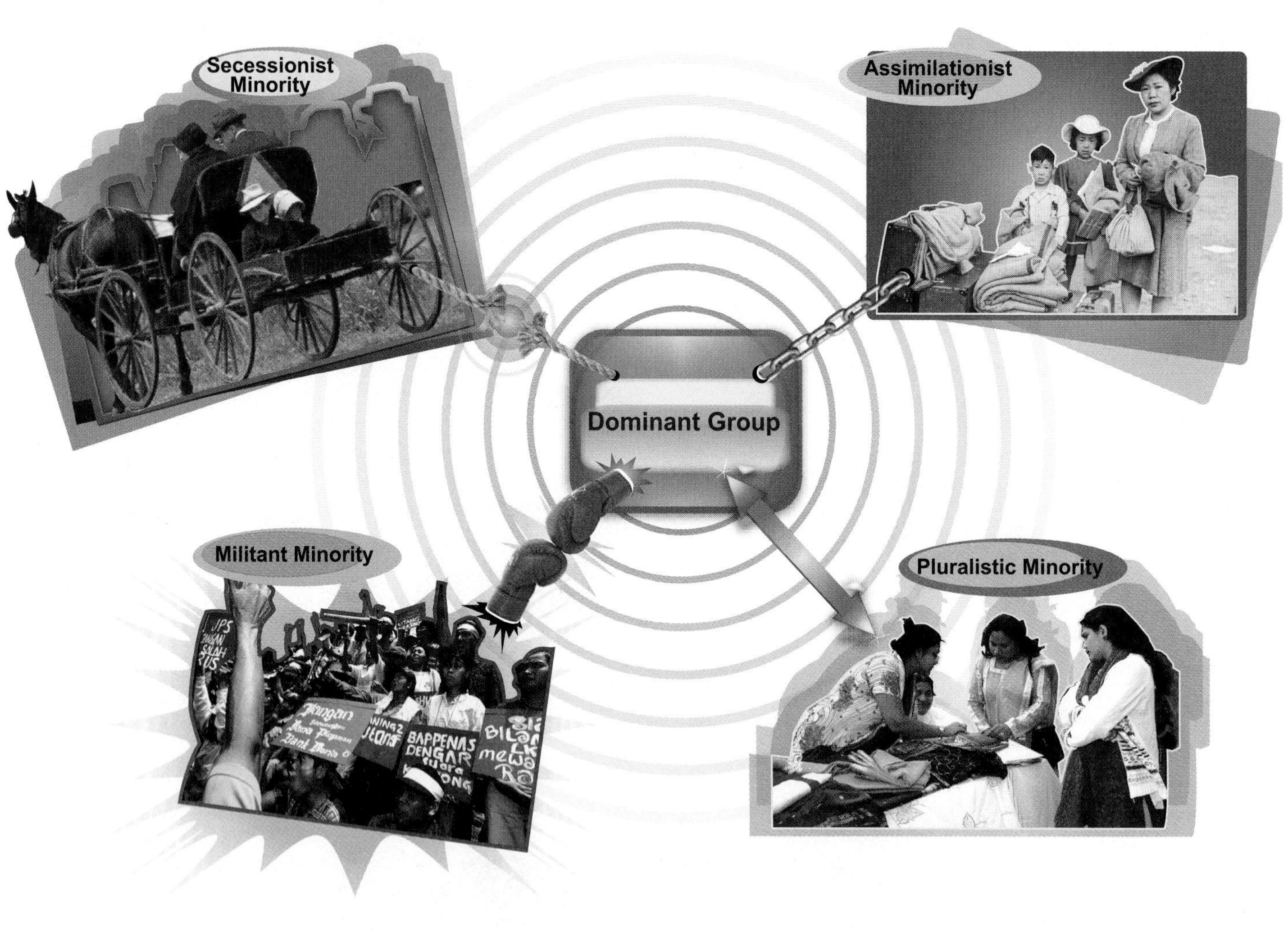

Secessionist Minority

Assimilationist Minority

Dominant Group

Militant Minority

Pluralistic Minority

Acceptance—Multiculturalism and Assimilation

Research suggests that racial and ethnic identity is related to four key factors: relative size, power, appearance, and discrimination.[24] These factors also tend to encourage a sense of solidarity among members of a single racial or ethnic group. In a sense, being different from the dominant group holds people together. The reason why many minority groups tend to cluster together in neighbourhoods is because their differences from the dominant group often lead to discrimination. Furthermore, the shared values of similar people make adjustment easier. Finally, their social capital increases their chances of success. On the other hand, belonging to a group that looks like the dominant group rarely leads to discrimination. Such people often let go of their ethnic heritage because their appearance makes it easier to assimilate into the dominant culture.

This lack of privilege to belong to the dominant group is the reason why many minority groups often bond together. This is especially true for new immigrants who are visible minorities. It is quite common for immigrants to live in neighbourhoods where people from similar cultures live together and assert cultural distinction, which are called **ethnic enclaves**, like a Chinatown or Little Italy. Such enclaves assist the new immigrant in making an easier transition into the new culture.

MILITANT MINORITIES are groups that seek to overthrow the existing system because they see it as unjust.

ETHNIC ENCLAVES are neighbourhoods where people from similar cultures live together and assert cultural distinction from the dominant group.

PREJUDICE refers to negative attitudes about an entire category of people.

STEREOTYPES are simplified perceptions people have of an entire group that are usually based on false assumptions.

DISCRIMINATION is the unfair treatment of people based on a prejudice.

PREJUDICE VS. DISCRIMINATION

To truly understand the complexity of race relations, it is vital to understand the differences between prejudice and discrimination. **Prejudice** usually refers to negative attitudes about an entire category of people. These prejudices are often reinforced by **stereotypes**: simplified perceptions people have of an entire group, usually based on a false assumption. Although negative stereotypes—such as believing all black people are prone to violence and crime, or that all Arabs are terrorists—are absolutely wrongheaded, so-called positive stereotypes can be just as damaging. While you may think you're offering a compliment when you assume your Asian Canadian classmate is a mathematical genius, the problem is that doing so confines that individual to a box that you have constructed in your mind. That is the danger of stereotypes. If we aren't careful, we might allow our prejudices to overtake our common sense.

These attitudes, if left unchecked, may lead to **discrimination**, or the unfair treatment of people based on a prejudice. Essentially, prejudice is an attitude, while discrimination is an action that stems from that attitude. The apartheid laws of South Africa were perpetuated by whites' attitudes toward black people. However, discrimination doesn't always have to be as blatant as the segregated water fountains and restaurants. A teacher with a prejudice against African Canadians may treat black students with contempt in the classroom. Similarly, a teacher who assumes the Asian Canadian student in class is a naturally studious person could overlook the fact that the student might actually need help.

Essentially, prejudice is an attitude, while discrimination is an action that stems from that attitude.

THINK SOCIOLOGICALLY

They're Coming to Canada

For centuries, immigrants have come to Canada. This trend continues to this day, constantly changing the face of the country.

Researchers are interested in what helps these immigrants not only survive but also thrive in a new country. They note that one key component of immigrant success is a successful neighbourhood, or enclave, in which they can live. Eric Fong and Milena Gulia studied different ethnic neighbourhoods in 20 Canadian cities. They found that new immigrants often form enclaves—that is, they all tend to live in the same neighbourhood. This is why there are Chinatowns, Little Italys, and Little Indias in cities across Canada. If new immigrants lack information about the new country and have low levels of language and work skills, they have a higher incentive to stay close to their countrymen for social, financial, and emotional support. Groups in which a large proportion of members are

recent immigrants also have a greater tendency to live close together. This is particularly important to groups with cultures which are significantly different from that of the dominant group, for example Southeast Asian immigrants.

British, northern Europeans, and western Europeans tend to live in relatively better neighbourhoods. These are characterized by households with a lower average number of residents per room, a higher percentage of neighbours who have completed university education, a higher median household income, a lower percentage of persons who do not speak either official language, a lower percentage of low-income families, and a lower percentage of unemployed residents.

On the other hand, southern Europeans and visible minority groups, such as South Asians, Southeast Asians, and blacks, tend to live in neighbourhoods with a poorer social environment. These neighbourhoods are characterized by higher density, lower educational attainment, a higher percentage

of low-income families, and a higher percentage of unemployed.[25]

As an immigrant group becomes established, members become more integrated into the dominant culture. They are more likely to speak English or French, and they probably earn a higher income. Once this happens, members of the group tend to move out into a better neighbourhood. In the late 1950s, a large number of Greek immigrants arrived in Montreal. Many settled in a district called "Park Extension," displacing the Jews who for years were the dominant ethnic group in that area. After about 20 years, as they became more financially successful, the Greeks started moving to the more prestigious suburbs, primarily Chomedy in Laval. As they moved out of Park Extension, new waves of immigrants from Pakistan, the West Indies, and Sri Lanka moved in.[26]

>>> **ACTIVITY** Locate the nearest ethnic enclave in your city or province. To what ethnicity does it cater?

Many of these prejudices and stereotypes are so prevalent it's difficult to trace exactly where they come from. Generally, sociologists agree that while we aren't born with prejudiced attitudes, we often learn prejudice from those around us.[27] We can even learn a prejudice against a group to which we belong. This self-loathing occurs when we internalize the values of the dominant group.[28] In my classes, I often have my students take an online test designed to measure biases. Generally, minorities hold similar beliefs to their non-minority counterparts. Recently a black student took the "Know Your Bias" test and was shocked to find that she held negative attitudes toward other blacks. This illustrates how we are all socialized to hold biases that are in accordance with the dominant society, even if we belong to a minority group.

INSTITUTIONAL DISCRIMINATION IN CANADA

While personal biases often cause individuals to view others negatively, those attitudes can carry over into the structures of society and often go unnoticed by others who don't even hold those views. When this happens, social institutions end up supporting racial and ethnic inequality. This **institutional discrimination** maintains the advantage for the dominant group, while providing the appearance of fairness to others. At various times in Canadian history, immigration policies have reflected direct institutional discrimination against certain groups such as the Chinese, blacks, and Jews. The *Canadian Charter of Rights and Freedoms* proscribes direct institutional discrimination, yet minority groups in Canada continue to suffer from indirect institutional discrimination. Indirect institutional discrimination maintains the advantage for the dominant group, while providing the appearance of fairness to all. It occurs when members of a minority group experience unequal treatment, not because of openly discriminatory policies, but because of unfair structural factors. In June 2003, Lucien Comeau filed a complaint against the City of Halifax for unequal funding which resulted in discrimination against him as a person of Acadian descent. He argued that a change to the taxation process meant that part of his property taxes went to provide additional funding for the English-language schools of the Halifax Regional School Board (HRSB), but not to the French-language schools of the Conseil Scolaire Acadien Provincial (CSAP). Mr. Comeau's children attended a CSAP school. The law has been changed so that both school boards now receive the same funding.[29]

Immigrants to Canada may experience indirect institutional discrimination. When their non-Canadian credentials are questioned and when their non-Canadian work experience is not recognized, immigrants are excluded from obtaining appropriate and rewarding jobs in Canada.

CAUSES FOR PREJUDICE AND DISCRIMINATION

So why does any kind of discrimination happen at all? John Dollard suggests that frustration leads to prejudice.[30] Often we don't have the ability to attack the real source of our irritation, and so we **scapegoat**, or unfairly accuse, another group as the cause of our problem. Usually a racial or ethnic minority becomes the target for a common societal problem like

∧
∧ **Lucien Comeau was upset that** the taxes he paid
∧ did not fund the French-language school where his
children attended.

widespread poverty. If you are poor, you may not be able to increase your salary, but you can blame others for your problems. This happened in 1982 in the United States when two white unemployed autoworkers, Ronald Ebens and Michael Nitz, beat Vincent Chin, a young Chinese American man, to death. What started as a barroom brawl—Ebens and Nitz reportedly used a racial slur to refer to Chin, after which a fistfight broke out—ended in murder. The two men blamed Japanese auto companies—and, by extension, all Japanese people—for the economic downturn and violently attacked Chin simply because they thought he was Japanese. To make matters worse, neither man ever spent a day in jail for Chin's murder. After they pled guilty to manslaughter, the judge sentenced Ebens and Nitz to three years' probation and fines totalling less than $4000. The judge later defended the light sentence by claiming, "These weren't the kind of men you send to jail. We're talking here about a man [Ebens] who's held down a responsible job with the same company for 17 or 18 years and his son [Nitz] who is employed and is a part-time student. . . . You don't make the punishment fit the crime; you make the punishment fit the criminal." In a civil trial later that year, Ebens was convicted of violating Chin's civil rights and sentenced to 25 years in jail. However, Ebens appealed the decision on the basis of a technicality and was later acquitted in a retrial, which was held in a different state.[31]

How could two men get away with committing such a hateful and racist act? Researchers often suggest the importance of education and intelligence in predicting a discriminatory type of personality. Generally, studies support the notion that people who are less educated and of lower intelligence are more likely to be prejudiced. This lends support to the idea that prejudice is learned, and can be unlearned.[32] Furthermore, structural issues such as the mix of racial and ethnic groups, as well as income inequality and differences in economic opportunities, may assist in the perpetuation of extreme forms of racism. White supremacist groups often cite these issues as evidence of minority group dominance and use these issues as a rallying cry for a white backlash against these groups.[33]

SEGREGATION

People who are discriminated against are often separated from the dominant group in terms of housing, workplace, and social settings. This enforced separation is called **segregation** when factors such as race, gender, or ethnicity are involved. Blacks and whites had separate schools, neighbourhoods, restaurants, and public restrooms in the southern United States in the 1960s and earlier. Although these and other forms of segregation are no longer legal, issues such as unofficial segregation continue to this day.

In a study of Canadian housing segregation, Harald Bauder and Bob Sharpe found that racial or ethnic segregation is linked to a number of factors. There may be "good segregation" and "bad segregation." Sometimes, minorities prefer to live in areas that are populated by their own groups. This is "good segregation," and is deliberately chosen because it is a protective measure that benefits the minority population. On the other hand, "bad segregation" is the result of racism and discrimination, and it does not benefit the minority group. A third explanation is that residential segregation is simply a reflection of socioeconomic status. Because some new immigrants are more likely to have lower incomes, they are also more likely to live in poor neighbourhoods.[34]

Racial Stratification in Canada

Now that you have a context in which to look at race and ethnicity, let's turn our attention to how these characteristics stratify our society. Although we live in a free society that claims to be equal, there are still

INSTITUTIONAL DISCRIMINATION maintains the advantage for the dominant group, while providing the appearance of fairness to all.

SCAPEGOAT means making an unfair accusation against a person or group as the cause of a problem.

SEGREGATION is forced separation because of factors such as race, gender, or ethnicity.

CYCLE OF POVERTY is a generational barrier that prevents poor people from breaking into the middle and upper classes.

injustices that occur because of race and ethnicity. How does the well-being of different racial and ethnic groups compare? Take a look at the chart below to find out. You've seen the numbers, so now let's take a closer look at racial and ethnic stratification.

INCOME

In Canada, minorities tend to be overrepresented in poverty statistics, particularly aboriginals and visible minorities. This is caused in part by the **cycle of poverty**, which makes it difficult for people to break into the middle class if their parents were poor. In 2006, the unemployment rate for aboriginals was 14.8 percent, over twice the Canadian rate of 6.6 percent. Not surprisingly, the median income for aboriginals ($18 962) was much lower than the Canadian median income ($25 615).[35] A study by Feng Hou and Simon Coulombe found that in the public sector whites and visible minorities received similar pay for similar jobs, but in the private sector visible minorities earned significantly less than whites doing comparable jobs.[36] Overall, Canadian-born visible minorities are not more likely than others born in Canada to experience low income. However, visible minority immigrants are more likely than other

Inequality in Canada

	Population Size (15 years and older)	Income	Labour Force
Visible Minorities	5 069 095	Median $22 395 Mean $30 385	Unemployment rate – 8.6%
Aboriginals	1 172 785	Median $18 962 Mean $25 961	Unemployment rate – 14.8%
Canada	31 241 030	Median $25 615 Mean $35 498	Unemployment rate – 6.6%

Source: Adapted from Statistics Canada, 2006 Census of Population, Statistics Canada catalogue no. 97-562-XCB2006017. Accessed at http://www12.statcan.gc.ca/census-recensement/2006/dp-pd/tbt/Rp-eng.cfm? LANG=E&APATH=3&DETAIL=0&DIM=0&FL=A&FREE=0&GC=0&GID=0&GK=0&GRP=1&PID=94183&PRID= 0&PTYPE=88971,97154&S=0&SHOWALL=0&SUB=0&Temporal=2006&THEME=80&VID=0&VNAMEE=&VNAMEF=; Adapted from Statistics Canada. 2007. Canada (Code01) (table). Aboriginal Population Profile. 2006 Census. Statistics Canada Catalogue no. 92-594-XWE. Ottawa. Released January 15, 2008. http://www12.statcan.ca/ census-recensement/2006/dp-pd/prof/92-594/index.cfm?Lang=E (accessed February 17, 2011).

immigrants to be poor. This may be because they have lower levels of education, or because they do not speak either English or French. It also suggests that there is persistent exclusion and discrimination in the labour market.

EDUCATION

One of the most important factors in determining income is education. Without formal education, it's difficult to get a well-paying job and advance in the workplace. There is a strong correlation between level of education and income, with people who have advanced degrees earning the most money. But who exactly is earning these advanced degrees? The graphs below show the educational attainment of visible minorities and aboriginals in Canada. Visible minorities are more likely than the average Canadian to have a university degree. Unfortunately, the picture is not so good for aboriginals. They are more than twice as likely to not finish high school, and only 6 percent complete a university degree.

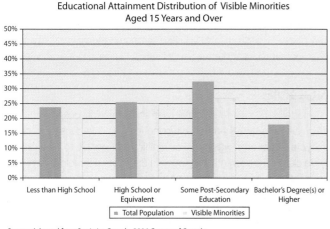

Source: Adapted from Statistics Canada, 2006 Census of Canada

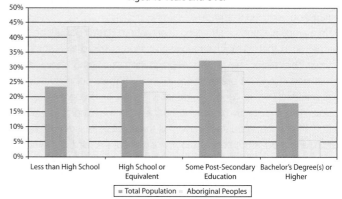

Source: Adapted from Statistics Canada, 2006 Census of Canada

MAKE CONNECTIONS

Justice Denied—The Donald Marshall Story

In the Canadian justice system, the accused is always presumed innocent until proven guilty. At least this is the principle. But in 1971, Donald Marshall wrongly received a life sentence for the murder of Sandy Seale in Sydney, Nova Scotia. He was just 17 years old when he was convicted. He was also a Mi'kmaq.

Marshall served 11 years in prison before a re-examination of the evidence led to the arrest and conviction of Roy Ebsary. Marshall was acquitted in May 1983, but his case had received much attention, and his name had become synonymous with the term *wrongful conviction*. There were powerful suggestions that prejudice may have been a factor.

In 1989, a royal commission completed its two-year investigation into the Marshall case. The commission concluded that "the criminal justice system failed Donald Marshall at virtually every turn," and that racism was a factor in the wrongful conviction. In compensation, Donald

Marshall was awarded a lifetime pension, which he received until he died in 2009.

While the Canadian justice system let Donald Marshall down, it did learn something from its mistakes. The royal commission that investigated his case recommended changes to the *Evidence Act*, such that the Crown Attorney is now obliged to present all evidence at a trial—rather than choosing to present only evidence that supports the Crown's case, as was done at Donald Marshall's trial. Sometimes it takes a dramatic travesty before changes are made to unfair practices.[37]

think sociologically: WHAT CAUSES RACIST ATTITUDES, AND HOW DO THESE ATTITUDES AFFECT PEOPLE?

Symbolic Interactionism: Colour-Blind Racism

Symbolic interactionists stress the importance of symbolism and language in the creation of society. In Canada, overtly racist language is socially unacceptable in most circles; however, sociologists don't believe that this means we have become a "colour-blind" society. In fact, **colour-blind racism**—the idea that racism still exists in more subtle ways—remains a part of Canadian society to this day. For example, there is no doubt that aboriginals in Canada remain in disadvantaged positions—they are poorer, achieve lower educational outcomes, live shorter lives, attend underfunded schools, experience problems with assimilation, and generally believe that the police and other social institutions work to increase their disadvantage.[38] Despite these facts, though, most whites in Canada claim these outcomes have nothing to do with racism. How can that be? Furthermore, most whites claim they are not racist.

Eduardo Bonilla-Silva suggests that this is because whites have developed a series of excuses for the status quo through four key factors: First, whites tend to hold on to ideals such as equality, individualism, and choice in an effort to explain why racial groups are disadvantaged.[39] In other words, people are only poor because they made bad choices, not because of some historical or cultural context that supports racism. Second, white people often use cultural stereotypes to explain racial inequality. Rather than understand the source of the problem, too many people simply latch on to stereotypes to explain the issue. The third factor is the false belief that segregation is a personal choice. The suggestion is that it's natural for racial groups to prefer "their own kind." Often, this attitude prevents white people from understanding the complex role institutionalized racism has on "segregated" communities. Fourth, and finally, many whites in Canada simply believe that racism is a thing of the past and deny that it has any impact on minorities' lives today.[40] Such thinking serves to defend the way things are, and excuses the dominant group from any responsibility to make things better.

Although racism is not as overt as it once was, that doesn't mean the problem has been eradicated. Racial prejudice still exists; it's just hidden behind a series of clever language constructions. For example, white college students rarely use racist terms such as "the n-word," but they might tell racist jokes. They usually first explain that the joke doesn't really reflect their beliefs, and conclude the joke with an apologetic comment— all to eliminate the perception of racism.[41]

Whites may try to prove they're not racist by claiming some of their "best friends are not white." This is supposed to

give the speaker an air of credibility for not being racist. Unfortunately, such disclaimers are usually followed by a negative stereotype. They might try to excuse a long history of structural racism or try to take all sides when it comes to matters of race. Whites may also excuse the long history of racism and a lack of equal opportunities by denying any personal responsibility for it. Comments like "I didn't steal land from the Indians; it's not my fault" lead the conversation away from structural problems that continue to exist regarding race, while excusing the speaker from any possible advantage based on his or her race.

W.E.B. Du Bois suggested that African Americans have a sort of **double consciousness**, meaning black people have to keep a foot in two worlds, one white and one black.[42] Minority group members must learn to integrate into the dominant group in order to successfully live in the society. They must also learn to live within their own culture. Many visible minorities are forced to "code switch"; that is, to speak and act one way among their own group and another in white society. Du Bois considered blacks to be in a unique position because they were accountable to white culture as well as their own. This influences their sense of self and affects how they live in the world. Only through understanding this position can blacks hope to navigate the world successfully.

Du Bois's classical ideas also apply to the study of other minority groups, including Hispanics and women.[43] Generally, sociologists find that members of the dominant group do not think much about race—but, as one student put it, "When you're a minority, race is always a factor."[44]

∧
∧ **Black Canadians,** and other visible
∧ minorities, **often have to live in two worlds—one black and the other white.**

These B.C. First Nations **protesters are fighting to have their** legal land rights recognized.

FUNCTIONALISM

Functionalists might view racism as having both intended and unintended consequences. For example, consider slavery in the United States. It was extremely functional to building wealth and a successful agricultural economy in the southern United States. Although not the only issue, slavery was a major cause of the American Civil War. The underlying horrors of slavery eventually became well known enough to push whites to make slavery illegal; however, it took more than 100 years for this to occur. Consider the institutional racism that occurs within the U.S. educational system today. What are the consequences of it? Are the tax savings that some receive really worth the costs of an under-educated future generation?

CONFLICT THEORY

From a conflict theorist's lens, racism is the result of one group wanting to keep its advantage over another. In 1928, a government official predicted that Canada would end its "Indian problem" within two generations. The "solution" was nothing less than an official policy of cultural genocide. Residential schools for aboriginal children were set up by the government and often run by religious orders. The schools were supposed to prepare the aboriginal children for life in white society. But the real impact was that aboriginal parents lost their children, aboriginal culture was demeaned and destroyed, and thousands of aboriginal children were subjected to forced separation from their families. Many also suffered physical, sexual and emotional abuse.[45]

HOW DO THE FOUR PARADIGMS VIEW RACISM?

SYMBOLIC INTERACTIONISM

Symbolic interactionists point to the micro interactions of our daily life and how they either support or attack an issue. Had I been teaching in a college classroom 100 years ago, I may have been willing and able to utter racial slurs in class. If I were to do that today, I would be reprimanded and could even lose my job. What has changed? Certainly tolerance for negative terms of racial groups has decreased dramatically in 100 years. Interactionists would suggest that by changing the acceptable terms, we can change the reality.

FEMINIST THEORY

While discrimination based on race or ethnicity can have powerful impacts on an individual, feminists point out that the effects are even more severe when the victim is also a woman. In the 1960s, a number of black feminists argued that, while sexism is certainly one form of discrimination, the types of oppression experienced by white, middle-class women were not representative of all women. A black woman in North America may suffer discrimination because she is a woman, but this is compounded by the fact that she is also black. In 1989, Kimberlé Crenshaw coined the term *intersectionality* to describe the fact that women experience oppression based on a variety of minority statuses, which may include not only gender, but also race, marital status, social class, religion, and sexual orientation. For example, a single black woman may have difficulty finding an apartment because many landlords believe the stereotype that she is less dependable.[46]

When Japan entered the Second World War, **more than 20 000 Canadians of Japanese descent were sent to internment camps** by the Canadian government.

In 1957, when nine African American students attended integrated schools in Arkansas, **they were met with resistance and racial slurs from the school's white population.**

discover sociology in action: HOW DOES AFFIRMATIVE ACTION HELP MINORITY GROUPS IN CANADA?

Affirmative Action

Affirmative action is a social policy designed to help minority groups gain opportunities through employment and education. In Canada, the *Canadian Charter of Rights and Freedoms* states that every individual is equal before the law. The *Charter* also includes a statement about affirmative action programs, which allow special provisions for individuals or groups disadvantaged because of race, national or ethnic origin, colour, religion, sex, age, or mental or physical disability. For example, in the Northwest Territories, aboriginal people are given preference for jobs and education. The logic behind this preference is based on hundreds of years of discrimination, as well as the obvious disadvantages that still exist for minorities.

A great deal of controversy surrounds affirmative action, because some believe that the policy would require universities and companies to establish quotas for minority groups. The Canadian *Employment Equity Act* requires employers in federally regulated industries to give preferential treatment to four designated groups: women, people with disabilities, aboriginal people, and visible minorities. In most Canadian universities, people of aboriginal background often have lower entrance requirements and are eligible to receive exclusive scholarships. The truth is that quotas are not part

> **AFFIRMATIVE ACTION** is a social policy designed to help minority groups gain opportunities through employment and education.

of acceptable affirmative action policies since that could encourage employers to hire minority members who are not qualified. While acknowledging the continuation of discrimination, sociologist William J. Wilson suggested that class-based policies should replace race-based ones.[47] He argued that financial needs and not race should determine advantage. This would allow poor whites, blacks, aboriginals, and so on to receive benefits—and, since visible minority groups and aboriginals are disproportionately poor, they would still reap the lion's share of these benefits. Basing the policies on class rather than on race would eliminate the perception of racial bias.

Do affirmative action policies work? Before affirmative hiring policies were introduced, visible minorities and aboriginals were underrepresented in the public service. Recent figures show that three of the four groups are now overrepresented in the federal government compared with the overall Canadian workforce. Only visible minorities are less represented in the federal government than in the workforce generally.[48]

ACTIVITIES

1. Engage someone not in this class in a conversation about race. See what you learn about his or her beliefs. Ask the following questions:
   - What are the races in Canada?
   - Are there any biological differences in races?
   - Does race play a role in opportunities?
2. Research ten ways to stop hate on a college campus.
   Follow this link to a list: www.tolerance.org/campus/index.jsp. Does your college do these things? If not, can you organize a group to address these problems?
3. Talk to your classmates about your own experiences of racial tension. Then visit this website to reveal your hidden biases: www.tolerance.org/hidden_bias/index.html.

From Classroom to Community ⟩ Feeding Knowledge

A student named Maryann confronted her own notions of white privilege when she assisted at a school that was located in a poor, urban neighbourhood. She was stunned to find a school filled with children who came to school without eating breakfast. The experience allowed Maryann to reflect on her own upbringing.

> "I never really thought that I was well-off when I was in school," see said. "What I found at this school shocked me."

One of the teachers told Maryann that one day she had sent a student to the principal, because he was not paying attention in class.

> "Later that day, the principal explained to her that the student has only one meal per day, and often comes to school hungry. She was so moved that now she brings lunch for this student every day."

Maryann spent most of her time trying to help the students learn to read English. Though the children were smart, outside factors were affecting their schoolwork. Many of the students were from poor immigrant families who were struggling with adapting to a new culture and a different language. Because English was not reinforced at home, these students had difficulty succeeding in class.

> "One child missed school one day because he had to translate for his father at a doctor's appointment,"

remembered Maryann. "I couldn't imagine being 8 years old and talking to a doctor for my dad."

The statistics show that many of these kids will never finish high school. The teachers hope to teach them enough so that they will be able to read and speak English, yet very few of them make it to college. After spending time among these students, Maryann concluded that society is not structured to help students in this situation.

> "I kept wondering how this was equal education. I decided that it wasn't."

WHAT **IS THE DIFFERENCE BETWEEN RACE AND ETHNICITY?** 161

race is the division of people based on certain physical character-istics, but *ethnicity* is the classification of people who share a common cultural, linguistic, or ancestral heritage

WHAT **CAUSES RACIST ATTITUDES, AND HOW DO THESE ATTITUDES AFFECT PEOPLE?** 170

colour-blind racism, racial stereotypes, belief that segregation is a personal choice, belief that racism is a thing of the past, which denies its impact on minorities; these lead to a feeling of double consciousness for minorities

HOW **DOES AFFIRMATIVE ACTION HELP MINORITY GROUPS IN CANADA?** 173

by allowing employers and educators to use minority status as a deciding factor if candidates are equal

get the topic: WHAT IS THE DIFFERENCE BETWEEN RACE AND ETHNICITY?

Theory

FUNCTIONALISM 172
- racism has both intended and unintended consequences
- slavery in the South functioned to build wealth and agriculture, but it also caused a civil war in the United States.

CONFLICT THEORY 172
- racism is a result of power conflicts among different groups
- the group with more power oppresses the weaker groups, a result of which can cause racism to occur
- internment of Japanese Canadians during the Second World War

SYMBOLIC INTERACTIONISM 170
- by changing what is acceptable in society, we change reality
- racial slurs that were acceptable 100 years ago are highly discouraged today
- acceptable terms lead to what is said and thought in society

FEMINIST THEORY 172
- women who are also visible minorities suffer from multiple forms of discrimination
- Kimberlé Crenshaw coined the term *intersectionality* to refer to this intersection of multiple forms of discrimination

Key Terms

race is the division of people based on certain physical characteristics. *161*

ethnicity is the classification of people who share a common cultural, linguistic, or ancestral heritage. *161*

visible minority is a person, other than an aboriginal, who is non-Caucasian in race or non-white in colour. *162*

aboriginal is a person who is Indian, Inuit, or Métis. *162*

minority group is a group that has less power than the majority group. *162*

dominant group is the group that has the greatest power, but not necessarily the greatest numbers. *162*

colonialism is the imposition of control over a weak nation by a more powerful country. *162*

racism is discrimination based on a person's race. *163*

genocide is the attempt to destroy or exterminate a people based on their race and/or ethnicity. *163*

hate groups are organizations that promote hostility or violence toward others based on race and other factors. *163*

conquest is the domination over a group of people by a superior force. *164*

annexation is the incorporation of one territory into another. *164*

voluntary immigration is the willing movement of people from one society to another. *164*

involuntary immigration is the forced movement of people from one society to another. *164*

ethnic cleansing refers to persecution through imprisonment, expulsion, or murder of members of an ethnic minority by a majority to achieve ethnic homogeneity in majority-controlled territory. *164*

migrant superordination is the conquest of a native population by a more powerful group. *165*

(continued)

indigenous superordination is the subordination of an immigrant group to a dominant group. *165*

pluralistic minorities are groups that enter into an area voluntarily but seek to maintain their own culture while also integrating into the dominant group. *165*

assimilationist minorities are groups that seek to shed their old ways and integrate themselves into mainstream society. *165*

secessionist minorities are groups that voluntarily separate themselves from the dominant group and view the dominant group with disdain, believing that it will corrupt the group's belief system. *165*

militant minorities are groups that seek to overthrow the existing system because they see it as unjust. *166*

ethnic enclaves are neighbourhoods where people from similar cultures live together and assert cultural distinction from the dominant group. *167*

prejudice refers to negative attitudes about an entire category of people. *167*

stereotypes are simplified perceptions people have of an entire group that are usually based on false assumptions. *167*

discrimination is the unfair treatment of people based on a prejudice. *167*

institutional discrimination maintains the advantage for the dominant group, while providing the appearance of fairness to all. *168*

scapegoat means making an unfair accusation against a person or group as the cause of a problem. *168*

segregation is forced separation because of factors such as race, gender, or ethnicity. *169*

cycle of poverty is a generational barrier that prevents poor people from breaking into the middle and upper classes. *169*

colour-blind racism is the idea that racism still exists in society in more subtle ways. *170*

double consciousness is the sense that a person must keep a foot in two worlds, one in the majority group's world and one in the minority group's world. *171*

affirmative action is a social policy designed to help minority groups gain opportunities through employment and education. *173*

Sample Test Questions

These multiple-choice questions are similar to those found in the test bank that accompanies this textbook.

1. Which term describes a group that tries to integrate itself into mainstream society?
   a. Annexation
   b. Migrant superordination
   c. Assimilation
   d. Conquest

2. Immigrants who learn their new home's language and culture while maintaining their own customs and beliefs are
   a. assimilationist minorities.
   b. secessionist minorities.
   c. pluralistic minorities.
   d. militant minorities.

3. Which term describes a social policy designed to help minority groups gain opportunities through employment and education?
   a. Ethnocentrism
   b. Ethnic segregation
   c. Colour-blind racism
   d. Affirmative action

4. A dominant group
   a. always has the most in number and in power.
   b. always has the least in number and in power.
   c. usually has the most in number and in power.
   d. usually has the least in number and in power.

5. Race is no longer an issue in Canada.
   a. True
   b. False

ANSWERS: 1. c; 2. c; 3. d; 4. c; 5. b

ESSAY

1. In Canada, who is considered a visible minority? Who is considered an aboriginal?

2. Why does Wilson believe that class-based affirmative action should replace our current race-based system?

3. Why do some people have a sort of "double consciousness"?

4. What is the difference between prejudice and discrimination?

5. What are some ways that Canada is trying to break the cycle of poverty for minority groups?

WHERE TO START YOUR RESEARCH PAPER

For more information on legislation against hate crime in Canada, go to www.media-awareness.ca/english/resources/legislation/canadian_law/federal/criminal_code/criminal_code_hate.cfm

To see the *Canadian Human Rights Act,* go to http://laws.justice.gc.ca/en/h-6/index.html

To find information about aboriginal initiatives in regards to discrimination, go to www.chrc-ccdp.ca/nai_ina/default-eng.aspx

To take the "Know Your Biases" test, go to https://implicit.harvard.edu/implicit

To learn more about the history of multiculturalism in Canada, watch archived footage, and read speeches and articles, go to http://archives.cbc.ca/society/celebrations/topics/3517/

To read more about what people are doing to stop genocide in the world today, go to www.genocidewatch.org

To read about how immigrants get help when settling in Canada, visit the City of Toronto's immigration help site; go to www.toronto.ca/immigration/

Find out ways countries are trying to stop discrimination; go to www.unesco.org/new/en/social-and-human-sciences/themes/human-rights/fight-against-discrimination/

To see what people are doing to break the cycle of poverty, go to www.makepovertyhistory.ca

To find more information on minority groups, go to www.minorityrights.org

To read about the World Conference against Racism, go to www.un.org/WCAR

Remember to check www.thethinkspot.ca **for additional information, downloadable flashcards, and other helpful resources.**

GENDER STRATIFICATION

Q WHAT IS THE DIFFERENCE BETWEEN SEX
AND GENDER?
WHAT ARE THE PERSPECTIVES ON GENDER
AND GENDER INEQUALITY?
WHAT POLICIES ARE IN PLACE TO PREVENT
SEXUAL HARASSMENT AND DOMESTIC
VIOLENCE?

"She is

not the same woman in each magazine advertisement, but she is the same idea. She has that working-mother look as she strides forward, briefcase in one hand, smiling child in the other. Literally and figuratively, she is moving ahead. Her hair, if long, tosses behind her; if it is short, it sweeps back at the sides, suggesting mobility and progress. There is nothing shy or passive about her. She is confident, active, 'liberated.' She wears a dark tailored suit, but with a silk bow or colorful frill that says, 'I'm really feminine underneath.' She has made it in a man's world without sacrificing her femininity. And she has done this on her own. By some personal miracle, this image suggests, she has managed to combine what 150 years of industrialization have split wide apart—child and job, frill and suit, female culture and male.

"When I showed a photograph of a supermom like this to the working mothers I talked to in the course of researching this book, many responded with an outright laugh."[1]

The Social Side *of* Sex

177

In their book *The Second Shift: Working Parents and the Revolution at Home,* sociologists Arlie Russell Hochschild and Anne Machung expound on the different expectations men and women have about women's roles in society.

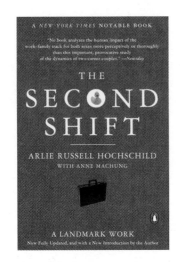

Nearly two decades after Dr. John Gray released *Men Are from Mars, Women Are from Venus,* it is still essential reading for anyone trying to figure out why his or her significant other is so annoying. The idea that the differences between men and women are so profound that we come from different planets may be a little extreme, but significant differences do exist between the sexes.

In *The Second Shift,* Hochschild and Machung contend that the women's liberation movement has actually created additional burdens for women. The movement opened up the world of work, but kept women in the world of domestic service. The image of the perfect woman involves brains, beauty, and toughness. However, as *The Second Shift* demonstrates, this image raises many problems for women. Even though women have excelled in the workforce and contributed mightily to the economy, society still expects them to fill the traditional role of mother.

In my household, we sometimes step out of our "traditional" roles. My wife and I both work, but instead of leaving all the domestic tasks to her, I pride myself on regularly doing what are typically viewed as "female" tasks. I care for our children, cook meals, and clean the house. Of course, are these really "female" tasks? Is there something biological about cleaning a toilet? Some men's attitudes have not evolved enough to share parental and domestic responsibilities. In Canada, only around 8 percent of men spend 30 hours or more on housework per week, whereas up to 20 percent of women clock those hours.[2] Even in households in which the wife works full-time, Hochschild shows how she is often expected to be a "supermom" when she comes home. Who created these ideas of men and women?

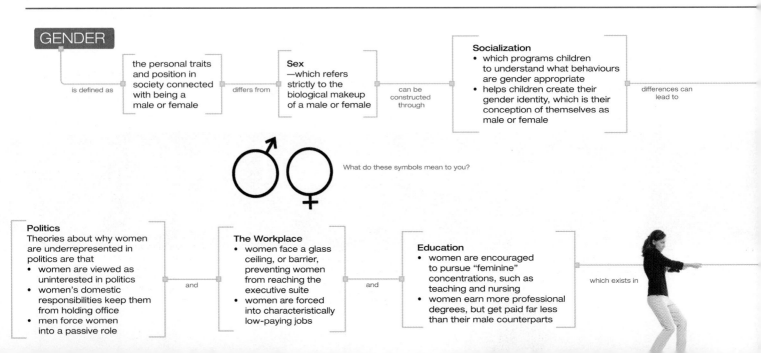

GENDER is defined as the personal traits and position in society connected with being a male or female differs from **Sex** —which refers strictly to the biological makeup of a male or female can be constructed through **Socialization**
• which programs children to understand what behaviours are gender appropriate
• helps children create their gender identity, which is their conception of themselves as male or female
differences can lead to

What do these symbols mean to you?

Politics
Theories about why women are underrepresented in politics are that
• women are viewed as uninterested in politics
• women's domestic responsibilities keep them from holding office
• men force women into a passive role
and **The Workplace**
• women face a glass ceiling, or barrier, preventing women from reaching the executive suite
• women are forced into characteristically low-paying jobs
and **Education**
• women are encouraged to pursue "feminine" concentrations, such as teaching and nursing
• women earn more professional degrees, but get paid far less than their male counterparts
which exists in

get the topic: WHAT IS THE DIFFERENCE BETWEEN SEX AND GENDER?

Gender vs. Sex

"Gender—it's bigger than sex."[3] Upon hearing this phrase, many television viewers were hooked to the *20/20* television special "It's More Than Just Sex: The Difference between Men and Women" in 2006.[4] During this broadcast, anchors John Stossel and Elizabeth Vargas attempted to find out why women flock to the bathroom in groups and why men just don't listen.[5] The name of this program brings up an interesting and often overlooked point: although related, one's gender and one's sex are not necessarily the same thing.

Gender is defined as the personal traits and position in society connected with being a male or female. For instance, in Canadian society, wearing a fancy dress is associated with the female gender, while wearing a tuxedo is associated with men. **Sex** refers strictly to the biological makeup of a male or female. The biological differences between men and women do correlate with some behavioural differences. For example, boys may be more aggressive, and girls more verbal. Such simple correlations support the notion that ideas about gender are based on sex.[6] However, sociologists suggest that socialization, rather than biology, determines gender.

GENDER CONSTRUCTION

In the second season of *Desperate Housewives*—a U.S. television series that enjoys "widespread, international success"[7]—Lynette Scavo's husband, Tom, was often seen taking care of the kids and doing housework while his wife climbed the corporate ladder. In reality, some men would scoff at Tom's actions. But why do we consider Tom's behaviour atypical? Probably because we've been socially programmed with ideas of how men and women should behave. The father as the primary caregiver contradicts our traditional cultural norm. But gender is not a set of traits or roles; "it is the product of social doings of some sort."[8] Sociologists Candace West and Don H. Zimmerman suggest that gender is developed in two ways: Not only do we "do gender" or participate in its construction, but we also have gender done to us as members of society.[9]

SEX is the biological makeup of a male or female.
GENDER IDENTITY is our perception of ourselves as male or female.

Childhood is the prime time for development of **gender identity**, or our perception of ourselves as male or female. During our childhood, we learn what behaviour is "appropriate" for each gender and how to fit in with others like us.

> **Gender** is not a set of traits or roles; "it **is the product of social doings of some sort.**"

To find out how children display or learn their gender, sociologist Michael Messner examined the interactions between two soccer teams—the all-boy Sea Monsters and the all-girl Barbie Girls.[10] Before a season-opening ceremony began, the Barbie Girls rallied together around a miniature Barbie float decorated with their team colours. A boom box on the float played music, and the girls gathered together to sing and dance. At first the little boys watched in confused awe, but soon took up a chant of "No Barbie!" When this chant failed to get the girls' attention, the little boys invaded their space, and a game of chase ensued. The parents observed this behaviour from the sidelines and remarked that little boys and little girls are like members of two different species.

Messner argues that the parents easily recognized the differences, but failed to recognize the similarities between the girls' and boys' teams during the rest of the season. Players on both teams regularly displayed many of the same behaviours—crying over skinned knees, racing to get snacks after the game, paying attention to birds or airplanes rather than to the coach—that would indicate a lack of major gender differences. Parents have no problem pointing out the differences between the boys

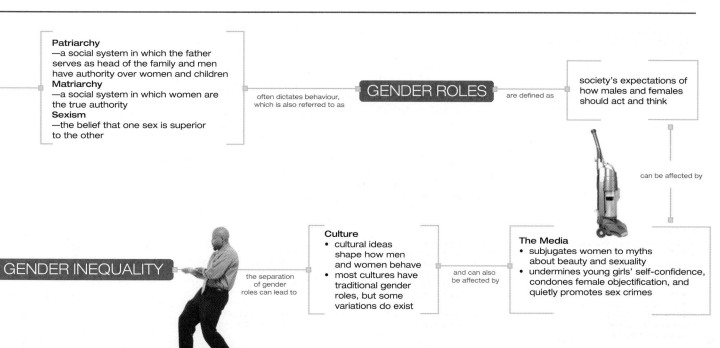

Patriarchy
—a social system in which the father serves as head of the family and men have authority over women and children
Matriarchy
—a social system in which women are the true authority
Sexism
—the belief that one sex is superior to the other

often dictates behaviour, which is also referred to as

GENDER ROLES

are defined as

society's expectations of how males and females should act and think

can be affected by

GENDER INEQUALITY

the separation of gender roles can lead to

Culture
• cultural ideas shape how men and women behave
• most cultures have traditional gender roles, but some variations do exist

and can also be affected by

The Media
• subjugates women to myths about beauty and sexuality
• undermines young girls' self-confidence, condones female objectification, and quietly promotes sex crimes

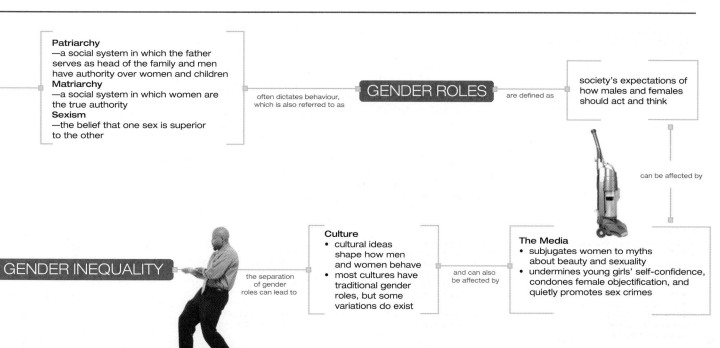

and girls, but have difficulty identifying similarities due to "an institutional context that is characterized by informally structured sex segregation among the parent coaches and team managers, and by formally structured sex segregation among the children."[11] In other words, the adults couldn't see the similarities because they were socialized to see boys and girls as different.

Patriarchy and Sexism

The English poet William Wordsworth once said, "Father—to God himself we cannot give a holier name." Wordsworth's sentiment was reflected in *Father Knows Best*—a definitive television program of the 1950s and 1960s. Humans have long considered the father the leader of the family unit. This role carries over into the rest of society through **patriarchy**, a social system in which men exert authority over women and children. The power position of men extends into government, business, and even religion. Few societies have been identified as a **matriarchy**, a social system in which women are the main authority and hold power over men.

The patriarchal system often results in **sexism**, or the belief that one sex is superior to the other. In many societies, attitudes often suggest women are the "weaker sex." This belief system may be adopted by women who seek jobs that fulfill these views. A few years ago, a very bright female student told me she wanted to be a medical doctor. I asked, "What's your major?" "Nursing" was the reply. She explained that her father, fiancé, and religious belief all dictated that women shouldn't be doctors. Clearly, these patriarchal beliefs possibly prevented a great mind from becoming a great doctor.

In *The Second Shift,* Hochschild finds that many married, working women have a "second shift" when they get home from work. Although their husbands may help around the house to some extent, women come home to the tasks of cooking dinner, doing laundry, and, if there are children, helping them with homework and getting them ready for the next day of school. However, most of the women stated they were satisfied with their marriages. This shows that the patriarchal system is deeply ingrained in people's minds.

Gender Roles

Television's female characters have come a long way since Wilma Flintstone and June Cleaver, for whom kissing their husbands good-bye and seeing the kids off to school started off a day of cleaning, baking, and homemaking. Today, we're used to seeing women portrayed as surgeons and attorneys and men actively participating in raising their children. What makes these arrangements acceptable to us now? The prevailing culture and the socialization that parents provide to their children shape ideas about gender-appropriate behaviours.

While women are succeeding in traditionally masculine fields like medicine and business, most of our children are still socialized to fit specific **gender roles**, or society's expectations of how males and females should act and think. Children's toys are an example of socialization at a young age. Manhattan Toy makes a line of dolls called Groovy Girls, which allows girls to "celebrate their own unique personalities," with various fashion options for the dolls.[12] The Hasbro Company's Nerf toys—geared toward more aggressive play, like football and mock war situations—continue to be popular among young boys.[13]

However, gender roles in North America are in a constant state of flux. This is not to say that we now encourage males to possess feminine characteristics, or vice versa, but that the differences between the sexes are less pronounced than they once were. Young girls race down soccer

∧∧∧ During our childhood, society shapes our gender identity. **What social cues might this young girl have picked up from the world around her?**

▶▶▶ GO GLOBAL

The Horrors of Female Circumcision

In some of the world's most patriarchal societies, it's traditional for men to control every aspect of a woman's life, including her body. Female circumcision, also referred to as female genital mutilation (FGM), is one such tradition. The procedure consists of the alteration or removal of parts of the female genital organs for no medical purpose.[14] The intention is to keep women sexually "pure," by ensuring that they will remain virgins until marriage.[15] Women who undergo FGM may suffer from a number of long-term medical consequences, including recurrent urinary tract infections, infertility, and increased risk of childbirth complications.[16]

This practice is most common in the western, eastern, and northeastern regions of Africa, some countries in Asia and the Middle East, and certain immigrant communities in Europe and North America.[17] It's estimated that between 100 and 140 million girls and women worldwide have undergone FGM.[18] Cultural tradition and ideas about proper sexual behaviour perpetuate the practice, subjecting new generations of female children to a painful and dangerous operation.

Although this practice is rooted in cultural tradition, many believe it's a violation of human rights and a sign of male domination over women. The practice represents an inequality between the sexes, and it is a major form of discrimination against women.[19]

fields or shoot hoops after school, and they're just as likely to wear jeans and T-shirts as skirts. The traditional roles of man as provider and woman as homemaker are shifting as well, since many households today have two breadwinners.

GENDER ROLES AND THE MEDIA

Although change is evident, we have not completely moved beyond old ideas about gender. Look no further than big-name reality shows like ABC's *The Bachelor,* and you'll see evidence that traditional gender roles are still in place. On these programs, women compete in order to win the affections of the man on the show. The shows also continue to perpetuate myths about beauty and sexuality, as the emphasis is placed on young, "sexy" girls. On the spin-off show *The Bachelorette,* a women chooses among several men—yet,

1

The Lolita Effect
MYTHS

Girls don't choose boys. Boys choose girls, but only sexy ones.

There's only one kind of sexy—slender, curvy, white beauty.

Girls should work to be that type of sexy.

The younger a girl is, the sexier she is.

Sexual violence can be attractive.

5

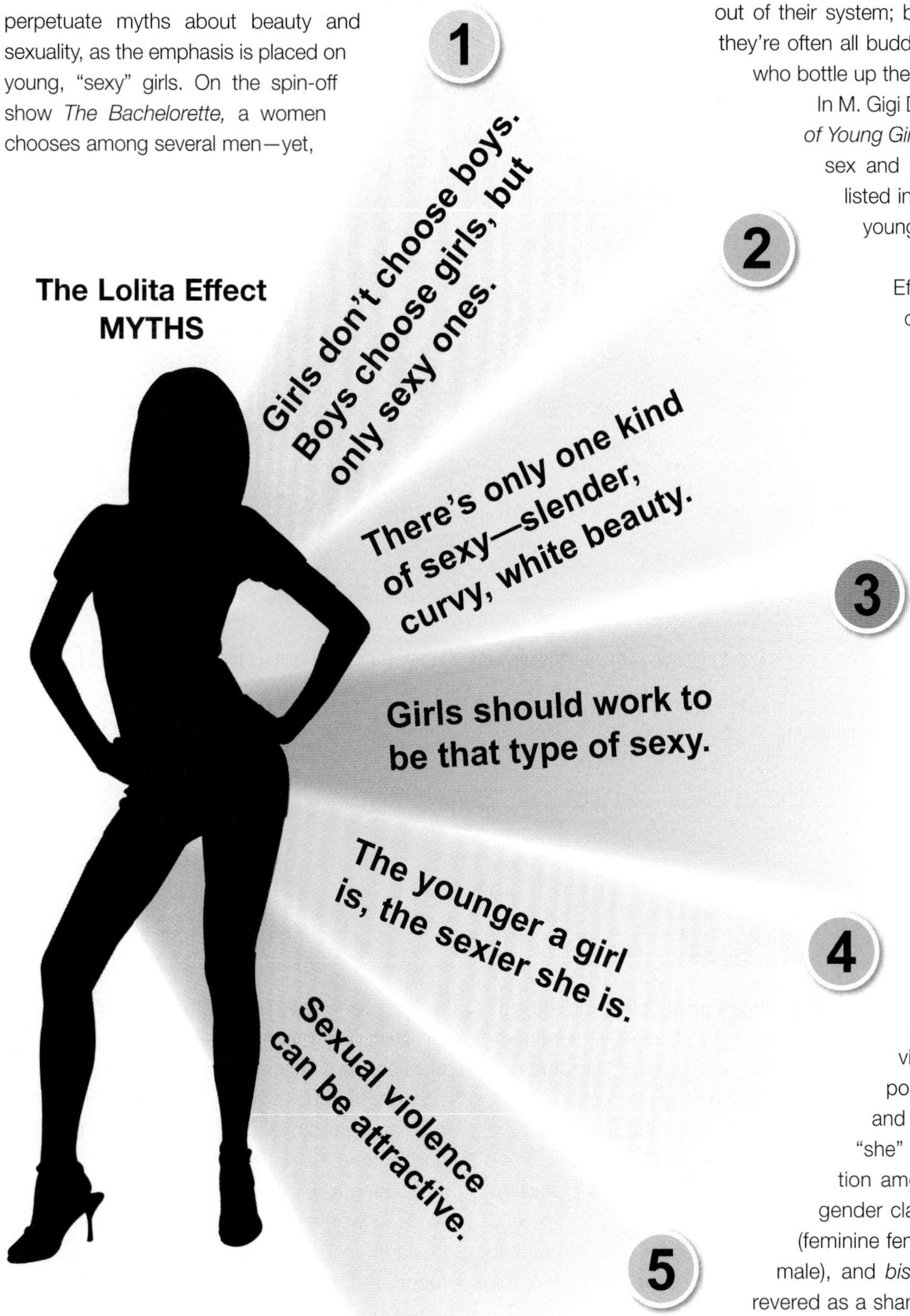

Source: Based on M. Gigi Durham, *The Lolita Effect: The Media Sexualization of Young Girls and What We Can Do About It* (Woodstock, NY: The Overlook Press, 2008).

PATRIARCHY is a social system in which the father serves as head of the family, and men have authority over women and children.

MATRIARCHY is a social system in which women are the main authority and hold power over men.

SEXISM is the belief that one sex is superior to the other.

GENDER ROLES are society's expectations of how males and females should act and think.

as one cyber-reviewer wrote, "gender and society expectations play a key role: Guys may have fist fights and hot arguments, but are quick to get it out of their system; by the time the 'Men Tell All' special is broadcast, they're often all buddies. In contrast, 'The Bachelor' shows have ladies who bottle up their anger and act catty."[20]

In M. Gigi Durham's *The Lolita Effect: The Media Sexualization of Young Girls and What We Can Do About It,* five myths about sex and sexuality are examined. These myths, which are listed in the graphic to the left, give many impressionable young women an "if you've got it, flaunt it" attitude.

2

Durham has labelled these myths the "Lolita Effect," which works to undermine girls' self-confidence, condones female objectification, and quietly promotes sex crimes.[21] The goal of Durham's book is to break down these myths in order to help girls recognize ideas about healthy, progressive sexuality, and to protect themselves from media degradation and sexual vulnerability.[22] Durham hopes to empower girls to make healthy decisions about their sexuality. Although the media's portrayal of sexuality is often a skewed one, people in the real world are not forced to abide by these views. However, the media play a big role in our culture, so we cannot help but be affected by the things we see on TV and in magazines. What other effect might culture have on our ideas of gender?

3

THE FLUIDITY OF GENDER ROLES: INDONESIA'S BUGIS PEOPLE

4

Some cultures, like the Bugis people living on the Indonesian island of Sulawesi, have a different view of gender and gender roles. Australian anthropologist Sharyn Davies studied the Bugis people and found that gender-specific pronouns like "he" and "she" don't exist in their language.[23] Gender stratification among the Bugis is complicated, with five different gender classifications: *oroané* (masculine male), *makkunrai* (feminine female), *calalai* (masculine female), *calabai* (feminine male), and *bissu* (embodying both male and female energies, revered as a shaman).[24] Each gender has specific behaviours, articles of clothing, social and religious roles, and sexual practices. The oroané and makkunrai genders are "normal," or comparable to what we know; the calalai, calabai, and bissu are what we might call "gender benders."

The **calalai** are anatomical females who assume the characteristics of men. They hold masculine jobs and dress as men, practise homosexuality, and typically live with female partners to adopt children.

The **calabai** are anatomical males who adhere to some of the responsibilities of women. Calabai males are homosexual and dress as women, yet they don't follow all cultural suggestions for women. They do, however, take on traditionally female responsibilities, like planning weddings.

The **bissu** embody the perfect mixture of male and female. A bissu that is externally male is considered to be internally female, and vice versa if the bissu is female. The Bugis people believe that bissu embody the best characteristics of both sexes, so they are able to communicate with the spirits and therefore occupy a special place in the community.

The Bugis have ideas about gender that are different from our own, but seem to be more accepting of different kinds of people. Men and women are allowed to live the gender role that suits them best in Bugis society.

Gender and Inequality

In many societies, the idea of gender is not as fluid as the Bugis people suggest, and a hierarchy of sorts exists between the sexes. In Canada, for example, men and women are ranked differently in terms of power and wealth. In 2008, the average total earnings for women was $30 200, and for men $46 900.[25] Because women are more likely to earn less than men, they're also more likely to live below the poverty line. Why is there such inequality between income levels and poverty status of men and women? We'll look into this further in the section relating to work. But first, let's look at a topic that should be relevant to everyone reading this book—gender and education.

In most societies, choosing a feminine style of dress will make a man stand out in a crowd. Why is it less conspicuous for calabai males to dress in a feminine style?

THINK SOCIOLOGICALLY

Culture's Effect on Gender Roles

Anthropologist Margaret Mead conducted a study of gender roles among three tribes in New Guinea: the Arapesh, the Mundgumor, and the Tchambuli.[26] She concluded that gender roles are largely dependent on culture. The men and women of the Arapesh tribe would both be considered "feminine" by our standards. The Mundgumor men and women were aggressive and violent, possessing "masculine" qualities. However,

among the Tchambuli people, men stayed home and raised the children, and women provided for the household.[27] This study drew much criticism; many accused Mead of doctoring her results to show what she had hoped to find.[28] Nevertheless, this study showed that gender is culturally constructed.

Other studies of gender roles have found that, in most societies, traditional gender roles have degrees of variation for any individual task. Anthropologist George Murdock's 1937 study of more than 200 societies found that

women performed farming tasks and construction of homes in almost as many societies as men. Although not every society is uniform, Murdock's findings showed definite cross-cultural similarities in the roles of men and women.[29]

Changes in gender roles have left working women with children in a tough position. In *The Second Shift,* Hochschild found that although gender roles in the working world may have changed, working women are still largely responsible for maintaining the home.

GENDER AND EDUCATION

A few years ago, my daughter went to her first day in grade two very excited, but came home feeling down. When I asked why she was so upset, she said it was because she had "a boy for a teacher." I had to explain to her that "boy teachers" could be just as smart and fun as "girl teachers." Two months later, she couldn't wait to catch the bus in the morning to get to his class. Male elementary school teachers don't break any major social taboos today, but 30 years ago, when I was in school, the only men at my school were the gym teacher, the principal, and the janitor.

Historically, men and women have received vastly different educations. In 1872, Mount Allison became the first Canadian university to grant degrees to women.[30] Although women were starting to be offered enrolment in post-secondary studies in North America, they were encouraged to study "feminine" concentrations, such as nursing and teaching. Men, conversely, focused on fields that involved either vocational or intellectual skills. These differences are becoming less pronounced today, but there is still a clear educational divide between men and women nationally.[31]

Even though higher education used to be a primarily masculine pursuit, women now earn the majority of associate's and bachelor's degrees. For example, Statistics Canada reported that in 2008, 60 percent of all degree, diploma, or certificate qualifications from Canadian universities had been awarded to women.[32] Women accounted for 55 percent of the students who received a master's-level qualification, and 44.2 percent of those who received doctorates. The doctorate figure was up from 36.1 percent a decade earlier.[33]

CALALAI are anatomical females in Bugis society who assume the characteristics of men.

CALABAI are anatomical males in Bugis society who adhere to some of the responsibilities of women.

BISSU are androgynous members of Bugis society who embody the perfect mixture of male and female.

Although this is a major improvement for women in education, the differences in choice of major still reflect traditional gender roles. For example, Statistics Canada's figures for 2008 show that women received about double the number of university qualifications than men in the fields of visual and performing arts and communications technologies, while men far outnumbered women in the fields of architecture, engineering, and related technologies.[34]

If women are earning degrees in greater numbers than men, shouldn't we see the income gap between men and women decrease? Census data show that the income gap between men and women actually becomes wider with higher levels of educational background (as shown in the "Gender Income Gap" figure). This seems curious. To investigate this further, let's turn to women in the workplace.

GENDER AND THE WORKPLACE

These days, women make up almost half of Canada's paid labour force,[35] and two-thirds of Canadian families depend on two incomes.[36] While it's now accepted and necessary for women to work, the types of jobs as

The Gender Income Gap by Level of Education in 2006

Median Earnings

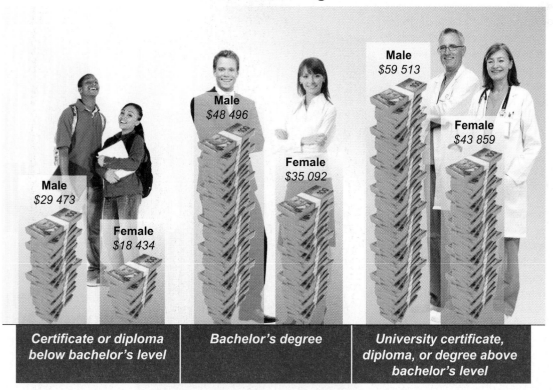

Male $29 473

Female $18 434

Male $48 496

Female $35 092

Male $59 513

Female $43 859

Certificate or diploma below bachelor's level

Bachelor's degree

University certificate, diploma, or degree above bachelor's level

Source: Statistics Canada, 2006 Census of Population, Statistics Canada catalogue no. 97-563-XCB2006008.
Accessed through www12.statcan.ca/census-recensement/index-eng.cfm

HUMAN CAPITAL MODEL assumes that men and women bring different natural skills to the workplace.

CHOICE MODEL explains the income gap by analyzing the kinds of jobs women choose.

PATRIARCHY MODEL assumes that we have a male-dominated society that doesn't allow women to hold upper-tier jobs.

GLASS CEILING is an invisible barrier preventing women from reaching executive-level positions in the workplace.

well as the compensation for these jobs remain different for men and women. Three theoretical models—the human capital model, the choice model, and the patriarchy model—attempt to explain these discrepancies.

The **human capital model** assumes that men and women bring different natural skills to the workplace. For example, society perceives men to have more mechanical skills, thus they make better engineers. Because society considers women to be more nurturing, they are assumed to be better teachers. Such an argument suggests it is not discrimination to hire men to do jobs for which they are more suited. This explains why men seem to have advantages in higher-income professions, such as medicine, engineering, and law.[37]

The **choice model** explains the income gap by analyzing the kinds of jobs women choose. Many women choose to major in social work or elementary education, therefore knowingly entering fields that traditionally pay less. This argument suggests that if you choose a career that you know pays very little, you have only yourself to blame.[38]

The **patriarchy model** assumes that we have a male-dominated society that doesn't allow women to hold upper-tier jobs or steers them away from such careers early in life. For example, when discussing majors with an academic adviser, students may experience stereotypical gender role expectations. Male students may be asked to consider business or engineering. Female students may be asked about education or communication fields as possible professions.

The patriarchy model also supports the idea of a **glass ceiling**, or the invisible barrier that prevents women from reaching the executive suite. For example, relatively few women become the CEOs of large companies. Women lead only 19 of the top 500 companies in Canada.[39] Sociology professor Shelley J. Correll studied labour distribution by sex and found that

cultural beliefs about gender shape both male and female attitudes about their abilities.[40] If this is the case, our ideas about gender may need to undergo a radical change before the income gap between men and women disappears.

GENDER AND POLITICS

Women are making huge political strides. Yet in 2010, Canada ranked 51st and the United States 73rd in terms of representation of women in national parliaments around the world.[41] In Canada, the lone woman who has served as prime minister did so for only a few months—Kim Campbell, in 1993. Women regularly hold high political office in other parts of the world. England has had several women in power, beginning in 1553 with Queen Mary I. Margaret Thatcher was prime minister from 1979 to 1990. Golda Meir was prime minister of Israel from 1969 to 1973, and Benazir Bhutto was prime minister of Pakistan from 1988 to 1990 and 1993 to 1996.[42] No woman has yet served as president of the United States, although Hillary Rodham Clinton received strong support in her bid for the 2008 Democratic presidential nomination.[43] Let's examine three theories that attempt to explain why women in North America are still not on an equal footing with men when it comes to the top political positions.

<<< **Women in the workplace often have to work twice as hard as men** to break through the glass ceiling above them.

Men Are a Gender, Too

It's important to remember that men are a gender, too. As noted earlier, men have many advantages in North American society. Christine Williams discusses how men have a "glass elevator" when it comes to getting jobs in traditionally female-dominated occupations. Men who sought jobs in the nursing, library, and elementary education fields said they felt they had an advantage over women applying for the same job because there were fewer men in those fields.[44]

However, it's important to know that with the male gender role come gender expectations. Recently, the son of a friend was going off to college. The boy complained when his parents refused to buy him a new car. His sister got a new car when she went to college, but my friend explained, "He's a boy. It's good for him to learn how to fix a junker car."

>>> ACTIVITY Write out as many household tasks as you can think of, and place an M next to those done primarily by men and a W next to those done primarily by women. Do you see any gender bias in your life?

Theory #1: Women, by nature, are uninterested in politics. This theory has been disproved time and again by data that show that women vote more regularly than men.[45] Women have also risen to political prominence, including the three women who have been appointed governor-general in Canada: Jeanne Sauvé (1984–1990), Adrienne Clarkson (1999–2005), and Michaëlle Jean (2005–2010).[46]

Theory #2: The structure of women's lives does not lend itself to the rigours of political office. I like to call this theory the "baby bias." Similar to Hochschild's "supermom" responsibilities, the theory assumes a woman in office would be too overwhelmed by her mothering duties to succeed in office. When Pat Carney announced in 2007 that she was resigning from her Canadian Senate seat—after more than a quarter century in Parliament—she was called "an example of how cultural and societal limitations on women were broken down, often through compelling competence, sheer acts of courage and personal will of the kind her career will always symbolize."[47] Carney played a "demanding role" in *Canada–U.S. Free Trade Agreement* negotiations and in 1991 voted against her own party to help defeat a bill that would have criminalized abortion.[48] She is the mother of two children.[49]

Theory #3. Society forces women into a politically passive role. Traditionally, this has been the case. But women are more independent today and have an increased interest in holding political office. Furthermore, politicians tend to often be lawyers and business people, traditionally "men's" worlds. Although this is changing, female representation in politics remains disproportionately low.

FEMINISM is the vast collection of social movements and theories about gender differences, proposing social equality for all people.

Feminism

Feminism refers to the vast collection of social movements and theories about gender differences. Feminism proposes social equality for all

Voter Turnout by Gender in 2008 Federal Election

Source: Numbers adapted from Elections Canada, "Estimation of Voter Turnout by Age Group at the 2008 Federal General Election," www.elections.ca/res/rec/part/estim/estimation40_e.pdf, page 10, accessed October 25, 2010.

people. Feminist thinkers believe that women should have the same rights as men and deserve the same opportunities as men.

The history of the feminist movement in Canada goes back to the nineteenth century, and can be divided into three "waves."

FIRST-WAVE FEMINISM

What is considered the first wave began in the late nineteenth and early twentieth centuries and revolved around the women's suffrage movement. One of the leading figures of this movement was Nellie McClung. In 1914, McClung and other Canadian suffragettes held a "mock parliament" in Winnipeg. This was a satirical parody on the dangers of giving men the right to vote, and drew attention to the cause of women's suffrage. The strategy worked—in 1916, Manitoba became the first Canadian province to grant women the right to vote, although only in provincial elections. Other provinces soon followed with similar laws, except Quebec, where women were not allowed to vote until 1940. In 1918, *An Act to Confer the Electoral Franchise upon Women* allowed Canadian women to vote in federal elections. However, women were still not allowed to hold a seat in the Canadian Senate. The *British North America Act,* Canada's constitution at that time, stated that one must be a "person" in order to serve in the Senate, but the term *person* did not include women, only men. In 1927, Nellie McClung, Emily Murphy, Irene Parlby, Louise McKinney, and Henrietta Edwards submitted to the British Privy Council, the highest constitutional court for Canada, what would famously become known as the "Persons Case." In October 1929 the Council's Judicial Committee ruled that Canadian women were, in fact, persons and could be appointed to the Senate.[50]

SECOND-WAVE FEMINISM

The second wave of feminism occurred during the women's liberation movement that began in the 1960s. While first-wave feminism protested legal inequality, second-wave feminism also included equality in the workplace, equality in education, and social independence from men.

In 1963, Betty Friedan published a book called *The Feminine Mystique,* bringing attention to the idea that a woman should seek personal fulfillment outside her home and family. The book attacked a social system in which women were treated as nothing more than homemakers and childbearers.[51] Friedan is said to have ignited the women's lib movement with this book, although she has also been criticized for focusing exclusively on the plight of white middle- and upper-class women.[52]

In addition to equal rights in education and the workplace, second-wavers demanded reproductive rights and protection from domestic and sexual violence. These demands caused a great deal of controversy, as many conservatives felt that contraceptives and abortion go against traditional morals.

In Canada, the *Royal Commission on the Status of Women* was established in 1967. In 1970, the Commission published a comprehensive report called the "Report of the Royal Commission on the Status of Women in Canada." The report made 167 recommendations that would address and correct many issues of women's inequality in Canadian society. In 1972, the National Action Committee on the Status of Women (NAC) was formed as an umbrella organization of women's organizations throughout Canada.[53]

THIRD-WAVE FEMINISM

Beginning in the early 1990s, the third wave of feminism branched out to include multiple racial and socioeconomic groups. Gloria Anzaldua, bell hooks (née Gloria Jean Watkins), Maxine Hong Kingston, and Audre Lorde are feminist leaders associated with the third wave in North America. Author and social activist bell hooks, for example, connected topics like race, capitalism, and gender within her works. She emphasized the fact that all three topics were interconnected and that they needed to be addressed at the same time.[54]

While the second wave of feminism pushed for changes to legislation, the third wave is about changing social attitudes. Despite many

The History of Feminism

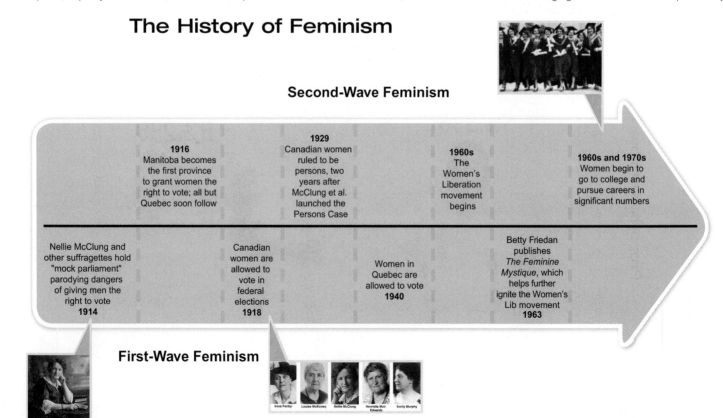

Second-Wave Feminism

1916
Manitoba becomes the first province to grant women the right to vote; all but Quebec soon follow

1929
Canadian women ruled to be persons, two years after McClung et al. launched the Persons Case

1960s
The Women's Liberation movement begins

1960s and 1970s
Women begin to go to college and pursue careers in significant numbers

Nellie McClung and other suffragettes hold "mock parliament" parodying dangers of giving men the right to vote
1914

Canadian women are allowed to vote in federal elections
1918

Women in Quebec are allowed to vote
1940

Betty Friedan publishes *The Feminine Mystique*, which helps further ignite the Women's Lib movement
1963

First-Wave Feminism

Irene Parlby   Louise McKinney   Nellie McClung   Henrietta Muir Edwards   Emily Murphy

improvements in the past 50 years, there still remain significant inequalities between men and women in Canada. The wage gap between men and women has narrowed only slightly since 1960. Women still hold fewer seats in the federal Parliament. The top boardrooms in the country are still dominated by men. It is clear that the goal of complete equality has not yet been achieved.

The discrepancy is even more pronounced for certain groups of women. Increasing attention is being paid to the situation of immigrant women and aboriginal women, two groups of Canadians who continue to experience significant discrimination and inequality in Canadian society.[55]

think sociologically: WHAT ARE THE PERSPECTIVES ON GENDER AND GENDER INEQUALITY?

Feminist Theory

Feminists study how gender affects the experiences and opportunities of men and women. Although feminists may not always agree about how to achieve gender equality, they do tend to adopt four general beliefs:

1 **Increasing equality in work and education.** Year after year women are earning more professional degrees than men and entering the workforce in large numbers. However, feminists continue fighting for equality in both the workplace and schools against the gender wage gap and the glass ceiling that women commonly face in the workplace.

2 **Expanding human choice for outcomes.** In the book *Woman Hating,* feminist Andrea Dworkin comments that "Being female in this world is having been robbed of the potential for human choice by men who love to hate us."[56] Not all feminists agree with Dworkin's suggestion, but virtually all feminists work to create a society in which men and women have equal opportunities. For example, by expanding enrollment in professional and graduate schools, women have greater opportunities to choose careers they enjoy.

3 **Eliminating gender stratification.** Feminism commits itself to ensure equal rights, equal opportunity, and equal pay for women. For example, about 15 percent of Canadian Forces personnel are women.[57]

4 **Ending sexual violence.** Feminist theorists believe that male violence against women perpetuates gender inequality in our society.[58] For example, the "rule of thumb" refers to the alleged British common law that allowed a man to beat his wife with a stick, as long as it was not any larger than the diameter of his thumb. It's important to note that this was never an actual law; however, men were allowed to punish their wives corporally.[59]

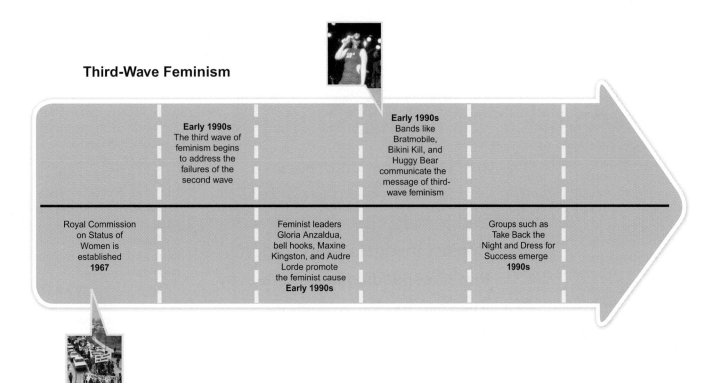

Third-Wave Feminism

Early 1990s
The third wave of feminism begins to address the failures of the second wave

Early 1990s
Bands like Bratmobile, Bikini Kill, and Huggy Bear communicate the message of third-wave feminism

Royal Commission on Status of Women is established **1967**

Feminist leaders Gloria Anzaldua, bell hooks, Maxine Kingston, and Audre Lorde promote the feminist cause **Early 1990s**

Groups such as Take Back the Night and Dress for Success emerge **1990s**

LIBERAL VS. RADICAL FEMINISM

Although there are many different kinds of feminism, and no universal agreement about the titles of the different types, we will address two types here—liberal feminism and radical feminism.

Liberal feminists tend to be in line with their historical roots, suggesting that women's equality is the primary motivation for the movement. If you believe that women should receive the same pay for the same work; have equal opportunities in education, the workplace, and political office; and be free from domestic violence, then you are a liberal feminist. As you can see, this group is the larger group, because most people agree that women should not be discriminated against based on their gender. As a result, they support the idea that women should be free to pursue their own interests and achieve equality.

Radical feminists agree with the liberal agenda, but generally carry the ideas further. They might focus on capitalism and the ways that men use their historical advantage over money to maintain control over women. Radicals see that patriarchy is firmly rooted in society. Some suggest that only an overthrow of capitalism can result in equality for women. Others suggest that women should avoid "traditional activities" such as childbearing, since this often leads women to subordinate their own goals for their husbands and families.

Functionalism

While feminists fight gender inequality in Canada, functionalists examine how the separation of gender roles actually functions in a society. Society places men and women in different spheres, and these differences help maintain society. Because men and women often play different roles, competition is eliminated between the sexes, and family life runs smoothly.[60] For example, if men are expected to go out and work to provide for the family, while women are expected to perform domestic tasks and care for the children, their roles are complementary to each other. Each is doing a job that must be done. As women steadily enter the workforce, the separation of gender roles becomes less distinct. Even so, women are generally expected to maintain the home.

Talcott Parsons studied the separation of gender roles in the context of the family. Parsons noted that as children, "sex discrimination is more than anything else a reflection of the differentiation of adult sex roles."[61] Girls at a young age are socialized to display expressive qualities, such as calmness and nurturing (qualities expected of lmany adult women), while boys are prone to be rational and competitive, which are instrumental qualities.[62]

According to Parsons, young girls are able to step into the adult feminine role early in their development.[63] These girls see their mothers performing domestic tasks and are often expected to help out. Young boys, however, have fathers who work outside the house. As a result, boys are trained to prepare for their futures in the workforce.

Conflict Theory

Conflict theorists argue that capitalism and patriarchy are deeply intertwined. In a capitalist society, women generally are at the bottom of the system, regardless of their job. Furthermore, they often engage in unpaid, domestic tasks that serve to maintain the status quo.[64] However, men devalue the work that women do, which reinforces the power that men have over women.[65]

Women who work tend to make less money than men in the workforce, so women are often subordinate to their better-paid husbands. Women are generally locked in a never-ending cycle that makes them submissive and subservient to men.

Symbolic Interactionism

Symbolic interactionists believe that people's definition of gender develops from everyday interactions with others from the same and the opposite sex.[66] Sociologists West and Zimmerman's idea of "doing gender" best illustrates the symbolic interactionists' point of view.[67] We all "do gender" every day, which means we act in a certain way that is associated with a particular gender. The way you style your hair, the mannerisms you have, and the way you talk are all part of the way you communicate your gender to others.

Sociologist Janet Chafetz argues that "doing gender" not only "(re)produces gender difference, it (re)produces gender inequality."[68] One way this happens is through conversation. Deborah Tannen's *You Just Don't Understand: Men and Women in Conversation* argues that our lives are essentially a series of conversations, and we pass on "different, asymmetrical assumptions about men and women" in these conversations.[69]

Chafetz would argue that men and women communicate differently. Men often dominate conversations, and women struggle to follow the sometimes arbitrary rules that men impose on the dialogue. Women use "verbal and body language in ways that weaken their ability to assert themselves," which makes them appear less powerful than their male

^
^
^ Notice the difference in dress between these male and female cheerleaders.

Conflict theorists would argue that cheerleading is just one way that men exploit women in our society.

counterparts.[70] For example, while eating out one day, I noticed a men's softball team and a few of their wives/girlfriends at a nearby table. The guys were talking and laughing, but the women were passive. Gender socialization generally teaches boys to make their voice heard, while girls are taught to be "good," meaning quiet and docile.

Men and women often follow scripted behaviour, acting in ways that are associated with their gender.[71] For example, men and women use

MACHISMO is overt and exaggerated displays of masculinity.

different types of language and gesture. Men tend to be more direct in describing their wants and desires, displaying **machismo**, overt and exaggerated displays of masculinity.[72]

Think about your conversations with people of the opposite sex. What patterns do you notice? **Do men and women really communicate differently?**

WRAP YOUR MIND AROUND THE THEORY

What functions might these boys serve in tomorrow's society? What characteristics might they have?

FUNCTIONALISM

The functionalists view society as a system of many parts, working in concert with one another to form a whole. Talcott Parsons believed that gender differences were essential in maintaining a properly function-ing society. Parents socialize boys and girls for their future roles of father and mother. Boys are taught to be confident, rational, and competitive because these charac-teristics are instrumental qualities for men to succeed. Parents socialize girls with the primary goal of preparing them to raise children. They learn nurturing qualities that Parsons refers to as expressive qualities. These complementary roles assist in the smooth functioning of society.

CONFLICT THEORY

Social conflict theorists are interested in the struggle for power between groups. In the case of gender, conflict theorists see the gender roles as beneficial to men, as their role as main breadwinner gives them power and control. Friedrich Engels, a contemporary of Karl Marx, suggested that women are the first oppressed group.[73] Although he agreed with Marx that the proletariat are oppressed, Engels points out that women, too, are exploited. This may not seem to be a major idea in today's world, but in 1884, it was staggering.

WHY DOES GENDER STRATIFICATION EXIST?

SYMBOLIC INTERACTIONISM

The symbolic interactionist perspective might focus on how people self-select by gender. For example, men may choose fields associated with "male-ness," whereas women select careers based on the types of work that are considered "normal" for them. Thus, women tend not to become engineers or work in other professions that require a mathematical background, in part, because it isn't expected of them. Gendered definitions influence career choices of men and women.[74] When I became a social worker, a job dominated by women, I had family members who actually said, "Isn't that a woman's job?" Such a definition might influence a career choice.

FEMINIST THEORY

Liberal feminists are the largest group of feminists, and they state that women should not be discriminated against based on their gender. They support the idea that women should be free to pursue their own interests and achieve equality. Radical feminists carry these ideas further. They believe that capitalism allows men to maintain control over women. Radical feminists say that patriarchy is firmly rooted in society, so only an overthrow of capitalism can result in real equality for women.

Why might capitalism give men and women **reason to fight?**

What are the **pros and cons of selecting a career** that falls **outside the traditional roles** for your gender?

discover sociology in action: WHAT POLICIES ARE IN PLACE TO PREVENT SEXUAL HARASSMENT AND DOMESTIC VIOLENCE?

Although more subtle forms of oppression can be damaging, physical, sexual, emotional, economic, and psychological abuse are all forms of oppression. In Canada, the General Social Survey 2009 (GSS) found that a large number of crimes go unreported: only 69 percent of violent victimizations (sexual assault, robbery, physical assault) are reported to police.[75] The most common reasons for not reporting sexual assaults were believing the incident was not important enough (68 percent), not believing the police could help them (59 percent), feeling the incident should be dealt with in an alternative way (42 percent), and feeling the incident was personal (34 percent).[76] It has been noted in the United States that because such victims begin to internalize their emotions, the women involved either believe they deserved the assault or believe that no one can help them.[77]

Resources are available to help the victims, but victims are often too scared or ashamed to come forward. In Canada, revisions to the *Criminal Code* have lengthened minimum sentences for certain sexual assault offences.[78] Canada also has a National Sex Offender Registry that is "a national registration system for sex offenders who have been convicted of designated sex offences and ordered by the courts to report annually to police."[79] A Public Safety Canada announcement in 2010 said that the federal government "is committed to strengthening the National Sex Offender Registry and the National DNA Data Bank so that they better protect Canadians from sexual offenders. Proposed changes will also enable police to prevent and investigate crimes of a sexual nature more effectively."[80]

ACTIVITIES

1. Research your province's sex offender laws. What is the suggested penalty for first-time rape offenders? Are sex offenders required to register and inform the neighbourhood in which they reside of their status?
2. Locate a battered women's shelter in your area. How is the shelter funded? What services does the shelter provide?

Social Policy—Stopping Sexual Harassment and Gender Violence

Sexual harassment and gender violence are persistent issues, as stories of office harassment, domestic violence, and rape are commonplace items in the news. In one of Canada's biggest recent sex murder stories, the country learned in 2010 that one of the two victims of Russell Williams, a colonel in the Armed Forces at the time, was a woman corporal who had been under his charge at CFB Trenton in Ontario. Williams was sentenced to two life terms in jail.[81]

The 2006 General Social Survey found that approximately 34 percent of women and 15 percent of men claim they were victims of sexual assault, and 51 percent of those assaults were done by a friend, acquaintance, or neighbour.[82]

Measures to help women victims include the creation of shelters for battered women, which give victims a place to stay to recuperate from domestic violence, and counselling services that help battered women with self-esteem issues, as well as other psychological trauma brought on by abuse. It is important to help men, women, and families suffering from abuse because damages extend far beyond a bruise. Abuse harms people on three levels: physical, financial, and emotional.[83]

From Classroom to Community } Visiting a Women's Shelter

Jane was in her late 40s when she decided to go back to school. As part of her class work, she volunteered some time in a local battered women's shelter, and she was surprised by how little things had changed since she was younger.

"When I was 22, I left an abusive man and lived with my son in a shelter for about six months. During that time, I learned a lot about the cycle of violence, and traced the roots of my willingness to tolerate this behavior with a counsellor."

For Jane, volunteering at the shelter brought all of those memories back. "Why is it that so many men think it is their right to beat the women in their lives? Why do they need to be so controlling? If girls aren't taught to behave this way, why are men?"

Jane answered phones, filed documents, and served meals from time to time. She was so determined to help these women because of her own experience.

"I escaped this lifestyle and never wish to return. I sure hope that I helped some of those women avoid falling back into abuse. No one deserves this."

WHAT IS THE DIFFERENCE BETWEEN SEX AND GENDER?   179

sex: the biological makeup of a male or female
gender: the personal traits and position in society connected with being a male or female

WHAT ARE THE PERSPECTIVES ON GENDER AND GENDER INEQUALITY?   187

feminist theory: feminists share the belief that equality in work and education should increase, human choice for outcomes should be expanded, gender stratification should be eliminated, and sexual violence should end
functionalism: the separation of gender roles eliminates competition between the sexes and makes family life run smoothly
conflict theory: capitalism and patriarchy are intertwined; as a result, women are locked in a never-ending cycle that makes them submissive and subservient to men
symbolic interactionism: people's definition of gender develops from everyday interactions with others from the same and opposite sex

WHAT POLICIES ARE IN PLACE TO PREVENT SEXUAL HARASSMENT AND DOMESTIC VIOLENCE?   191

campaigns against sexual assault and domestic violence, shelters, and counselling services

get the topic: WHAT IS THE DIFFERENCE BETWEEN SEX AND GENDER?

Theory

FUNCTIONALISM   188

- gender differences help maintain a functioning society
- parents socialize boys and girls to their future roles of fathers and mothers
- boys are taught to be competitive and confident; girls are taught to be nurturing and caring

CONFLICT THEORY   188

- gender roles are beneficial to men, as their role as main breadwinner gives them power and control
- capitalism emphasizes male domination, as women are encouraged to spend money on goods
- Engels: women are the first oppressed group

SYMBOLIC INTERACTIONISM   188

- women select careers based on the types of work that are considered "normal" for women to perform

- certain careers are perceived as "masculine," which drives many capable women away from even attempting to enter these fields
- differences in the career choices of men and women begin early in life
- people "do gender" every day, which creates gender differences and inequality

FEMINIST THEORY   187

- gender affects the experiences and opportunities of men and women
- there is increasing equality in work and education
- there is expanding human choice for outcomes
- feminists are committed to eliminating gender stratification
- male violence against women perpetuates gender inequality in our society

Key Terms

sex is the biological makeup of a male or female. *179*

gender identity is our perception of ourselves as male or female. *179*

patriarchy is a social system in which the father serves as head of the family, and men have authority over women and children. *180*

matriarchy is a social system in which women are the main authority and hold power over men. *180*

sexism is the belief that one sex is superior to the other. *180*

gender roles are society's expectations of how males and females should act and think. *180*

calalai are anatomical females in Bugis society who assume the characteristics of men. *182*

calabai are anatomical males in Bugis society who adhere to some of the responsibilities of women. *182*

bissu are androgynous members of Bugis society who embody the perfect mixture of male and female. *182*

human capital model assumes that men and women bring different natural skills to the workplace. *184*

choice model explains the income gap by analyzing the kinds of jobs women choose. *184*

patriarchy model assumes that we have a male-dominated society that doesn't allow women to hold upper-tier jobs. *184*

glass ceiling is an invisible barrier preventing women from reaching executive-level positions in the workplace. *184*

feminism is the vast collection of social movements and theories about gender differences, proposing social equality for all people. *185*

machismo is overt and exaggerated displays of masculinity. *189*

Sample Test Questions

These multiple-choice questions are similar to those found in the test bank that accompanies this textbook.

1. Gender identity is mostly developed at which stage in life?
   a. Childhood
   b. Middle age
   c. Adolescence
   d. Late adulthood
2. Children are socialized to fit specific
   a. gender roles.
   b. social classes.
   c. gender inequities.
   d. occupational roles.
3. Which of the following is *not* one of M. Gigi Durham's myths about sexuality?
   a. Girls don't choose boys. Boys choose girls, but only sexy ones.
   b. There's only one kind of sexy—slender, curvy, white beauty.
   c. Girls should be satisfied with their current body type.
   d. The younger a girl is, the sexier she is.
4. Which of the following is a major cause of the increase in working mothers?
   a. More educational opportunities for women
   b. Increase in homosexuality
   c. Rising divorce rate
   d. Lack of children
5. According to functionalist analysis, children are socialized in order to
   a. keep men in a dominant position in society.
   b. maintain a society that runs properly.
   c. establish a clear career path.
   d. entertain their parents.

ESSAY

1. How have gender roles in Canada changed and stayed the same since the 1950s?
2. What are the underlying causes of sexism, and will society ever be able to overcome them?
3. How might society be different if traditional gender roles were reversed?
4. Which of the three models explaining inequality in the workplace do you think is the strongest?
5. How effective do you the think the feminist movement has been in championing women's equality?

WHERE TO START YOUR RESEARCH PAPER

To learn about government's role in the status of women in Canada, go to www.swc-cfc.gc.ca/index-eng.html

To read about women in business and government, visit *The Globe and Mail*'s "Women in Power" section; go to www.theglobeandmail.com/news/national/time-to-lead/women-in-power/

For information about December 6, the National Day of Remembrance and Action on Violence against Women in Canada, go to www.swc-cfc.gc.ca/dates/vaw-vff/index-eng.html

For information about ending violence against women worldwide, go to www.un.org/events/women/iwd/2007/

To learn more about Take Back the Night, go to www.takebackthenight.org/

To learn more about Dress for Success, go to www.dressforsuccess.org/

Remember to check www.thethinkspot.ca **for additional information, downloadable flashcards, and other helpful resources.**

ANSWERS: 1. a; 2. a; 3. c; 4. a; 5. b

AGING AND HEALTH

HOW DO HEALTH AND AGING AFFECT
STRATIFICATION?
WHAT THEORIES EXIST ABOUT THE
AGING PROCESS?
HOW DO WE TAKE CARE OF RETIRED
CANADIANS?

"During

my medical school years, a major topic of discussion was the embryonic development of what Canadians now commonly know as Medicare. From 1970 to 1990, universal access to hospital and physician services became a practical reality in Canada. Medical school admissions grew. People sensed that quality of care was increasing and outcomes were improving. This era might be considered the golden age of Medicare. Certainly, during this time, Medicare entered the Canadian pantheon of values, alongside such concepts as hockey and fair play, woven into the fabric of our country. It remains so.

"During the nineties, the cost of care, an important driver in the health system, became an urgent concern. Those responsible for managing health costs saw restricting access to products and services as an easy way to control costs. Thus began what might be called the restructuring era of Medicare.

"More recently, restricting access has had the unintended but adverse effect of reducing the quality of health care. The Canadian public now has a widespread perception that the quality of health care has decreased and continues to decline. This has driven several governmental task forces, the Romanow Commission most notable among them, to seek out the underlying problems and make corrective recommendations for Medicare. One common insight from these commissions is the realization that there is no single, simple legislative solution."[1]

195

The Greying
of Society

CHAPTER 11

Doctor Terrence Montague **takes a critical look at the health-care system in Canada** in the book *Patients First: Closing the Health Care Gap in Canada.*

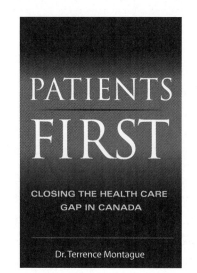

Most of you reading this textbook were born after the introduction of **Medicare** in Canada. Free universal health care is a powerful, almost sacred value in Canadian society. But this system has been in place only since the mid-1960s, and as Dr. Montague describes, it is now under threat because of the enormous financial costs of maintaining it.

After 50 years, anxiety is growing among Canadians about the future of our precious health-care system. The issue consistently tops the polls as a primary political concern for Canadians. For patients, health-care providers, academics, policy-makers, bureaucrats, and politicians alike, fixing Medicare has become an endless challenge.[2] Cracks have started to appear in the form of private clinics, in which individuals pay from their own pocket in order to receive faster care. The next few years will be a real test of our desire and ability to maintain free universal health care for all.

Canada's population is aging, placing even more strain on an already fragile system. This is true not just in Canada, but all over the world. In fact, the world's elderly population is increasing by approximately 800 000 people per month.[3] The rising number of elderly people brings a new dilemma: How do we support and take care of our aging population? What does the growing elderly population mean to society as a whole?

HEALTH is defined as → a state of complete physical, mental, and social well-being and not merely the absence of disease or infirmity

is often studied by using →

Social Epidemiology—the study of the distribution of diseases and health throughout a society's population

can be affected by one's →

- Age
- Gender
- Social Class
- Race

concerns include

New Health-Care Strategies—user fees and a parallel private health-care system are among the new strategies being debated

and

Aging Population—a growing number of seniors will place additional strains on the health-care system

health-care systems in Canada characterized by

Sustainability—a series of economic recessions have made it more difficult to maintain Canada's health care

get the topic: HOW DO HEALTH AND AGING AFFECT STRATIFICATION?

Health Defined

When you are asked about your health, your response is likely to explain how you're feeling physically. However, there's more to health and being "healthy" than whether or not you're battling a cold or nursing a fever. According to the World Health Organization, **health** is "a state of complete physical, mental, and social well-being and not merely the absence of disease or infirmity."[4] In other words, several social factors determine one's health.

SOCIAL EPIDEMIOLOGY

In the 2007 movie *The Bucket List,* Morgan Freeman and Jack Nicholson play two elderly, terminally ill patients who jet off to exotic places to fulfill their lifelong goals. The movie entertains while teaching about patterns of health in the United States. For example, Freeman's character is a lower-middle-class African American man, and Nicholson's character is an upper-class white owner of several hospitals. Nicholson gets the best care possible, while the doctors and nurses often ignore Freeman. Age, gender, social class, and race all have an effect on health care in the United States. Do you think that this is true in Canada as well?

Social epidemiology is the study of the distribution of diseases and health throughout a society's population. Social epidemiologists want to find a link between health and the social environment. How does one's age affect his or her health? Are there health differences between the genders? Are race and social class connected to the treatment a patient receives? These are all questions that social epidemiologists seek to answer.

Age and Health

In Canada—unlike other parts of the world, particularly developing countries—death is rare among the young. The Canadian infant mortality rate

MEDICARE is the term used to describe Canada's government-run health-care insurance program that provides health coverage for all Canadians.

HEALTH is a state of complete physical, mental, and social well-being and not merely the absence of disease or infirmity.

SOCIAL EPIDEMIOLOGY is the study of the distribution of diseases and health throughout a society's population.

is low; only about 5 infants are expected to die per 1000 births. While this may sound very good, there are 35 countries, mostly in Western Europe, but also including Japan and South Korea, with lower rates.[5] For the most part, Canadians are healthy—or at least we think we are. In 2007, 88 percent of Canadians reported their health to be "good" or "very good."[6] However, as people age, they experience more and more serious health problems. Chronic conditions such as arthritis, diabetes, heart disease, lung disease, and mental illness are major problems for older people. These conditions limit their activities, meaning that work, socializing, and exercise are often limited or become impossible to pursue.

Gender and Health

You've probably heard that, on average, men die before women virtually everywhere in the world.[7] In Canada, women are expected to live an average of 83.9 years, while men live only 78.7 years.[8] Sociologists attribute many factors to this trend. For example, young men have higher testosterone levels than young women, which may make them more likely to abuse alcohol and tobacco, drive aggressively, and engage in other life-threatening behaviours. Men often choose riskier types of work, which is also connected to men's decreased life expectancy. Studies show that women are less likely to experience life-threatening illnesses and health problems than men are.[9]

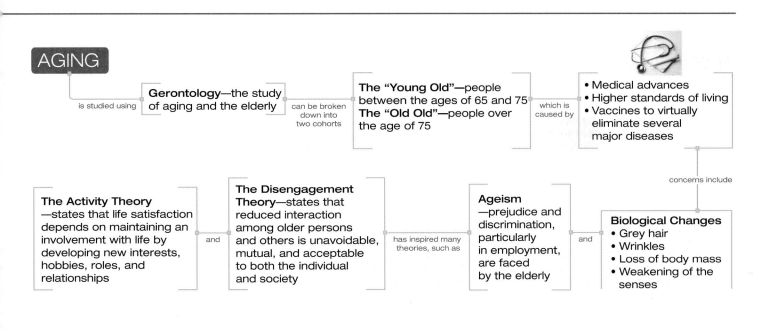

Infant Mortality Rates, by Province and Territory (Both Sexes)

	2003	2004	2005	2006	2007
Canada	5.3	5.3	5.4	5.0	5.1
Newfoundland and Labrador	5.0	5.1	6.2	5.3	7.5
Prince Edward Island	4.9	4.3	2.2	2.1	5.0
Nova Scotia	5.7	4.6	4.0	4.0	3.3
New Brunswick	4.1	4.3	4.1	4.0	4.3
Quebec	4.4	4.6	4.6	5.1	4.5
Ontario	5.3	5.5	5.6	5.0	5.2
Manitoba	8.0	7.0	6.6	6.0	7.3
Saskatchewan	6.3	6.2	8.3	6.1	5.8
Alberta	6.6	5.8	6.8	5.3	6.0
British Columbia	4.2	4.3	4.5	4.1	4.0
Yukon	6.0	11.0	0.0	8.2	8.5
Northwest Territories	5.7	0.0	4.2	10.2	4.1
Nunavut	19.8	16.1	10.0	13.4	15.1

Note: The infant mortality rate is calculated as the number of deaths of children less than one year of age per 1000 live births in the same year.
Source: Adapted from Statistics Canada. Accessed at http://www40.statcan.gc.ca/l01/cst01/health21a-eng.htm.

Men and women differ in their desire for health care. Women are twice as likely to get preventive care and have regular checkups,[10] while men are less likely to discuss health issues with their doctors.[11]

Despite this discrepancy in doctor visits, most past research was centred on middle-class white men. However, recent studies show that some treatments are more effective for different races, like an AIDS drug that was tested in 1991. The study initially said the drug would help everyone, but the studied cohort was mostly gay white men. Further studies indicated that the drug worked better for white men than black men. Feminists also criticize the tendency to think that research conducted on males can be generalized to females. Today, studies are more likely to include women and visible minorities in testing, which could positively impact their health.[12]

Social Determinants of Health

In May 2010, Juha Mikkonen and Dennis Raphael published *Social Determinants of Health: The Canadian Facts*. In this publication, they make the bold statement that "the primary factors that shape the health of Canadians are not medical treatments or lifestyle choices but rather the living conditions they experience. These conditions have come to be known as the social determinants of health."[13]

The authors identified 14 social factors that affect the health of Canadians. These are aboriginal status, gender, disability, housing, early life, income and income distribution, education, race, employment and working conditions, social exclusion, food insecurity, social safety net, health services, and unemployment and job security. How important are these factors? The authors claim that each of these social determinants can have a stronger effect on a person's health than traditional risk factors such as poor diet, lack of physical activity, and even tobacco and excessive alcohol use.

As you can see, health depends on a number of factors that surround individuals, families, and whole societies. Getting to the root cause of an

individual's illness or other health problem requires more than just medical knowledge—it requires a sociological understanding as well.

The following story was included as part of a report titled "Toward a Healthy Future: Second Report on the Health of Canadians." It illustrates the complex set of factors and conditions that determine the health of every Canadian:

> *"Why is Jason in the hospital?*
> Because he has a bad infection in his leg.
> *But why does he have an infection?*
> Because he has a cut on his leg and it got infected.
> *But why does he have a cut on his leg?*
> Because he was playing in the junk yard next to his apartment building and there was some sharp, jagged steel there that he fell on.
> *But why was he playing in a junk yard?*
> Because his neighbourhood is kind of run down. A lot of kids play there and there is no one to supervise them.
> *But why does he live in that neighbourhood?*
> Because his parents can't afford a nicer place to live.
> *But why can't his parents afford a nicer place to live?*
> Because his Dad is unemployed and his Mom is sick.
> *But why is his Dad unemployed?*
> Because he doesn't have much education and he can't find a job.
> *But why . . .?"*[14]

Source: The Federal, Provincial and Territorial Advisory Committee on Population Health, "Toward a Healthy Future: Second Report on the Health of Canadians," www.phac-aspc.gc.ca/ph-sp/report-rapport/toward/pdf/toward_a_healthy_english.PDF, accessed October 12, 2010. This is a copy of an official work that is published by the Government of Canada and the reproduction has not been produced in affiliation with, or with the endorsement of the Government of Canada.

Neighbourhoods

Neighbourhoods in particular can have an effect on health. Neighbourhoods that house poor, poorly educated, unemployed, and single mothers with little government assistance adversely affect the health of the people living there.[15] Similarly, people living in neighbourhoods with high crime and drug use also report poor health.[16] These threatening environments can lead to stress, which can in turn lead to more serious health problems.

This raises the issue of environmental justice. Environmental justice studies the impact of environmental factors on social classes. The poor often live in environmentally dangerous areas[17] that experience regular interaction with toxins, unclean water, and/or air.[18] For example, many of Toronto's poorest residents live near industries that spew high levels of toxic chemicals and pollutants into the air. The low-income families who live in these neighbourhoods already face diminished health from stress, bad nutrition, diabetes, and poor dental care. They are placed at further risk because they breathe air contaminated with pollutants suspected of causing cancer and reproductive disorders.[19]

Aboriginal Health

When Europeans arrived in Canada, they brought with them many foreign diseases that had a devastating effect on the First Nations Peoples. Because of widespread ethnocentrism and overt racism, many aboriginal people were excluded from the health-care system, and at the same time, their traditional medical practices were generally regarded as

Comparison: Poor Neighbourhoods vs. Rich Neighbourhoods

- Image of Crime Infestation and Danger
- Dilapidated Houses
- Dirty, Littered Streets

- Image of Safety and Security
- Immaculate Houses
- Clean Streets

inferior to those of the Europeans. This racism and discrimination has taken its toll on the aboriginal population.

While the life expectancy of all Canadians is a bit over 81 years, an aboriginal man will die about seven years earlier than a non-aboriginal man, and an aboriginal woman will die about five years earlier than a non-aboriginal woman.[20] The infant mortality rate is 1.5 times higher among First Nations Peoples than among Canadians overall.

The prevalence of diabetes in the First Nations population is at least three times the national average, and tuberculosis rates are 8 to 10 times higher than those for the Canadian population. Although aboriginal peoples make up only 5 percent of the total population in Canada, they represent 16 percent of new HIV infections.[21]

Social factors go a long way in explaining this awful situation. Although the Canadian health-care system has been praised as one of the best and most progressive in the world, quality health care is out of reach for many aboriginal Canadians. Jurisdictional disputes, cultural barriers, and geographic isolation have impeded aboriginal peoples' access to the health-care system.[22] People who have low incomes and who live in disadvantaged neighbourhoods are at an increased risk of having health problems. In many aboriginal communities, the living conditions are comparable to those of a developing nation, as measured by the United Nations' Human Development Index.

The Medicalization of North American Society

One way to consider the sociology of health is to look at how health and health care influence people's lives. Talcott Parsons believed that sickness can become a social role.[23] A **sick role** is the expected behaviours and responsibilities appropriate for someone who is ill. For example, part of an ill person's role is to go to the doctor in an attempt to get rid of the illness. Physicians have a primary position in society, allowing them to

∧
∧ Look at these two neighbourhoods.
∧ **How might each one affect the health of its residents?**

> **SICK ROLE** is the expected behaviours and responsibilities appropriate for someone who is ill.
>
> **MEDICALIZATION** is the idea that the medical community is the centre of many aspects of our society.

label sickness and health, which gives them great power over those with whom they come into contact.

This has led to what many consider the **medicalization** of North American society, or the idea that the medical community is the centre of many aspects of our society.[24] North Americans tend to believe that we can find the right pill for anything. I attended a funeral where the widow was quite distraught, saying, "He was my whole life." Her son, a medical professional, gave her an antidepressant. Our society believes that if you take a pill, all will be okay.

One of my favourite books is *The Myth of Mental Illness* by Thomas Szasz.[25] Dr. Szasz suggests that mental illness is not really a disease at all. In fact, the diagnosis of mental illness is often used as a means of social control.[26] Paula Caplan argues that the *Diagnostic and Statistical Manual of Mental Disorders* used for the diagnosis of all mental illness, relies on personal ideology and political manoeuvring.[27] In the course of 10 years, the committee added more than 70 "new" mental illnesses. In fact, according to the DSM, many women are "mentally ill" for one week a month when they menstruate.[28]

North America has many issues associated with the medicalization of our society. Keeping this in mind, let's look in depth at the epidemic of obesity.

Health in Canada: Living Off the Fat of the Land

With free health care, you would think that Canada would be a country of healthy citizens. However, all affluent nations face a host of health concerns, including obesity. Part of the problem is in the foods we eat. Food options in Canada run the gamut from healthy (organic arugula) to unhealthy (bacon cheddar cheeseburgers). Many consumers, including myself, prefer the latter. Shopping for healthier food takes more time, effort, and money. Fast food is convenient and inexpensive, making it hugely popular, despite being unhealthy.

CHILDHOOD OBESITY

Although it's a relatively new phenomenon, Canada is in the grips of what some are calling an obesity epidemic. This is the term that was used in a report called "Healthy Weights for Healthy Kids." Canada now has one of the highest rates of childhood obesity, ranking fifth out of 34 OECD countries. Twenty-six percent of Canadians between 2 and 17 years old are overweight or obese. The numbers are even worse among aboriginal children, where nearly half are either overweight or obese.[29]

A 2006 study determined that the increase in childhood obesity was a direct result of the availability of energy-dense foods and drinks combined with a lack of energy expenditure.[30] That is, children are getting bigger because they are taking in more calories than they are burning. Kids today face many challenges in keeping their weight down that didn't necessarily exist before, including:

- Poor diet—only one-third of Canadian children aged 4–18 consume the number of servings of fruits and vegetables recommended by *Canada's Food Guide*.[31]
- Dual-income and single-parent families create the need for children to eat packaged, prepared meals, which are typically unhealthy. These busy working parents are more likely to rely on takeout to feed their families. A lack of supervision also makes it difficult to monitor how much their children eat.[32]

- Television, computers, and video games are many children's primary modes of entertainment, creating sedentary behaviour. This has led to a decrease in active, outdoor play.[33]

STIGMATIZATION OF THE OBESE

Another consequence of childhood obesity is that overweight children are often targets of scorn and ridicule among their peers. Numerous studies have shown that people hold prejudicial attitudes about the obese. These perceptions can cause discrimination against an obese person. This loss of status could have harmful psychological, economic, and physical consequences.[34]

Sociologists Deborah Carr and Michael Friedman performed a study to determine whether obesity is in fact a stigma. The factor that separates a stigma from a prejudice is the attitude of the group in question toward their treatment. They found that obese individuals believed that other members of society treated them unfairly, which contributed to their poor self-esteem and lack of psychological well-being. Carr and Friedman found that obese professional workers were 2.5 times more likely to report work-related discrimination than their thinner counterparts.[35]

OBESITY AND RACE

We saw above that in Canada, aboriginal children are nearly twice as likely to be obese compared to the overall Canadian average. Research in the United States has also shown that African Americans have a substantially higher rate of obesity than whites. But does this mean certain races are more likely to be obese? We know that race is a social construct and not a biological trait. So what contributes to this statistic? One study by Jason D. Boardman and colleagues found that socioeconomic status plays a major role in the relationship between race and obesity.[36] According to this study, black communities in the United States are almost four times as likely as white communities to have obesity rates greater than 25 percent. However, when comparing black and white communities in more affluent areas, this relative risk drops. So essentially, it would appear that level of affluence, not race, is a determinant of obesity. Among Canadian First Nations children, those who live on a reserve had obesity rates of 55 percent, while those who live off reserve have rates of about 40 percent—quite a bit less.[37] An eight-year-long study on obesity in Canada found that members of the

> **While it is often not the healthiest choice,** why is fast food so popular with so many people?

Is Keeping Kids Safe Hurting Their Health?

We know that unhealthy foods, inactivity, and lack of parental control are contributing factors to childhood obesity, but location also plays a big part in packing on the kilograms. In an article about contributing factors to childhood obesity, Arielle Concilio and colleagues assert that where a child grows up is a crucial factor in the child's health. The article explains that children growing up in poor, urban communities are more likely to suffer from obesity than kids in sub-urban areas. Their reasoning? It's too dangerous for kids to go outside and play.[38]

These kids are growing up in an area where fast food is cheaper than healthy food, and their parents might be working long hours. Add to this the fact that they live in neighbour-hoods where space is tight and the available outdoor areas aren't safe places to play. To stay safe, kids look for indoor activities, which tend to be

more sedentary. Schools may be too poor to afford physical education equipment for students, meaning that students have to find other ways to entertain themselves, and activities at home are equally limited.[39]

>>> **ACTIVITY** Do some research on youth centres where kids can go after school. What kinds of activities are available? Would these activities help or hinder a child with weight issues?

>>> **How can kids get the exercise they need** when it's too dangerous to go outside and play?

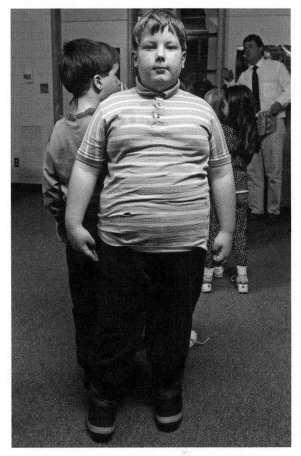

highest-income households were 40 percent less likely than those in the lowest-income households to become obese. Why are the poor more likely to be obese? Part of the reason is the high cost of healthier food options. Unhealthy, inexpensive foods are often necessary for those who cannot afford healthier food options. Also, a lack of education about nutrition can lead people to make uninformed choices about what they eat.

Health Care in Canada

The Canadian health-care system is often (mistakenly) called socialized medicine. In fact, it is a system of *socialized insurance,* and is best described as an interlocking health insurance plan. Each of the ten provinces and three territories has its own system of health insurance. The basics, however, remain the same—universal coverage for health-care services provided on the basis of need, rather than the ability to pay. Known to Canadians as Medicare, the system provides access to universal, comprehensive coverage for medically necessary hospital and physician services.[40]

The system is funded through income tax—all citizens contribute according to their income rather than the benefits they expect to derive. Public health-care insurance in Canada is based on the principle of transferring resources from the richer to the poorer and pooling the risks among the healthy and the less healthy. Another advantage to this kind of system is that it costs less. Public insurance eliminates the cost of marketing and selling private health-care insurance policies and evaluating insurance risks. This is one of the reasons why the Canadian health-care

system costs less to administer than the privately funded U.S. system.[41] For these reasons, Canadians have favoured public health-care insurance over private insurance since 1966, the year of the first *Medical Care Act.* This does not mean, though, that the private sector is totally absent from health-care in Canada. Private health-care insurance exists, but it is limited to providing additional coverage for health services that are not insured by the public plan, or that are only partially insured by it.[42]

The fundamental ideology behind the Canadian health-care system is the principle of economic and social equity. In addition, there are five other specific principles that define the Canadian health-care system:

- *Public administration:* each province administers a health insurance plan on a non-profit basis by a public authority, which is accountable to the provincial government.
- *Comprehensiveness:* the health-care insurance plan of a province must insure all services that are "medically necessary." Each provincial government defines what these are, so the range of insured services may vary among provinces.
- *Universality:* all residents must have access to public health-care insurance and insured services on equal terms and conditions.
- *Portability:* citizens are still insured even if they are temporarily absent from their province of residence or from Canada.
- *Accessibility:* everyone must have reasonable and uniform access to insured health services, free of financial or other barriers. No one may be discriminated against on the basis of such factors as income, age, and health status.[43]

HEALTH CARE—AN INTERNATIONAL COMPARISON

Health care in the United States operates under a very different system than ours in Canada. Health-care insurance is provided almost entirely by the private sector. Because the costs are very high, large numbers of Americans have no medical insurance. If they need to see a doctor, they have to pay out of their own pocket. According to the American Medical Association, people without health insurance "tend to live sicker and die younger than people with health insurance."[44] With the high numbers of uninsured persons in the United States, this trend is true for a lot of the nation's population, and many question the fairness of the U.S. system.

In 2000, the World Health Organization (WHO) released a report that identified five characteristics that a good and fair health system should have. According to WHO, a good and fair health system has:

- overall good health (low infant mortality rates and high life expectancy)
- a fair distribution of good health (low infant mortality and high life expectancy across the entire population)
- a high level of overall responsiveness
- a fair distribution of responsiveness
- a fair distribution of financing health care (the health-care costs are evenly distributed based on a person's ability to pay).[45]

After creating a list of criteria, **WHO compared the health systems of 191 of the world's countries. The United States was first in overall responsiveness,** meaning that its health-care system does an excellent job in responding to the desires of consumers. **However, other variables present a different story.**

The world map below shows the per-capita costs, life expectancy, and infant mortality of selected countries around the globe. Those selected are nations similar to Canada and the United States in that they are wealthy, industrialized, capitalist democracies.

The U.S. health-care system ranks rather low compared to other wealthy democracies around the world. The United States is the only one of these countries that doesn't provide some form of universal government health care. So, it scores lower than other wealthy countries in fairness in financing and people's satisfaction with the health-care system. The United States ranks 37th, leaving many policymakers wondering what can be done to improve the system.[46] One possibility could be extending the U.S. Medicare program.

The rising elderly population affects not just health-care, but also society as a whole. With people living longer than ever, we have to understand the aging process and figure out what impact aging has on the individual.

Aging: The Greying of Canada

The population of Canada is getting older. This trend has been called the "greying" of the population. In 1956, the median age of Canadians was 27.2 years. In 2009, it was 39.5 years, and by 2056, the median age is expected to reach 46.9 years.[47] The number of senior citizens could more than double, outnumbering children for the first time.[48]

A Global Look at Health-Care Systems in 2005

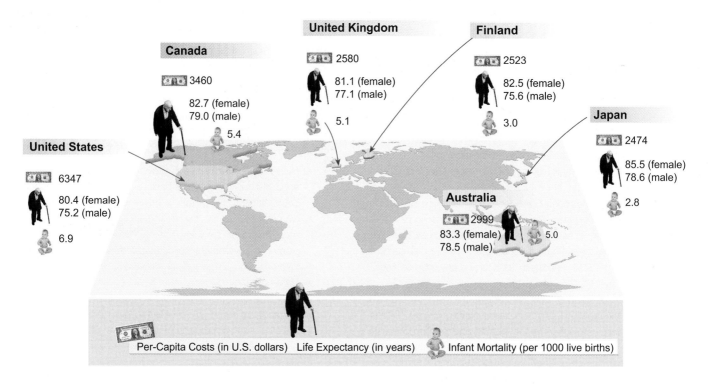

Canada — 3460 — 82.7 (female) / 79.0 (male) — 5.4

United Kingdom — 2580 — 81.1 (female) / 77.1 (male) — 5.1

Finland — 2523 — 82.5 (female) / 75.6 (male) — 3.0

Japan — 2474 — 85.5 (female) / 78.6 (male) — 2.8

United States — 6347 — 80.4 (female) / 75.2 (male) — 6.9

Australia — 2999 — 83.3 (female) / 78.5 (male) — 5.0

Per-Capita Costs (in U.S. dollars)   Life Expectancy (in years)   Infant Mortality (per 1000 live births)

Source: Data based on Health Statistics under Health from OECD.Stat Extracts. Accessed at http://stats.oecd.org.

Canada's Aging Population—Percentage of Population Aged 65 Years or Older in Canada, 1956–2006	
1956	7.7%
1966	7.7%
1976	8.7%
1986	10.7%
1996	12.2%
2006	13.7%

Source: Adapted from Statistics Canada, 2006 Census: Portrait of the Canadian Population in 2006, by Age and Sex: Provincial/Territorial populations by age and sex, 2006 Analysis series, 97-551-XWE2006001, July 2007; http://www.statcan.gc.ca/bsolc/olc-cel/olc-cel?catno=97-551-XWE2006001&lang=eng#olcinfopanel

AGING AND DEMOGRAPHIC CHANGE IN CANADA

Concerns about the increasing percentage of elderly people in society have drawn the attention of psychologists, medical professionals, and sociologists. The study of aging and the elderly is officially known as **gerontology**. This field of study is critically important to our future.

The elderly have been broken down into two major cohorts: the "young old" and the "old old." The **young old** cohort consists of people between the ages of 65 and 75, while the **old old** refers to those over the age of 75. The "young old" are generally in good health, live alone, and are financially independent. The "old old" tend to have failing health, live with family or in a retirement home, and rely on others for financial support. Approximately 53 percent of the elderly population fall into the "young old" category. However, living past the age of 75 is not uncommon.

Life Expectancy

Medical advances and higher standards of living dramatically increase life expectancy. At the beginning of the twentieth century, the average life expectancy was 47.3 years. In 2009, the average life expectancy in Canada was 81.23 years.[49] The development of vaccines for many infectious diseases, such as measles, diphtheria, and smallpox, virtually eliminated these diseases, allowing many more people to live longer, healthier lives.

Origins of the Baby Boomers

After the Second World War, social and economic restraints that were keeping couples from starting families were removed, leading to a "boom" in childbirths. Men who served in the war returned home, married, and started families. Generally, wages were high enough to support a family, so women stayed home and raised children. A period of economic prosperity also contributed to the "baby boom" that lasted from about 1946 until 1964. Between 1940 and 1965 the annual number of births in Canada rose from 253 000 in 1940 to 419 000 in 1965. Over this period of 25 years, the baby boom produced about 1.5 million more births than would otherwise have occurred. By 1965, the boom was fading, as people married at a later age and waited longer to have children.[50]

The decline in female fertility was the main factor that contributed to the end of the baby boom. Women who married after the war ended in 1945 were typically in their twenties, giving them approximately 20 more years of fertility. The introduction of the birth control pill in 1960 also contributed to the slowing birth rate, as it became the most widely used contraceptive method.[51]

The "Sandwiched" Generation

The baby boomer generation is unique in that it is the first **"sandwiched" generation**—it takes care of its children and its elderly parents. Most future generations will probably also be sandwiched between their children and their parents because of longer lives and delays in childbearing. This can keep families closer together. The elderly can help their adult

<<< With advances in medical technology and new vaccines popping up every day, **the life expectancy of these children could lengthen considerably in the future.**

The Elderly in Japan

We often see the elderly as weak or bothersome if they need to rely on others for help. We live in a culture that values youth and self-sufficiency to the point that many of us fear growing old and losing our independence.

However, in countries like Japan, the elderly are revered because age is associated with wisdom. Respect for the Aged Day, celebrated on September 15, has been an annual holiday in Japan since 1966. Three-generation homes, common in Japan, encourage respect for the elderly by making children feel more connected to their grandparents.[52]

With 21 percent of the population over the age of 65, Japan is the oldest society in the world. The elderly are expected to account for 40 percent of the population by 2050.[53] As in Canada, in Japan the birth rate is going down and life expectancy is going up. But three-generation homes are becoming less common as more elderly people live independently. At the same time, suicide rates among the elderly are soaring in Japan.[54]

Aside from depression, worries about finances and health care have been cited as the main causes of suicide among Japan's elderly. With less family support, elderly people are isolated and have to rely on their own incomes or pensions. Japan's declining economy and growing elderly population have made it difficult to supply them with affordable health care. Perhaps the Japanese elderly are having more of a difficult time adjusting to changes because they were raised in a culture that revered the elderly as beacons of wisdom.[55]

>>> ACTIVITY How do the changes in Japan reflect the trends in aging on an international level? Are similar trends appearing in Canada and other developed countries?

∧
∧ In what ways **could the decline of the three-generation home in Japan be**
∧ **detrimental to the elderly population?**

children in times of crisis by watching grandchildren, providing temporary housing, giving loans, and offering advice to their adult children.[56] This allows the elderly to stay involved in family life and increases overall life satisfaction.

Gender and Aging: Where Are the Men?

If studies were done about the gender differences between elderly Japanese men and women, the focus would probably concentrate on Japanese women. According to sociologists John Knodel and Mary Beth Ofstedal, concerns about gender inequality have taken too much precedence, and the situation of elderly men is not being considered.[57] The Second World Assembly on Aging produced a report called the "Madrid International Plan of Action" that is almost solely concerned with the situation of aging women. Knodel and Ofstedal were taken aback by the assembly's lack of "willingness to acknowledge that the relationship between gender and aging varies across settings and over time."[58] Although it is a noble goal to promote gender equality and empowerment of women, a one-sided view of the situation fails to actually promote gender equality. Knodel and Ofstedal suggest that research should also examine the "experiences of older men and women within the contexts in which they live."[59]

Data from the Philippines, Singapore, Taiwan, Thailand, and Vietnam suggest a relative equality of satisfaction with income for elderly men and women. Vietnam has the greatest disparity, with 52 percent of elderly men satisfied with their income, compared to 40 percent of elderly women. Thailand actually has a higher percentage of elderly women who are satisfied with their income than men, with 74 percent and 68 percent, respectively. Developing countries such as these are home to a large portion of the elderly population and provide useful data about the relative situation of elderly men and women.[60]

The study's authors feel that gender should not be placed above all other markers of disadvantage in old age. A more balanced approach that addresses the disadvantages of both elderly men and women would be better suited to aid current and future generations of the elderly.

CONCERNS ABOUT AGING

Biological Changes

Everyone knows that as you age, certain biological changes take place. Grey hair, wrinkles, and loss of body mass are all physical signs of aging. As you age, your senses also decline. Your senses of vision, hearing, taste, touch, and smell all become weaker. In fact, in 2006, more than 17 percent of people over the age of 65 reported that their vision was failing, while 11.4 percent reported having trouble hearing.[61] These percentages were higher than those for persons in any other age group.

Many people in our society associate aging with being weaker and less capable of doing normal, everyday activities. It's sentiments like these that can lead to prejudices and discrimination toward the elderly.

Ageism

Steve Richardson has worked as a contractor for Dynamic Solutions since the age of 25. Now that Steve is approaching his 65th birthday, his younger supervisor is pressuring him to retire. The company is offering him good retirement benefits, but he feels that they are attempting to gently push him out the door. However, Steve's work is an essential part of his life, and he has no desire to retire now. Dynamic Solutions views Steve as an outdated employee, who served his purpose when he was younger, but is of no use anymore. Although Steve Richardson and

Dynamic Solutions don't actually exist, situations like this happen every day in Canada. With an aging population and workforce, the new concern of ageism has come into play. **Ageism** is prejudice and discrimination based solely on age.

The workplace is the main forum for ageism. Employers seek workers who are energetic and willing to work for a long duration. If an employer feels that someone is too old, the employer may be thinking that the prospective employee is going to be too slow on the job and is more likely to quit because he or she does not really need the job. It is technically illegal to discriminate in hiring on the basis of age, but many elderly people have difficulty finding new employment or find themselves being asked to leave their jobs.

Television and film are major sources of ageism, as entertainment tends to focus on the young and attractive. The elderly are typically shown as senile and frail or are just ignored. Aging movie stars, particularly women, have voiced their discontent at not getting roles. Aging actresses must deal with what is known as "double jeopardy," or the two factors that contribute to the downfall of their career: gender and age.[62]

Generally, in film and television women have been on relatively equal footing with men, both in employment and compensation. However, the entertainment industry values physical attractiveness first and foremost, and seems to have little or no place for older, less attractive females. When a society values beauty and youth, the elderly are cast aside. This negative perception of growing old can lead to dissatisfaction in old age.

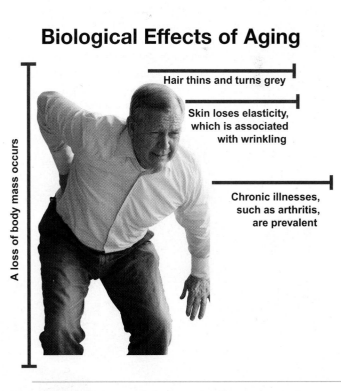

Biological Effects of Aging

A loss of body mass occurs

Hair thins and turns grey

Skin loses elasticity, which is associated with wrinkling

Chronic illnesses, such as arthritis, are prevalent

∧∧∧ Aging brings along with it certain biological changes. **Grey hair, wrinkles, and liver spots are the inevitable physical markers of the aging process.**

think sociologically: WHAT THEORIES EXIST ABOUT THE AGING PROCESS?

Functionalism—Disengaging from Society

What happens to people's social roles as they reach old age? Many functionalists would suggest that elderly people begin to shed their old social roles and begin to take on new roles in society. Their roles as worker or spouse drop off as they retire or become widowed. Functionalists use the disengagement theory to describe the aging process. The **disengagement theory** states that reduced interaction between older persons and others is unavoidable, mutual, and acceptable to both the individual and society.[63]

Society disengages people from important positions as they get older so that the social system does not get disrupted. The disengagement theory suggests that the functions of retirement are to make older people less important in society since they are about to die, which, in turn, makes society function better. The older people move out of the way so that the younger population can take their place.

Social distance is provided between death and daily life. Death disrupts many social functions, and retirement decreases the chances that a vital person will be eliminated. Retirement allows for new generations with new ideas to move society forward. The young are promoted and expensive older workers are let go.

According to Cumming and colleagues, the disengaging process is intrinsic and is desirable for most older people.[64] However, some sociologists would disagree. Some sociologists have found that elderly people who take part in activities such as volunteering are "happiest and have the greatest expressed life satisfaction."[65] Symbolic interactionists, whom we will discuss next, often agree with this idea. Other critics of this theory suggest that elderly people don't often vacate their social roles willingly. Instead, they are often forced out of their positions through an exercise of power, because employers feel they're too old for the job or cannot afford to keep them on.

Symbolic Interactionism—Living an Active Lifestyle

Symbolic interactionists study how factors like environment and relationships with others affect how people experience aging. Sociologist Charles H. Cooley suggested that people develop the "self" through their interactions with others in the social world. This development of self is a lifelong process, so social interactions continue to be important to us as we age. Symbolic interactionists believe that successful aging is a "multifaceted phenomenon that encompasses not only health but also psychological well-being, role integration, and social engagement."[66] In other words, these theorists believe in the **activity theory**, which states that life satisfaction depends on maintaining an involvement with life by developing new interests, hobbies, roles, and relationships.

One way that the elderly population can remain active is through volunteer work. Sociologists Yunqing Li and Kenneth Ferraro suggest that volunteer work is beneficial for social life and gives people the opportunity to remain socially engaged throughout their entire lives.[67] Volunteering can reduce depression among the elderly population and improve life satisfaction. Why does volunteering have such a positive effect? Like any activity that involves helping others, volunteering provides the elderly with a sense of meaning and purpose in life. Interacting with others can also help the elderly cope with bereavement of a spouse or close friend, and helps strengthen their relationships with others.

Conflict Theory—Aging and Inequality

Conflict theorists, unlike functionalists and symbolic interactionists, examine how power and economic forces influence aging in society. Those who accept a conflict perspective of aging might consider a number of issues. First, they note that ageism is no different than any other *ism,* like racism and sexism. By placing a negative stigma on the elderly, society segregates them from others.

If you consider retirement, for example, whose benefit does it serve? A few years ago, the college at which I teach had an early retirement buyout. Faculty members were given a bonus to retire early. Why would an organization do this? Because it was significantly cheaper to hire younger faculty at an entry-level salary than to continue to pay some who had been on campus for 25 to 30 years.

One reason for increased conflict could be changes in the **dependency ratio**. The dependency ratio is the ratio of the youth population (0 to 19 years) and senior population (65 or older) to the working-age population (20 to 64 years). It is expressed as the number of "dependants" for every 100 "workers."[68] As the population ages, the dependency ratio will increase. In 2006, the dependency ratio was 60 dependants per 100 workers, but is projected to rise to 84 dependants for every 100 workers by 2056, as the proportion of seniors increases.

Conflict theorists suggest that age can play an important role in the formation of social policies. As

How might volunteering at a school **help the elderly cope with the aging process?**

the number of seniors increases, this group will have more political power. This will probably result in changes to mandatory retirement policies, health-care funding, and government pensions.

Feminist Theory—Gender Differences in Aging

Feminist theorists point out that aging impacts men and women differently. For example, while older people generally are not well represented in the media, feminist Betty Friedan found that older women are basically "invisible" in the media. Out of a sample of nearly 300 photographs of faces in the magazine *Vogue,* only one depicted a woman who might be over 60 years old.[69] The message is that older women are not important.

We have seen that women live longer than men, but this is a mixed blessing. A woman who is married will most probably become a widow. Older women are also more likely to experience poverty. Part of the reason is that retired people live off their pensions. Because pensions are

DISENGAGEMENT THEORY states that reduced interaction between older persons and others is unavoidable, mutual, and acceptable to both the individual and society.

ACTIVITY THEORY states that life satisfaction depends on maintaining an involvement with life by developing new interests, hobbies, roles, and relationships.

DEPENDENCY RATIO is the ratio of the youth population (0 to 19 years) and senior population (65 or older) to the working-age population (20 to 64 years).

related to the individual's lifetime earnings, and because women are more likely to take time off to care for children, or to work part-time, their pensions are often quite low. The Old Age Security pension given by the federal government was never designed to be the sole source of income in old age. Even the provincial retirement pensions are often very limited. The result is that many older women live at or below the poverty line.[70]

THINK SOCIOLOGICALLY

AIDS Orphans

UNAIDS estimates that around the world, more than 16 million children have lost one or both parents to AIDS. Around 14.8 million of these children live in sub-Saharan Africa. In some countries, the rate of AIDS orphans is staggering. For example, 16 percent of children in Zimbabwe and 12 percent of children in Botswana are orphaned due to AIDS.[71]

Beyond the incredible emotional tragedy of losing one or both parents, these children also face numerous social challenges. The first is a drop in their standard of living. Because of the loss of a principal income-earner, the family's financial situation usually worsens. Children may have to provide financial support to the household by working or begging. They may also have to provide other kinds of care such as doing more household chores, or taking care of younger siblings or the

remaining parent, who is often also infected. The additional pressure to provide financial support plus fewer financial resources often means that orphaned children can no longer go to school.

Children whose parents are infected with HIV or who have died of AIDS are often stigmatized by society. Whether it is true or not, in many cases these children are assumed to be HIV positive themselves. They seldom receive any social support, and even face open discrimination. The extended family is often the only safety net for most orphaned children.

AIDS is a terrible disease that has wreaked havoc among an entire generation of parents in Africa. It has also created millions of AIDS orphans. These children will grow up with much greater hardship, much less education, and incomprehensible suffering. The long-term social impact on these countries is worrying to many governments and organizations.

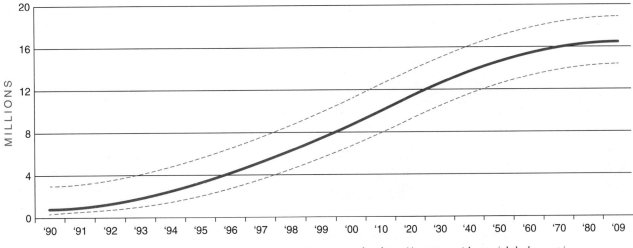

Number of orphans due to AIDS

Source: UNAIDS Report on the Global AIDS Epidemic - 2010. Accessed at http://www.unaids.org/globalreport/

WRAP YOUR MIND AROUND THE THEORY

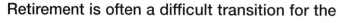

Retirement is often a difficult transition for the elderly, as maintaining a sense of self-worth while not working can present a challenge.

FUNCTIONALISM

Functionalists believe that removing the elderly, whom they consider to be near death anyway, serves society well. Therefore, retirement helps both society and the elderly person disengage from jobs and other social tasks. Functionalist Elaine Cumming has written about the disengagement theory of aging. The sight of elderly people slowing down physically and approaching death disrupts the work ethic of younger people and inhibits society's ability to function. To avoid this, society gradually transfers responsibilities to younger workers, and older workers are phased out of the workplace. The federal and provincial governments provide Canadians with pensions to assist the elderly once they have left the workplace.[72]

CONFLICT THEORY

Because society is stratified by age, middle-aged people have the greatest power and access to social resources. The dependency ratio indicates the number of dependants, both young and old, per working adult. Young people and the elderly are often pushed to the side and run a greater risk of living in poverty. The elderly are perceived as washed-up, incapable workers and are removed from jobs in favour of younger, more capable workers. This type of ageism reminds one of the ideas of Karl Marx, who states that a capitalist society, with a focus on profit, has no place for less-productive workers. As the elderly become less productive, their importance to society diminishes, so they are removed from positions of importance and are largely ignored.

WHY DOES AGE STRATIFICATION EXIST?

SYMBOLIC INTERACTIONISM

The symbolic interactionist perspective on aging focuses on the life satisfaction of the elderly. The activity theory states that the elderly are more likely to have a high degree of life satisfaction if they engage in plenty of activities. When the workplace is no longer an option, it is important to replace the time and effort that was focused on work with something else. A study by Soleman Abu-Bader and colleagues found four core components of life satisfaction in the elderly: physical status, emotional health, social support, and locus of control. Their findings indicated that physical health was the most important indicator of overall life satisfaction in the elderly.[73]

FEMINIST THEORY

The feminist perspective points out that men and women experience aging in different ways, and face different challenges. Betty Friedan found that older women are virtually invisible in the media. Many women end up alone after their husband dies. Because women often accumulated a lower pension during their working lives, if they worked at all, there is a higher risk that they will end up in poverty.

Grey hair and wrinkles— **symbols of wisdom, or weakness?**

Maintaining a high level of activity is crucial to satisfaction at all ages, but particularly **in the elderly.**

discover sociology in action: HOW DO WE TAKE CARE OF RETIRED CANADIANS?

Taking Care of Retired Canadians

Before 1952, when someone in Canada retired, they often either lived off what they had saved over a lifetime of working, or became dependent on their family or others to provide for them. In Chapter 3, you saw that some of the fundamental values of Canadian culture are compassion and generosity. In 1952, the *Old Age Security Act* was passed. This is the first of the "three pillars" of the Canadian retirement system. The OAS is available to most Canadians after they turn 65 years old. Employment history is not a factor, and the applicant does not even need to be retired. However, this pension is taxable, so if the person has other pensions, or continues to work, he or she may pay back some or all of the OAS. However, if an individual has little or no other retirement income, he or she is eligible for the Guaranteed Income Supplement.[74]

The second pillar of the system is the Canada Pension Plan/Quebec Pension Plan (CPP/QPP). In 1966, Parliament passed legislation creating the Canada Pension Plan, a national social insurance plan funded by the contributions of employers, employees, and the self-employed. The CPP operates in all provinces and territories except Quebec, which established its own Quebec Pension Plan. The CPP/QPP was designed to provide workers and their families with a modest pension upon retirement. Payments are based on how much an individual contributed over his or her lifetime of working.[75]

The third pillar consists of private pensions and savings. This includes company pensions and Registered Retirement Savings Plans (RRSPs).

The government pension system is a pay-as-you-go system. This means that the present retirees are being paid from future contributions of later generations. We have seen that Canada's population is aging. This means that there will be an increasing number of retirees, and therefore more people receiving government pensions. As early as the 1990s, people began to worry about the sustainability of the Canadian pension system. It was calculated that if no changes were made, working Canadians in 2030 will need to contribute nearly twice as much as those currently working in order to sustain the system. In 1998, changes were introduced to the CPP which increased contributions modestly. By planning and making changes now, the CPP can remain operational for future generations.[76]

ACTIVITIES

1. Visit a nursing home or retirement centre. Talk with a few residents about aging, and listen to their perceptions about how it influences them.
2. Does your college practise ageism? Do you offer discount tuition and other offers to senior citizens who want to enrol?
3. Do you think universal health care is a right or a privilege? If you think health care is a right, then what do you think must be done to provide it to those who need it? If you think it is a privilege, then rationalize why paying for it is acceptable.
4. Take a magazine such as *Maclean's* and analyze all the pictures that show people. How many of these pictures show seniors? How many pictures show older women?

From Classroom to Community } Volunteering at a Hospital

Jin did his community learning in a hospital. He thought volunteering in a hospital would be a valuable learning experience. So, Jin welcomed people at the front desk and helped them find their way around the building.

"As I walked the hospital halls, I noticed that the rooms were primarily filled with the elderly and many of them seemed to have long-term problems related to their age.

"One day, I was asked to escort a patient's family up to his room. The patient was in his eighties and his brother, also elderly, needed my help finding his way through the maze that was the hospital. When we got to the room, we discovered that the patient was in cardiac arrest. A nurse ushered us to a waiting room to wait. Sadly, the patient died.

"A doctor walked toward us and informed us the patient had died. Understandably, his brother was really upset, but said something to me that I'll never forget. He said, 'When you're young, you think about dying as something far off. When you get this old, you really know that every day could be the last, and you have to learn to live with it.'"

HOW DO HEALTH AND AGING AFFECT STRATIFICATION? 197

Race, age, social class, and gender affect health; example: people from higher social classes generally have better health

WHAT THEORIES EXIST ABOUT THE AGING PROCESS? 206

functionalism: as people grow older, they reduce their interactions with others—a practice that is unavoidable, mutual, and acceptable to the individual and society
conflict theory: society places a negative stigma on the elderly, which segregates them from others
symbolic interactionism: successful aging encompasses health, psychological well-being, role integration, and social engagement
feminism: men and women experience aging differently, partly because society treats older men and women differently

HOW DO WE TAKE CARE OF RETIRED CANADIANS? 209

first pillar: the Old Age Security pension is given to most Canadians over 65 years old. It is not based on employment earnings, and it is taxable
second pillar: the Canada Pension Plan and Quebec Pension Plan pay a modest pension to working Canadians when they retire. Benefits are based on lifetime earnings contributions
third pillar: company pensions and private savings, such as Registered Retirement Savings Plans, are another source of retirement income for Canadians

get the topic: HOW DO HEALTH AND AGING AFFECT STRATIFICATION?

Theory

FUNCTIONALISM 206

- as people age, they shed old social roles and take on new roles
- seeing the elderly slow down and approach death inhibits society's ability to function at full capacity
- retirement makes older people less important because they are close to death
- new generation moves forward

SYMBOLIC INTERACTIONISM 206

- Cooley suggests that people develop the "self" through interaction
- life improves by developing new activities, hobbies, roles, and relationships
- volunteer work is socially engaging and gives a sense of purpose in life

FEMINIST THEORY 207

- men and women experience aging differently
- older women are almost "invisible" in society
- older women are more likely to be alone and to experience poverty

CONFLICT THEORY 206

- middle-aged people have the most power
- as the elderly become less productive, their importance in society diminishes
- the elderly are not respected and ageism occurs

Key Terms

Medicare is the term used to describe Canada's government-run health-care insurance program that provides health coverage for all Canadians. *196*

health is a state of complete physical, mental, and social well-being and not merely the absence of disease or infirmity. *197*

social epidemiology is the study of the distribution of diseases and health throughout a society's population. *197*

sick role is the expected behaviours and responsibilities appropriate for someone who is ill. *199*

medicalization is the idea that the medical community is the centre of many aspects of our society. *199*

gerontology is the study of aging and the elderly. *203*

young old is a cohort that consists of people between the ages of 65 and 75. *203*

old old is a cohort that consists of people over the age of 75. *203*

"sandwiched" generation is the generation that takes care of both its children and its elderly parents. *203*

ageism is prejudice and discrimination based solely on age. *205*

disengagement theory states that reduced interaction between older persons and others is unavoidable, mutual, and acceptable to both the individual and society. *206*

activity theory states that life satisfaction depends on maintaining an involvement with life by developing new interests, hobbies, roles, and relationships. *206*

dependency ratio is the ratio of the youth population (0 to 19 years) and senior population (65 or older) to the working-age population (20 to 64 years). *206*

Sample Test Questions

These multiple-choice questions are similar to those found in the test bank that accompanies this textbook.

1. According to Juha Mikkonen and Dennis Raphael, which of the following is a primary determinant of health?
   a. Diet
   b. Education
   c. Physical activity
   d. Medical treatments

2. Which of the following is *not* a reason why children are struggling with obesity?
   a. Dual-income homes
   b. Nutritious school lunches
   c. The price of healthy food
   d. The popularity of sedentary activities

3. Obesity is most affected by
   a. race.
   b. gender.
   c. social epidemiology.
   d. socioeconomic status.

4. What was the main factor that contributed to the end of the baby boom?
   a. Women entering the workforce
   b. A period of economic decline
   c. A decline in female fertility
   d. The end of the Second World War

5. Which of the following is a physical characteristic of aging?
   a. Loss of body mass
   b. Heightened senses
   c. A hunched back
   d. Senility

ESSAY

1. How does social class affect health?
2. How can television perpetuate stereotypes about people who are obese?
3. Describe the Canadian health-care insurance system.
4. Why has life expectancy increased?
5. What benefits are available to Canadian seniors?

WHERE TO START YOUR RESEARCH PAPER

To learn more about aging using an interactive map to view demographics from countries around the world, go to www.aarpinternational.org/map

To watch a population pyramid representing Canada's aging population, go to www.statcan.gc.ca/kits-trousses/animat/edu06a_0000-eng.htm

To see the world population clock and more international demographic graphs, go to www.census.gov/ipc/www/idb/worldpopinfo.php

To learn more about health in Canada, go to www.hc-sc.gc.ca/index-eng.php

To learn more about First Nations, and Inuit, health, go to www.hc-sc.gc.ca/fniah-spnia/index-eng.php

To learn more about obesity, and its effects on health, go to www.participaction.com/en-us/TheInactivityCrisis/FactsAndStats.aspx, and www.obesity.org

To learn more about baby boomers and their concerns, go to www.babyboomers.com

Remember to check www.thethinkspot.ca **for additional information, downloadable flashcards, and other helpful resources.**

ANSWERS: 1. b; 2. b; 3. d; 4. c; 5. a

CRIME AND THE LEGAL SYSTEM

"There are

various approaches to understanding youthful offending. These approaches translate, to some extent, into different models of what a youth justice system should look like. Looking at each of these models on its own, in isolation from others, creates something of a caricature of youthful offending. Nevertheless, it is useful as a way of looking at differences.

"In the first place, one can look at offending as a symptom of some kind of underlying problem. This problem could be biological or psychological, or it could be social (e.g., a symptom of inadequacy in child rearing or the impact of poverty). Second, one can see youthful offending as a symptom of an inadequate crime control system (e.g., inadequate numbers of police, inadequate severity of punishments, or inadequate forms of social control in the community). Third, one could look at youthful offending as being a natural consequence of growing up.

"These different 'models' of understanding youthful offending are not simply part of an academic exercise. They suggest quite different approaches for responding to youthful offending. The first model would suggest a focus on the characteristics of individual offenders. If 'offending' is a symptom of a problem, then official responses should focus on the problem, not the symptom. This assumes, of course, that one's goal is 'fixing' the problem. It further assumes that courts, not those responding to youthful offending, both know how to intervene effectively and have adequate available resources.

"If on the other hand, youth crime is seen as the result of an inadequate justice system . . . then the focus of society would be largely on the youth justice system as a 'crime control' system. The underlying justification of a youth justice system would be to stop youth crime. The specific focus would be on the tools available within that system to address this goal.

"Finally, a model that is based on the assumption that youthful offending is, to a large extent, a 'natural' consequence of growing up would have a quite different orientation. Such a system might focus more on responding in a measured way to offending rather than on the traditional utilitarian purposes. If part of what we see as being 'just' in our society is that inappropriate behaviour has consequences, the focus of youth justice would be on ensuring not only that there are consequences, but that these consequences are seen as being appropriate."[1]

213

How Do Societies Respond *to* Crime and Deviance?

Responding to Youth Crime in Canada **by Anthony Doob and Carla Cesaroni** reflects the sociological understanding that the youth justice system is just one of many factors affecting youth criminal behaviour.

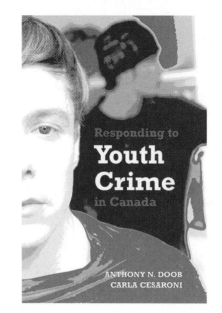

In 2008, the Conservative party campaigned with a promise to "get tough" on young offenders. The Conservative leader, Stephen Harper, said "the proposed changes would make young criminals more accountable and therefore help deter them from a life of crime."[2] Do tougher penalties reduce the level of crime? What are the consequences of crime? What can be done about it? In this chapter, we will investigate these and other questions so you can see how sociologists look at these issues.

get the topic: WHAT IS CRIME?

Deviance vs. Crime

Most prisoners are incarcerated because they've broken a law. But how do we determine which behaviours are criminal? **Deviance** is the violation of norms that a society agrees upon. For example, teens who dye their hair in neon colours would be considered deviant in most parts of society. However, some acts that may be considered socially deviant, like refusing to bathe, for instance, aren't necessarily illegal, no matter how much you might wish they were. For something to be considered a **crime**, it has to be a violation of norms that have been written into law. Driving while impaired by alcohol or a drug is an example of a crime. Sociologists who specialize in **criminology** scientifically study crime, deviance, and social policies that the criminal justice system applies.

Everyday Crime and Deviance

Crime
Stealing a Car
Speeding
Cheating on a Test
Deviance

Crime and the Legal System

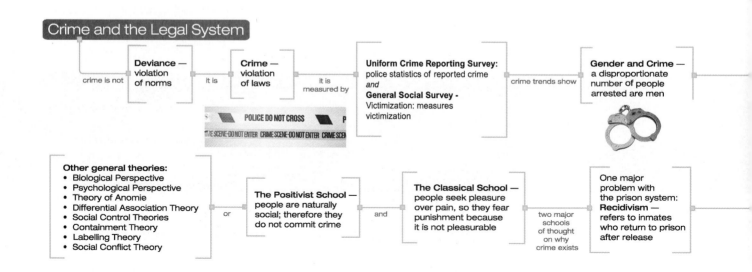

crime is not — **Deviance —** violation of norms

it is — **Crime —** violation of laws

it is measured by — **Uniform Crime Reporting Survey:** police statistics of reported crime *and* **General Social Survey -** Victimization: measures victimization

crime trends show — **Gender and Crime —** a disproportionate number of people arrested are men

POLICE DO NOT CROSS   P
CRIME SCENE-DO NOT ENTER   CRIME SCENE-DO NOT ENTER   CRIME SCE

Other general theories:
- Biological Perspective
- Psychological Perspective
- Theory of Anomie
- Differential Association Theory
- Social Control Theories
- Containment Theory
- Labelling Theory
- Social Conflict Theory

or — **The Positivist School —** people are naturally social; therefore they do not commit crime

and — **The Classical School —** people seek pleasure over pain, so they fear punishment because it is not pleasurable

two major schools of thought on why crime exists

One major problem with the prison system: **Recidivism —** refers to inmates who return to prison after release

WHAT IS DEVIANCE?

If deviance refers to violating socially agreed upon norms, then how do we determine what is and what isn't considered deviant? There are four specific characteristics that sociologists use to define deviance:

1 **Deviance is linked to time.** History changes the definition of deviance, so what is considered deviant today may not be deviant tomorrow. One hundred years ago, it was considered deviant for women to wear trousers. Today, it's normal for women to dress in trousers.

2 **Deviance is linked to cultural values.** How we label an issue determines our moral point of view. Cultural values come from religious, political, economic, or philosophical principles. For example, in Holland, active euthanasia for the terminally ill, or "mercy killing," is legal within some circumstances. In Canada, euthanasia is considered murder and is punished accordingly. Each culture defines euthanasia differently.

> **DEVIANCE** is the violation of norms that a society agrees upon.
>
> **CRIME** is the violation of norms that have been written into law.
>
> **CRIMINOLOGY** is the scientific study of crime, deviance, and social policies that the criminal justice system applies.
>
> **STREET CRIME** refers to many different types of criminal acts which occur in public places, such as burglary, drug dealing, and pick-pocketing.

3 **Deviance is a cultural universal.** You can find deviants in every culture on the planet. Regardless of what norms a society establishes, you can always find a small number of nonconformists who will break those rules.

4 **Deviance is a social construct.** Each society views actions differently. If society tolerates a behaviour, it is no longer deviant. For example, Prohibition in the 1920s and early '30s made drinking alcohol illegal in many parts of Canada, but today it's commonplace.

MAKE CONNECTIONS

Crime and Media

Real-world police work is nothing like television crime solving. Most real-world crime involves public disturbances or missing property, but most news reports are about gang shootings or drug busts. The primetime shows don't exactly help either. Marcus Felson uses the phrase "the dramatic fallacy of crime" to describe how the media, both in news coverage and entertainment shows, paint an unreal picture of the reality of crime.[3]

Most officers never shoot their guns. They spend the majority of their time doing tedious tasks such as "driving around a lot, asking people to quiet down, hearing complaints about barking dogs, filling out paperwork, meeting with other police officers, and waiting to be called up in court."[4]

Most crime is actually rather boring and petty, like a teenager getting drunk and stealing money to buy more alcohol. Since that's not much of a story to broadcast, the media producers prefer something more sensational.

>>> **ACTIVITY** Spend two or three nights watching a variety of police shows and local newscasts. Record the types of crimes being described in each type of show. What differences do you see?

Street Crime

Although there are many different types of crime, when most people talk about "crime," they're likely talking about **street crime**, which refers to types of criminal acts which occur in public places, such as burglary, drug dealing, and pick-pocketing. Street crime has been the focus of most criminological research, but you may wonder how much street crime actually exists. The next section will discuss street crime and how it is measured.

CRIME STATISTICS

After spending an hour watching a show like *CSI*, you'd think the police are able to solve crimes like they do on TV. Unfortunately, real life isn't as convenient as television. For example, when someone stole my wife's bicycle right out of our garage, I asked the police officer when we might get it back. She said, "Probably never. These kinds of crimes are difficult to solve."

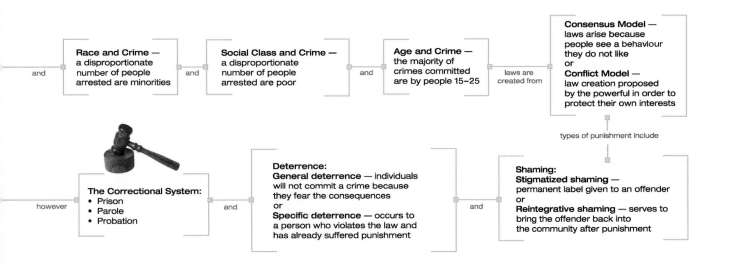

The Uniform Crime Reporting Survey and the General Social Survey—Victimization

Another aspect of detective work often omitted from television is the paperwork that officers must file. The information in those files is vital to understand crime statistics. Criminologists use two primary sources of data to measure the amount of crime: the UCR Survey and the General Social Survey—Victimization. Statistics Canada creates the **Uniform Crime Reporting (UCR) Survey** using the official police statistics of reported crimes. Statistics Canada's **General Social Survey (GSS)—Victimization** measures crime victimization by contacting a representative sample of nearly 20 000 Canadians over 15 years old.

UCR surveys contain data only on reported crimes, so when a bicycle is reported as stolen, it becomes a UCR Survey statistic. These data are used to calculate the **crime rate**.[5] In this calculation, all offences are counted equally—for example, one incident of murder equals one incident of bicycle theft. The crime rate is expressed as number of crimes per 100 000 population.[6] Since 2009, another measure has also been produced by Statistics Canada. The **Crime Severity Index** assigns a weight to each type of crime. More serious crimes are given a higher weight.[7]

Criminologists understand that many crimes go unreported, so they also refer to the GSS—Victimization statistics. Victimization data always indicate more crime than UCR Survey data. In 2004, only about 34 percent of criminal incidents were reported to police.[8] This supports the criminologist's general estimation that more than half the crimes that are committed go unreported.

CRIME TRENDS

UCR Survey and victimization data are also used to determine crime trends—and the trend that seems most constant is that the crime rates change over time. The majority of crime in Canada is property crime. In 2009, property crimes made up 56 percent of all reported crimes, whereas violent crimes constituted about 18 percent.[9] These trends are in stark contrast to the media's portrayal of crime.

Gender and Crime

Throughout history, men have traditionally committed more crime than women. This demographic characteristic of offenders in Canada has not changed much over time. In 2008, men were considered the accused in 81 percent of cases of violent victimization against women, and in 79 percent of cases of violent victimization against men.[10] This is a significant statistic because men make up less than 50 percent of the population. However, several other factors also figure in crime trends.

Ethnicity and Crime

Although the gender differences in crime statistics are fairly easy to distinguish, discussing a link between ethnicity and crime is controversial. The major problem is the long history of racism in Canada. In 2008, aboriginal adults accounted for 22 percent of new prisoners while representing just 3 percent of the Canadian population.[11] Does this disproportionate representation suggest aboriginals commit more crimes, or does the criminal justice system unfairly pursue them?

Some argue that the police's different enforcement practices are responsible for these data. Racial profiling is a controversial police practice of targeting criminals based on their race or ethnicity. David Cole shows that traffic police disproportionately stop members of visible minorities.[12] Jeffrey Reiman suggests that the police seek out the poor for arrest because the poor are easier to catch and easier to convict of crimes.[13] Wealthy people can hire expensive lawyers; poor people must use the public defender system. This increases the odds that official statistics have an inherent ethnic bias because visible minorities disproportionately represent the poor in Canada.

Social Class and Crime

Although crime rates are higher in poorer neighbourhoods, that doesn't necessarily mean people in lower classes actually commit more crime. This makes data on the link between social class and crime difficult to interpret. A number of studies have shown that poorer people are arrested at higher rates,[14] but that doesn't mean everyone who lives in poor neighbourhoods breaks the law or is more likely to break the law.[15]

Reiman believes that social class makes a huge difference in who gets caught and who goes to prison. He argues that laws are applied differently and that dangerous activities performed by the "elite" are not even considered crimes.

For example, doctors who accidentally kill a patient during an unnecessary surgery are not accused of manslaughter. Similarly, Reiman suggests that white-collar crimes often are not reported because people want to avoid a scandal.

Age and Crime

Essentially, crime is a young person's game. This idea is supported by the relationship between age and crime. It indicates that the majority of arrests peak between the ages of 15 and 25. After that point, they follow a slow but steady decrease throughout life.[16] Arrest data from other cultures and times in history also support this claim.[17]

The link between age and crime is very clear in criminology. Since the early 1970s, declining Canadian fertility rates have resulted in a drop in the proportion of young people aged 15 to 24. A Statistics Canada study found that this demographic shift may be associated with a decline in rates of breaking and entering.[18] Clearly, age matters when discussing crime.

International Comparisons of Crime

To gain a better perspective on crime in Canada, sociologists often make international comparisons. However, making international comparisons of crime data creates certain problems for the researcher. Here is a list of potentially complicating factors:

1. Crime numbers may or may not be accurate. Some countries deliberately skew their data to show lower crime rates in order to keep tourism high.
2. Legal definitions of crimes differ among nations. For example, some nations do not recognize marital rape as a crime; others have legalized drugs that are illegal in Canada.
3. Different methods of collecting data can result in differences in reported crimes. Some nations have extraordinarily reliable data collection systems, while others do not.
4. Cultures vary, as do programs to prevent, punish, and curb crime.

Number One with a Bullet

Why does the United States have the highest murder rate in the industrialized world? Some blame easy access to guns, and others claim it's their violent history as a nation. Still others argue that it is the level of inequality in that country. Whatever the reasons, one thing is clear: U.S. citizens are three times more likely to be murdered compared to people in other developed nations.[19]

However, the graph below presents a somewhat different picture of violence with regard to international rates of rape and robbery. The countries selected are similar to the United States and give you a quick way to compare crime in the United States to that of other countries. As you can see from these data, England leads these nations in robbery, and Canada has the highest rate of rape. Japan stands out among these countries because of its very low rates of violent crime.

Property crimes present a different picture. The graph below provides data on four nonviolent crimes: theft, motor vehicle theft, drug offences, and burglary. Generally speaking, occurrences of theft are higher in other industrialized nations than in Canada.

These data leave a mixed picture for the international comparison of crime. Living in the United States increases the odds that one might be murdered, but it also decreases the chance of being a victim of most property crimes.[20]

Comparing international crime rates shows that crime is common to all industrial societies. Some suggest this occurs because industrial societies have more high-value, lightweight items—such as smartphones or laptops—that are easily stolen and sold.[21]

International Violent Crime Rates

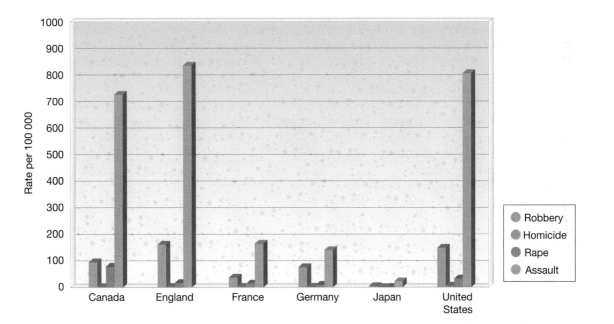

International Nonviolent Crime Rates

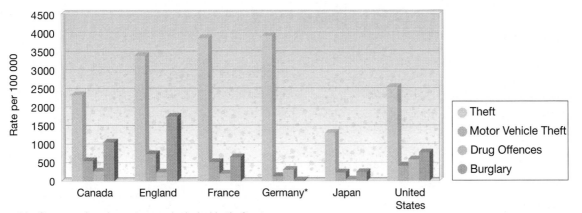

* In Germany, burglary rates are included in theft rates.

Source: *Criminal Victimisation in Seventeen Industrialized Countries: Key-findings from the 2000 International Crime Victims Survey*, Kesteren et al., 2000.

CONSENSUS MODEL OF LAW suggests that laws arise because people see a behaviour they do not like, and they agree to make it illegal.

CONFLICT MODEL OF LAW proposes that powerful people write laws to protect their own interests while punishing the actions of those they wish to control.

SHAMING is a deliberate effort to attach a negative meaning to a behaviour.

STIGMATIZED SHAME is a permanent label given to an offender, which could actually increase the chances of reoffending because the guilty person is forever labelled.

REINTEGRATIVE SHAMING is an effort to bring an offender back into the community after punishment.

SOCIETAL RESPONSES TO CRIME AND DEVIANCE

Why are certain things illegal and not others? There are two primary models as to how laws are created: the consensus and conflict models. The **consensus model of law** suggests that laws arise because people see a behaviour they do not like, and they agree to make it illegal. For example, virtually everyone thinks child abuse is wrong. Laws against it arise out of a general agreement about the treatment of children.

The **conflict model of law** proposes that powerful people write laws to protect their own interests while punishing the actions of those they wish to control. For example, laws prohibiting vagrancy, loitering, trespassing, and theft are designed primarily to protect the wealthy from attacks by the poor.

Punishment

All societies must deal with rule breakers. Historically, punishments were often harsh and included physical torture, exile, forced slavery, or death. Alternative punishments included shaming an offender by placing him in the pillory and stocks in the town square.

Shaming is a deliberate effort to attach a negative meaning to a behaviour. John Braithwaite suggests shame can either stigmatize or reintegrate.[22] **Stigmatized shame** is a permanent label given to an offender, which could actually increase the chances of reoffending because the guilty person is forever labelled. In Canada, we stigmatize former inmates when we require them to admit their prior convictions on job applications and housing forms. **Reintegrative shaming** serves to bring the offender back into the community after punishment.

In Canada, being sent to prison is the most severe form of punishment. Probation, community service, and fines are other forms of punishment that are often used. The principles underlying the punishment of criminals have changed over time. These changes reflect how criminals are viewed

> Who do you think posted this sign? Whom is it meant to keep out?

by society, and changes in what people think are the causes of crime and criminal behaviour. There are five goals of punishment:

Retribution reflects the belief that someone who commits a crime is responsible for their actions, and deserves to be punished. The expression "an eye for an eye" is an example of the retribution goal of punishment.

Incapacitation usually means sending an offender to prison. Society needs to protect its law-abiding members from criminal behaviour. One way to do this is to incapacitate offenders so that they are unable to commit further crimes. When offenders are sent to prison, being locked up, away from the general public, serves to incapacitate them. They are no longer a threat as long as they are behind bars.

Deterrence tries to prevent a person from doing something because of fear of the consequences. **General deterrence** ensures individuals will not commit a crime because they see the negative consequences applied to others, and they fear experiencing these consequences. Prison is a general deterrent for many people. **Specific deterrence** occurs to individuals who have violated the law and have already been punished. When we send an offender to prison, we hope he or she will be specifically deterred from committing future offences because of the fear of returning to prison.

Rehabilitation tries to reform offenders so that they can be returned to society, but will no longer choose to engage in criminal behaviour. Prison programs that include counselling or vocational training reflect the rehabilitation goal of punishment.

Restoration attempts to make the victim, and the community, whole again. In Canada, victim impact statements are used to give victims a voice in the criminal justice process. It allows them to participate in the sentencing of an offender by explaining to the court, and the offender, how the crime has affected them.[25]

PRISON AND THE CHARACTERISTICS OF PRISON INMATES

Prison is a last resort in the criminal justice system. The guilty party is locked in a facility for a period of time depending on the crime. In 2009, on any given day, over 37 000 adults and nearly 2000 youth aged 12 to 17 were in custody in Canada. This resulted in an incarceration rate of 117 people in custody for every 100 000 people.[26] However, the rate is much higher for some groups. Aboriginals represent 18 percent of all those in custody. In all the Canadian provinces and territories, the proportion of aboriginal adults in correctional services exceeds their representation in the general population. The overall incarceration rate is highest for adults aged 25 to 34 years old. Females account for only 11 percent of the total population in custody, but this proportion has been increasing in the last ten years.[27]

RETRIBUTION is based on the belief that offenders should be punished.

INCAPACITATION means preventing the offender from causing further harm.

DETERRENCE is a measure that prevents a person from doing something because of fear of the consequences.

GENERAL DETERRENCE is a measure that ensures individuals will not commit a crime because they see the negative consequences applied to others, and they fear experiencing these consequences.

SPECIFIC DETERRENCE is a measure that changes the attitude of individuals who have already violated the law and have been punished, by causing them never to commit crime again.

REHABILITATION tries to reform the offender so that he or she can be returned to society.

RESTORATION uses impact statements so that victims can participate in the sentencing process.

RECIDIVISM is the tendency for inmates released from prison to return to prison.

Since most inmates are eventually released from prison, what will happen to them? Unfortunately, the most likely outcome for inmates released from prison is to return to prison. This is called **recidivism**. If a return to prison is a failure of the prison system, then clearly the system is failing—37 percent of all inmates will return to prison.[28]

Costs of Incarceration

The actual costs to incarcerate an individual are difficult to determine. Although a dollar amount can be calculated, there are hidden costs associated with the incarcerated—the children left behind in the foster-care system, or families who must use the welfare system to survive. These social costs can't be factored in the prison budget, so the reported cost of incarceration never includes them. Nevertheless, taxpayers are left to pay for all the direct and indirect costs. A Statistics Canada report estimated the average daily cost to be $143.03 per prisoner[29]; this amounts to more than $52 000 per year.

Canadian Incarceration Rates vs. International Incarceration Rates

Canada's incarceration rate has tended to be higher than rates in most Western European countries, yet lower than that of the United States.[30] The United States has the highest incarceration rate in the world. Policies like the three-strikes law have contributed to the United States' much higher incarceration rate in comparison to similar countries' rates.

THINK SOCIOLOGICALLY

Reintegrative Justice

Criminal justice programs throughout the world are experimenting with new or traditional ideas of justice. In New Zealand, police officers use family conferencing with young offenders and their parents instead of juvenile detention. The goal is to heal the problems in the family and avoid labelling the teen. Teens return to the community as teens who have made a mistake, and not young offenders.[23]

In Canada, aboriginal justice is based on the concept of restoring peace in communities through compensation, restitution, rehabil-itation, reconciliation, and balance. While all Canadians are subject to the *Criminal Code of Canada* and the Canadian legal system, some First Nations communities have adopted a process called *sentencing circles*. A sentencing circle is composed of fellow community members, the victim, and often the offender. The circle will make sentencing recommendations, and in many cases the trial judge will accept these recommendations. Through this process, the entire community can be involved and is given the chance to contribute to the rehabilitation of the offender and the healing of the community as a whole.[24]

Crime Severity Index, 2009

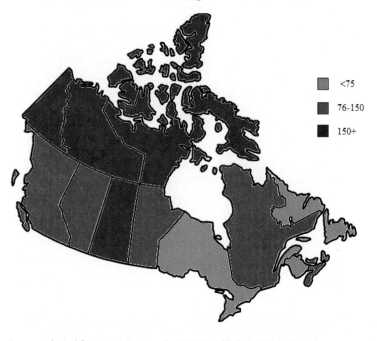

<75

76-150

150+

Source: Adapted from Statistics Canada, CANSIM table 252-0052 and Catalogue no. 85-002-X. Last modified: 2010-07-29. www40.statcan.ca/l01/cst01/legal51a-eng.htm.

International Incarceration Rates

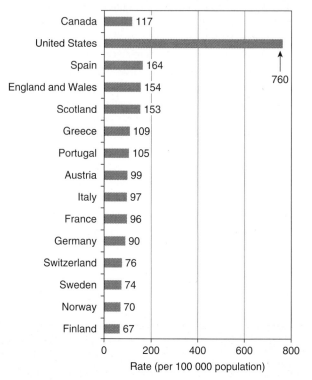

Rate (per 100 000 population)

Source: Statistics Canada, "Adult and Youth Correctional Services: Key Indicators," *The Daily*. References to incarceration rates from countries other than Canada are based on data from World Prison Brief, prepared by the International Centre for Prison Studies, King's College London. The rate for Canada is based on data for the fiscal year 2008/2009, and the rate for the United States is based on the calendar year 2008 and excludes youth. The data for other countries are based on the most recent data published by World Prison Brief, and reference years range from between 2008 and 2009. These rates are based on each country's total population and include, with the exception of the United States, the total number of adults and youth in custody. In Canada, a youth is considered to be aged between 12 and 17. The definition of youth may vary from one country to another. www.statcan.gc.ca/daily-quotidien/091208/dq091208a-eng.htm, accessed October 23, 2010.

In fact, the United States incarcerates at a rate six times higher than Canada and ten times higher than Switzerland. It's important to remember that, just as with crime rates, you should use caution when interpreting international data regarding prison populations. Think about what you already know about international crime and murder rates. What factors do you think contribute to the role of the United States as the world's leader in crime and incarceration?

think sociology: WHY DOES CRIME EXIST?

Historical Roots of Deviance and Crime Theories

Most crime theories arise from two philosophical schools of thought: Positivists ask why people commit crimes, and classicists ask what keeps people from committing them.

THE POSITIVIST SCHOOL

Positivists assume that people are naturally social beings and are not prone to act criminally unless some biological, psychological, or social factor is involved. To a positivist, the world is orderly and follows natural laws. And since natural law dictates that everything must have a cause, positivists are interested in what factors cause people to commit crime.

BIOLOGICAL PERSPECTIVES ON CRIME AND DEVIANCE

In the nineteenth century, physician Cesare Lombroso believed that "criminals" could be distinguished by physical characteristics: big ears, protruding jaws, and deep-set eyes.[31] While this idea is clearly preposterous, scientists believe there might be a biological element to crime. The search for biological causes for criminality continues to this day in recent investigations, including the study of hormonal differences between men and women and how they impact criminal behaviour. For example, higher testosterone levels make men more aggressive than women. Could this account for some of the difference between men and women's delinquent behaviours?[32]

Many modern-day positivists continue to seek the biological causes of crime. Some test chemical imbalances in the brain caused by genetic predisposition,[33] low blood sugar,[34] and low levels of serotonin.[35] All of these factors are shown to have connections to criminal behaviour, but the statistical links are often weak. The search for a biological cause for crime is far from complete and often fails to isolate social factors from genetic ones.

THE CLASSICAL SCHOOL

While positivists look for the underlying causes of criminal behaviour, the classical school assumes all people are self-interested by nature. Classical thinkers also suggest that people are rational and make free-will choices of how to behave. Their primary question asks what keeps us from being criminal.

The classical school emphasizes that individuals make rational choices based on pleasure/pain calculations. To a classicist, the reason why most people do not commit crime is because they fear being punished. So, if the goal of the criminal justice system is to deter crime, classicists believe that the punishments must be swift, certain, and severe enough to deter people's actions.

Cesare Beccaria's 1764 essay *On Crimes and Punishments* had a great impact on the way the Western world looks at justice and crime. Beccaria argued that a legal system must treat everyone equally to protect people against excessive government power. In fact, many ideas contained in our *Charter of Rights and Freedoms* come from Beccaria. He believed that in order to truly deter crime, we needed a fair legal system.[36]

Another classicist, Jeremy Bentham, believed people were inherently *hedonistic,* seeking pleasure over pain. Being a strong supporter of the idea of deterrence, Bentham felt that people would avoid the pleasure of crime only if they feared the pain of punishment. However, the punishment must be severe enough to deter them, but not so severe as to alienate them from society. In other words, the punishment should fit the crime.[37]

PSYCHOLOGICAL PERSPECTIVES ON CRIME AND DEVIANCE

The American Psychiatric Association (APA) claims that criminals suffer from an "antisocial" personality disorder that causes them to "fail to conform to social norms with respect to lawful behaviours as indicated by repeatedly performing acts that are grounds for arrest."[38] According to the APA, criminals are impulsive, aggressive, and irritable, and they tend to lie about their behaviours and feel no remorse for their actions.

Travis Hirschi and Michael J. Hindelang[39] support the idea that criminals have low IQs because the relationship between IQ and crime to official delinquency is strong. Stanton Samenow[40] proposes that criminals actually have thinking errors, including chronic lying, viewing others' property as their own, unfounded optimism, fear of injury or insult, and inflated self-image.

Psychological theories of criminality tend to be positivistic, placing the blame on something abnormal in the individual, such as a low IQ, or a thinking error. Sociological theories tend to view criminality as a social construct. Let's look at some of these theories of criminality.

Classical View

Pleasure > Pain = Crime

Functional Explanations of Crime and Deviance

Functional theories describe crime as a response to some social factor, and theorists look for what causes crime to grow. Émile Durkheim noted that crime and deviance are needed social realities because they meet one of these three needs:

1. Crime marks the boundaries of morality. Frequently, we do not know what we like until we see something we don't like.
2. Crime promotes social solidarity because it unites people against it. People unify against a common enemy, and criminals are often a common enemy.
3. Deviance can bring about needed change in a social system.[41] Acts of civil disobedience are performed to change laws for the betterment of society.

THEORY OF ANOMIE

Robert Merton's theory of anomie—social instability caused by a wearing away of standards and ethics—questions whether social structures cause deviance. Poor individuals have limited opportunities for success.

Merton suggests that most of us have common goals, including wealth, a home, career, cars, and family. Achieving these goals usually involves education, hard work, entrepreneurship, and some luck. Many in the lower classes have blocked access to these goals, so they adapt to their plight in one of five ways:

1 **Conformists** accept society's goals and use socially acceptable means to try to achieve them. They obey rules and work at low-paying jobs with little chance of advancement. One example is a janitor who works three jobs, but can't get ahead because of low pay.

2 **Innovators** accept common goals but not the traditional means of reaching them, using socially unacceptable and often illegal means to achieve those goals instead. For example, an innovator might steal goods and sell them at a pawnshop instead of getting a job.

3 **Ritualists** accept the traditional means of achieving the goals, but are not as interested in the material goals. Social workers use their advanced degrees to pursue humanitarian efforts rather than monetary benefits.

4 **Retreatists** reject both the means and the goals of society. These people often live in isolation or deal with issues of drug and alcohol abuse, mental illness, or homelessness.

5 **Rebels** use their own means to create new goals, often seeking major societal changes.[42] Gandhi was a rebel who sought to change society through nonviolent methods.

Few sociologists accept Merton's theory today as it stands; however, it clearly draws a connection between social structures and crime, and it provokes more thinking about the relationships between poverty and crime. The theory is criticized for the assumption of universal goals and its inability to explain violent or white-collar crimes.

>>> Though the acts in which Martin Luther King, Jr., and his followers engaged were considered illegal at the time, **these "deviant" acts helped bring about much-needed change to the racist laws of the United States.**

Social Interaction Theories

Is it how we interact with people that influences our criminality? Criminals engage in social interactions that influence the likelihood of their violation of the law. Criminologists often divide such theories into social process theories and social reaction theories. Social process theories review how criminal behaviours develop, while social reaction theories examine how societal reactions affect criminal behaviour.

DIFFERENTIAL ASSOCIATION THEORY

Edwin Sutherland proposed the **differential association theory**, which emphasizes that criminal and deviant behaviour is learned. For instance, a teen might sneak out at night to go hang out with friends. If that teen has a younger sibling, the sibling might learn that it is acceptable to sneak out, and how to do so. Similarly, criminals pass on their attitudes, values, mechanisms, and beliefs about crime to others. People commit crimes because they learn that criminal activity is acceptable and/or normal. Sutherland makes this theory clear with nine propositions listed below. Clearly he is a positivist, asserting that crime must be learned from others.

Sutherland's Nine Propositions

1. Criminal behaviour is learned, not inherited.
2. Criminal behaviour is learned through communication.
3. The principal part of learning behaviour occurs within intimate personal groups.
4. The learning includes the techniques of committing the crime and the special direction/motives, drives, rationalizations, and attitudes necessary to carry it out.

5. The specific direction of motives and drives is learned from definitions of the legal codes as favourable and unfavourable.
6. A person becomes delinquent because of an excess of definitions favourable to the violation of the law.
7. Differential associations may vary in frequency, duration, priority, and intensity.
8. The process of learning criminal behaviour by association with criminal and noncriminal patterns involves all the same mechanisms that are involved in any other learning.
9. Although criminal behaviour is an expression of general needs and values, it is not explained by those general needs and values.[43]

SOCIAL CONTROL THEORIES

Social control theories suggest that people are hedonistic and self-interested. Walter Reckless[44] argued that internal and external factors control behaviour. His **containment theory** argues that criminals cannot resist the temptations that surround them. Everyone has different levels of internal controls, including the ability to withstand temptations, morality, integrity, self-esteem, fear of punishment, and the desire to be and do good. External forces such as the police, our family, and/or our friends also control us. However, it is the internal control that influences criminality; for example, few people speed in front of a police car.

Travis Hirschi[45] agrees that internal controls predict criminality and suggests that four social bonds—attachment, commitment, involvement, and belief—affect our inner controls. Strong bonds indicate less likelihood toward criminality.

The first bond, **attachment**, refers to our relationship to others. If a teen hangs out with conformists, friends who do not drink, smoke, or use illegal drugs, they are less likely to engage in these behaviours themselves. **Commitment** refers to our dedication to live a socially acceptable life. By attending school, you are committed to a socially acceptable behaviour. Thus, as we age, we are often more committed to responsible behaviour. Could this explain the age-crime connection? **Involvement** refers to the level of participation in conventional activities. Teens who are involved in their schools or have extracurricular activities are less likely to be delinquent. This is in part because they have less time for deviance. The final bond, **belief**, refers to a person's conviction of truth. If we believe that living a conventional life is good, then we are unlikely to deviate from that path.

Each of these bonds can act together or independently to influence a person's inner control. For example, the theory would say that cross-dressing occurs because people attach themselves to nonconformists (other cross-dressers). They involve themselves in non-normative behaviours by cross-dressing, and believe this is normal and "okay." Involvement in conforming activities may raise the level of attachment to conventional values that could increase a person's belief in those values. Likewise, low levels on these bonds might increase the likelihood that a person will engage in nonconventional activity.

Symbolic Interactionist Theory

LABELLING THEORY

Some theorists believe that certain punishments can actually contribute to future deviance or crime. Edwin Lemert[46] proposes two types of deviance: primary and secondary. **Primary deviance** refers to the initial deviant act itself, such as when a group of teenagers decides to buy beer illegally. Many people can be primarily deviant, but not get caught in the act. When they get caught, they are secondarily deviant. **Secondary deviance** refers to the psychological reorientation that occurs when the system catches a person and labels him or her. The beer-buying teens become "delinquents" when they are sent to juvenile hall. Their friends' and family's perceptions of them have changed, making them secondarily deviant. According to Lemert, secondary deviance often encourages future misdeeds.

DIFFERENTIAL ASSOCIATION THEORY emphasizes that criminal and deviant behaviour is learned.

CONTAINMENT THEORY argues that criminals cannot resist the temptations that surround them.

ATTACHMENT is the social bond that refers to our relationship to others.

COMMITMENT is the social bond that refers to our dedication to live a socially acceptable life.

INVOLVEMENT is the social bond that refers to the level of participation in conventional activities.

BELIEF is the social bond that refers to a person's conviction of truth.

PRIMARY DEVIANCE is the initial deviant act itself.

SECONDARY DEVIANCE refers to the psychological reorientation that occurs when the system catches a person and labels him or her as a deviant.

>>> **According to Sutherland, crime must be taught.** Only then will criminal behaviours develop.

CHIVALRY HYPOTHESIS suggests that female offenders are treated more leniently by male police officers and judges.

Social Conflict Theory

Reiman states that "the rich get richer and the poor get prison," meaning if you are part of the upper class, you can get away with criminal acts.[47] Social conflict theories usually focus on issues of social class, power, capitalism, and their relation to crime. For instance, Willem Bonger[48] argues that capitalism causes crime by emphasizing selfishness in individuals. Capitalism pits people against each other in a struggle for possessions. It also doesn't help that wealthy people who commit crimes often face more lenient punishment than poor people who commit crimes. Income and wealth inequality lead to abuses of the system, and this structural inequality leads to crime.

Modern conflict criminologists continue Bonger's stand that power and wealth inequality leads to crime. Reiman[49] suggests that the inequalities of the justice system are rooted in social class. Although conflict theories focus on the structural reasons for crime, they don't explain why certain individuals commit them.

General Theories of Crime Causation

Figuring out the motivation behind criminal behaviour is the job of causation theorists. General theories of crime causation attempt to explain a broad range of criminal behaviours. Some integrate concepts from various theories such as Robert Agnew's[50] general strain theory, or Michael Gottfredson and Travis Hirschi's[51] general theory of crime.

The general strain theory takes the basic concepts of Merton's anomie and adds a more psychological bent. According to Agnew, a person experiences strain from three sources. First, a person can suffer from a failure to achieve positively valued goals, such as the common goals proposed by Merton. Second, individuals experience strain from unpleasant life events such as losing a job or loved one. The third source of strain results from negative events such as abuse, punishment, and pain. All or any of these strains can lead a person to behave criminally. Agnew believes that everyone experiences strain, but criminality is linked to the individual's coping skills. By learning to cope with stress, people are less likely to turn to crime.[52]

Michael Gottfredson and Travis Hirschi[53] propose a general theory of crime, which states that **self-control, the ability to delay gratification, affects all criminality.** Those who trade short-term rewards for long-term consequences have low self-control. **Most crimes and other criminal-like behaviours involve spur-of-the-moment decisions; this demonstrates their lack of self-control.**

These people often engage in excessive drinking, speeding, drug use, crime, accidents, marital infidelity, and a host of other risky behaviours.[54] Thus, the solution to crime is to teach children self-control.

Feminist Theory

Crime is primarily a male activity—females account for only a small proportion of all offenders. As a result, the theories we have seen so far have tended to focus on explaining the causes of male criminal behaviour. From the feminist perspective, the gender differences in crime are largely due to differences in power and control. This is why males are more likely than females to commit crimes, but women are more likely to be the victims.

Feminists also point out that when women do commit crimes, they are more likely to commit only certain crimes, and to do so for different reasons. In 2005, the most frequent offences committed by women in Canada were theft, common assault, bail violations, and fraud.[55]

Feminist theorists argue that because of the androcentric bias, women are often treated differently within the criminal justice system. Historically, female criminals have been treated like delinquent children. Their criminal behaviour has been seen to be the result of an illness or psychological imbalance. This reflects the patriarchal ideology that women need to be protected, and the **chivalry hypothesis** states that female offenders are treated more leniently by male police officers and judges.[56]

The feminist perspective has also brought attention to crimes in which women are often the victims. In 2008 the overall rates of police-reported violent victimization were comparable between men and women, but the nature of their victimization differed. Females were over ten times more likely than males to be victims of a police-reported sexual assault.[57] Women are far more likely than men to be the victims of intimate violence. Finally, women working as police officers, attorneys, and judges often face very different issues than their male counterparts.[58] These are just some of the topics addressed by feminist criminologists.

WRAP YOUR MIND AROUND THE THEORY

These students chose society's traditional means to reach their goals of success.

FUNCTIONALISM

For functionalists, crime is a part of society. Durkheim notes that crime always exists in society, and therefore must serve some function. For Merton, crime results because the pursuit of socially desirable goals is blocked for some people. Therefore, people must adapt. Only one of these modes of adaptation leads to crime, but all occur because the system blocks some people from the goals to which they aspire.

CONFLICT THEORY

Bonger argues that capitalism causes crime in society because it teaches people to be selfish and to do what is best for themselves instead of thinking of others. The inherent competition of capitalism results in inequality of wealth and power. This leads some to strike out in criminal ways. Reiman's statement "the rich get richer, the poor get prison" points out that laws are written in the best interest of the wealthy. The wealthy often make the laws that punish poor people who might steal to survive. Meanwhile, illegal acts of the wealthy are often not considered crimes. Businessmen with power who break the law often receive little more than a slap on the wrist.

WHAT CAUSES CRIME IN OUR SOCIETY?

SYMBOLIC INTERACTIONISM

Edwin Lemert's labelling theory clearly shows the power of symbols in people's lives. Although he has no explanation for primary deviance, he argues that secondary deviance occurs as a result of the way society reacts to the first act. Thus, people learn that others see them only as criminals and so they behave in that way. Such a self-fulfilling prophecy can be enhanced by differential association theory. Sutherland suggests that we learn criminality from others, through social interactions. If, for example, your friends are "gangbangers," you may believe behaving that way is acceptable. Why? Because your friends teach you that committing crimes is no big deal.

FEMINIST THEORY

Power imbalances in society mean that women are more likely to be the victims of male perpetrators of crime. The reasons why women commit crimes are different from those that explain male criminal behaviour. Feminist theorists also draw attention to how female offenders, as well as female police, lawyers, and judges, are treated differently within the criminal justice system.

The police enforce laws written by the wealthy. These **laws often benefit the wealthy and exploit the poor.**

Society and our own social interactions influence our tendencies toward **crime.**

discover sociology in action: HOW DO WE DEAL WITH CRIME?

> **DISCRETION** is the ability to make decisions.
> **SUMMARY CONVICTION OFFENCES** are less serious offences.
> **INDICTABLE OFFENCES** are more serious offences.

Crime Control: The Criminal Justice System

The Canadian justice system has three parts: *police, courts,* and *corrections*. Each of these parts of the system responds to violations of the law and each reflects the social policies of our country toward crime.

POLICE

Today, there are more than 67 000 police officers across Canada.[59] Police are the ones on the front line against crime. This role requires police officers to have **discretion**, or the ability to make decisions, which often involves whether or not they will enforce the law. If you've ever received a warning instead of a ticket for speeding through a school zone, you've reaped the benefit of a police officer's discretion.

COURTS

The courts are the second part of the criminal justice system. The basic role of courts in Canada is to help people resolve disputes fairly and with justice. There are four levels of courts in Canada. The provincial and territorial courts handle the majority of cases that come into the system. Second are the provincial/territorial superior courts, which deal with more serious crimes and also hear appeals from provincial/territorial court judgments. At the third level are the provincial/territorial courts of appeal, while the highest level is the Supreme Court of Canada.[60]

Since a crime is considered to be an offence against society as a whole, it is usually the state that starts a criminal trial. The person charged with a crime is called the "accused," and is always presumed innocent until proven guilty. In Canada, there are two types of criminal offences. **Summary conviction offences** are less serious. The accused appears before a provincial court for a trial. The maximum penalty for this type of offence is normally a $5000 fine, six months in prison, or both.

More serious offences are called **indictable offences**. There is often a "preliminary hearing" for indictable offences during which a judge examines the case to decide whether there is enough evidence to proceed with the trial. If the judge decides there is not enough evidence, the case is dismissed. Otherwise, a full criminal trial is ordered. During the trial, the prosecution must prove that the accused is guilty of the charge beyond a reasonable doubt.

If the accused is found not guilty, he or she is acquitted and is free to go. If the accused is found guilty of the crime, a judge must then decide on an appropriate sentence, which may include a fine, community service, or jail time.[61]

CORRECTIONAL SERVICES

The correctional system is the last leg of the criminal justice system. It supervises those who are convicted of crimes. Correctional Service Canada is the department responsible for carrying out any sentence imposed by a judge.

The name Correctional Service suggests that prisons are supposed to correct the offender and assist in his or her successful reintegration into society. There are six services under the responsibility of Correctional Service Canada:

1. Custodial remands—after a person has been arrested and charged with an offence, he or she may be kept in remand (prison) until trial and sentencing. If the trial judge imposes a custodial sentence (a prison term), the time spent in remand is usually deducted from the sentenced time.

2. Custodial sentences—at trial, the judge may impose a sentence of custody in prison. In Canada, any custodial sentence longer than two years is served in a federal penitentiary, while sentences of less than two years are served in provincial or territorial facilities.

3. Conditional sentences—at the discretion of the trial judge, a conditional sentence may be ordered that allows the offender to serve his or her time in the community under supervision.

4. Probation—this may be ordered as the sole condition of the sentence, or it may be required following a term in custody. Probation is a sentence that is served in the community, and the offender is usually required to report to a probation officer.

5. Conditional release—this includes temporary leaves for family visits, medical services, or on humanitarian grounds. It also includes day parole or full parole.

6. Parole boards—these are administrative tribunals that oversee all issues related to parole. They decide whether a prisoner may be granted parole, and they also can revoke parole if certain conditions are violated.[62]

> ### ACTIVITIES
>
> 1. Read stories about prison inmates. Do you see any commonalities in their stories?
> 2. Research prisons in your province. What are the demographics of the inmates?
> 3. What types of community service programs are available in your community for inmates to participate in?

Bill was an inmate in a local correctional centre who participated in the Adult Basic Education program while serving his sentence. At about the midpoint of the semester, students were offered the chance to earn extra credit by doing community learning. Bill wanted to participate, too. The program had never had an inmate do community service, so the teacher spoke with his educational officer, who agreed that community learning could occur anywhere.

Bill wrote in his paper, "My prison is a community of inmates, most of whom committed no violent offences like me. I spent my time volunteering to help with the drug and alcohol group, meaning that each day I would set up the chapel for the meetings, and after the meetings I would put it back in order. Initially, I didn't stay for the meetings because it didn't seem to be important: I have no drug addiction, I haven't used since I was incarcerated. But one time the group leader invited me to stay. I was stunned to hear the stories of how alcohol and drugs caused so much damage in these men's lives. Almost all of them were under the influence when they committed their crimes.

"It made me decide that I wanted to be a drug and alcohol counsellor when I got out of prison. It also made me see that a lot of inmates are just like me: normal guys trying to do their time without getting hurt, and hoping for a better life on the outside when they get released."

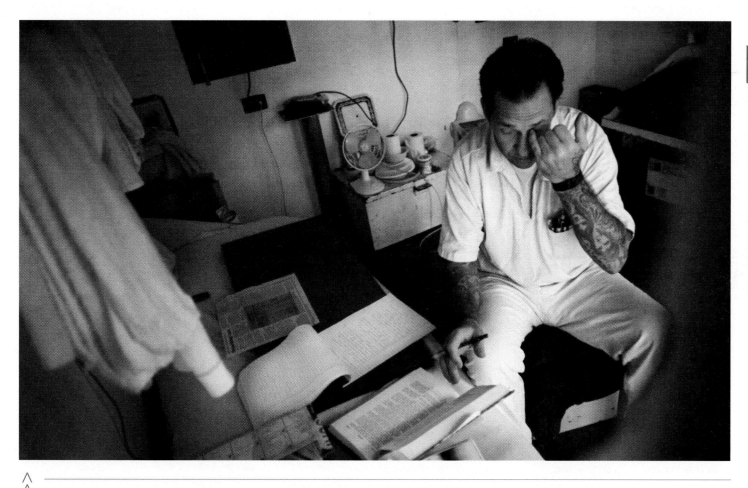

How do you think community service programs, like a support group for alcoholics, could be beneficial to inmates trying to turn their lives around?

get the topic: WHAT IS CRIME?

Theory

FUNCTIONALISM   221

- crime is a response to some social factor
- Durkheim's three functions of crime and deviance: they mark the boundaries of morality, promote social solidarity, and bring about needed change
- theory of anomie: social instability caused by a wearing away of standards and ethics
- Merton: crime results because the pursuit of socially desirable goals is blocked for some people

SYMBOLIC INTERACTIONISM   223

- labelling theory
- people react to how others view them
- people learn criminality through social interactions

CONFLICT THEORY   224

- capitalism teaches people to be selfish and competitive, resulting in inequality
- the wealthy create the laws that punish the poor, while many illegal acts committed by the wealthy are often not considered crimes
- "the rich get rich, the poor get prison"

FEMINIST THEORY   224

- androcentric bias in explaining the causes of criminal behaviour
- chivalry hypothesis means female offenders are treated more leniently
- women experience the justice system differently

Key Terms

deviance is the violation of norms that a society agrees upon.   *214*

crime is the violation of norms that have been written into law.   *214*

criminology is the scientific study of crime, deviance, and social policies that the criminal justice system applies.   *214*

street crime refers to many different types of criminal acts which occur in public places, such as burglary, drug dealing, and pick-pocketing.   *215*

Uniform Crime Reporting Survey measures the incidence of crime using police statistics of

reported crimes gathered from police reports and paperwork.   *216*

General Social Survey—Victimization is the measurement of crime victimization based on a representative sample of nearly 20 000 Canadians over 15 years old.   *216*

crime rate measures the volume of crime reported to the police.   *216*

Crime Severity Index measures the seriousness of crime reported to the police.   *216*

consensus model of law suggests that laws arise because people see a behaviour they do not like, and they agree to make it illegal.   *218*

conflict model of law proposes that powerful people write laws to protect their own interests while punishing the actions of those they wish to control.   *218*

shaming is a deliberate effort to attach a negative meaning to a behaviour.   *218*

stigmatized shame is a permanent label given to an offender, which could actually increase the chances of reoffending because the guilty person is forever labelled.   *218*

reintegrative shaming is an effort to bring an offender back into the community after punishment.   *218*

retribution is based on the belief that offender should be punished. *219*

incapacitation means preventing the criminal from causing further harm. *219*

deterrence is a measure that prevents a person from doing something because of fear of the consequences. *219*

general deterrence is a measure that ensures individuals will not commit a crime because they see the negative consequences applied to others, and they fear experiencing these consequences. *219*

specific deterrence is a measure that changes the attitude of individuals who have already violated the law and have been punished, by causing them never to commit crime again. *219*

rehabilitation tries to reform the offender so that he or she can be returned to society. *219*

restoration uses impact statements so that victims can participate in the sentencing process. *219*

recidivism is the tendency for inmates released from prison to return to prison. *219*

differential association theory emphasizes that criminal and deviant behaviour is learned. *222*

containment theory argues that people who commit crimes cannot resist the temptations that surround them. *222*

attachment is the social bond that refers to our relationship to others. *222*

commitment is the social bond that refers to our dedication to live a socially acceptable life. *223*

involvement is the social bond that refers to the level of participation in conventional activities. *223*

belief is the social bond that refers to a person's conviction of truth. *223*

primary deviance is the initial deviant act itself. *223*

secondary deviance refers to the psychological reorientation that occurs when the system catches a person and labels him or her as a deviant. *223*

chivalry hypothesis suggests that female offenders are treated more leniently by male police officers and judges. *224*

discretion is the ability to make decisions. *226*

summary conviction offences are less serious offences. *226*

indictable offences are more serious offences. *226*

Sample Test Questions

These multiple-choice questions are similar to those found in the test bank that accompanies this textbook.

1. Deviance is not linked to
   a. time.
   b. society.
   c. legal norms.
   d. cultural values.
2. Which type of crime is most common?
   a. Violent crime
   b. Property crime
   c. White-collar crime
   d. Drug-related crime
3. Which of the following is an alternative punishment?
   a. Prison
   b. Death
   c. Torture
   d. Shaming
4. What is the last resort in the criminal justice system?
   a. Counselling
   b. Probation
   c. Parole
   d. Prison
5. According to Robert Merton, which type of lower-class person obeys social rules and works with little chance of advancement?
   a. Conformist
   b. Innovator
   c. Retreatist
   d. Ritualist

ESSAY

1. Which groups are more likely to be overrepresented in Canadian prisons?
2. Do the poor commit more crimes than other members of society?
3. Why is it difficult to make international comparisons about crime statistics?
4. Why are only certain things illegal?
5. What are the different sentencing options in the Canadian justice system?

WHERE TO START YOUR RESEARCH PAPER

To learn more about crime in Canada, go to
www.justice.gc.ca/eng/index.html

To learn about the *Youth Criminal Justice Act,* go to
www.justice.gc.ca/eng/pi/yj-jj/

To learn more about positive deviance, go to
www.positivedeviance.org

To see statistics about crime in Canada, go to
www.statcan.gc.ca/bsolc/olc-cel/olc-cel?catno-85-002-XIE⟨=eng

To read about victimization as part of the General Social Survey, go to
www.statcan.gc.ca/daily-quotidien/100928/dq100928a-eng.htm

To learn more about prisons and their administration in Canada, go to
www.csc-scc.gc.ca/text/index-eng.shtml

To learn more about international police organizations, go to
www.interpol.int

ANSWERS: 1. c; 2. b; 3. d; 4. d; 5. a

Remember to check out www.thethinkspot.ca **for additional information, downloadable flashcards, and other helpful resources.**

MARRIAGE AND FAMILY

"Social scientists

often get carried away with a definition of terms, discussing fine distinctions between 'statistical families,' 'economic families' and 'extended families.' But the family in our experience is clear. It is the coming together of two adults, usually but not always a man and a woman, usually but not always legally married, to express their mutual love and commitment. If the relationship lasts, children are often produced, and then the family is made of mother, father, and children living together under one roof, developing a long-term economic, social, and emotional unit. Sometimes as the years advance, the family expands to include aging grandparents.

"The big things are commitment, obligation, responsibility. Recognizing that we all must age and that our sexual currency on the love market must decline, physical love is replaced by deeper bases of understanding and support and, often most importantly, the shared love and excitement of raising children. The establishment of the family is an effort to find assured meaning and solace, as well as to express our emotional selves in more fundamental and lasting ways. That was the family. That is the family. And that will be the family in the future. The human species has not yet produced an alternative as fulfilling or as rewarding.

"That fundamental marriage, or common-law, relationship that brings two adults together sets the stage for the bearing and raising of children, for the care and comfort of the old and dying, and for emotional and financial support in our declining years. In the distant past, marriage and the family were the social structure of the species. And today they remain the central social experience of our day-to-day lives.

"The family in this sense is in crisis. It has been in crisis before—when feudalism declined and collapsed; when industrial capitalism emerged; when war, famine, and plague swept a land. But the crisis today, just like previous crises, is specific and needs focussed attention, if only because new embryonic family forms are emerging and urgently appealing for midwives."[1]

How Do Societies Perpetuate Themselves?

CHAPTER 13

In his book *The Canadian Family in Crisis,* John Conway looks at Canadian families in the past, the present, and the future. He examines how changes in the family have different impacts on children, on women, and on men.

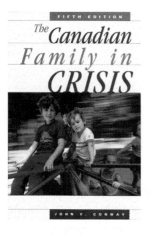

Here's the story of a lovely lady, who was bringing up three very lovely girls. . . That lovely lady met a man named Brady and soon one of the most beloved sitcoms of all time—*The Brady Bunch*—was born. Families watching the show back then wanted to be just like them. In fact, the Bradys are still an ideal for many viewers. However, today's family sitcom is more likely to feature a dysfunctional family than a happy, loving family. What happened?

John Conway suggests that most people carry with them a misconception of what the family "ought" to be, which influences their thinking. Each semester, I ask my students to draw the "ideal family." They draw something like the image to the right. Rarely does anyone draw his or her own family. This exercise usually helps us launch into a discussion that most people never consider. What is a family? Who taught us what a family is? We will address these questions and further investigate families and marriage in this chapter.

get the topic: WHAT IS A FAMILY?

Marriage and Family

The concept of family exists in all societies and comes in all shapes and sizes. But what is a family? The term is difficult to define, but generally a **family** is two or more people who are related by blood, marriage, or adoption. Often we think of marriage as the legal institution that defines family, with **marriage** being the union of two people that is typically recognized by law or cultural norms. However, like family, marriage is a social construct, so the status of people who commit to each other for life is often related to social institutions and cultures.[2]

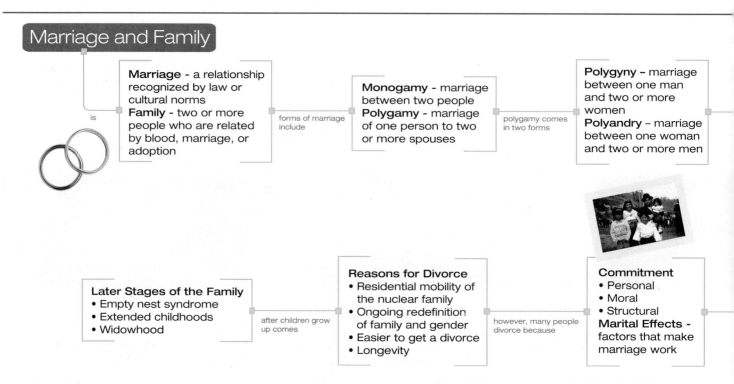

Marriage and Family

is →

Marriage - a relationship recognized by law or cultural norms
Family - two or more people who are related by blood, marriage, or adoption

forms of marriage include →

Monogamy - marriage between two people
Polygamy - marriage of one person to two or more spouses

polygamy comes in two forms →

Polygyny – marriage between one man and two or more women
Polyandry – marriage between one woman and two or more men

Later Stages of the Family
• Empty nest syndrome
• Extended childhoods
• Widowhood

after children grow up comes →

Reasons for Divorce
• Residential mobility of the nuclear family
• Ongoing redefinition of family and gender
• Easier to get a divorce
• Longevity

however, many people divorce because →

Commitment
• Personal
• Moral
• Structural
Marital Effects - factors that make marriage work

My Ideal Family

>>> When I ask my students to draw their "ideal family," I get images that look like this. Neat, tidy families with a mother, father, and two-and-a-half kids. However, **few families in our society come in such tidy packages.**

DAUGHTER DAD MOM SON BRUNO

FORMS OF MARRIAGE AND FAMILY

Take a look around and you'll notice that families come in all shapes and sizes. Some families have only one parent in the home, while others have stepparents helping to raise the children. Still others have two parents of the same sex. The drawings my students generally create consist of a husband, wife, and their children—a group that can also be referred to as a **nuclear family**. But other forms of family exist. For various reasons, another relative, like a grandparent or an uncle, may live with a nuclear family, which creates an **extended family**.

FAMILY is two or more people who are related by blood, marriage, or adoption.

MARRIAGE is the union of two people that is typically recognized by law or cultural norms.

NUCLEAR FAMILY is a household consisting of a husband, wife, and children.

EXTENDED FAMILY is a household consisting of a nuclear family plus an additional relative.

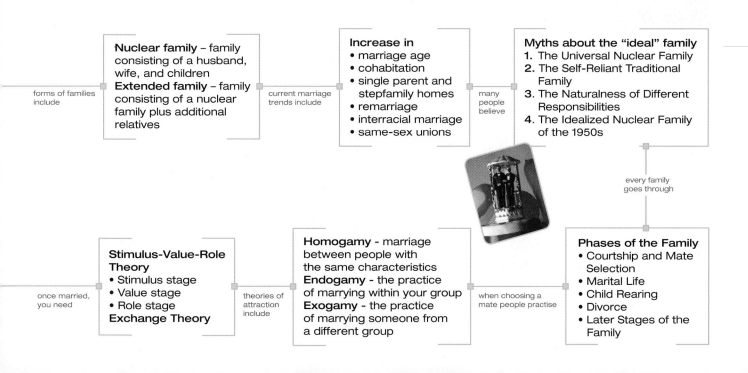

forms of families include

Nuclear family – family consisting of a husband, wife, and children
Extended family – family consisting of a nuclear family plus additional relatives

current marriage trends include

Increase in
• marriage age
• cohabitation
• single parent and stepfamily homes
• remarriage
• interracial marriage
• same-sex unions

many people believe

Myths about the "ideal" family
1. The Universal Nuclear Family
2. The Self-Reliant Traditional Family
3. The Naturalness of Different Responsibilities
4. The Idealized Nuclear Family of the 1950s

every family goes through

once married, you need

Stimulus-Value-Role Theory
• Stimulus stage
• Value stage
• Role stage
Exchange Theory

theories of attraction include

Homogamy - marriage between people with the same characteristics
Endogamy - the practice of marrying within your group
Exogamy - the practice of marrying someone from a different group

when choosing a mate people practise

Phases of the Family
• Courtship and Mate Selection
• Marital Life
• Child Rearing
• Divorce
• Later Stages of the Family

Most of you probably grew up under a family system of **monogamy**, which is the practice of being married to one person at a time. However, some societies allow **polygamy**, the practice of having more than one spouse at a time. Polygamy is illegal in Canada, but you will recall that in Chapter 6 we described the fundamentalist Mormon community of Bountiful, B.C., where polygamy is practised in violation of this law. Two leaders of this group—Winston Blackmore and James Oler—were each charged with practising polygamy, but in September 2009 the charges were thrown out.

Polygamy itself comes in two forms: polygyny and polyandry. **Polygyny** is more common and consists of a man marrying two or more women. This ancient practice is illegal in most developed countries, although it still exists in many developing countries around the world. **Polyandry** allows a woman to take two or more husbands. Anthropologists determined that polyandry is practised to concentrate labour and maintain a comfortable standard of living while limiting animosity. For example, Tibetans practise fraternal polyandry, meaning a woman is married to brothers.[3] All the brothers maintain their land while limiting the number of heirs, which prevents family infighting.[4]

Most of these family types fall under the patriarchal system, which you will recall from Chapter 10 means that men have power over women and children. In contrast, several First Nations groups were originally organized as matriarchal societies.

>>> I live with my mom, Jeffrey, and my new baby brothers, Kevin and Scott. **On the weekends, I see my dad, his wife, Anita, and my half-sister, Kylie.**

TRENDS OF THE CANADIAN FAMILY

Ideologies regarding the family are also changing. Years ago, female students were in a race to "get pinned," or engaged, before the end of their last semester of college. As one faculty member put it, "Springtime was for engagement parties." Today, things are different. It's no longer unusual for a woman to graduate from college without having a fiancé.

In 1921, the average age people married was 28 for men and 24.5 for women. By 1971, Canada was in an era that recognized the family as *the* social

institution. The average age at first marriage lowered to 25 for men and 22.6 for women. In 2003, the average ages hit an all-time high with the average age being 30.6 for men and 28.5 for women.[5] These delays in marriage may be due to a number of factors. One of these is an increase in couples who choose to live together without being legally married.[6]

It's increasingly common for unmarried, cohabiting couples to have children. Just look at Brad Pitt and Angelina Jolie. This unmarried celebrity couple continues to add to their ever-expanding brood. It has been estimated that 40 percent of all children will spend time in a cohabiting family before their sixteenth birthdays.[7] Some researchers point out that many cohabitating couples of today resemble families of the past.[8] However, there are other forms of families that have arisen as well.

New Forms of Families

Remarriage and stepfamilies are also part of the everyday norm. Both of these trends take the traditional idea of a nuclear family and rework it to fit new forms of family. Since the 1950s, traditional roles and rules associated with families have become more varied and complex.[9] For example, I've often heard children say to an adult who is not their biological parent but is living with and providing for them, something like this: "You're not my real mom (or dad), you can't tell me what to do!" If that's true, what is that person's role in the household? Cohabitants and stepfamilies often experience such questions and stresses over these changing roles in the family.

Some children may grow up in **blended families**, which are families composed of children and some combination of biological parents. Some children grow up in a single-parent home. In fact, although the percentage of births for married women has decreased in the last 15 years, the percentage of births for unmarried women has increased.[10] These are really two different things. First, some children live in a single-parent household because their parents are divorced. Other children live in unmarried households due to cohabitation. Either way, social norms are more accepting of unmarried women raising children today than they used to be. In fact, a growing number of children today are expected to live in a single-parent home at some time.[11]

Other changes in the family form include same-sex couples and interracial/interethnic marriages. Compared to the past, stigma surrounding these unions has declined significantly, so that many people no longer keep such unions a secret.[12] What has caused such a change in family forms?

One structural event may help explain what happened. Throughout the 1950s, most children lived with their parents before getting married. During this time, the power of the parents to help select an "acceptable mate" reigned supreme. Now there is an independent life stage as people delay marriage and often live independently from their parents prior to getting married.[13] This geographic split decreases the parents' ability to control the behaviour of their grown children,[14] perhaps leading to greater diversity and partner selection. This, along with changing social norms, seems to allow people to couple in a way that would not have been imaginable 40 years ago.[15]

Myths about the "Ideal" Family

In the opening excerpt, John Conway discusses how people have idealized the traditional family. He points out that many myths exist about family structure and family life. For example, I thought I lived in a typical home when I was growing up. My mother cooked Sunday dinners, and my father mowed the lawn. However, both of my parents worked outside the home and everyone helped with chores. In college, I visited a friend's house, and his mother waited on us hand and foot. When I got up to help with the dishes, my friend's father said, "That's women's work." That's how I learned that my family wasn't typical. Conway discusses similar myths about families in Canada.

MONOGAMY is the practice of being married to one person at a time.

POLYGAMY is the practice of having more than one spouse at a time.

POLYGYNY is the practice of a man marrying two or more women.

POLYANDRY is the practice of a woman marrying two or more men.

BLENDED FAMILIES are families composed of children and some combination of biological parents.

> The idealized 1950s family did exist, but was perpetuated by television. Shows such as *Father Knows Best* and *The Adventures of Ozzie and Harriet* depicted picture-perfect families whose problems were resolved in the span of a half-hour program.

MYTH 1 The Universal Nuclear Family

Although common belief is that all families take the form of the traditional nuclear family, the reality is that families vary in organization, membership, life cycle, social networks, and function. What many people consider the "ideal family" only came about with industrialization. When people left the farm, they often didn't take their extended family with them and created smaller family units.

MYTH 2 The Self-Reliant Traditional Family

Some people believe that family units carved out their lives on their own and that returning to a more self-reliant family structure would solve many of today's issues. The idealized image of families striking out on their own to settle the west overstates the reality of self-reliance. These families received both government support as well as support from others in the area. Early settlers relied on military protection and government programs designed to move First Nations Peoples off the lands that they were to eventually inhabit. Finally, local families often banded together for childcare, construction projects, and mutual protection and support. In a complex society, no one makes it on his or her own.

MYTH 3 The Naturalness of Different Responsibilities for Wives and Husbands

We touched on this subject in the gender chapter, but many people believe that there has always been a clear division between men and women when it comes to childcare and other family roles. Some suggest that if mothers stayed home and "did their jobs" (raising the children), families would function better. The truth is that prior to industrialization, men and women shared almost equally in childcare tasks. Men often worked at home and their children helped them. My mother learned farming techniques from her dad. He taught her to be innovative and never afraid to try new things. So, men did take responsibility for raising their children. Women also worked hard. My grandmother worked with my grandfather and when he died, she remained on the farm, raising the children and working the fields. The notion that family roles were different is not so clear when we look at history.

MYTH 4 The Idealized Nuclear Family of the 1950s

During the 1950s, an image of the family emerged. It was a middle-class family with a stay-at-home mom and a working dad. This image came to be idealized in television shows, and people started buying into this thinking that this is what families should look like. However, there is historical evidence to suggest that for many, this "ideal" family was far from real.

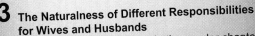

Image of the Perfect Family

Stephanie Coontz argues that the image of the perfect family is just that—an image.[16] In fact, the romanticized family portrait of the past often covered up a life of discontent and conformity. Families like the Cleaver family in the 1950s sitcom *Leave It to Beaver* did exist, but only for a tiny blip in history and only for a small portion of the population.

Looking back on it, the 1950s seemed like the golden age of happiness for many North Americans. Divorce rates were down, out-of-wedlock births were low, and marriage was universally esteemed as an institution.[17] Not only was there a housing boom, but the gross national product (the estimated total value of all the goods created in the country) and per-capita income also rose. Even though there is a measure of truth to these points, they don't provide a clear picture of average

families. Before people were ever married, they knew exactly what to expect from their lives. After a brief courtship, a couple was married, had sex, and started a family. They purchased a house, with the husband as breadwinner. His salary was high enough for the wife to stay at home as a homemaker. This routine led some women to believe life consisted of the four Bs: booze, bowling, bridge, and boredom.[18]

In fact, "[b]y 1960, almost every major news journal was using the word *trapped* to describe the feelings of the North American housewife."[19] To dull the pain and tedium, some women began drinking and taking tranquillizers to make it through the day.

Men were also dissatisfied with family life and became resentful of women. Publications like *Playboy* encouraged men to take power over areas that women previously governed. Men were encouraged to have a say in the clothes they wore and the food they ate. In

Playboy's debut issue it published an article titled "Miss Gold-Digger of 1953," promoting the idea that women were interested in men for material reasons.[20] These negative stereotypes were damaging to both men and women.

Trying to gauge the frequency of events such as violence and incest is difficult because many instances were never reported. These topics were not considered appropriate for conversation. Many women suffered from physical abuse and just dealt with it, rather than face the stigma of being a member of a dysfunctional family. In the 1950s, a victim of domestic violence was often viewed "as a masochist who provoked her husband into beating her."[21]

>>> **ACTIVITY** What do current family sitcoms say about the role of the family in our culture? After conducting research, compare this image to reality. Do you see any discrepancies?

>>> In the 1950s sitcom *The Honeymooners,* New York bus driver Ralph Kramden wants to strike it rich, but his wife knows it's not going to happen. **Ralph threatens her by saying, "One of these days, Alice, right in the kisser . . . pow!" Scenes like this trivialized domestic violence in a comedic sketch.**

Networks and Family Change in Japan

Many of the family demographic changes in Canada—increased age at marriage, decreased marital stability, and lower birthrate—have been mirrored by Japan. Traditionally, Japanese family values strongly discouraged these behaviours. However, a survey conducted by Ronald R. Rindfuss and colleagues suggested that Japan might be on the cusp of a major demographic change.[22]

The traditional Japanese family is patriarchal: men are the authority figure, lineage is traced through the father, and fathers pass wealth on to their sons.[23] Women are left with the bulk of the housework. In 2000, Japanese women spent 29 hours per week on household labour; husbands spent just three.[24]

However, times are changing. More women are attaining higher levels of education and entering the labour force.[25] As more women enter the full-time workforce, Japan faces an increased need for daycare situations. Some suggest that cohabitation may become more common.[26] In fact, recent studies indicate that 92 percent of Japanese citizens know someone who has engaged in non-traditional behaviours.[27] Japan should anticipate more changes in the future.

∨
∨
∨ Some societies feel a strong need to preserve traditional culture.

What motivates societies to cling to traditional values?

PHASES OF THE FAMILY

Although every family is different and complex in its own right, there are commonalities that emerge in most unions. Traditionally speaking, people court, choose a mate, get married, have children, and experience the later stages of family life. Let's look at these issues.

Courtship and Mate Selection

I understand that there are possibly millions of women on the planet with whom I could have a satisfying marriage. Yet, I married someone who lived in the same town I did and who happened to go to my church. Feelings of attraction and affection were part of this decision, but choosing a mate often has to do with finding people who live near you and who share similar values and social traits. Propinquity or proximity is a major factor to interpersonal attraction. It makes sense that you are attracted to people who live near you.[28]

Finding a mate comes with many unspoken or spoken rules that society, your family, or even you dictate. So, when choosing a mate, what kind of cultural questions arise?

Common Cultural Practices

Finding someone to marry can be a daunting prospect, but in Canada the options are relatively open. There are only a few rules: potential mates cannot already be married, must be of legal age, and must not be closely related. In fact, most cultures have similar restrictions regarding age and other social issues.

HOMOGAMY is marriage between people with similar backgrounds, such as religion, ethnicity, class, or age.

ENDOGAMY is the practice of marrying within your social group.

EXOGAMY is the practice of marrying someone from a different social group.

MARITAL EFFECTS are factors that make marriage work.

Despite this relative freedom in choosing marital partners, many people practise **homogamy**, or marriage between people with the same characteristics. This occurs when people choose a partner with a similar background: religion, ethnicity, class, geographic location, or age. Partners of similar backgrounds are likely to socialize their children the same way,

which avoids conflict. Also, coming from similar backgrounds increases the likelihood that the couple will have things in common, which can increase the longevity of the relationship. I married someone with homogenous traits in that we shared similar educational backgrounds and social class expectations.

Some cultures and groups strive to enforce marrying within a group, which is a practice known as **endogamy**. If, for example, your religion requires you to marry a person of the same faith, endogamy becomes a primary predictor of whom you might marry. For example, a former student of mine often talked about how important it was to her and her family that she marry someone from within the same culture. Although this was not a "rule" to which she had to adhere, the attitudes of her family and friends provided a clear directive that she needed to follow. On the other hand, **exogamy** is the practice of marrying someone from a different group. The best example is the incest taboo, which prohibits marriage between certain relatives. Remember, the appropriateness of a spouse is dependent on cultural norms and regulations. Treatment of this issue in different cultures ranges from unspoken disapproval to "illegal" unapproved marriages.

Stimulus-Value-Role Theory of Mate Selection

STIMULUS STAGE

In this stage two people are attracted to each other by some kind of stimulus. This could be something like looks, cool shoes, or a nice car. These are superficial characteristics, which are noticed before two people get to know one another. If a couple stays attracted, they move to the second stage.

VALUE STAGE

In this stage the compatibility of the relationship is tested regarding a variety of mutually held beliefs/values (religion, politics, familial expectations, attitudes about money). If a couple talks and manages to find common ground in some of these areas, then they may choose to move on to stage three.

ROLE STAGE

After realizing that they share a mutual attraction and a similar set of beliefs, people decide to act out the roles of a couple. This includes dating and sexual behaviour, possibly leading to a long-term relationship.

Exchange Theory

Take a look at the stimulus-value-role theory of mate selection shown in the graphic to the left. This theory, created by sociologist Bernard Murstein, suggests that we select our friends and close partners through a three-stage model. At each stage, we weed out those who do not fit. Compared to the stimulus-value-role theory, the social exchange theory takes more of a practical approach to dating and marriage. The entire courtship process is like a negotiation to find the best deal. Exchange theory essentially states that people seek to maximize rewards and minimize costs. A student of mine told me that he was deeply in love with his girlfriend, but that in the end he had to break it off because she was too jealous. He got tired of the constant phone calls, text messages, and her constant need to be by his side. In the end, it was just "too much work." Relationships are started and maintained as long as they are rewarding for us. This does not mean it is always "fun," but only that some type of reward, emotional, social, or financial, outweighs the cost. When we cease to benefit from the relationship, we end it.

Issues in the Family

One of the biggest worries people have before they get married is whether or not they are going to be happy. Don't be blinded by movies or novels into thinking you are going to be swept away by your soul mate. In order to be happy, you need to have a solid commitment to one another and understand the variables that make a marriage work.

According to Johnson and colleagues, commitment is made up of more than a single component. Instead, he suggests that there are three types of commitment that strengthen a couple's marriage: personal, moral, and structural.[29] Take a look at the chart on page 239 summarizing the types of commitment.

In addition to having a solid commitment to your spouse there are **marital effects**, or factors that make marriage work. Research shows that one of the easiest ways to stay satisfied is to spend time together doing activities both of you enjoy.[30] This means you are engaging in companionship with your

Three Types of Commitment

Type of Commitment	Why It Keeps You Married	Characterized by the Sentence
Personal—a desire to stay married based on love and marital satisfaction	You stay married because you want to.	I want . . .
Moral—a duty to stay married based on your attitudes toward divorce and the contract you made with your partner	You stay married because you feel obligated.	I should . . .
Structural—a feeling of constraint based on alternatives, social pressure, and investments	You stay married because of the barriers you feel around you.	I have to . . .

Source: Based on Michael P. Johnson, John P. Caughlin, and Ted L. Huston, "The Tripartite Nature of Marital Commitment: Personal, Moral, and Structural Reasons to Stay Married," *Journal of Marriage and the Family*, Feb. 1999. 61, 1:160–177.

spouse while also enjoying a leisure activity. However, spending time pursuing activities that only one of you enjoys can create feelings of dissatisfaction over the long term.[31]

"Satisfaction" is difficult to gauge since outside factors such as gender ideologies make satisfaction a social construct. Using data from two-earner, married couples, Daphne Stevens and colleagues studied the relationships between marital satisfaction and labour in marriages. For them, marital work has three components: the level of household labour, the division of the emotional work of the marriage, and how individuals provide status enhancement to each other.[32]

According to Stevens and colleagues, both husbands and wives have increased marital satisfaction when they perceive the household labour to be "fair." If one feels overworked, marital satisfaction decreases. Although women usually did more of the housework than the men, generally speaking, the more work the husband did around the house, the happier the wife reported she was with her marriage. The same appears to be true for the balance of emotional work. As long as the couple perceived the balance to be at an acceptable level, marital satisfaction increased. With regard to status enhancement, men were happiest in their marriages when they reported their wives supported their careers. However, women's marital satisfaction was more related to their own ability to improve their status at work than to their husbands' support.[33]

Generally speaking, the more a woman is allowed to work in her career and the less household labour she is required to do, the happier she will be in her marriage. For men, similar findings follow; however, men tended to base their marital satisfaction on their wives' happiness. Interestingly, the study controlled for the number of children, income, and many other variables, but showed that marital satisfaction is linked to the couple's comfort with their arrangement.[34]

Child Rearing

Child rearing influences a married couple's life. In Chapter 5, we discussed the importance of child-rearing practices and socialization. Here, let us consider the influence of social class.

∨
∨
∨ Many factors that help make a marriage work—like compromising and spending time together—seem simple. **Why do you think so many marriages end in divorce?**

Taking care of a child is expensive. Based on estimates from 2004, the average cost of raising a daughter to age 18 in Canada was $166 549. The amount was slightly higher for boys due to extra costs for food.[35] So, how are children from low-income families affected? Remember, inequality is a vicious cycle. Children from wealthy families remain wealthy, and children from poor families continue to be poor.[36] Sociologist Lisa Strohschein studied the mental health and social behaviour of children from low-income families. She found that "low household income is associated with higher levels of depression and antisocial behaviour; subsequent improvements in household income reduce child mental health problems."[37] However, having children is often seen as a status symbol, and many lower-class families want children because they are a valuable social resource.[38]

Divorce

Frequently, stress stemming from marital troubles causes couples to break up. Divorce is now an accepted and viable option for these couples and is perhaps the single biggest change in the state of marriage in Canada today. In 1901, there were only three divorces per 10 000 marriages. That is far less than one percent.[39] When asked what the rate is now, students say that 50 percent of marriages end in divorce. They suggest that "everyone knows that." However, is that really true? People get the 50 percent number after comparing the number of marriages and divorces in a given year. Are those getting married really the same people getting divorced? Those getting married are adding more people to the pool of married people, and those getting divorced are subtracting from it. For this reason, sociologists usually do not take this simple calculation seriously.

The table below shows marriage rates and divorce rates for various countries. For example, the Canadian divorce rate of 3.2 in 2005 means that in that year, 3.2 Canadians between 15 and 64 years old got a divorce. The United States has the highest divorce rate in this group, but it also has the highest marriage rate. The more marriages you have, the more potential you have for divorces. When a common-law relationship ends, this does not count as a divorce.

Marriage and Divorce Rates by Country, 1980 to 2005

Country	Marriage Rate*				Divorce Rate**			
	1980	1990	2000	2005	1980	1990	2000	2005
Canada	11.5	10.0	7.5	6.8	3.7	4.2	3.4	3.2
United States	15.9	14.9	12.5	11.2	7.9	7.2	6.2	5.4
Japan	9.8	8.4	9.3	8.4	1.8	1.8	3.1	3.1
Denmark	8.0	9.1	10.8	10.1	4.1	4.0	4.0	4.3
France	9.7	7.7	7.9	7.1	2.4	2.8	3.0	3.5
Germany		8.2	7.6	7.0		2.5	3.5	4.0
Ireland	10.9	8.3	7.6	7.2			1.0	1.2
Italy	8.7	8.2	7.3	6.5	0.3	0.7	1.0	1.2
Netherlands	9.6	9.3	8.2	6.7	2.7	2.8	3.2	2.9
Spain	9.4	8.5	7.9	7.0		0.9	1.4	1.7
Sweden	7.1	7.4	7.0	7.5	3.7	3.5	3.8	3.4
United Kingdom	11.6	10.0	8.0	8.0	4.1	4.1	4.0	3.9

* The number of marriages per 1000 people in the population aged 15 to 64, per year.
** The number of divorces per 1000 people in the population aged 15 to 64, per year.

[grey box] = Data Not Available

Source: U.S. Bureau of Labor Statistics, updated and revised from "Families and Work in Transition in 12 Countries, 1980–2001," Monthly Labor Review, September 2003, with unpublished data. Accessed at http://www.bls.gov. Adapted from Statistics Canada, CANSIM database http://cansim2.statcan.gc.ca, Table 101-6501, February 17, 2011.[40]

If you consider Canada's divorce rate of 3.2 for every 1000 members of the population between 15 and 64 years of age, less than one percent of that population experienced a divorce in 2005. Of course, not everyone gets married, but it's clear that married couples' chances of divorce are far lower than the media's projected 50 percent.

Sociological Reasons for the High Divorce Rate

For the first half of the twentieth century, divorce rates in Canada were quite low. Then in 1968 the rate spiked dramatically, and reached an all-time high in 1987. It has been declining ever since.[41] Why?

1 **Residential Mobility of the Nuclear Family.** Moving around a lot, people don't find the external support for their marriages in the form of family and community. The family becomes isolated from extended family and old friends, and this isolation causes more stress.

2 **Ongoing Redefinition of Family and Gender Roles.** Changing gender roles create tension, which can lead to conflict and the dissolution of relationships.

3 **Ease of Filing for a Divorce.** In 1968, Parliament enacted the federal *Divorce Act* making it easier for couples to end a marriage. This law was revised in 1985, making it even easier.[42]

4 **Longevity.** People live longer, making it harder to maintain a stable relationship. It increases the chance that you and your spouse will encounter stresses that could lead to your divorce. Generally, as the population ages, the percentage of those who experience divorce increases.

5 **Social Acceptance.** Today, divorce is socially acceptable in Canada. In grade school, I didn't know anyone living in a home of divorce. In my children's school, there are many students with divorced parents. Divorce is much more common today, so the social acceptance may also increase the likelihood of it.[43]

∧∧∧ **When children leave home, some parents feel sad, while others feel satisfied.** How did your parents react when you left home for the first time?

Later States of the Family

Family dynamics often shift when children move out of the house. When the last child leaves the house, mothers may have a difficult period of adjustment, called "empty nest syndrome." However, many couples report increased marital satisfaction and companionship after their children leave. Sociologist Lillian Rubin says that empty nest syndrome is largely a myth.[44]

A more modern issue is the phenomenon of "extended childhood." Some children wait until a later age to leave home or move back in after college. Tough job markets and high costs of living sometimes make this necessary.[45] However, sociologist Michael Rosenfeld suggests that a certain percentage of adult children have always lived at home.[46]

Finally, there is the inevitability of death. Women generally live longer than men, so aging women are more likely to contend with issues associated with widowhood. We saw in Chapter 11 that older women are also at a higher risk of ending up in poverty.

<<< **Getting a divorce in Canada is much easier than getting a divorce in Europe.** Some European countries have up to a six-year waiting period, while most divorces in Canada are finalized in less than three months.[47]

think sociologically: IS THE FAMILY IN DECLINE?

Symbolic Interactionism

Symbolic interactionists investigate how values and definitions of reality influence the way in which society sees an issue. What exactly is marriage? Is the importance of the family decreasing? What exactly is a "traditional marriage"?[48]

Conway points out that marriage as a tradition has changed a great deal over time. In his book *The Canadian Family in Crisis,* he provides a comprehensive study of how marriages have changed over time. The only constant in marriage has been the constant change in its form. In earlier historical periods, living in extended families was normal, while cohabitation and divorce were rare. One hundred years ago, people would have defined marriage differently than they do today. Over time, society has shifted to see nuclear families, divorced families, and cohabitating families as families. The definition of what is and is not a family has changed, and it will likely continue to do so.[49]

THINK SOCIOLOGICALLY

Marriage and Men's Lives

Does marriage have special benefits for men? Steven L. Nock, director of the Marriage Matters project, believes so. In *Marriage in Men's Lives,* Nock argues that marriage is a positive force in men's lives, making them less likely to frequent bars and engage in risky behaviours. Men who are married live longer and are healthier overall. Furthermore, they express greater satisfaction in their lives. In a sense, marriage plays an important role for men's happiness, and it also can help them define their masculinity.

Adult males' masculinity is developed and sustained when men enter a marriage characterized by fairly traditionally gendered beliefs and practices. In this environment, they are able to fulfill and express their sense of manhood. Nock suggests that this is rooted in a long history in which men play the roles of hunter/gather, protector, and supporter of family. These primitive roles are linked to modern family roles as men now see economic achievement as their obligation and role.[50]

If we are to believe, as Nock argues, that much of men's sense of masculinity comes from the traditional family form, this poses a question: How is masculinity surviving the changing norms of society? Simply put, am I still a man even if I am economically dependent upon my wife to do housework and cook meals?

Nock suggests a new system in which it is necessary for both partners to feel as though they are contributing equally to the household. However, these new roles are going to be difficult to fill for some men since they had no role models in this form of family. The gender-role stereotype is deeply ingrained in society, so acceptance of new gender roles will take time.

Feminist Theory

While the feminist movement has made significant gains for women in the public domain, such as paid employment and education, the family still remains a place of unequal division of labour. As a married person, I can

Erosion of the American TV Family

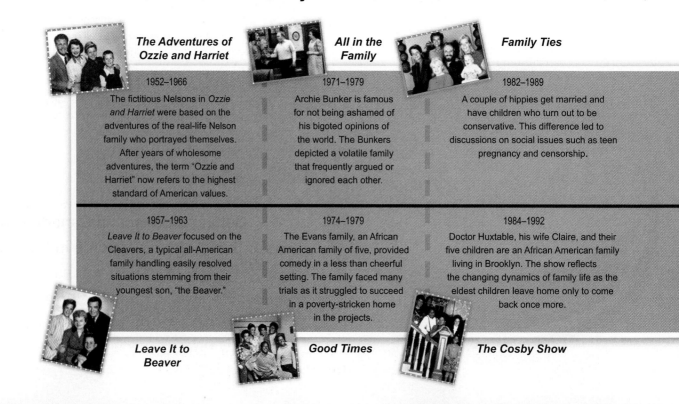

The Adventures of Ozzie and Harriet

1952–1966

The fictitious Nelsons in *Ozzie and Harriet* were based on the adventures of the real-life Nelson family who portrayed themselves. After years of wholesome adventures, the term "Ozzie and Harriet" now refers to the highest standard of American values.

All in the Family

1971–1979

Archie Bunker is famous for not being ashamed of his bigoted opinions of the world. The Bunkers depicted a volatile family that frequently argued or ignored each other.

Family Ties

1982–1989

A couple of hippies get married and have children who turn out to be conservative. This difference led to discussions on social issues such as teen pregnancy and censorship.

1957–1963

Leave It to Beaver focused on the Cleavers, a typical all-American family handling easily resolved situations stemming from their youngest son, "the Beaver."

1974–1979

The Evans family, an African American family of five, provided comedy in a less than cheerful setting. The family faced many trials as it struggled to succeed in a poverty-stricken home in the projects.

1984–1992

Doctor Huxtable, his wife Claire, and their five children are an African American family living in Brooklyn. The show reflects the changing dynamics of family life as the eldest children leave home only to come back once more.

Leave It to Beaver

Good Times

The Cosby Show

safely say that marital disagreements sometimes centre on the division of household labour, and our two most scarce resources: energy and free time. Historically, men would control these resources, but with changes in the form of family, this is not always true.

Modern times have created many dual-career households. But with both partners working, who's taking care of the house? In *The Second Shift: Working Parents and the Revolution at Home,* Arlie Hochschild argues that working wives end up doing most of the housework. Stevens and colleagues also note the dissatisfaction wives feel when the division of household work is unequal.[51]

In general, the women in *The Second Shift* seem to accept this role as something they cannot change. But some women find difficulties in their "first shift," which frequently doesn't honour their desires to be mothers, employees, and wives. Likewise, some women feel stuck because they realize a divorce will leave them with less income and more work.[52]

Conflict Theory

In the pre-industrial age, the family was both a producer and a consumer of goods. With industrialization, work shifted from the home to the factory. It was often the husband/father who would leave the home to work for a wage, and the money earned was used to buy goods and services in the market. The family became a consumption unit of society, and since it was primarily the man who provided the income, this gave him more power over his dependent wife and children.

Conflict theory also suggests that work and family are incompatible due to their different norms and responsibilities. These different norms and responsibilities cause intrusion and spill-over from one domain to the other. For example, if an individual spends many hours at work, this will probably interfere with his or her family life. On the other hand, an individual who has problems at home will often bring them to work.[53]

Functionalism

According to Durkheim, families are functional institutions that increase one's ability to function in society. People must get along with others in their family, which in turn prepares them for getting along with others in

society.[54] At the beginning of the twentieth century, historian Arthur Calhoun proclaimed, "The child is becoming the center of life"; however, sociologist David Popenoe believes "the family" has gone downhill fast.[55]

POPENOE'S EROSION OF THE FAMILY

Popenoe believes that the traditional nuclear family has been in decline for a long time, but the erosion of the family has accelerated over the past 25 years. During this time, the strengths that make up family institutions have weakened significantly. Popenoe claims that the three key strengths of families are cohesion, the performance of familial functions, and the power family has over other social institutions.[56]

Individuals have become more autonomous, leaving family members less connected. Families once spent days on end with each other; this is far less likely to occur now. When families lose cohesion, they are unable to perform their functions. Furthermore, after the Industrial Revolution, families couldn't provide their children with a means to live because they generally left the farm and worked for someone else.[57] Mandatory education relieved parents from the responsibility of educating their children. The size of the family is smaller, weakening traditional functions. For Popenoe, these prove that family is losing its importance in the United States. These same factors are weakening the traditional functions of Canadian families as well.

Popenoe believes that **the traditional nuclear family has been in decline for a long time, but the erosion of the family has accelerated over the past 25 years.** During this time, the strengths that make up family institutions have weakened significantly.

One just has to look at the evolution of TV sitcoms to witness the family's erosion. Many family sitcoms emerged in the 1950s depicting the ideal nuclear family: a strong father figure, caring mother, and respectful, docile children. Over time, sitcoms began showing women working and children being more assertive in their views. Soon, the strong patriarch devolved into a comical imbecile, and the mother started wearing the pants in the family.

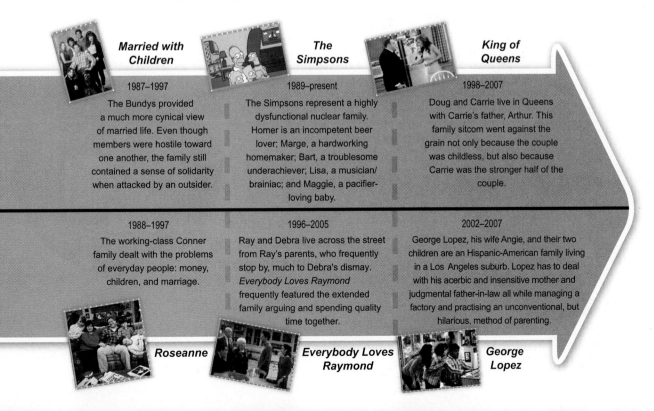

Married with Children

1987–1997

The Bundys provided a much more cynical view of married life. Even though members were hostile toward one another, the family still contained a sense of solidarity when attacked by an outsider.

The Simpsons

1989–present

The Simpsons represent a highly dysfunctional nuclear family. Homer is an incompetent beer lover; Marge, a hardworking homemaker; Bart, a troublesome underachiever; Lisa, a musician/brainiac; and Maggie, a pacifier-loving baby.

King of Queens

1998–2007

Doug and Carrie live in Queens with Carrie's father, Arthur. This family sitcom went against the grain not only because the couple was childless, but also because Carrie was the stronger half of the couple.

1988–1997

The working-class Conner family dealt with the problems of everyday people: money, children, and marriage.

1996–2005

Ray and Debra live across the street from Ray's parents, who frequently stop by, much to Debra's dismay. *Everybody Loves Raymond* frequently featured the extended family arguing and spending quality time together.

2002–2007

George Lopez, his wife Angie, and their two children are an Hispanic-American family living in a Los Angeles suburb. Lopez has to deal with his acerbic and insensitive mother and judgmental father-in-law all while managing a factory and practising an unconventional, but hilarious, method of parenting.

Roseanne

Everybody Loves Raymond

George Lopez

WRAP YOUR MIND AROUND THE THEORY

David Popenoe suggests that **the traditional nuclear family is practically extinct.**

FUNCTIONALISM

The family serves as a mechanism for maintaining order. The traditional functions of the family include: (1) *Reproduction and socialization of children.* The species can't go on and the group can't exist without replacing members and training them. (2) *Affection, companionship, and recreation.* Families provide a social structure that gives us support. (3) *Sexual regulation.* A lack of sexual regulation can result in conflicts within society, both between members as well as in determining the lineage of a child. (4) *Economic cooperation.* It is cheaper to live with someone else than to live alone. (5) *Care for the sick and aged.* When you had your wisdom teeth taken out, who took care of you? Throughout history, people have had these needs and used the family to solve them.

CONFLICT THEORY

Industrialization pushed the family from producing goods to primarily consuming goods. Since it was usually the father/husband who worked outside the home and earned a wage in order to buy goods and services, he held more power. Working outside the home involves different norms and responsibilities. These different norms and responsibilities may conflict with each other.

IS THE FAMILY IN DECLINE?

SYMBOLIC INTERACTIONISM

Interactionists look at the family on a micro level, by studying the relationships between individual family members. The expectation of different roles played out by men and women help determine the success of a marriage. Traditionally, men played the role of "breadwinner," while women played "homemaker." Since these roles are in a state of constant change, the way in which couples adjust to these changes defines the structure of the family. Furthermore, Coontz points out that change in ideologies shows that the institution of the family is simply changing, not declining.

FEMINIST THEORY

In *The Second Shift,* Hochschild discusses the disparity between men and women in terms of housework and how this leads to conflict between husbands and wives. This argument is about time, energy, and leisure. Wives tend to get stuck with the bulk of the work, leaving many disgruntled. This does not show a breakdown in marriage, but instead, according to Coontz, is a socioeconomic problem. Both parents are forced to work outside the home to survive, unlike many families of the past, and this change creates conflict.

Many **couples fight over** who gets more **free time and leisure.**

As **families evolve in order to keep up with social trends,** ideologies associated with the family also need to evolve.

discover sociology in action: HOW ARE FAMILIES CHANGING?

Same-Sex Marriage in Canada

In 1965, Everett Klippert was being interrogated by police in the Northwest Territories about an arson case. During the interrogation, he admitted that he had had sex with men. Because homosexual acts were illegal under the *Criminal Code,* Klippert was sent to prison indefinitely as a "dangerous sex offender." Two years later, in 1967, Justice Minister Pierre Trudeau proposed a revision of the *Criminal Code,* and made his famous statement that "There's no place for the state in the bedrooms of the nation." In 1969 the amendments were passed, and homosexuality was decriminalized in Canada. Two years later, Everett Klippert was released.

In 1988, Svend Robinson of the New Democratic Party publicly announced that he was gay, becoming the first member of Parliament to do so. In 1995, an Ontario judge ruled that four lesbians had the right to adopt their partners' children. Ontario became the first province to make it legal for same-sex couples to adopt, and the other provinces soon adopted similar legislation. In May 1999 the Supreme Court of Canada ruled that same-sex couples should have the same social benefits as opposite-sex common-law couples. A year later, Parliament passed a bill that gave same-sex couples the same social and tax benefits as heterosexuals in common-law relationships.

On July 12, 2002, the Ontario Superior Court became the first Canadian court to rule in favour of recognizing same-sex marriages under the law. Later that year, a nation-wide poll found that 45 percent of Canadians would vote Yes if there were a referendum to change the definition of marriage to one that could include same-sex couples. The next year, Prime Minister Jean Chrétien proposed legislation that would make same-sex marriages legal, while at the same time permitting religious groups to "sanctify marriage as they see it." In July 2003, British Columbia became the second province to legalize same-sex marriages; a year later, Quebec became the third. Same-sex marriages were now legal in three Canadian provinces, but there was still no national legislation on this issue.

It was bound to happen, and in June 2004 a lesbian couple in Ontario filed for the first same-sex divorce. By 2005, eight provincial courts had passed legislation recognizing same-sex marriages. On July 20, 2005, Bill C-38, a law giving same-sex couples the legal right to marry, received royal assent and became law. Canada was the fourth country in the world to legalize same-sex marriage.[58]

When we discuss this issue in class, some students raise concerns over the sanctity of marriage and the welfare of children involved. However, students who raise concerns over the sanctity of marriage almost never propose eliminating divorce, which is far more common. Also, children raised by gay or lesbian parents have lower rates of child abuse and neglect and better educational attainment compared to their peers in households with heterosexual parents.[59] Regardless of whether a person believes one's sexual orientation is a choice or not, the question is, really, should government restrict that choice or give benefits to some but not to others? In Canada, we said no.

> ### ACTIVITIES
>
> 1. Watch a prime-time sitcom or drama and analyze the depiction of family life on that show. Are the characters married or unmarried? What roles do men and women play in their relationships? Write a paragraph analyzing the show.
> 2. Interview an elderly family member or acquaintance. Discuss what family life was like when he or she was your age. How did his or her experience differ from your own?

From Classroom to Community | Adoption for Same-Sex Couples

Josephine did her community learning at a group home for orphaned children. She was assigned the task of greeting prospective foster parents and playing with the children in the home.

"The foster children are excited when prospective parents come to visit, because they all want to be part of a loving, caring home.

"Most of the foster parents were married heterosexual couples, but occasionally a gay or lesbian couple would come in. I was upset by the attitude of some of my fellow volunteers. Several felt that same-sex couples should not be allowed to adopt children.

"I tried explaining that children raised by homosexuals were no more likely to be gay than those raised by heterosexuals. But willing, adoptive parents were rejected based on their sexual orientation. It's sad because many children await adoption, and a home is surely a better place than a shelter."

13

get the topic: WHAT IS A FAMILY?

Theory

SYMBOLIC INTERACTIONISM   242

- expectations of roles help determine the success of the family
- the way couples respond to changes in their environment affect the structure of the family

FEMINIST THEORY   242

- Hochschild's *The Second Shift*; family is a system in which women are generally stuck doing the majority of the work
- husbands and wives argue over time, energy, and leisure
- both people work because of socioeconomic problems, which causes tension

CONFLICT THEORY   243

- industrialization changed families from producers and consumers to primarily consumers.
- it was usually the husband/father who would go out to work and earn a wage that was used to buy goods and services
- work and family have different norms and responsibilities that may influence each other

FUNCTIONALISM   243

- family serves as a way to maintain order
- parents teach children how to behave and what is acceptable
- Popenoe: the family is no longer cohesive, functional, or powerful

Key Terms

family is two or more people who are related by blood, marriage, or adoption.   *232*

marriage is the union of two people that is typically recognized by law or cultural norms.   *232*

nuclear family is a household consisting of a husband, wife, and children.   *233*

extended family is a household consisting of a nuclear family plus an additional relative.   *233*

monogamy is the practice of being married to one person at a time.   *234*

polygamy is the practice of having more than one spouse at a time.   *234*

polygyny is the practice of a man marrying two or more women.   *234*

polyandry is the practice of a woman marrying two or more men.   *234*

blended families are families composed of children and some combination of biological parents.   *234*

homogamy is marriage between people with similar backgrounds, such as religion, ethnicity, class, or age.   *238*

endogamy is the practice of marrying within your social group.   *238*

exogamy is the practice of marrying someone from a different social group.   *238*

marital effects are factors that make marriage work.   *238*

Sample Test Questions

These multiple-choice questions are similar to those found in the test bank that accompanies this textbook.

1. Which of the following is one of the four *Bs* of marriage?
   a. Billing
   b. Business
   c. Boredom
   d. Breakup
2. What is someone who marries within his or her social group practising?
   a. Homogamy
   b. Endogamy
   c. Polyandry
   d. Exogamy
3. Women who work a "second shift"
   a. come home to hours of housework.
   b. must work two jobs to make ends meet.
   c. go back and get new jobs when they marry.
   d. equally divide responsibilities with their spouses.
4. The "appropriateness" of a spouse is dependent upon
   a. marital effects in a marriage.
   b. cultural norms and regulations.
   c. gender ideologies and gender roles.
   d. physical and mental characteristics.
5. Which of the following is *not* one of the listed reasons for the increased divorce rate in Canada?
   a. Longer life spans
   b. More mobile families
   c. Easier paperwork
   d. Lax marriage laws and tax breaks

ANSWERS: 1. c; 2. b; 3. a; 4. b; 5. d

ESSAY

1. Why do so many people consider the 1950s an ideal time for the traditional nuclear family?
2. What are some of the causes in the changing of the traditional nuclear family?
3. Why do some couples wait to have children?
4. What is the stimulus-value-role theory?
5. What are some of Conway's myths of marriage?

WHERE TO START YOUR RESEARCH PAPER

To find information about Canadian families and the challenges they face in their structural, demographic, economic, cultural, and social diversity, go to www.vifamily.ca

To learn about same-sex marriage in Canada, legislation and definitions, go to www.chrc-ccdp.ca/legislation_policies/submission_marriage-eng.aspx

For statistical information about marriage, common-law unions, and family types, go to www.statcan.gc.ca/subject-sujet/theme-theme.action?pid=40000&lang=eng&more=0

To learn about marriage and family therapy, go to www.marriageandfamily.ca

To find more information about the divorce rates in Canada, go to www.divorceincanada.ca

Remember to check www.thethinkspot.ca **for additional information, downloadable flashcards, and other helpful resources.**

EDUCATION AND RELIGION

"A majority

of Canadians believe that their children will attend a post-secondary educational institution when they finish high school. Further education after high school education is increasingly seen as a vitally important part of a person's life, both for participation and success in the knowledge economy. Human Resources Development Canada has estimated that by 2004 more than 70% of new jobs created will require a college or university education, with nearly half of those new jobs requiring at minimum a Bachelor's degree. . . .

"According to recent reports, Canada has the greatest proportion of citizens with post-secondary education of all the OECD [Organisation for Economic Co-operation and Development] countries. . . . Recognizing the importance

of an increasingly educated population, the Canadian Government pledged in 2002 to ensure that '. . . one hundred percent of high school graduates have the opportunity to participate in some form of post-secondary education. . . .' However, questions remain about how accessible post-secondary education really is in Canada. Although participation in post-secondary education has remained strong in the face of rising up-front costs to individual students, it is not clear that particular groups of people are being represented in all aspects of post-secondary education. . . .

"Researchers point to a number of factors, related to socio-economic status or family background, that impact an individual's decision to attend a post-secondary institution. Parental expectations of attendance, attitudes of family and friends, knowledge of costs and funding options, gender, and academic achievement are all related to whether or not individuals are able to choose to further their education after high school."[1]

How Do Societies Pass on Information?

CHAPTER 14

As Andrea Rounce writes—in *Access to Post-secondary Education: Does Class Still Matter?*—despite an official pledge to achieve 100 percent participation in post-secondary education, there are still many social barriers to achieving this goal.

Access to Post-secondary Education: Does Class Still Matter?

By Andrea Rounce

ISBN: 0-88627-381-1   August 2004

I sometimes ask my students why they are in college. The most common answer is "to get a better job." Upon further questioning, a better job is inevitably one that pays well. Students seem to equate education with higher income, and they are right to do so, because this is a social fact that is well-established in our society.

After discussing all the benefits of post-secondary education, we end up agreeing that post-secondary education is a good thing. I then ask them "Well, if getting a college degree is such a great thing, why doesn't everyone get one?" After a bit of reflection, some will answer "College isn't for everyone." Almost always, they point to individual decisions not to attend.

Perhaps they are right. Some people may decide that high school was difficult enough, and post-secondary education is just not for them. And some of these people go on to do very well. But let's hope that by now, you have enough sociological imagination to appreciate that "decisions" that may seem personal are often taken within a social context that has a powerful influence over us. A student whose family and friends don't encourage post-secondary education may more easily "decide" that college is not for him, while another student whose family and friends do encourage it will just as easily "decide" to go to college.

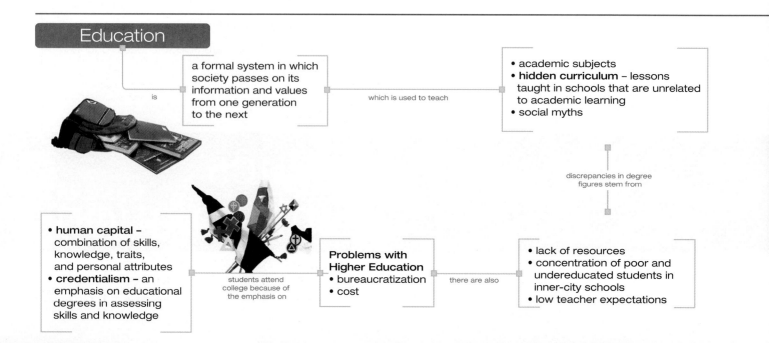

Education

is — a formal system in which society passes on its information and values from one generation to the next

which is used to teach —
• academic subjects
• **hidden curriculum** – lessons taught in schools that are unrelated to academic learning
• social myths

discrepancies in degree figures stem from

• **human capital** – combination of skills, knowledge, traits, and personal attributes
• **credentialism** – an emphasis on educational degrees in assessing skills and knowledge

students attend college because of the emphasis on

Problems with Higher Education
• bureaucratization
• cost

there are also

• lack of resources
• concentration of poor and undereducated students in inner-city schools
• low teacher expectations

get the topic: HOW DO SOCIETIES PASS ON INFORMATION?

Education in Society

> **EDUCATION** is the formal system in which society passes its knowledge, skills, and values from one generation to the next.

I often ask my students, "If I promised all of you an A, then asked those genuinely interested in learning to return, how many of you would be here tomorrow?" Rarely do I have more than five percent of my students raise their hands. Why is that? I've always found that students tend to be pragmatic about their reasons for education. They ask themselves, "What can I do with this degree?"

Since the Industrial Revolution, there has been a link between economic advancement and **education**, the formal system in which society passes on its knowledge, skills, and values from one generation to the next. Schools connect to the job system because they train individuals for specific types of work. For example, in order to become a surgeon, students must go through years of schooling and training. However, when they complete school, they have the benefit of a high salary, and the community benefits from their medical knowledge. In order to reach this point, students need to make an extended commitment to their education.

Educational Attainment of the Population 15 Years and Older, 2006

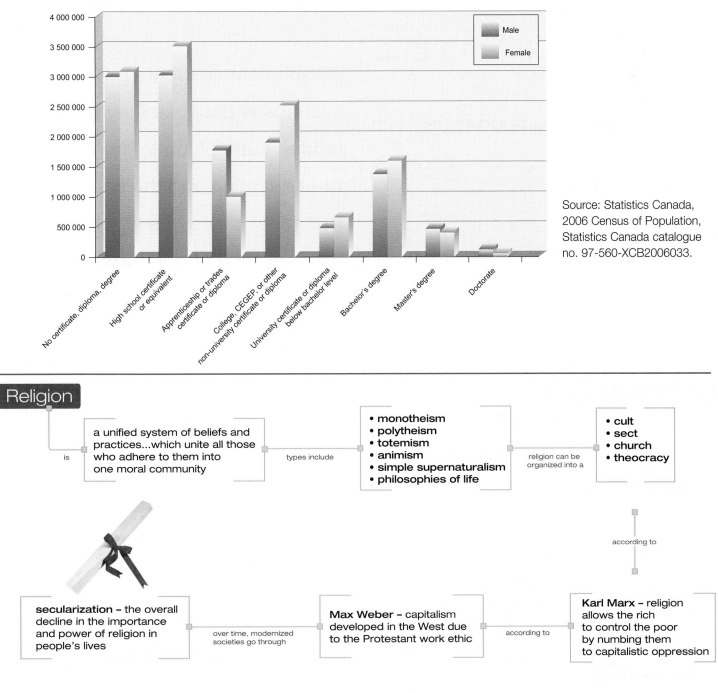

Source: Statistics Canada, 2006 Census of Population, Statistics Canada catalogue no. 97-560-XCB2006033.

Religion

is a unified system of beliefs and practices...which unite all those who adhere to them into one moral community

types include
- monotheism
- polytheism
- totemism
- animism
- simple supernaturalism
- philosophies of life

religion can be organized into a
- cult
- sect
- church
- theocracy

according to

secularization – the overall decline in the importance and power of religion in people's lives

over time, modernized societies go through

Max Weber – capitalism developed in the West due to the Protestant work ethic

according to

Karl Marx – religion allows the rich to control the poor by numbing them to capitalistic oppression

HIDDEN CURRICULUM

When I was in elementary school, our school did not have air conditioning. With the sponsorship of a teacher, myself, and another student, we started a small school store, the proceeds of which went toward installing air conditioners throughout the school. In less than two years, we earned enough money selling school supplies to provide air-conditioners for the entire school. Through this experience, I learned about capitalism, hard work, and service.

Schools teach more than just academic subjects. If you think back to elementary school, you'll remember that you learned all kinds of things that are unrelated to academic life, like sharing and communication. Sociologists suggest that the education system plays an important role in society, because it teaches individuals the values of a community.

Certainly we want to transfer academic knowledge to the next generation, but schools also socialize students in what some call the "hidden curriculum." The term *hidden curriculum* refers to lessons taught in schools that are unrelated to academic learning. Schools teach children about citizenship when they have mock elections, and they teach us to follow orders, routines, and other seemingly arbitrary regulations. The hidden curriculum also applies to students' socialization of one another. Students learn how to negotiate their neighbourhoods and how to deal with peers and peer conflicts successfully. This prepares students for stresses that will occur later in life.[2]

ROOTS OF MODERN EDUCATION SYSTEMS

People began going to school to learn the three Rs—reading, 'riting, and 'rithmetic—right? Actually, the expansion of education systems is a social movement that stems from the ideas of building a nation and building the ideology of a nation's identity. This means that education also serves to ensure that certain "myths" are spread throughout society. These "myths" may or may not be factually true, but they are vital to the success of building a unified nation. Thinking back, do you remember any school activities that supported these myths?

Myth of the individual. The primary unit in society is the individual, not the family, clan, or ethnic group. Therefore, it is up to the individual to improve his or her place in society.

Myth of the nation as a group of individuals. The nation is no longer the property of a king or some group of elites. Individuals make up society and the nation. Therefore, by developing your skills and knowledge, you are bettering yourself and your community.

Myth of progress. Society's goal is to improve the status of both current and future residents. Thus, education for children is one way a nation can support the idea that it is working toward self-improvement.

Myth of socialization and life cycle continuity. Childhood socialization leads to adult character. Therefore, if children are socialized properly, this will lead to good character that ultimately benefits the nation in the long run. Thus, educating children plays a vital role in this endeavour.

Myth of the state as the guardian of the nation. It is the state's job to raise good, loyal, patriotic children, who will then be the next generation of good, loyal, and patriotic adults. In this way, socializing children into the nation becomes the role of the state, not the family.[3]

However, you should note that these myths are not universal. Certain groups see this forced homogenization as detrimental to their way of life. The Africentric Alternative School in Toronto, for example, is working to give students more "culturally relevant resources."[4] (For more on the Africentric Alternative School, see page 264.)

By looking at these five myths, you can see that **state-sponsored schools are an essential part of any strong nation.** Notice that nowhere on this list is the idea that everyone should learn to read. **One reason nations create educational systems is because they foster the hidden curriculum. In the long run, the education and the socialization that takes place in schools paves the way for a strong future.**

EDUCATION THROUGHOUT THE WORLD

Every nation has some type of educational system; however, not all educational systems are equal. The amount of resources, funding, and worth placed on education varies, which in turn creates inequalities in global education. A country's socioeconomic status has a huge effect on its education system. Systems in developing countries often fail to provide children with basic educational needs and struggle to sustain stable educational institutions. Paraguay, Sri Lanka, and the Philippines are all countries where one in five students goes to a school with no running water.[5]

Poor education systems often result in low literacy rates, or low percentages of people in the population who can read and write. In Sierra Leone, only 47 percent of men and 24 percent of women over the age of 15 are literate. This falls far below the world literacy rate of 88 percent of men and 79 percent of women.[6] Aside from showing you how poor education systems affect literacy rates, these figures also show you the imbalance of education between men and women. The number of women educated is almost half the number of men educated in Sierra Leone. Similarly, as you can see in the literacy rates map on the next page, in every region of the world, male literacy rates are higher than female literacy rates. In Chapter 10, you learned about gender stratification and how men and women have been treated differently throughout history. Unfortunately, this is still true today.

A country's wealth plays a central role in education, so lack of funding and resources from a nation-state can weaken a system. Governments in sub-Saharan Africa spend only 2.4 percent of the world's public resources on education, yet 15 percent of the school-age population lives there. Conversely, North America and Western Europe spend 55.1 percent of all the money spent in the world on education, yet they house only about 8 percent of the world's school-age population.[7]

Total expenditure on education in Canada—that is, including private as well as public sources—came to $72.3 billion, or $2305 per person, in 2002–2003. Of that, 59 percent was for elementary-school education and 41 percent for post-secondary education. (Note that public expenditure includes money from the federal, provincial/territorial, and municipal governments.) Canada's total public and private spending on education accounted for 6.4 percent of the GDP in 2002–2003. Exact comparisons between different jurisdictions in the country can't be made easily; nevertheless, education spending relative to GDP ranged from 18.5 percent in Nunavut to 5.3 percent in Alberta.[8]

As the above figures indicate, colleges and universities receive taxpayer benefits to keep their doors open. I often ask my students, "Who's on welfare in here?" Usually, no one raises a hand. However, attending college or university almost guarantees you are on educational welfare because taxpayers subsidize some part of your education.

No matter what kind of college or university you attend, you'd probably agree that the main goal of attending is to receive a degree. Between 1991 and 2004, the number of degrees issued by higher education institutions in Canada increased from 28 percent to 33 percent.[9] But who exactly is receiving these degrees? Does ethnicity, gender, or socioeconomic status affect educational attainment? You bet it does.

EDUCATIONAL DISCREPANCIES OF NOTE IN CANADA

"Unfortunately, most Canadians are not aware of the many issues which brought about the need for First Nations Peoples to assert their rightful position in Canadian society. Many are unaware of conditions that aboriginal people experience in Canada—discrimination, exploitation, and violations against basic human rights. Furthermore, all of these infractions are grossly ignored and glossed over by standard Canadian history textbooks." This statement appears on the Assembly of First Nations website.[10] Think back to Chapter 4 and the deliberate moves aimed at weakening the structure and culture of the First Nations Peoples in Canada, such as residential schools (the last one of which closed in 1996).

It's no secret that socioeconomic background is one of the facts that can influence the way a person's education will develop. Aboriginal peoples in Canada today are overcoming an extremely difficult background, and, in the words of one recent study, while many aboriginal people are doing "quite well," the fact is that "on average the aboriginal population suffers from higher unemployment, lower levels of education, below average incomes and many other indicators of limited socioeconomic circumstances." The way to turn this around, the study says, "is through education."[11]

The breakdown of post-secondary educational figures in Canada shows the following: aboriginal peoples lag behind non-aboriginal Canadian-born people in terms of the percentage with college and university credentials, and recent immigrants far outdo both groups on the university front. Focusing on those aged 25 to 64, the 2006 census revealed that, among aboriginal people, 19 percent had a college diploma and 8 percent a university degree, compared with 22 percent and 20 percent, respectively, of the non-aboriginal Canadian-born population. For recent immigrants, the figures were 51 percent and 11 percent, respectively. (Of immigrants who entered Canada before 2001, 28 percent had a university degree.[12])

Discrepancies at the post-secondary level are a reflection of discrepancies down the line. A 2008 Vancouver newspaper headline read "Study Gives Aboriginal Education a Failing Grade." The study concerned was conducted by Simon Fraser University economist John Richards for the C.D. Howe Institute, and it concluded, in the newspaper's words, that "Aboriginal education is falling further behind schooling for other Canadians, and all levels of government . . . are failing to do much about it."[13] If things don't change, Richards warned, there will be economic losses due to low productivity, as well as an "impact on poverty and racial tension."[14]

Regional Literacy Rates for Adults (15+), 2005–2007

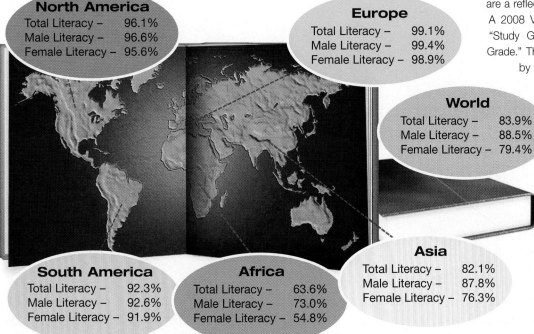

North America
Total Literacy –	96.1%
Male Literacy –	96.6%
Female Literacy –	95.6%

Europe
Total Literacy –	99.1%
Male Literacy –	99.4%
Female Literacy –	98.9%

World
Total Literacy –	83.9%
Male Literacy –	88.5%
Female Literacy –	79.4%

South America
Total Literacy –	92.3%
Male Literacy –	92.6%
Female Literacy –	91.9%

Africa
Total Literacy –	63.6%
Male Literacy –	73.0%
Female Literacy –	54.8%

Asia
Total Literacy –	82.1%
Male Literacy –	87.8%
Female Literacy –	76.3%

Source: Data from United Nations Educational, Scientific, and Cultural Organization (UNESCO) Institute for Statistics.

TEACHER EXPECTANCY EFFECT is the impact of a teacher's expectations on a student's performance.

GRADE INFLATION is the trend of assigning higher grades than previously assigned to students for completing the same work.

TEACHER EXPECTANCY AND ATTAINMENT

The phenomenon known as the **teacher expectancy effect**—the impact of a teacher's expectations on a student's performance—is not just applied to poor and minority students.[15] If a teacher expects that a student will love the class and do well, the student generally does well. Of course, measuring teacher expectations is a difficult thing to do. Some studies show that expectancies influence not only individual student performance, but also the performance of the entire school.[16] Other studies suggest that teachers may indeed influence students' self-perception, but that it is that perception that influences academic achievement.[17]

When I discuss this issue in class, I usually ask my students, "Who is afraid of math?" Many students sheepishly raise their hands. When we discuss why they fear mathematics, students usually say that they "don't get it," and they "hate it." When I ask the math-haters what grade they expect in their math course, the answer is usually "low." Such a self-fulfilling prophecy forms the core of most research on how educational expectations influence academic outcomes.

ACADEMIC ACHIEVEMENT

Grades

It's only in recent years that grade inflation has started to get serious attention in connection with Canadian campuses.[18] **Grade inflation** is the trend of assigning higher grades than previously assigned to students for completing the same work. "Many students now expect high grades for relatively little effort," James Côté and Anton Allahar state in their 2007 Canadian book *Ivory Tower Blues*. "Indeed, grade inflation has become rampant in many institutions throughout Canada and the United States, from high school through university."[19] In one of the first major studies of its kind in Canada, economics professors Paul M. Anglin and Ronald Men looked at grade patterns over 20 years at seven Ontario universities and concluded that "grade point averages rose in 11 of 12 arts and sciences

---

In the movie *Freedom Writers*, **Erin Gruwell's at-risk students were not expected to pass her class,** let alone graduate from high school. **However, all of her students graduated from high school, and many went on to college.**

courses between 1973–74 and 1993–94."[20] (The exception? Sociology.[21]) The study found that a higher percentage of students were getting As and Bs and fewer were getting Cs, Ds, and Fs.[22]

"It starts in high school," *Ivory Tower Blues* co-author James Côté has said. "Giving higher grades is one way to reward kids fairly easily, boost their self-esteem and stop them from dropping out." Grades, he said, have risen steadily since the 1970s "and have reached a crisis point."[23] Professors face pressure to conform to the trend.[24]

One of my own students recently approached me to discuss her grade. She was very upset because she had received a B in my course. This young woman was visibly distraught, breathing hard, brow furrowed, and she rapidly began to tell me that she had "never gotten a B" in her life. She felt like a failure. Couldn't she "write an extra paper" or "do some other assignment?"

"Everyone in my high school makes As," she said. "I'm not used to failing." I pointed out that a B was not failing and thought about grade inflation. When a student views a B as failure, what do grades mean? As I said to this student, "If everyone makes an A, then an A means nothing."

Some teachers claim that grade inflation is a result of the pressure that students are under to receive high marks that is then projected onto the instructor. Côté is one of those who believe that standardized testing might help in Canada.[25]

Home Schooling

Some parents choose to forgo the offerings of a traditional school education. Around 70 000 students are homeschooled across Canada each year.[26] As a professor I have taught some first-year students who were homeschooled. When I ask them why they were homeschooled, I hear a variety of reasons. Some say their parents were concerned about the quality of education at the public school they were assigned, but they couldn't afford a private school. Others cite religious reasons as the primary factor for learning at home. Still others report that a parent was an educator, and simply felt that a caring parent could do a better job of teaching his or her own children than an overworked stranger. These reports follow the general findings of researchers who study parents who homeschool. Such parents are generally motivated by a desire to be active in their children's learning, and although issues of value and quality are relevant, the strongest motivator of parents who homeschool appears to be a desire to be more deeply involved with their children.[27]

Higher Education: Bureaucratization and Cost

Traditional schools are formal organizations that have many of the aspects of any bureaucracy. Recall in Chapter 6 our discussion of Max Weber and formal organizations. The basic characteristics of bureaucracy are division of labour, rules and regulations, impersonality, hierarchy of authority, and technical qualifications. In your school, I'm sure you're aware that there is a hierarchy of authority, a division of labour among teachers, administrators, and support staff, and that most schools have student and faculty handbooks to make sure that everyone knows the rules and regulations. Schools can also take on these aspects of bureaucracy when they are impersonal to their students. For example, how many of you had to learn a unique student identification number upon entering college? Often when you enter a large population of students, you simply become a number.

Of course, by the time you reach college, you are probably used to the bureaucratic nature of education. However, I've heard some of my students say that a large part of their decision for choosing a college is

HUMAN CAPITAL is a person's combination of skills, knowledge, traits, and personal attributes.

CREDENTIALISM is an emphasis on educational degrees in assessing skills and knowledge.

based on personalization, but this is not always the case. What made you select where you go to college?

Costs can be a factor. Students sometimes base their college choice on factors such as accommodation costs and distance from family or friends, in part to help cut down on their overall expenses.

In Canada, the federal government supports post-secondary education only indirectly, through (a) financial transfers to the provinces and (b) funding of university research and student assistance.[28] In 2005–2006, undergraduate university tuition cost an average of $3788.[29] The percentage of graduates who had borrowed from any source to finance their higher education stood at 57 percent in 2005 (compared with 49 percent in 1995), and the average amount borrowed was $18 000 (up from $15 200 in 1995). As well, 27 percent of student borrowers had debt loads of $25 000 or more at graduation, compared with 17 percent in 1995.[30]

In some industrialized countries, education at all levels is free. For example, in Sweden, government and institutionally managed schools—primary, secondary, and post-secondary—are free of tuition courtesy of the Swedish government and taxpayers. This allows all students who meet certain academic standards to attend any school regardless of their economic status.[31]

Theories Behind Higher Education

Even though college can bring cost concerns and bureaucratization, you still decided to go. Why? Sociologists propose a few theories. First, students seek an education as a way to improve their **human capital**, or their combination of skills, knowledge, traits, and personal attributes. Generally, you know that an employer will reward a worker who performs better. Education improves your attractiveness to an employer and perhaps your output for that job. Such skills are important to employers, and you understand that it improves your place in the market for jobs. Thus, through education you can improve your social status, and the education system becomes the vehicle by which you come closer to acquiring that status.

Similarly, I know many people who chose to go to college because of the reality of **credentialism**—an emphasis on educational degrees in assessing skills and knowledge. Many jobs today require a post-secondary degree, but this was not always true. Neither of my parents had college degrees, but with hard work they held white-collar jobs in business management and accounting. Such a climb with a high school degree would be impossible in today's world. Employers use education as a type of litmus test to determine who is and who is not qualified. In North America, the status of holding a degree can be essential for success.[32]

EDUCATION AND RELIGION

It's no secret that indoctrinational religious instruction is not permitted in public schools in either Canada or the United States. Teachers are not allowed to promote one religion over another. Nevertheless, sociologists have found that a student's religious affiliation and involvement play a big role in his or her educational outcome.

The Five Most Expensive Canadian and American Universities in 2008

Most Expensive Canadian Universities		Most Expensive American Universities		
School	Tuition in C$	School	Tuition in $US	Converted to C$
1. Trinity Western University, Langley, BC	17 460	1. Sarah Lawrence College, Bronxville, NY	54 066	57 688
2. Redeemer University College, Ancaster, ON	11 924	2. Georgetown University, Washington, D.C.	50 700	54 097
3. The King's University College, Edmonton, AB	8 091	3. George Washington University, Washington, D.C.	50 537	53 923
4. Dalhousie University, Halifax, NS	6 990	4. New York University, New York City, NY	50 282	53 651
5. Royal Roads University, Victoria, BC	6 915	5. Johns Hopkins University, Baltimore, MD	49 778	53 124

Source Canadian data: msn.Money, Most Expensive Canadian Universities, by Jason Buckland, November 21, 2009, http://money.ca.msn.com/savings-debt/gallery/gallery.aspx?cp-documentid=22656953, accessed October 25, 2010.

Source U.S. data: http://www.fortunesmallbusiness.com/galleries/2009/news/0910/gallery.most_expensive_colleges/index.html, accessed February 16, 2011.

Studies have shown that educational attainment and religious practice generally have a positive correlation.[33] In other words, religiously active students are apt to perform well in school and to graduate. For example, the findings of one recent Canadian study suggested that—across all school grades—attending religious services is linked to both lower levels of substance use and higher academic achievement over time.[34]

In an earlier study, Texan Mark Regenerus found that intensely religious students scored better on standardized tests, "even after accounting for other predictors of academic success."[35] He argued that religious involvement gave students "a level of social control and motivation toward education."[36] This trend held up across all types of neighbourhoods—affluent and poor—and across many different ethnicities. In fact, the more disadvantaged the neighbourhood, the more beneficial a student's church attendance was on educational attainment.[37]

This research points to a possible connection between education and religion. Although certainly not causal, it does show that both of these social institutions perform a similar task—to socialize a person into society. Churches do this by socializing us into a value system, and schools do this through their academic mission and their transmission of the hidden curriculum.

MAKE CONNECTIONS

Scheduling Around the Holidays

In 2007, members of the New York Muslim community called for a change in the school holiday schedule when standardized state tests were scheduled on Id al-Adha, a Muslim holy day. Although students could take excused absences, parents argued that it was unfair that children were off for Christian and Jewish holidays. However, the New York Department of Education refused to add any additional holidays to the school schedule. Many U.S. school districts require that students be in school a certain number of days per school year, so any additional holidays would cause the school year to run even longer.[38]

Thoughts of altering the school calendar can get people worked up in Canada, too. There was a stir early in 2010 after the Quebec government moved toward changing the province's school calendar so that schools could stay open on weekends—and, it was initially thought, so that they could substitute their own religious holidays for the standard Christmas, Thanksgiving, and Easter. The Quebec education minister made headlines when she denied that any of the regular statutory holidays would change in the move, which she said was aimed at curbing Quebec's dropout problem.[39]

>>> ACTIVITY Create a new school calendar for your province that includes major religious holidays for the top three religions in the province. Remember that most school systems require that students be in school a set number of days, and that religious populations vary from province to province. Research the demographics of your province, and research the holidays of the three largest religious populations in your area. How difficult is it to create a schedule that meets everyone's religious needs?

Religion

Sociologist Émile Durkheim defined **religion** as a "unified system of beliefs and practices relative to sacred things, that is to say, things set apart and forbidden—beliefs and practices which unite into one single moral community called a Church, all those who adhere to them."[40] Although most societies have some sort of dominant religion, there are many different religions, each of which comes with its own set of beliefs and customs.

> **RELIGION** is a unified system of beliefs and practices, relative to sacred things.
>
> **THEISM** is the belief in a god or gods.
>
> **MONOTHEISM** is the belief that there is only one God.
>
> **POLYTHEISM** is the belief in multiple gods and demigods.
>
> **PHILOSOPHIES OF LIFE** are ways of life that focus on a set of ethical, moral, or philosophical principles.
>
> **TOTEMISM** is the practice of honouring a totem or a sacred object.

TYPES OF RELIGION

The three major religious groups of the West—Christians, Jews, and Muslims—all practise **theism**, the belief in a god or gods. More specifically, these religions practise **monotheism**, meaning they believe that there is only one God.[41]

Not all religions believe that there is one powerful God. Some religions believe in multiple gods or demigods; this belief is called **polytheism**. Instead of having multiple gods be all-powerful, many polytheistic cultures have a single god to represent a specific power or object. For example, in ancient Nordic mythology, Odin was the god of wisdom, and Thor was the warrior god.[42] In some cases, each village in a particular area may have its own god along with a particular place or a sacred object reserved for worshipping that god.[43]

Some cultures do not have religions per se, but have philosophies that help guide people throughout life. **Philosophies of life** are ways of life that focus on a set of ethical, moral, or philosophical principles. Buddhism, Confucianism, and Taoism are all philosophies of life and are dedicated to achieving a kind of moral enlightenment. This enlightenment is attained by following a specific set of rules, such as the teachings of Buddha or the laws of Confucius. The processes of being and becoming are key aspects of these ways of life.[44]

Preliterate societies practised **totemism** by honouring a totem or a sacred object. These totems were symbolic objects that often depicted animals or plants that were important to the community. The totem itself was thought to have divine and mystical powers. In addition to

World Religious Affiliations 2007

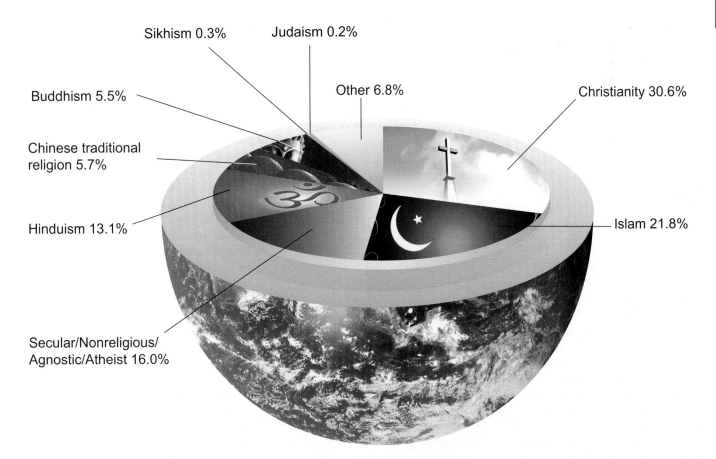

- Sikhism 0.3%
- Judaism 0.2%
- Buddhism 5.5%
- Chinese traditional religion 5.7%
- Other 6.8%
- Christianity 30.6%
- Hinduism 13.1%
- Islam 21.8%
- Secular/Nonreligious/Agnostic/Atheist 16.0%

Source: Major Religions of the World Ranked by Number of Adherents, Adherents.com

Hinduism in Canada

It should be no surprise that recent immigration patterns influence religious preferences in Canada. The 2001 census—the most recent one dealing with religion—reflected trends toward more immigrants coming from areas outside Europe, especially Asia and the Middle East. One of the religions it showed to have grown "substantially" in Canada was Hinduism.[45] Between 1991 and 2001, the number of people in Canada who identified themselves as Hindu rose by 89 percent, to 297 200—representing about 1 percent of the population. Hindus accounted for almost 7 percent of the new immigrants who came to Canada in the 1990s.[46]

Hinduism has existed for thousands of years. It's the world's third largest religion, after Christianity and Islam, and the majority of people in India practise it.[47] Different sources label Hinduism in different ways. But most forms of Hinduism are "henotheistic religions," according to ReligiousTolerance.org. **Henotheistic** religions "recognize a single deity, and view other Gods and Goddesses as manifestations or aspects of that supreme God."[48] In 2001, 73 percent of the Hindu population in Canada lived in Ontario.[49] There are more than 50 Hindu temples in the province, mostly around Toronto.[50]

HENOTHEISM is the worship of one god while recognizing the existence of other deities.

SIMPLE SUPERNATURALISM is the belief in a variety of supernatural forces that affect and influence people's lives.

ANIMISM is the belief that recognizes that animate spirits live in natural objects and operate in the world.

CULTS are new religious movements led by charismatic leaders with few followers.

SECTS are religious groups that have enough members to sustain themselves and go against society's norms.

CHURCH is a large, highly organized group of believers.

THEOCRACY is a government which is controlled by religious leaders.

totemism, preliterate societies also practised simple supernaturalism. **Simple supernaturalism** is the belief in a variety of supernatural forces that affect and influence people's lives. Similarly, **animism** is the belief that recognizes that animate spirits live in natural objects and operate in the world. For example, in Shinto, which is practised in Japan, the natural world is filled with *kami*—spirits that can bring luck or cause mischief.[51]

ORGANIZATION IN RELIGION

Have you ever come across a televised religious service while flipping channels? If so, you know that these gatherings can boast thousands of worshippers in the audience and maybe even millions at home. How do religious followings get so large?

Religions go through a series of stages before they become an integrated part of society. Sociologically, all religions begin as cults. **Cults** are new religious movements led by charismatic leaders with few followers. The teachings and practices of the religion are often at odds with the dominant culture and religion, so society is likely to reject the cult. Cults demand intense commitment and involvement by members, and they acquire new members through outside recruitment. Most cults fail because they cannot attract enough followers to sustain themselves.

Once a cult has enough members to sustain itself, it becomes a sect. **Sects** still go against society's norms. Often, members have greater social standing and are usually better integrated into society. As a result, they are less likely to be persecuted by the dominant society. As time passes and the sect grows, the members tend to become respectable members of society.[52]

Eventually, sects can evolve into a church. The term **church** does not specifically refer to a building or a denomination of a religion; instead, it is a large, highly organized group of believers. Churches are bureaucratized institutions and may include national and international offices, and leaders must undergo special training to perform established rituals.

If a church becomes highly integrated into the dominant culture, it may join with the state. A **theocracy** is a government which is controlled by religious leaders. For example, Iran has a theocratic government,

<<< Cows are considered sacred beasts in Hindu culture, and as such are not to be harmed. **In India, you can sometimes see a cow sitting in the middle of traffic as cars and bikes move around it.**

going so far as placing religious leaders at the pinnacle of executive government decisions.[53]

RELIGION IN SOCIETY

Durkheim argues that religion and society are so connected that the elementary forms of religion are actually expressions of the importance of the social group. A united group accomplishes more than an individual, and religion became a way that primitive people sought to express and explain this mystery. Concepts of divinity or the supernatural were a means of explanation.[54]

Religions also function to provide cultural norms like values and beliefs that societies hold important. Religions divide the **sacred** (things connected to God or dedicated to a religious purpose) from the **profane** (things related or devoted to that which is not sacred) by labelling certain objects, events, and people as sacred. For example, few people might take offence if I burned this textbook. What if I burned a sacred book like the Bible, the Torah, or the Koran? An object's sacredness is related to the perception of the believer.

Likewise, religious rituals develop around these sacred objects further strengthening the social norm. **Rituals** are an established pattern of behaviour closely associated with experience of the sacred. This allows the followers to come together and contribute to these rituals, strengthening the group's common understanding and belief. This in turn helps strengthen the group's bonds and further integrates the individuals into the group. This unity created by religion allows members to integrate by increasing cohesion and functioning as a social control mechanism.

SACRED means connected to God or dedicated to a religious purpose.

PROFANE means related or devoted to that which is not sacred.

RITUALS are established patterns of behaviour closely associated with experience of the sacred.

RELIGION AND THE ECONOMY

Karl Marx

Karl Marx didn't view religion as a way to unify people and answer questions. Instead, he viewed religion as the "opium of the people." In other words, Marx believed religion was often used as a tool by the wealthy to mislead the poor about their true social class. He suggested that religion gave people an illusion of happiness but nothing of real, long-lasting value.[55]

Remember, Marx believed that the rich controlled the poor through a variety of means, one of which was ideology. If people believed that something was fair or justified, then they were unlikely to bring about change in the system. Marx thought religions did very little to change the corrupt system of capitalism; instead, they often found harmony within it.

Marx believed the wealthy used their power and influence to ensure that the poor believed their plight was divinely inspired, and that some heavenly afterlife would make everything better. Marx suggested that religion helped people feel better by numbing them to their true pain. In short, religion causes people to ignore the real problem—capitalist oppression.[56]

>>> **A church choir is a ritual that strengthens bonds for the entire church.** When the choir sings, both the singers and churchgoers are participating in the activity for the same reason—to celebrate their faith together.

▶▶▶ GO GL🌐BAL

The Golden Rule Around the World

Even though many religions hold different beliefs, some ideas are practically universal. An example is the Golden Rule, which states, "Treat others as you want to be treated." You can see that this rule manifests itself in many societies regardless of the specific belief system.

Buddhism (Udana-Varga 5:18): Hurt no others in ways that you yourself would find hurtful.

Christianity (Matthew 7:12): In everything do to others as you would have them do to you; this is the law and the prophets.

Confucianism (Analects 15:23): Surely it is the maxim of loving-kindness: do not unto others what you would not have done unto you.

Hinduism (Mahabharata 5:1517): This is the sum of duty: do naught unto others, which would cause you pain if done to you.

Islam (Fourth Hadith of an-Nawawi 13): Not one of you is a believer until you wish for others what you wish for yourself.

Judaism (Talmud Shabbat 31a): What is hateful to you, do not to your fellow man, this is the entire law: all the rest is commentary.[57]

Max Weber

Max Weber agreed with Marx's idea that there is a link between the economy and religion, but he believed the opposite is true. He pointed out a connection between Protestant and capitalist values. Weber proposed that John Calvin's teachings laid the foundation for capitalism. Therefore, Weber believed capitalism developed in the West primarily because the Calvinist Protestant belief system supported it.[58]

One of Calvin's important philosophical points was the belief in pre-destination. This teaching suggests that God knows in advance who will and who will not go to Heaven because God is all-knowing. Prosperity is seen as a mark of God's favour because blessings would not be given to the "damned." So hard work and the creation of wealth are positive attributes and signs that you are a "chosen one." While not explicitly stated, notice how this infers that poverty is a sign of God's disfavour. In order to avoid poverty, people have to work hard, save money, and be thrifty. Weber termed this idea the Protestant Ethic.

Furthermore, the Protestant work ethic emphasizes individuality. Protestantism often supports the notion of individual salvation, which lays the groundwork for individuals to focus on their own well-being first and the good of others second. Both of these components—prosperity and individuality—laid the foundation for capitalism.[59]

Notice how both Marx and Weber saw a connection between the economy and religion. However, Marx saw religion as a tool to keep the rich wealthy, while Weber saw it as a tool to make people work hard to become prosperous.

CHANGES IN RELIGION

As societies modernized, religions began going through **secularization**,[60] which is the overall decline in the importance and power of religion in people's lives. Institutional religion weakens as societies become more scientifically advanced.

Secularization theorists generally agree that as society becomes more complex people become less tied to the "old ways" and more inclined to pursue other avenues.[61] This seems to indicate that secularization is inevitable for society; however, many developing parts of the world show no obvious decline in religious influence.[62]

Religion in Canada

Canada is one of the world's most religiously diverse countries.[63] In our southern neighbour, the United States, sociologist Robert Bellah and colleagues argue that there is a "civil religion."[64] A **civil religion** is a binding force that holds society together through political and social issues. Civil religion elevates democracy to sacredness by giving democracy religious undertones. The flag and the cross become equally sacred.

In Canada, though, the parliamentary system—as opposed to the U.S. presidential and congressional system—has not fostered that kind of nationalistic civil religion, *The Canadian Encyclopedia* notes. In fact, "Today, our sacred places may include the Arctic or the Prairie sky as the horizon of our sense of identity."[65]

Frequency of Religious Attendance, 1985–2005

Legend:
- At least once a week
- Less Frequently
- Never

Source: Canadians attend weekly religious services less than 20 years ago. Colin Lindsay. June 2008. Component of Statistics Canada Catalogue no. 89-630-X. www.statcan.gc.ca/pub/89-630-x/2008001/article/10650-eng.pdf, p. 1.

<<< **There was a nine percent decline in two decades in the number of people over age 15 in Canada who attended weekly religious services,** Statistics Canada's 2005 General Social Survey showed.

If we look at the statistics, we see signs of change in Canada's religious makeup in recent years. For example, the percentage of Christians has been dropping at about 0.9 percentage points a year—or almost 10 percent in a decade.[66] However, Canada's biggest single religious group, Catholics, has been growing since it outstripped Protestants in 1971 for the first time since Confederation. In 2001, Catholics made up 43.2 percent of the population, up 4.8 percent in a decade.[67] Just under half of Canada's Catholics lived in Quebec in 2001, making up 83 percent of that province's population (the highest in Canada).[68]

The second biggest religious denomination measured in the 2001 census was "No religion"—16 percent of the population. That group made up less than 1 percent of the population before 1971.[69] Statistics Canada cited immigration as a factor in the blossoming of the "no religion" group, especially because of newcomers from China, Hong Kong, and Taiwan.[70]

However, as suggested when we focused on Hinduism earlier, "The largest gains in religious affiliations occurred among faiths consistent with changing immigration patterns toward more immigrants from regions outside of Europe, in particular Asia and the Middle East."[71] Those identifying themselves as Muslim showed the biggest increase in this group, more than doubling from 1991 to 2001, to represent 2 percent of the country's population and take eighth spot in the ranking of Top 10 religious denominations in the country. Every other group on the list, apart from those with "No religion," was Christian. A total of 61 percent of all Muslims lived in Ontario.[72]

The number of people identifying themselves as Jewish made up 1.1 percent of Canada's population in 2001, almost unchanged from a decade beforehand. For more than half of them, Ontario was home.[73]

think sociologically: HOW DOES RELIGION AFFECT SOCIETY?

Symbolic Interactionism

Religious believers feel that everything in the world can be interpreted or defined as either sacred or profane. Almost anything—trees, animals, even bodies of water—can be considered sacred. However, what is sacred to one group may be profane to another. An element can be both sacred and profane for the same religious group. For example, for some Christians, red wine is profane when consumed during an ordinary meal, but the wine is sacred when consecrated by a priest or minister during the ritual of Holy Communion. The setting influences the reverence of an object.

A **system of beliefs** relates sacred objects to religious rituals and defines and protects the sacred from the profane. It labels what is a virtue and what is a sin. These labels provide meaning and morals for specific actions. For example, certain belief systems tell people that sex within marriage is acceptable, but sex outside marriage is sinful. A religion's system of beliefs is maintained by an **organization of believers**, which is a group of people who ensure the prosperity and effectiveness of the religious experience.

An organization of believers is composed of religious leaders and followers who define and guard the sacred. The organization determines possible conflicts with the religion's moral code. For example, there are said to be about 200 000 "Old Order Amish" in Canada and the United States. The Amish community (sometimes known as Amish Mennonites) does not permit its followers to use modern technology. However, some orders show a little leniency toward their members, such as allowing communal telephones and riding in cars when there is an emergency.[74] Without an organization of believers to keep abreast of current developments, a religion becomes extinct.

Functionalism

Durkheim believed that religion binds the community together through ritual and tradition. Followers gather to celebrate the power of things that

SYSTEM OF BELIEFS relates sacred objects to religious rituals, and defines and protects the sacred from the profane.

ORGANIZATION OF BELIEVERS is a group that ensures the prosperity and effectiveness of the religious experience.

are sacred and supernatural. Rituals unite the group as they celebrate and perform the actions together. For example, in the United States Martin Luther King, Jr., was president of the Southern Christian Leadership Conference, an organization that combined religion and politics to promote the 1960s civil rights movement. Thousands of activists joined together to share their faith and beliefs while working toward equality and unity.[75]

Religion also strengthens society's norms and values by including society's values in its own lessons. Religion influences a person's actions in society, often acting as a means of social control. All religions provide rules for adherents to live by, and most suggest that disobedience of these rules leads to negative consequences.

Religion reconciles people to the hardships and inequities of society. It offers the poor and oppressed strong moral codes as a conduit to salvation after death. Religion provides both the reason and the reward to conform to social rules.

However, religion promotes stability, even if the status quo is unfair and unequal. Religion can perpetuate practices like slavery, racism, and sexism. People in power use religion to enforce social hierarchy, maintain social order, and prevent the likelihood of rebellion. Furthermore, technological advancements may go against religious beliefs. When Galileo proposed that Earth orbits the Sun, this conflicted with the geocentric views of the Christian Church at that time. The church forced Galileo to retract his claims and then placed him under house arrest.[76]

Religion can also make it more difficult to resolve political struggles. Think about modern "religious wars." The Jewish/Muslim conflicts in the Middle East and the Protestant/Catholic tensions in Northern

∧
∧ ∧   The Promise Keepers is an international organization committed to
∧   helping men lead a Christian life. **When people are going through periods
of uncertainty, religion can bring them together for support.**

Ireland appear to be about religion when, in fact, they are mostly about land—who lives on it, and who controls it.

Conflict Theory

Conflict theorists believe that religion legitimizes social inequalities. Think about slavery in the Americas. The practice of owning and abusing another human being was accepted, in part, because some churches condoned it. In the hierarchy of faith, God was at the top of the list, followed by whites. Blacks and other non-whites were viewed as being worth less than whites.[77]

Marx believed that religion promotes capitalism and inequality because churches often support the idea that the wealthy deserve privileges. Weber's ideology that God blesses those who will go to Heaven also indicates that religion and economics are intertwined.

Religion also promotes obedience and legitimizes governments that are not in the best interests of everyone concerned. For example, the imperial family of Japan claims lineage from Amaterasu, Shinto goddess of the Sun. Therefore, to attack the emperor is to attack Amaterasu. Such a system guarantees faithful obedience to political leaders.[78]

Feminist Theory

Many of the world's religions are deeply and formally patriarchal. In studying the topic of religion, Johanna Stuckey has described four approaches to religious engagement taken by women. Revisionists accept the basic messages of religions, and seek only more gender neutrality. Reformists (or renovationists) expose and refuse to accept any part of the religious tradition that is sexist. Revolutionaries seek a deeper change to sexist traditions, and Rejectionists believe that traditional religions are irremediably sexist, so they seek a new spirituality.[79]

Another feminist writer, Linda Woodhead, also identified four types of reaction to religion in relation to gender. First, religion can serve to reproduce and legitimate the gender inequality that exists within that religion as well as in the wider society (consolidating). Second, religion can be used to subvert the existing gender order; for example, church groups for women in which they actually exercise considerable power and influence (tactical). Third, religion may be used by women for their own personal and spiritual purposes, without challenging the status quo (questing). Finally, religion may become a site in which women openly challenge the gendered distribution of power (counter-cultural).[80]

WRAP YOUR MIND AROUND THE THEORY

One of the functions of religion is to bring people together through ritual. This family unites to read from the Koran.

FUNCTIONALISM

Functionalists believe that religion binds members of the community together through participation in rituals that celebrate the supernatural. Religion also strengthens society's norms and values by teaching these beliefs in a religious context. In this way, religion also strengthens and supports the governmental authority. People tend to accept the norms of society and religion, which effectively creates social stability. This stability means that people are less likely to oppose the leadership of those in power.

SYMBOLIC INTERACTIONISM

Symbolic interactionists focus on labelling things as either "sacred" or "profane." Almost anything can be considered sacred, including locations, trees, caves, and animals, and these sacred objects are usually involved in rituals. The rituals themselves can also become sacred over time. Believers separate things that are sacred from things that are profane using their systems of beliefs. These systems of beliefs give sacred meaning to specific actions. In addition to this belief system, there is an organization that ensures the continuing effectiveness of the religious experience.

CONFLICT THEORY

Conflict theorists see religion as a tool used by powerful groups to legitimate their authority and to control the prevailing ideology. Consider how the church used residential schools in Canada to try to convert First Nations children to Christianity (more in Chapter 4).

HOW DOES RELIGION AFFECT SOCIETY?

FEMINIST THEORY

Feminist theorists believe that religion often serves only to further the inequalities of gender. One aspect often discussed is the position of female ministers in churches. Feminist theorists might point out that for centuries women have been excluded from leadership in organized religions, often for reasons that are more cultural than religious. Thus, why does the system perpetuate these ideas? When I discuss this with a class, I refer to God as "She" and "Her." Some students become uncomfortable, while others laugh. Eventually, someone will say, "God is a man." Feminists would suggest that the reason people believe God is a man is because men run most religions, and they wish to maintain their positions.

Religion is one way that those in power stay in control. Monarchies can use the power of the people's faith to maintain order and quell any rebellions that could threaten their thrones.

Some religions use totems to portray sacred objects and ideas. In this Tsimshian ceremony, the totems are used as a backdrop for the ritual being performed.

discover sociology in action: WHAT SOCIAL POLICIES HELP CHILDREN GET A BETTER EDUCATION?

Improving Education with Africentric Schooling

Finding a way to counter high dropout rates for black students in Toronto led to a controversial solution: the city's first Africentric public school opened its doors in September 2009 with 85 students.[81]

Enrolment for the school's second year soared to 160. And along the way, the Africentric Alternative School's 16 Grade 3 students "significantly outperformed" the Toronto District School Board and the province as a whole in 2009–2010 EQAO tests, with 69 percent of the Grade 3 students at the new school reaching Ontario's Level 3 standard in reading, 80 percent in writing, and 81 percent in math. The respective figures were 60, 70, and 71 percent for the board, and 62, 70, and 71 percent for all of Ontario.[82] (Ontario's Education Quality and Accountability Office, or EQAO, is responsible for province-wide assessments.[83])

The school is not just for black students, University of Toronto Professor George Dei explained just before the school first opened.

"We're talking about looking at the world through the eyes of African peoples—their experiences, their cultural knowledge and their history." Africentric education regards school as a community endeavour, he said, and instead of treating students as individual learners, "We want them to see themselves as a community of learners with a responsibility to those who are struggling."[84]

Two women—Angela Wilson and Donna Harrow—pushed for the school in order to help black youth succeed. The proposal to create the school was approved 11:9 at a Toronto District School Board meeting in January 2008. School board statistics showed that 40 percent of black youth in the board's schools do not graduate, compared with about 25 percent board-wide. One detractor voiced concern about the decision to "segregate" the education system; another called the school idea "half-baked."[85]

Africentric school principal Thando Hyman-Aman stressed from the beginning that children would learn the same curriculum as other schools in Ontario. "What makes this school different are the culturally relevant resources that we use," she said.[86]

ACTIVITIES

1. Research details of the Africentric school idea. Do you think the Toronto school is helping struggling students? Do you think the idea could work in any other part of Canada? Do you think it could—or should—be applied for any other segment of society?
2. Have a class debate over the pros and cons of the Africentric Alternative School.

From Classroom to Community } Basic Problems

"Greg" is a 16-year-old black high school student in Toronto. He is in the "basic" level program and he is having problems. This is abbreviated from Lennox V. Farrell's "Greg Is Not His Real Name"[87]:

He is very much for real about his feelings of being in grade ten Basic classes. He is for real about arriving a couple of minutes late each day for class. He hides until the hallway is clear so that other students . . . will not know that he is entering the hated Basic class. He also rushes to leave class before the dismissal bell for the same reason.

And he schemes to get non-Basic texts to display on the outside of the Basic texts. He carries these defensive texts—a shield against the barbs, name-calling, and the possibility that others, especially girls will know the grim truth:

That Greg is Basic!

Greg is sent to the office so often that he will sometimes refuse on other occasions to go there and get something as innocuous as some chalk. If the Principal sees him, no matter what, he will get in trouble, he says.

Later in life, he will also have the same relationship with Police.

His is a life in which every new day is another ambush. And days reach to months, and months to years in which there is an evolution of declining expectations, for him by all others; of him for himself.

He is given options that are constantly being diminished and diminishing. And he does what a normal human being, faced with abnormality would do. He rebels. He becomes obnoxious. He may traffic in illegal drugs. He could use a weapon on another Black youth. For a buck, or less.

In spite of this, he is so much for real that he is among the young Black people who, while being streamed into Basic level programmes because authorities judge them unable to 'understand' Advanced poetry in school, go on, outside of school to create international art forms like Rap, and Breakdancing!

Despite this, too, he does not think much of his own opinions.

Nobody listens to him, he says.

HOW **DO SOCIETIES PASS ON INFORMATION?**   251

through education and religion

HOW **DOES RELIGION AFFECT SOCIETY?**   261

functionalism: religion binds people together through ritual and tradition

conflict theory: religion legitimizes social inequalities; for example, the practice of owning slaves was accepted in part because some churches condoned the practice

symbolic interactionism: everything in the world can be interpreted as profane or sacred, but the setting influences the reverence of objects or acts

feminist theory: religion, like all social institutions, is very patriarchal, but feminists are looking at how women can increase their participation

WHAT **SOCIAL POLICIES HELP CHILDREN GET A BETTER EDUCATION?**   264

the opening of an Africentric alternative school in Toronto is aimed at reducing the dropout rate of African and Caribbean Canadian students

get the topic: HOW DO SOCIETIES PASS ON INFORMATION?

Theory

FUNCTIONALISM   261

- religion strengthens norms and values
- rituals unite the group when they celebrate or perform actions
- created social stability that supports governmental authority
- acts as a means of social control by influencing a person's actions

CONFLICT THEORY   262

- religion strengthens the inequalities of social classes
- dogma created to benefit the wealthy and condemn the poor
- Marx: religion promotes obedience and legitimizes governments that are not in the best interest of everyone

SYMBOLIC INTERACTIONISM   261

- everything is either sacred or profane
- system of beliefs define meaning and morals to specific actions
- organization that supports belief system ensures continuation and effectiveness of the religious experience

FEMINIST THEORY   262

- religious organizations often reflect the gender inequality of the wider society
- women can adopt different strategies to engage with religion
- Stuckey called these revisionist, reformist, revolutionary, and rejectionist
- Woodhead described the engagement of women as consolidating, tactical, questing, or counter-cultural

Key Terms

education is the formal system in which society passes its knowledge, skills, and values from one generation to the next. *251*

teacher expectancy effect is the impact of a teacher's expectations on a student's performance. *254*

grade inflation is the trend of assigning higher grades than previously assigned to students for completing the same work. *254*

human capital is a person's combination of skills, knowledge, traits, and personal attributes. *255*

credentialism is an emphasis on educational degrees in assessing skills and knowledge. *255*

religion is a unified system of beliefs and practices, relative to sacred things. *257*

theism is the belief in a god or gods. *257*

monotheism is the belief that there is only one God. *257*

polytheism is the belief in multiple gods and demigods. *257*

philosophies of life are ways of life that focus on a set of ethical, moral, or philosophical principles. *257*

totemism is the practice of honouring a totem or a sacred object. *257*

henotheism is the worship of one god while recognizing the existence of other deities. *258*

simple supernaturalism is the belief in a variety of supernatural forces that affect and influence people's lives. *258*

animism is the belief that recognizes that animate spirits live in natural objects and operate in the world. *258*

cults are new religious movements led by charismatic leaders with few followers. *258*

sects are religious groups that have enough members to sustain themselves and go against society's norms. *258*

church is a large, highly organized group of believers. *258*

theocracy is a government which is controlled by religious leaders. *258*

sacred means connected to God or dedicated to a religious purpose. *259*

profane means related or devoted to that which is not sacred. *259*

rituals are established patterns of behaviour closely associated with experience of the sacred. *259*

secularization is the overall decline in the importance and power of religion in people's lives. *260*

civil religion is a binding force that holds society together through political and social issues. *260*

system of beliefs relates sacred objects to religious rituals, and defines and protects the sacred from the profane. *261*

organization of believers is a group that ensures the prosperity and effectiveness of the religious experience. *261*

Sample Test Questions

These multiple-choice questions are similar to those found in the test bank that accompanies this textbook.

1. Which of the following is *not* a myth associated with education?
   a. Society is the primary unit.
   b. A nation is merely a group of individuals.
   c. Childhood socialization leads to adult character.
   d. Learning increases individual and national future progress.

2. Some parents decide to homeschool their children because they are concerned with
   a. school size.
   b. lack of resources.
   c. school segregation.
   d. academic instruction.

3. Which of the following statements is *true*?
   a. Improvements in student performance are directly related to religious practice.
   b. Religious students from all backgrounds are apt to perform well in school.
   c. Intensely religious students do not perform as well on standardized tests.
   d. Religious practice only benefits poor students.

4. A type of religious organization is a
   a. synagogue.
   b. mosque.
   c. temple.
   d. church.

5. What is Max Weber's view of religion?
   a. Scientific advancement weakens religion.
   b. Protestant teachings laid the foundation for capitalism.
   c. Religion is a way to unite people and answer questions.
   d. Elementary forms of religion express the importance of social groups.

ANSWERS: 1. a; 2. d; 3. b; 4. d; 5. b

ESSAY

1. What is the hidden curriculum?
2. How can a country's socioeconomic status affect education?
3. What factors affect educational attainment?
4. How do religions become integrated into society?
5. How can religion be related to capitalism?

WHERE TO START YOUR RESEARCH PAPER

To look at more educational statistics, go to
www.unesco.org/en/efareport

To read more about Canada's First Nations Peoples, go to
www.afn.ca

To learn more about grade inflation, go to
http://economics.ca/cgi/jab?journal=cpp&view=v26n3/CPPv26n3p361.
pdf, www.macleans.ca/article.jsp?content=20070605_153207_13228

To learn more about home schooling in Canada, go to
www.flora.org/homeschool-ca/index.html www.hslda.ca
www.hslda.ca/images/HomeEdinCanadaEnglish.pdf

To learn more about university costs, go to
www.canadianbusiness.com/my_money/planning/education/
university_cost/tool.jsp

To learn more about education and religion, go to
www.edu.gov.on.ca/eng/document/curricul/religion/religioe.html

To learn about Freedom of Religion and Religious Symbols in public
areas such as schools, go to
www2.parl.gc.ca/Content/LOP/ResearchPublications/
prb0441-e.htm#overview

To learn more about Africentric research and education, go to
http://fcis.oise.utoronto.ca/~gpieters/afrocentricschools/index.html

Remember to check www.thethinkspot.ca for additional
information, downloadable flashcards, and other helpful resources.

SOCIAL MOVEMENTS, COLLECTIVE BEHAVIOUR, AND SOCIAL CHANGE

"Rodriguez

de Gerada is widely recognized as one of the most skilled and creative founders of culture jamming, the practice of parodying advertisements and hijacking billboards in order to drastically alter their messages. Streets are public spaces, adbusters argue, and since most residents can't afford to counter corporate messages by purchasing their own ads, they should have the right to talk back to images they never asked to see. In recent years, this argument has been bolstered by advertising's mounting aggressiveness in the public domain. . . . Adding even greater urgency to their cause is the belief among many jammers that concen-

tration of media ownership has successfully devalued the right to free speech by severing it from the right to be heard.

"All at once, these forces are coalescing to create a climate of semiotic Robin Hoodism. A growing number of activists believe the time has come for the public to stop asking that some space be left unsponsored, and to begin seizing it back. Culture jamming baldly rejects the idea that marketing—because it buys its way into our public spaces—must be passively accepted as a one-way information flow."[1]

How Do Societies Change?

In *No Logo: Taking Aim at the Brand Bullies,* Naomi Klein describes a number of issues that have been raised by the "anti-globalization movement."

Pervasive advertising (including ads in schools), sweatshops, and censorship are just some of the corporate actions that Klein criticizes in *No Logo.* But in addition to condemning the large multinational corporations that seem to rule the world, Klein offers suggestions for how ordinary citizens can reclaim power and a voice. *Culture jamming* is a term used to describe one such strategy.

Jammers such as Rodriguez de Gerada wage a small but persistent war against the ubiquitous corporate logo. They are expressing their social discontent. It is people such as Rodriguez de Gerada who can bring about change in society. Throughout this book, you have seen how society has a powerful impact on you as an individual. In this final chapter, we will look at how individuals can form groups in order to change society. What drives changes, and how do we react to those changes? In this chapter, we review these and other questions as we study social change, collective behaviour, and social movements.

Social Movements and Cultural Change

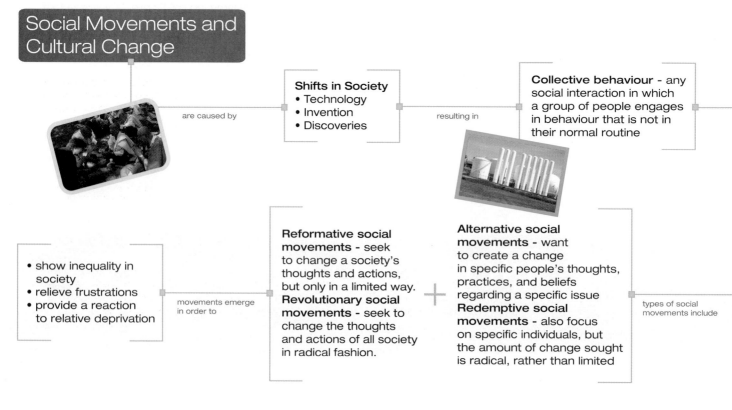

are caused by

Shifts in Society
• Technology
• Invention
• Discoveries

resulting in

Collective behaviour - any social interaction in which a group of people engages in behaviour that is not in their normal routine

• show inequality in society
• relieve frustrations
• provide a reaction to relative deprivation

movements emerge in order to

Reformative social movements - seek to change a society's thoughts and actions, but only in a limited way.
Revolutionary social movements - seek to change the thoughts and actions of all society in radical fashion.

Alternative social movements - want to create a change in specific people's thoughts, practices, and beliefs regarding a specific issue
Redemptive social movements - also focus on specific individuals, but the amount of change sought is radical, rather than limited

types of social movements include

get the topic: WHAT DRIVES SOCIAL CHANGE?

Shifts in Society

Changes in society are often caused by reactions to events and new opportunities, like the Industrial Revolution. This event brought about great **social change**, the way in which culture, interaction, and innovation change social institutions over time. Recall how the Industrial Revolution brought about changes in social classes. Capitalists became more powerful and wealthy than the old landed aristocracy, while workers struggled to make ends meet.[2]

Around the same time, new ways to think about the world arose, including the science of sociology. Some of these ideas helped form the intellectual basis for creating a new nation, based on common ideals. One merely needs to look at the *Canadian Charter of Rights and Freedoms* to read some of these ideas. Ideas often drive social change. For example, no one recycled in my neighbourhood when I was growing up. Someone realized that people were wasting too many natural resources and came up with the idea to reuse these materials. Today, recycling is a common practice.

Populations also grew, bringing about demographic changes such as immigration. Immigration and internal migration have changed Canada. Canada is one of the world's three main immigrant-receiving nations.[3] This has shaped the history of Canada. Immigration had helped to push the population up to 3.4 million by 1867.[4] Canada's future Prairie provinces were opened to settlement in the late nineteenth century, and the national population is now spread out across the vast country, with about 90 percent of the population living within 160 kilometres of the Canada–United States border.[5] The country's population has roughly

> **SOCIAL CHANGE** is the way in which culture, interaction, and innovation change social institutions over time.

doubled every 40 or so years since 1867, and these days roughly a quarter of a million immigrants enter the country each year.[6]

The population of aboriginal peoples in what is now Canada is estimated to have been roughly 350 000 at the time Europeans first arrived, but dropped to 137 000 or fewer by 1867 due to disease, starvation, and warfare.[7]

The country's current population was estimated in July 2010 to be 33 759 742.[8] Despite interprovincial migration, more than 13 million people—or about one in three Canadians—currently live in the province of Ontario.[9]

Currently we are experiencing globalization, a new trend in the world in which we are more interconnected to other nations than ever before. I've discussed this issue at length in previous chapters, but recall that the world is becoming smaller through technology and globalization. **For example, the Disney Channel is available all over the world, including Canada, Japan, Australia, France, Southeast Asia, India, Germany, the United Kingdom, and Mexico. What's the significance of this?**

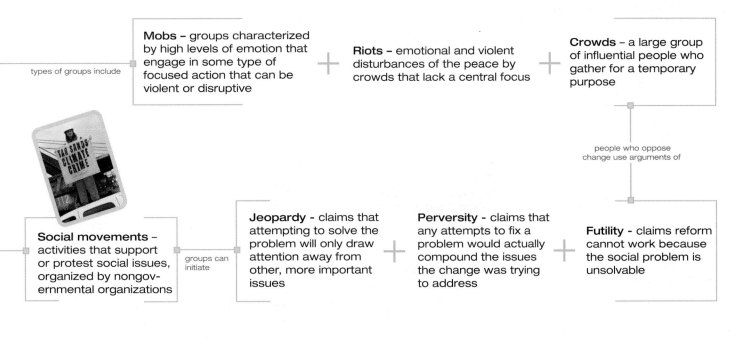

types of groups include

Mobs – groups characterized by high levels of emotion that engage in some type of focused action that can be violent or disruptive

Riots – emotional and violent disturbances of the peace by crowds that lack a central focus

Crowds – a large group of influential people who gather for a temporary purpose

people who oppose change use arguments of

Social movements – activities that support or protest social issues, organized by nongovernmental organizations

groups can initiate

Jeopardy - claims that attempting to solve the problem will only draw attention away from other, more important issues

Perversity - claims that any attempts to fix a problem would actually compound the issues the change was trying to address

Futility - claims reform cannot work because the social problem is unsolvable

Well, the Disney Channel's television programs pass along American information, ideals, and beliefs to children all over the world. Kids around the globe learn about U.S. culture from the teen crews on *Hannah Montana* and *Wizards of Waverly Place*. How could this affect foreign cultures and bring about social change?

TECHNOLOGY

One specific vehicle of social change is technology. **Technology** deals with the creation, use, and application of knowledge and its interrelation with life, society, and the environment. Technology often inspires change because it offers new possibilities for people to improve their environment and their lifestyles. Sociologist William Ogburn suggests that all social change is a result of technology.[10] Technology is usually the product of invention. An **invention** is the creation of a new device or way of thinking. Look at the graphic to the right to see how a simple invention can change society.

The term *technology* is not simply restricted to objects and things. Systems are also considered technologies, and new systems offer similar opportunities and changes that new objects might bring. The capitalist system offers the opportunity to rise in society's ranks by gathering material wealth and power. Similarly, the democratic system changes society by providing everyone a chance to be involved in the political process.

Technology also leads to new discoveries, which mean new opportunities. A discovery does not just have to be a place or object. A discovery can be a new way to see the world. However, discoveries cannot have a big impact on society unless they are made known. This is done by **diffusion**. It's by this process that new technologies, discoveries, and ideas are shared and spread from one person to another, extending the knowledge far beyond its point of origin. This in turn creates opportunities for someone to improve upon these ideas, further advancing and improving the original technologies while creating new technologies and discoveries.

Effects of Invention on Society: Tractors

The tractor was invented by combining two already existing technologies, the steam engine and the plough.

This provided farmers with a new tool that made it easier to tend to their crops.

This in turn led to better crop production, which meant that there was more food readily available for people to buy.

More food meant people were better fed and healthier. Now people could spend more energy thinking up new inventions than worrying about food.

Take, for instance, the automobile. Karl Benz created the first gasoline-fuelled automobile in 1885 in Germany. Ten years later, U.S. inventor George Selden improved on this design by combining an internal combustion engine with a carriage. In 1893, brothers Charles and Frank Duryea created the first successful gas-powered car, and the two set up an automobile-manufacturing company.[11] Fast-forward to today's automotive industries. Automobiles continue to change as rising gas prices spur interest in new fuels and alternative energy. Technology changes and improves as new ideas and inventions from around the world are put into practice.

The rapid pace at which technology spreads and changes can leave some cultures lagging behind. *Cultural lag,* as we discussed in Chapter 3, occurs when some parts of a culture cannot keep up with the inventions, discoveries, and diffusion of ideas. Technology changes first, leaving other parts of the culture scrambling to keep up. For example, India's rapid industrialization has created a new affluence for some members of society, but other parts of the culture suffer from cultural lag. Trash piles up behind buildings because of the pressure on the area's resources and inability to keep up with industrial progress. People are fighting to keep up with the technological and societal changes that industrialization brings.[12]

Resistance to Change

Change happens in a culture, whether it is directly related to technology or not. However, although many people might be pushing for this change to occur, there may be some people who wish to resist it. They are happy with the way things are, and they strive to maintain the status quo. Sociologist Albert Hirschman noted that every new idea for constructive change is met with three types of attack by people who want things to stay the way they are.

First, Hirschman says that these protesters will argue **futility**, which claims that the reform cannot work because the social problem is unsolvable. One example of this type of argument can be heard from people who criticize efforts to find cleaner, more efficient alternative energy sources for our motor vehicles. They claim that we're stuck with oil because it's the only thing that really works and that changing to alternative fuels would make transportation unreliable and more costly. People using this and the other forms of attack are often those who benefit from the use of oil and other fossil fuels and desire to maintain the status quo to protect their profits.

Another form of attack that protesters might choose as their argument is **perversity**, which claims that any attempt to fix a problem would actually compound the issues the change was trying to address. This argument is often used in the debate for electric cars. Although plugging in your car might sound like a cleaner solution for the environment, these protesters point out that this electricity must come from somewhere. In many countries, electricity comes from power plants that burn coal, the process of which releases harmful gases and fumes into the air. More electric cars mean that there will be a greater demand for electricity, and more demand for electricity means more coal burning. Their argument is that the additional burning of coal would be worse than the damage we are already doing with oil.

Yet another way to attack change is the argument of jeopardy. **Jeopardy** claims that attempting to solve the problem will only draw attention away from other, more important issues. People who support the use of oil might say that researching alternative fuels not only is costly, but also is a waste of time. They say that there is plenty of oil and that

TECHNOLOGY deals with the creation, use, and application of knowledge and its interrelation with life, society, and the environment.

INVENTION is the creation of a new device or way of thinking.

DIFFUSION is the spreading of something more widely.

FUTILITY is the claim that a reform cannot work because the social problem is unsolvable.

PERVERSITY claims that any attempts to fix a problem would actually compound the issues the change was trying to address.

JEOPARDY is the claim that attempting to solve a problem will only draw attention away from other, more important issues.

we do not need to worry about shortages; instead, we need to drill more. Spending money to find new energy sources then draws our attention away from other more important issues such as national security, education, or some other social problem.[13]

Attack Strategies

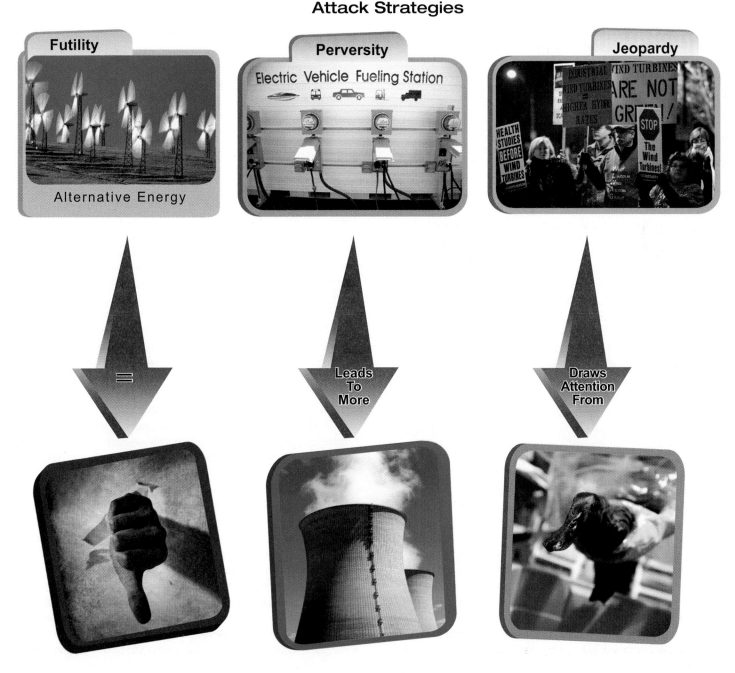

Internet Petitions

Many people who want society to change will sign a petition. Traditionally, this entails someone going around with a piece of paper for others to sign or mark up as a way to show their views on a subject. In recent years, petitions and polls have switched from paper to online. The internet is beneficial because it allows for thousands of replies, as well as links to further information about the topics being addressed.

However, these internet petitions are not as effective as people would think. For instance, the distinct handwriting of many participants you find on paper petitions proves that many people signed the petition. However, once a petition is moved to an online format, the individual writing styles become typed text, indistinguishable from one person to the next. Another issue is that the intended audience is often not explicitly mentioned, or the topic itself is too vaguely outlined for readers to understand everything that is being proposed in the petition. There is no guarantee that the petition will reach its intended audience or that the specified recipient actually has the credentials or ability to act upon the petition's results. There's also the fact that signing a petition doesn't actually get anything accomplished. People can sign a petition stating that they want something to be done about global warming, but they themselves do not take the initiative to go out and do something about it with this petition.[14]

Despite these issues, the internet is still a potential way to reach a broader voting population and audience. Online petition companies like www.ipetitions.com, www.thepetitionsite.com, and www.gopetition.com/petition-campaigns/Canada/ have sprung up around the Web, allowing anyone to create a petition. These companies may offer to "make sure" that the petition gets to the person it needs to get to. However, even if the petition doesn't get signed, it may still influence people's opinions. Online petitions can expose people to opinions and causes that they had never thought about before. Even if people don't end up signing the petition, they might be interested in the cause. This may encourage them to go out and do something about the issue themselves, which in effect accomplishes what the petition set out to do in the first place.[15]

>>> **ACTIVITY** Find and read through an online petition. What is the issue the petition is trying to address? Is this an effective petition? Why or why not?

COLLECTIVE BEHAVIOUR

People who gather in groups often react and think in the same way when they gather together. **Collective behaviour** is any social interaction in which a group of people engages in behaviour that is not in their normal routine. Depending on the type of collective behaviour, this can be harmful and dangerous.

Violence

When discontent and tempers run high, violence often follows. Riots and mobs are likely to break out when people assemble in anger, and chaos ensues. **Mobs** are groups characterized by high levels of emotion that engage in some type of focused action that can be violent or disruptive. In June 2010, a peaceful march by about 10 000 protesters against the G-20 political summit in Toronto was followed by violence, riot squad deployment, tear gas, and 412 arrests.[16] Mobs can lead to **hysteria**, a heightened emotional state that can lead a group to violence.

Riots are emotional and violent disturbances of the peace by a crowd. Riots involve high levels of emotion and violence, but unlike mobs the people taking part in riots have no centralized focus and lash out at any- and everything. Rioters express rage and anger and often spontaneously attack property and people. For example, two fires blazed in the yard of the Edmonton Institution on the evening of Canada Day 2008, after inmates broke into a fenced-off area where wood was kept for sweat-lodge use. By the time a nine-hour standoff was over, eight inmates had been stabbed and one shot by a guard. This all apparently started with a clash between rival prison gangs during a recreational period. As many as 40 inmates were involved.[17]

Consumerism

Consumerism, rather than hate, often causes people to go out in droves, but to buy things en masse instead of protesting social injustice. For instance, people might buy into the newest fad, like the latest smartphone or gaming console. A **fad** is a temporary fashion, notion, or action that the public embraces. Fads can take many forms. One year, my daughter wanted a Wii gaming system for Christmas, and I was thrown into the midst of an object fad. Finding a Wii was nearly impossible. (Fortunately, Santa was able to get one.)

Fads may also include popular ideas, such as using feng shui to increase the chi, or energy, in one's home. They can also include activities, like in-line skating. Finally, fads can be people. The latest teen sensation, Canadian pop singer Justin Bieber, is a human fad who has been taking tween girls by storm.

Sociologist Joel Best suggests that fads such as the hula hoop are one thing, but fads in institutions are another.[18] Institutional fads follow a predetermined cycle: *emerging, surging,* and *purging*. At the emerging and surging stages, we embrace institutional change because we are optimistic and believe in progress. Thus, the latest trends take over the way we do business, regardless of their effectiveness.[19] Look at the DARE—Drug Abuse Resistance Education—program, developed in Los Angeles and now used in both Canada and the United States.[20] Police officers teach children about the dangers of drugs, but the results are dubious at best, and some studies actually show that the program makes drug use worse, not better.[21]

The problem with institutional fads is that at the time they are surging, no one really knows if they will work. Usually, the media publicize someone or something as the latest trend in business, education, or medicine. This fad promises to solve a problem or change society. North Americans tend to jump on the bandwagon of the latest institutional fad, so it's only after the fad has proved itself to be a total failure that this changes.

But some fads can actually leave lasting effects on a society. When this occurs, we call it a **craze**. When I was in college, you had to go to video arcades to play games. They were so new that people actually took dates to the arcade. Such a craze has largely ended, but the lasting effect of this video game craze is that many homes have some type of gaming system.

Fear also instigates consumerism. A **panic** is an extreme fear based on something that might happen. You may have heard of the Y2K panic, when many people were convinced that modern life would stop because computers would fail to recognize "00" as 2000. However, when January 1, 2000, came and went without incident, people realized that they'd panicked for nothing.[22] The panic caused by the 9/11 terrorist attacks led the U.S. government to encourage Americans to buy duct tape and plastic to seal doors and windows against a chemical attack. This panic caused a large increase in purchases of these items.[23]

Crowds

You might not join in the latest fad, craze, or panic, but at some point everyone is part of a large group of influential people, called a crowd. A **crowd** is a large group of people who gather for a temporary purpose. When you attend a football game, you're in a crowd. Members can easily influence each other. For example, when you cheer, others will often join in with you. Other crowds may focus on a cause, like those protesting a political or social issue. Protest crowds can be large or small. For instance, on October 27, 1995, about 100 000 Canadians from across the country gathered in Montreal for a huge Unity Rally. Held just a few days before a referendum on separatism, the rally appealed to French Canadians to "vote for Canada." Separatism was narrowly defeated in the referendum.[24]

Rumours

People connect in other ways, too. Sociologists suggest that passing on **rumours**, stories or statements that lack confirmation or certainty, is part of modern culture. A common type of rumour is an urban legend. **Urban legends** are rumours that are presented as true stories and act as cautionary tales. These are stories that circulate that claim to have happened to other people, but are actually false. We spread them as if we really saw or heard the event personally to entertain our listeners.[25] One of my favourite rumours is one I call "How long must I wait?"

This legend deals with the supposed rules pertaining to how long students must wait for a tardy professor. When a professor is late, students worry that they might miss something if they leave too soon. The rumour suggests that there's a tardiness policy that dictates how long students must wait before they can assume they will not be penalized for leaving class. Wait times vary depending on the rank of the professor: graduate assistants get the shortest leeway, while full doctoral professors receive the most patience. Truthfully, few colleges have an official faculty tardiness policy. Of those that do, academic rank doesn't affect how long you must wait. To be safe, check your student handbook or ask your professor what policy he or she has about this matter.[26]

NATURE OF SOCIAL MOVEMENTS

Social movements are activities that support or protest social issues, organized by nongovernmental organizations. In other words, social movements allow regular folks to participate in the political process, diffusing ideas and beliefs. Many social movements want to bring about social change, while others seek to maintain the status quo. According to sociologist Charles Tilly, there are three elements that exist in all social movements.[27]

The first element in a social movement is the promotional campaign. **Campaigns** are organized and ongoing efforts to achieve a specific goal. For instance, when it's time for elections, politicians have campaigns geared to the voters. They make claims of what they will do if they are elected to office and try to convince the voter that they would be the best candidate for the position.

COLLECTIVE BEHAVIOUR is any social interaction in which a group of people engages in behaviour that is not in their normal routine.

MOBS are groups characterized by high levels of emotion that engage in some type of focused action that can be violent or disruptive.

HYSTERIA is a heightened emotional state that can lead a group to violence.

RIOTS are emotional and violent disturbances of the peace by crowds that lack a central focus.

FAD is a temporary fashion, notion, or action the public embraces.

CRAZE occurs when a fad leaves a lasting effect on society.

PANIC is an extreme fear based on something that might happen.

CROWD is a large group of influential people who gather for a temporary purpose.

RUMOURS are stories or statements that lack confirmation or certainty.

URBAN LEGENDS are rumours that are presented as true stories that act as cautionary tales.

SOCIAL MOVEMENTS are activities that support or protest social issues, organized by nongovernmental organizations.

CAMPAIGNS are organized and ongoing efforts to achieve a specific goal.

∧
∧ **The 1995 Unity Rally drew** 100 000
∧ people **to the streets in Montreal in**
a successful bid to defeat a referendum
on separatism.

Rescuing Rainforests

As sociologists, it's important to study and understand the effects that humans have on the environment. Deforestation, pollution, and poaching are just three ways that humans have negatively impacted their environment.[28] It's no surprise, then, that conservation movements are gaining popularity around the world.

One conservation movement is rainforest conservation. Rainforests clean the air, provide food and raw materials, and are home to half of the world's population of plants and animals.[29] To maintain and protect these vital areas, organizations like the World Wildlife Foundation (WWF) and the Rainforest Alliance work alongside individuals, governments, and other organizations. Members can help by donating money to the conservation projects or by volunteering in local and national conservation efforts.[30] The WWF also focuses on helping the people who live in the area surrounding the rainforests. These people rely on the forest for their livelihood, so they work with organizations to safely harvest items from the forest while protecting its valuable natural resources.[31]

Activist groups like the Rainforest Action Network (RAN) employ different methods to get their point across. In 1987, RAN's successful boycott against Burger King stopped the fast-food chain's practice of buying cheap beef from areas that were once rainforests.[32] The group calls for nonviolent protests to make the public aware of important issues.

Another element used is repertoire. **Repertoires** are actions used to promote interest and involvement within the movement. For example, several hundred people marched on Parliament Hill in Ottawa in March 2009 as part of international lobbying to mark the fiftieth anniversary of the Raise the Tibet Flag Campaign, which aims to "generate awareness and solidarity amongst Tibetans and Tibet supporters alike" for the recognition of Tibet as an occupied country and the recognition of the Tibetan government in exile as the sole legitimate government of Tibetans. Other Canadian demonstrations included gatherings at the Chinese Consulates in Vancouver and Toronto.[33]

Finally, you have the members of a movement who want to show the public the worthiness, unity, numbers, and commitments of their movement (**WUNC**). They're the people who organize the events, participate in the activities, and do what they can to get the word out about their organization. Remember, people committed to a cause do not constitute a movement. Movements need WUNC members to help lead and keep it focused.

Tilly suggests that before the eighteenth century, there was no such thing as a true "social movement." It's true that there were violent revolutions and rebellions demanding changes in society before this period; however, these movements were not social movements because they didn't bring about organizations. It was not until the 1800s that movements arose over issues such as unionism in response to capitalism, women's suffrage, and many other issues.

Stages of Social Movements

All social movements go through a set of predictable stages of development. In the first stage, **emergence**, people become aware of a problem and begin to notice that others feel the same way. Fifty years ago, few Canadians were concerned about the environment. But after a few people began to take notice in the 1960s, they took the first steps for any social movement—making people aware of the problem. The 1971 actions of Don't Make a Wave (see the Think Sociologically feature on Greenpeace on the next page) are a good example.

In the next stage, social movements seek to define their goals and design a plan to get their goals met. This state is known as **coalescence**. In this stage, groups reach out to other groups and individuals to gain membership. The movement then grows and increases the public awareness of the problem. In Canada, environmental organizations such as Greenpeace were born out of the first major wave of environmentalism and continued growing. By the late 1980s, interest in the environment had surged throughout North America.[34]

<<< **Parliament Hill was one of several Canadian demonstration sites during the international fiftieth anniversary of the Raise the Tibet Flag Campaign, held in March 2009.** Participants want freedom for Tibet, which has been under China's rule since 1959.

The environmental movement has become a political force internationally, and has moved into **bureaucratization.** The myriad social movements dedicated to the environment show that this concern will not go away. Organizations like Greenpeace International now strive to achieve what Don't Make a Wave dreamed possible in Vancouver in 1971.

When an organization completes its goal or is seen as irrelevant, it falls into the final stage, **decline.** If and when the day comes that we have clean energy and recycling becomes the norm, the clean air movement may decline because it will have achieved some of its goals.[35]

TYPES OF SOCIAL MOVEMENTS

Although all social movements are essentially sustained campaigns that support a goal, there is no standard type of social movement. They have different methods of approaching their goals and identifying potential followers. David F. Aberle developed an early typology of social movements in 1966.[36] He categorized movements based on two dimensions: the orientation of change (society as a whole or individuals) and the amount of change sought (limited or radical). This classification created four categories of social movement: alternative, redemptive, reformative, and revolutionary.[37] Each category seeks a different combination of target audience and level of change.

REPERTOIRES are actions used to promote interest and involvement within the movement.

WUNC refers to the members of a movement who want to show the public the worthiness, unity, numbers, and commitment of their movement.

EMERGENCE is the first stage of a movement when people become aware of a problem and begin to notice that others feel the same way.

COALESCENCE is the second stage of a movement when groups reach out to other groups and individuals to gain membership.

BUREAUCRATIZATION is the third stage of a movement when it becomes a political force.

DECLINE is the final stage of a movement when an organization completes its goal or is seen as irrelevant.

ALTERNATIVE SOCIAL MOVEMENTS want to create a change in specific people's thoughts, practices, and beliefs regarding a particular issue.

Alternative Social Movements

Alternative social movements want to create a change in specific people's thoughts, practices, and beliefs regarding a specific issue. Their goal is to encourage a small, defined change in the way a particular group of people think and act in order to solve a problem. Mothers

THINK SOCIOLOGICALLY

Greenpeace

It started with a small group of activists sailing out of Vancouver in a leaky fishing boat in 1971, to "bear witness" to U.S. nuclear testing in the northerly Aleutian Islands. Four decades later, the international organization that grew out of that first step is known as "the world's leading environmental watchdog" and has more than 2.9 million members.[38]

Greenpeace describes itself as "an independent, non-profit, global campaigning organization that uses non-violent, creative confrontation to expose global environmental problems and their causes." The organization's goal is "to ensure the ability of Earth to nurture life in all its diversity."[39]

Among its substantial successes, Greenpeace Canada lists the 1982 European Council ban on the import of seal pup skins after Greenpeace actions in Canada and the resulting public outcry, and the 2006 provincial government announcement of an agreement that should ensure the protection of the Great Bear Rainforest in British Columbia.

On the international front, Greenpeace organizations had started in a number of countries before Greenpeace International was formed in 1979. Today the international organization is based in Amsterdam. A Greenpeace list highlighting close to 100 international successes includes such events

How a Group of Ecologists, Journalists and Visionaries Changed the World

REX WEYLER

GREENPEACE

as the shelving in 2009—after a three-year Greenpeace campaign—of plans to build what would have been the first new coal power plant in the United Kingdom in 20 years, and Iceland's stepping back in 2004 from plans to kill 500 minke, sei, and fin whales over two years, announcing instead a quota of just 25 minkes for the year. Greenpeace Web activists "fuelled domestic opposition" by getting 50 000 pledges from around the world to visit Iceland if the government would stop whaling.

<<< The photo on the cover of Greenpeace co-founder Rex Weyler's book *Greenpeace* shows **underdog activists at work on the high seas.**

And the very first leaky boat trip from Vancouver in 1971? That forerunner to Greenpeace was called Don't Make a Wave, and comprised Vancouver environmentalists who wanted to stop the second planned U.S. nuclear test on the tiny island of Amchitka, in the Aleutians. Thousands of protesters had gathered on the Canada–United States border before the first test, because they feared the blast would cause an earthquake, but the initial test went ahead anyway. Greenpeace never made it to the actual test zone—despite two attempts—but it managed to stir up public concern about the second test. Five months after Don't Make a Wave sailed out from Vancouver, the United States announced it was stopping Aleutian Island nuclear testing. Today, the island is a bird sanctuary.

Incidentally, the nonviolent protest style Greenpeace uses to "bear witness" is based on a Quaker tradition of silent protest.[40]

The Four Categories of Social Movements

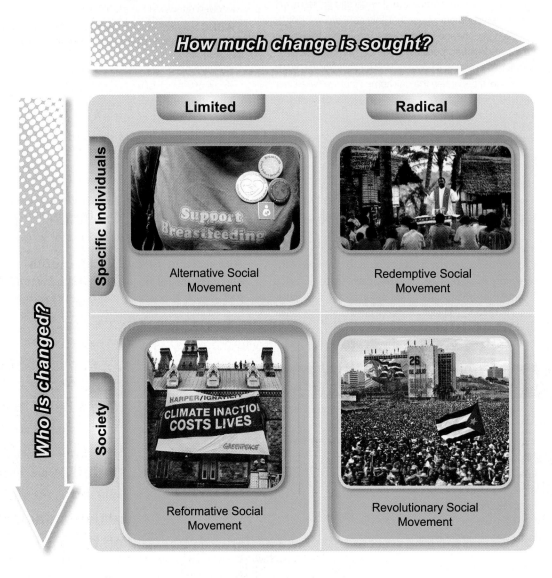

How much change is sought?

Who is changed?

	Limited	Radical
Specific Individuals	Alternative Social Movement	Redemptive Social Movement
Society	Reformative Social Movement	Revolutionary Social Movement

Against Drunk Driving (MADD) Canada is an alternative social movement organization whose mission is "To stop impaired driving and to support victims of this violent crime."[41]

MADD Canada was formed in 1990. Using a method developed by James Fell, the organization calculates that the number of lives saved due to reduction in alcohol-related fatal crashes in Canada rose from 221 in 1982 to 1151 in 2007, for a 1982–2007 total of 32 883 lives. "The figures provide us with an important perspective on the progress that has been made since the founding of MADD Canada and its predecessor organizations," one MADD research document states.[42] In an April 2008 news release, the organization noted that Transport Canada had reported a total of 39 487 alcohol-related fatalities on Canadian roads since 1982. "Had there been no effort to reduce impaired driving deaths, MADD Canada estimates the number could have been 70 000 in alcohol-related fatalities."[43]

Redemptive Social Movements

Redemptive social movements also focus on specific individuals, but the amount of change sought is radical, rather than limited. Religious movements, such as those involving evangelical Christians, are typically categorized as redemptive because they encourage a specific group of nonbelievers to make a dramatic lifestyle change by converting to or adopting a new religion. Christian missionaries have held a quiet presence in traditionally Islamic states in the Middle East for centuries.

However, this missionary movement has surged in recent years. According to the Center for the Study of Global Christianity at Gordon-Conwell Theological Seminary in South Hamilton, Massachusetts, the number of missionaries to Islamic countries has increased from about 15 000 in 1982 to more than 27 000 in 2001.[44] The 9/11 attacks pushed the movement even farther. Some Christian missionaries enter Islamic countries with the sole intention of providing aid to the region's struggling communities; however, evangelical missionaries proceed with the primary goal of converting Muslims to Christianity. This practice is controversial in both Muslim and Christian communities.

Reformative Social Movements

Not all social movements are targeted to specific individuals or groups. Some social movements attempt to tether all of society to their mission. **Reformative social movements** seek to change a society's thoughts and actions, but only in a limited way. This type of movement can be **progressive,** favouring or promoting change, or **regressive,** seeking to stop change. Progressive reformative social movements ask society to accept something new into the social order. For example, environmental groups ask society to participate in or support conservation efforts like recycling programs, clean air legislation, or alternative fuel funding. This movement has grown by leaps and bounds, as conservation has become a growing global concern.

REVOLUTIONARY SOCIAL MOVEMENTS

The most ambitious type of social movement is the **revolutionary social movement**, sometimes called the *transformative social movement*. This type of movement seeks to change the thoughts and actions of all society in radical fashion. Social movement groups that are considered revolutionary aim to completely restructure society. While the anti-globalization movement espoused by Naomi Klein covers a broad spectrum, some elements of that movement would certainly be considered revolutionary. When a revolutionary social movement organization attempts to fulfill its missions, it is called a revolution.

On July 26, 1953, Fidel Castro organized rebel forces and launched an attack on the Moncada military barracks in Santiago de Cuba. The revolution was an attempt to spark an uprising against Fulgencio Batista's regime. After the attack failed to dismantle the existing government, Castro moved his efforts to Mexico, where he organized Cuban exiles into a revolutionary group called the 26th of July Movement. After gaining the support of numerous Cuban citizens through the distribution of

political propaganda, the movement's guerrilla forces defeated the existing Cuban government and enlisted Castro as president in 1960. The movement asked all citizens on the island of Cuba to change their ideology and support a government that would reinstate full civil and political liberties and assume moderate reforms. Unfortunately, the initial goals of the movement were never realized as Castro changed his policies once he was in power.[45]

<<< Groups protest the presence of Christian missionaries in many countries. **New Delhi inhabitants protest against Christian missionary conversions, which increase violence and tension between India's Christians and Hindus.**

think sociologically: WHAT ARE THE THEORIES BEHIND SOCIAL MOVEMENTS?

Conflict Theory

Conflict theorists believe that social movements are normative events in a social world that has inequality. This can be because of social inequalities or because of a perceived inequality. As Marx suggested, inequality makes social change not only necessary, but likely. Why? Because people eventually notice their plight and decide to do something about this. Sociologists such as Charles Tilly suggest that discontent is always present because there will always be haves and have-nots in every society.[46] This applies to social movements.

Social movements are in competition with each other for resources. Resource mobilization theory suggests that those organizations that are best able to gain access to money, media, and larger audiences are more likely to succeed. The nature of the scarcity of resources causes movements to compete for those resources. The ones that compete most effectively are the ones that are going to survive.[47]

Functionalism

Functionalists do not believe that social movements are actually activities per se. Instead, they are a way for participants to relieve the frustrations and emotions they have about a particular subject. In this way, social movements challenge the equilibrium of society, and change is likely to occur.

Sociologists Robert E. Park and Ernest W. Burgess discuss how successful social movements become more organized and eventually institutionalized.[48] First, crowds gather together to protest something they object to or something that is stressful or uncertain. Within this crowd, leaders eventually emerge to take on the responsibility of guiding the crowds toward their purpose. In this way, the crowd begins to organize under the leadership, and an organization will begin to form. This organization is based on ideology, and more people may join the organization's ranks. Eventually, the mainstream accepts this ideology, and the organization becomes institutionalized.

RELATIVE DEPRIVATION points to the gaps between what people have and what they expect.

FRAME ALIGNMENT PROCESS occurs when social movement organizations link their goals to the goals of other organizations.

FRAME BRIDGING occurs when two or more groups that may be somewhat opposed to each other join forces.

AMPLIFICATION occurs when ideas become elaborated and sometimes exaggerated.

EXTENSION refers to the way social movement organizations seek to align their interests with those of other groups that are related, sometimes furthering ideas that were not originally in their frame.

TRANSFORMATION changes the old meanings and understandings of the problem and creates new and innovative ones.

For example, a diverse group of people went to my town's city council meetings to complain about the lack of bike lanes on the roads. At the meetings, we met others who had similar feelings, and, over time, leaders began to emerge from our group. We formed an organization to promote bicycling as an alternative mode of transportation. The group now meets regularly with the park's board and the city council to discuss progress on new bike lanes.

William Kornhauser supports Park and Burgess's idea. He went on to say that not only do social movements bring together people who are like-minded, these movements also allow people who feel less important or isolated in society to come together with others. These people relish the idea of being a part of something bigger, and they feel fulfilled because they take part. Therefore, social movements take on a personal, individualistic component, filling the need of those who feel separate from the rest of society.[49]

Symbolic Interactionism

Symbolic interactionists believe that social movements are less of a unifying force of individuals and more of a reaction to relative deprivation. **Relative deprivation** points to the gaps between what people have and what they expect. For example, you may have a cheap car, but you believe that you should have an expensive car. This makes you feel deprived when you see cars that you think are better than your own. You forget to consider the people who drive cars that are not as nice as your car or the people who don't have cars at all. You focus on the envy you feel when you see people with things that are "better" than yours.[50]

James Chowning Davies applies this theory to social movements by explaining that when people's expectations are met, they are unlikely to organize and work to make changes.[51] They are satisfied with what they have and are unlikely to complain. So, it's only natural to assume that people will be unhappy and more willing to rebel when their expectations are not being met. Collective violence will most likely occur after a period of rising expectations, and a steep decline and reversal of the people's fortunes follows increased gratification.

Ted Gurr suggests that deprivation creates discontent, which leads to civil strife. If social institutions can absorb some of the stress or channel it into something other than violence, revolution is unlikely. Nonviolent strife consists of turmoil such as riots and demonstrations. Violent strife consists of revolution and terrorism.[52]

Feminist Theory

Feminism itself is the product of a social movement. For feminist theorists, the fundamental inequality in most societies that needs to be redressed is gender inequality. As we have seen in earlier chapters, the feminist movement in Canada has achieved many significant changes in Canadian society. Because of women like Nellie McClung, Dorothy Smith, and Margaret Eichler, Canadian women are able to vote, hold political office, and go to school and work alongside men. In Canada, equality of the sexes is a fundamental principle in the *Canadian Charter of Rights and Freedoms*.

The principle of gender equality has been won on many fronts. It has resulted in changes to many laws. But gender equality is more than just a legal issue. True gender equality will be achieved when there is a fundamental change in society—in the ideology that guides our behaviour. Feminist theory has been included as a sociological perspective in this book because it draws attention to issues that concern women, and because it offers yet another way of looking at our social world.

FRAMING PROCESSES

In social movement studies, the idea of frames in social movements has its root in the work of Erving Goffman.[53] Frames provide the individual the opportunity to identify, understand, and label events as they occur in the social world. Frames are templates that organize how we behave publicly. They do not completely limit our understanding of social events, like a

<<< For years activists have written and spoken about the state of the environment. **In 2006, Al Gore's *An Inconvenient Truth* gave a huge boost to environmental awareness.**

Overview of Politicized Communal Groups by Region and Type of Group in 1990

WORLD REGIONS	Number of countries with politicized groups	Number of politicized groups	Ethno-classes	Types of Groups			
				Ethno-nationalists	Militant sects*	Indigenes	Communal contenders
Advanced industrial democracies (21)	12	23	8	10	3 (1)	4	0
Eastern Europe and the USSR (9)	5	32	4	17	14 (1)	11	0
East, Southeast, and South Asia (21)	15	42	7	19	8 (2)	25	3
North Africa and the Middle East (19)	11	29	5	13	9 (5)	11	8
Africa South of the Sahara (36)	29	72	10	21	5	12	51
Latin America and the Caribbean (21)	17	29	9	1	0 (1)	19	0
Totals (127)	89	227	43	81	39 (10)	82	62

*Listed first are numbers of Muslim minorities; numbers in parentheses are non-Muslim religious minorities: Northern Irish Catholics, Jews (in the ex-USSR and Argentina), Copts in Egypt, Maronites in Lebanon, Hindus (in Pakistan and Bangladesh), Sikhs in India, Baháʼís in Iran, and Ahmadis in Pakistan. The latter two have been condemned as non-Muslim heresies in Iran and Pakistan, respectively, which is a warrant for discrimination against their followers. The total number of sects is 49.
Source: Ted Robert Gurr, International Political Science Review (volume 14, issue 2). Pp. 161–201, copyright © 1993 by Sage Publications. Reprinted by Permission of SAGE.

∧
∧ This table shows the number of political groups in different countries around the world. Notice how
∧ more industrialized areas have fewer politicized groups and no contenders for resources, **but in poorer regions like southern Africa, there are as many as 72 political groups and 51 contending groups. Do you think the number and types of groups have anything to do with social stratification and strife?**

picture frame limits the end of a photo; instead, they provide the building blocks by which we understand the world. Frames exist before us, and we become part of them through social processes that teach us how to dress, communicate, and interact within them.[54] For example, if you're on an elevator, you probably do not speak to strangers. At a sporting event, you might hug a stranger if you're caught up in the moment. The frames of the events provide the parameters for understanding that interaction.

Successful social movements use frames to further their cause. If a movement hopes to bring about a change, it must frame its argument successfully. There are three core tasks in framing:

1 **Diagnostic framing:** Creates a frame that states the problem clearly. Is this really a problem? Why? For example, the movement to move the economy away from petroleum relies on accurately and effectively pointing to the problems associated with continued dependence on oil.[55]

2 **Prognostic framing:** Provides the solution to this problem. Currently, there are a host of social movements competing to be the solution to the problem. Is natural gas the best alternative, or are hydroelectric, solar, wind, nuclear energy, or bio-fuels the better choice? Each group competes against the other and provides a prognosis of how its solution will be the best one.[56]

3 **Motivational framing:** This calls people to take action. It makes an argument that people need to do more than merely talk about a problem—they must also take action. When groups urge you to buy a hybrid car or put up a windmill, they are using the motivational frame.[57]

Of course, in an environment such as this, where energy concerns continue to take centre stage in the national debate, it is not surprising that some groups are coming together to provide answers. This **frame alignment process** occurs when social movement organizations link their goals to the goals of other organizations. Four processes occur when organizations are involved in the frame alignment process: bridging, amplification, extension, and transformation.[58]

Frame bridging occurs when two or more groups that may be somewhat opposed to each other join forces. Within the public debate over the oil-based economy, solar and natural gas power proponents have bridged, suggesting that both sources of energy are renewable and clean and they should work together to change the country's collective understanding about how to power their homes and cars.[59]

Amplification occurs when ideas become elaborated and sometimes exaggerated. Groups seek to engage people by illuminating the social issue. The closer this issue is to an already existing value or cultural belief, the more likely amplification can work.[60] For example, in the 1980s, I was a member of a group that proposed using wind power for electricity generation. However, we had little success because the price of oil was still cheap, and energy seemed plentiful. As times change, North Americans are warming up to the idea of wind power if that means they can continue to have air conditioning they can afford.

Extension of the frame alignment refers to the way in which social movement organizations seek to align their interests with those of other groups that are related, sometimes furthering ideas that were not originally in their frame. For example, the solar movement is often connected in the public discourse to the use of biological fuels. Finally, frames can experience transformation when they become aligned.[61]

Transformation changes the old meanings and understandings of the problem and creates new and innovative ones. To push our example further, the energy independence frame is transforming into an organization that once sought to foster only renewable and clean energy, but now often includes a discussion of coal and nuclear power as well.[62]

WRAP YOUR MIND AROUND THE THEORY

These South Koreans are protesting the import of U.S. beef after a mad cow disease scare. **Emotions often run high when people gather to protest something.**

FUNCTIONALISM

Functionalists tend to focus on how systems find balance. In general, they would suggest that social movements cause imbalance, but that they will be short term. For example, Talcott Parsons suggested that social movements follow a predictable pattern that eventually leads the movement into harmony and balance with the rest of society.[63] If you consider the environmental movement, it has become a much more accepted part of society today compared to its status 25 years ago. According to Paul Hawken, over two million organizations worldwide are organizing and uniting because of people's concerns for the environment.[64] These groups are not a part of the status quo.

CONFLICT THEORY

Conflict theorists believe that social structures are the cause of social movements. Inequality causes discontent. This discontent causes people to seek out change, either from within the system or with outside forces. Opposing parties fight for resources, so social movements are a way for groups to mobilize and seize power and resources. Whichever group is most effective at mobilizing "wins" the conflict. An exception to this rule would be with regard to climate concerns. The origin of environmental organizations is a much more organic creation marked by concern for ecological degradation.

SYMBOLIC INTERACTIONISM

Some believe that social movements are caused by the perception of relative deprivation. When a person's expectations are not met, they are discontent. If their expectations are continually not met, they are likely to resort to social movements. For example, environmental hazards seen in countries with few safety regulations can spur people to make a change. Perception is the big key: What do people perceive as unfair? In addition, people react differently because of different framing situations. Bridging, amplification, extension, and transformation are all ways in which organizations react to a framing situation and problem.

WHAT ARE THE RESULTS OF SOCIAL MOVEMENTS?

FEMINIST THEORY

Feminist theory focuses on gender inequality as a prevalent source of discontent in many societies. Feminism is also itself a social movement. It arose because women perceived relative deprivation compared to men. The feminist movement continues to bring change to society's institutions that are unfair to women. Many legal battles have been won, and the resulting changes are now fully acceptable features of society. For example, few people in Canada would suggest that boys and girls be given different educational opportunities.

Conflict theorists believe that **social movements are a result of people wanting what others have.**

Workers will often strike if their expectations are not met. Thousands went on strike in 1986 when the Newfoundland Association of Public Employees (NAPE) was caught up in a battle with the province over legislation limiting the right to strike.[65]

discover sociology in action: HOW DO SOCIAL MOVEMENTS INFLUENCE SOCIOLOGICAL THEORY AND STUDY?

Social Policy: Government Cash for Clunkers

Blessed Unrest author Paul Hawken discusses how people and organizations are working without a formal system of leadership to oversee their actions.[66] Together, these people and organizations make up groups that focus on human rights, the environment, and a plurality of other issues dedicated to improving the people's lives. They make up a loose configuration of groups dedicated to change. These independent movements have a strong force behind them, despite their unconventional structure. So, what would happen if government decided to take part, too?

One way the government is joining in is by providing incentives to help put more fuel-efficient cars on the roads. In British Columbia, for instance, the Scrap-It program allows car owners to trade in their old vehicles for cash. A car owner can save or receive up to $550 when trading in an old clunker for a new, efficient car. Those who want to replace the old clunker with a bicycle instead can receive $500 toward its purchase. Additional incentives include car-sharing and transit passes.[67]

On the national level, the federal government was set to begin regulating fuel consumption of vehicles in 2011. Fuel consumption standards have existed in Canada for several decades, but until now were only voluntary for vehicle manufacturers. In 2008 federal Transport Minister Lawrence Cannon announced: "Our government recognizes that the transportation sector is one of the largest sources of greenhouse gas [GHG] and air pollutant emissions in Canada, accounting for 25 per cent of all Canada's GHG emissions. That's why we are taking action now to make sure that, into the future, we have the most environmentally responsible cars and trucks on Canadian roads." The new regulated standards, which began with 2011 models, aim to match, and possibly exceed, the U.S. fuel consumption target of 6.7 litres of gas per 100 kilometres by 2020. (In 2006, the average fuel consumption for new vehicles in Canada was 8.6/100 km).[68]

More fuel-efficient cars are already in production, and companies like Nissan and Chevrolet were expected to introduce their more environmentally friendly, electric vehicles in Canada for the 2012 model year.[69] In January 2010, General Motors did its last run of the H3 and H3T, the only remaining Hummers that were still being produced. The Hummer, an SUV, was "the perfect target for the green movement."[70] It's predicted that in the future, people will drive smaller, more efficient vehicles and use less gas.[71]

As you fill your car with expensive gas, think how glad you would be to have increased fuel efficiency. Of course, what will happen to those large SUVs and gas-guzzling pickups? Who will be able to afford these new, more efficient cars? Are there sources of energy that we could use other than gasoline? These and other questions remain to be answered, but the policy of rewarding moves to more fuel-efficient cars is one way governments are trying to help reduce fuel consumption and GHG emissions.

ACTIVITIES

1. Think about some of the social policies in Canada. Choose three and look for information about when they came into effect, and what spurred the movement.
2. Use the internet to find out the popular fads in Canada beginning with the 1900s and continuing today. Create a timeline or graphic showing what the latest fads were from each decade.
3. Research an environmental group that is located in your community or province. Find out what the group's mission statement is and what steps it has taken to improve the environment. Design an advertisement for the group that might inspire others to join.

From Classroom to Community ⟩ Carpooling

With gas prices increasing all the time, many of my students were complaining about their decreasing funds. Some students decided that biking to school would be their best money-saving option. Devante, who drove 20 minutes to get to class, suggested a campus-wide carpool. Using the school's online community board, he set up a page where commuters could find other students in their area.

"I wanted one or two other people to share the cost of travel. I didn't expect to hear back from more than 20 people. The online community board made it easy for us to get in touch and figure out scheduling details. It also helped us form a commuter community on campus. We ended up creating a commuter's lounge where students could relax between classes and wait for their rides.

"Then, the campus' conservation club wrote an article for the school newspaper about how carpooling helps the environment by decreasing pollution. Even more students joined our online group. It was great to see so many people in one group for so many different reasons. I got to meet a lot of really interesting people, and I felt closer to our school community. By the end of the semester, the money I saved on gas was just one of the many perks I received by starting this group."

get the topic: WHAT DRIVES SOCIAL CHANGE?

Theory

FUNCTIONALISM   279
- social movements are not the actual activities, but are ways for people to vent their frustrations and emotions
- venting upsets the balance of society
- movements also bring individuals together, allowing those who feel isolated and alone to feel as though they are part of something bigger

CONFLICT THEORY   279
- social structures are the cause of social movements
- people concentrate on the things that they do not have, and inequality causes discontent
- discontent causes people to seek out change, either from within the system or with outside forces
- opposing parties fight for resources, so social movements are a way for groups to mobilize and seize power and resources

SYMBOLIC INTERACTIONISM   280
- social movements are caused by relative deprivation
- when people's expectations are not met, they are discontent
- if their expectations are continually not met, they are likely to resort to social movements
- perception is key

FEMINIST THEORY   280
- feminist theory is the product of a social movement
- gender equality is the basic inequality in most societies that needs redressing
- true gender equality will exist when there has been a fundamental change in the ideology that guides our behaviour

Key Terms

social change is the way in which culture, interaction, and innovation change social institutions over time.   271

technology deals with the creation, use, and application of knowledge and its interrelation with life, society, and the environment.   272

invention is the creation of a new device or way of thinking.   272

diffusion is the spreading of something more widely.   272

futility is the claim that a reform cannot work because the social problem is unsolvable.   272

perversity claims that any attempts to fix a problem would actually compound the issues the change was trying to address.   273

jeopardy is the claim that attempting to solve a problem will only draw attention away from other, more important issues.   273

(continued)

collective behaviour is any social interaction in which a group of people engages in behaviour that is not in their normal routine. *274*

mobs are groups characterized by high levels of emotion that engage in some type of focused action that can be violent or disruptive. *274*

hysteria is a heightened emotional state that can lead a group to violence. *274*

riots are emotional and violent disturbances of the peace by crowds that lack a central focus. *274*

fad is a temporary fashion, notion, or action the public embraces. *274*

craze occurs when a fad leaves a lasting effect on society. *274*

panic is an extreme fear based on something that might happen. *275*

crowd is a large group of influential people who gather for a temporary purpose. *275*

rumours are stories or statements that lack confirmation or certainty. *275*

urban legends are rumours that are presented as true stories that act as cautionary tales. *275*

social movements are activities that support or protest social issues; organized by nongovernmental organizations. *275*

campaigns are organized and ongoing efforts to achieve a specific goal. *275*

repertoires are actions used to promote interest and involvement within the movement. *276*

WUNC refers to the members of a movement who want to show the public the worthiness, unity, numbers, and commitment of their movement. *276*

emergence is the first stage of a movement when people become aware of a problem and begin to notice that others feel the same way. *276*

coalescence is the second stage of a movement when groups reach out to other groups and individuals to gain membership. *276*

bureaucratization is the third stage of a movement when it becomes a political force. *277*

decline is the final stage of a movement when an organization completes its goal or is seen as irrelevant. *277*

alternative social movements want to create a change in specific people's thoughts, practices, and beliefs regarding a particular issue. *277*

redemptive social movements focus on specific individuals, but the amount of change sought is radical, rather than limited. *278*

reformative social movements seek to change a society's thoughts and actions, but only in a limited way. *278*

progressive means favouring or promoting change. *278*

regressive means seeking to stop change. *278*

revolutionary social movements, sometimes called transformative social movements, seek to change the thoughts and actions of all society in radical fashion. *279*

relative deprivation points to the gaps between what people have and what they expect. *280*

frame alignment process occurs when social movement organizations link their goals to the goals of other organizations. *281*

frame bridging occurs when two or more groups that may be somewhat opposed to each other join forces. *281*

amplification occurs when ideas become elaborated and sometimes exaggerated. *281*

extension refers to the way social movement organizations seek to align their interests with those of other groups that are related, sometimes furthering ideas that were not originally in their frame. *281*

transformation changes the old meanings and understandings of the problem and creates new and innovative ones. *281*

Sample Test Questions

These multiple-choice questions are similar to those found in the test bank that accompanies this textbook.

1. Which of the following statements about mobs is *false*?
   a. They are violent and disruptive.
   b. They have high levels of emotions.
   c. They have no central focus or intent.
   d. They are one form of collective behaviour.
2. Social protesters who argue perversity claim that
   a. there is no solution to the problem.
   b. any change will only make the problem worse.
   c. the "so-called problem" is not really a problem at all.
   d. focusing on the problem means ignoring more important things.
3. Which of the following statements about technology is *false*?
   a. Technology encompasses more than objects and things.
   b. As technology changes, culture remains the same.
   c. Technology is the product of invention.
   d. Technology leads to new discoveries.
4. Which of the following is an example of a craze?
   a. People redecorating their home using feng shui techniques
   b. People going on a date at a video arcade.

   c. People attending a DARE presentation
   d. People waiting in line to buy a Wii
5. Which type of social movement seeks to create limited change for the entire society?
   a. An alternative social movement
   b. A redemptive social movement
   c. A reform social movement
   d. A revolutionary social movement

ESSAY

1. Discuss the four types of social movements and the features of each one.
2. How does new technology affect society?
3. What is relative deprivation?
4. How do sociologists from the four sociological paradigms view social movements?
5. How does the culture jamming movement that Naomi Klein discusses differ from other social movements?

ANSWERS: 1. c; 2. b; 3. b; 4. b; 5. d

WHERE TO START YOUR RESEARCH PAPER

To learn more about the United Nations environmental report, including data on environmental trends, go to www.unep.org/Evaluation/default.htm

For examples of social movements and groups in Canada, go to Greenpeace www.greenpeace.org/canada

Gwen Jacobs (Ontario law for women to be topless) www.fcn.ca/Gwen.html

David Suzuki Foundation www.davidsuzuki.org

October Crisis in Quebec, 1970 www.historyofrights.com/events/flq.html, Separatism in Quebec http://thecanadianencyclopedia.com/index.cfm?PgNm=TCE&Params=A1ARTA0007291

Aboriginal rights in B.C. www.bctreaty.net/files/about_us.php

Universal health care in Canada www.cupe1975.ca/bursary/burs5.html

For international earth science information, including numerous reports and various data sources, go to www.ciesin.org

To find information on health indicators, international comparisons or health-care systems, and health-related data, go to www3.who.int/whosis/menu.cfm

For data on income and inequality throughout the world, go to www.wider.unu.edu/wiid/wiid.htm

To find international data and analysis of poverty and wealth throughout the world, go to www.worldbank.org

Remember to check www.thethinkspot.ca for additional information, downloadable flashcards, and other helpful resources.

GLOSSARY

aboriginal is a person who is North American Indian Inuit, or Métis. (162)

absolute poverty is poverty so severe that one lacks resources to survive. (126)

achieved status is a type of position that you earn or do something to attain. (70)

activity theory states that life satisfaction depends on maintaining an involvement with life by developing new interests, hobbies, roles, and relationships. (206)

affirmative action is a social policy designed to help minority groups gain opportunities through employment and education. (173)

ageism is prejudice and discrimination based solely on age. (205)

agents of socialization are the people and groups who shape our self-concept, beliefs, and behaviour. (94)

alternative social movements want to create a change in specific people's thoughts, practices, and beliefs regarding a particular issue. (277)

altruistic suicides are suicides that occur when the level of solidarity is exceptionally high and when the individual views the group's interests as superior to all other interests. (7)

amplification occurs when ideas become elaborated and sometimes exaggerated. (281)

androcentric bias a focus on men which influences sociology in terms of how social research is done and which issues and topics are studied. (21)

animism is the belief that recognizes that animate spirits live in natural objects and operate in the world. (258)

annexation is the incorporation of one territory into another. (164)

anomic suicides are suicides that occur as a result of social unrest. (8)

ascribed status is a position in society that is given or assigned. (70)

assimilation is the process by which minority groups adopt the patterns of the dominant culture. (57)

assimilationist minorities are groups that seek to shed their old ways and integrate themselves into mainstream society. (165)

attachment is the social bond that refers to our relationship to others. (222)

authoritarian style is a parenting style with which children experience high levels of social control but low levels of emotional support. (94)

authoritative style is a parenting style in which parents listen to their children's input while consistently enforcing the preset rules. (94)

autocratic leaders are leaders who determine the group policies and assign tasks. (110)

backstage is the demeanour that incorporates our true feelings and beliefs. (77)

belief is the social bond that refers to a person's conviction of truth. (223)

bissu are androgynous members of Bugis society who embody the perfect mixture of male and female. (182)

blended families are families composed of children and some combination of biological parents. (234)

bounded relationships are relationships that exist only under specific conditions. (107)

bourgeoisie refers to members of the capitalist class. (14)

brain drain occurs when the best talent leaves poor countries and thereby provides an even greater advantage to wealthy countries. (151)

bureaucracies are formal organizations that are organized into a hierarchy of smaller departments. (115)

bureaucratization is the third stage of a movement when it becomes a political force. (277)

bureaucrats are managers of business and government agencies. (149)

calabai are anatomical males in Bugis society who adhere to some of the responsibilities of women. (182)

calalai are anatomical females in Bugis society who assume the characteristics of men. (182)

campaigns are organized and ongoing efforts to achieve a specific goal. (275)

case studies are investigations of one person or event in detail. (39)

caste systems are systems in which a person's position may be a position of power and privilege or of disadvantage, but in either case his or her place is permanently fixed. (147)

causal relationship is a relationship in which one condition leads to a certain consequence. (34)

causation is the relationship between cause and effect. (34)

central tendency is the middle of the distribution of a variable. (40)

chattel slavery is a form of slavery in which a slave is considered property. (146)

chivalry hypothesis suggests that female offenders are treated more leniently by male police officers and judges. (224)

choice model explains the income gap by analyzing the kinds of jobs women choose. (184)

church is a large, highly organized group of believers. (258)

civil religion is a binding force that holds society together through political and social issues. (260)

class consciousness is an understanding of one's position in the class system. (14)

coalescence is the second stage of a movement when groups reach out to other groups and individuals to gain membership. (276)

coercive organizations are organizations that people are forced to join. (114)

cognitive development is a person's ability to think and reason. (90)

cohort is a specific group of people used in a study. (35)

collective behaviour is any social interaction in which a group of people engages in behaviour that is not in their normal routine. (274)

colonialism is the imposition of control over a weak nation by a more powerful country. (162)

colour-blind racism is the idea that racism still exists in society in more subtle ways. (170)

commitment is the social bond that refers to our dedication to live a socially acceptable life. (223)

community learning occurs when individuals and groups work to identify and address issues of public concern. (26)

comparative studies use data from different sources in order to evaluate them against each other. (35)

concepts are abstract ideas that are impossible to measure. (35)

concrete operational stage is the stage (ages 7 through 12 years) at which children can think about objects in the world in more than one way and start to understand causal connections in their surroundings. (90)

conflict model of law proposes that powerful people write laws to protect their own interests while punishing the actions of those they wish to control. (218)

conflict theory is a theoretical framework that views society as an unequal system that brings about conflict and change. (9)

conformity is the degree to which we will alter our behaviour, attitudes, and points of view to fit into our perceived expectation of what is appropriate. (111)

conquest is the domination over a group of people by a superior force. (164)

consensus model of law suggests that laws arise because people see a behaviour they do not like, and they agree to make it illegal. (218)

contagion is a rapid, irrational mode in which people do not think rationally or clearly. (19)

containment theory argues that people who commit crimes cannot resist the temptations that surround them. (222)

content analysis is a type of research in which the sociologist looks for common words or themes in newspapers, books, or structured interviews. (43)

contract slavery is a form of slavery in which a person signs a work contract, receiving food and shelter from an employer, but is threatened when he or she tries to leave the contract. (147)

control variables are variables that are kept constant to accurately test the impact of an independent variable. (34)

conventional level is the second stage of moral development that arises before puberty and uses the lens of norms and rules to determine what is right and wrong. (92)

correlation is an indication that one factor might be the cause for another factor. (34)

countercultures are groups with value systems that are in opposition to the dominant group's values. (57)

craftspeople are the skilled labourers such as plumbers or carpenters. (149)

craze occurs when a fad leaves a lasting effect on society. (274)

credentialism is an emphasis on educational degrees in assessing skills and knowledge. (255)

crime is the violation of norms that have been written into law. (214)

crime rate measures the volume of crime reported to the police. (216)

Crime Severity Index measures the seriousness of crime reported to the police. (216)

criminology is the scientific study of crime, deviance, and social policies that the criminal justice system applies. (214)

cross-sectional studies look at one event at a single point in time. (35)

crowd is a large group of influential people who gather for a temporary purpose. (275)

cults are new religious movements led by charismatic leaders with few followers. (258)

cultural lag occurs when social and cultural changes occur at a slower pace than technological changes. (57)

cultural relativism means making a deliberate effort to appreciate a group's ways of life without prejudice. (56)

cultural transmission is culture passing from one generation to the next through language. (52)

culture is the language, beliefs, values, norms, behaviours, and material objects that are important enough to pass on to future generations of a society. (50)

culture shock occurs when a person encounters a culture foreign to his or her own and has an emotional response to the differences between the cultures. (57)

cycle of poverty refers to the vicious circle where poor children are more likely to be poor as adults. (131, 169)

debt bondage is a form of slavery in which someone borrows money in order to repay a different debt, and works off the new debt. (147)

decline is the final stage of a movement when an organization completes its goal or is seen as irrelevant. (277)

delegated means given or assigned. (127)

democratic leaders are leaders who strive to set group policy by discussion and agreement. (110)

demographic similarity refers to shared characteristics such as race, gender, or age. (77)

dependency ratio is the ratio of the youth population (0 to 19 years) and senior population (65 or older) to the working-age population (20 to 64 years). (206)

dependent variables are the response to the manipulated variable. (33)

deterrence is a measure that prevents a person from doing something because of fear of the consequences. (219)

deviance is the violation of norms that a society agrees upon. (214)

differential association theory emphasizes that criminal and deviant behaviour is learned. (222)

diffusion is the spreading of something more widely. (272)

discreditable stigma is a stigma that can be concealed from others. (71)

discredited stigma is a stigma that cannot be hidden from others or is no longer hidden from others. (71)

discretion is the ability to make decisions. (226)

discrimination is the unfair treatment of people based on a prejudice. (167)

disengagement theory states that reduced interaction between older persons and others is unavoidable, mutual, and acceptable to both the individual and society. (206)

dominant group is the group that has the greatest power, but not necessarily the greatest numbers. (162)

double consciousness is the sense that a person must keep a foot in two worlds, one in the majority group's world and one in the minority group's world. (171)

dramaturgy is a theory of interaction in which all social life is like acting. (19)

dyad is a group consisting of only two people. (110)

education is the formal system in which society passes its knowledge, skills, and values from one generation to the next. (251)

egoistic suicides are suicides that result from a lack of solidarity, occurring among those who have few social connections, feel isolated and alone, and are more likely to fall into despair. (7)

elite class see upper class

embarrassment is a state that occurs when we realize our act has failed. (77)

emergence is the first stage of a movement when people become aware of a problem and begin to notice that others feel the same way. (276)

endogamy is the practice of marrying within your social group. (238)

entrepreneurs are the business class, as identified by Weber. (149)

ethics is a system of values or principles that guide one's behaviour. (42)

ethnic cleansing refers to persecution through imprisonment, expulsion, or murder of members of an ethnic minority by a majority to achieve ethnic homogeneity in majority-controlled territory. (164)

ethnic enclaves are neighbourhoods where people from similar cultures live together and assert cultural distinction from the dominant group. (167)

ethnicity is the classification of people who share a common cultural, linguistic, or ancestral heritage. (161)

ethnocentrism occurs when a person uses his or her own culture to judge another culture. (56)

ethnography is a research method that aims to understand the social perspective and cultural values of a particular group by participating in or getting to know their activities in detail. (39)

exchange mobility is a concept suggesting that, within a country, each social class contains a relatively fixed number of people. (132)

exogamy is the practice of marrying someone from a different social group. (238)

extended family is a household consisting of a nuclear family plus an additional relative. (233)

extension refers to the way social movement organizations seek to align their interests with those of other groups that are related, sometimes furthering ideas that were not originally in their frame. (281)

face-saving work is a reaction to embarrassment in the form of either humour, anger, or retreat. (77)

fad is a temporary fashion, notion, or action the public embraces. (274)

false consciousness is a person's lack of understanding of his or her position in society. (14)

family is two or more people who are related by blood, marriage, or adoption. (232)

fatalistic suicides are suicides that result from a lack of social control. (8)

feminism is the vast collection of social movements and theories about gender differences, proposing social equality for all people. (185)

feminist theory is a theoretical framework that focuses on gender inequalities which are built in to the social structure. (10)

feminization of poverty refers to the fact that around the world women experience poverty at far higher rates than men. (133)

feral means wild. (88)

field research is research conducted in a natural setting. (39)

folkways are informal types of norms. (55)

formal operational stage is the stage (ages 12 years and above) at which people become able to comprehend abstract thought. (90)

formal organizations are groups created for a certain purpose and built for maximum efficiency. (114)

formal rationality is the reasonable actions that organizations and bureaucracies take to achieve goals in the most effective way. (115)

formal structures are the explicit rules, goals, and guidelines of an organization. (114)

frame alignment process occurs when social movement organizations link their goals to the goals of other organizations. (281)

frame bridging occurs when two or more groups that may be somewhat opposed to each other join forces. (281)

front stage is what the audience sees, or the part of ourselves that we present to others. (77)

functionalism is a theoretical framework that defines society as a system of interrelated parts. (9)

functions are social factors that affect people in a society. (13)

futility is the claim that a reform cannot work because the social problem is unsolvable. (272)

game stage is Mead's third stage of development, which never truly ends, and is the stage in which we begin to understand that others have expectations and demands placed upon them. (89)

Gemeinschaft refers to community connections involving personal relationships based on friendship and kinship ties, such as family. (74)

gender is the expectations of behaviour and attitude that a society considers proper for males and females. (97)

gender identity is our perception of ourselves as male or female. (179)

gender roles are society's expectations of how males and females should act and think. (180)

gender socialization teaches members of society how to express their masculinity or femininity. (97)

general deterrence is a measure that ensures individuals will not commit a crime because they see the negative consequences applied to others, and they fear experiencing these consequences. (219)

General Social Survey—Victimization measures crime victimization based on a representative sample of nearly 20,000 Canadians over 15 years old. (216)

generalization is the extent that what is learned from a sample can be applied to the population from which the sample is taken. (36)

generalized other is our sense of others. (89)

genocide is the attempt to destroy or exterminate a people based on their race and/or ethnicity. (163)

gerontology is the study of aging and the elderly. (203)

Gesellschaft refers to societal connections that are more formal and impersonal. (75)

gestures are symbols we make using our bodies, such as facial expressions, hand movements, eye contact, and other types of body language. (52)

glass ceiling is an invisible barrier preventing women from reaching executive-level positions in the workplace. (184)

global stratification is the categorization of countries based on objective criteria, such as wealth, power, and prestige, which highlights social patterns and inequality throughout the world. (142)

global village refers to the "shrinking" of the world through immediate electronic communications. (58)

globalization is a complex process by which the world and its international economy are becoming more and more intertwined. (151)

grade inflation is the trend of assigning higher grades than previously assigned to students for completing the same work. (254)

groups are any number of people with similar norms, values, and behaviours who frequently interact with one another. (69)

groupthink is the term for group decisions that are made without objective thought. (111)

hate groups are organizations that promote hostility or violence toward others based on race and other factors. (163)

Hawthorne effect occurs when people behave differently because they know they are being studied. (39)

health is a state of complete physical, mental, and social well-being and not merely the absence of disease or infirmity. (197)

hedonism is seeking pleasure over pain. (92)

henotheism is the worship of one god while recognizing the existence of other deities. (258)

hidden curriculum refers to the lessons taught in school that are unrelated to academic learning. (96)

homogamy is marriage between people with similar backgrounds, such as religion, race, class, or age. (238)

horizontal mobility refers to moving within the same status category. (130)

human capital is a person's combination of skills, knowledge, traits, and personal attributes. (255)

human capital model assumes that men and women bring different natural skills to the workplace. (184)

hypothesis involves a suggestion about how variables relate. (34)

hysteria is a heightened emotional state that can lead a group to violence. (274)

"I" self is the subjective part of the self. (89)

imitation stage is Mead's first stage of development, which is the period from birth to about age 2, and is the stage at which children merely copy the behaviours of those around them. (89)

impression management is management of the impression that the performer makes on others. (77)

incapacitation means preventing the offender from causing further harm. (219)

income is the money received for work or through investments. (124)

independent variables are variables that are deliberately manipulated in an experiment. (33)

indictable offences are more serious offences. (226)

indigenous superordination is the subordination of an immigrant group to a dominant group. (165)

informal structures are friendships, allegiances, and loyalties among members of an organization. (114)

in-group is a group to which we feel an affinity or closeness. (108)

in-group bias is the feeling that a person's in-group is superior to others. (108)

institutional discrimination maintains the advantage for the dominant group, while providing the appearance of fairness to all. (168)

intergenerational mobility refers to the change that family members make from one social class to the next through generations. (131)

intimate distance is distance reserved for those with whom we are very close. (76)

intragenerational mobility occurs when an individual changes social standing, especially in the workforce. (131)

invention is the creation of a new device or way of thinking. (272)

involuntary immigration is the forced movement of people from one society to another. (164)

involvement is the social bond that refers to the level of participation in conventional activities. (223)

iron cage is a concept introduced by Max Weber that refers to the way in which bureaucracies make workers feel trapped and turn them into little more than robots accomplishing tasks. (115)

jeopardy is the claim that attempting to solve a problem will only draw attention away from other, more important issues. (273)

laissez-faire leaders are leaders who lead by absence and may in fact not want to be leaders at all. (110)

language is a system of speech and/or written symbols used to convey meaning and communicate. (51)

latent functions are functions that lead to unforeseen or unexpected consequences. (13)

leadership style is a behavioural mode that leaders use to influence group members. (110)

literature review is a study of relevant academic articles and information. (34)

longitudinal studies include data from observations over time using a cohort. (35)

looking-glass self is the theory that the self develops through a process of reflection, like a mirror. (89)

lower class is a social class living in poverty. (129)

machismo is overt and exaggerated displays of masculinity. (189)

macro means large-scale. (6)

macrosociology is the study of large-scale society, focusing on the social structures that exist within a society and examining how those structures create the social world. (69)

manifest functions are functions that lead to an expected consequence or outcome. (13)

marginal poverty is a state of poverty that occurs when a person lacks stable employment. (126)

marital effects are factors that make marriage work. (238)

marriage is the union of two people that is typically recognized by law or cultural norms. (232)

mass media include any print or electronic resource that is used to communicate to a wide audience. (98)

master status is the status toward which we gravitate. (70)

material culture consists of items within a culture that you can taste, touch, and feel. (50)

matriarchy is a social system in which women are the main authority and hold power over men. (180)

"me" self is the objective part of the self. (89)

mean is an average. (40)

mechanical solidarity refers to the state of community bonding in traditional societies in which people share beliefs and values and perform common activities. (12)

median refers to the midpoint in a distribution of numbers. (40)

medicalization is the idea that the medical community is the centre of many aspects of our society. (199)

Medicare is the term used to describe Canada's government-run health-care insurance program that provides health coverage for all Canadians. (196)

meritocracy argument states that those who get ahead do so based on their own merit. (132)

micro means small-scale. (6)

microsociology is the study of the small interactions of daily life. (69)

middle class is a social class that consists of those who have moderate incomes. (129)

migrant superordination is the conquest of a native population by a more powerful group. (165)

militant minorities are groups that seek to overthrow the existing system because they see it as unjust. (166)

minority group is a group that has less power than the majority group. (162)

mobs are groups characterized by high levels of emotion that engage in some type of focused action that can be violent or disruptive. (274)

mode refers to the most common value in a distribution. (40)

monogamy is the practice of being married to one person at a time. (234)

monotheism is the belief that there is only one God. (257)

morality of care is morality decided by a standard of how best to help those who are in need. (93)

morality of justice is morality based on the rule of law. (93)

mores are norms that represent a community's most important values. (55)

multiculturalism is a concept that supports the inherent value of different cultures within society. (57)

nature theory states that the genes we get from our parents at conception are the primary causes of human behaviours. (87)

needs assessment is an analysis that studies the needs of a specific group and presents the results in a written statement. (45)

negative correlation occurs when variables move in opposite directions. (34)

neocolonialism is a process in which powerful nations use loans and economic power to maintain control over poor nations. (151)

nonmaterial culture consists of the nonphysical products of society, including our symbols, values, rules, and sanctions. (51)

normative organizations are organizations that exist to achieve a worthwhile goal. (114)

normative relativism is the evaluation of a society based on that society's norms. (56)

norms are rules developed for appropriate behaviour based on specific values that are conditional; they can vary from place to place. (54)

nuclear family is a household consisting of a husband, wife, and children. (233)

nurture theory states that our environment influences the way we think, feel, and behave. (87)

objectivity is the ability to conduct research without allowing personal biases or prejudices to influence you. (33)

old old is a cohort that consists of people over the age of 75. (203)

operationalizing is turning abstract ideas into something measurable. (35)

organic solidarity occurs when people live in a society with a diverse division of labour. (12)

organization of believers is a group that ensures the prosperity and effectiveness of the religious experience. (261)

organizations are formal groups that exist to achieve a desired goal. (114)

out-group is a group from which we are disconnected. (108)

oversampling is the process of taking a bigger sample if the group you wish to study makes up a small percentage of the whole population. (36)

panic is an extreme fear based on something that might happen. (275)

paradigm refers to a theoretical framework through which scientists study the world. (9)

parsimony is extreme unwillingness to use resources. (35)

participant observation is a type of field research in which the researcher poses as a person who is normally in the environment. (39)

patriarchal refers to a social system that benefits men. (10)

patriarchy is a social system in which the father serves as head of the family, and men have authority over women and children. (180)

patriarchy model assumes that we have a male-dominated society that doesn't allow women to hold upper-tier jobs. (184)

peer groups are made up of people who are generally the same age and who share the same interests. (96)

permissive style is a parenting style in which parents provide high levels of support but an inconsistent enforcement of rules. (94)

personal distance is distance that ranges from 45 centimetres to 1.2 metres; this distance is for normal conversations. (76)

personal space is the invisible bubble that each of us has around us that insulates us from others. (76)

perversity claims that any attempts to fix a problem would actually compound the issues the change was trying to address. (273)

petite bourgeoisie are small-business owners in Weber's class system. (149)

philosophies of life are ways of life that focus on a set of ethical, moral, or philosophical principles. (257)

play stage is Mead's second stage of development, which occurs around the ages of 2–4 years, during which children play roles and begin to take on the characteristics of important people in their world. (89)

pluralistic minorities are groups that enter into an area voluntarily but seek to maintain their own culture while also integrating into the dominant group. (165)

polyandry is the practice of a woman marrying two or more men. (234)

polygamy is the practice of having more than one spouse at a time. (234)

polygyny is the practice of a man marrying two or more women. (234)

polytheism is the belief in multiple gods and demigods. (257)

populations are target groups from which researchers want to get information. (35)

positive correlation includes two variables that move in a parallel direction. (34)

postconventional level is the third stage of moral development that refers to a morality based on abstract principles. (92)

power is the ability to carry out your will and impose it on others. (127)

power elite is a small group of people who hold immense power. (127)

preconventional level is the first stage of moral development that lasts through the elementary school years; at this level, children make their moral judgments within a framework of hedonistic principles. (92)

prejudice refers to negative attitudes about an entire category of people. (167)

preoperational stage is the stage (ages 2 through 7 years) at which the ability to speak grows rapidly. (90)

prestige is the level of esteem associated with one's status and social standing. (127)

primary deviance is the initial deviant act itself. (223)

primary groups are groups that are small, intimate, and enduring. (69)

primary socialization is socialization that occurs during childhood. (87)

profane means related or devoted to that which is not sacred. (259)

progressive means favouring or promoting change. (278)

proletariat refers to members of the poor working class. (14)

psychosocial crisis is a crisis occurring during each of Erikson's stages that will be resolved either positively or negatively, and each outcome will have an effect on our ability to deal with the next one. (90)

public distance is the zone of interaction that is used in highly formal settings; this distance includes everything greater than 3.6 metres. (76)

qualitative data include words, pictures, photos, or any other type of information that comes to the researcher in a non-numeric form. (43)

quantitative data refer to data based on numbers. (43)

quintile is one of five groups of households, ranked by income. (125)

race is the division of people based on certain physical characteristics. (161)

racism is discrimination based on a person's race. (163)

random sample is a group of subjects arbitrarily chosen from a defined population. (36)

recidivism is the tendency for inmates released from prison to return to prison. (219)

redemptive social movements focus on specific individuals, but the amount of change sought is radical, rather than limited. (278)

reference group is the group that you use to evaluate yourself. (109)

reformative social movements seek to change a society's thoughts and actions, but only in a limited way. (278)

regressive means seeking to stop change. (278)

rehabilitation tries to reform the offender so that he or she can be returned to society. (219)

reintegrative shaming is an effort to bring an offender back into the community after punishment. (218)

relative deprivation points to the gaps between what people have and what they expect. (280)

relative poverty is a state of poverty that occurs when we compare ourselves to those around us. (126)

reliable means able to be trusted. (35)

religion is a unified system of beliefs and practices, relative to sacred things. (257)

rentiers are the wealthy members of a society, as identified by Weber. (149)

repertoires are actions used to promote interest and involvement within the movement. (276)

research design refers to the process used to find information. (35)

research methods are the scientific procedures that sociologists use to conduct research and develop knowledge about a particular topic. (32)

residual poverty is chronic and multigenerational poverty. (126)

resocialization is the process of learning new norms, values, attitudes, and behaviours, and abandoning old ones. (95)

restoration uses impact statements so that victims can participate in the sentencing process. (219)

retribution is based on the belief that offenders should be punished. (219)

revolutionary social movements, sometimes called transformative social movements, seek to change the thoughts and actions of all society in radical fashion. (279)

riots are emotional and violent disturbances of the peace by crowds that lack a central focus. (274)

rituals are established patterns of behaviour closely associated with experience of the sacred. (259)

role is the behaviour of a specific status. (70)

role conflict is a phenomenon occurring when one is forced to choose between the competing demands of multiple roles. (71)

role expectations are the anticipated behaviours for a particular role. (70)

role performance is the degree to which a person plays the role in a manner we expect. (70)

role set is the variety of roles an individual plays. (71)

role strain occurs when the demands and expectations of one role are impossible for us to satisfy. (71)

rumours are stories or statements that lack confirmation or certainty. (275)

sacred means connected to God or dedicated to a religious purpose. (259)

sample is a subset of the population. (35)

sample of convenience is a nonrandom sample available to the researcher. (38)

sanction is a reward or punishment you receive when you either abide by a norm or violate it. (54)

"sandwiched" generation is the generation that takes care of both its children and its elderly parents. (203)

Sapir-Whorf hypothesis is a hypothesis, first advanced by Edward Sapir in 1929 and subsequently developed by Benjamin Whorf, that the structure of a language determines a native speaker's perception and categorization of experience. (52)

scapegoat means making an unfair accusation against a person or group as the cause of a problem. (168)

secessionist minorities are groups that voluntarily separate themselves from the dominant group and view the dominant group with disdain, believing that it will corrupt the group's belief system. (165)

secondary data are data that others have already collected and published. (39)

secondary data analysis is the process of using and analyzing data that others have collected. (39)

secondary deviance refers to the psychological reorientation that occurs when the system catches a person and labels him or her as a deviant. (223)

secondary groups are groups that are formal, superficial, and temporary. (69)

secondary socialization is the dynamic whereby socialization continues throughout our lives. (87)

sects are religious groups that have enough members to sustain themselves and go against society's norms. (258)

secularization is the overall decline in the importance and power of religion in people's lives. (260)

segregation is forced separation because of factors such as race, gender, or ethnicity. (169)

selection effects are the likelihood that a nonrepresentative sample may lead to inaccurate results. (38)

self refers to a person's identity and what makes that person different from others. (18)

self-focused impression management refers to techniques that include acting modest about your accomplishments (even if that modesty is false), boasting occasionally about your successes, and showing your friendliness and self-assuredness through smiles and eye contact. (77)

semi-skilled manual workers are the workers who have some training and may work in factories. (149)

sensorimotor stage is the stage (birth to 2 years) at which infants learn to experience and think about the world through their senses and motor skills. (90)

sex is the biological makeup of a male or female. (179)

sexism is the belief that one sex is superior to the other. (180)

shaming is a deliberate effort to attach a negative meaning to a behaviour. (218)

sick role is the expected behaviours and responsibilities appropriate for someone who is ill. (199)

simple supernaturalism is the belief in a variety of supernatural forces that affect and influence people's lives. (258)

slavery is the total control over people who have no choice about their status. (146)

social capital is a sociological concept that refers to the individual and collective resources available to a person. (113)

social change is the way in which culture, interaction, and innovation change social institutions over time. (271)

social control refers to the social mechanisms that regulate a person's actions. (7)

social Darwinism is a notion that suggests strong societies survive and weak ones become extinct. (12)

social distance is distance that ranges from about 1.2 metres to 3.6 metres and is usually reserved for formal settings. (76)

social dynamics are the change in the existing structural elements of society. (10)

social epidemiology is the study of the distribution of diseases and health throughout a society's population. (197)

social groups are groups that consist of two or more people who interact with one another and share a common identity. (106)

social institutions are structures that provide for patterned relationships. (73)

social laws are statements of fact that are unchanging under given conditions and can be used as ground rules for any kind of society. (10)

social mobility is the ability to change social classes. (130)

social movements are activities that support or protest social issues, organized by nongovernmental organizations. (275)

social network is the web of ties you have with others. (113)

social policies are deliberate strategies designed to correct recognized social problems. (100)

social research is investigation conducted by social scientists. (34)

social statics are the existing structural elements of society. (10)

social stratification is the ranking of people and the rewards they receive based on objective criteria often including wealth, power, and/or prestige. (124)

social stratification systems are slavery, caste, and class systems. (146)

social structures are patterns of relationships that endure from one generation to the next. (69)

socialization is the process that teaches the norms, values, and other aspects of a culture to new group members. (86)

sociological imagination is the ability to look beyond the individual as the cause for success and failure and see how one's society influences the outcome. (6)

sociology is a science guided by the basic understanding that our lives are affected, not only by our individual characteristics but by powerful social forces and our place in the social world. (5)

solidarity refers to the level of connectedness a person feels to others in the environment. (7)

specific deterrence is a measure that changes the attitude of individuals who have already violated the law and have been punished, by causing them never to commit crime again. (219)

spurious correlation occurs when two variables appear to be related, but actually have a different cause. (34)

stereotypes are simplified perceptions people have of an entire group that are usually based on false assumptions. (167)

stigma is a mark of disgrace associated with a particular status, quality, or person. (71)

stigmatized shame is a permanent label given to an offender, which could actually increase the chances of reoffending because the guilty person is forever labelled. (218)

street crime refers to many different types of criminal acts which occur in public places, such as burglary, drug dealing, and pick-pocketing. (215)

structural mobility occurs when social changes affect large numbers of people. (131)

subculture is a subset of the dominant culture that has distinct values, beliefs, and norms. (57)

summary conviction offences are less serious offences. (226)

supervisor-focused impression management refers to techniques that involve flattering your boss and agreeing with your boss's opinions (or at least avoiding disagreements whenever possible). (77)

survey is an investigation of the opinions or experience of a group of people by asking them questions. (35)

symbolic interactionism is a theoretical framework that focuses on how people interact with others in their everyday lives. (9)

symbols represent, suggest, or stand for something else. (51)

system of beliefs relates sacred objects to religious rituals, and defines and protects the sacred from the profane. (261)

taboo is an act that is socially unacceptable. (55)

teacher expectancy effect is the impact of a teacher's expectations on a student's performance. (254)

technology deals with the creation, use, and application of knowledge and its interrelation with life, society, and the environment. (272)

theism is the belief in a god or gods. (257)

theocracy is a government which is controlled by religious leaders. (258)

theory is a comprehensive and systematic explanation of events that lead to testable predictions. (34)

total institutions are places in which the most effective forms of resocialization can occur because they isolate people from outside influences so they can be reformed and controlled. (95)

totemism is the practice of honouring a totem or a sacred object. (257)

transformation changes the old meanings and understandings of the problem and creates new and innovative ones. (281)

transitional poverty is a temporary state of poverty that occurs when someone loses a job for a short time. (126)

triad is a group consisting of three people. (110)

triangulation is the process of using multiple approaches to study a phenomenon. (44)

Uniform Crime Reporting Survey measures the incidence of crime using police statistics of reported crimes gathered from police reports and paperwork. (216)

unskilled workers are the lowest class, consisting of people who frequently perform manual labour jobs that are often unpleasant and sometimes dangerous. (149)

upper class is a social class that is very small in number and holds significant wealth; also called **elite class**. (128)

upper middle class is a social class that consists of high-income members of society who are well educated but do not belong to the elite membership of the super wealthy. (128)

urban legends are rumours that are presented as true stories that act as cautionary tales. (275)

urban underclass is a social class living in disadvantaged neighbourhoods that are characterized by four components: poverty, family disruption, male unemployment, and lack of individuals in high-status occupations. (130)

utilitarian organization is an organization in which people receive wages in exchange for work. (114)

validity assures that you're actually measuring the thing you set out to measure in the first place. (35)

value clusters are two or more values that support each other. (53)

value conflict occurs when two or more values are at odds. (53)

value pairs help us define values, usually in terms of opposites. (53)

values are a part of a society's nonmaterial culture that represent cultural standards by which we determine what is good, bad, right, or wrong. (53)

vertical mobility refers to moving from one social status to another. (131)

visible minority is a person, other than an aboriginal, who is non-Caucasian in race or non-white in colour. (162)

voluntary association is the act of joining an organization that offers no pay and that expands social networks through interaction. (114)

voluntary immigration is the willing movement of people from one society to another. (164)

wealth is all of your material possessions, including income. (124)

working class is a social class generally made up of people with high school diplomas and lower levels of education. (129)

WUNC refers to the members of a movement who want to show the public the worthiness, unity, numbers, and commitment of their movement. (276)

xenocentrism is perceiving other groups or societies as superior to your own. (56)

xenophobia refers to fear and hostility toward people who are from other countries or cultures. (56)

young old is a cohort that consists of people between the ages of 65 and 75. (203)

ENDNOTES

CHAPTER 1

1. Dennis Raphael, *Poverty and Policy in Canada: Implications for Health and Quality of Life* (Toronto: Canadian Scholars' Press Inc., 2007).

2. C. Wright Mills, *The Sociological Imagination* (New York: Oxford, 1959).

3. Ibid.

4. Ibid.

5. Émile Durkheim, *Suicide*, George Simpson (ed.), translated by John A. Spaulding and George Simpson (New York: The Free Press, 1897/1966).

6. Ibid.

7. Ibid.

8. Durkheim, *Suicide*; Robert Travis, "Halbwachs and Durkheim: A Test of Two Theories of Suicide," *British Journal of Sociology*, 1990. 41: 225–243.

9. Jean Stockard and Robert M. O'Brien, "Cohort Effects on Suicide Rates: International Variations," American Sociological Association, *American Sociological Review*, 2002. 67(6): 854–872.

10. Stéphanie Langlois and Peter Morrison, "Suicide Deaths and Suicide Attempts," *Health Reports*, 2002. 13: 9–22. http://www.statcan.gc.ca/studies-etudes/82-003/archive/2002/6060-eng.pdf, Accessed August 28, 2008.

11. Raphael, *Poverty and Policy in Canada*.

12. Daphne Bramham, "Charges Laid Against B.C. Polygamist Leaders," *Vancouver Sun*, January 9, 2009, http://www.canada.com/life/Charges+laid+against+polygamist+leaders/1151592/story.html.

13. Kenneth Thompson, *Auguste Comte: The Foundation of Sociology* (New York: Halsted Press, 1975).

14. Jonathan Turner, Leonard Beeghily, and Charles H. Powers, *The Emergence of Sociological Theory* (Albany, NY: Wadsworth Publishing Company, 1998).

15. Émile Durkheim, *The Division of Labor in Society*, with introduction by Lewis A. Coser, translated by W.D. Halls (New York: Free Press, 1893/1997).

16. Ibid.

17. Ibid.

18. Talcott Parsons, *The Social System* (Glencoe, IL: The Free Press, 1951).

19. Ibid.

20. Robert K. Merton, *Social Theory and Social Structure* (Glencoe, IL: Free Press, 1957).

21. Ibid.

22. "Conrad Black: Tracking the Media Tycoon's Career and Conviction," *CBC News*, http://www.cbc.ca/canada/story/2010/06/25/f-conrad-black-timeline.html. August 27, 2010.

23. Karl Marx, *Selected Writings in Sociology & Social Philosophy*, T. B. Bottomore and Maximilien Rubel (eds.), translated by T. B. Bottomore (New York: McGraw-Hill, 1964); Karl Marx, "Economic and Philosophic Manuscripts of 1844," pp. 37–42 in *Readings in Social Theory: The Classical Tradition to Post-Modernism*, 4th ed. James Farganis (ed.) (New York: McGraw-Hill, 1844/2004); Karl Marx, *Capital: A Critique of Political Economy, Vol. 1* (New York: International Publishers, 1867/1967); Karl Marx and Friedrich Engels, "Manifesto of this Communist Party" pp. 26–36 in *Readings in Social Theory: The Classical Tradition to Post-Modernism*, 4th ed. James Farganis (ed.) (New York: McGraw-Hill, 1845/2004); Karl Marx and Friedrich Engels, "The German Ideology," pp. 43–46 in *Readings in Social Theory: The Classical Tradition to Post-Modernism*, 4th ed. James Farganis (ed.) (New York: McGraw-Hill, 1974/2004).

24. "W.E.B. Du Bois," NAACP, http://www.naacp.org/about/history/dubois/, Accessed October 21, 2008.

25. W.E.B. Du Bois (William Edward Burghardt), "The Philadelphia Negro: A Social Study," pp. 167–170 in *Readings in Social Theory: The Classical Tradition to Post-Modernism*, 4th ed. James Farganis (ed.) (New York: McGraw-Hill, 1899/2004).

26. Tukufu Zuberi, "Being Here and Being There: Fieldwork Encounters and Ethnographic Discoveries: W.E.B. Du Bois's Sociology: *The Philadelphia Negro* and Social Science," *The Annals of the American Academy of Political and Social Science*, 2004. 595: 146–156.

27. Joseph P. DeMarco, *The Social Thought of W.E.B. Du Bois* (Lanham, MD: University Press of American Inc., 1983).

28. Ralf Dahrendorf, *Class and Class Conflict in Industrial Society* (London: Lowe & Brydone (Printers) Ltd., 1959).

29. John Bellamy Foster, "The End of Rational Capitalism," *Monthly Review*, March 2005, http://findarticles.com/p/articles/mi_m1132/is_10_56/ai_n16126168/ pg_1?tag5artBody;col1, Accessed September 11, 2008.

30. George H. Mead, *Mind, Self, and Society: From the Standpoint of a Social Behaviorist* (Chicago: University of Chicago Press, 1934/1962).

31. Herbert Blumer, "Society as Symbolic Interaction," in Arnold M. Rose, *Human Behavior and Social Process: An Interactionist Approach* (Boston: Houghton-Mifflin, Reprinted in 1969).

32. Suzanne Speak and Graham Tipple, "Perceptions, Persecution, and Pity: The Limitations of Interventions for Homelessness," *International Journal of Urban and Regional Research*, 2006. 30(1): 172–188.

33. Erving Goffman, *The Presentation of Self in Everyday Life* (Edinburgh: University of Edinburgh, Social Sciences Research Centre, 1958).

34. Catalyst, *Women CEOs and Heads of the Financial Post 500*. http://www.catalyst.org/publication/271/women-ceos-and-heads-of-the-financial-post-500, Accessed September 2, 2010.

35. Susan Hoecker-Drysdale, *Harriet Martineau: First Woman Sociologist* (New York: St. Martin's Press, 1992).

36. Ibid.

37. Allen F. Davis, *American Heroine: The Life and Legend of Jane Addams* (New York: Oxford University Press, 1973).

38. Mary Jo Deegan, *Jane Addams and the Men of the Chicago School, 1892–1918* (New Brunswick, NJ: Transaction Books, 1988).

39. Dorothy Smith, *The Conceptual Practices of Power: A Feminist Sociology of Knowledge* (Toronto: University of Toronto Press, 1990).

40. Ibid.

41. Jonathan Turner, Leonard Beeghily, and Charles H. Powers, *The Emergence of Sociological Theory* (Albany, NY: Wadsworth Publishing Company, 1998).

CHAPTER 2

1. From Eileen Barker, "The Scientific Study of Religion? You Must Be Joking!" pp. 9–10, in *Cults and New Religious Movements: A Reader*, Lorne L. Dawson (ed.) (Oxford: Blackwell, 2003).

2. Ibid., p. 7.

3. "Cult Killer Denied Parole," *CBC News*, July 11, 2002, http://www.cbc.ca/canada/new-brunswick/story/2002/07/11/sv_parol071102.html, Accessed September 27, 2010; "Quebec Cult Leader Theriault Denied Parole," *CTV News*, July 11, 2002, http://www.ctv.ca/CTVNews/CTVNewsAt11/20020711/theriault_cult_parole_020711/, Accessed September 27, 2010.

4. Lorne L. Dawson, "The Study of New Religious Movements," *Cults and New Religious Movements*, p. 5.

5. Max Weber, "Class, Status, Party," in *Readings in Social Theory: The Classical Tradition to Post-Modernism*, 4th ed. James Farganis (ed.) (New York: McGraw-Hill, 1978/2004).

6. Statistics Canada and Council of Ministers of Education, Canada. 2007. *Education Indicators in Canada: Report of the Pan-Canadian Education Indicators Program*. Catalogue no. 81-582-XIE. Ottawa. Updated June 16, 2008.

7. Earl Babbie, *The Practice of Social Research*, 8th ed. (Belmont, CA: Wadsworth Publishing Company, 1998).

8. Steven Stack and Jim Gundlach, "The Effect of Country Music on Suicide," *Social Forces* 1992. 72: 211–218.

9. Jeffrey B. Snipes and Edward R. Maguire, "Reassessing the Link Between Country Music and Suicide," *Social Forces* 1994. 72: 1239–1243.

10. Snipes and Maguire, "Reassessing the Link"; Jeffrey B. Snipes and Edward R. Maguire, "Country Music, Suicide, and Spuriousness," *Social Forces* 1995. 74: 327–330; Stack and Gundlach, "The Effect of Country Music on Suicide"; Steven Stack and Jim Gundlach, "Country Music and Suicide, A Reply to Maguire and Snipes," *Social Forces* 1994. 72: 1245–1248; Steven Stack and Jim Gundlach, "Country Music, Suicide—Individual, Indirect, and Interaction Effects: A Reply to Snipes and Maguire," *Social Forces* 1995. 74: 331–336.

11. United Nations Office on Drugs and Crime, graph on "Seizures of Cannabis Herb in kg and %—by Region—in 2008," on p. 1 of "Global and Regional Seizure Totals," part of the *World Drug Report 2010* package at http://www.unodc.org/en/data-and-analysis/WDR-2010.html, Accessed September 24, 2010.

12. *World Drug Report 2010*, main document, pp. 8–9, http://www.unodc.org/unodc/en/data-and-analysis/WDR-2010.html, Accessed September 24, 2010.

13. Drug Policy Alliance, "Drug Policy Around the World," http://www.drug-policy.org/global/drugpolicyby/westerneurop/thenetherlan/, Accessed May 21, 2008.

14. Ibid.

15. "Should He Be Extradited? Arrest of 'Prince of Pot' Seeds a Political Uproar: Marijuana Party Leader Wanted by U.S. Authorities," by Tracey Tyler, from *The Toronto Star,* August 8, 2005, reproduced at http://osgoode.yorku.ca/media2.nsf/releases/732A9DD2CE3A28DC8525705700567AD8, Accessed September 27, 2010.

16. "Pot Activist Marc Emery Gets 5 Years in U.S. Jail," by CTV.ca News Staff, Sept. 10, 2010, http://www.ctv.ca/CTVNews/TopStories/20100910/marc-emery-sentenced-100910/, Accessed Sept. 27, 2010.

17. "An Open Letter to Rob Nicholson, Canada's Minister of Justice," by Karen Selick, from longer version of article that ran in *National Post* on Jan. 2, 2008; http://www.karenselick.com/NP080102.html, Accessed September 27, 2010.

18. "WeBeHigh.com: A Traveler's Guide to Getting High," http://www.webehigh.com/city/detail.php?CITYID=2024, Accessed September 27, 2010.

19. Chris Clarke, "Canada Bans Pot But Taxes Seeds," Jan. 28, 2005. Capital News Online, http://carleton.ca/Capital_News/28012005/n6.shtml, Accessed September 24, 2010.

20. Statistics Canada, "Police-Reported Crime for Selected Offences, Canada," table, *The Daily,* July 20, 2010, http://www.statcan.gc.ca/daily-quotidien/100720/t100720a1-eng.htm, Accessed September 12, 2010.

21. Statistics Canada, "Canada's Population by Age and Sex" (figures as of July 1, 2008), *The Daily,* Jan. 15, 2009, http://www.statcan.gc.ca/daily-quotidien/090115/dq090115c-eng.htm Accessed September 12, 2010.

22. Stanley Milgram, *Obedience to Authority: An Experimental View* (New York: Harper & Row, 1974).

23. Fritz J. Roethlisberger and William J. Dickson, *Management and the Worker* (Cambridge, MA: Harvard University Press, 1939).

24. *Covert Observation in Practice: Lessons from the Evaluation of the Prohibition of Smoking in Public Places in Scotland,* Petticrew et al., 2007, licensee BioMed Central Ltd., http://www.biomedcentral.com/1471-2458/7/204, Accessed September 27, 2010.

25. Anthony R. Ward, "Isabelle," *Feral Children,* http://www.feralchildren.com/en/showchild.php?ch5isabelle, Accessed August 26, 2008.

26. Robert Yin, *Applications of Case Study Research,* 2nd ed. (Thousand Oaks, CA: Sage Publishing, 2003).

27. Morris Freilich, "Scientific Possibilities in Iroquoian Studies: An Example of Mohawks Past and Present," *Anthropologica,* New Series, Vol. 5, No. 2 (1963). Published by Canadian Anthropology Society, pp. 180–181. http://www.jstor.org/stable/25604582, Accessed September 14, 2010.

28. *Social Research Methods: Qualitative and Quantitative Approaches,* by H. Russell Bernard (Thousand Oaks, CA; London; New Delhi: Sage Publications, 2000), p. 357. http://books.google.ca/books, Accessed September 10, 2010.

29. Morris Freilich, "Scientific Possibilities in Iroquoian Studies," pp. 182–183.

30. Joint United Nations Programme on HIV/AIDS (UNAIDS) and World Health Organization (WHO) 2009, http://data.unaids.org/pub/Report/2009/JC1700_Epi_Update_2009_en.pdf, Accessed Oct. 3, 2010.

31. *Tri-Council Policy Statement [TCPS]: Ethical Conduct for Research Involving Humans,* Draft 2nd ed., December 2009, a joint policy of the Canadian Institutes of Health Research, the Natural Sciences and Engineering Research Council of Canada, and the Social Sciences and Humanities Research Council of Canada. http://pre.ethics.gc.ca/pdf/eng/Revised%20Draft%202nd%20Ed%20PDFs/Revised%20Draft%202nd%20Edition%20TCPS_EN.pdf, Accessed September 14, 2010.

32. Ibid.; points that follow are abbreviated from pp. 4–7.

33. Abbreviated from "Statement of Professional Ethics," Canadian Sociological Association, approved June 1994, revised August 2010, pp. 4–9. http://www.csa-scs.ca/code-of-ethics, Accessed September 14, 2010.

34. *TCPS,* p. 1.

35. Norman K. Denzin, *The Research Act in Sociology* (Chicago: Aldine Publishing Company, 1970).

36. "Statement of Professional Ethics," p. 3.

37. Factcheck.org, "Misstatement of the Union: The President Burnishes the State of the Union through Selective Facts and Strategic Omissions," http://factcheck.org/article376.html#, Accessed August 26, 2008.

CHAPTER 3

1. Thomas Homer-Dixon, "A Canadian Is..." in Irvin Studin (ed.), *What Is a Canadian? Forty-Three Thought-Provoking Responses* (Toronto: McClelland & Stewart Ltd., 2006).

2. The World Factbook, "Rank Order—Electricity—Consumption," Central Intelligence Agency, https://www.cia.gov/library/publications/the-worldfactbook/rankorder/2042rank.html, Accessed March 30, 2006; The World Factbook, "Rank Order—Oil—Consumption," Central Intelligence Agency, https://www.cia.gov/library/publications/the-world-fact-book/rankorder/2174rank.html, Accessed March 30, 2006; The World Factbook, "Rank Order—Population," Central Intelligence Agency, https://www.cia.gov/library/publications/the-world-factbook/rankorder/2174rank.html, Accessed March 30, 2006.

3. "Crucifix Has Deep Constitutional Roots in Quebec," *Montreal Gazette,* May 26, 2008.

4. Jan Kavan, "International Mother Language Day: Address to the Fifty-seventh Session of the United Nations General Assembly," Office of the President of the General Assembly, http://www.un.org/ga/president/57/pages/speeches/statement 210203-MotherTongue.htm, Accessed September 18, 2008.

5. Noam Chomsky, *Reflections on Language* (New York: Pantheon Books, 1975).

6. Marie Coppola and Elissa L. Newport, "Grammatical Subjects in Home Sign: Abstract Linguistic Structure in Adult Primary Gesture Systems without Linguistic Input," *Proceedings of the National Academy of Sciences of the United States,* 2005. 103(52): 19249–19253.

7. Benjamin L. Whorf, *Language, Thought, and Reality* (New York: Wiley, 1956).

8. Richard Monastersky, "Speak Before You Think," *Chronicle of Higher Education,* 00095982, 2002. 48(29): A17–A19.

9. Peter Gordon, "Numerical Cognition without Words: Evidence from Amazonia," *Science,* 2004. 306(5695): 496–499.

10. Spicer Commission, "1991 Citizen's Forum on Canadian Unity," http://www.uni.ca/initiatives/spicer.html, Accessed September 3, 2010.

11. Peijia Zha, Jeffrey J. Walczyk, Diana A. Griffith-Ross, Jerome J. Tobacyk, Daniel F. Walczyk, "The Impact of Culture and Individualism-Collectivism on the Creative Potential and Achievement of American and Chinese Adults," *Creativity Research Journal,* 2006. 18(3): 355–366.

12. B. Quiroz, P. M. Greenfield, and M. Altchech, "Bridging Cultures with a Parent-Teacher Conference," *Educational Leadership,* 1999. 56 (7): 68–70.

13. Chuansheng Chen, Shin-ying Lee, and Harold W. Stevenson, "Response Style and Cross-cultural Comparisons of Rating Scales Among East Asian and North American Students," *Psychological Science,* 1995. 6(3): 170–175.

14. Ibid.

15. William Sumner, *Folkways and Mores* (New York: Schocken Books, 1911/1979).

16. Bronislaw Malinowski, *Magic, Science, and Religion and Other Essays* (Garden City, NY: Doubleday, 1954).

17. Elizabeth Cashdan, "Ethnocentrism and Xenophobia: A Cross-cultural Study," *Current Anthropology,* 2001. 42(5): 760–765.

18. Robert B. Edgerton, *Sick Societies: Challenging the Myth of Primitive Harmony* (New York: Free Press, 1992).

19. Daniel M. Kammen, "Cookstoves for the Developing World," *Scientific American,* 1995. 273(1): 72–76.

20. Elections Canada: http://www.elections.ca/content.aspx?section=ele&dir=turn&document=index&lang=e.

21. Ibid.

22. Marshall McLuhan, *The Gutenberg Galaxy: The Making of Typographic Man* (Toronto: University of Toronto Press, 1962).

23. Stanley Milgram, "The Small-World Problem," *Psychology Today,* 1967. 1: 61–67.

24. Peter Sheridan Dodds, Roby Muhamad, and Duncan J. Watts, "An Experimental Study of Search in Global Social Networks," *Science,* 2003. 301(5634): 827–829.

25. Marshall Fishwick, *Probing Popular Culture: On and Off the Internet* (Binghamton, NY: The Haworth Press, Inc, 2004).

26. Andrew Murphie and John Potts, *Culture and Technology* (New York: Palgrave McMillian. 2003).

27. Seymour Martin Lipset, *Continental Divide: The Values and Institutions of the United States and Canada* (New York: Routledge, Chapman and Hall, Inc., 1990).

28. Canadian Radio-television and Telecommunications Commission, "About the CRTC," http://www.crtc.gc.ca/eng/backgrnd/brochures/b29903.htm, Accessed October 5, 2010.

29. George Ritzer, *The McDonaldization of Society,* Revised New Century Edition (Thousand Oaks, CA: Pine Forge Press, 2004).

30. Josh Fineman and David Scanlan, "Tim Hortons Raises C$783 Million in Initial Offering," http://www.bloomberg.com/apps/news?pid=newsarchive&sid=aVbau_WUTixk&refer=news_index, Accessed September 17, 2010.

31. Nancy Théberge, *Higher Goals: Women's Ice Hockey and the Politics of Gender* (Albany, NY: State University of New York Press, 2000).

32. Philip Resnick, "Quebecers Signal a Return to the Two Solitudes," *The Vancouver Sun,* May 13, 2010; and Benoit Aubin, "Bill 101: A Gift We Never Expected," *Maclean's,* 2007. 120(31/32), 18–20.

CHAPTER 4

1. From Francis Adu-Febiri and Everett Ofori, *Succeeding from the Margins of Canadian Society: A Strategic Resource for New Immigrants, Refugees and International Students* (British Columbia: CCB Publishing, 2009), pp. xi–xii.

2. Charles H. Cooley, *Human Nature and Social Order,* Revised ed. (New York: Scribner and Sons, 1922).

3. Linda L. Lindsay, Stephen Beach, and Bruce Ravelli, *Core Concepts in Sociology,* 2nd Canadian in-class ed. (Toronto: Pearson Education Canada, 2009).

4. Yanjie Bian, "Chinese Social Stratification and Social Mobility." *Annual Review of Sociology,* 2002. 28: 91–116.

5. Andrew Chung, "Cop Helps Halle Berry Jump Line at Airport," *Toronto Star,* Jan. 9, 2010, http://www.thestar.com/news/canada/article/748479—cop-helps-halle-berry-jump-line-at-airport, Accessed Sept. 16, 2010; CTV.ca News Staff, "Montreal Police Admit Berry Skipped Airport Line," Jan. 8, 2010, http://www.ctv.ca/CTVNews/TopStories/20100108/ent_hallee_airport_100108/, Accessed Sept. 16, 2010.

6. Julian A. Oldmeadow, Michael J. Platow, Margaret Foddy, and Donna Anderson, "Self-categorization, Status, and Social Influence," *Social Psychology Quarterly,* 2003. 66(2): 138–152.

7. Ibid.

8. Ibid.

9. Robert K. Merton, "The Role-Set: Problems in Sociological Theory," *British Journal of Sociology,* 1957. 8: 106–120; Robert K. Merton, *Social Theory and Social Structure,* Revised and Enlarged ed. (New York: Free Press, 1968).

10. Iran Chamber Society, "The Structure of Power in Iran," http://www.iran-chamber.com/government/articles/structure_of_power.php, Accessed Oct. 4, 2010.

11. Erving Goffman, *Stigma: Notes on the Management of Spoiled Identity* (Englewood Cliffs, NJ: Prentice-Hall, 1963).

12. Gerhard Lenski, Jean Lenski, and Patrick Nolan, *Human Societies* (New York: McGraw-Hill, 1990).

13. Douglas S. Massey, "A Brief History of Human Society: The Origin and Role of Emotion in Social Life: 2001 Presidential Address," *American Sociological Review,* 2002. 67(1): 1–29.

14. Gerhard E. Lenski, *Power and Privilege: A Theory of Social Stratification* (Chapel Hill, NC: University of North Carolina Press, 1966).

15. Jared Diamond, *Collapse: How Societies Choose to Fail or Succeed* (New York: Viking Penguin Press, 2005).

16. Massey, "A Brief History of Human Society."

17. Lenski, Lenski, and Nolan, *Human Societies.*

18. Ibid.

19. Ibid.

20. Massey, "A Brief History of Human Society."

21. Lenski, Lenski, and Nolan, *Human Societies.*

22. Ibid.

23. Massey, "A Brief History of Human Society."

24. Daniel Bell, *The Coming of Post-Industrial Society: A Venture in Social Forecasting* (New York: Basic Books, 1973, 1999).

25. Stephanie Coontz, *Marriage, A History: How Love Conquered Marriage* (New York: Penguin Publishing, 2005).

26. Information in this paragraph is from Library and Archives Canada, http://www.collectionscanada.gc.ca/sos/002028-5100-e.html, and The Weather Doctor, http://www.islandnet.com/~see/weather/almanac/arc2008/alm08jan.htm, both Accessed Sept. 19, 2010.

27. Ferdinand Tönnies, *Community and Society (Gemeinschaft und Gesellschaft).* Translated and edited by Charles P. Loomis (East Lansing, MI: Michigan State University Press, 1887).

28. Steven Brint, "*Gemeinschaft* Revisited: A Critique and Reconstruction of the Community Concept," *Sociological Theory,* 2001. 19(1): 1–23.

29. James FitzGerald, *Old Boys: The Powerful Legacy of Upper Canada College* (Toronto: Macfarlane, Walter & Ross, 1994). http://jamesfitzgerald.info/Excerpts.html, Accessed September 29, 2010.

30. Ibid.

31. Ibid.

32. Edward T. Hall, *The Hidden Dimension* (New York: Anchor Books, 1966, 1982). Hall's study was conducted in the United States. However, Canada and the U.S. are both "low-context" cultures where such features as personal space are alike.

33. Ibid.

34. Erving Goffman, *The Presentation of Self in Everyday Life* (Edinburgh: University of Edinburgh, Social Sciences Research Centre, 1958).

35. Sandy J. Wayne and Robert C. Liden, "Effects of Impression Management on Performance Ratings: A Longitudinal Study," *The Academy of Management Journal,* 1995. 38(1): 232–260.

36. "Nude Photos of Judge Contained in Complaint," *CBC News,* Aug. 31, 2010, http://www.cbc.ca/canada/manitoba/story/2010/08/31/judge-manitoba-douglas.html and *Winnipeg Free Press,* "Judge Embroiled in Sex Scandal Removes Self from Bench," Aug. 31, 2019, both accessed Oct. 4, 2010.

37. Wayne and Liden, "Effects of Impression Management."

38. W. I. Thomas and Dorothy Swaine Thomas, *The Child in America: Behavior Problems and Programs* (New York: Alfred A. Knopf, 1928).

39. Émile Durkheim, *Rules of Sociological Method,* George E. G. Catlin, (ed.), translated by Sarah A. Solovay & John H. Mueller (New York: The Free Press of Glenco, 1895).

40. Jared Diamond, *Collapse: How Societies Choose to Fail or Succeed* (New York: Viking Penguin Press, 2005).

41. Jared Diamond, *Guns, Germs, and Steel: The Fates of Human Societies* (New York: W.W. Norton and Company, 1999).

42. Durkheim, *Rules of Sociological Method*; D. F. Aberle, A. K. Cohen, A. K. Davis, M. J. Levy Jr., and F. X. Sutton, "The Functional Prerequisites of a Society," *Ethics,* 1950. 60(2): 100–111; Raymond W. Mack and Calvin P. Bradford, *Transforming America: Patterns of Social Change,* 2nd ed. (New York: Random House, 1979); Diamond, *Guns, Germs, and Steel*; Diamond, *Collapse.*

43. Bruce Ravelli, Michelle Webber, and John Patterson, *Sociology for Everyone* (Toronto: Pearson Canada, 2011), p. 281.

44. "A New Future" (broadcast March 13, 1955, last updated Sept. 29, 2010), CBC Digital Archives, http://archives.cbc.ca/version_print.asp?page=1&IDLan=1&IDClip=4003&IDDossier=0&IDCat=355&IDCatPa=262, Accessed September 30, 2010.

45. Ibid.

46. J.R. Miller, "Residential Schools" entry in *The Canadian Encyclopedia,* http://www.thecanadianencyclopedia.com, Accessed Sept. 30, 2010.

47. "A New Future."

48. Miller, "Residential Schools."

49. Ibid.

50. Indian Residential School Survivors Society, http://www.irsss.ca/history.html, Accessed September 30, 2010.

51. Ibid.

52. Miller, "Residential Schools."

53. Indian and Northern Affairs Canada, "Backgrounder, Indian Residential Schools Settlement Agreement," 2008. http://www.ainc-inac.gc.ca/ai/rqpi/nwz/2008/20080425b_is-eng.asp, Accessed Sept. 30, 2010.

54. Colin G. Calloway, *First Peoples: A Documentary Survey of American Indian History,* 2nd ed. (Boston: Bedford/St. Martin's, 2004).

55. Statistics Canada, "Average Hourly Wages of Employees by Selected Characteristics and Profession, Unadjusted Data, by Province (monthly)." http://www40.statcan.ca/l01/cst01/labr69a-eng.htm, Accessed Oct. 4, 2010.

56. HRSDC, 2006. "Gender Composition and Wages: Why Is Canada Different from the United States?" http://www.hrsdc.gc.ca/eng/cs/sp/hrsd/prc/publications/research/2000-000181/page04.shtml, Accessed September 30, 2010.

57. Marie Drolet, "New Evidence on Gender Pay Differentials: Does Measurement Matter?" *Canadian Public Policy,* March 2002. 28(1), 1–16. http://www.jstor.org/stable/3552156, Accessed Oct. 4, 2010.

58. Adu-Febiri and Ofori, *Succeeding from the Margins of Canadian Society,* p. 35.

59. "Police Target Black Drivers: Star Analysis of Traffic Data Suggests Racial Profiling," *Toronto Star,* Oct. 20, 2002. http://www.thestar.com/specialsections/raceandcrime/article/761200—police-target-black-drivers, Accessed Oct. 2, 2010.

60. Cleveland Gordon, Barry Forer, Douglas Hyatt, Christa Japel, and Michael Krashinsky. *New Evidence about Child Care in Canada: Use Patterns, Affordability and Quality, IRPP Choices,* 2008. 14(12), p. 8.

61. Lynn Robson, "A Snap Shot of Child Care," *The National, CBC News,* Feb. 9, 2005. http://www.cbc.ca/news/background/daycare/canada_snapshot.html, Accessed September 19, 2010.

62. *New Evidence about Child Care in Canada,* p. 7.

63. Ibid.

64. *New Evidence about Child Care in Canada,* p. 12.

65. "Budget 2010 Proposes Changes to Universal Child Care Benefit," Government of Canada, Accessed September 19, 2010 at http://www.universalchildcare.ca/eng/messages/2010/100603.shtml.

66. "Daycare: The Debate over Space," *CBC News*. Feb. 11, 2009. Accessed September 19, 2010 at http://www.cbc.ca/consumer/story/2009/02/06/f-daycare.html.

CHAPTER 5

1. Gwynne Dyer, *War: The New Edition* (Toronto: Vintage Canada, 2005), pp. 38–44.

2. Talcott Parsons, *The Social System* (New York: Free Press, 1951).

3. Talcott Parsons and Robert Bales, *Socialization and the Interaction Process* (New York: Free Press, 1955).

4. Orville G. Brim, Jr., "Socialization through the Life Cycle," in Orville Brim and Stanton Wheeler (eds.), *Socialization after Childhood: Two Essays* (New York: Wiley, 1966).

5. Theodore E. Long and Jeffrey K. Hadden, "Reconception of Socialization," *Sociological Theory*, 1985. 3(1): 39–49.

6. Brim, "Socialization through the Life Cycle."

7. Richard Dawkins, *The Selfish Gene* (Oxford: Oxford University Press, 1989).

8. W. L. Reese, *Dictionary of Philosophy and Religion: Eastern and Western Thought* (Atlantic Highlands, NJ: Humanities Press Inc., 1987).

9. Paul R. Ehrlich, *Human Natures: Genes, Cultures, and the Human Prospect* (Washington, D.C.: Island Press, 2000), p. 6, at http://books.google.com/books?id5mHFsScY8ewMC&dq5Human1Natures1Paul1Ehrlich&pg5PP1&ots5XW4w7TDMLU&sig5MjKy9QADe0TPCKe0fZZ8h_ahKLM&hl5en&sa5X&oi5book_result&resnum51&ct5result.

10. Harry F. Harlow and Margaret Harlow, "Social Deprivation in Monkeys," *Scientific American*, 1962. November: 137–146.

11. Susan Donaldson James, "Wild Child Speechless after Tortured Life," *ABC News*, May 7, 2008, at http://abcnews.go.com/Health/story?id54804490; "What Drove Father Who Built House of Horror?" *CNN News*, April 29, 2008, at http://www.cnn.com/2008/WORLD/europe/04/29/austria.cellar.profile/, Accessed November 12, 2008.

12. Public Broadcasting Service, "Secret of the Wild Child," *Nova*, aired March 4, 1997. http://www.pbs.org/wgbh/nova/transcripts/2112gchild.html, Accessed Oct. 3, 2010.

13. Russ Rymer, *Genie: An Abused Child's Flight from Silence* (New York: HarperCollins Publishers, 1993).

14. Ibid.

15. Ibid.

16. Louis De Maio, "Stages of Language Development," at http://www.mnstate.edu/pccp/stages%20of%20%20language%20development.pdf, Accessed June 5, 2008; "Isabelle," http://www.feralchildren.com/en/showchild.php?ch5isabelle, Accessed June 26, 2008.

17. Charles H. Cooley, *Human Nature and the Social Order* (New York: Schocken Books, 1902, 1964).

18. King-To Yeung and John L. Martin, "The Looking Glass Self: An Empirical Test and Elaboration," *Social Forces*, 2003. 81(3): 843–879.

19. Ibid.

20. George Herbert Mead, *Mind, Self, and Society*, Charles W. Morris (ed.) (Chicago: University of Chicago Press, 1934, 1962).

21. Ibid.

22. Ibid.

23. Erik Erikson, *Childhood and Society* (New York: Norton Press, 1963).

24. Public Broadcasting Service, "Secret of the Wild Child."

25. Jean Piaget and Barbel Inhelder, *The Psychology of the Child* (New York: Basic Books, 1969, 2000).

26. Ibid.

27. Ibid.

28. Ibid.

29. Ibid.

30. Lawrence Kohlberg, *The Psychology of Moral Development: The Nature and Validity of Moral Stages* (New York: Harper & Row, 1981).

31. Ibid.

32. Ibid.

33. Ibid.

34. "Jim Crow" entry, *Canadian Oxford Dictionary*, 2nd ed., Katherine Barber (ed.) (Toronto: Oxford University Press, 2004).

35. Charles Helwig and Urszula Jasiobedzka, "The Relation between Law and Morality: Children's Reasoning about Socially Beneficial and Unjust Laws," *Child Development*, 2001. 72: 1382–1394.

36. Anne Colby and William Damon, *Some Do Care: Contemporary Lives of Moral Commitment* (New York: Free Press, 1992).

37. Carol Gilligan, *In a Different Voice: Psychological Theory and Women's Development* (Cambridge, MA: Harvard University Press, 1982).

38. Ibid.

39. Elliott Turiel, "The Development of Morality," in W. Damon (ed.), *Handbook of Child Psychology*, 5th ed., vol. 3, 863–932 (New York: Wiley, 1998).

40. Eva A. Skoe and Alethia Gooden, "Ethics of Care and Real-Life Moral Dilemma Content in Male and Female Early Adolescents," *Journal of Early Adolescence*, 1993. 13(2): 154–167.

41. Eva A. Skoe and Rhett Diessner, "Ethics of Care, Justice, Identity and Gender: An Extension and Replication," *Merrill–Palmer Quarterly*, 1994. 40: 102–119; Eva A. Skoe and Anna L. von der Lippe, "Ego Development and the Ethics of Care and Justice: The Relations among Them Revisited," *Journal of Personality*, 2002. 70(4): 485–508.

42. Andrew J. Cherlin, *Public and Private Families: An Introduction*, 2nd ed. (Boston: McGraw–Hill College, 1999).

43. Diana Baumrind, "Current Patterns of Parental Authority," *Developmental Psychology Monographs*, 1971. 4(1, pt. 2):103; Diana Baumrind, "Parental Disciplinary Patterns and Social Competence in Children," *Youth and Society*, 1978. 9: 239–276; Diana Baumrind, "The Discipline Controversy Revisited," *Family Relations*, 1996. 5(4): 405–415.

44. The show was included in the 2010 program schedule at MTV.ca. Note that the Media Awareness Network carries a 1998 reference to MTV being the most watched network for girls aged 11 to 19 in Canada. (See "1998: Girls and TV [Canada]" section, using figures from Saatchi & Saatchi, SmartGirl Internette and Teenage Research Unlimited, cited in *KidScreen*, August 1998. http://www.media-awareness.ca/english/resources/research_documents/statistics/television/tv_viewing_habits.cfm, Accessed Oct. 3, 2010.)

45. Ibid.

46. Ruth K. Chao, "Beyond Parental Control and Authoritarian Parenting Style: Understanding Chinese Parenting through the Cultural Notion of Training," *Child Development*, 1994. 65(4): 1111–1119.

47. Ibid.

48. Min Zhou, *Chinatown: The Socioeconomic Potential of an Urban Enclave* (Philadelphia, PA: Temple University Press, 1992).

49. Min Zhou and Carl L. Bankston, III, "Social Capital and the Adaptation of the Second Generation: The Case of Vietnamese Youth in New Orleans," *The New Second Generation*, Alejandro Portes (ed.) (New York: Russell Sage Foundation, 1996), 197–220.

50. Erving Goffman, *Asylums: Essays on the Social Situation of Mental Patients and Other Inmates* (Chicago: Aldine, 1961).

51. Harold Garfinkel, "Conditions of Successful Degradation Ceremonies," *American Journal of Sociology*, 1956. 61(2): 420–424.

52. Howard S. Becker, "The Politics of Presentation: Goffman and Total Institutions," *Symbolic Interaction*, 2003. 26(4): 659–669.

53. Charles Tittle and Michael Welch, "Religiosity and Deviance: Toward a Contingency Theory of Constraining Effects," *Social Forces*, 1983. 61(3): 653–682.

54. Harold Grasmick, Karyl Kinsey, and Kent Smith, "Framing Justice: Taxpayer Evaluations of Personal Tax Burdens," *Law and Society Review*, 1991. 25: 845–873.

55. "Prisoners of Time," Education Commission of the States, April 1994, http://www.eric.ed.gov/ERICDocs/data/ericdocs2sql/content_storage_01/0000-019b/80/1b/b9/60.pdf, Accessed November 12, 2008.

56. Annette Hemmings, "The 'Hidden' Corridor Curriculum," *High School Journal*, 2000. 83(2): 1–10.

57. Philip Jackson, *Life in Classrooms* (New York: Holt, Rinehart, and Winston, 1968).

58. Melvin L Kohn, "Social Class and Parent-Child Relationships: An Interpretation," *American Journal of Sociology*, 1963. 571–580.

59. William J. Wilson, *The Truly Disadvantaged: The Inner City, The Underclass, and Public Policy* (Chicago: University of Chicago Press, 1987).

60. Jeanne Brooks–Gunn, Greg Duncan, Pamela Klebanove, and Naomi Sealand, "Do Neighborhoods Influence Child and Adolescent Development?" *American Journal of Sociology*, 1993. 99(2): 353–395.

61. Ibid.

62. Gary Solon, Marianne Page, and Greg J. Duncan, "Correlations Between Neighboring Children and Their Subsequent Educational Attainment," *Review of Economics and Statistics*, 2000. 82(3): 383–393.

63. John D. Carl, "Social Capital and Sport Participation," Ph.D. dissertation, Department of Sociology, University of Oklahoma, Norman, OK, 2002.

64. S. Laberge and M. Albert, "Conceptions of Masculinity and of Gender Transgressions in Sport among Adolescent Boys: Hegemony, Contestation, and Social Class Dynamic," *Men and Masculinities*, January 1999. 1(3), 243–267. Retrieved from Sage database.

65. Alvin Powell, "Former Canadian Leader Campbell Addresses Gender Bias: Discusses 'If She Knew Then What She Knows Now' with Harvard Women's Group," *Harvard University Gazette*, 2007. http://www.news.harvard.edu/gazette/2003/02.27/03-campbell.html, Accessed Oct. 5, 2010.

66. Ibid.

67. Kirstie Farrar, Dale Kunkel, Erica Biely, Keren Eyal, Rena Fandrich, and Edward Donnerstein, "Sexual Messages During Primetime Programming," *Sexuality & Culture*, 2003. 7(3): 7–38.

68. The Fundamental Freedoms Project interactive ("Impact" section), Accessed through http://charterofrights.ca/en/02_00_01 on Oct. 3, 2010.

69. David Hutton, "'Just Society' Has Evolved, Justin Trudeau Says," *The Vancouver Sun,* http://www.vancouversun.com/news/Just+society+evolved+Justin+Trudeau+says/3599384/story.html#ixzz11JedbBv7, Accessed Oct. 3, 2010.

70. The Fundamental Freedoms Project interactive ("History" section).

71. The Fundamental Freedoms Project interactive ("Impact" section).

72. Canadian Human Rights Commission, http://www.chrc-ccdp.ca/en/timePortals/milestones/113mile.asp, Accessed Oct. 3, 2010.

CHAPTER 6

1. Daphne Bramham, *The Secret Lives of Saints: Child Brides and Lost Boys in Canada's Polygamous Mormon Sect* (Toronto: Vintage Canada, 2009), pp. 9–17.

2. Information in this paragraph and the next is from Petti Fong, "'Bountiful' Sect Leaders Charged with Polygamy," *Toronto Star,* Jan. 8, 2009 (http://www.thestar.com/article/563546) and *CBC News,* "Polygamy Charges in Bountiful, B.C., Thrown Out," Sept. 23, 2009 (http://www.cbc.ca/canada/british-columbia/story/2009/09/23/bc-polygamy-charges-blackmore-oler-bountiful.html), both accessed Oct. 12, 2010.

3. Charles H. Cooley, *Human Nature and the Social Order* (New York: Schocken Books, 1902/1964).

4. Ibid.

5. Henry Tajfel, "Social Categorization, Social Identity, and Social Comparison," in *Differentiation between Social Groups: Studies in Social Psychology of Intergroup Relations,* Henry Tajfel (ed.) (London: Academic Press, 1978), 61–76; Robert K. Merton, *Social Theory and Social Structure* (New York: Free Press, 1968).

6. Merton, *Social Theory and Social Structure.*

7. Daan Scheeners, Russell Spears, Bertjan Doosje, and Antony S.R. Manstead, "Diversity in In-group Bias: Structural Factors, Situational Features, and Social Functions," *Journal of Personality and Social Psychology,* 2006. 90(6): 944–960.

8. B. Ann Bettencourt, Kelly Charlton, and Nancy Dorr, "Status Differences and In-Group Bias: A Meta-analytic Examination of the Effects of Status Stability, Status Legitimacy, and Group Permeability," *Psychological Bulletin,* 2001. 127(4): 520–542.

9. Henry Tajfel and John Turner, "The Social Identity Theory of Intergroup Behavior," in S. Worschel and W. G. Austin (eds.), *Psychology and Intergroup Relations* (Chicago: Nelson-Hall, 1986), pp. 7–24.

10. Courtney D. Von Hippel, "When People Would Rather Switch Than Fight: Out-group Favoritism Among Temporary Employees." *Group Processes and Intergroup Relations,* 2006. 9(4): 533–546.

11. Ibid.

12. Ibid.

13. Charles H. Cooley, *Human Nature and the Social Order.*

14. Ron Adams, "Hikikomori/Otaku Japan's Latest Out-Group," eclip5e.visualassault.org/assets/Hikikomori_Japans_Latest_Outcasts.pdf, Accessed June 11, 2008.

15. Ibid.

16. Ibid.

17. Ibid.

18. Georg Simmel, *The Sociology of Georg Simmel,* Kurt Wolfe (ed.) (New York: Free Press, 1902/1950).

19. Ibid.

20. Henry Hamburger, Melvin Guyer, and John Fox, "Group Size and Composition," *The Journal of Conflict Resolution,* 1975. 19(3): 503–531.

21. James Tucker and S. Thomas Friedman, "Population Density and Group Size," *American Journal of Sociology,* 1972. 77(4): 742–749.

22. Kurt Lewin, Ronald Lippit, and Ralph K. White, "Patterns of Aggressive Behavior in Experimentally Created Social Climates," *Journal of Social Psychology,* 1939. 10: 271–299.

23. Ibid.

24. Ibid.

25. Ibid.

26. Litsa Nicolaou-Smokovita, "Business Leaders, Work Environment, and Leadership Styles." *Current Sociology,* 2004. 52(3): 404–427.

27. Solomon Asch, *Social Psychology* (Englewood Cliffs, NJ: Prentice-Hall, 1952).

28. Irving L. Janis, *Victims of Groupthink: A Psychological Study of Foreign-Policy Decisions and Fiascoes* (Boston: Houghton Mifflin, 1972); Irving L. Janis, *Groupthink: Psychological Studies of Policy Decisions and Fiascoes* (Boston: Houghton Mifflin, 1983).

29. Janis, *Groupthink.*

30. Janis, *Victims of Groupthink.*

31. Ibid.

32. "Shock and Awe Campaign Launched in Iraq," *CNN.com,* March 22, 2003, http://www.cnn.com/2003/fyi/news/03/22/iraq.war/, Accessed November 12, 2008.

33. Dan Glasiter, "Bush Voices Regret for Macho Rhetoric in Run-up to Iraq War," *Guardian.co.uk,* June 11, 2008, http://www.guardian.co.uk/world/2008/jun/11/georgebush.usforeignpolicy.

34. George W. Bush, "Address to a Joint Session of Congress and the American People," September 20, 2001, http://www.whitehouse.gov/news/releases/2001/09/20010920-8.html, Accessed November 12, 2008.

35. Bob Woodward, *Plan of Attack* (London: Simon and Schuster, 2004).

36. Mike Celizic, "Network Anchors Differ on Iraq War Coverage," *msnbc.com,* May 28, 2008, http://www.msnbc.msn.com/id/24855902/, Accessed November 12, 2008.

37. "Colin Powell on Iraq, Race, and Hurricane Relief," *ABC News,* September 8, 2005, http://abcnews.go.com/2020/Politics/story?id51105979&page51, Accessed November 12, 2008.

38. James S. Coleman, "Social Capital in the Creation of Human Capital," *American Journal of Sociology,* 1988. 94(S): 95–120.

39. Coleman, "Social Capital in the Creation of Human Capital"; Pierre Bourdieu, "The Forms of Capital," *Handbook of Theory and Research for the Sociology of Education,* John G. Richardson (ed.) (New York: Greenwood, 1986), pp. 241–258.

40. Li Xue, L., *Social Capital and Employment Entry of Recent Immigrants to Canada: Evidence from the Longitudinal Survey of Immigrants to Canada (LSIC) Wave 1 and Wave 2.* 2007. Retrieved from http://ceris.metropolis.net/9thMetropolisConference/WorkshopPresentations/B1_Xue.pdf on Oct. 12, 2010.

41. Mark S. Granovetter, "The Strength of Weak Ties," *American Journal of Sociology,* 1973. 78(6): 1360–1380.

42. Robert D. Putnam, "Bowling Alone: America's Declining Social Capital," *Journal of Democracy,* 1995. 6(1): 65–78.

43. Jennifer Barber, Lisa D. Pearce, Indra Chaudhury, and Susan Gurung, "Voluntary Associations and Fertility Limitation," *Social Forces,* 2002. 80(4): 1369–1401.

44. Amitai Etzioni, *A Comparative Analysis of Complex Organizations: On Power, Involvement, and Their Correlates* (New York: Free Press, 1975).

45. Ibid.

46. Ibid.

47. Ibid.

48. Amitai Etzioni and Edward W. Lehman, *A Sociological Reader on Complex Organizations,* 3rd ed. (New York: Holt, Rinehart and Winston, 1980).

49. Max Weber, "Max Weber Bureaucracy," in *Readings in Social Theory: The Classical Tradition to Post-Modernism,* 4th ed., James Farganis (ed.) (New York: McGraw-Hill, 1978/2004), pp. 99–108; Max Weber, *Max Weber: Essays in Sociology.* Translated and edited by Hans H. Gerth and C. Wright Mills (New York: Oxford University Press, 1946).

50. Ibid.

51. George Ritzer, *The McDonaldization of Society,* Revised New Century Edition (Thousand Oaks, CA: Pine Forge Press, 2004).

52. John C. Maxwell, *Leadership 101: What Every Leader Needs to Know* (Nashville, TN: Thomas Nelson Publishers, 2002).

53. Ibid.

54. Martin O'Malley, CBC News Online, "One of Our Best and Brightest," http://www.canadahistory.com/sections/Politics/pm/pierretrudeau.htm, Accessed Oct. 13, 2010.

55. Ibid.; and "The October Crisis," at *Historica,* http://www.histori.ca/peace/page.do?pageID=342, Accessed Oct. 13, 2010.

56. "Pierre Elliott Trudeau: Philosopher and Prime Minister," CBC Digital Archives, http://archives.cbc.ca/politics/prime_ministers/topics/2192/, Accessed Oct. 13, 2010.

57. Critique of Hegel's *Philosophy of Right Karl Marx, 1843,* http://www.marxists.org/archive/marx/works/1843/critiquehpr/ch03.htm#027, Accessed August 28, 2008.

58. Richard D. Rosenberg and Eliezer Rosenstein, "Participation and Productivity: An Empirical Study," *Industrial and Labor Relations Review,* 1980, 33(3): 355–367; Henry Levin, "Worker Democracy and Worker Productivity," *Social Justice Research,* 2006. 19(1): 109–121.

59. Tove H. Hammer, Steven C. Curral, and Robert N. Stern, "Worker Representation on Boards of Directors: A Study of Competing Roles," *Industrial and Labor Relations Review*, 1991. 44(4): 661–680.

60. "Health Reports: Job Satisfaction, Stress and Depression," *The Daily*, Oct. 17, 2006, Statistics Canada, http://www.statcan.gc.ca/daily-quotidien/061017/dq061017a-eng.htm, Accessed Oct. 13, 2010. (Note that the study, released in 2006, was based on the 2002 Canadian Community Health Survey.)

61. "Most U.S. Workers Not Living the Dream," *msnbc.com*, Jan. 25, 2007, http://www.msnbc.msn.com/id/16795881/, Accessed Oct. 13, 2010. (Note that the survey was conducted in late 2006 by CareerBuilder.com, an online job site, and The Walt Disney Co.)

62. Randy Hodson, *Working with Dignity* (Cambridge: Cambridge University Press, 2000).

63. Joyce Rothschild-Whitt and J. Allen Whitt, *Cooperative Workplace: Potentials and Dilemmas of Organizational Democracy and Participation* (New York: Cambridge University Press, 1986).

64. Ibid.

65. Ibid.

66. Joyce Rothschild, "Utopian Visions: Engaged Sociologies for the 21st Century: Creating a Just and Democratic Workplace: More Engagement and Less Hierarchy," *Contemporary Sociology*, 2000. 29(1): 195–213.

67. K. L. Ferguson, *The Feminist Case Against Bureaucracy* (Philadelphia: Temple University Press, 1984).

68. Oprah Fansite, http://www.oprah-fansite.com/, Accessed August 29, 2008.

69. Robert D. Putnam, "Bowling Alone: America's Declining Social Capital," *Journal of Democracy*, 1995. 6(1): 65–78.

70. Abdolmohammad Kazemipur, *Social Capital and Diversity: Some Lessons from Canada* (Bern, Switzerland: Peter Lang AG, International Academic Publishers, 2009), p. 60. Accessed at Google Books on Oct. 13, 2010.

71. Daniel A. McFarland and Reuben J. Thomas, "Bowling Young: How Youth Voluntary Associations Influence Adult Political Participation," *American Sociological Review*, 2006. 71: 401–425.

72. Ibid.

73. Ibid.

CHAPTER 7

1. John Porter, *The Vertical Mosaic: An Analysis of Social Class and Power in Canada*, (Toronto: University of Toronto Press, 1965), p. xiii).

2. Philip Carl Salzman, "Is Inequality Universal?" *Current Anthropology*, 1999. 40: 31–61.

3. Statistics Canada, "Table 202-0405: Upper Income Limits and Income Shares of Total Income Quintiles, by Economic Family Type, 2008 Constant Dollars, Annual." CANSIM (database). http://estat.statcan.gc.ca/cgi-win/cnsmcgi.exe?Lang=E&EST-Fi=EStat/English/CII_1-eng.htm, Accessed September 20, 2010.

4. Statistics Canada, "Table 202-0701: Market, Total and After-Tax Income, by Economic Family Type and Income Quintiles, 2008 Constant Dollars, Annual." CANSIM (database), http://estat.statcan.gc.ca/cgi-win/cnsmcgi.exe?Lang=E&EST-Fi=EStat/English/CII_1-eng.htm, Accessed September 20, 2010.

5. Statistics Canada, "Income of Canadians," http://www.policyalternatives.ca/sites/default/files/uploads/publications/National_Office_Pubs/2008/Quarter_Century_of_Inequality.pdf, Accessed September 22, 2010.

6. Conference Board of Canada, "Income Inequality," http://www.conferenceboard.ca/hcp/details/society/income-inequality.aspx.

7. Statistics Canada, "The Wealth of Canadians: An Overview of the Results of the Income Statistics Division," http://dsp-psd.pwgsc.gc.ca/Collection/Statcan/13F0026M/13F0026MIE2006001.pdf. Accessed September 23, 2010.

8. Human Resources and Skills Development Canada, "Indicators of Well-Being in Canada," http://www4.hrsdc.gc.ca/h.4m.2@-eng.jsp, Accessed September 24, 2010.

9. Human Resources and Skills Development Canada, "Low Income in Canada: 2000–2006 Using the Market Basket Measure," http://www.hrsdc.gc.ca/eng/publications_resources/research/categories/inclusion/2008/sp-864-10-2008/page00.shtml, Accessed September 23, 2010; and Statistics Canada, "Low Income Lines: 2008–2009," http://www.statcan.gc.ca/pub/75f0002m/75f0002m2010005-eng.htm, Accessed September 22, 2010.

10. C. Wright Mills, *The Power Elite* (New York: Oxford University Press, 1956).

11. Wallace Clement, "Elites," *The Canadian Encyclopedia*, http://www.thecanadianencyclopedia.com/index.cfm?PgNm=TCE&Params=A1ARTA0002573, Accessed September 20, 2010.

12. Michael D. Martinez, "Voters and nonvoters in Canadian federal elections," http://www.clas.ufl.edu/users/martinez/cpsa08/martinez_cpsa08.pdf, Accessed September 22, 2010.

13. Monica Boyd, "A Socioeconomic Scale for Canada: Measuring Occupational Status from the Census," *Canadian Review of Sociology*, 45: 51–91.

14. John Goyder, "The Dynamics of Occupational Prestige: 1975–2000." *Canadian Review of Sociology & Anthropology*, 2005. 42: 1–23.

15. Lee Rainwater and William Yancey, *The Moynihan Report and the Politics of Controversy* (Cambridge, MA: The MIT Press, 1968).

16. Feeding America, "Hunger and Poverty Statistics", http://feedingamerica.org/faces-of-hunger/hunger-101/hunger-and-poverty-statistics.aspx, Accessed January 20, 2011.

17. Ibid.

18. *ChildStats.gov*, "America's Children in Brief: Key National Indicators of Well-Being, 2008," http://www.childstats.gov/americaschildren/econ_fig.asp, Accessed July 21, 2008.

19. Ibid.

20. Sean Alfano, "Senators are in the money, 54 are millionaires, according to financial disclosure records," New York Daily News. October 28, 2010, http://www.nydailynews.com/news/politics/2010/10/28/2010-10-28_senators_are_in_the_money_54_are_millionaires_according_to_financial_disclosure_.html, Accessed January 20, 2011.

21. Ibid.

22. Monica Boyd, "A Socioeconomic Scale for Canada: Measuring Occupational Status from the Census, Canadian Review of Sociology, 45: 51-91.

23. Porter, *The Vertical Mosaic*.

24. Harold R. Kerbo, *Social Stratification and Inequality: Class Conflict in Historical, Comparative and Global Perspective*, 6th ed. (New York: McGraw-Hill, 2006).

25. Ashbury College, "An International Education in the Heart of the Nation's Capital," http://www.ashbury.on.ca/Page.aspx?pid=594, Accessed September 19, 2010.

26. Dennis Gilbert, *The American Class Structure in an Age of Growing Inequality*, 6th ed. (Belmont, CA: Wadsworth, 2003).

27. Ross, Reynolds, and Geis, "The Contingent Meaning of Neighborhood Stability."

28. Catherine S. Ford, "Concentrated Poverty in Urban Canada: Health Issues for Consideration," http://www.fp.ucalgary.ca/chaps/Ford.pdf, Accessed September 19, 2010.

29. Jeanne Brooks-Gunn, Greg Duncan, Pamela Klebanove, and Naomi Sealand, "Do Neighborhoods Influence Child and Adolescent Development?" *American Journal of Sociology*, 1993. 99: 353–395.

30. Gary Solon, "Intergenerational Income Mobility in the United States," *The American Economic Review*, 1992. 82: 393–408;

31. David J. Zimmerman, "Regression Toward Mediocrity in Economic Stature," *American Economic Review*, 1992. 82: 409–429.

32. Kingsley Davis and Wilbert E. Moore, "Some Principles of Stratification," *American Sociological Review*, 1944. 10: 242–249.

33. Minister of Education, Leisure, and Sports, "Average salary of teachers in school boards," http://www.mels.gouv.qc.ca/STAT/indic03/indic03A/ia03110.pdf, Accessed September 23, 2010.

34. Statistics Canada, "Average Annual Employment Income in Constant 2005 Dollars, Canada," http://www.statcan.gc.ca/pub/85-002-x/2008010/article/10730/tbl/tbl04-eng.htm, Accessed September 20, 2010.

35. Blackhawkzone.com, "NHL Salaries," http://www.blackhawkzone.com/salaries/teams.php?TeamID=28, Accessed September 21, 2010.

36. Melvin Tumin, "On Inequality," *American Sociological Review*, 1963. 28: 19–26.

37. Edward G. Grabb and Ronald D. Lambert, "The Subjective Meanings of Social Class among Canadians," *The Canadian Journal of Sociology*, 7: 297–307.

38. Statistics Canada, "Table 202-0102: Average Female and Male Earnings, and Female-to-Male Earnings Ratio, by Work Activity, 2008 Constant Dollars, Annual." CANSIM (database). http://estat.statcan.gc.ca/cgi-win/cnsmcgi.exe?Lang=E&EST-Fi=EStat/English/CII_1-eng.htm, Accessed September 20, 2010.

39. "Que. Doctors Lagging in Fee-for-Service Payments," *CTV News*, December 21, 2006, http://www.ctv.ca/CTVNews/Health/20061221/quebec_doctors_061221/.

40. Grabb and Lambert, "The Subjective Meanings of Social Class."

41. Senate of Canada, *In from the Margins: A Call to Action on Poverty, Housing, and Homelessness*, http://www.parl.gc.ca/40/2/parlbus/commbus/senate/com-e/citi-e/rep-e/rep02dec09-e.pdf, Accessed September 20, 2010.

42. "Minimum Wage Laws—The State of Pay in Canada," *CBC News,* January 23, 2009 http://www.cbc.ca/money/story/2009/01/23/f-money-minimum-wage.html.

43. Ibid.

CHAPTER 8

1. Stephen Lewis, *Race Against Time* (Toronto: House of Anansi Press, 2005), pp. 2–5. Accessed at http://books.google.com on Oct. 14, 2010.

2. "The Millennium Development Goals Report: Statistical Annex 2006," *United Nations,* http://unstats.un.org/unsd/mdg/Default.aspx, Accessed April 23, 2007.

3. "Country Comparison: Population" and "Country Comparison: Area," CIA World Factbook, Accessed at https://www.cia.gov/library/publi-cations/the-world-factbook/rankorder/2119rank.html and https://www.cia.gov/library/publications/the-world-factbook/rankorder/2147rank.html on Oct. 15, 2010. (Note: All figures used here and in the next reference are latest actual or estimated in 2010.)

4. Population density figures from WorldAtlas.com, http://www.worldatlas.com/aatlas/populations/ctypopls.htm, Accessed Oct. 15, 2010.

5. "The Millennium Development Goals Report: Statistical Annex 2006," *United Nations,* http://unstats.un.org/unsd/mdg/Default.aspx, Accessed April 23, 2007.

6. *Trends in Maternal Mortality: 1990 to 2008*, World Health Organization, UNICEF, UNFPA and The World Bank, 2010, pp. 1, 42.

7. Ibid, p. 42 (Appendix 12). (Note: WHO defines maternal death as: "The death of a woman while pregnant or within 42 days of termina-tion of pregnancy, irrespective of the duration and site of the preg-nancy, from any cause related to or aggravated by the pregnancy or its management but not from accidental or incidental causes."—p. 4).

8. "Poverty" entry in *Canadian Oxford Dictionary,* 2nd ed. (Don Mills, ON: Oxford University Press, 2004).

9. Bruce Ravelli, Michelle Webber, and John Patterson, *Sociology for Everyone* (Toronto: Pearson Canada Inc., 2011), p. 209; and Linda L. Lindsey, Stephen Beach, and Bruce Ravelli, *Core Concepts in Sociology,* 2nd Canadian in-class ed. (Toronto: Pearson Education Canada, 2009), p. 259.

10. "The 7 Facts You Need to Know about Extreme Poverty," *The Praxis Ethiopia Foundation,* http://www.praxisethiopia.org/ep/extreme_poverty.htm, Accessed Oct. 15, 2010.

11. Timothy M. Smeeding and Lee Rainwater, *Comparing Living Standards Across Nations: Real Incomes at the Top, the Bottom, and the Middle,* Social Policy Research Centre, December 2002, http://www.sprc.unsw.edu.au/dp/DP120.pdf.

12. "Quality of Living Worldwide City Rankings 2010—Mercer Survey," Mercer LLC, May 26, 2010, http://www.mercer.com/press-releases/quality-of-living-report-2010, Accessed Oct. 8, 2010.

13. Ibid.

14. "Country Comparison: Life Expectancy at Birth," CIA Factbook, https://www.cia.gov/library/publications/the-world-factbook/rankorder/2102rank.html, Accessed Oct. 15, 2010.

15. Daniel J. Slottje, Gerald W. Scully, Joseph Gerald Hirschberg, and Kath Hayes "Measuring the Quality of Life Across Countries," *Review of Economics and Statistics,* 1991. 73(4): 684–693.

16. Kai Müller, "The World Economic and Social Development Ranking List," *Global Policy Forum,* March 18, 2000, http://www.globalpolicy.org/nations/kaiswork.htm.

17. Slottje et al., 1991 table reproduced in Myles I. Friedman, "Improving the Quality of Life: A Holistic Scientific Strategy" (Westport, CT: Praeger Publishers, 1997), p. 27. Accessed at Google Books on Oct. 15, 2010.

18. Li Lian Ong and Jason D. Mitchell, "Professors and Hamburgers: An International Comparison of Real Academic Salaries," *Applied Economics,* 2000. 32: 869–876.

19. Kevin Bales, *Disposable People: New Slavery in the Global Economy* (Berkeley, CA: University of California Press, 1999).

20. "Country Comparison: Population," CIA World Factbook.

21. Bales, *Disposable People.*

22. Michael Overall, "Workers Allege Abuses," *Tulsa World,* February 1, 2002, p. 1; Michael Overall, "Workers Free to Leave, Pickle Testifies," *Tulsa World,* September 11, 2003, p. A1; Michael Overall, "Verdict: Guilty: Judgment Exceeds $1 Million," *Tulsa World,* May 25, 2006, p. A1.

23. John Henry Hutton, *Caste in India, Its Nature, Function and Origin,* 4th ed. (Oxford: Oxford University Press, 1963).

24. David K. Shipler, *The Working Poor: Invisible in America* (New York: Vintage Books, 2005).

25. Karl Marx, "Economic and Philosophic Manuscripts of 1844," *Readings in Social Theory: The Classical Tradition to Post-Modernism,* 4th edition, edited by James Farganis (New York: McGraw-Hill, 1844/2004), 37–42; Karl Marx, *Capital: A Critique of Political Economy,* Vol. 1. (New York: International Publishers, 1867/1967); Karl Marx and Friedrich Engels, "Manifesto of this Communist Party," *Readings in Social Theory: The Classical Tradition to Post-Modernism,* 4th edition, edited by James Farganis (New York: McGraw-Hill, 1845/2004), 26–36.

26. Robin W. Winks, "Slavery," *The Canadian Encyclopedia,* Accessed through http://www.thecanadianencyclopedia.com on Oct. 17, 2010.

27. "Sex Slaves Staffed Brothels, Police Say," *CBC News,* Oct. 13, 2010, http://www.cbc.ca/canada/british-columbia/story/2010/10/13/bc-metro-vancouver-brothels-sex-slaves.html, Accessed Oct. 17, 2010.

28. Winks, "Slavery," *The Canadian Encyclopedia.*

29. "Black History in Canada," Owen Sound's Black History website, http://www.osblackhistory.com/history.php, Accessed Oct. 17, 2010.

30. Winks, "Slavery"; Lindsey, Beach, and Ravelli, *Core Concepts in Sociology,* p. 191; and "Black History in Canada," Owen Sound's Black History website.

31. John Henry Hutton, *Caste in India: Its Nature, Function, and Origins* (Bombay: Oxford University Press, 1963); Narendra Jadhav, *Untouchables: My Family's Triumphant Journey Out of the Caste System in Modern India* (New York: Scribner, 2007).

32. Karl Marx, "Economic and Philosophic Manuscripts of 1844," *Readings in Social Theory: The Classical Tradition to Post-Modernism,* 4th ed., James Farganis (ed.) (New York: McGraw-Hill, 1844/2004), 37–42; Karl Marx, *Capital: A Critique of Political Economy,* Vol. 1. (New York: International Publishers, 1867/1967); Karl Marx and Friedrich Engels, "Manifesto of this Communist Party," *Readings in Social Theory: The Classical Tradition to Post-Modernism,* 4th ed., James Farganis (ed.) (New York: McGraw-Hill, 1845/2004), 26–36.

33. Ibid.

34. Max Weber, *Economy and Society: An Outline of Interpretive Sociology,* 2 Volumes, Guether Rothe and Claus Wittich (eds.) (Berkeley: University of California Press, 1978); Max Weber, "Class, Status, Party," *Readings in Social Theory: The Classical Tradition to Post-Modernism,* 4th ed., James Farganis (ed.) (New York: McGraw-Hill, 1978/2004), 116–126.

35. Marx, "Economic and Philosophic Manuscripts of 1844"; Marx, *Capital: A Critique of Political Economy;* Marx and Engels, "Manifesto of this Communist Party."

36. Immanuel Wallerstein, *The Modern World System: Capitalist Agriculture and the Origins of the European World-Economy in the Sixteenth Century* (New York: Academic Press, 1974); Immanuel Wallerstein, *The Capitalist World-Economy* (New York: Cambridge University Press, 1979).

37. "Nigeria," The World Factbook, https://www.cia.gov/library/publica-tions/the-world-factbook/print/ni.html, Accessed July 24, 2008; "Iraq," The World Factbook, https://www.cia.gov/library/publications/the-world-factbook/print/iz.html, Accessed July 24, 2008.

38. Richard H. Robbins, *Talking Points on Global Issues: A Reader* (Boston: Allyn and Bacon, 2004); Richard H. Robbins, *Global Problems and the Culture of Capitalism* (Boston: Allyn and Bacon, 1999).

39. Michael Harrington, *The Vast Majority: The Journey to the World's Poor* (New York: Simon and Schuster, 1977).

40. Margaret Hanson and James J. Hentz, "Neocolonialism and Neoliberalism in South Africa and Zambia," *Political Science Quarterly,* 1999. 114(3): 479–502.

41. Leslie Sklair, "The Transnational Capitalist Class and Global Politics: Deconstructing the Corporate State Connection," *International Political Science Review,* 2002. 23(2): 159–174.

42. Günseli Berik, Yan van der Meulen Rodgers, and Joseph E. Zveglich, "International Trade and Gender Wage Discrimination, Evidence from East Asia," *Review of Development Economics,* 2004. 8(2): 237–254.

43. A. Aboubakr Badawi, "The Social Dimension of Globalization and Health," *Perspectives on Global Development and Technology,* 2004. 3(1–2): 73–90.

44. Jonathan Crush, "The Global Raiders: Nationalism, Globalization and the South African Brain Drain," *Journal of International Affairs,* 2002. 56(1): 147–173.

45. Ibid.

46. Jared Diamond, *Guns, Germs, and Steel: The Fates of Human Societies* (New York: W.W. Norton & Company, 1997).

47. Ibid.

48. Ibid.

49. Ibid.

50. Ibid.

51. Jacques Diouf, "Food Security and the Challenge of the MDGs," *UN Chronicle,* No. 4, 2007.

52. Ibid.

53. Diamond, *Guns, Germs, and Steel.*

54. Vilfredo Pareto, *The Rise and Fall of Elites: An Application of Social Theory* (New Brunswick, NJ: Transaction Publishers, 1901/2000).

55. Gaetano Mosca, *The Ruling Class* (New York: McGraw-Hill, 1895/1965).

56. Fernando Cardosa and Enzo Faletto, *Dependency and Development in Latin America,* Translated by Marjory Mattingly Urquidi (Berkeley, CA: University of California Press, 1979).

57. Fernando Enrique Cardosa, *The Accidental President of Brazil: A Memoir* (New York: Public Affairs, 2006).

58. Caspar W. Weinberger, "Brazil in 1997," *Forbes*, July 28, 1997. 160(2): 37.

59. T. R. Reid, *The United States of Europe: The New Superpower and the End of American Supremacy* (New York: Penguin, 2004).

60. Jeremy Rifkin, *The European Dream* (New York: Jeremy P. Tarcher/ Penguin, 2005).

61. Reid, *The United States of Europe.*

62. UNFPA (n.d.), *Gender Equality Fact Sheet,* http://www.unfpa.org/swp/ 2005/presskit/factsheets/facts_gender.htm, Accessed Oct. 18, 2010; M. Buvinic, "Women in Poverty: A New Global Underclass," *Foreign Policy* (1997), 108. Retrieved from Ebsco database.

63. USAID, "New Frontiers in U.S. Foreign Aid," http://www.usaid.gov/ policy/, Accessed July 9, 2007.

64. "Canadian Foreign Aid," *Maps of the World* website, http://finance.mapsof-world.com/aid/foreign/canadian.html, Accessed Oct. 18, 2010.

65. Anup Shah, "Foreign Aid for Development Assistance," *Global Issues,* updated April 25, 2010. Accessed Oct. 18, 2010 at http://www.glob-alissues.org/article/35/foreign-aid-development-assistance.

66. Ibid. (using OECD figures).

67. "Development Aid Rose in 2009 and Most Donors Will Meet 2010 Aid Targets," OECD, April 14, 2010. Accessed through http://www.oecd. org on Oct. 18, 2010.

CHAPTER 9

1. Carl E. James, "Race, Ethnicity, and Cultural Identity," pp. 43–56 in *Identity and Belonging: Rethinking Race and Ethnicity in Canadian Society,* Sean P. Hier and B. Singh Bolaria (eds.) (Toronto: Canadian Scholars' Press, 2006).

2. Leo Driedger and Shivalingappa S. Halli, *Race and Racism: Canada's Challenge,* (Montreal: McGill-Queen's University Press, 2000).

3. Statistics Canada, "Census Variables," http://www12.statcan.ca/ census-recensement/2006/ref/dict/overview-apercu/pop5-eng.cfm, Accessed September 29, 2010.

4. Louis Wirth, "The Problem of Minority Groups," in *The Science of Man in the World Crisis,* Ralph Linton (ed.) (New York: Columbia University Press, 1945).

5. Apartheid, *Africana: The Encyclopedia of the African and African American Experience,* Kwame Anthony Appiah and Henry Louis Gates, Jr., (eds.) in *Featured Selections,* http://www.africanaencyclopedia.com/apartheid/ apartheid.html, Accessed August 12, 2008.

6. Canadian Index of Well-Being, "Fact Sheet—How Are Canadians Really Doing? A Closer Look at Select Groups," http://www.ciw.ca/en/ Media/09-12-16/df39996f-52af-4c21-a004-823133c15744.aspx, Accessed October 9, 2010.

7. Statistics Canada, "Study: Canada's Visible Minority Population in 2017," *The Daily,* http://www.statcan.gc.ca/daily-quotidien/050322/ dq050322b-eng.htm, Accessed October 9, 2010.

8. Human Rights Watch, "Children Targeted in the Genocide," http://hrw. org/reports/2003/rwanda0403/rwanda0403-03.htm, Accessed September 10, 2008.

9. Library and Archives Canada, "The Anti-Slavery Movement in Canada," http://www.collectionscanada.gc.ca/anti-slavery/index-e.html, Accessed October 5, 2010.

10. Stopracism.ca, "Groups and Individual Cases," http://www.sto-pracism.ca/content/groups-and-individual-cases, Accessed October 8, 2010.

11. Ralph T. Pastore, "The Beothuks," http://www.heritage.nf.ca/aborigi-nal/beothuk.html, Accessed October 3, 2010.

12. Jared Diamond, *Guns, Germs, and Steel: The Fates of Human Societies* (New York: W.W. Norton and Company, 1999).

13. Canadiana.org, "Canada in the Making: 1867–1931: Territorial Expansion," http://www1.canadiana.org/citm/themes/constitution/ constitution14_e.html#manitoba, Accessed October 8, 2010.

14. Chinese Canadian National Council, "History: The Chinese Head Tax and Exclusion Act," http://www.ccnc.ca/redress/history.html, Accessed October 7, 2010.

15. Public Broadcasting Service, "Srebrenica: A Cry from the Grave," http://www.pbs.org/wnet/cryfromthegrave/massacre/massacre.html, Accessed August 12, 2008.

16. Marcus Cox, "The Right to Return Home: International Intervention and Ethnic Cleansing in Bosnia and Herzegovina," *The International and Comparative Law Quarterly,* 1998. 47(3): 599–631.

17. Chris Stephen, "Court Wants Exemplary Karadzic Trial," *BBC News,* July 24, 2008, http://news.bbc.co.uk/2/hi/europe/7522908.stm, Accessed August 12, 2008.

18. "Speaking out: Quebec's Debate over Language Laws," *CBC News,* http://www.cbc.ca/canada/story/2009/10/22/f-quebec-language-laws-bill-101.html, Accessed October 7, 2010.

19. Gerhard P. Bassler, "Germans," *The Canadian Encyclopedia,* http:// www.thecanadianencyclopedia.com/index.cfm?PgNm=TCE&Params= A1ARTA0003238, Accessed October 8, 2010.

20. Harry Loewen, "Mennonites," in *Multicultural Canada,* http://www. multiculturalcanada.ca/Encyclopedia/A-Z/m6, Accessed October 8, 2010.

21. "Separation Anxiety: The 1995 Quebec Referendum," *CBC News,* http://archives.c.ca/politics/federal_politics/topics/1891/, Accessed October 8, 2010.

22. "Castro, Fidel," *Encyclopædia Britannica, 2008,* Encyclopædia Britannica Online, http://search.eb.com/eb/article-9020736, Accessed September 30, 2008.

23. "Gandhi, Mohandas Karamchand," *Encyclopædia Britannica, 2008,* Encyclopædia Britannica Online, http://search.eb.com/eb/article-22639, Accessed September 30, 2008.

24. Ashley W. Doane, Jr., "Dominant Group Ethnic Identity in the United States: The Role of 'Hidden' Ethnicity in Intergroup Relations," *The Sociological Quarterly,* 1997. 38(3): 375–397.

25. Eric Fong and Milena Gulia, "Differences in Neighborhood Qualities among Racial and Ethnic Groups in Canada," *Sociological Inquiry,* 1999. 69(4): 575–598.

26. Efie Gavaki, "Greek Immigration to Quebec: The Process and the Settlement." http://thesis.haverford.edu/dspace/bitstream/handle/10066/ 5554/Gavaki_17_1.pdf, Accessed February 12, 2011.

27. Kathryn Blee, *Inside Organized Racism: Women in the Hate Movement* (Berkeley, CA: University of California Press, 2002).

28. Mark E. Hill, "Skin Color and Perception of Attractiveness Among African Americans: Does Gender Make a Difference?" *Social Science Quarterly,* 2002. 65(1): 77–91.

29. Supreme Court of Canada, SCC Case Information, May 22, 2009, http://www.scc-csc.gc.ca/case-dossier/cms-sgd/sum-som-eng.aspx?cas=33651, Accessed January 23, 2011.

30. John Dollard, *Frustration and Aggression* (New Haven, CT: Yale University Press, 1939).

31. "Vincent Chin," Vincent Who?, posted June 14, 2007, http://vin-centchin.net/vincent/, Accessed August 12, 2008.

32. M. Brewster Smith, "The Authoritarian Personality: A Re-review 46 Years Later," *Political Psychology,* 1997. 18(1): 159–163; John Levi Martin, "The Authoritarian Personality, 50 Years Later: What Lessons Are There for Political Psychology?" *Political Psychology,* 2001. 22(1): 1–26.

33. Rory McVeigh, "Structured Ignorance and Organized Racism in the United States," *Social Forces,* 2004. 82(3): 895–936.

34. Harald Bauder and Bob Sharpe, "Residential Segregation of Visible Minorities in Canada's Gateway Cities," *Canadian Geographer,* 2002. 46(3): 204–222.

35. Canadian Index of Well-Being, "Fact Sheet—How Are Canadians Really Doing? A Closer Look at Select Groups," http://www.ciw.ca/en/ Media/09-12-16/df39996f-52af-4c21-a004-823133c15744.aspx, Accessed October 9, 2010.

36. Feng Hou and Simon Coulombe, "Earnings Gaps for Canadian-Born Visible Minorities in the Public and Private Sectors," *Canadian Public Policy,* 2010. 36(1): 29–43.

37. CBC, "Reluctant Hero: The Donald Marshall Story," http://www.cbc.ca/ lifeandtimes/marshall.html, Accessed October 9, 2010; and Edward Butts, "Marshall, Donald, Jr.," *The Canadian Encyclopedia,* http://www .canadianencyclopedia.ca/index.cfm?PgNm=TCE&Params=A1ARTA000 5123, Accessed October 9, 2010.

38. Jonathan Kozol, *Savage Inequalities: Children in America's Schools* (New York: Crown Publishers, 1991); Mary C. Waters and Karl Eschbach, "Immigration and Ethnic and Racial Inequality in the United States," *Annual Review of Sociology,* 1995. 21: 419–446; Grace Kao and Jennifer S. Thompson, "Racial and Ethnic Stratification in Educational Achievement and Attainment," *Annual Review of Sociology,* 2003. 29: 417–443; Rory McVeigh, "Structured Ignorance and Organized Racism in the United States," *Social Forces,* 2004. 82(3): 895–936.

39. Eduardo Bonilla-Silva, "The Linguistics of Color Blind Racism: How to Talk Nasty about Blacks Without Sounding 'Racist,'" *Critical Sociology,* 2002. 28(1–2): 41–64.

40. Ibid.

41. Constance Backhouse, *Colour-Coded: A Legal History of Racism in Canada, 1900–1950* (Toronto: Osgoode Society for Canadian Legal History, 1999).

42. W.E.B. Du Bois, *The Souls of Black Folk* (New York: Penguin, 1903/1996).

43. Patricia Hill Collins, *Black Feminist Thought* (New York: Routledge, 1990); Darlene Clark Hine, "In the Kingdom of Culture: Black Women and the Intersection of Race, Gender, and Class," in *Lure and Loathing: Essays on Race, Identity and the Ambivalence of Assimilation,* Gerald Early (ed.) (New York: Penguin Press, 1993).

44. Ibid.

45. CBC Archives, "A Lost Heritage: Canada's Residential Schools," http://archives.cbc.ca/society/education/topics/692/, Accessed October 9, 2010.

46. Barbara Bagilhole, *Understanding Equal Opportunities and Diversity: The Social Differentiations and Intersections of Inequality* (Bristol, UK: The Policy Press, 2009).

47. William J. Wilson, *The Declining Significance of Race: Blacks and Changing American Institutions,* 2nd ed. (Chicago: University of Chicago Press, 1980).

48. Eduardo Ramirez, "Revision of Minority Advantage," http://imprint.uwaterloo.ca/2010/jul/30/cover/revision-minority-advantage/, Accessed October 9, 2010; and Nick Aveling, "Tories to Review Affirmative-Action Hiring Practices," *Vancouver Sun,* July 23, 2010.

CHAPTER 10

1. Arlie Russell Hochschild and Anne Machung, *The Second Shift: Working Parents and the Revolution at Home* (New York: Penguin Books, 1989/2003).

2. "Men Doing More Housework, StatsCan Says," CBC News Online, last updated March 4, 2008, Accessed October 19, 2010 at http://www.cbc.ca/consumer/story/2008/03/04/housework-men.html.

3. "20/20: The Difference between Men and Women: 9/29/06," *ABC News,* http://abcnewsstore.go.com/webapp/wcs/stores/servlet/DSIProductDisplay?catalogId511002&storeId520051&productId52003060&langId5-1&categoryId5100032.

4. Ibid.

5. Ibid.

6. Ivy Kennelly, Sabine N. Merz, and Judith Lorber, "What Is Gender?" *American Sociological Review,* 2001. 66(4): 598–605.

7. Natalie Braine, "Feature: Desperate Housewives. Why Has This Series About Life in American Suburbia Become Such a Phenomenon?" (taken from *The Works,* Jan. 2006 issue), Accessed at *Visimag.com,* http://www.visimag.com/theworks/a02_feat01.htm on Oct. 20, 2010.

8. Candace West and Don H. Zimmerman, "Doing Gender," *Gender and Society,* 1987. 1(2): 125–151.

9. Ibid.

10. Michael A. Messner, "Barbie Girls versus Sea Monsters: Children Constructing Gender," *Gender and Society,* 2000. 14(6): 765–784.

11. Ibid.

12. Manhattan Toy Online Store, http://store.manhattantoy.com, Accessed July 28, 2008.

13. Nerf, http://www.hasbro.com/nerf, Accessed July 28, 2008.

14. "Female Genital Mutilation," World Health Organization, http://www.who.int/mediacentre/factsheets/fs241/en/, Accessed July 28, 2008.

15. Ibid.

16. Ibid.

17. Ibid.

18. Ibid.

19. Ibid.

20. "jlewis77-1," user review for *The Bachelorette* TV series on the Internet Movie Database, http://www.imdb.com/title/tt0348894/, Accessed Oct. 20, 2010.

21. M. Gigi Durham, *The Lolita Effect: The Media Sexualization of Young Girls and What We Can Do About It* (Woodstock, NY: The Overlook Press, 2008).

22. Ibid.

23. Sharyn Graham Davis, *Challenging Gender Norms: Five Genders Among the Bugis in Indonesia* (Belmont, CA: Thomson Wadsworth, 2007).

24. Ibid.

25. Carmen DeNavas-Walt, Bernadette D. Proctor, and Jessica Smith, *Income, Poverty, and Health Insurance Coverage in the United States: 2006,* U.S. Census Bureau, Current Population Reports, P60–233, U.S. Government Printing Office, Washington, DC, 2007.

26. Margaret Mead, *Sex and Temperament* (New York, Harper Perennial, 1935).

27. Ibid.

28. Derek Freeman, *Margaret Mead and Samoa: The Making and Unmaking of an Anthropological Myth* (Cambridge, MA: Harvard University Press, 1983).

29. G. P. Murdock, "Comparative Data on the Division of Labor by Sex." *Social Forces,* 1937. 15: 551–553.

30. Marie Hammond Callaghan, *We Were Here: Exploratory Essays on Women's History at Mount Allison University.* 2006. Accessed Oct. 20, 2010 at http://www.mta.ca/wewerehere/06/intro.html.

31. "Colleges for Women," National Women's History Museum, http://www.nmwh.org/exhibits/education/1800s_6.htm, Accessed August 18, 2008.

32. Statistics Canada, "University Degrees, Diplomas and Certificates Awarded, 2008," *The Daily,* July 14, 2010, http://www.statcan.gc.ca/daily-quotidien/100714/dq100714b-eng.htm, Accessed Oct. 20, 2010. (Note that some of the data were preliminary or based on estimates, and StatsCan said University of Regina data were not included but would not alter the trend analysis.)

33. Ibid.

34. Ibid, Table 2.

35. Statistics Canada, "Labour Force Survey, 2009," Accessed Oct. 21, 2010 at http://www40.statcan.gc.ca/l01/cst01/labor05-eng.htm. (Women make up 47 percent of the paid labour force.)

36. *Families Count: Profiling Canada's Families, 2010,* p. 83, Accessed Oct. 21, 2010 at http://www.vifamily.ca/media/webfm-uploads/Publications/FamiliesCount/Families_Count.pdf. (About 68 percent of families have two incomes.)

37. Brian L. Rich, "On Inequality," *Sociological Perspectives*: Papers from the 56th Annual Meeting, Autumn 1995. 38(3): 357–380.

38. Miriam David, "Choice, Diversity and Equity in Secondary Schooling," *Oxford Review of Education,* 1997. 23(1): 77–87.

39. "Women CEOs and Heads of the Financial Post 500," updated July 6, 2010 on Catalyst.org, Accessed Oct. 21, 2010 at http://www.catalyst.org/publication/271/women-ceos-and-heads-of-the-financial-post-500.

40. Shelley J. Correll, "Gender and the Career Choice Process: The Role of Biased Self-Assessments." *The American Journal of Sociology,* 2001. 106(6): 1691–1730.

41. "Women in National Parliaments: Situation as of 30 September 2010," Inter-Parliamentary Union, Accessed Oct. 22, 2010 at http://www.ipu.org/wmn-e/classif.htm.

42. "Prime Minister Golda Meir," The President and Prime Minister Memorial Council, http://www.pmo.gov.il/PMOEng/Government/Memorial/PrimeMinisters/Golda.htm, Accessed August 15, 2008; "Benazir Bhutto," *Benazirbhutto.org,* http://www.benazirbhutto.org/mbb-profile.html, Accessed August 15, 2008; "Benazir Bhutto," Encyclopædia Britannica Online, 2008, http://search.eb.com/eb/article-9079076, Accessed August 27, 2008.

43. Hendrik Hertzberg, "Exhillaration," *The New Yorker,* June 23, 2008, http://www.newyorker.com/talk/comment/2008/06/23080623taco_talk_hertzberg, Accessed August 26, 2008.

44. Christine Williams, "The Glass Escalator: Hidden Advantages for Men in the 'Female' Professions." *Men's Lives,* 2007, http://jan.ucc.nau.edu/hdh9/ereserves/Williams_-_The_glass_escalator_PDF-1.pdf, Accessed August 15, 2008.

45. Susan Carroll, "Women Voters and the Gender Gap," http://www.apsanet.org/content_5270.cfm, Accessed August 18, 2008.

46. "Former Governors General," The Governor General of Canada website, Accessed Oct. 22, 2010 at http://www.gg.ca/document.aspx? id=55.

47. Hugh Segal, quoted in *Debates of the Senate (Hansard),* 2nd Session, 39th Parliament, Vol. 144, Issue 23, Dec. 12, 2007. Accessed Oct. 22, 2010 at www.patcarney.ca/pdf/RetirementTributesDecember12,2007.pdf.

48. Ibid.

49. "Hon. Pat Carney, P.C.: Official Biography," Accessed Oct. 22, 2010 at http://www.patcarney.ca/officialbio.html.

50. Information in this section from Joanne Goodrich (ed.), *Famous Women in Canada,* The Centre for Canadian Studies at Mount Allison University, 2001, "Introduction" and "Nellie McClung," Accessed Oct. 21, 2010 through http://www.mta.ca/about_canada/study_guide/famous_women/index.html; and "Women's Right to Vote in Canada," Parliament of Canada compilation, rev. 2007, Accessed Oct. 21, 2010 at http://www2.parl.gc.ca/parlinfo/compilations/provinceterritory/ProvincialWomenRightToVote.aspx.

51. Betty Friedan, *The Feminine Mystique* (New York: W.W. Norton and Company, 1963).

52. Barbara Epstein, "Feminist Consciousness After the Women's Movement," *Monthly Review,* 2002. 54(4). http://www.monthlyreview.org/0902epstein.htm.

53. Information in this section from Dawn Elizabeth Monroe, "Famous Canadian Women's Historical Timeline," updated 2009, on FamousCanadianWomen.com, Accessed Oct. 22, 2010 at http://www.famouscanadianwomen.com/timeline/timeline1910-1919.htm; Dominique Clément, "The Royal Commission on the Status of Women" (n.d.), *Canada's Rights Movement: A History,* Accessed Oct. 22, 2010 at http://www.historyofrights.com/events/rcsw.html; and Royal Commission on the Status of Women in Canada, *Report of the Royal Commission on the Status of Women in Canada* (Ottawa: Information Canada, 1970).

54. "bell hooks," *Contemporary Educational Thought,* University of Miami, http://www.education.miami.edu/ep/contemporaryed/Bell_Hooks/bell_hooks.html, Accessed August 15, 2008.

55. Tobi Cohen, "Second Wave of Feminism Revisited at Rideau Hall," *Postmedia News,* Sept. 9, 2010, Accessed Oct. 22, 2010 at http://www.canada.com/news/Second+wave+feminism+revisited+Rideau+Hall/3501518/story.html.

56. Andrea Dworkin *Woman Hating,* (Boston: Dutton, 1974), p. 139.

57. Department of National Defence figures, cited in "Women in the Military," *CBC News,* last updated May 30, 2006. Accessed Oct. 22, 2010 at http://www.cbc.ca/news/background/cdnmilitary/women-cdnmilitary.html.

58. Janet Saltzman Chafetz, "Feminist Theory and Sociology: Underutilized Contributions for Mainstream Theory," *Annual Review of Sociology,* 1997. 23: 97–120.

59. "Rule of Thumb," The Phrase Finder, http://www.phrases.org.uk/meanings/rule-of-thumb.html, Accessed August 28, 2008.

60. Talcott Parsons, "Age and Sex in the Social Structure of the United States," *American Sociological Review,* 1942. 7(5): 604–616.

61. Ibid.

62. Ibid.

63. Ibid.

64. Janet Saltzman Chafetz, "Feminist Theory and Sociology: Underutilized Contributions for Mainstream Theory," *Annual Review of Sociology,* 1997. 23: 97–120.

65. Ibid.

66. Ibid.

67. Candace West and Don H. Zimmerman, "Doing Gender," *Gender and Society,* 1987. 1(2): 125–151.

68. Saltzman Chafetz, "Feminist Theory and Sociology."

69. Deborah Tannen, *You Just Don't Understand: Women and Men in Conversation* (New York: HarperCollins Publishers, 2007).

70. Saltzman Chafetz, "Feminist Theory and Sociology."

71. Ibid.

72. Gloria Gonzalez-Lopez, "Beyond Machos and Machoism: Mexican Immigrant Men, Sexuality, and Intimacy," *Men's Lives,* July 11, 2003, http://www.allacademic.com/meta/p_mla_apa_research_citation/1/0/9/1/5/pages109159/p109159-1.php.

73. Friedrich Engels, *The Origin of the Family, Private Property and the State* (Resistance Books, 1884).

74. Shelley J. Correll, "Gender and the Career Choice Process: The Role of Biased Self-Assessments." *The American Journal of Sociology,* 2001. 106(6): 1691–1730.

75. Samuel Perreault and Shannon Brennan, "Criminal Victimization in Canada, 2009" (Ottawa: Published by authority of the minister responsible for Statistics Canada, September 2010). http://www.statcan.gc.ca/pub/85-002-x/2010002/article/11340-eng.pdf.

76. Ibid.

77. United States Department of Justice, "About Domestic Violence," http://www.ovw.usdoj.gov/domviolence.htm, Accessed August 15, 2008.

78. "Differences in Response to Long-Term Imprisonment: Implications for the Management of Long-Term Offenders," prepared by Frank J. Porporino, Correctional Service Canada, mod. Nov. 25, 2008, Accessed Oct. 22, 2010 at http://www.csc-scc.gc.ca/text/rsrch/reports/r10/r10e-eng.shtml.

79. "Canada Takes Action to Strengthen the National Sex Offender Registry and the National DNA Data Bank," Public Safety Canada notice, mod. March 17, 2010, Accessed Oct. 22, 2010 at http://www.publicsafety.gc.ca/media/nr/2010/nr20100317-1-eng.aspx.

80. Ibid.

81. "Williams's Murder Victims Pleaded for Their Lives," *CBC News,* Oct. 19, 2010, Accessed Oct. 22, 2010 at http://www.cbc.ca/canada/story/2010/10/19/russell-williams-day-2.html.

82. Perreault and Brennan, *Criminal Victimization in Canada,* Table 7, p. 25. http://www.statcan.gc.ca/pub/85-002-x/2010002/article/11340/tbl/tbl7-eng.htm, Accessed February 12, 2011.

83. "Cost of Intimate Partner Violence against Women in the United States," Centers for Disease Control and Prevention, http://www.cdc.gov/ncipc/pubres/ipv_cost/01_executive.htm, Accessed September 17, 2008.

CHAPTER 11

1. Terrence J. Montague, *Patients First: Closing the Health Care Gap in Canada* (Toronto: Canadian Copyright Licensing Agency, 2004).

2. Canadian Museum of Civilization, "Making Medicare: The History of Health Care in Canada, 1914–2007," http://www.civilisations.ca/cmc/exhibitions/hist/medicare/medic00e.shtml, Accessed October 12, 2010.

3. Kevin Kinsella and Victoria A. Velkoff, U.S. Census Bureau, Series P95/01-1, *An Aging World: 2001* (Washington, D.C.: U.S. Government Printing Office, 2001).

4. Preamble to the Constitution of the World Health Organization as adopted by the International Health Conference, New York 19–22 June, 1946; signed on 22 July 1946 by the representatives of 61 States (Official Records of the World Health Organization, no. 2, p. 100) and entered into force on 7 April 1948.

5. Index Mundi, "Canada Infant Mortality Rate," http://www.indexmundi.com/canada/infant_mortality_rate.html, Accessed October 12, 2010.

6. Conference Board of Canada, "Health: Self-Reported Health Status," http://www.conferenceboard.ca/hcp/details/health/self-reported-health-status.aspx#past, Accessed October 12, 2010.

7. John Knodel and Mary Beth Ofstedal, "Gender and Aging in the Developing World: Where Are the Men?" *Population and Development Review,* 2003. 29: 677–698.

8. Index Mundi, "Canada Life Expectancy at Birth," http://www.index-mundi.com/canada/life_expectancy_at_birth.html, Accessed October 12, 2010.

9. Knodel and Ofstedal, "Gender and Aging in the Developing World."

10. "Women Visit Doctors More Than Men," *CNN.com,* http://transcripts.cnn.com/TRANSCRIPTS/0606/17/hcsg.01.html, Accessed August 28, 2008.

11. Clarian Health, "Healthy Living for Men," *The Commonwealth Fund News Release,* http://www.clarian.org/portal/patients/healthyliving?paf_gear_id5200001&paf_dm5full&paf_gm5content&task_name5articleDetail&articleId59764&sectionId59, Accessed August 28, 2008.

12. Gina Kolata, "Ideas & Trends: In Medical Research Equal Opportunity Doesn't Always Apply," *New York Times,* March 14, 1991.

13. Juha Mikkonen and Dennis Raphael, *Social Determinants of Health: The Canadian Facts* (Toronto: York University School of Health Policy and Management, 2010), p. 7.

14. The Federal, Provincial and Territorial Advisory Committee on Population Health, "Toward a Healthy Future: Second Report on the Health of Canadians," http://www.phac-aspc.gc.ca/ph-sp/report-rapport/toward/pdf/toward_a_healthy_english.PDF, Accessed October 12, 2010.

15. Terrence D. Hill, Catherine E. Ross, and Ronald J. Angel, "Neighborhood Disorder, Psychophysiological Distress, and Health," *Journal of Health and Social Behavior,* 2005. 46: 170–186.

16. Ibid.

17. Robert E. Bullard, *Confronting Environmental Racism: Voices from the Grass Roots* (Boston: MA: South End Press, 1993); Robert E. Bullard, "Anatomy of Environmental Racism and the Environmental Justice Movement," in *The Environment and Society Reader,* R. Scott Free (ed.) (Needham Heights, MA: Allyn and Bacon, 2001).

18. Natan Keyfitz, "Population Growth, Development, and the Environment," *Population Studies,* 1996. 50: 335–359; Beverly H. Wright, "Endangered Communities: The Struggle for Environmental Justice in Louisiana's Chemical Corridor," *Journal of Public Management and Social Policy,* 1998. 4: 181–191.

19. Moira Welsh, "Poorest areas also most polluted, report shows," *The Toronto Star,* Nov. 27, 2008.

20. Assembly of First Nations, "Fact Sheet," http://www.afn.ca/article.asp?id=764, Accessed October 12, 2010.

21. Ibid.

22. Centre for Social Justice, "Aboriginal Issues," http://www.socialjustice.org/index.php?page=aboriginal-issues, Accessed October 12, 2010.

23. Talcott Parsons, "The Sick Role and the Role of Physicians Reconsidered," *Milbank Medical Fund Quarterly Health and Society,* 1975. 53: 257–278.

24. Ivan Illich, *Medical Nemesis* (New York: Pantheon Books, 1975); Peter Conrad and Joseph Schneider, *Deviance and Medicalization: From Badness to Sickness* (Philadelphia: Temple University Press, 1992).

25. Thomas Szasz, *The Myth of Mental Illness: Foundations of a Theory of Personal Conduct* (New York: Harper & Row, 1974).

26. Ibid.

27. Paula Caplan, *They Say You're Crazy: How the World's Most Powerful Psychiatrists Decide Who Is Normal* (New York: Perseus Books Group, 1995).

28. Ibid.

29. Rob Merrifield, "Healthy Weights for Healthy Kids: Report of the Standing Committee on Health," http://www.ccfn.ca/pdfs/healthyweights-forhealthykids.pdf, Accessed October 12, 2010.

30. Pamela M. Anderson and Kristin F. Butcher, "Childhood Obesity: Trends and Potential Causes," *The Future of Children,* 2006. 16: 19–45.

31. Centre for Science in the Public Interest (Canada), "A National Nutritious School Meal Program for Canadian Children," http://cspinet.org/canada/pdf/child-nutrition-backgrounder-jan2009-budget.pdf, Accessed October 12, 2010.

32. Ibid.

33. Ibid.

34. Deborah Carr and Michael A. Friedman, "Is Obesity Stigmatizing? Body Weight, Perceived Discrimination, and Psychological Well-Being in the United States," *Journal of Health and Social Behavior,* 2005. 46: 244–259.

35. Ibid.

36. Jason D. Boardman, Jarron M. Saint Onge, Richard G. Rogers, and Justin T. Denney, "Differentials in Obesity The Impact of Place," *Journal of Health and Social Behavior,* 2005. 46: 229–243.

37. Rob Merrifield, "Healthy Weights for Healthy Kids: Report of the Standing Committee on Health," http://www.ccfn.ca/pdfs/healthyweights-forhealthykids.pdf, Accessed October 12, 2010.

38. Arielle Concilio, Sydney Lake, and Gabrielle Milner, "Lack of Resources and Outdoor Space Lead to High Rate of Obesity in Bronx," *New York Daily News,* August 19, 2008.

39. Ibid.

40. Health Canada, "Health Care System," http://www.hc-sc.gc.ca/hcs-sss/index-eng.php, Accessed October 12, 2010.

41. Odette Madore, "The Canada Health Act: Overview and Options," http://www2.parl.gc.ca/content/lop/researchpublications/944-e.htm, Accessed October 12, 2010.

42. Ibid.

43. Ibid.

44. Ronald M. Davis, "Resolutions for a Healthy New Year," *American Medical Association,* January 3, 2008, http://www.ama-assn.org/ama/pub/category/18240.html.

45. World Health Organization, *The World Health Report 2000—Health Systems: Improving Performance* (Geneva: WHO, 2000).

46. World Health Organization, "World Health Organization Assesses the World's Health Systems," http://www.who.int/whr/2000/media_centre/press_release/en/, Accessed August 28, 2008.

47. Statistics Canada, "Population and Demography," http://www41.statcan.gc.ca/2009/3867/cybac3867_000-eng.htm, Accessed October 15, 2010.

48. Statistics Canada, "Population Projections: Canada, the Provinces and Territories," *The Daily,* http://www.statcan.gc.ca/daily-quotidien/100526/dq100526b-eng.htm, Accessed October 15, 2010.

49. Statistics Canada, "Population and Demography."

50. Jacques Henripin, "Baby Boom," *Canadian Encyclopedia,* http://thecanadianencyclopedia.com/index.cfm?PgNm=TCE&Params=A1ARTA0000437, Accessed October 15, 2010.

51. Charles F. Westoff and Elise F. Jones, "The End of 'Catholic' Fertility," *Demography,* 1979. 16(2): 209–217.

52. Global Action on Aging, "Moving Beyond Respect for Age," *The Yomiuri Shimbun Daily,* September 15, 2000, http://www.globalaging.org/elderrights/world/respect.htm.

53. Mari Yamaguchi, "Number of Elderly in Japan Hits High Record," *USA Today.com,* May 20, 2008, http://www.usatoday.com/news/world/2008-05-20-1807510551_x.htm; "Elderly Suicides Surge in Japan," *BBC News,* June 19, 2008, http://news.bbc.co.uk/2/hi/asia-pacific/7463139.stm.

54. U.S. Library of Congress, "Japan: The Elderly," http://countrystudies.us/japan/74.htm, Accessed August 28, 2008.

55. Ibid.

56. Berit Ingersoll-Dayton, Margaret B. Neal, and Leslie B. Hammer, "Aging Parents Helping Adult Children: The Experience of the Sandwiched Generation," *Family Relations,* 2001. 50: 262–271.

57. John Knodel and Mary Beth Ofstedal, "Gender and Aging in the Developing World: Where Are the Men?" *Population and Development Review,* 2003. 29: 677–698.

58. Ibid.

59. Ibid.

60. Ibid, p. 693.

61. National Center for Health Statistics, *Health, United States, 2007 with Chartbook on Trends in the Health of Americans* (Hyattsville, MD: Author, 2007).

62. Anne E. Lincoln and Michael Patrick Allen, "Double Jeopardy in Hollywood: Age and Gender in the Careers of Film Actors, 1926–1999," *Sociological Forum,* 2004. 19: 611–631.

63. Elaine Cumming, Lois R. Dean, David S. Newell, and Isabel McCaffrey, "Disengagement—A Tentative Theory of Aging," *Sociometry,* 1960. 23: 23–35.

64. Ibid.

65. *Aging and Everyday Life,* eds. Jaber F. Gubrium and James A. Holstein (Malden, MA: Blackwell Publishers Ltd, 2000).

66. Robert Crosnoe and Glen H. Elder, Jr., "Successful Adaptation in the Later Years: A Life Course Approach to Aging," *Social Psychology Quarterly,* 2002. 65: 309–328.

67. Yunqing Li and Kenneth F. Ferraro, "Volunteering and Depression in Later Life: Social Benefit or Selection Processes?" *Journal of Health and Social Behavior,* 2005. 46: 68–84.

68. Statistics Canada, "Dependency Ratio," http://www.statcan.gc.ca/pub/82-229-x/2009001/demo/dep-eng.htm, Accessed October 15, 2010.

69. Betty Friedan, *The Fountain of Age* (New York: Simon and Shuster, 1993).

70. Statistics Canada, "Women in Canada: A Gender-based Statistical Report," http://www.statcan.gc.ca/pub/89-503-x/89-503-x2005001-eng.htm, Accessed October 15, 2010.

71. UNAIDS, "Report on the Global AIDS Epidemic - 2010," http://www.unaids.org/en/media/unaids/contentassets/documents/unaidspublication/2010/20101123_globalreport_en.pdf, Accessed January 11, 2011.

72. Service Canada, "Overview of the Old Age Security Program," http://www.servicecanada.gc.ca/eng/isp/oas/oasoverview.shtml, Accessed October 15, 2010.

73. Soleman H. Abu-Bader, Anissa Rogers, and Amanda S. Barusch, "Predictors of Life Satisfaction in Frail Elderly," *Journal of Gerontological Social Work,* 2002. 38: 3–17.

74. Service Canada, "Overview of the Old Age Security Program," http://www.servicecanada.gc.ca/eng/isp/oas/oasoverview.shtml, Accessed October 15, 2010.

75. Human Resources and Skills Development Canada, "Canada Pension Plan and Old Age Security," http://www.hrsdc.gc.ca/eng/oas-cpp/index.shtml, Accessed October 15, 2010.

76. Human Resources and Skills Development Canada, "Making the Canada Pension Plan Secure," http://www.rhdcc-hrsdc.gc.ca/eng/oas-cpp/cpp_disability/future/5thpg3.shtml, Accessed October 15, 2010.

CHAPTER 12

1. Anthony N. Doob and Carla Cesaroni, *Responding to Youth Crime in Canada* (Toronto: University of Toronto Press, 2004), pp. 6–7.

2. "Conservative Plan Would Name Violent Young Offenders," *CTV News,* http://www.ctv.ca/servlet/ArticleNews/story/CTVNews/20080920/election2008_harper_crime_080921/20080922?s_name=election2008, Accessed October 23, 2010.

3. Marcus Felson, *Crime & Everyday Life* (Thousand Oaks, CA: Pine Forge Press, 1998).

4. Ibid.

5. Mia Dauvergne and John Turner, "Police-Reported Crime Statistics in Canada, 2009," http://www.statcan.gc.ca/pub/85-002-x/2010002/article/11292-eng.htm, Accessed October 23, 2010.

6. Ibid.

7. Ibid.

8. Maire Gannon and Karen Mihorean, "Criminal Victimization in Canada, 2004," http://www.statcan.gc.ca/pub/85-002-x/85-002-x2005007-eng.pdf, Accessed October 23, 2010.

9. Roxan Vaillancourt, "Gender Differences in Police-reported Violent Crime in Canada, 2008," http://www.statcan.gc.ca/pub/85f0033m/85f0033m2010024-eng.htm, Accessed October 23, 2010.

10. Ibid.

11. Statistics Canada, "Study: Exploring Crime Patterns in Canada," *The Daily,* http://www.statcan.gc.ca/daily-quotidien/050629/dq050629b-eng.htm, Accessed October 23, 2010.

12. David Cole, *No Equal Justice: Race and Class in the American Criminal Justice System* (New York: New Press, 1999).

13. Jeffrey Reiman, *The Rich Get Richer and the Poor Get Prison* (New York: Allyn & Bacon, 2008).

14. John Braithwaite, "The Myth of Social Class and Criminality Reconsidered," *American Sociological Review*, 1981. 46: 36–57; Margaret Farnsworth, *Social Background and the Early Onset of Delinquency: Exploring the Utility of Various Indicators of Social Class Background* (Albany, NY: Hindelang Criminal Justice Research Center, 1990).

15. Elijah Anderson, "Ideologically Driven Critique," *American Journal of Sociology*, 2002. 197(6): 1533–1550.

16. Valerie Pottie Bunge, Holly Johnson, and Thierno A. Baldé, "Exploring Crime Patterns in Canada," http://www.statcan.gc.ca/pub/85-561-m/85-561-m2005005-eng.pdf, Accessed October 23, 2010.

17. Michael Gottfredson and Travis Hirschi, *A General Theory of Crime* (Stanford, CA: Stanford University Press, 1990).

18. Statistics Canada, "Study: Exploring Crime Patterns in Canada," *The Daily*, http://www.statcan.gc.ca/daily-quotidien/050629/dq050629b-eng.htm, Accessed October 23, 2010.

19. J. N. van Kesteren, P. Mayhew, and P. Nieuwbeerta, *Criminal Victimization in Seventeen Industrialized Countries: Key Findings from the 2000 International Crime Victimization Survey* (The Hague, Ministry of Justice, WODC, 2000).

20. Ibid.

21. Marcus Felson, *Crime & Everyday Life* (Thousand Oaks, CA: Pine Forge Press, 1998).

22. John Braithwaite, *Crime, Shame, and Reintegration* (New York: Cambridge University Press, 1989).

23. L. Thomas Winfree, Jr., "New Zealand Police and Restorative Justice Philosophy," *Crime and Delinquency*, 2004. 50: 189–213.

24. Melanie Spiteri, "Sentencing Circles for Aboriginal Offenders in Canada: Furthering the Idea of Aboriginal Justice within a Western Justice Framework," http://www.sfu.ca/crj/fulltext/spiteri.pdf, Accessed October 24, 2010.

25. Frank Schmalleger, David MacAlister, Paul F. McKenna, and John Winterdyk, *Canadian Criminal Justice Today: An Introductory Text for the Twenty-First Century* (Toronto: Prentice-Hall Canada Inc., 2000); and Canadian Resource Centre for Victims of Crime, "Victim Impact Statements," http://www.crcvc.ca/docs/VictimImpactStatements.pdf, Accessed October 24, 2010.

26. Statistics Canada, "Adult and Youth Correctional Services: Key Indicators," *The Daily*, http://www.statcan.gc.ca/daily-quotidien/091208/dq091208a-eng.htm, Accessed October 23, 2010.

27. Samuel Perreault, "The Incarceration of Aboriginal People in Adult Correctional Services," *Juristat*, http://www.statcan.gc.ca/pub/85-002-x/2009003/article/10903-eng.htm, Accessed October 23, 2010.

28. Correctional Services Canada, "FORUM on Corrections Research," http://www.csc-scc.gc.ca/text/pblct/forum/e053/e053h-eng.shtml, Accessed October 24, 2010.

29. Laura Landry and Maire Sinha, "Adult Correctional Services in Canada, 2005/2006," http://www.statcan.gc.ca/pub/85-002-x/85-002-x2008006-eng.pdf, Accessed October 24, 2010.

30. Statistics Canada, "Adult and Youth Correctional Services: Key Indicators," *The Daily*, http://www.statcan.gc.ca/daily-quotidien/091208/dq091208a-eng.htm, Accessed October 23, 2010.

31. Cesare Lombroso, "Introduction," in Gena Lombroso-Ferrero, *Criminal Man According to the Classification of Cesare Lombroso* (Montclair, NJ: Patterson Smith, 1911/1972).

32. Alan Booth and D. Wayne Osgood, "The Influence of Testosterone on Deviance in Adulthood: Assessing and Explaining the Relationship," *Criminology*, 1993. 31: 93–117; J. R. Sanchez-Martin, E. Fano, L. Ahedo, J. Cardas, P. F. Brain, and A. Azpiroz, "Relating Testosterone Levels and Free Play Social Behavior in Male and Female Preschool Children," *Psychoneuroendocrinology*, November 25, 2000, 773–783.

33. James J. Hudziak and Lawrence P. Rudiger, "A Twin Study of Inattentive, Aggressive and Anxious/Depressed Behaviors," *Journal of American Academy of Child and Adolescent Psychiatry*, 2000. 39: 469–476.

34. William Duffy, *Sugar Blues* (Pandor, PA: Childton Book Co., 1975).

35. Abdulla Badawy, "Alcohol and Violence and the Other Possible Role of Serotonin," *Criminal Behaviour and Mental Health*, 2003. 12: 31–45.

36. Cesare Beccaria, *Essays on Crimes and Punishments*, translated by Henry Paolucci (Indianapolis, IN: Bobbs-Merrill, 1764/1963).

37. Jeremy Bentham, *An Introduction to the Principles of Morals and Legislation*, J. H. Burns and H. L. A. Hart (eds.) (London: Athlone Publishing, 1789/1970).

38. DSM, *Diagnostic and Statistical Manual of Mental Disorders*, 4th ed. (Washington, D.C.: American Psychiatric Association, 1994).

39. Travis Hirschi and Michael J Hindelang, "Intelligence and Delinquency: A Revisionist Review," *American Sociological Review*, 1977. 42: 57–87.

40. Stanton E. Samenow, *Inside the Criminal Mind: Revised and Updated Edition* (New York: Crown Publishers, 2004).

41. Émile Durkheim, *The Rules of Sociological Method*, 8th ed., edited by George E. G. Catlin, translated by Sarah A. Solovay and John H. Mueller (New York: Free Press, 1895/1964).

42. Robert K. Merton, "Social Structure and Anomie," *American Sociological Review*, 1938. 3: 672–682.

43. Edwin Sutherland and Donald Cressey, *Principles of Criminology*, 10th ed. (Philadelphia: Lippincott, 1978).

44. Walter C. Reckless, *The Crime Problem* (New York: Appleton-Century-Crofts, 1955).

45. Travis Hirschi, *Causes of Delinquency* (Berkeley, CA: University of California Press, 1969).

46. Edwin M. Lemert, *Social Pathology* (New York: McGraw-Hill, 1951); Edwin M. Lemert, *Human Deviance, Social Problems and Social Control* (Englewood Cliffs, NJ: Prentice-Hall, 1967).

47. Jeffrey Reiman, *The Rich Get Richer and the Poor Get Prison: Ideology, Class and Criminal Justice* (Needham Heights, MA: Pearson Education, 1998).

48. Willem A. Bonger, *Criminality and Economic Conditions* (Bloomington, IN: Indiana University Press, 1969).

49. Reiman, *The Rich Get Richer and the Poor Get Prison*.

50. Robert Agnew, "Foundation for a General Strain Theory of Crime and Delinquency," *Criminology*, 1992. 30: 47–66.

51. Michael Gottfredson and Travis Hirschi, *A General Theory of Crime* (Stanford, CA: Stanford University Press, 1990).

52. Agnew, "Foundation for a General Strain Theory."

53. Gottfredson and Hirschi, *A General Theory of Crime*.

54. H. Grasmick, C. R. Tittle, R. Bursik, and B. Arnkelev, "Testing the Core Empirical Implications of Gottfredson and Hirschi's General Theory of Crime," *Journal of Research in Crime and Delinquency*, 1993. 30: 5–29; Marianne Junger and Richard E. Tremblay, "Self-Control, Accidents, and Crime," *Criminal Justice and Behavior*, 1999. 26: 485–502; Carter Hay, "Parenting Self-Control, and Delinquency: A Test of Self-Control Theory," *Criminology*, 2001. 39: 707–736; Richard Tremblay, Frank Vitaro, Lucie Bertrand, Marc Leblanc, Helene Beauchesne, Helene Boileau, and Lucille David, "Parent and Child Training to Prevent Early Onset Delinquency: The Montreal Longitudinal Experimental Study," *Life-Course Criminology: Contemporary and Classic Readings*, Alex Piquero and Paul Mazerolle (eds.) (Belmont, CA: Wadsworth Publishing Co., 2001); Charles R. Tittle, David Ward, and Harold Grasmick, "Gender, Age, and Crime/Deviance: A Challenge to Self Control Theory," *Journal of Research in Crime and Delinquency*, 2003. 40: 426–454.

55. Statistics Canada, "Study: Female Offenders," *The Daily*, http://www.statcan.gc.ca/daily-quotidien/080124/dq080124a-eng.htm, Accessed October 24, 2010.

56. Sally S. Simpson and Denise C. Herz, "Gender, Crime, and Criminal Justice," *Handbook of the Sociology of Gender*, Janet Saltzman Chafetz (ed.) (New York: Kluwer Academic/Plenum Publishers, 1999).

57. Laura Landry and Maire Sinha, "Adult Correctional Services in Canada, 2005/2006," http://www.statcan.gc.ca/pub/85-002-x/85-002-x2008006-eng.pdf, Accessed October 24, 2010.

58. Susan F. Sharp, "Editorial," *Feminist Criminology*, 2006. 1(1): 3–5.

59. Statistics Canada, "Police Officers, by Province and Territory," http://www40.statcan.gc.ca/l01/cst01/legal05a-eng.htm, Accessed October 24, 2010.

60. Justice Canada, "Canada's Court System," http://www.justice.gc.ca/eng/dept-min/pub/ccs-ajc/page2.html, Accessed October 24, 2010.

61. Justice Canada, "Canada's System of Justice," http://www.justice.gc.ca/eng/dept-min/pub/just/08.html, Accessed October 24, 2010.

62. Statistics Canada, "Adult Correctional Services in Canada," http://www.statcan.gc.ca/pub/85-002-x/85-002-x2006005-eng.pdf, Accessed October 24, 2010.

CHAPTER 13

1. John Frederick Conway, *The Canadian Family in Crisis* (Toronto: James Lorimer & Company Ltd., 2003).

2. Ted L. Huston, "Social Ecology of Marriage and Other Unions," *Journal of Marriage and Family*, 2000. 62: 298–320.

3. Melvyn C. Goldstein, "Pahair and Tibetan Polyandry Revisited," The Center for Research on Tibet, http://www.case.edu/affil/tibet/tibetanSociety/marriage.htm, Accessed July 28, 2008.

4. Ibid.

5. Human Resources and Skills Development Canada, "Family Life—Marriage," http://www4.hrsdc.gc.ca/.3ndic.1t.4r@-eng.jsp?iid=78, Accessed October 27, 2010.

6. Statistics Canada, "Marriages," *The Daily,* http://www.statcan.gc.ca/daily-quotidien/070117/dq070117a-eng.htm, Accessed October 27, 2010.

7. Urban Institute, "Introduction," http://www.urban.org/publications/310962.html, Accessed July 20, 2008.

8. Larry L. Bumpass, James A. Sweet, and Andrew Cherlin, "The Role of Cohabitation in Declining Rates of Marriage," *Journal of Marriage and the Family,* 1991. 53: 913–927.

9. Andrew J. Cherlin and Frank F. Furstenberg, Jr., "Stepfamilies in the United States: A Reconsideration," *Annual Review of Sociology,* 1994. 20: 359–381.

10. Statistics Canada, "Table 102-4506—Live Births, by Marital Status of Mother, Canada, Provinces and Territories, Annual, CANSIM (database)," http://cansim2.statcan.gc.ca/cgi-win/cnsmcgi.exe?Lang=E&CNSM-Fi=CII/CII_1-eng.htm, Accessed October 27, 2010.

11. Anne-Marie Ambert, "One Parent Families: Characteristics, Causes, Consequences, and Issues," http://www.vifamily.ca/media/node/396/attachments/oneparent_families.pdf, Accessed October 27, 2010.

12. Michael J. Rosenfeld and Byung-Soo Kim, "The Independence of Young Adults and the Rise of Interracial and Same-Sex Unions," *American Sociological Review,* 2005. 70: 541–562.

13. Ibid.

14. David Popenoe, "American Family Decline, 1960–1990: A Review and Appraisal," *Journal of Marriage and the Family,* 1993. 55: 527–542.

15. Rosenfeld and Kim, "The Independence of Young Adults."

16. Stephanie Coontz, *The Way We Never Were: American Families and the Nostalgia Trap* (New York: Basic Books, 2000).

17. Ibid., p. 24.

18. Ibid., p. 37.

19. Ibid.

20. Ibid., p. 172.

21. Ibid., p. 35.

22. Ronald R. Rindfuss, Minja Kim-Choe, and Larry L. Bumpass, "Social Networks and Family Change in Japan," *American Sociological Review,* Dec. 2004. 69: 838–861.

23. Ibid.

24. Noriko O. Tsuya, "Gender, Employment, and Housework in Japan," Paper presented at the annual meeting of the Population Association of America, Boston, MA, April 1–3, 2004.

25. Minja Kim-Choe, Larry L. Bumpass, and Noriko O. Tsuya, "Employment," from *Marriage, Work, and Family Life in Comparative Perspective: Japan, South Korea, and the United States,* Noriko O. Tsuya and Larry L. Bumpass (eds.) (Honolulu, HI: University of Hawaii Press, 2004), 95–113.

26. Rindfuss, Kim-Choe, and Bumpass, "Social Networks and Family Change in Japan."

27. Ibid.

28. Maurice R. Davie and Ruby Jo Reeves, "Propinquity of Residence Before Marriage," *The American Journal of Sociology,* 1939. 44: 510–517; Joseph R. Marches and Gus Turbeville, "The Effect of Residential Propinquity on Marriage Selection," *The American Journal of Sociology,* May 1953. 58: 592–595; James H. S. Bossard, "Residential Propinquity as a Factor in Marriage Selection," *The American Journal of Sociology,* 1932. 38: 219–224.

29. Michael P. Johnson, John P. Caughlin, and Ted L. Huston, "The Tripartite Nature of Marital Commitment: Personal, Moral, and Structural Reasons to Stay Married," *Journal of Marriage and the Family,* 1999. 61(1): 160–177.

30. Duane W. Crawford, Renate M. Houts, Ted L. Huston, and Laura J. George, "Compatibility, Leisure, and Satisfaction in Marital Relationships," *Journal of Marriage and the Family,* 2002. 64(2): 433–449.

31. Ibid.

32. Daphne Stevens, Gary Kiger, and Pamela Riley, "Working Hard and Hardly Working: Domestic Labor and Marital Satisfaction among Dual-Earner Couples," *Journal of Marriage and Family,* 2002. 63: 514–526.

33. Ibid.

34. Ibid.

35. Canadian Council on Social Development, "Families: A Canadian Profile," http://www.ccsd.ca/factsheets/family/, Accessed October 27, 2010.

36. Sara McLanahan and Christine Percheski, "Family Structure and the Reproduction of Inequalities," *The Annual Review of Sociology,* 2008. 34: 12.1–12.19.

37. Lisa Strohschein, "Household Income Histories and Child Mental Health Trajectories," *Journal of Health and Social Behavior,* 2005. 46: 359–375.

38. Robert Schoen, Young J. Kim, Constance A. Nathanson, Jason Fields, and Nan Marie Astone, "Why Do Americans Want Children?" *Population and Development Review,* June 1997. 23: 333–358.

39. Anne Milan, "One Hundred Years of Families," *Canadian Social Trends,* http://www.statcan.gc.ca/pub/11-008-x/1999004/article/4909-eng.pdf, Accessed October 27, 2010.

40. Adapted from Statistics Canada, CANSIM database http://cansim2.statcan.gc.ca, Table 101-6501, February 17, 2011.

41. Milan, "One Hundred Years of Families."

42. Mary Bess Kelly, "The Processing of Divorce Cases through Civil Court in Seven Provinces and Territories," *Juristat,* http://www.statcan.gc.ca/pub/85-002-x/2010001/article/11158-eng.htm, Accessed October 27, 2010.

43. Stephanie Coontz, *Marriage, A History: How Love Conquered Marriage* (New York: Penguin, 2006).

44. Kelly, "The Processing of Divorce Cases through Civil Court in Seven Provinces and Territories."

45. Lillian B. Rubin, "Women of a Certain Age: The Midlife Search for Self," *Contemporary Sociology,* May 1981. 10: 460–462.

46. Arlene Saluter and Terry Lugaila, "Marital Status and Living Arrangements: March 1996," *Current Population Reports: Population Characteristics,* http://www.census.gov/prod/3/98pubs/p20-496.pdf, Accessed August 21, 2008.

47. Michael J. Rosenfeld, *The Age of Independence: Interracial Unions, Same Sex Unions and the Changing American Family* (Cambridge, MA: Harvard University Press, 2007).

48. A. Kroska, "The Division of Labor at Home: A Review and Reconceptualization," *Social Psychology Quarterly,* 1997. 60: 304–322.

49. Stephanie Coontz, *Marriage, A History: From Obedience to Intimacy, or How Love Conquered Marriage* (New York: Viking Adult, 2005); Stephanie Coontz, *The Way We Never Were: American Families and the Nostalgia Trap* (New York: Basic Books, 2000), 18.

50. Steven L. Nock, *Marriage in Men's Lives* (New York: Oxford University Press, 1998).

51. Stevens, Kiger, and Riley, "Working Hard and Hardly Working."

52. Arlie Russell Hochschild with Anne Machung, *The Second Shift: Working Parents and the Revolution at Home* (New York: Penguin Books, 1989/2003).

53. Kristin Byron, "A Meta-Analytic Review of Work–Family Conflict and its Antecedents," *Journal of Vocational Behavior,* 2005. 67: 169–198.

54. Herbert Bynder, "Émile Durkheim and the Sociology of the Family," *Journal of Marriage and Family,* 1969. 31: 527–533.

55. David Popenoe, "American Family Decline, 1960–1990: A Review and Appraisal," *Journal of Marriage and the Family,* Aug. 1993. 55: 527–542.

56. Ibid.

57. Ibid.

58. "Same-Sex Rights: Canada Timeline," *CBC News,* March 1, 2007, http://www.cbc.ca/news/background/samesexrights/timeline_canada.html, Accessed October 27, 2010.

59. William Meezan and Jonathan Rauch, "The Future of Children," *Marriage and Child Wellbeing,* 2005. 15: 97–115.

CHAPTER 14

1. Andrea Rounce, *Access to Post-secondary Education: Does Class Still Matter?* (Canadian Centre for Policy Alternatives, 2004), pp. 1, 8, Accessed Sept. 28, 2010 at https://www.policyalternatives.ca/sites/default/files/uploads/publications/Saskatchewan_Pubs/pse.pdf.

2. Annette Hemmings, "The 'Hidden' Corridor Curriculum," *High School Journal,* 2000. 83(2): 1–10.

3. Francisco O. Ramirez and John Boli, "The Political Construction of Mass Schooling: European Origins and Worldwide Institutionalization," *Sociology of Education,* 1987. 60: 2–17.

4. "Toronto's 1st Africentric School Set to Open," *CBC News,* updated Sept. 4, 2009. Accessed Oct. 28, 2010 at http://www.cbc.ca/canada/toronto/story/2009/09/04/africentric-school.html

5. "Under-privileged Children Also Disadvantaged in the Classroom," *UNESCO Institute for Statistics,* May 29, 2005, http://www.uis.unesco.org/ev.php?ID57200_ 201&ID25DO_TOPIC.

6. "Literacy Rates," *UNESCO Institute for Statistics,* http://stats.uis.unesco.org/unesco/TableViewer/document.aspx?ReportId5121&IF_Language5eng&BR_Country56940, Accessed August 12, 2008; "Sierra Leone," The Central Intelligence Agency's *World Fact Book,* https://www.cia.gov/library/publications/the-worldfactbook/print/sl.html, Accessed July 17, 2008.

7. *Global Education Digest 2007,* "Global Distribution of Public Expenditure on Education, GDP and Population Aged 5 to 25 Years, by Region and for Selected Countries, 2004," UNESCO Institute for Statistics, http://unesdoc.unesco.org/images/0015/001536/153607e.pdf, pp. 11–12, Accessed Oct. 26, 2010.

8. *Education Indicators in Canada: Report of the Pan-Canadian Education Indicators Program 2007,* Statistics Canada, 2007, Catalogue 81-582-X, pp. 29–31.

9. *Education Indicators in Canada,* p. D2.

10. "Assembly of First Nations—The Story," *Assembly of First Nations* website, http://www.afn.ca/article.asp?id=59, Accessed Oct. 25, 2010.

11. Michael Mendelson, *Aboriginal Peoples and Postsecondary Education in Canada* (Ottawa: Caledon Institute of Social Policy, 2006), p. 35.

12. Statistics Canada, 2006 Census, analysis series, 97-560-XIE2006001.

13. "Study Gives Aboriginal Education a Failing Grade," *Vancouver Sun,* Oct. 29, 2008, Accessed Oct. 25, 2010 at http://www.canada.com/vancouversun/news/westcoastnews/story.html?id=6fafa6b0-7366-4d77-bc1a-66a151a4e194.

14. Ibid., quoting John Richards' report.

15. Robert Rosenthal and Lenore Jacobson, *Pygmalion in the Classroom* (New York: Holt, 1968).

16. Hussain Al-Fadhili and Madhu Singh, "Teachers' Expectancy and Efficacy as Correlates of School Achievement in Delta, Mississippi," *Journal of Personnel Evaluation in Education,* 2006. 19(1–2): 51–67.

17. Margaret R. Kuklinksy and Rhona S. Weinstein, "Classroom and Developmental Differences in a Path Model of Teacher Expectancy Effects," *Child Development,* 2001. 72(5): 1554–1579.

18. Paul M. Anglin and Ronald Meng, "Evidence on Grades and Grade Inflation at Ontario's Universities," *Canadian Public Policy,* 2000. 26(3): 361.

19. James E. Côté and Anton L. Allahar, *Ivory Tower Blues: A University System in Crisis* (Toronto: University of Toronto Press, 2007), p. 9.

20. Daniel Girard, "Prof Says Pressure Is on to Accept 'Grade Inflation,'" *Toronto Star,* June 11, 2007, Accessed Oct. 23, 2010 at http://www.thestar.com/article/223884.

21. Anglin and Meng, "Evidence on Grades and Grade Inflation," p. 362.

22. Girard, "Prof Says Pressure Is On."

23. Quoted in Michael Woods, "Making the Grade," Queen's University's *The Journal,* Sept. 19, 2008, Accessed Oct. 23, 2010 at http://www.queensjournal.ca/story/2008-09-19/features/making-the-grade/.

24. Girard, "Prof Says Pressure Is On."

25. Quoted in Woods, "Making the Grade."

26. Deani Van Pelt, *Home Education in Canada: A Summary of the Pan-Canadian Study on Home Education 2003,* Canadian Centre for Home Education and Home School Legal Defence Association, p. 1, Accessed Oct. 26, 2010 at http://www.hslda.ca/cche_research/SummaryFinal.pdf.

27. Crista L. Green and Kathleen Hoover-Dempsey, "Why Do Parents Homeschool?" *Education & Urban Society,* 2007. 39(2): 264–285.

28. "Higher Education Finance and Cost-Sharing in Canada" (updated April 9, 2010), p. 1, part of The International Comparative Higher Education and Finance Project, operated through the State University of New York at Buffalo, Accessed Oct. 24, 2010 at http://gse.buffalo.edu/org/inthigheredfinance/project_profiles.html.

29. "Educational Indicators in Canada: Report of the Pan-Canadian Education Indicators Program 2007," Statistics Canada, Catalogue No. 81-582-XPE, page xiii.

30. "Higher Education Finance and Cost-Sharing in Canada," p. 2. (Figures in Canadian. dollars.)

31. "Higher Education," Estia in Sweden, http://www.estia.educ.goteborg.se/svestia/edu/edu_sys5.html, Accessed September 2, 2008.

32. Randall Collins, *The Credential Society* (New York: Academic Press, 1979); Randall Collins, "Functional and Conflict Theories of Educational Stratification," *American Sociological Review,* 1971. 36: 1002–1019.

33. Mark D. Regenerus, "Religion and Positive Adolescent Outcomes: A Review of Research and Theory," *Review of Religious Research,* 2003. 44(4): 394–413.

34. Marie Good and Teena Willoughby, "Evaluating the Direction of Effects in the Relationship between Religious versus Non-Religious Activities, Academic Success, and Substance Use," *Journal of Youth and Adolescence,* pub. online August 14, 2010, Accessed Sept. 29, 2010 through http://www.springerlink.com/.

35. Regenerus, "Religion and Positive Adolescent Outcomes."

36. Ibid.

37. Min Zhou and Carl L. Bankston, III, "Social Capital and the Adaptation of the Second Generation: The Case of Vietnamese Youth in New Orleans," in *The New Second Generation,* Alejandro Portes (ed.) (New York: Russell Sage Foundation, 1996), 197–220.

38. "Selected Characteristics of Public School Teachers: Selected Years, Spring 1961 Through Spring 2001," *Digest of Educational Statistics,* http://nces.ed.gov/programs/digest/d05/tables/dt05_068.asp, Accessed July 9, 2008; "Secondary Education: Teacher's Characteristics," *Institute of Educational Sciences,* http://nces.ed.gov/surveys/international/intlindicators/index.asp?SectionNumber53&SubSectionNumber56&IndicatorNumber 584, Accessed July 9, 2008; "2008 Federal Holidays," *National Archives News,* http://www.archives.gov/news/federal-holidays.html, Accessed July 9, 2008; Emily Brady, "For Muslim Students, A Drive to Deem Holy Days as Holidays," *The New York Times,* April 29, 2007, http://www.nytimes.com/2007/04/29/nyregion/thecity/29holi.html.

39. "Schools Won't Lose Stat Holidays: Minister," *CBC News,* March 24, 2010, Accessed Oct. 26, 2010 at http://www.cbc.ca/canada/montreal/story/2010/03/24/mtl-courchesne-holidays.html.

40. Émile Durkheim, *Elementary Forms of the Religious Life,* translated by Karen Fields (New York: Free Press, 1912/1995).

41. Ibid.

42. Huston Smith, *The World's Religions: Our Great Wisdom Traditions* (New York: HarperCollins, 1958/1991).

43. Ibid.

44. Durkheim, *Elementary Forms of the Religious Life;* Smith, *The World's Religions.*

45. "Religion Data from the 2001 Canadian Census," ReligiousTolerance.org, Accessed Oct. 27, 2010 at http://www.religioustolerance.org/can_rel0.htm; and *2001 Census: Analysis Series, Religions in Canada,* Statistics Canada, 2003, catalogue no. 96F0030XIE2001015, p. 5.

46. *2001 Census: Analysis Series, Religions in Canada,* p. 8.

47. *Religions in Canada,* 2nd ed. (Ottawa: Directorate of Human Rights and Diversity, 2008), p. 47, catalogue no. D2-147/2003.

48. "Hinduism: The World's Third Largest Religion," ReligiousTolerance.org, Accessed Oct. 27, 2010 at http://www.religioustolerance.org/hinduism.htm.

49. *2001 Census: Analysis Series, Religions in Canada,* p. 8.

50. David J. Goa and Harold G. Coward, "Hinduism," *The Canadian Encyclopedia,* Accessed Oct. 27, 2010 through www.thecanadianencyclopedia.com.

51. Durkheim, *Elementary Forms of the Religious Life;* Smith, *The World's Religions;* Mark Schumaker, "Shintoism—The Way of the Gods," *Gods of Japan: A-to-Z Photo Dictionary,* February 26, 2008, http://www.onmarkproductions.com/html/shinto.shtml.

52. Benton Johnson, "On Church and Sect," *American Sociological Review,* 1963. 28: 539–549.

53. Hoa Omid, "Theocracy or Democracy? The Critics of 'Westoxification' and the Politics of Fundamentalism in Iran," *Third World Quarterly,* 1992. 13(4): 675–690.

54. Durkheim, *Elementary Forms of the Religious Life.*

55. Karl Marx, *Karl Marx: Selected Writings,* 2nd ed., David McLellan (ed.) (Oxford: Oxford University Press, 1844/2000).

56. Ibid.

57. "A Humanist discussion of . . . The Golden Rule," *British Humanist Association,* February 2006, http://www.humanism.org.uk/site/cms/contentViewArticle.asp? article51222.

58. Max Weber, *The Protestant Ethic and a Spirit of Capitalism: And Other Writings,* translated by Peter Caehr and Gordon C. Wells (New York: Penguin Books, 2002).

59. Ibid.

60. Peter Berger, *The Sacred Canopy: Elements of the Sociology of Religion* (Garden City, NY: Doubleday, 1969).

61. Ibid.

62. Peter Berger, "The Desecularization of the World, a Global Overview," in *The Desecularization of the World: Resurgent Religion and World Politics,* Peter Berger (ed.) (Grand Rapids, MI: Eerdmans, 1999), pp. 1–18.

63. "Information about Religion in Canada," ReligiousTolerance.org, Accessed Oct. 27, 2010 at http://www.religioustolerance.org/can_rel.htm.

64. Robert Bellah, Richard Madsen, William M. Sullivan, Ann Swidler, and Steve Tipton, *Habits of the Heart: Individualism and Commitment in American Life* (Berkeley, CA: University of California Press, 1996).

65. Harold Coward and Roland Chagnon, "Religion," *The Canadian Encyclopedia.*

66. "Information about Religion in Canada," ReligiousTolerance.org.

67. *2001 Census: Analysis Series, Religions in Canada,* pp. 6, 20.

68. Ibid, p. 7.

69. Ibid, p. 9.

70. Ibid.

71. Ibid, p. 8.

72. Ibid, pp. 8, 20.

73. Ibid, p. 9.

74. "The Amish," *ReligionFacts,* Accessed Oct. 27, 2010 at http://www.religionfacts.com/christianity/denominations/amish.htm; and "The Amish," *Encyclopedia Britannica,* http://search.eb.com/eb/article-233461, Accessed July 11, 2008.

75. "Martin Luther King, Jr.: Biography," The Nobel Foundation, http://nobelprize. org/nobel_prizes/peace/laureates/1964/king-bio.html, Accessed September 3, 2008.

76. Megan Wilde, "Galileo and the Inquisition," *The Galileo Project,* http://galileo.rice.edu/bio/narrative_7.html, Accessed September 2, 2008.

77. Shirley Ann Rainey, "Great Chain of Being," *Encyclopedia of Race and Racism* (New York: MacMillan, 2007), http://personal.uncc.edu/jmarks/pubs/Encpercent20race percent20GCOB.pdf.

78. "Amaterasu," *Encyclopedia Britannica,* http://search.eb.com/eb/article-9006019, Accessed September 2, 2008; "Religion & Ethics: Shinto—The Imperial Family," *BBC.com,* http://www.bbc.co.uk/religion/religions/shinto/texts/stories_5.shtml, Accessed September 2, 2008.

79. Giselle Vincett, "Why Are Women Attracted to Goddess Feminism?" *MatriFocus Quarterly,* 2009, Accessed Sept. 21, 2010 at http://www.matrifocus.com/LAM09/goddess-feminism.htm.

80. Linda Woodhead, "Gender Differences in Religious Practice and Significance," in J. Beckford and N. J. Demerath III (eds.), *The Sage Handbook of the Sociology of Religion* (Los Angeles: Sage, 2007), pp. 550–570.

81. "Toronto's 1st Africentric School Set to Open," *CBC News.*

82. Moira MacDonald, "Africentric School Shines: MacDonald," *Toronto Sun,* updated Sept. 25, 2010, Accessed Oct. 28, 2010 at http://www.torontosun.com/comment/columnists/moira_macdonald/2010/09/24/15469271.html.

83. Information from report abbreviated as "Elementary School Report" under 2009–2010 EQAO Provincial Reports, at http://www.eqao.com/.

84. Quoted in Scott Anderson, "Afrocentric Schools," *University of Toronto Magazine,* Autumn 2009, Accessed Oct. 28, 2010 at http://www.magazine.utoronto.ca/leading-edge/afrocentric-schools/.

85. Natalie Alcoba, "Toronto Trustees Vote in Favour of Afrocentric School," *National Post,* Jan. 29, 2008, Accessed Oct. 28, 2010 at http://www.nationalpost.com/news/story.html?id=272389.

86. Toronto's 1st Africentric School Set to Open," *CBC News.*

87. Abbreviated extract from Lennox V. Farrell, "Greg Is Not His Real Name," 1998, *TimBookTu: Stories, Poetry & Essays with an African-American Flavor,* Accessed Oct. 23, 2010 at http://www.timbooktu.com/lennox/ythprobl.htm.

CHAPTER 15

1. Naomi Klein, *No Logo: Taking Aim at the Brand Bullies* (Toronto: Vintage Canada, 2000), pp. 280–281.

2. Pat Hudson, *The Industrial Revolution: Reading History* (New York: Hodder Arnold, 1992).

3. Warren E. Kalbach, "Population," *The Canadian Encyclopedia,* Accessed Oct. 30, 2010 through http://www.thecanadianencyclopedia.com.

4. Warren E. Kalbach, "Population."

5. Harold Troper, "Immigration," *The Canadian Encyclopedia,* http://www.thecanadianencyclopedia.com; and "Canada," WorldRover.com, citing CIA statistics, http://www.worldrover.com/vital/canada.html (both Accessed Oct. 30, 2010).

6. Irvin Studin, "Canada—Population 100 Million," June 14, 2010 feature in *Global Brief,* published out of the Glendon School of Public and International Affairs at Toronto's York University, Accessed Oct. 30, 2010 at http://globalbrief.ca/blog/2010/06/14/canada-%E2%80%93-population-100-million/.

7. Frank Trovato, "Native People, Demography," *The Canadian Encyclopedia,* Accessed Oct. 30, 2010 through http://www.thecanadianencyclopedia.com.

8. Central Intelligence Agency, *World Factbook,* Accessed Oct. 30, 2010 at https://www.cia.gov/library/publications/the-world-factbook/geos/ca.html.

9. "People and Culture—Population Densities," Government of Ontario, Accessed Oct. 30, 2010 at http://www.ontario.ca/en/about_ontario/EC001035.

10. William Fielding Ogburn, *Social Change with Respect to Cultural and Original Nature* (New York: Dell Publishing Co., 1923/1966).

11. Library of Congress, "Everyday Mysteries: Who Invented the Automobile?" March 1, 2007, http://www.loc.gov/rr/scitech/mysteries/auto.html.

12. "India: Environmental Issues," Energy Information Administration, February 2004, http://www.earthscape.org/p1/ES2_6242/6242.pdf, Accessed November 6, 2008.

13. Albert Hirschman, *The Rhetoric of Reaction: Perversity, Futility, Jeopardy* (Cambridge, MA: Harvard University Press, 1991).

14. "Internet Petitions," *Snopes.com,* http://www.snopes.com/inboxer/petition/internet.asp, Accessed September 11, 2008.

15. Ibid.

16. "G20 Protest Violence Prompts over 400 Arrests," *CBC News,* updated June 27, 2010, Accessed Oct. 30, 2010 at http://www.cbc.ca/canada/story/2010/06/26/g20-saturday-protests.html.

17. "Violent Riot Ends in Shooting at Edmonton Prison," *Edmonton Journal,* July 2, 2008, Accessed Oct. 30, 2010 at http://www.canada.com/globaltv/national/story.html?id=025998f4-9969-4b7f-806e-7ddbcbaa0ea3.

18. Joel Best, *Flavor of the Month: Why Smart People Fall for Fads* (Berkeley, CA: University of California Press, 2006).

19. Ibid.

20. Drug Abuse Resistance Education, Saint John, NB, Accessed Oct. 30, 2010 at http://www.daresj.com/dare_in_canada.php.

21. Joel Best, *Flavor of the Month.*

22. "FEMA for Kids: Y2K for Kids," *Federal Emergency Management Agency,* http://www.fema.gov/kids/y2k.htm, Accessed September 11, 2008; "Are You Ready?" *The White House,* February 3, 2003, http://www.whitehouse.gov/news/releases/2003/02/20030207-10.html; Jeanne Meserve, "Duct Tape Sales Rise Amid Terror Fears," *CNN.com,* February 11, 2003, http://www.cnn.com/2003/US/02/11/emergency.supplies/.

23. Meserve, "Duct Tape Sales Rise."

24. "1995 Referendum," Canada History, part of The History Project, http://www.canadahistory.com/sections/eras/moderncanada/1995_referendum.htm.

25. Bernard Guerin and Yoshihiko Miyazaki, "Analyzing Rumors, Gossip, and Urban Legends through Their Conversational Properties," *Psychological Record,* Winter 2006. 56(1): 23.

26. "The Obligatory Wait," *Snopes.com,* http://www.snopes.com/college/admin/wait.asp, Accessed August 5, 2008.

27. Charles Tilly, *Social Movements, 1768–2004* (Boulder, CO: Paradigm Publishers, 2004).

28. Rhett Butler, "Rainforests Face Array of Emerging Threats," *Mongabay.com,* June 15, 2008, http://news.mongabay.com/2008/0614-laurance.html.

29. Rainforest Alliance, "Research & Resources: Tropical Forests in Our Daily Lives," http://www.rainforest-alliance.org/resources.cfm?id5daily_lives, Accessed September 11, 2008; J. Louise Mastrantonio and John K. Francis, "A Student Guide to Tropical Forest Conservation," October 1997, http://www.fs.fed.us/global/lzone/student/tropical.htm.

30. World Wildlife Fund, http://wwf.worldwildlife.org/site/PageServer?pagename5can_home&JServSessionIdr01256kimssfum2.app13a, Accessed September 11. 2008; The Nature Conservancy 2008, http://www.nature.org/?src5logo, Accessed September 11, 2008.

31. WWF Amazon Project 2008, http://www.worldwildlife.org/what/wherewework/amazon/item1376.html, Accessed September 11, 2008.

32. Rainforest Action Network: Our Mission and History, http://ran.org/who_we_ are/our_mission_history/, Accessed September 11, 2008.

33. All information from the International Tibet Support Network, Accessed Oct. 30, 2010 at http://www.tibetnetwork.org.

34. George Hoberg, "Governing the Environment," in Keith G. Banting, George Hoberg, and Richard Simeon (eds.), *Degrees of Freedom: Canada and the United States in a Changing World* (McGill-Queen's University Press, 1997), pp. 343–345.

35. Charles Tilly, *From Mobilization to Revolution* (Reading MA: Addison-Wesley, 1978).

36. David F. Aberle, *The Peyote Religion Among the Navaho* (Norman, OK: University of Oklahoma Press, 1966).

37. Frances A. DellaCava, Norma Kolko Phillips, and Madeline H. Engel, "Adoption in the U.S.: The Emergence of a Social Movement," *Journal of Sociology and Social Welfare,* Dec. 2004, http://findarticles.com/p/articles/mi_m0CYZ/is_4_31/ai_n8681413.

38. "History," Greenpeace Canada, http://www.greenpeace.org/canada/en/About-us/History/; and "Greenpeace: Always Bearing Witness," CBC, broadcast 1971–2003, http://archives.cbc.ca/environment/environmental_protection/topics/867/, both Accessed Oct. 30, 2010.

39. Information taken from Greenpeace Canada and Greenpeace International websites, http://www.greenpeace.org/canada/en/ and http://www.greenpeace.org/international/, and from "The Birth of Greenpeace," CBC Digital Archives, http://archives.cbc.ca/environment/environmental_protection/clips/5000/, all accessed Oct. 30, 2010.

40. Ibid.

41. 2009/2010 Annual Report, *MADD, Mothers Against Drunk Driving Canada*, p. 1, Accessed Oct. 31, 2010 at http://www.madd.ca/english/about/annualreports.html.

42. "Lives Saved," MADD Canada, Accessed Oct. 31, 2010 at http://www.madd.ca/english/research/lives_saved.pdf.

43. "Over 30,000 Lives Saved Fighting Impaired Driving Since 1982," MADD Canada, April 24, 2008, Accessed Oct. 31, 2010 at http://www.madd.ca/english/news/pr/p20080424.htm.

44. Danuta Otfinowski, "Should Christians Convert Muslims?" *Time*, June 22, 2003, http://www.time.com/time/magazine/article/0,9171,1101030630-460157,00. html?CNN5yes.

45. "Fidel Castro," Encyclopedia Britannica Online, http://www.britannica.com/EBchecked/topic/98822/Fidel-Castro, Accessed September 11, 2008.

46. Tilly, *From Mobilization to Revolution*.

47. David A. Locher, *Collective Behavior* (Upper Saddle River, NJ: Prentice-Hall, 2002).

48. Robert E. Park and Ernest W. Burgess, *Introduction to the Science of Society*, 3rd ed. (Chicago: University of Chicago Press, 1921/1969).

49. William Kornhauser, *The Politics of Mass Society* (New York: Free Press, 1959).

50. Denton E. Morrison, "Some Notes Toward Theory on Relative Deprivation, Social Movements and Social Change," *American Behavioral Scientists*, 1971, 14(5): 675–690; Locher, *Collective Behavior*.

51. James Chowning Davies, "The J-Curve and Power Struggle Theories of Collective Violence," *American Sociological Review*, 1974. 39(4): 607–610; James Chownng Davies, *When Men Revolt and Why: A Reader in Political Violence and Revolution* (New York: Free Press, 1970).

52. Ted Robert Gurr, *Why Men Rebel* (Princeton, NJ: Princeton University Press, 1970).

53. Erving Goffman, *Frame Analysis: An Essay on the Organization of Experience* (Cambridge, MA: Harvard University Press, 1974).

54. David A. Snow, E. Burke Rochford, Jr., Steven K. Worden, and Robert D. Benford, "Frame Alignment Processes, Micromobilization, and Movement Participation," *American Sociological Review*, 1986. 51: 464–481.

55. Robert D. Benford and David A. Snow, "Framing Processes and Social Movements: An Overview and Assessment," *Annual Review of Sociology*, 2000. 26: 611–639.

56. Ibid.

57. Ibid.

58. Snow, Rochford, Worden, and Benford, "Frame Alignment Processes."

59. Ibid.

60. Ibid.

61. Ibid.

62. Ibid.

63. Talcott Parsons, *The Social System* (Glencoe, IL: The Free Press, 1951).

64. Paul Hawken, *Blessed Unrest: How the Largest Social Movement in History Is Restoring Grace, Justice, and Beauty to the World* (New York: Viking Penguin, 2007).

65. Sean Thomas Cadigan, *Newfoundland and Labrador: A History* (Toronto: University of Toronto Press, Scholarly Publishing Division, 2009), p. 273.

66. Hawken, *Blessed Unrest*.

67. *BC SCRAP-IT Program*, Accessed Oct. 29, 2010 at http://www.scrapit.ca/p4incentivechoices.htm.

68. "Canada's First Motor Vehicle Fuel Consumption Regulations: Consultations Begin," Transport Canada news release, Jan. 17, 2008, Accessed Oct. 29, 2010 at http://www.tc.gc.ca/eng/mediaroom/releases-nat-2008-08-h006e-4909.htm.

69. John LeBlanc, "Nissan Leaf: Driving to the Sounds of Silence," *Toronto Star*, Oct 22, 2010, http://www.wheels.ca/article/792217; and Alain Morin, "Chevrolet Volt: Get a Charge out of It!" March 9, 2010, *The Car Guide*, http://www.carguideweb.com/articles/7131/, both Accessed Nov. 1, 2010.

70. "GM Says Hasta la Vista to Hummer," *MSN Money* staff, Jan. 1, 2010, Accessed Nov. 1, 2010 at http://articles.moneycentral.msn.com/SavingandDebt/SaveonaCar/gm-halts-hummer-production.aspx.

71. Hawken, *Blessed Unrest*.

PHOTO CREDITS

313

Dawn. **143:** John Wilkes/CORBIS All Rights Reserved; Tim Ridley © Dorling Kindersley; Dorling Kindersley © Bethany Dawn. **144:** Christopher Jones/Shutterstock; jossnat/Shutterstock; Dmitriy Shironosov/Shutterstock; Christopher Conrad/Getty Images, Inc./PhotoDisc. **146:** "Returning from the Cotton Fields in South Carolina", ca. 1860, stereograph by Barbard, negative number 47843. © Collection of The New-York Historical Society; Malcolm Linton/Getty Images, Inc./Liaison. **148:** Getty Images. **149:** © Michael Newman/PhotoEdit Inc. **150 (Clockwise from top left):** Robert St-Coeur/Shutterstock; © RobHowarth/iStockPhoto; MarFot/Shutterstock; © George Clerk/iStockPhoto; Wade H. Massie/Shutterstock; Shutterstock; © Sascha Burkard/iStockPhoto; Gilmanshin/Shutterstock. **151:** © Michael S. Yamashita/CORBIS All Rights Reserved. **153:** Jose Elias da Silva Neto/Shutterstock; vgstudio/Shutterstock. **154 (Clockwise from top left):** Victor Englebert/Photo Researchers, Inc.; Dorling Kindersley © Jamie Marshall; © Jon Hicks/CORBIS All Rights Reserved; Eric Lansner/Black Star. **156:** J.P. Laffont/ZUMA Press—Gamma; © Michael S. Yamashita/CORBIS All Rights Reserved; Victor Englebert/Photo Researchers, Inc.

CHAPTER 09 PAGE 158: © Daniel Koebe/Corbis. **160:** Identity and Belonging: Rethinking Race and Ethnicity in Canadian Society, edited by Sean P. Hier and B. Singh Bolaria © 2006 Canadian Scholars' Press. Reprinted with permission of Canadian Scholars' Press Inc; Tony Souter © Dorling Kindersley; Scott Cunningham/Merrill Education. **161:** Chad Ehlers/Stock Connection. **163:** Source: Library and Archives Canada/Shananditti : the last of the Beothucks/AMICUS 84794/nlc-8715. **165:** Library and Archives Canada/British Columbia Securities Commission collection/C-046355. **166:** © Nik Wheeler/CORBIS; Morgan Lane Photography/Shutterstock; Jozsef Szasz-Fabian/Shutterstock; Library and Archives Canada/British Columbia Securities Commission collection/C-046355; Munshi Ahmed/Munshi Ahmed Photograhy; Eduardo Miller/Shutterstock; Kayte M. Deioma/PhotoEdit Inc. **168:** David Martin/AP Wide World Photos. **171:** Stephanie Carter/Stock Illustration Source. **172:** Kamloops Daily News/Stf/The Canadian Press; Corbis/Bettmann; Library and Archives Canada/British Columbia Securities Commission collection/C-046355. **174:** © Daniel Koebe/Corbis; Library and Archives Canada/British Columbia Securities Commission collection/C-046355; Stephanie Carter/Stock Illustration Source.

CHAPTER 10 PAGE 176: Alan Becker/Getty Images, Inc.—Image Bank. **178:** Penguin Group USA, Inc.; © Dorling Kindersley; iofoto/Shutterstock. **179:** Clive Streeter © Dorling Kindersley, Courtesy of the Design Museum, London. **180:** Felicia Martinez/PhotoEdit Inc. **181:** Zoom Team/Shutterstock. **182:** Christine Chew /Landov. **183:** Orange Line Media/Shutterstock; Yuri Arcurs/Shutterstock; vgstudio/Shutterstock; Yuri Arcurs/Shutterstock; Yuri Arcurs/Shutterstock; © Alex Slobodkin/iStockPhoto. **184:** Charly Franklin/Getty Images, Inc.—Taxi. **185:** © Ariel Skelley/CORBIS All Rights Reserved; iStockphoto/Thinkstock; Somos Images/CORBIS All Rights Reserved. **186 (from the left):** National Archives of Canada/C.Jessop/The Canadian Press; Calgary Herald/The Canadian Press; Getty Images. **187 (from the left):** Globe and Mail/Denis Robinson/The Canadian Press; Lindsay Brice/Getty Images Inc.—Michael Ochs Archives. **188:** © Trinette Reed/CORBIS. **189:** Jupiterimages/Brand X Pictures/Thinkstock. **190 (from the top):** Bill Bachmann/The Image Works; Ryan McVay/Getty Images, Inc.—PhotoDisc; Darrin Klimek/Getty Images. **192:** Alan Becker/Getty Images, Inc.—Image Bank; Christine Chew/Landov; Charly Franklin/Getty Images, Inc.—Taxi.

CHAPTER 11 PAGE 194: Veit Mette/laif/Redux. **196:** Patients First: Closing the Health Care Gap in Canada by Terrence J. Montague. Copyright © 2004 John Wiley & Sons Canada, Ltd. Reprinted with permission of John Wiley & Sons Canada, Ltd., a subsidiary of John Wiley & Sons, Inc.; Corbis Digital Stock. **197:** Dave King © Dorling Kindersley. **199:** Richard Lord/PhotoEdit Inc.; Michael Newman/PhotoEdit Inc. **200:** John A. Rizzo/Getty Images, Inc.—PhotoDisc. **201:** Scott Cunningham/Merrill Education. **202:** © Joseph Sohm/Visions of America/CORBIS All Rights Reserved; Digital zoo/Corbis Royalty Free; Olga Sapegina/Shutterstock. **203:** Laima Druskis/Pearson Education/PH College. **204:** Kyodo News/AP Wide World Photos. **205:** Creatas Images/Thinkstock. **206:** Elizabeth Crews/Elizabeth Crews Photography. **208:** Michael Newman/PhotoEdit Inc.; Ian O'Leary/Getty Images, Inc.—Stone Allstock; Dennis Kitchen/Getty Images, Inc.—Stone Allstock. **210:** Veit Mette/laif/Redux; Elizabeth Crews/Elizabeth Crews Photography; Michael Newman/PhotoEdit Inc.

CHAPTER 12 PAGE 212: Rich Pedroncelli/AP Wide World Photos. **214:** © John A. Rizzo/Photodisc/Getty Images; Cover from Responding to Youth Crime in Canada by Anthony N. Doob and Carla Cesaroni. © University of Toronto Press Inc., 2004. Reprinted with permission of the publisher; © Andy Green/iStockPhoto; VladKol/Shutterstock; Digital Vision/Thinkstock; Andy Crawford © Dorling Kindersley; Dave King © Dorling Kindersley. **215:** Steve Gorton © Dorling

Kindersley. **218:** Jupiterimages/Thinkstock. **221:** Andrew Wakeford/Getty Images, Inc.—PhotoDisc. **222:** © Wally McNamee/CORBIS All Rights Reserved. **223:** John Francis Bourke/Corbis Zefa Collection. **225:** Patrick White/Merrill Education; AP Wide World Photos; Ken Lax/Photo Researchers, Inc. **227:** David Leeson/The Image Works. **228:** John Francis Bourke/Corbis Zefa Collection; Ken Lax/Photo Researchers, Inc.; Rich Pedroncelli/AP Wide World Photos.

CHAPTER 13 PAGE 230: ©H.Armstrong Roberts/CORBIS All Rights Reserved. **232:** Cover from The Canadian Family in Crisis by John Frederick Conway. © James Lorimer & Company Ltd., 2003. Reprinted with permission by the publisher; Janice Morris/Pearson Education/PH College. **233:** Bomshtein/Shutterstock; Justin Slide© Dorling Kindersley. **234:** Shutterstock; Shutterstock. **235:** Katrina Brown/Shutterstock; Lori Martin/Shutterstock; Getty Images Inc.—Hulton Archive Photos. **236:** Getty Images Inc.—Hulton Archive Photos. **237:** Jeremy Sutton-Hibbert/Getty Images. **238:** Greg Hinsdale/CORBIS All Rights Reserved; Richard Lord/The Image Works; © Randy Faris/CORBIS All Rights Reserved. **239:** Greg Huglin/Stock Connection. **241:** David Young-Wolff/PhotoEdit Inc.; iQoncept/Shutte rstock. **242 (From top):** Hulton Archive by Getty Images, Inc.; Corbis/Bettmann; UBU Productions/Picture Desk, Inc./Kobal Collection; CBS Photo Archive/Hulton Archive/Getty Images; CBS Photo Archive/Hulton Archive/Getty Images; Picture Desk, Inc./Kobal Collection. **243 (From top):** Hulton Archive/Getty Images; TM and © Twentieth Century Fox Film Corp./Photofest; Getty Images; Lynn Goldsmith/Corbis/Corbis/Bettmann; HBO/Worldwide Pants Inc/The Kobal Collection/Voets, Robert; © Richard Cartwright/American Broadcasting Companies, Inc. **244:** David Ellis/Getty Images/Digital Vision; Paul Conklin/PhotoEdit Inc.; Stephanie Rausser/Getty Images, Inc.—Taxi. **246:** Getty Images Inc.—Hulton Archive Photos; David Ellis/Getty Images/Digital Vision; iQoncept/Shutterstock.

CHAPTER 14 PAGE 248: © Andrew Rich/iStockPhoto. **250:** Access to Post-Secondary Education: Does Class Still Matter? by Andrea Rounce © 2004. Printed with permission from the Canadian Centre for Policy Alternatives—Saskatchewan; Richard Haynes/Prentice Hall School Division; Philip Gatward © Dorling Kindersley. **251:** Jo Foord © Dorling Kindersley. **253:** Torian/Shutterstock; © Denis Scott/CORBIS. **254:** Jaimie Trueblood/Paramount/Picture Desk, Inc./Kobal Collection. **257 (Clockwise from top right):** Joy Fera/Shutterstock; aispl/Shutterstock; Shutterstock; Videowokart/Shutterstock; hfng /Shutterstock; © NASA/CORBIS All Rights Reserved. **258:** © Robert Wallis/CORBIS All Rights Reserved. **259:** Andy Sacks/Getty Images Inc.—Stone Allstock. **260:** Shutterstock. **262:** Mark Richards/PhotoEdit Inc. **263:** Corbis Royalty Free; Getty Images; Lawrence Migdale/Lawrence Migdale/Pix. **265:** Jaimie Trueblood/Paramount/Picture Desk, Inc./Kobal Collection; Andy Sacks/Getty Images Inc.—Stone Allstock; © Andrew Rich/iStockphoto.com.

CHAPTER 15 PAGE 268: Dennis Brack/Black Star. **270:** Reprinted by permission of Knopf Canada; Laima Druskis/Pearson Education/PH College; Pearson Education/PH College. **271:** Greenpeace/EM. **272:** Geoff Brightling © Dorling Kindersley, Courtesy of the Museum of English Rural Life, The University of Reading; Mike Dunning © Dorling Kindersley, Courtesy of the Science Museum, London; Andy Crawford © Dorling Kindersley, Courtesy of the Museum of the Revolution, Moscow; Bruce Forster © Dorling Kindersley; Getty Images. **273:** Glen Allison/Getty Images Inc.—Stone Allstock; Joe Sohm/Chromosohm/Stock Connection; John Rennison, The Hamilton Spectator; Benny De Grove/Getty Images, Inc.—Image Bank; iStockphoto/Thinkstock; Andre J. Jackson/MCT/Landov. **275:** © Christopher J. Morris/CORBIS. **276:** Courtesy of Students for a Free Tibet Canada. **277:** Courtesy of Rex Weyler. **278:** Getty Images; Friedrich Stark/Das Fotoarchiv/Peter Arnold, Inc.; Fred Chartrand/The Canadian Press; Getty Images Inc.—Hulton Archive Photos. **279:** © Kamal Kishore/CORBIS All Rights Reserved. **280:** © Paramount Classics/Photofest. **282:** Getty Images; Getty Images; Greg Locke Photo. **284:** Greg Locke Photo; © Paramount Classics/Photofest; © Kamal Kishore/CORBIS All Rights Reserved.

TEXT, TABLE AND FIGURE CREDITS

CHAPTER 01 PAGE 3: Poverty and Policy in Canada: Implications for Health and Quality of Life, Dennis Raphael. © 2007 Canadian Scholars' Press Inc. Reprinted with permission of Canadian Scholars' Press Inc.

CHAPTER 02 PAGE 31: Cults and New Religious Movements: A Reader, Lorne L. Dawson (Editor). © 2003, Blackwell Publishing Ltd. Reproduced with permission of Blackwell Publishing Ltd.

CHAPTER 03 PAGE 49: Courtesy of Thomas Homer-Dixon.

INDEX

THINK

SOCIOLOGY Study Card — PEARSON

The Sociological Perspective

What Is Sociology?

Discovering Sociology

- **Social forces:** Forces that influence our behaviour.
- **Social facts:** Social patterns that endure or recur over time.
- **Social location:** The factors (e.g., class, gender, age, ethnicity) that define our membership in social groups.
- **Social inequality:** Differences in the way rewards, opportunities, and other social resources are allocated.
- Human behaviour on a **micro level** (small scale or group) as well as a **macro level** (whole populations).
- **Social change:** Examining the means through which culture and society change over time.
- **Globalization:** The increasing interconnectedness of contemporary cultures and societies.

Thinking Sociologically

- The **"sociological imagination"** (**C. Wright Mills**, 1916–1962): An ability to see the connections between "biography" (individual lives) and "history" (larger social forces).
- *Verstehen* (understanding) (**Max Weber**, 1864–1920): The notion that social reality can be discovered only by seeing the world empathically through the lived experiences of people.
- Individual behaviour must be examined and understood in its **social context.**
- People tend to behave in **predictable ways.**
- People are products of their **time and place** in **history and society.**
- People construct their own society and **social reality.**
- Social behaviour is **complex** and has **multiple causes and effects.**
- Look below the surface of **common sense explanations** to discover the true nature of behaviour.

Founders of Sociology and Sociological Theory

The Functionalists (Social Order)

August Comte (1798–1857)

- Founded sociology as a field that scientifically investigates the social world **(positivism).**

- Society is made up of social structures and social relations that function together for the good of the whole society.
- Believed that societies are social "organisms" that more or less adhere to the natural laws of evolution.

Émile Durkheim (1858–1917)

- Societies achieve **social solidarity** (integration) through **normative consensus,** in which people share a set of values and expectations for appropriate behaviour **(collective conscious).**
- People who do not share the underlying moral order, or **social conscience,** experience **anomie** (alienation) from the society.

Robert Merton (1910–2003)

- Some social behaviours are **dysfunctional,** meaning that they have negative consequences for society instead of contributing to its smooth functioning.
- Social structures and behaviour have **manifest** (intended) as well as **latent** (unintended) functions.

The Conflict Theorists (Social Disorder)

Karl Marx (1818–1883)

- Social change is driven by **class conflict.**
- Wealth generated by the rise of industrial capitalism is enjoyed by the **bourgeoisie** (owners of the means of production) but not the **proletariat** (workers).

Max Weber

- **Religion,** not social conflict, is the main force behind social change.
- Societies that move from traditional to modern undergo **rationalization,** emphasizing efficiency over tradition.
- **Bureaucracies** that dehumanize social life are a central feature of modern society. Weber called this the **iron cage** of bureaucracies.

W.E.B. DuBois (1868–1963)

- Poverty among African Americans in the United States is primarily the result of prejudice and discrimination.

C. Wright Mills

- A small number of people, the **power elite,** control the dominant social institutions and amass great wealth, power, and prestige.

- The power elite draws its power, wealth, and/or influence from the **military–industrial complex,** an overarching social structure composed of elite members of the government, military, and industrial structures.

The Symbolic Interactionists (Social Interactions)

Charles H. Cooley (1864–1929)

- Coined the phrase **"looking-glass self"** to emphasize how we see ourselves and develop a sense of self through others' eyes.

George Herbert Mead (1863–1931)

- Social order is based on our ability to distinguish between the **"I"** (the spontaneous, expressive self) and the **"me"** (the self that acts on social norms and values).

Erving Goffman (1922–1982)

- Introduced the idea of **dramaturgy**—the way we "perform" our lives, acting out scripts that are appropriate for us and monitoring and managing the impression we make on others.

Harold Garfinkel (1917–)

- Developed a research method, called **ethnomethodology,** for analyzing the social construction of rules for social behaviour.

The Feminist Theorists (Gender)

Harriet Martineau (1802–1876)

- Some people do not have the same opportunities as others.
- Focused on the inequality between the sexes.

Jane Addams (1860–1935)

- In order to understand the poor, Addams felt that she must live among them.
- Hull House became a laboratory for the application of sociological principles.

Dorothy Smith (1926–)

- Critiqued traditional sociology for adopting an "objectifying discourse."
- Sociologists should recognize the everyday experiences of ordinary people, including women, workers, and other marginalized groups.

Social Science Research

- Examines empirical data gathered from the social world via social research methods.
- Research looks for positive and negative correlations between social variables.
- Two types of data are collected:

The Sociological Perspective (continued)

- **Quantitative:** Involving the statistical analysis of numerical data collected on social variables. Examine the cause-and-effect relationship between social variables.
- **Qualitative:** Involving the analysis of nonnumeric data collected through observations of the social environment.

Steps in the Research Process

- Choose a subject.
- State the research problem.
- Formulate a hypothesis.

- Operationalize definitions of the variables under study.
- Review the literature.
- Design the study.
- Develop instruments for data collection.
- Choose the sample.
- Collect the data.
- Analyze the data.
- Report findings and conclusions.

Research Methods

Survey: Typically quantitative in nature.

Field observation: Actively participating in social environment under study; typically qualitative in nature.

Experiment: The collection of data in an environment controlled by the researcher in a laboratory setting; typically quantitative in nature.

Content analysis: Examination of cultural artifacts (magazines, movies, music, etc.), which allows for insight into a society's culture; typically quantitative in nature.

Secondary analysis: The examination of preexisting databases; typically quantitative in nature.

Individuals and Society

Society and Culture

Society: A group of interacting people who share the same culture.

Culture: The language, beliefs, values, behaviours, and material objects that are passed from one generation to the next. Culture can be divided into two types:

- **Material culture:** Physical pieces of culture, such as jewellery, hairstyles, books, and the like.
- **Nonmaterial culture:** A group's ways of thinking (beliefs, values) and doing (common behaviour, language, and gestures).

Sociologists must practise cultural relativism in which each culture is examined on its own terms, eliminating judgments of one culture being better or worse than another.

Types of Societies

- Hunting-gathering
- Pastoral
- Horticultural
- Agrarian
- Industrial
- Postindustrial

Language and Culture

- Language is vital for **cultural transmission,** the preserving and communicating of culture.
- Language allows ideas and experiences to be passed down from one generation to another.
- Language allows for shared understanding of concepts that are the basis of social life.
- **Sapir-Whorf Hypothesis** (**Edward Sapir,** 1884–1939, and **Benjamin Whorf,** 1897–1941): The idea that language influences or even determines our conscious perceptions of the world.

Groups Outside of Dominant or Mainstream Cultures

Subculture: System of values, attitudes, modes of behaviour, and lifestyles of a social group

that is distinct from, but related to, that of the dominant culture.

Counterculture: System of values, attitudes, modes of behaviour, and lifestyles of a social group that is radically different from that of the dominant culture.

Social Structure and Interaction

Groups within Society

Social group: Two or more people who interact on a regular basis; they share interests and expectations.

Primary group: Long-term group associations with strong emotional attachments.

Secondary group: Larger, more formal, and more impersonal than primary groups.

In-group: A group to which an individual feels a strong allegiance.

Out-group: A group that competes with or rivals an individual's in-group.

Reference groups: A group that provides personal standards of dress, success, attitudes, and beliefs for an individual.

Networks: A chain of associations that link people with common interests.

Group Composition and Leadership

Leader: Someone who influences the behaviours, opinions, or attitudes of others.

Instrumental leader: Keeps a group moving toward its goals.

Expressive leader: Typically not recognized as a formal leader yet contributes to improving group morale and keeping the group intact.

Types of Leadership

Authoritarian leader: A leader who gives orders to bring the group to action.

Democratic leader: A leader who attempts to gain a consensus to bring the group to action.

Laissez-faire leader: A leader who is highly permissive or laid-back with the group.

Key Research on Groups and Leaders

Solomon Asch (1880–1957)

- Conducted experiments to determine the effect of groups on conformity.
- Results suggested that a majority of individuals will submit to group consensus even if it means giving the wrong answer to a question.

Stanley Milgram (1933–1984)

- Conducted experiments to determine the effect of an authority (leader) on a subordinate.
- Found that a majority of individuals would submit their will to that of the authority, even to the point of hypothetically killing another person.

Theories of Development

Sigmund Freud (1856–1939): Explored the relationship between the id (inborn drive to seek satisfaction), ego (balancing force between the id and the demands of society), and superego (the conscience, also balanced by the ego).

Cooley: Coined the term **looking-glass self** to describe the process by which a sense of self is developed. Three elements of the looking-glass self:

1. we imagine how we appear to those around us,
2. we interpret others' reactions, and
3. we develop a self-concept.

Mead: Explored the manner in which children and adults explore, come to understand, and eventually take on (as adults) various roles in society.

Jean Piaget (1896–1980): Explored the process through which humans gain the ability to reason logically. Described four stages for learning the ability to reason (the sensorimotor, preoperational, concrete operational, and formal operational stages).

continued next page

continued next page

Matriarchy: A system of family in which most power and authority are held by a female.

Egalitarian family: A system of family in which power is shared by family members.

Family Diversity

Cohabitation: A couple living together without legal marriage (domestic partnership).

Civil union: Officially sanctioned cohabitation.

Blended families: Families composed of children and some combination of biological parents.

Same-sex marriage: Has been legally recognized in Canada since 2005.

Sociological Perspectives

Functionalism: Family fulfills many social functions: regulating sexual activity, providing new members for society, education, and socialization.

Symbolic interactionism: Focuses on the meaning of the marriage for its members.

Feminist theory: Marriage and family reflect the social inequalities between men and women.

Conflict theory: Industrialization pushed the family from producing goods to primarily consuming goods.

Religion

Religion: System of shared beliefs, rituals, and symbols that address fundamental questions of human existence.

- **Animism:** The belief that spiritual beings inhabit the world alongside, but invisible to, human beings.
- **Totemism:** The practice of honouring a totem or a sacred object.
- **Theism:** The belief in one or more supreme beings or gods.
- **Monotheism:** The belief in one supreme being or god.
- **Polytheism:** The belief in many supreme beings or gods.
- **Ethical religions:** Philosophical ideals that illustrate how to attain enlightenment, peace, and harmony.

Social Organization

Denominations or churches: Established religious organization that coexists peacefully with other denominations.

Sects: Small informally organized religious group that is sometimes in conflict with society.

Cults: Religious sect that is generally considered to be extremist or false and is often in direct conflict with the dominant social order.

Sociological Perspectives

Functionalism: Religion provides for functions for society: social solidarity, social control, meaning and purpose for individuals, and psychological/emotional support.

Conflict theory: Because of a lack of any other support, people turn to religion for answers to hardship and pain effected by the economic system.

Symbolic interactionism: Tends to focus on the symbols of religions and their shared meanings and interpretations.

Feminist theory: Many of the world's religions are deeply and formally patriarchal.

Contemporary Trends

Secularization: The process by which religion becomes less influential over time.

Fundamentalism: Religious orientation that denounces secularization and attempts to return to beliefs and doctrines of the past.

Liberation theology: Christian groups actively engaged in promoting social justice.

Education

Education involves instructing society's members in knowledge, values, and skills that are deemed important.

Acculturation: Early societies' means of passing on cultural skills and understanding.

Formal education: Instruction given by specially trained teachers in designated settings.

Sociological Perspectives

Functionalism: Education prepares the young with the skills necessary to fill adult roles.

Symbolic interactionism: Focuses on the identity an individual forms through the process of education.

Conflict theory: The education system ensures the maintenance of the unequal class and power structure in the society.

Feminist theory: Boys and girls have different experiences in education.

Contemporary Trends

Multicultural education: Recognizes cultural diversity and promotes appreciation for all cultures.

Lifelong learning: Technological innovation requires the continuous learning of new skills.

Home schooling: The education of a child by parents in a private home.

Health and Medicine

Measures of Health

Infant mortality: A rate of the number of deaths in the first year of life per 1000 live births a year.

Life expectancy: Number of years a person born in a certain year can expect to live.

Public health: Government-sponsored health systems usually working on a community level.

The Canadian Health Care System

Medicare: A system of interlocking health insurance plans.

Public administration: Each province administers a health insurance plan.

Comprehensiveness: All services that are "medically necessary" are covered.

Universality: All residents are covered.

Portability: Citizens are still insured even if they are temporarily absent from their province of residence or from Canada.

Accessibility: Everyone must have reasonable and uniform access.

Current Trends and Problems

Wellness movement: An emphasis on preventive care with a focus on diet and exercise.

AIDS: Caused by HIV; destroys the body's immune system.

Greying of the population: The Canadian population is getting older.

Sociological Perspectives

Functionalism: Health of individuals is of utmost important to maintaining the proper functioning of society, as disease will affect one's ability to fill one's role in society.

Symbolic interactionism: Interested in health care on an individual level, such as the interaction between doctor and patient and the roles that each fills in that interaction.

Conflict theory: Focuses on the unequal distribution of health care depending on the class to which an individual belongs.

Feminist theory: Men and women have different health issues and differ in their desire for health care.

Collective Behaviour

Collective behaiour: Social interaction in which a group of people engages in behaviour that is not in their normal routine.

continued next page

Mobs: Groups characterized by high levels of emotion that engage in some type of focused action that can be violent or disruptive.

Hysteria: A heightened emotional state that can lead a group to violence.

Riots: Emotional and violent disturbances of the peace by crowds that lack a central focus.

Fad: A temporary fashion, notion, or action the public embraces.

Craze: Occurs when a fad leaves a lasting effect on society.

Panic: An extreme fear based on something that might happen.

Crowd: A large group of influential people who gather for a temporary purpose.

Rumours: Stories or statements that lack confirmation or certainty.

Urban legends: Rumours that are presented as true stories that act as cautionary tales.

Types of Social Movements

Alternative social movements: Want to create a change in specific people's thoughts, practices, and beliefs regarding a particular issue.

Redemptive social movements: Focus on specific individuals, but the amount of change sought is radical, rather than limited.

Reformative social movements: Seek to change a society's thoughts and actions, but only in a limited way.

Revolutionary social movements: Sometimes called transformative social movements, seek to change the thoughts and actions of all society in a radical fashion.

Copyright ©2012 Pearson Canada Inc., Toronto, Ontario

www.thethinkspot.ca